THE TELECOM MOSAIC:
ASSEMBLING THE NEW INTERNATIONAL STRUCTURE

Robert R. Bruce
Jeffrey P. Cunard
Mark D. Director

Debevoise & Plimpton
Washington, D.C.

BUTTERWORTHS

All rights reserved. No part of this publication may be reproduced or transmitted in
any form or by any means, including photocopying and recording, without the
written permission of the copyright holder, application for which should be
addressed to the Publishers, or in accordance with the provisions of the Copyright
Act 1956 (as amended), or under the terms of any licence permitting limited copying
issued by the Copyright Licensing Agency, 7 Ridgemount Street, London WC1E
7AE, England. Such written permission must also be obtained before any part of this
publication is stored in a retrieval system of any nature.

Any person who does any unauthorized act in relation to this publication may be
liable to criminal prosecution and civil claims for damages.

This book is sold subject to the Standard Conditions of Sale of Net Books and may
not be re-sold in the UK below the net price given by the Publishers in their current
price list.

First published, 1988 by Butterworth Scientific

© International Institute of Communications, 1988

British Library Cataloguing in Publication Data

Bruce, Robert R.
  The telecom mosaic : assembling the
  new international structure.
  1. International telecommunication services
  I. Title II. Cunard, Jeffrey P.
  III. Director, Mark D.
  384

ISBN 0-408-02670-7

Library of Congress Cataloging in Publication Data

Bruce, Robert R., 1944-
  The telecom mosaic.

  1. Telecommunication policy. 2. Telecommunication.
I. Cunard, Jeffrey P. II. Director, Mark D.
III. Title.
HE7645.B78   1988   384   88-14661
ISBN 0-408-02670-7

Photoset by Butterworths Litho Preparation Department
Printed and bound in Great Britain by Butler & Tanner, Frome, Somerset

SPONSORS

AMERICAN TELEPHONE & TELEGRAPH COMPANY (United States)

BELLSOUTH (United States)

BRITISH TELECOM (United Kingdom)

CABLE & WIRELESS plc (United Kingdom)

CITICORP (United States)

COMMISSION OF THE EUROPEAN COMMUNITIES

DEPARTMENT OF COMMUNICATIONS (Australia)/OTC (Australia)

DEPARTMENT OF COMMUNICATIONS (Canada)/Teleglobe Canada

DEPARTMENT OF TELECOMMUNICATIONS (India)

DIRECTION GÉNÉRALE DES TÉLÉCOMMUNICATIONS (France)

FEDERAL MINISTRY OF POSTS AND TELECOMMUNICATIONS (Federal Republic of Germany)

IBM (United States)

INIZIATIVA Me.t.a OF GRUPPO MONTEDISON (Italy)

INTELSAT

MTV OY/NOKIA OY/TALOUDELLINEN TIEDOTUSTOIMISIO (Finland)

NIPPON TELEGRAPH AND TELEPHONE (Japan)

REUTERS plc (United Kingdom)

SOCIÉTÉ INTERNATIONALE DE TÉLÉCOMMUNICATIONS AÉRONAUTIQUES (France)

This book reflects the views of its authors and not necessarily those of the sponsors nor of the International Institute of Communications and its members.

Note

The ICC is an independent, non-profit organization with members in over 70 countries. It has an active research and conference programme on telecommunications, broadcasting and development communications issues. The Institute is based in London.

Readers interested in further information about the IIC should direct queries to the Executive Director, John Howkins, or the Director of Projects, Gregory Staple, at the following address: Tavistock House South, Tavistock Square, London, WC1 H9LF. Tel: 01-388 0671; Telex: 24578 IICLDN G.

FOREWORD

Each of the five reports which constitute the major chapters of this book on telecommunications makes a distinct contribution to our understanding of this key sector of the world economy. Readers will find that one of their main strengths is their ability to integrate signal themes. Thus, while each report is self-contained, it complements the others.

The reports range widely in focus, from the continuing problem of defining monopoly services, to international facilities planning in a competitive age, to the tariff and interconnection issues confronting European policymakers, to the impact which new electronic financial services are having on the banking and securities industries. Regardless of the subject addressed, however, all the reports share common themes (*e.g.* the pressures for and against liberalization, rate rebalancing, technical standardization and multilateral co-operation—to cite but a few of the issues discussed). They also stress the impossibility of developing domestic telecommunications policies without taking into account changes in the international arena.

The reports are the culmination of the second phase of the Study of Telecommunications Structures (STS) which was begun by the International Institute of Communications (IIC) in 1984. The initial phase of STS was completed in August 1985 with the book-length study, *From Telecommunications to Electronic Services*. The current reports build effectively upon the national studies compiled there by more fully exploring the policy options and business strategies appropriate to the changing telecommunications environment of the 1980s.

As with the first phase of STS, the IIC has benefitted greatly from the commitment of the law firm Debevoise & Plimpton and especially its partner, Robert R. Bruce. The energy, skill and insight which Mr Bruce and his associates Jeffrey P. Cunard and Mark D. Director have brought to this project are clearly reflected in the reports. Their contribution has justly won the Institute's appreciation and respect.

I also want to offer a personal word of thanks to the special group of organizations from Europe, North America and the Pacific that sponsored these reports. The willingness of key officers and staff members from these organizations to meet with one another, often at a considerable individual sacrifice in time and travel, so as to explore the common questions facing tomorrow's communications and information service industries has given this study much of its unique value. It has been a privilege, as President of the IIC, to participate in that process as Chairman of the steering group of sponsors that guided the work.

The support of the sponsors also enabled telecommunication issues from developing countries to be addressed. The individual report on telecommunications structures in selected developing countries provides a particularly useful complement to the study's prior review of OECD countries. The broad scope of STS's work thus reflects the Institute's view that telecommunications progress is a global concern.

Thomas P. Hardiman
President, IIC
May 1987

TABLE OF CONTENTS

		Page
Chapter I	SUMMARY AND INTRODUCTORY OBSERVATIONS	1
Chapter II	BOUNDARY LINES: A FURTHER EXPLORATION OF ENHANCED OR VALUE-ADDED SERVICES	41
Chapter III	TELECOMMUNICATIONS AND TRANSACTIONAL SERVICES: A CASE STUDY OF EMERGING STRUCTURAL AND REGULATORY ISSUES IN THE FINANCIAL SECTOR	183
Chapter IV	THE FUTURE OF EUROPEAN TELECOMMUNICATIONS POLICY	271
Chapter V	THE CHANGING ENVIRONMENT FOR PLANNING INTERNATIONAL FACILITIES: RESPONDING TO COMPETITIVE PRESSURES IN THE TELECOMMUNICATIONS MARKET	337
Chapter VI	TELECOMMUNICATIONS STRUCTURES IN THE DEVELOPING WORLD: AN ESSAY ON TELECOMMUNICATIONS AND DEVELOPMENT	407
	ABOUT THE AUTHORS	447

CHAPTER I
SUMMARY AND INTRODUCTORY OBSERVATIONS

TABLE OF CONTENTS

		Page
I.	Introduction and a Caution	3
II.	Overarching Themes: Linkages Among the Papers	4
III.	Issues Raised by "Boundary Lines"	6
	A. United States	7
	B. United Kingdom	7
	C. France	8
	D. Federal Republic of Germany	9
	E. Elsewhere in Europe	10
	F. Tariffing as an Adjunct to Liberalization	10
	G. The Development of Procedures and Oversight Institutions	11
	H. Regulation and Competition Policy	13
	I. A Dialogue Among Regulators	14
	J. Telecommunications and Trade: Market Access	14
	K. Access to Underlying Services: CEI and ONA in the USA	15
	L. Enhanced or Value-Added Services: The International Dimension	16
IV.	Issues Raised by "Transactional Services"	18
	A. The Interdependence of Two Sectors	18
	B. The Development of Electronic Networks and Markets	19
	C. Different Sectors, Different Issues	20
	D. Should Telecommunications Regulation be Applied to New Transactional Networks?	20
	E. Electronic Markets, the CCITT, and the Use of Leased Circuits	21
	F. Market Access and Two-Tier Regulation	22
	G. The Development of Electronic Markets for Securities and Other Financial Instruments	23

		Page
V.	Issues Raised by "European Telecommunications Policy"	25
	A. A Broad and Independent Perspective	25
	B. Economic Pressures on the PTTs	25
	C. European Approach to ISDN	26
	D. European Satellite Policies	27
	E. The Role of the European Commission: What Options are Available?	28
	F. Role of European Competition Policy and Exercise of Treaty of Rome Powers	29
	G. The Commission and Trade Issues	30
VI.	Issues Raised by "International Facilities"	31
	A. Increasing Capacity, Emerging Competition	31
	B. Strains in Existing Processes	32
	C. Improving Information Flow	32
	D. Committing to Intelsat Capacity	33
	E. Broadening Involvement in Intelsat	33
	F. New Roles — and Changes — for Intelsat	33
VII.	Issues Raised by "Telecommunications and Development"	35
	A. A Lack of Resources	35
	B. The Relationship Between Economic Development and Telecommunications	36
	C. Private Networks: The Cost of Insufficient Supply	37
	D. Structural Innovation and Reform	37
	E. The Framework for New Services	38
	F. Sensitivity to International Considerations	38
	G. Development of New Fora	39
VIII.	Conclusion	39

CHAPTER I
SUMMARY AND INTRODUCTORY OBSERVATIONS

I. INTRODUCTION AND A CAUTION

The work of the second phase of the Study of Telecommunications Structures, which has been conducted under the auspices of the International Institute of Communications, has been organized around five principal themes. Though the work has been interrelated, exploration of each of the five issues has produced a separate paper, each of which is a chapter of this book. This introductory essay is an attempt by the authors of the Study to offer some observations on the issues that are discussed in the following chapters.

The five central themes of this second phase, and of the papers produced, are as follows:

1) the evolution of national and international regulatory policies that distinguish between "basic" and "enhanced" or value-added services and seek to create a framework in which such services can be provided ("Boundary Lines: A Further Exploration of Enhanced or Value-Added Services", hereinafter referred to as " Boundary Lines");

2) the legal and regulatory issues raised by the emergence of electronic financial and transactional services that may constitute the infrastructure for the global trading of the future in securities, commodities, foreign exchange or other financial instruments ("Telecommunications and Transactional Services: A Case Study of Emerging Structural and Regulatory Issues in the Financial Services Sector," hereinafter referred to as "Transactional Services");

3) an overview of European telecommunications and information policies, with a special focus on the role of the Commission of the European Communities ("The Future of European Telecommunications Policy," hereinafter referred to as "European Telecommunications Policy");

4) the present—and possible future—arrangements for developing the infrastructure of international telecommunications facilities—cables and satellite—with an exploration of the role of Intelsat ("The Changing Environment for Planning International Facilities: Responding to Competitive Pressures in the Telecommunications Market," hereinafter referred to as "International Facilities"); and

5) the relevance of industry structure and reform to the developing world, with some observations on the perspectives and reactions of the less developed countries to changes in the telecommunications sectors of the industrialized world ("Telecommunications Structures in the Developing World: An Essay on Telecommunications and Development," hereinafter referred to as "Telecommunications and Development").

Obviously, the range of issues addressed in this second phase was enormously diverse and highly complex. The group of sponsors and others who actively collaborated in the second phase—constituted of service providers, users, and policymaking bodies—made significant contributions to the presentation and analysis of these issues. Ultimately, however, the four papers, and the essay on telecommunications and development, are a synthesis of perspectives that have been influenced by the somewhat idiosyncratic views of the Study's authors.

The caution, therefore, is that each paper be evaluated in its entirety so that individual observations made in the papers can be read in the context of the overall set of documents. This is necessary if the reader is to take complete account of the full range and diversity of views on a particular theme or issues, of the complexity of the questions addressed, and of any possible distortions introduced in the process of capturing the complexity of those issues in what are, relatively, short papers.

The general cautions for the reader of the Study must be underscored with respect to this introductory essay, given both its summary nature and its brevity. Despite what are likely to be inevitable biases, an introduction to the four papers and the final essay seems necessary. This introductory essay is intended to encourage spirited pursuit of the issues touched on here and in the fuller exposition of those issues in the work product of the second phase.

II. OVERARCHING THEMES: LINKAGES AMONG THE PAPERS

One further, important objective of this introductory essay is to breach the artificial boundaries between the different issues addressed in the separate papers. As this essay notes throughout, though the five themes were explored in five distinct documents, the papers are linked in many ways.

At the outset, the close nexus between the issues raised by the offering of value-added services, discussed in "Boundary Lines", and the regulatory questions provoked by the emergence of electronic financial services, discussed in "Transactional Services", should be specially highlighted. A threshold question is whether electronic transactional services are merely a subset of value-added services or whether regulators should treat them altogether differently.

Each of the four papers and the essay treats, to a varying extent, the future institutional arrangements needed for international telecommunications and information services. "Boundary Lines" examines how agreements might be reached between countries that have already decided to allow new value-added or enhanced services. The paper looks critically at the role of international institutions, such as that of the Consultative Committee on International Telegraph and Telephone ("CCITT") of the International Telecommunication Union ("ITU"), in devising such arrangements. It also assesses the possible influence of including trade in services in the new round of the General Agreement on Tariffs and Trade ("GATT") on the future ways of offering services to the public.

Both "European Telecommunications Policy" and "International Facilities" explore the possible options for reaching agreements relating to international telecommunications services and facilities.

Several of the papers address the impact of changes in the competitive environment and industry structure on regulatory policy. In particular, "Boundary Lines", "European Telecommunications Policy", "International Facilities", and "Telecommunications and Development" focus on the procedures for formulating substantive policies. They examine the process of separating responsibility for the operation and the regulation of telecommunications services.

The papers as a whole reflect a certain preoccupation with process as much as with substantive policy. The Study explored the procedures through which policy initiatives are identified and disputes are resolved. The advantage of a focus on procedures is that they do not necessarily dictate specific policy outcomes. Rather, an attention to procedures can lead to the formation of a structure by which conflicts and pressures can be mediated and resolved.

The attention of the second phase of the Study to the advantages of a procedurally-oriented approach, a perspective running throughout much of the work, is by no means intended to minimize the significance of economic or technological factors in shaping policies. Virtually no telecommunications markets are influenced entirely by past regulation or by transitional arrangements designed to increase the role of marketplace forces in providing services. Rather, procedures work as an adjunct to changes in technology to stimulate or regulate markets. In particular, "Boundary Lines", "European Telecommunications Policy" and "International Facilities" explore the interplay between regulation and marketplace forces in structuring the national and international telecommunications sectors.

Given that the initial impetus for the Study was the pace of change in the telecommunications sector, it is not surprising that the papers explore in considerable detail the problems of transition: telecommunications policy today is fundamentally concerned not just with the provision of service but with the movement from traditional industry or institutional arrangements toward a sector reflective of, and responsive to, emerging technological and economic pressures. For example, "International Facilities" is keenly attentive to the challenges faced by Intelsat in attempting to adapt to a new, competitive international environment. Similarly, "Boundary Lines" examines the flexibility of the CCITT—and the ITU itself—to develop the processes for assuring the inter-operability of information-based services that are now springing up around the world. In the same way, "European Telecommunications Policy" looks at some options faced by the Commission of the European Communities as it is forced to react to the shifts in telecommunications policy in several European countries.

One additional point that suffuses the papers is the convergence of telecommunications and trade policies. Both "Boundary Lines" and "Transactional Services" address how the consensus on industry structures and services is collapsing; they focus on the increased role for negotiated arrangements reached on an *ad hoc* basis.

Several of the papers—"Boundary Lines", "International Facilities" and "European Telecommunications Policy"—explore the differences between "negotiated" policy outcomes and policies that derive from traditional regulatory procedures or processes for setting international norms. They examine how new national procedures may complement the trend toward hammering out international telecommunications arrangements in trade negotiations.

One additional important point is the erosion of the never-too-clear boundary between telecommunications and related industry sectors dependent on telecommunications. This convergence of sectors is examined in both "Boundary Lines" and "Transactional Services". Some of the issues that have been raised concern the role of entities traditionally active in the telecommunications sector, the terms by which they can expand into other sectors and, particularly, the safeguards that must be adopted to ensure fair competition in information businesses.

Increasingly, too, there is regulatory attention being paid to the converse proposition: to what extent should a non-telecommunications entity be subject to telecommunications-related regulation? A crucial question concerns the circumstances under which it is appropriate to focus on the nature of the business activity rather than the functional means by which such services are offered. For example, it is important for regulatory purposes to examine whether an entity is primarily involved in offering a banking or brokerage service, which uses telecommunications capabilities, or is engaged principally in the offering of a transmission service.

Having very briefly surveyed some overlapping issues, and the relationship among the papers, the remainder of this introductory essay will identify the principal issues within each of the four separate papers and the essay. As noted above, the discussion here must be rather summary. For a more extended discussion of the issues, the papers and the essay themselves should be examined. To facilitate such examination, a cross-reference to the section in each paper in which such discussion appears has been placed at the end of the subsections of this essay, or wherever else might be appropriate.

III. ISSUES RAISED BY "BOUNDARY LINES"

The paper entitled "Boundary Lines" is the most direct continuation of the work of the first phase of the Study. The discussion in this paper highlights developments in telecommunications policy since the completion of the first phase in mid-1985. In addition, it focuses in some depth on the environment in Australia, which was not examined in Phase I, on the arrangements for structuring international value-added services, and on the importance of new mechanisms—bilateral and multilateral—for addressing new complexities in the international sector.

A. United States

In almost all the major industrialized countries, policymakers have continued to wrestle with the problems of defining, and regulating, value-added or enhanced services. Even in the United States, where it had been thought that the *Computer II* distinction seemed entrenched, the Federal Communications Commission ("FCC") has expended considerable resources in the *Computer III* proceeding. Initially thinking that it might move toward a marketplace scheme for assessing the appropriate regulatory framework, the FCC ultimately retained the "basic"/"enhanced" dichotomy. In its ongoing examination in the *Computer III* proceeding and in its docket aimed at options for deregulating basic services, the Commission continues, however, to be intrigued by the role of marketplace forces in guiding the need for regulation, if not supplanting it altogether. "Boundary Lines", Sections II.B and II.D.

B. United Kingdom

Outside the U.S., much of the emphasis of the efforts to achieve definitional harmony seems to have moved from attempting to identify services subject to a more liberal regime toward developing regulatory policies that prescribe services that may not be offered competitively. In the United Kingdom, for example, the Department of Trade and Industry ("DTI") abandoned an effort to delineate two categories of services that were to be offered under a liberalized framework: value-added services and managed data network services ("MDNS"). The DTI intended MDNS to embrace value-added services that use leased lines to serve a broad and undifferentiated group of customers.

In the end, however, it proved too confusing to distinguish between value-added and MDNS. Therefore, the DTI's Value-Added and Data Services Class Licence, finally released in April 1987, applies basically the same regulatory requirements to all value-added services. While liberalizing data services, the DTI continues, however, to restrict the resale of voice services, in particular switched voice services, and various types of "telex" services. A Licence also imposes special regulatory requirements on large service providers and on those offering "trilateral services", which are services offered to unaffiliated third parties.

The relatively straightforward approach taken by the British has nevertheless raised difficulties for large groups of customers who wish to continue their special corporate networking activities. These activities initially had been included in the Branch Systems General Licence. Finally, however, the government decided that regulatory restrictions relating to shared voice networks used by particular companies or groups of companies with similar interests should be included in the Value-Added and Data Services Class Licence. Nevertheless, the result of fusing the value-added licence and the set of restrictions applicable to private networks has resulted in what is a highly complex regulatory document indeed. "Boundary Lines", Section III.B.

One other major step taken by the British was to treat all providers of value-added services essentially alike. Thus, entities that offer specialized services to a particular business sector—such as banking, brokerage or electronic publishing—are regulated much like providers of services such as format or protocol conversion, which are more closely related to traditional telecommunications services. Entities in both categories are subject to regulatory strictures that govern pricing practices and proscribe rate discrimination.

Large and "trilateral service" providers subject to the Value-Added and Data Services Class Licence are required to comply with the standards of Open Systems Interconnection. They must do so within a particular period of time after the adoption of the internationally accepted standard. This requirement has been imposed despite the fact that many specialized entities serving particular industry groups may also, as a commercial matter, be required to conform with norms that have evolved in their particular industry sector.

C. France

In France, policymakers have begun exploring the possible liberalization of services by adopting a distinction between open and closed groups. This approach aims to impose greater regulatory burdens—or possibly higher tariffs—on networks that are oriented, like most PTT services, toward the general public.

Regulatory policies based on distinctions between open and closed networks, however, face all the definitional and practical questions that have confronted—and confounded—efforts to define value-added services. Should closed networks be defined on the basis of an existing ownership interest between a company and its subsidiaries? Between a company and other companies linked through contractual or other ties? Should the groups be limited to a particular industry sector, such as airlines or banking? If the dichotomy between "open" and "closed" does, to some extent, turn on whether the members of the group are engaged in a similar business activity, such a regulatory boundary line will be hard put to take account of the fact that the distinctions between industrial sectors are collapsing. The business of a sector, such as airlines, is inevitably entangled with other sectors, such as the provision of credit card or tourism-oriented services. "Boundary Lines", Section V.C.

Some of the discussion in "Transactional Services", which highlights the use of telecommunications networks to create new markets, is most relevant to the French effort to regulate on the basis of "open" or "closed" groupings. "Transactional Services", Section IV. These electronic markets tie together many of the entities involved in a particular sector and they facilitate services among corporate entities that have transactional ties. This flexibility may have to extend beyond merely according more leeway to create a single network linking different entities with transactional ties. It may have to accommodate the interconnection of different specialized corporate networks including one or more entities in a particular industry sector. Such practices are now discouraged by the D-Series Recommendations of the CCITT and could lead to difficulties under the proposed French scheme.

In France, keen attention is paid to the need for infusing information systems into the activities of other business sectors. Much of French policy has been predicated on the advantages of liberalizing the information services sector. Nevertheless, even the French have an inclination to deal with new information-based services as a regulatable activity akin to a telecommunications service rather than as an activity of a customer of the telecommunications provider. The distinction between the provider of a telecommunications service and a customer, however, remains important for several reasons. Telecommunications providers must adhere to pricing and other norms. As a "customer", the offeror of a service may be able to avoid disclosing information about the structure of an information network—details about services and protocols—to the provider (and would-be competitor) of an underlying service. "Transactional Services", Section IV.

D. Federal Republic of Germany

In the Federal Republic of Germany, the pace of change has been more deliberate. The Deutsche Bundespost has proceeded with developing tariffing changes. At the same time, many questions concerning the scope of competition in value-added services are being considered by the Witte Commission, a government commission which has been studying the future role of the Bundespost since it was constituted in early 1985.

One important element of the German approach has been to predicate liberalization of value-added services that use leased lines on shifts in tariffs. These policy changees would not necessarily mean the adoption of a new, license-based regime. Rather, they would allow broad leeway to resell or share private leased lines that are priced on the basis of usage. "Boundary Lines", Section XI.A.

Many observers note that usage-based pricing is intended to compensate for the fact that German intercity tariffs for public switched services are determined on a basis that includes substantial subsidies to maintain postal services and a rate structure aimed at ensuring universal service. Faced with a difficult political problem in removing these entrenched subsidies, German policymakers have declined to differentiate between value-added services, as have some other European policymakers. Instead, they insist that any distinction between pure resale of voice circuits and other types of services is inherently unworkable. They rely instead on a policy favoring liberalization of all uses of private line services, provided that a usage-sensitive tariff is adopted to remove the incentive to skim off the cream.

The problem with the German approach is, however, that, while it may discourage cream skimming by resellers, it may also discourage innovation in the use of new information services by other entities in industry sectors highly dependent on telecommunications. Indeed, many observers see German tariff policies as likely to discourage investment by major multinational entities in hubs for their international networks. "Boundary Lines", Section XI.B.

E. Elsewhere in Europe

Several other countries in Europe seem to be following the approach being staked out in the U.K. toward defining value-added services. For example, the Dutch seem to be keeping a watchful competitive eye on policy changes in the U.K. that might affect the likelihood that London—as opposed to Amsterdam—would gain the edge as a hub for European services. "Boundary Lines", Section VI.

In Spain, new legislation is being considered that would liberalize value-added services considerably. Resale would be proscribed and a monopoly would be maintained over transmission services. "Boundary Lines", Section X.

F. Tariffing as an Adjunct to Liberalization

The German attempt to liberalize network usage on the basis of a new, usage-based tariff structure is an alternative approach to the drawing of boundary lines. Nevertheless, it may be difficult to sustain usage-based tariffs in light of the current environment of rivalry in Europe.

Recently, for example, British Telecom informed many of its major international customers that it would no longer apply the D.6 Recommendations of the CCITT (which imply the imposition of usage-sensitive tariffs) to joint services, or services involving related customers. This practical step by British Telecom may chill the willingness of European administrations other than the Bundespost to impose new tariff structures on providers or configurations of value-added services.

Influenced, in part by the German policies, by the need to develop new economic or regulatory arrangements for the provision of value-added services, and by an interest in increasing network utilization, other countries are reviewing the possibility of installing new tariff structures. The French, for example, in exploring the distinction between "open" and "closed" networks seem to believe that incremental tariff charges should be imposed on networks open to "third parties", howsoever that term may come to be defined. "Boundary Lines", Section XIII.A, "European Telecommunications Policy", Sections II.A and II.B.

The adoption of new tariff structures raises a series of complex issues for telecommunications administrations and for economic planners outside the telecommunications sector itself. Should different types of users of leased lines be subject to different rate structures? Would new, usage-based structures create disincentives to innovate in developing new electronic markets or new techniques of disseminating information within an industry sector? Would what users view as the economic disincentives of usage-based tariffs discourage new uses of the networks, thereby forestalling increased utilization of transmission services and, consequently, preventing increased revenues?

Might the development of usage-based rate structures affect the interest of telecommunications providers that would otherwise be keen to compete in the provision of new services? If such providers do wish to offer competitive offerings (*i.e.*, other than transmission), how can comparable rates be charged to entities both within and outside the administration intending to provide similar services? In some countries, the adoption of new tariff structures might encourage the development of regulatory pressure—in bodies concerned with competition or economic policy—to oppose expansion by the telecommunications administration into other sectors. Might there be a trade-off between the implementation of new tariff structures and permitting the administration to diversify into new fields?

These difficult questions are now being considered in many policy circles—by national policymakers and at the European Commission. Many of the answers are still in the process of being formulated.

The lines of the argument are beginning to crystallize. Some telecommunications administrations—in Germany, perhaps in France—believe that they should, through the implementation of new tariff structures, be able to take advantage of the business opportunities made possible by the demand for new information services. Other policymakers question whether such a stance is consistent with the traditional concept of the role of a "carrier".

G. The Development of Procedures and Oversight Institutions

A significant development noted in the first phase of the Study was the interrelationship between changes in industry structure and policies and in the mechanisms charged with regulatory oversight. The preceding discussion, which focused on the debate about the advantages and disadvantages of new tariff structures, is integrally related, for example, to questions about the procedures by which such new tariffs might be established.

In this connection, if there are departures from historic rate levels, what is the basis of establishing any new rates? What overall pricing principles might apply? How might these principles be applied in practice in particular countries or to particular sets of services? To what extent will the carriers articulate questions about the procedures by which any such new pricing arrangements might be established? Will carriers be in a position to gather and supply to regulators the relevant economic information—cost and pricing data—necessary for an open discussion of pricing alternatives? *See, e.g.,* "Boundary Lines", Sections III.C (U.K.), IV.B (Japan), and XIII.B.

In many countries the means for overseeing transitions in pricing policies are not well developed. Historically, pricing has been entirely internal to the the PTTs. With the tendency to separate regulatory and operational functions, issues of pricing may be addressed on an arm's-length basis between operators and regulators; additionally, there might be leeway for participation by the spectrum of interests affected by rate adjustments.

Procedural adjustments in pricing practices are, however, only part of the trend toward developing new regulatory mechanisms that is being accelerated by policies liberalizing value-added services. Worldwide, there has been much attention paid to creating new regulatory bodies that are separated formally from the provision of telecommunications services. "Boundary Lines", Section XIII.C.

Oftel in the U.K. has, of course, taken a leading role in formulating the necessary transitional arrangements in the aftermath of the 1984 Telecommunications Law. It assisted in negotiating access arrangements between British Telecom and Mercury for switched voice services. Oftel has also been a focal point for discussion of the various proposals for, and drafts of, the value-added licenses. In the same way, it has become increasingly entangled in pricing issues, especially in connection with oversight of British Telecom's proposals to restructure rates to establish a new balance between local and intercity charges. "Boundary Lines", Section III.B.

Oftel has carried out its tasks in a manner significantly different from that of the FCC or even the Canadian Radio-television and Telecommunications Commission. Oftel has acted as a mediator or arbiter between differing interests; far more so than has the FCC, it has avoided the introduction of formalized administrative procedures such as formal rulemaking proceedings, the retention of comments in public files, and the issuance of lengthy administrative orders detailing the contentions of parties and explaining in detail the reasons for rejecting or accepting such contentions. Proceeding as it has, Oftel has crisply addressed the agenda of issues raised by the transition in the U.K.

In France, the newly-established Commission Nationale des Communications et Libertés ("CNCL") has sometimes been viewed as the regulatory institution closest in concept to the FCC. Yet, the CNCL has still to be vested with significant jurisdiction to oversee the emergence of value-added services or to establish any of the regulatory conditions that might affect the role of the Direction Générale des Télécommunications ("DGT") regarding such services. The nature and focus of any such regulatory responsibilities will be determined when—and if—a telecommunications law is adopted by the end of 1987 or after the French Presidential elections in 1988. "Boundary Lines", Section V.C.

A special directorate within the office of the French Minister of Posts and Telecommunications is examining the possible provisions of this law. This office, which is independent of but is working closely with the DGT, is now facing some difficult practical problems regarding the structure of any regulatory process.

Several issues must be addressed. Can a regulatory body with a membership of thirteen—many without extensive experience in the telecommunications field—devise the transitional measures necessary to broaden the competition faced by the DGT? Where will the expert staff come from? Should the CNCL merely advise the Minister on options for developing policy? If so, how could the CNCL and policymakers avoid substantial delay in formulating the issues to be resolved? Where would the real center for decisionmaking reside? Would affected interests have to cope with two separate sets of procedures? Would the same decisionmaking criteria and administrative processes be followed by each body?

These issues are not yet resolved in France. Elsewhere, in Finland, the Netherlands, Spain, and even in the developing world, administrations will face similar issues as they seek to introduce new mechanisms for regulation. "Boundary Lines", Sections VII.C, VI.C and X.B; "European Telecommunications Policy", Section VII.A; and "Telecommunications and Development", Section IV.B.

H. Regulatory and Competition Policy

In addition to developing procedures and institutions, policymakers must establish a relationship between regulatory and competition policy. The critical issues concern what safeguards might be necessary to assure the emergence of fair competition between the established service providers and new competitors. More specifically, on what basis will the established provider be able to obtain access to the underlying services and facilities necessary to expand into new value-added, information-related, or data services? What transmission services, and what components of such services, will be available to competitors of the facilities providers?

Such issues must be faced in specific, substantive terms. Often overlooked, however, is the fact that they raise institutional concerns about the relationship of telecommunications authorities and officials charged with competition policy.

In the U.K. for example, Oftel must consult with the Office of Fair

Trading and the Monopolies and Mergers Commission when the terms of a license for a public telecommunications operator ("PTO") are modified substantially. The Deutsche Bundespost has an ongoing dialogue with the Monopolies Commission. In the U.S., of course, in the aftermath of the Modified Final Judgment—but more significantly long before that time—the Department of Justice regularly offered its views on the competitive implications of the new rules of the game. In Europe, within the European Commission, D.G. XIII, which has jurisdiction over telecommunications policy, and D.G. IV, vested with responsibility for competition policy, engage in an ongoing dialogue.

The point is, of course, a direct and simple one. It is difficult to devise new regulatory structures without discussing competition policy. *See e.g.,* "Boundary Lines", Section II.D; "European Telecommunications Policy", Sections VI.A and VIII.D.

I. A Dialogue Among Regulators

In Phase II of the Study developments concerning regulatory policies are noted and discussed with emphasis. Specifically, in structuring international services, "Boundary Lines" suggests that it might be useful for regulatory bodies developing nationally to meet or to exchange information. Further, "European Telecommunications Policy" points out the advantages of an approach centered around having national policymakers, perhaps under the auspices of the European Commission, participate in such discussions. "Boundary Lines", Section XIV.F; "European Telecommunications Policy", Section XIII.D.

J. Telecommunications and Trade: Market Access

In structuring international services, and in developing national regulatory arrangements, "Boundary Lines" highlights the importance of paying close attention to the relationship between market access for providers of telecommunications and related services and regulatory institutions. The regulatory process can be used as an outlet for dealing with transitional issues, once framework agreements are established for relationships in telecommunications trade.

For example, if an entity faces difficulties in entering a foreign market based on problems with access to facilities, pricing issues, or concerns about competition, such issues will best be resolved through a forum where such foreign-owned entities can present their views openly and freely. A regulatory forum is also likely to put foreign-owned and domestic competitors in an equivalent position. Indeed, it may allow or encourage the formation of groups or coalitions of similarly situated industry participants, *e.g.,* providers of value-added services who are, in a parallel way, attempting to influence the regulatory process. "Boundary Lines", Section XIV.F.

K. Access to Underlying Services: CEI and ONA in the USA

The discussions about enhanced or value-added services in the international arena have moved away from attempts to "define" such services. Much of the thrust of the discussions has been focused on the operational relationship between the providers of underlying transmission facilities and the provision of value-added, information-based, or transactional services that rely on such facilities.

The FCC's *Computer III* decision was the first effort at addressing these issues of access to underlying facilities. As detailed at some length in Sections II.B and II.C of "Boundary Lines", the FCC has established two new regulatory concepts known as comparably efficient interconnection ("CEI") and Open Network Architecture ("ONA"). Essentially, CEI requires that a dominant provider of underlying or basic services offer an enhanced service provider interconnection arrangements that are "comparably efficient" to those provided by such underlying service provider to an enhanced service provider with which it is affiliated.

The CEI obligations have been imposed primarily on the Bell Operating Companies ("BOCs") because of their role in providing local exchange services. (The FCC initially concluded that CEI obligations should be imposed on AT&T; however, in response to AT&T's Petition for Reconsideration to its initial decision in the *Computer III* proceeding, the FCC eased this requirement.) In short, a carrier subject to CEI requirements does not have to offer a specified set of network functionalities, nor must it offer interconnection that is "equal" or at its central switching premises—just interconnection that is comparable to that of which it avails itself in offering an enhanced service.

By contrast, ONA requires the elaboration of a set of "network primitives" that a carrier intends to make available. ONA obligations are now being defined through a series of informal meetings known as the ONA Forum, where carriers and users meet to hammer out future arrangements. Inasmuch as the FCC has declined to take an active role in this process, it is, in principle, possible for each BOC's ONA plan to differ from that of the others. There are, however, certainly strong pressures from users and the BOCs themselves to assure inter-operability for new services.

It is proving fairly difficult in practice to give concrete meaning to the FCC's concept of ONA. Without referring to specific services or applications it is difficult to define interconnection configurations. Nevertheless, the FCC's effort is likely to stimulate the provision of value-added services. "Boundary Lines", Sections II.B and II.C.

The ONA concept is now being examined overseas. A group within the European Commission is reviewing the relevance of ONA in the European context. "European Telecommunications Policy", Section VIII.C.

One issue of particular importance is how the emergence of ONA will affect the provision of international value-added services. Great efforts have been made to assure that new services can be uniformly offered among the various BOCs and across the United States. Less attention has been directed at how value-added services that are based on network components—such as would be made available in an ONA environment—might evolve internationally. Such inattention is largely due to the fact that most information-based services will not be offered only within a single market. "Boundary Lines", Section XIV.B.

Policymakers in the U.S. and elsewhere will have to determine whether the concept of ONA should be expanded internationally. The CCITT or some other *ad hoc* process, by contrast, could be used as the basis for assuring that value-added and other new services are provided internationally. As a threshold matter, more attention must be paid to the international dimension of the ONA discussions now under way in the U.S. Ultimately, the issues of compatibility—or lack thereof—of interconnection arrangements for new services may have to be resolved in a bilateral negotiating process. "Boundary Lines", Sections XIV.B and XIV.F.

L. Enhanced or Value-Added Services: The International Dimension

As described in "Boundary Lines", until recently policymakers were virtually solely preoccupied with the problems raised by devising and refining new national policies for the provision of value-added services. With the development of new, liberalizing policies in the U.S., U.K., Japan, and other countries, policymakers are coming to understand that the national approaches differ: the definitions of "enhanced services" in the U.S., "value-added services" in the U.K., and "Type II" entities in Japan are not congruent.

Specifically, the scope of activities of Type II entities in Japan is broader than the categories of enhanced services in the U.S. or value-added services in the U.K. That is, in principle, Type II services could include many types of services that could be classified as "basic" in the U.S., which common carriers would be likely to offer.

These discrepancies between national regulatory policies—even among countries with liberal or open entry policies—make the task of establishing a framework for international value-added services extremely vexing. The most fundamental issues concern how such services should be perceived or classified. Are they like traditional carrier services? Or, do they most closely resemble the activities of users or "customers" of international carriers?

One of the critical questions with which policymakers are wrestling is whether new offerings that serve third parties might be inconsistent with the D-Series Recommendations of the CCITT; these Recommendations restrict the use of a leased line to the business of the "customer" of those lines (*i.e.*, the lessee). Several different approaches for dealing with this question are considered in "Boundary Lines". "Boundary Lines", Section XIV.

On the one hand, some administrations stress that the CCITT Recommendations are not binding and that they need not be applied by administrations that reach bilateral arrangements. Such arrangements are viewed as fully consistent with the International Telecommunication Convention, which emphasizes the essential place of agreements among administrations in the international regime.

On the other hand, other administrations, and the Japanese in particular, seem to be reluctant to depart from the CCITT Recommendations, sometimes even characterizing them as binding. Certainly, the Japanese place great stress on maintaining an international consensus with regard to the structure of service arrangements. Thus, they have been exploring the extent to which the provider of an international value-added service might be acting differently from the traditional activity of a "customer" of a carrier. One important study group in Japan has recommended that operators of international value-added services should be treated as recognized private operating agencies ("RPOAs"). "Boundary Lines", Section XIV.D.

The FCC and others in the U.S. have been reluctant to resort to a scheme that would impose, on a mandatory basis, RPOA status on the providers of international value-added services. Among the concerns about relying on RPOA status has been the fact that the adoption of such a formal regulatory designation might encourage administrations to impose restrictions on entry or other telecommunications-related regulations. In countries with open entry policies, such burdens might not be significant; elsewhere, however, they might result in serious impediments. "Boundary Lines", Section XIV.C.

The reluctance on the part of U.S. policymakers to embrace the RPOA concept (due to the triggering effect it might have in other administrations) stems, in part, from the fact that many value-added services encompass a broad range of activities which, it is believed, ought not to be subject to telecommunications-based regulations. Such services include offerings by entities in the financial services or electronic publishing sectors. As discussed in greater depth in Section IV of this essay, the very proliferation of different regulatory regimes could itself establish barriers to the provision of such services.

One approach that does not rely on the concept of an RPOA might hinge on examining the provision of value-added services as part of the range of activities carried out by the users—the "customers"—of carriers. Such activities increasingly depend on flexibility in network usage; in the case of an electronic trading system, a customer of a leased line—and the manager of a trading service—might want the ability to connect clients to a source supplying pricing information that would then allow them to enter into transactions. Such a trading system also may require connecting different private networks.

Such activities create considerable pressure for a more liberal approach to the terms and conditions under which leased lines are made available. Because such flexibility may not be available where a restrictive reading of the CCITT Recommendations obtains, this approach would focus those

Recommendations on simple or pure resale rather than on various specialized or value-added services.

Discussions over the appropriate framework for the provision of international value-added services are of extraordinary importance. They are taking place in both bilateral and multilateral settings; they may require re-examination of the distinction between a "carrier" and its "customer". It is likely that pressure will build for the recognition of "hybrid" regulatory categories. These developments will warrant close attention to assure the development of a coherent future framework for new electronic services. "Boundary Lines," Section XIV.F.

IV. ISSUES RAISED BY "TRANSACTIONAL SERVICES"

The genesis of the paper entitled "Transactional Services" is the growing interrelationship between the telecommunications and financial services industries. The paper is intended to open a dialogue between these two sectors, the future development of which is clearly intertwined.

A. The Interdependence of Two Sectors

In many countries, such as the Netherlands and the U.K. for example, liberalization of the telecommunications and financial sectors is moving in step, with developments in one sector reinforcing those in the other. On the one hand, it is undoubtedly the case that enhanced flexibility in the telecommunications field has created new opportunities for electronic financial services. On the other hand, pressures for telecommunications services from the financial sector are forcing changes in telecommunications policies. By way of illustration, observers note that the financial community is setting the pace for the development of international telecommunications services—just as the maritime and aviation communities had been the prime movers for international communications in the past.

Despite the interdependence of the two sectors, however, there is still little real dialogue between their business leaders and policymakers. Telecommunications, until recently, had been considered only a "back office concern", one not essential to the future profitability and competitiveness of financial institutions. Likewise, from the wary perspective of the providers of telecommunications services, banks and other financial institutions are merely another set of large customers with ambitions to infringe on the PTT's turf.

"Transactional Services" aims to be a basis for exploratory talks between the sectors. The financial community needs to take a more active role in influencing telecommunications policy. It can work with providers of telecommunications services to assure that pricing is more cost-based and internationally competitive and to develop efficient, modern management structures that encourage efficient financing practices and permit administrations to recruit and retain skilled marketing and software engineering personnel.

In turn, telecommunications officials would benefit from a better understanding of the evolving nature of electronic financial markets. The financial community needs a certain autonomy to structure and organize these markets, to assure the security and integrity of transactions over these new systems. By their nature, transactional systems link groups of customers across industry lines; thus, they often defy the past benchmarks devised by telecommunications regulators.

Telecommunications officials, by grasping more concretely the nature of these services—and regulatory issues outside the telecommunications field that may influence or inhibit the introduction of new electronic techniques—can adopt strategies and build alliances that facilitate the emergence of new services. In so doing, they can stimulate new market activities, new and innovative uses of telecommunications services, and thus increase usage of the network itself. Increasing the exchange of information may, therefore, be of mutual benefit to the telecommunications and related sectors. "Transactional Services," Sections III.F and IV.

B. The Development of Electronic Networks and Markets

As "Transactional Services" notes, it is not just the financial sector that is now providing both challenges and opportunities for the telecommunications sector. More broadly, electronic networks are becoming the basis for transactional systems linking manufacturers, distributors, and retailers. Such distribution systems are, of course, evolving independently through financial institutions; these are installing electronic networks to facilitate payment through credit or debit cards, or to allow customers to obtain cash or execute banking transactions at locations remote from the main bank office or at home.

The paper also traces the rapid emergence of electronic markets that link financial institutions. Such electronic markets facilitate trading in foreign exchange, securities, commercial paper, or other financial instruments. The evolution of these markets is just beginning; however, they are changing the traditional structure of markets by moving trading away from a specific place or geographic location. Links among the trading rooms of major financial houses—and through connections between national markets that were once separate from each other—comprise the future of national and international trading. "Transactional Services," Section II.

As a first step toward building a bridge among disparate communities, "Transactional Services" largely focuses on attempts to piece together impressionistic evidence of these developments. Some practical observations are offered in the paper; a summary of some of these follows.

C. Different Sectors, Different Issues

The term electronic financial services embraces a host of many different offerings in different sectors. It is, therefore, extremely difficult to generalize about the telecommunications implications of those services or to address the issues that they raise in abstract terms. "Transactional Services" notes that there are several disparate kinds of services, each of which raises its own set of regulatory issues. "Transactional Services," Section II.E.

Systems intended to facilitate electronic payments by consumers, for example, often raise issues involving access to local distribution facilities. The structure of tariffs for local services—or the availability of bypass or non-wireline services—are often of great importance for new electronic financial services.

Many such localized consumer- or retailer-oriented services do evolve through co-operation among financial institutions; such services might make use of common point-of-sale terminals or cash dispensers. For such services, telecommunications-related concerns relating to the shared use of private lines and the interconnection of different networks operated by separate financial institutions can be significant.

By contrast, in reviewing the telecommunications-based issues raised by links among national exchanges or financial institutions in different countries, more importance arises from the availability, pricing, and flexibility of use of leased circuits. "Transactional Services", Section III.E.

D. Should Telecommunications Regulation be Applied to New Transactional Networks?

The newly-developing regulatory schemes for value-added services are increasingly likely to collide with the development of electronic transactional services. If such transactional networks are deemed to be value-added services, should telecommunications-oriented regulation apply to several of their key operational aspects?

One issue involves the pricing of the electronic transactional services. Should issues relating to pricing, which may implicate fair trading or price discrimination in the telecommunications sector, be addressed from the standpoint of a telecommunications regulator or from that of a regulator overseeing the financial or transactional service itself? Similarly, should network and protocol standardization be dealt with as telecommunications issues or as properly determined by the providers of what are, essentially, other-than-telecommunications services?

Put more simply, who should determine the future operational standards for electronic financial or transactional services? Telecommunications regulators, or regulators for the industry in which the service is provided? This fundamental question cannot be readily answered in black and white terms. What is certain is that regulators in each sector will need to establish a dialogue relating to the interfaces and operating protocols that are necessary to deliver electronic services to customers. "Transactional Services", Sections III.F and IV.

E. Electronic Markets, the CCITT, and the Use of Leased Circuits

A principal focus of "Transactional Services" beyond issues raised at the national level is the restrictions imposed by the CCITT Recommendations on the use of leased circuits. Increasingly, the tension between the emergence of electronic transactional markets and the Recommendations is causing points of stress that are identified in the paper.

The markets of the future will be assembled by linking a large number of intermediaries and then connecting the clients of the intermediaries into an "electronic market". That is, such a market may not necessarily be organized around a specific co-operative entity—a stock exchange or an organization such as the Society for Worldwide Interbank Financial Telecommunication ("SWIFT"). Rather, a market may result from the connection of unaffiliated players—different banks or securities firms. Indeed, whereas markets have been defined along classic industry lines—banking or securities, for example—sectoral reforms are now eroding these boundaries.

Practically speaking, these developments may well mean that the private line networks of separate firms or organizations will eventually be connected. Moreover, once these inter-institutional markets are brought into existence, they will then need to be tied with customers. In turn, customers will have to obtain access to such markets through the switched network.

These developments create substantial friction with the D-Series CCITT Recommendations. Based on these Recommendations, many administrations discourage the interconnection of private line networks. They also look askance at connecting both ends of a leased circuit to the public switched network. "Transactional Services", Section III.E.

Conventionally, of course, such restrictions have been applied to maintain distinctions between private leased circuits and public switched services—which have often been priced on a different basis and to preserve the monopoly of an administration. To ensure that leased circuits are not substituted for public switched services, telecommunications officials impose such tariff-related restrictions to prevent arbitrage of private line networks. The justification offered by administrations is the prevention of cream-skimming by predatory resellers.

However, "Transactional Services" points out that many of the new electronic market services are not intended to substitute for the public switched network. Rather, they are, deliberately, activities different from telecommunications. Instead of drawing traffic away from existing services, they will increase usage and generate revenues for administrations. "Transactional Services", Section III.F.

The ultimate question, of course, is not how to interpret or apply the CCITT Recommendations to the new electronic market services. As noted earlier in this essay, in Section III.F, the real focus of discussion concerns pricing: instead of imposing regulatory conditions on the usage of leased lines, can the potential for arbitrage be minimized through repricing—either by moving the prices of public switched services closer to costs or by adopting policies aimed at harmonizing the rates of switched and leased line services?

Users view tariff harmonization and the adoption of usage-based pricing as disrupting and impeding the introduction of services. Departing from the flat-rate structures of today is seen as hampering the emergence of electronic markets, to the detriment of the revenue flow of administrations. In the years ahead, both telecommunications and other policymakers will increase their attention to these core economic issues.

F. Market Access and Two-Tier Regulation

The issues of national regulation involved in developing an electronic financial or market service are difficult. However, the complexities are increased manifold in attempting to establish such services on a transnational basis.

The complexity is introduced by the fact that such arrangements may involve two tiers of regulation and negotiation in each country in which the service is to be provided. The first tier involves the infrastructure of facilities and services—*i.e.*, the element of "value" added to the transmission service. The second tier involves the specific service (brokerage, or commodities trading, for example), which may itself be subject to non-telecommunications regulation. At the first tier, for example, a provider of an electronic financial service may need to obtain approval to use a leased line network from overseas; at the second tier, it usually has to secure necessary approvals from a ministry of finance. "Transactional Services", Section IV.

Policymakers should examine the implications for the provision of service in having to deal with the hurdles posed by two tiers of regulation. If it is too difficult or complex for a provider to obtain access to the infrastructure, progress in offering specific services may be impeded significantly. Particular attention should be paid to the problems created by the presence of an array of discordant requirements for the provision of an international value-added service.

"Transactional Services" notes that there are two possible approaches to minimizing the entry barriers for new electronic services. One would deal with such services as activities of a "customer" of a leased line and reduce or eliminate altogether regulation by telecommunications authorities. What would be left would be the second tier: any regulation would originate in the sector in which the service is provided.

A second approach, which is also discussed in "European Telecommunications Policy", examines whether national regulators might be able to rely on regulation imposed by the country in which the service originates. Inconsistent regulations imposed by both the country of origination and delivery may, if this approach is not adopted, make it impossible to develop transnational services. "Transactional Services", Section IV; "European Telecommunications Policy", Section VI.E.

The existence of troubling inconsistencies between regulatory schemes at either the first or second tier is a fact that is only now beginning to emerge. Officials charged with responsibilities for negotiating away barriers to trade are still grappling with the general principles that should apply to trade in services. They have not yet begun to confront the complexities of harmonizing or co-ordinating the differences between national regulatory regimes that govern the terms by which electronic transactional services can be provided.

To date, there is little dialogue between trade officials having responsibility for market access in the telecommunications and information services sectors and officials with responsibility for similar issues in the financial or other sectors. In the United States, for example, the responsibility for dealing with access in the financial sector is vested in the Treasury Department; other trade in services issues are handled by the U.S. Trade Representative and by the Department of Commerce. Inevitably, questions of how to co-ordinate national, let alone international, policymaking for trade in electronic services will arise outside the U.S. as well.

G. The Development of Electronic Markets for Securities and Other Financial Instruments

Much attention is given in "Transactional Services" to the various scenarios by which new electronic financial services and markets are emerging. One section of the paper, for example, examines in detail the problems in linking various European stock exchanges to form an integrated market. The barriers to such integration are complex; they impede even the prospects for a common quotation system, such as the European Inter Bourse Data Information System ("IDIS"). These issues arise owing to substantial differences in quotation systems among the European exchanges—some are auction-based and others have moved toward continuous pricing. In addition, the national exchanges establish their own requirements regarding the type of financial institution that can participate in trading activities. Diverse national regulations also apply to the arrangements for clearing transactions. "Transactional Services", Section III.C.

These restrictions are now subject to intense pressures due to fierce and growing inter-market competition. Nevertheless, some European exchanges, in France and Italy, for example, have essentially limited trading to *agents de change* or brokers; the role of banks in dealing in securities is confined, though this is now changing in France. In other markets, in the Federal Republic of Germany, in particular, the banks play a major role.

Parallel with the activities carried out on the well-established trading floors, a substantial amount of informal trading outside the formal arrangements has emerged both in various national environments and internationally. Such off-floor trading is carried out among major banks and financial institutions by telephone or via other telecommunications-based contacts. Thus, electronic capabilities have significance for both traditional trading activity and the more informal business networks that are now evolving. "Transactional Services", Section II.E.

Informal information-based trading systems may overtake traditional exchanges if national regulators are not able to resolve differences in trading and clearing rules. It may not be possible to establish a wholly integrated quotation and trading system. In the absence of such a system, however, large traders will have substantial incentives to assemble different systems of quotation either from the national exchanges themselves or from independent vendors of financial information. The movement toward off-market execution and clearing will slowly accelerate as international networks expand to facilitate transactions by participants from outside a national market. In short, informal systems will intensify pressures for harmonization and integration of diverse national trading systems.

Another factor of importance is the extent to which pressures will intensify to formalize and regulate informal systems of dealing once they become centered around computer systems. It may be harder to assert jurisdiction over an informal market, created by telephonic and telex links, than to regulate a market with a computer system at its core.

Several novel and difficult policy issues will be presented to regulators. As computer-based markets develop, what should be the "situs" of the market for purposes of regulation? Should it be where the processing system is located? Or, should it depend on where the transaction is initiated? When should a national regulator deem that a security is offered in a market via an electronic exchange? Does the offering take place when the quotation service is available on a screen through a local concentrator or does it occur when access is obtained to an off-shore data base? What are the implications of extending national regulation to foreign exchanges or broker dealers operating within a jurisdiction via a telecommunications network? "Transactional Services", Section III.D.

Although "Transactional Services" does not address these questions comprehensively, it does begin to identify some of the issues that will be faced. That these issues are not simply academic is demonstrated by the recent announcement of the Association of International Bond Dealers ("AIBD") that it was delaying implementation of a new electronic exchange for Eurobonds; traders had been concerned that the impact of the new system on their traditional trading practices would be adverse. To date, the Eurobond market has been unregulated, informal, and international in scope. Had the AIBD system come on-line, it would have been subject to the jurisdiction of the U.K. Financial Services Act—an outcome that might have resulted in some hard scrutiny of non-U.K. participants in the market.

In summary, "Transactional Services" addresses a highly complex, rapidly evolving area in which there are far more questions than answers. Indeed, many questions have not yet been formulated. The paper is a first, tentative look at some of the issues and is intended to stimulate further discussion and analysis.

V. ISSUES RAISED BY "EUROPEAN TELECOMMUNICATIONS POLICY"

The first phase of the Study contained an initial look at the problems of, and issues raised by, the need for and emergence of a European telecommunications policy. The changes in national European policies, the growing divergence in national schemes, the intensified level of global competition in the international telecommunications sector, and the increasing activity of the European Commission (as manifested in its soon-to-be-released Green Paper on European telecommunications policy) all warranted a more detailed exploration of developments in Europe in Phase II.

A. A Broad and Independent Perspective

The product of this examination, "European Telecommunications Policy", addresses, therefore, from both a broad and a very independent perspective, some of the options and approaches toward European policies. In large part, it seeks to take into account, but essentially to stand back from, the precise details of national developments or alternatives currently being considered by the European Commission.

It should be noted that the paper articulates views that have been distilled from a great number of discussions with observers of the European scene. However, more than some of the other papers in Phase II, it is suffused with the perspectives of its authors, who, as non-Europeans, still attach enormous importance to the struggle to establish an integrated market in Europe for telecommunications and information services. Although there may be advantages to such independence, the paper no doubt suffers somewhat from being detached from the political pressures with which the European Commission must now wrestle.

B. Economic Pressures on the PTTs

At the outset, "European Telecommunications Policy" describes some of the economic pressures faced by European PTTs as they are confronted with constructing new integrated digital infrastructures. By and large, these PTTs are placed in a most difficult position. While having to upgrade infrastructures, international competitive pressures are forcing them to reduce prices of—and profits from—international and interexchange services. "European Telecommunications Policy", Section II.A.

PTTs are seeking to offset such lost revenues by increasing rate levels and instituting new rate structures for local services. In many countries, however, it is difficult to implement such rate adjustments without encountering political resistance.

Consequently, PTTs can examine a series of options for increasing efficiency of network utilization and cutting costs. Many administrations are engaged in an internal reorganization; they are attempting to act more like traditional businesses and to compensate marketing and software engineers at levels commensurate with salaries in the private sector. Similarly, they are trying to maintain control over internally generated funds and financing sources and to free themselves from excessive demands by officials in the Ministries of Finance who would like contributions by the PTTs to support other governmental activities. "European Telecommunications Policy", Section II.B.

With regard to the pricing of international services, many PTTs see themselves in an environment more characterized by rivalry than at any time in the past. Corporations are increasingly deciding where to locate based on the rate levels and terms and conditions upon which telecommunications services are available. In an attempt to respond to these more vociferous users, therefore, PTTs are vying with each other to become the hub for international networks. Such rivalries may also be manifested in national efforts to market national satellite capacity on a transborder basis.

The PTTs also find themselves wrestling with the question of whether and how they can diversify into new markets and services that are dependent on—but are not—telecommunications services. Many are concerned that they might be restricted to offering only core transmission services. They believe that entities offering value-added or other specialized, industry-specific services are infringing on their monopolies or right to provide such services.

For the PTTs, however, the risks of developing new services are not inconsequential. The long-term potential of many such services remains uncertain. The capital costs and operating expenses that must be borne during the start-up phase are significant. Some administrations, therefore, may be receptive to strategies whereby the risks of developing new services can be shared with firms in the private sector. Such a strategy would be predicated on attempts to stimulate use of the network to generate revenues. "European Telecommunications Policy", Section II.B.

C. European Approach to ISDN

"European Telecommunications Policy" also examines some of the perspectives within Europe on the development of new integrated digital networks. Some policymakers stress that new broadband networks must be financed and supported before, and until, the development of demand for the services that they will make possible. Others emphasize that it is imperative to assess potential demand for such new services before massive investments are made in a universal infrastructure.

The paper points out that many large users are skeptical about the need for new integrated digital networks. They are fearful that they will have to pay for wasteful investment based on the PTTs' supply-driven—as opposed to demand-driven—investment policies. "European Telecommunications Policy" also notes that, despite the efforts of the European Commission to harmonize developments in Integrated Services Digital Networks ("ISDN") within Europe, it will still be necessary to establish *ad hoc* arrangements among administrations to assure the regional inter-operability of integrated digital services. "European Telecommunications Policy", Section III.B.

D. European Satellite Policies

"European Telecommunications Policy" also addresses the question of how satellite servicees can—and are likely to—become integrated in the planning for digital services. Some observers stress that planning for future ISDN services is based on an expectation that international connections will be made through major gateways, and not through connections via satellite earth stations that are located on or close to the premises of large customers. "European Telecommunications Policy", Section III.A.

Many of these users have noted their continuing difficulties in obtaining flexible access to Eutelsat's Satellite Multiservices System for multipoint data distribution. Administrations continue to follow a variety of practices with regard to ownership of small earth stations, location at the user's premises, and the pricing of multipoint circuits on a basis independent of existing terrestrial services. "European Telecommunications Policy", Section III.A.

Some observers in Europe stress the extent to which satellite services can effectively complement the planning for international digital networking. High-speed digital connections can be made to dispersed locations and to regions where it might be impractical to overbuild a new terrestrial network of integrated digital facilities.

The paper places some stress on the conditions necessary for new satellite developments, largely owing to the predilection toward new terrestrial services in existing European facilities planning mechanisms. Terrestrial services can often be planned on a bilateral basis; they remain under the control of individual administrations. By contrast, the planning, marketing, and use of satellites—especially in the European context—require a regional and potentially more political orientation.

Usage of satellite services might be stimulated through efforts to create a liberalized, European market for value-added services. Should this occur, new European-wide ventures might want to take advantage of capacity on the Eutelsat system and on existing or future national systems to offer new information-based services on a transborder basis. "European Telecommunications Policy", Sections III.A and IV.C.

E. Role of the European Commission: What Options are Available?

Perhaps the principal thrust of "European Telecommunications Policy" is an examination of some of the options by which the European Commission could address the process of liberalization, and the increasing disharmonies in national approaches, among the Member States of the European Community. As noted above, rivalries are increasing in Europe, with countries vying with one another to become hubs for international traffic. The rapid pace of change represents both a challenge and an opportunity for the European Commission. "European Telecommunications Policy", Section VIII.

Many observers fear that the national reviews and shifts in policy, if not directed or channeled in some way by the Commission, will lead to discordant policies that may make the task of integrating the European market even more difficult. Others, by contrast, believe that the set of movements at the national level constitute an impetus for a more integrated European policy.

The complexity of policy reform will turn many administrations inward, preoccupying them with the national process of transition. Thus, in some respects, pressures will increase on national administrations to maintain their independence and autonomy from external forces. The result may make it even harder to convince national policymakers and administrations of the need to work together to develop an outward-looking, European-wide set of policies.

In this setting, the European Commission is in the midst of considering a series of options for creating a more integrated market. One course of action being assessed would involve it in trying to establish a uniform approach to distinguishing between "basic" and "enhanced" services. This latter approach would focus on defining as a "basic" service one that is offered on similar terms and conditions by several different administrations. There would be broad leeway for competition in the provision of non-basic services; however, administrations would have some advantages over third-party competitors with respect to the terms and conditions by which they could avail themselves of underlying services.

The viability of an approach based on trying to achieve definitional uniformity throughout Europe is examined in the paper. There are drawbacks to the proposed definition of basic services; it might have the effect of discouraging the provision of non-basic services by entities other than administrations. "European Telecommunications Policy", Section VIII.B.

The European Commission might encourage new cross-border services even without establishing universal definitions. This more "procedural" approach would have the Commission intervene to block obstacles to the interconnection of value-added or non-basic services among different European countries. "European Telecommunications Policy", Section VIII.C.

It is important that new service agreements be negotiated on an *ad hoc* basis rather than trying to establish some *a priori* scheme focused on regulatory norms for which there is an international consensus. The European Commission, in defining for itself a role in stimulating the development of new information-based services, faces a task not unlike that confronting the CCITT, which is also essaying to define for itself an appropriate role regarding such services. "European Telecommunications Policy", Sections VIII.C and VIII.E.

The Commission must also develop some mechanism for dealing with the restructuring of prices. For example, among the options under its consideration might be policies to restructure the tariffs for leased lines, to lower them for pure point-to-point services but to encourage some volume-related charges for other services involving third parties. Given the significant impact any such restructuring would have on carriers and users, the Commission must be in a better position to evaluate the consequences of any changes in tariff structure that might be implemented within a Member country.

As a practical matter, it is difficult for the European Commission to assert a role in influencing the terms and conditions of tariffs without having some capacity to deal with issues relating to rate levels or rate structures. Pricing issues may, *de facto*, operate to inhibit the interconnection of services on a European-wide basis. Moreover, the Commission can hardly divorce itself from the consideration of pricing, if it concludes that it should deal with issues of access or barriers to the interconnection of services. "European Telecommunications Policy", Sections VI.D, VIII.B, and VIII.D.

F. Role of European Competition Policy and Exercise of Treaty of Rome Powers

The European Commission may have substantial powers under the Treaty of Rome to encourage a new legal framework for the provision of value-added services on a transborder basis. The *British Telecom* case held that administrations are subject to the Treaty's competition provisions. Thus, the Commission might be able to forge a European-wide policy by applying its authority under Articles 85 and 86 of the Treaty. "European Telecommunications Policy", Section VI.B.

Article 86 can be read as barring PTTs from abusing and extending their dominant position. The Commission might use this Article to prevent administration tying practices—in linking together equipment and services. In addition, it might be able to employ the Article in examining tariff provisions that it views as restrictive or discriminatory. New value-added service providers might be affordeed some leeway in using leased circuits if restrictions on resale are subject to review under Article 86. "European Telecommunications Policy", Section VI.C.

Under Article 85, the Commission may have the authority to review agreements among administrations. It might also be able to impose conditions necessary to ensure that any such agreements do not inhibit the development of effective competition within Europe. Article 85 may well confer on the Commission far-reaching powers to examine many facets of the European telecommunications sectors—including tariffing arrangements. "European Telecommunications Policy", Section VI.D.

The Commission need not implement a traditional regulatory process, one that would, in any event, gain little support from administrations. Instead, it could exercise its authority to block restrictive practices that inhibit the interconnection of new services within Europe. It could, for example, establish benchmarks relating to access to underlying facilities or to provision of an open network architecture.

The primary responsibility for such policies would rest with national administrations. However, the Commission could review access or ONA policies upon complaint or based on its own initiative in the event of national policies thwarting guidelines promulgated by the Commission.

As part of its attempt to create a "level playing field" based on its powers under the Treaty, the Commission could play a role in encouraging the development of regulatory mechanisms within Europe. Competition policy could be used as a vehicle for assisting various countries as they proceed to separate the operational and regulatory roles of the PTTs. The Commission could act as a catalyst among such new bodies. Indeed, it might well encourage its own competition directorate—D.G. IV—to take an active part in such a consultative group and to encourage the participation of national officials dealing with competition policy. "European Telecommunications Policy", Sections VIII.C and VIII.D.

G. The Commission and Trade Issues

The Commission will be in the vanguard of those addressing the issues which are now emerging relating to trade in telecommunications and electronic services. As mentioned in the context of 'Transactional Services", the Commission might be at the forefront of establishing a legal regime for the evolution of trade in electronic financial services. Traditionally, the Commission has questioned how services could be offered on a transborder basis subject to conflicting regulatory regimes. In focusing on transborder services, it has attempted to delineate the circumstances in which a service could be subject to regulation in the jurisdiction where the service is provided as well as in that where it originates. "European Telecommunications Policy", Sections VIII.E and VI.E; "Transactional Services", Section IV.

VI. ISSUES RAISED BY "INTERNATIONAL FACILITIES"

Many of the national and international shifts in policy are having an impact on the process of planning for international facilities. Changes in the arrangements for providing the infrastructure of international cable and satellite facilities are documented in "International Facilities". The paper also explores how existing planning processes—and that of Intelsat in particular—may have to be modified to cope with the new players and new competition that are emerging in the international arena.

A. Increasing Capacity, Emerging Competition

Among the most important of these changes is the rapid increase in the capacity of the international infrastructure. One significant element of this growth is the underseas fiber optic cable links that now serve the world's major international traffic streams. These cables are being constructed through multilateral agreements among the major PTTs and carriers in North America, Europe, and Japan. The cable circuits can be priced to reflect the high volume of traffic routed over them. In this respect, the emergence of these new fiber optic cable systems is creating great pressure on Intelsat's traditional price structures, which are based on a commitment to universal service for all its members. "International Facilities", Section II.B.

In addition, the U.S. decision to open up competition in international public switched telephone services has increased pressure on the FCC to modify or eliminate the requirement that AT&T balance the loading of traffic in the North Atlantic between satellite and cable facilities. The FCC has already accorded AT&T some flexibility in loading circuits; it is re-examining the circuit loading policy in light of the fact that AT&T's competitors are now able to choose least-cost facilities. If the loading requirements are relaxed altogether, significant traffic may move to underseas cables, which will further increase pressure on Intelsat to reprice its services. "International Facilities", Section II.E.

Although no private satellite system has yet established any firm correspondent agreement, it is increasingly likely that national or regional satellite systems can be utilized to offer international services. Users of such services will put increased pressure on carriers and service providers to handle national, regional, and international traffic over the same satellite system—if it is operationally feasible to do so. "International Facilities", Sections II.C and II.D.

The increasing diversity and competitive nature of national structures for the provision of telephone services have complicated the process of establishing arrangements for satellite and cable services. In the U.K., Mercury, in addition to British Telecom, provides international switched voice services. Soon, KDD in Japan will face at least one other provider of switched services. In addition, users and providers of value-added service will also account for an increasing volume of international traffic; they have been seeking ways to make known their need for new international facilities. "International Facilities", Sections II.E and III.F.

Traditionally, differing national interests have been represented in Intelsat through signatory organizations; these have been responsible for offering international satellite services at the national level. Increasingly, these representative organizations are confronting competitive pressures. In the U.S., AT&T, the largest user of the Intelsat system, has no direct role in Intelsat planning. Comsat, the U.S. in representative Intelsat, is now faced with the prospect of direct participation or representation by other U.S. entities in Intelsat. In the U.K. and Japan, as a result of the new competitive industry structure, the arrangements for representation in Intelsat may become subject to policy review. "International Facilities", Sections II.E and III.E.

In addition to the diversification of industry structure, the trend toward separating operational and regulatory responsibilities has made the process of formulating policy more intricate. In the past, it was only in the U.S. that regulatory bodies participated in meetings on facilities planning with operating entities. The DTI in the U.K. and the Ministry of Posts and Telecommunications in Japan, however, will increasingly take a more active role in addressing issues relating to facilities planning. "International Facilities", Section IV.

These changes in the international environment affect the processes that can be used to plan future cable and satellite facilities. Several important implications for policymakers are identified in "International Facilities".

B. Strains in Existing Processes

The emergence of competition is putting increasing strain on the existing institutions for facilities planning. At present, there are numerous decentralized centers for decisionmaking. It is not realistic, therefore, to assume that any co-ordinated or centralized planning process can or should be implemented. Past efforts to deal with facilities planning—such as the North Atlantic Consultative Process—have been put under considerable stress by the private fiber optic cables projects, which the FCC authorized outside the consultative process. "International Facilities", Sections II.C and III.A.

C. Improving Information Flow

It may not be either possible or desirable to implement a centralized planning process. Nevertheless, decisionmaking about future facilities may be made more efficient and rational by improving the flow of information relating to the current (and proposed) configurations of facilities and pricing. "International Facilities", Section III.B.

Intelsat, for example, it is widely assumed, may have to adjust its pricing to respond to competition from new fiber optic cable systems. Intelsat has had some difficulty in achieving a consensus within the organization that some kind of comprehensive reappraisal of pricing policies is required. Until the future direction of Intelsat pricing policies becomes clear, and uncertainties concerning the competitiveness of the international environment are resolved, it may be difficult for investors in new private cables or satellites to obtain the financing they need. "International Facilities", Section III.E.

D. Committing to Intelsat Capacity

Intelsat's planning for future needs is made difficult because administrations can project needs for future capacity without making any financial commitments for such capacity. In the future, it will be both necessary and useful to encourage Intelsat members to make commitments for satellite circuits in the same way that commitments are made for cable circuits. "International Facilities", Sections II.F and III.E.

E. Broadening Involvement in Intelsat

Both in terms of advancing national policies and of improving the Intelsat planning process itself, not just signatories to the Intelsat Treaty but important users—both carriers and customers—of the system should become more involved in the organization. It may well be impractical for Comsat to be obligated to meet U.S. projections of use of Intelsat without also according AT&T a greater role in the process of planning and making commitments for new satellite capacity. More broadly, Intelsat may need to be freer to have more direct contact with users and other entities who are likely to use some of its new business-oriented services that are intended to provide connections at the customer's premises. "International Facilities", Section III.E.

F. New Roles—and Changes—for Intelsat

Faced with the installation of fiber optic cables, Intelsat may have to accelerate the pace at which it is assessing new configurations of satellite capacity that can offer competitive services to large users. Any such reorientation will intensify pressure between Intelsat and investors in cable facilities.

To minimize such frictions, it may be useful for Intelsat to re-examine the way it approaches the process of acquiring satellite capacity. Rather than procuring satellites directly from manufacturers, Intelsat might profitably weigh the option of becoming a clearinghouse for satellite capacity by acquiring, where appropriate or available, satellite circuits from national or regional systems. "International Facilities", Section III.E.

As the potential for rivalry among Intelsat and national providers of satellite service increases, more attention will have to be placed on separating Intelsat's operational and regulatory roles. As "regulator", it now has important responsibilities in assessing both the technical and the economic impacts of private satellites on the global system. "International Facilities", Section III.E.

Similarly, as Intelsat begins to reappraise its pricing policies, its decisions may have an important impact on the plans of national and regional satellite systems—some of them with the potential to compete with its own services. Thus, it may well have to develop a more open and transparent approach to cost accounting and cost allocation. Although it may be infeasible to subject Intelsat pricing to formal regulatory oversight, some mechanisms for channeling and resolving complaints about pricing may be useful.

A separation of responsibilities does not necessarily imply that Intelsat ought to be split into two distinct organizations. Rather, the suggestion is that autonomy should be accorded to its officials with responsibility for the co-ordination of separate systems and for addressing disputes over pricing. It is important that such decisions not be seen as influenced by what could be viewed as Intelsat's entrepreneurial priorities.

Finally, although Intelsat clearly cannot assume any central role in the process of planning facilities, its activities do bear significantly on the efficiency and responsiveness of arrangements for such facilities. In the past several years, it has adopted a very aggressive posture in opposing competitive private satellite systems. Such attention to the question of private satellite systems, however, deflected attention from the need for a comprehensive overhaul of its own pricing and facilities planning processes. Rather than developing a consensus regarding the need for change among its broad membership, Intelsat used its political contacts and global support to resist any attempts to discuss change; in the process, it may well have hindered prospects for a sweeping reappraisal of its own role. "International Facilities", Section III.E.

Perhaps one of the most important tasks for policymakers worldwide, then, is to find a way of beginning a far-reaching review of Intelsat's future role and activities. Such a review can be either formal or informal. What is critical, however, is that Intelsat's members understand the need to afford institutional and operational flexibility to the organization if it is to thrive in the new, competitive international environment. In particular, the perceptions of the developing world will be crucial. Thus, the industrialized countries must make concerted attempts to reach out to the less developed countries, to persuade them that it is imperative that this review of Intelsat be undertaken as quickly as possible.

VII. ISSUES RAISED BY "TELECOMMUNICATIONS AND DEVELOPMENT"

The Study began its work by focusing on policy and structural changes in the telecommunications sectors of the major industrialized nations. It soon became apparent, however, that the factors contributing to such changes were not confined to the developed countries. Indeed, the imperatives of efficiency, improved performance, stimulation of related sectors, sensitivity to trade-related concerns and political exigencies—all of which constitute the incentives for shifts in policies in the industrialized world—are equally relevant to the less developed nations.

Similarly, changes in the industrialized world have a direct impact on the less developed world. The "International Facilities" paper demonstrates the extent to which competition spawned by the industrialized nations in the national and international arenas can profoundly affect institutions, such as Intelsat, that are charged with serving all the countries of the world. In an attempt to explore the relevance for developing countries of changes—and the factors forcing such changes—in the developed world, Phase II of the Study examined the perspectives of the developing world in the essay "Telecommunications and Development".

At the outset, of course, it should be said that, while the developing countries have much in common, they should not be viewed as having uniform needs, concerns or resources. In general, the countries of Asia that were visited have better infrastructures—and resources—than those of Africa. India, for example, has a sizeable manufacturing base, a software sector, a satellite, large users and little foreign debt. Indonesia's concerns focus on the archipelagic nature of the country (hence the impetus for its own satellite system), the need to bind a widely dispersed population together and the fact that there is only one major city to serve—and to generate urban revenues. Malaysia has had resources in the past, has a significant educated populace, and has a population essentially concentrated in one region around Kuala Lumpur.

A. A Lack of Resources

Although only three countries in the developing world were visited in the course of Phase II—India, Indonesia, and Malaysia—it seems obvious that the overarching problem faced by the less developed countries is a scarcity of resources. The nature and extent of the scarcity can vary, of course, but the crucial problem in the developing world is that demand far exceeds supply and that inadequate resources exist to satisfy that demand. "Telecommunications and Development", Section II.

Extraordinary demands are placed on the local plant. The absence of adequate facilities increases utilization literally beyond the capacity of the system. Such over-use strains switches and hastens the overall breakdown of the physical plant. Thus, the installed infrastructure is, in many cases, deteriorating rapidly—far outstripping the resources or ability to replace outmoded or worn-out switches or subterranean cables which have never been protected by conduits. Urban congestion can make it nearly impossible to replace existing cables. "Telecommunications and Development", Section III.B.

Obviously, administrations do all they can to upgrade or expand the network. Nevertheless, such administrations face two principal problems in obtaining the resources necessary for the job.

First, concerns arising from scarce foreign exchange create restrictions on the ability of administrations in the developing world to invest in new equipment and transmission facilities. Ministries of Finance are cautious about authorizing expenditures that will consume foreign exchange; telecommunications, unlike tourism, for example, is not seen as directly bringing compensatory foreign exchange into the country. "Telecommunications and Development", Section III.F.

Second, telecommunications expenditures are competing with basic human needs. It is difficult for administrations to convince central planners that resources should be taken from health, sanitation, or education to upgrade telecommunications facilities or to introduce new services. This may particularly be the case where the administration is interested in spending a substantial part of such resources in urban areas—where it may be possible to reap greater profits—but at the price of substantially underserving the poor or rural areas. "Telecommunications and Development", Section IV.A.

On this last point, the allocation of resources to the sector overall is only the prelude to the further allocation between the rural and urban areas. The decision whether to extend services to unserved rural areas—a costly proposition that is supported by important social concerns—must be balanced against the likelihood that greater revenues will flow from improving services in urban areas. Such revenues, of course, might then be used to serve rural areas. Thus, the decision on how to allocate within the sector is caught up in a complex web of political, economic, technological and social factors. "Telecommunications and Development", Section IV.B.

B. The Relationship Between Economic Development and Telecommunications

The case for increasing the allocation of resources to the telecommunications sector has been difficult to make. In the developing world there is some skepticism about the direct benefits to the economy of improving the telecommunications infrastructure. Although there is some economic literature demonstrating the relationship between investing in telecommunications and boosting the overall economic health of a country, much of it is too general, or not precisely directed at a particular national situation, to be seen as relevant.

As an adjunct to offering aid to the developing countries for their telecommunications sectors, multilateral institutions and bilateral donors or lenders ought to make the case as forcefully as possible that economic improvement—which will ultimately lead to improvements in health, sanitation, and education—will follow from investing in telecommunications. "Telecommunications and Development", Sections II, III.F, and III.G.

C. Private Networks: The Cost of Insufficient Supply

In India, the insufficiency of service has created incentives for large users—state-owned corporations such as the railway and steel authorities—to construct their own networks. Such networks are viewed as siphoning additional resources from the telecommunications sector. They are criticized as duplicative and inefficient, largely owing to the fact that it is anticipated that they will not be fully utilized. In addition, any revenues that might have been obtained from such users, in the absence of the construction of private networks, would certainly be welcomed by the Indian administration. "Telecommunications and Development", Section III.B.

D. Structural Innovation and Reform

As is the case in many of the industrialized countries, several nations in the developing world are attempting to increase efficiency and accountability by pursuing a variety of approaches to structuring the sector.

In India, institutional innovation has placed the telephone systems of two of the major urban areas—New Delhi and Bombay—in a separate corporate entity—Mahanagar Telephone Nigam Ltd ("MTN") within the Indian Department of Telecommunications ("DOT"). At the same time, the entity providing international services, which historically has been separate from the domestic organization, was placed in a similar corporate entity.

This bold step had several objectives. First, MTN now has the ability to go to the financial markets to obtain and develop its own financing resources. In part, the institutional reorganization addresses the political problem of allocating resources between the urban and rural sectors. Second, much as has been the case in France, the separate "subsidiary" is thought to increase its efficiency by having commercial decisions made in a business setting. Finally, by separating local services, the DOT will gradually force the development of more sophisticated cost accounting mechanisms. "Telecommunications and Development", Section III.D.

In Malaysia, the telecommunications department has been privatized. Though the stock continues to be held by the state, the privatization of Jabatan Telekom Malaysia ("JTM") is seen as achieving several important goals. First, it has freed the administration somewhat from the bureaucratic supervision of the Treasury and liberated it to pursue various financing options. Second, the new entity, Syarikat Telekom Malaysia Berhad ("STM"), is able to create separate units or subsidiaries to enhance efficiencies and, possibly, to divide services between urban and rural areas along the lines of the Indian experiment with MTN. Third, STM can enter into joint ventures for business networks. "Telecommunications and Development", Section IV.B.

E. The Framework for New Services

Business users in the developing world are clamoring for new services. In India, the DOT is contemplating offering a Business Subscriber Network—possibly through a separate subsidiary within the Department. The services would be offered over narrowband and, perhaps, satellite facilities. Various innovative financing options are being explored—including the possibility of raising capital from subscribers. The Indians have also been responsive, where resources permit, to requests for leased line services and are sensitive to large users' needs to have access to foreign information services. "Telecommunications and Development", Section III.E.

Various business and data services would be opened to competition in Malaysia, with the monopoly on transmission being retained by STM. The definitional approach is *ad hoc* and no new legislation would be needed to liberalize the services sector. "Telecommunications and Development", Section IV.B.

By contrast, in Indonesia the model being considered to introduce new value-added services is more "regulatory" than structural in focus. A pending legislative proposal would permit some liberalization of the services sector: private sector companies would be able to provide new services in co-operation with the domestic provider, Perumtel, and the international provider, Indosat. Such a joint-venture model, for example, has been adopted in Italy for the STET-Montedison joint venture, Televas. "Telecommunications and Development", Section V.C.

F. Sensitivity to International Considerations

National policymaking in the less developed world is keenly attentive to the international environment. In India, the vigorous software sector and expertise in developing switches for rural areas may be taken into account in a trade-oriented telecommunications policy. Already, the DOT's consulting subsidiary has a visible presence throughout much of the Third World. The Indian satellite as well might eventually come to play a role in regional telecommunications. "Telecommunications and Development", Section III.G.

Not unlike their colleagues in Europe, the Malaysians are interested in the possibility of having their country serve as a regional and Pacific Basin hub for services. They have concluded an agreement for a submarine fiber optic cable between Peninsular and East Malaysia that could become part of a Pacific system. The competition posed by Singapore, Hong Kong, and Australia will be tough, especially in light of the relatively small size and now depressed state of the Malaysian economy. However, the new, entrepreneurial structure of STM, and the new cable, may well make Malaysia a force with which its neighbors ought to reckon. "Telecommunications and Development", Section IV.C.

G. Development of New Fora

Given the magnitude of the problems facing telecommunications policymakers in the developing world, it could be useful to develop new institutions to exchange perspectives with both the developed and the less developed world. Existing institutions—the World Bank, the ITU, the United Nations, and donor countries—have done a commendable job of sharing information about technical and financial options with the developing world. What is needed, however, (in both the developed and developing countries) is an exchange of views on various regulatory and structural issues. An international forum could be a valuable adjunct to ongoing work in the area of telecommunications and development. "Telecommunications and Development", Section VI.

VIII. CONCLUSION

The material produced by the work of Phase II is, admittedly, voluminous and detailed. This summary is intended to be useful, not only to signal what seem to be the issues of greatest significance that were addressed in the second phase of the Study but also as a signpost to the papers themselves.

These relatively brief summary observations have necessarily required the omission of many important points that are analyzed in the papers. The fuller treatment of some of these issues in the papers will, it is hoped, compensate for any inevitable oversights here.

The principal lesson of the work of both phases of the Study is that change in the telecommunications sector is both inevitable and rapid. Throughout both phases, the pace of global developments has been relentlessly at odds with efforts to document the process of change. Inevitably, much of this material will become dated, though an effort has been made to be current up to May 1987, when Phase II was completed. It is certain, however, that many issues addressed in both Phases I and II of the Study will themselves remain the subject of lively discussion and debate.

The original—and ongoing—goal of the IIC's Study of Telecommunications Structures has been to lay the groundwork for others who will conduct their own, more detailed research and policy studies. It is hoped that the Study will make at least some small but continuing contribution to discussions of national, regional, and global telecommunications policies in the months and years ahead.

CHAPTER II
BOUNDARY LINES: A FURTHER EXPLORATION OF ENHANCED OR VALUE-ADDED SERVICES

TABLE OF CONTENTS

		Page
I.	Introduction	43
II.	United States	43
	A. Background: *Computer I* and *Computer II*	43
	B. *Computer III*	43
	C. Problems	55
	D. Prospects	61
III.	United Kingdom	75
	A. Background	75
	B. Problems	76
	C. Prospects	82
IV.	Japan	83
	A. Background	83
	B. Problems	88
	C. Prospects	91
V.	France	93
	A. Background	93
	B. Problems	95
	C. Prospects	97
VI.	The Netherlands	99
	A. Background	99
	B. Problems	100
	C. Prospects	101
VII.	Finland	101
	A. Background	101
	B. Problems	103
	C. Prospects	103
VIII.	Canada	105
	A. Background	105
	B. Problems	107
	C. Prospects	108

		Page
IX.	Italy	109
	A. Background	109
	B. Problems	109
	C. Prospects	109
X.	Spain	110
	A. Background	110
	B. Problems	110
	C. Prospects	111
XI.	The Federal Republic of Germany	112
	A. Background	112
	B. Problems	114
	C. Prospects	114
XII.	Australia	116
	A. Background	116
	B. Problems	120
	C. Prospects	135
XIII.	The Convergence of National Approaches	144
	A. Facing Common Economic Pressures	144
	B. Regulatory and Technical Convergences	148
	C. New Regulatory and Industry Structures	150
XIV.	International Value-Added or Enhanced Services: How to Develop Arrangements for Interconnection	153
	A. Overview of International Issues	153
	B. The Impact of ONA on International Services	156
	C. RPOAs and IRUs in the United States	159
	D. The Evolving Japanese Approach to VANs	162
	1. Introduction	162
	2. The May 1987 Amendments to the Telecommunications Business Law	163
	3. Continuing Problems and General Policy Considerations in Japan	167
	E. A Process for Developing Arrangements for International Value-Added Services–Part I: The ITU	171
	F. A Process for Developing Arrangements for International Value-Added Services–Part II: A New Bilateralism	174

CHAPTER II
BOUNDARY LINES: A FURTHER EXPLORATION OF ENHANCED OR VALUE-ADDED SERVICES

I. INTRODUCTION

This paper takes a closer, more focused look at the boundary lines that were examined in Phase I of the Study of Telecommunications Structures. In particular, it focuses on the evolution of the boundary line between "basic" and "enhanced" or "value-added" services. A great variety of national approaches is developing—even since the first phase of the Study was completed in 1985.

The approaches of the following nations are analyzed in detail: the United States, the United Kingdom, Japan, France, the Netherlands, Finland, Canada, Italy, Spain, the Federal Republic of Germany and Australia. The paper continues with an examination of the rationale for, and problems with, distinctions between services and the process of classifying services. From the national approaches, it seeks to elicit some trends and draw some conclusions with respect to future directions. In particular, it concludes with some observations on the international treatment of value-added services and on how to structure arrangements for interconnecting them.

II. UNITED STATES

A. Background: *Computer I* and *Computer II*

1. In its 1971 *Computer I* decision, the Federal Communications Commission (the "FCC" or the "Commission") sought to distinguish between "data processing" and "communications services". *Regulatory and Policy Problems Presented by the Interdependence of Computer and Communications Services and Facilities*, 28 F.C.C.2d 267 (1971) (Final Decision and Order), *aff'd in part sub nom. GTE Service Corp. v. FCC*, 474 F.2d 724 (2d Cir. 1973), *decision on remand*, 40 F.C.C. 2d 293 (1973) (*Computer I*). It also adopted distinctions between "hybrid communications" and "hybrid data processing" services, both of which were mixed services involving elements of both data processing and communications

capabilities. A service would be classified as "hybrid communications"—and subject to regulation—if the data processing features were incidental to the communications capabilities. The FCC decided to forbear from regulating a "hybrid data processing" service, in which communications capabilities were incidental to the data processing functions.

2. The *Computer II* proceeding attempted to draw new boundary lines between "basic" and "enhanced" services. *Amendment of Section 64.702 of the Commission's Rules and Regulations*, 77 F.C.C.2d 384 (1980) (Final Decision), *modified on recon.*, 84 F.C.C.2d 50 (1980) (Reconsideration Order), *further modified on recon.*, 88 F.C.C.2d 512 (1981) (Further Reconsideration Order), *aff'd sub nom. Computer and Communications Industry Ass'n v. FCC*, 693 F.2d 198 (D.C. Cir. 1982), *cert. denied*, 461 U.S. 938 (1983), *aff'd on further recon.*, FCC No. 84-190 (released May 4, 1984) (*Computer II*). The basic/enhanced distinction was intended to resolve the policy dilemma that the FCC faced, owing to the application of the then-effective 1956 Consent Decree to the service offerings of AT&T. The Consent Decree prohibited AT&T from offering services that were not "subject to public regulation under the Communications Act of 1934". By exercising jurisdiction over enhanced services to require that AT&T provide enhanced services only through a fully separated subsidiary, the FCC concluded that it had brought such enhanced services within the realm of those that were "subject to public regulation" and thus could be offered by AT&T.

3. In the aftermath of *Computer II*, the FCC was confronted with numerous requests for *ad hoc* rulings to classify new services as either basic or enhanced.

4. In January 1984, AT&T was compelled to divest its Bell Operating Companies (the "BOCs") under the terms of the Modification of Final Judgement (the "MFJ"), which was approved by Federal District Court Judge Harold H. Greene in 1982, in settlement of the government's antitrust suit against AT&T. The 22 BOCs were grouped into seven Regional Holding Companies ("RHCs"). (In this paper, the term "RHC" will be used to refer collectively to the RHCs and the BOCs that they own.)

a. As a result of the divestiture, the FCC faced questions about how to apply *Computer II* to services offered by the RHCs and about whether such application would be consistent with the terms of the MFJ. A potential conflict between *Computer II* and the MFJ existed because the MFJ prohibits the RHCs from providing "information services", but *Computer II* permitted the RHCs to provide enhanced services, some or all of which might be considered "information services".

b. To date, the MFJ has not been applied to prevent an RHC from providing an enhanced service, although a number of the RHCs believe the MFJ blocks their involvement in much of the enhanced services market and, therefore, have decided not to offer many enhanced services.

5. The AT&T divestiture and changes in industry structure, including consolidation in the interexchange telecommunications market

(such as IBM's acquisition of an interest in MCI Communications Corp. and MCI's simultaneous purchase from IBM of Satellite Business Systems, the merger of GTE Sprint Communications Corp. and U.S. Telecom Inc. to form US Sprint Communications Co., and the merger of Allnet and Lexitel to form ALC) and the growth and dispersion of affordable, increasingly powerful processing capabilities, have prompted the FCC to revisit and relax certain of the competitive safeguards applicable to AT&T and the RHCs under *Computer II*.

6. The safeguards contained in the FCC's *Computer II* decision include:

    a. The requirement that the carriers use separate transmission facilities and separate corporate entities to provide basic and enhanced services ("structural separation").

    b. Restrictions on the exchange of information between the "basic" and "enhanced" operations.

    c. The requirement that enhanced service providers affiliated with AT&T and the RHCs obtain facilities and services from their affiliated carriers under tariff and on the same terms and conditions as are available to unaffiliated service providers.

B. Computer III

1. On May 15, 1986, the FCC adopted a new regulatory scheme in its Report and Order in the *Computer III* proceeding. *Amendment of Section 64.702 of the Commission's Rules and Regulations (Third Computer Inquiry)*, 60 Rad. Reg. 2d (P&F) 603 (1986) [hereinafter referred to as *Computer III Phase I Order*], *modified in part*, FCC No. 87-102 (released May 22, 1987) [hereinafter referred to as *Phase I Reconsideration Order*]. Under the *Computer III* regime, AT&T and the RHCs will be freed from the structural separation requirements of *Computer II* when they comply with a new set of non-structural safeguards applicable to their enhanced service offerings. The FCC identified as dual goals of the non-structural safeguards "advancing the availability of efficient enhanced services while not unduly perturbing competition". *Computer III Phase I Order*, 60 Rad. Reg. 2d at 663.

    a. In adopting this new set of safeguards, the Commission rejected a plan that had been offered in its Notice of Proposed Rulemaking in the *Computer III* proceeding. This plan would have eliminated the dichotomy between "basic" and "enhanced" services as the boundary line between regulated and unregulated activities. The proposal called for the adoption of a new way of distinguishing among services. Under this proposed scheme, the FCC would have relied on economic or market-power criteria, rather than on technological distinctions, to determine whether a particular service should be subject to various competitive safeguards.

b. In place of structural separation, the Commission adopted a set of non-structural rules that are intended to ensure that AT&T, the RHCs, their affiliates, and unaffiliated service providers have access to the carriers' transmission networks on the same (or virtually identical) terms and conditions. The safeguards are intended to balance concerns for competitive equality without so burdening AT&T and the RHCs that they are unable to provide users with efficient enhanced services that take advantage of the various capabilities of these carriers' networks.

2. As a first step, AT&T and the RHCs will be required to offer comparably efficient interconnection ("CEI") in conjunction with each enhanced service that they want to provide on an unseparated basis. Each CEI offering will be subject to full public notice and comment procedures. Under the CEI concept, AT&T and the RHCs must make available to unaffiliated service providers roughly the same gateway into the network that they use for their own enhanced services (or the services of an affiliate).

3. Each carrier also must file an accounting plan that will allow the FCC to review allocation of joint and common costs among the components of the carrier's network, the CEI gateway, and any enhancements that the carrier may provide as part of a separate enhanced service offering. The accounting plan must comply with the guidelines developed in a separate FCC proceeding. *Separation of Costs of Regulated Telephone Service from Costs of Nonregulated Activities*, 61 Rad. Reg. 2d (P&F) 163 (1987).

a. Under these guidelines, costs are to be assigned directly to regulated or non-regulated activities, to the greatest extent possible. Costs that cannot be assigned directly are to be grouped into specific categories and attributed to regulated and non-regulated activities in accordance with particular mechanisms designed to measure cost "causation". (In the case of transmission plant, for example, costs are to be attributed to particular services that use that plant in proportion to the relative projected peak demands for each service.) Residual costs that cannot be attributed to specific activities will be allocated according to the same ratio as directly assigned and otherwise attributed costs.

b. The RHCs are required to file with the FCC cost allocation manuals complying with these guidelines no later than September 1, 1987. AT&T has filed its manual with the FCC, as required by the cost allocation decision.

4. Finally, the carriers must not discriminate between affiliated and unaffiliated service providers in the provision of network and customer information.

5. Over the longer term, the emphasis of the new safeguards will shift from being service-specific to requiring an extensive reorganization (and at least some redesign) of the basic transmission networks of AT&T and the RHCs. The *Computer III* scheme required AT&T and the RHCs to adopt open network architecture ("ONA") plans by February 1, 1988. The

ONA plans of the RHCs will be subject to FCC approval after completion of formal public notice and comment proceedings. An ONA plan must "permit all users of the basic network, including the enhanced service operations of the carrier and its competitors, to interconnect to specific basic network functions and interfaces on an unbundled and 'equal access' basis". *Computer III Phase I Order*, 60 Rad. Reg. 2d at 646. ONA will implement, in the form of an overall network design, many of the objectives of CEI that carriers will be required to provide on a service-by-service basis prior to implementation of their ONA plans.

6. AT&T will be permitted to meet its "ONA obligations" in a rather different—and less rigorous—fashion. In the *Phase I Reconsideration Order*, the FCC decided to modify the ONA requirements applicable to AT&T. This issue is discussed more fully below in Section II.B.14. AT&T is still required to comply with the CEI provisions of the *Computer III* rules before offering an enhanced service on an unseparated basis.

7. The FCC specified nine CEI "parameters", all of which must be satisfied by each CEI plan that a carrier submits for the unseparated offering of an enhanced service. These parameters require that a carrier:

    a. Provide standardized network interfaces (both hardware and software) to support transmission, signalling, and switching functions identical to those made available to the carrier's own enhanced services.

    b. Separate from other basic network services the basic service components used by the carrier to provide each enhanced service, and make them available to other enhanced service providers on an unbundled basis pursuant to a specific rate element in the CEI plan tariff.

    c. Acquire basic services for its enhanced service offerings at the tariffed rate.

    d. Offer basic services to other enhanced service providers that have the same technical characteristics as the basic services used by the carrier's own enhanced service operation.

    e. Provide installation, maintenance, and repair services to other enhanced service providers that are as timely as the services the carrier receives for the basic network facilities used for its enhanced services.

    f. Offer all users of enhanced services that rely on the carrier's network equal means of access to those services, including dial-up access or access through derived channels such as data-over-voice.

    g. Make CEI available and fully operational on the same date that the carrier first offers the enhanced service covered by the particular CEI plan. Prior to this date, the carrier must make the CEI facilities available to other service providers for testing.

    h. Minimize the cost of any transmission facilities, which may be charged for on a distance-sensitive basis, that are required to connect the third-party provider's equipment with the carrier's network. The cost of any multiplexing or other concentration equipment located at the carrier's facility is to be allocated on an averaged basis so that all entities, including the carrier, will pay a basic concentration charge as part of the CEI tariff.

i. Make CEI available both to enhanced service providers and to large end-users.

8. The FCC identified four cost elements for CEI and devised a pricing scheme intended to maximize incentives for the development of efficient interconnection arrangements, while minimizing cost disparities between carriers and non-carrier users.

a. Carriers are not required to permit enhanced service providers to collocate their enhanced service equipment with the carrier's network. They may impose on CEI users a distance-sensitive charge for transmission facilities needed to connect the user's facility with the carrier's network. This cost element may impose a competitive disadvantage on some non-carriers; however, the FCC concluded that transmission costs were only a small component of the overall cost of providing an enhanced service and that, therefore, any disadvantage was likely to be minimal. In addition, a cost-based charge would encourage users to locate their equipment as close to a carrier's CEI facility as possible, unless non-transmission costs in that neighborhood made it more economical to locate such equipment farther away. If transmission costs were averaged, individual users would have no incentive to minimize the distance of the required loop.

b. Interconnection costs—the costs of interfaces—are required to be identical for all users, including the carrier's own enhanced service operation.

c. Traffic concentration costs are required to be averaged for equipment located on the CEI carrier's facilities; cost-based pricing may be applied to equipment located at the user's facility.

d. Various basic services used to provide an enhanced service must be acquired at tariffed rates.

9. The FCC views CEI as an improvement over the structural separation rules developed in the *Computer II* proceeding because CEI permits carriers to use the most efficient network configuration possible to provide enhanced services, even if such efficiency requires the collocation of enhanced and basic service equipment, which was prohibited by the *Computer III* rules.

10. The FCC also considers CEI necessary because, without it, facilities providers might have an inherent advantage over third-party service providers in offering enhanced services that require the use of underlying basic transmission facilities.

a. The FCC recognized that mandatory collocation for all enhanced service providers could not be implemented for pragmatic reasons, including lack of central office space and various administrative and security concerns. However, the Commission also was unwilling to deny carriers—and, in turn, their customers—the potential efficiencies of integrated or collocated enhanced service offerings.

b. As a result, the FCC has permitted AT&T and the RHCs to collocate or integrate their enhanced service equipment on the condition that they comply with the CEI requirements.

c. In rejecting mandatory collocation, the FCC noted that collocation may not always be the most efficient form of interconnection, both for carriers and non-carriers. It was feared that mandatory collocation would inhibit the development of possibly superior interconnection and network usage arrangements. Thus, the specifics of such interconnection are left to the discretion of carriers, subject to the requirement that they produce results consistent with the CEI parameters.

11. The FCC may allow a carrier to provide an enhanced service on an unseparated basis without satisfying all of the nine CEI "parameters" in "rare" instances where a carrier can demonstrate, in a "detailed explanation" submitted to the FCC, which CEI parameters cannot be fulfilled and why. In such a case, if the carrier can provide a CEI plan that meets the CEI requirements "in a manner that is minimally different from that required", the FCC has said it may be willing to permit deviations. *Computer III Phase I Order*, 60 Rad. Reg. 2d at 658.

12. As of March 31, 1987, Bell Atlantic had filed the only CEI plan submitted since adoption of the *Computer III Phase I Order*. Bell Atlantic filed the plan as part of a proposal to offer message storage service on an unseparated basis.

a. Under the CEI plan, Bell Atlantic will offer third-party vendors a standard voice-grade business dial tone line to connect message storage equipment with a central office switching facility. Bell Atlantic will use the same line-side connection, although its message storage equipment will be collocated within a central office and, therefore, will require a "shorter" connecting line. Neither Bell Atlantic nor third-party vendors will obtain additional functions through the connection. The standard business line is currently offered as an "unbundled" basic service under tariff; Bell Atlantic will subscribe to the offering at the tariffed rate, and no additional unbundling is contemplated.

b. Bell Atlantic argued that decisions about whether its connections and the connections of third-party vendors are of equal quality should be judged by whether customers can "reasonably perceive" any difference, not by whether "sophisticated testing equipment" can measure differences. *Id.* at 4. Because third-party vendors not using collocated equipment will require longer wires to connect to the Bell Atlantic switch, they will suffer some additional signal degradation. Bell Atlantic contends, however, that any degradation is limited and that voice-storage equipment typically is designed to adjust output volume to compensate for the effects of transmission; thus, equal quality service should result. *Id.* at 4–5.

c. The CEI filing says that existing tariffs "reflect economies realized through use of subscriber loop carriers and other multiplexing and concentration systems". *Id.* at 6. Thus, Bell Atlantic concludes, its CEI offering minimizes transmission costs.

d. Bell Atlantic has committed itself to monitoring the installation and maintenance of the basic services included in the CEI offering to comply with the FCC's non-discrimination requirements. It will submit quarterly reports of complaints received from third-party vendors using the CEI offering.

e. To meet the FCC's rules regarding customer proprietary network information ("CPNI"), Bell Atlantic will inform affected customers of their right to restrict access to their records. Any restricted customer records will be marked accordingly, and Bell Atlantic sales personnel will be "administratively prohibited from attempting to sell Bell Atlantic's enhanced service to any customer whose record is so marked". *Id.* at 9.

f. This particular CEI plan does not raise many of the potentially difficult issues that surround the CEI and ONA processes because it involves a relatively uncomplicated offering. Because existing voice-grade service is being used to make the connection to the central office switch, Bell Atlantic is not required to disclose in advance complex proprietary network specifications developed specifically to offer the proposed enhanced service. The CEI offering also does not propose any additional unbundling of network elements. Thus, the Bell Atlantic filing does not indicate how the *Computer III* rules would apply to a complicated, novel offering in which an RHC was attempting to introduce a particularly innovative enhanced service into the market.

g. The *Computer III* rules may be tested more fully as the FCC reviews Bell Atlantic's CEI filing. Initial comments on the CEI plan, which pointed to the precedential impact of the plan, were highly critical of Bell Atlantic's filing. They contended that Bell Atlantic failed to unbundle its basic network adequately, did not properly price the CEI service to minimize price disparities between Bell Atlantic's service and the services of third-party vendors, and did not properly safeguard CPNI.

13. With the implementation of ONA, the RHCs will be relieved of having to provide CEI on a service-by-service basis. In theory, ONA will result in a reconfiguration of the basic service network—and the way in which the RHCs use that network and make it available to others—so that technology will implement the objectives that CEI's service-specific regulation is intended to achieve. In theory, a network configured according to ONA principles should have CEI engineered into it.

14. As a result of the *Phase I Reconsideration Order*, AT&T will not be required to offer basic service elements ("BSEs") on an unbundled basis to the same extent as the RHCs to comply with the ONA requirements.

a. Rather, AT&T will be required to file a "modified" ONA plan on February 1, 1988, in which it is required to demonstrate "the manner in which it intends to respond to the needs of enhanced service providers for equal and efficient access to its basic services". This modified plan must demonstrate specifically (*i*) AT&T's capabilities "to transport such signals and other information associated with the BSEs of the BOCs or other local exchange carriers", (*ii*) its plan to provide such transport in a non-discriminatory manner, and (*iii*) procedures for responding to requests by carriers for "new forms of transport". FCC No. 82–107, slip op. at paras. 51–52.

b. After filing its modified ONA plan, AT&T will be permitted to continue to rely on CEI service-specific plans for any enhanced services it decides to offer on an unseparated basis. Thus, it appears that unbundling of the AT&T network will be controlled by AT&T's decisions about what enhanced services it wants to offer on an unseparated basis; the FCC's unbundling requirements, which are part of the ONA rules, will not dictate the way in which the AT&T network will be pieced out.

15. Unlike CEI, which carriers must elect to follow because of a desire to offer an enhanced service on an unseparated basis, ONA is a uniform regulatory requirement that permits the FCC—rather than the carriers—to control the way in which access to carrier networks will have to be made available in the future. CEI is keyed to the enhanced service offerings of a carrier and is intended to ensure that the network features or capabilities that are offered by a dominant carrier to its affiliated enhanced service entity are made available to unaffiliated entities on an "equal access" basis. By contrast, ONA requires the carrier to identify a series of network elements and capabilities (BSEs) to be offered on an unbundled basis and to design a network configuration that provides CEI as part of its technology. These capabilities are to be independent of any decision by the dominant carrier to offer a service dependent on such features. A number of parties, including AT&T, have objected to ONA as providing the regulatory process with too much control over network design decisions.

16. The FCC was not specific in identifying the BSEs that an ONA plan would have to include as part of its initial unbundled package of "primitives"; this lack of specificity is in stark contrast to the detailed nine-item list of CEI parameters contained in the *Computer III Phase I Order*. The FCC has said only that some initial set of BSEs must be identified and made available to the public within one year of approval of a carrier's ONA plan. The services included in the initial set and in all its augmentations are to be determined by the carrier; however, all basic services used by a carrier to provide enhanced services must be offered generally as BSEs. Each time an enhanced service is introduced that uses a basic service not covered by the ONA plan, the ONA plan must be amended to include this basic service as one of the BSEs.

17. At the same time that it released its *Computer III Phase I Order*, the FCC also issued a Supplemental Notice of Proposed Rulemaking requesting comment on five issues that it was not able to resolve. *Amendment of Section 64.702 of the Commission's Rules and Regulations (Third Computer Inquiry)*, FCC No. 86–253 (released June 16, 1986) [hereinafter referred to as *Phase II Notice*]. The *Phase II Notice* concerned the following issues:

a. Whether protocol processing functions should remain within the category of enhanced services, meaning that their provision would be subject to the CEI, accounting, and non-discrimination requirements of the *Computer III* rules, or whether they should be defined as a new category of service (regulated as a basic service when provided as an "adjunct" to a basic service and as an enhanced service when offered as part of an enhanced service).

    b. Whether the FCC should impose on the RHCs slightly different competitive safeguards from those it would impose on AT&T, owing to differences between the operations and competitive situations in the exchange and interexchange service markets.

    c. Whether *Computer III* should be applied to certain of the independent local telephone companies.

    d. Whether carriers should be permitted to offer certain functions generally considered part of unrelated customer premises equipment as part of the tariffed offering of network services.

    e. Whether the *Computer III* rules should be applied to international communications (the FCC tentatively concluding, and proposing, that they should).

18. At the same time that it adopted the *Phase I Reconsideration Order*, the FCC adopted a decision in response to the *Phase II Notice*. *Amendment of Section 64.702 of the Commission's Rules and Regulations (Third Computer Inquiry)*, FCC No. 87–103 (released May 22, 1987) [hereinafter referred to as *Phase II Order*].

19. The most complex of the issues considered in the *Phase II Notice*—and the focus of the bulk of the comments in response to the Notice—was the appropriate regulatory treatment of protocol processing.

    a. Under the *Computer II* rules, protocol processing was considered to be within the FCC's definition of "enhanced services". Therefore, protocol processing could be provided by AT&T and the RHCs only through separate subsidiaries. In the *Computer III Phase I Order*, the FCC decided to retain the enhanced services definition and to continue waivers of the structural separation requirements for the RHCs for the provisions of X.25/X.75 and asynchronous/X.25 conversions. The *Phase II Notice*, however, offered three new options for regulating protocol processing services. Under two of these options, carriers would have been permitted to offer protocol processing services that did not alter the information contained in a subscriber's message as a tariffed basic service offering that would be an adjunct to its other basic services.

    b. More specifically, Alternative A would have classified as basic all protocol processing services that did not (*i*) alter the information content of a subscriber's message, (*ii*) provide the subscriber with additional information, or (*iii*) permit the subscriber to interact with stored information. Under Alternative B, the FCC would have continued to classify protocol processing services generally as enhanced services, but it would have used its discretion to identify specific services that could "be classified with certainty as adjuncts to basic service". *Phase II Notice*, FCC No. 86–253 at para. 35. Initially, four services would have been classified as adjuncts to basic service: (*i*) call initiation, routing, and termination, (*ii*)

X.25/X.75 conversion, (*iii*) asynchronous/X.25 conversion, and (*iv*) "protocol conversion in connection with the introduction of new technology to implement existing services". *Id.*

c. Either approach might have had the consequence of subjecting some currently unregulated service providers to the possibility of increased state regulation—if they provided an intrastate protocol processing service classified as basic that states would view as a common carrier offering subject to state regulation. A number of value-added network ("VAN") operators opposed Alternative A because of a fear that their packet-switched network offerings would have become subject to regulation by state public utility commissions. The states might have required VAN operators to obtain certificates of public convenience and necessity before offering their services on an intrastate basis and to offer their services under tariffs approved by regulatory authorities. Such state regulation might have been used to limit the number of VAN operators permitted to enter a specific intrastate market or to prevent VAN operators from competing with local telephone companies.

d. Under the third option (Alternative C), which the FCC adopted (although in a modified form) in its *Phase II Order*, the FCC will continue to treat all protocol processing activities as enhanced services. This approach reflects the FCC's concern for promoting the development of a competitive services market and its recognition that certain protocol processing functions are vital components of competitive services.

e. A concern about Alternative C that was expressed to the FCC in comments was whether CEI could be provided for protocol processing efficiently or effectively. Several commenters argued that if the unbundling requirements of CEI and ONA were made applicable to enhanced protocol processing functions, carriers would face potentially far-reaching technical obstacles. In the view of some carriers, the unbundling of protocol conversion features would require the separation of "inseparable" elements. In a packet-switched network, for example, carriers claimed that they would find it extremely difficult—if not impossible—to provide a CEI interface within the packet assembler/disassembler (the "PAD") that performs an asynchronous/X.25 conversion.

f. This concern may be somewhat alleviated by the contentions of certain VAN operators and large users that experience gained in implementing the FCC's policy on waivers for asynchronous/X.25 conversion demonstrates the feasibility of a specific approach for the provision of CEI. Such operators do not view CEI as requiring an interface within the PAD; that interface could be provided at some point in the network before the PAD. These assurances, however, do not offset the concern of some carriers that one or more aggressive users might attempt to have CEI or ONA requirements applied more broadly.

g. The FCC seems to have recognized these concerns by deciding in the *Phase II Order* to impose a modified form of non-structural safeguards on protocol processing offerings. As a result, the RHCs will continue to be required to comply with the conditions of the *Asynchronous/X.25 Waiver Order*, 100 F.C.C.2d 1057 (1985), when providing protocol processing offerings on a collocated or unseparated basis. These conditions, which the *Computer III Phase I Order* made applicable pending resolution of the Phase II proceeding, require the RHCs (*i*) to make available to competitors, without discrimination, the inter-office channels from which they assemble underlying packet networks, (*ii*) to include in their tariffs for these underlying circuits a rate element applicable to users of the asynchronous/X.25 conversion offering that reflects the costs (in terms of decreased efficiency in the packet network) of having collocated the protocol conversion functions, (*iii*) to offer to end users access to competitors' protocol conversion offerings equal to the access available to RHC offerings, and (*iv*) to take under tariff the intra-office connection by which the RHCs connect with subscribers to their protocol conversion offerings.

h. AT&T is subject to a less rigorous set of requirements in connection with its unseparated protocol processing offerings. AT&T will have to make available on a non-discriminatory basis any digital transmission services and facilities used in connection with integrated protocol processing offerings. It will also have to acquire such transmission services at a tariffed rate.

i. It remains to be seen whether VAN operators and other service providers will feel that the FCC's treatment of protocol processing serves their best interests. In the *Computer III* proceedings, these groups contended that the FCC should treat protocol processing as an enhanced service because, in this event, the inclusion of protocol processing in the network would trigger the applicability of non-structural safeguards. If such activities had not been classified as enhanced services, carriers would not have been required to observe non-structural safeguards when providing protocol processing. What is less clear, however, is whether VAN operators will find the requirements of the *Asynchronous/X.25 Waiver Order* and the special safeguards applied to AT&T to be satisfactory substitutes for CEI.

20. With respect to the remaining issues, the FCC (*i*) decided to impose on the RHCs competitive safeguards that are essentially identical to those imposed on AT&T (except insofar as the FCC responded to AT&T's petition for reconsideration by modifying the ONA requirements applicable to AT&T); (*ii*) decided—at least for now—not to apply the *Computer III* requirements to the independent local telephone companies or to the local telephone companies owned by GTE; (*iii*) decided to permit the RHCs to offer loopback testing as part of the tariffed offering of basic network services (*i.e.*, at the point of demarcation between the network and the terminal, rather than within the terminal, thereby permitting a carrier to determine whether a technical problem is located within the network wiring) and to allow RHCs to apply for waivers to provide other functions under similar conditions; and (*iv*) decided to apply its *Computer III* policies to international communications.

C. Problems

1. There is some doubt that the theory of ONA can be implemented.

a. In the FCC's view, ONA development will involve the compilation (probably through some broad-based industry fora) of a set of BSEs that will balance carrier and non-carrier needs. Within the industry, however, and particularly among network engineers, there is substantial doubt about whether a satisfactory set of BSEs can be identified in the abstract.

b. According to carriers, enhanced service providers and other facilities users do not have a "shopping list" of desirable BSEs; the carriers contend that the specifics of any ONA plan will necessarily depend on what services are to be provided using the carriers' networks. Competing enhanced service providers, however, have understandably voiced some reluctance to disclose plans for future services. Carriers, on the other hand, do not want to offer up a long list of all possible BSEs for fear that this approach will either prompt users to dream up new services they had never before considered or encourage them to request an unreasonably large number of BSEs. As a result, the process of turning the ONA concept into a reality seems likely to involve more turmoil than the FCC may have anticipated.

2. The ONA development process also appears likely to involve the FCC in a closer ongoing supervision of carrier decisionmaking than the *Computer III Phase I Order* seems to have contemplated. Planning for a future generation of network facilities may require the FCC to become deeply involved in issues of carrier co-ordination and the relative effectiveness of disparate ONA plans. It is not clear that the FCC envisioned ONA as a way of injecting regulation into the process of network design; ONA seems intended to move issues of network configuration out of the realm of regulators and into the arena of industry technicians, consistent with the general belief by the FCC that market mechanisms are the most appropriate forum for the resolution of competitive issues. Nonetheless, the ONA requirements, rather than market developments, are triggering the redesign and reconfiguration of carrier networks now in process as the February 1, 1988 deadline for filing ONA plans approaches.

3. In an effort to develop some commonality in their ONA plans—and to offer some organized way of gaining user and customer input—the RHCs have organized an Open Network Architecture Forum (the "ONAF"). There can be no assurance, however, that this voluntary collaborative effort will produce uniform or compatible ONA plans, although a number of the RHCs have stressed the need for "national" discussions to ensure compatibility between regions.

a. The RHCs sponsored the first ONAF in October 1986. Participants included enhanced service providers, information service providers, the RHCs, and other local exchange carriers. Other members of the telecommunications industry, such as interexchange carriers, vendors, consultants, and research organizations also participated.

b. The sponsors of the ONAF said that the goal of the forum was to gain broad industry input on the ONA development process by fostering a free exchange of information among the ONAF participants. This goal proved elusive at the first meeting primarily because of the conflict described above about how ONA plans should be designed. Participants other than the RHCs asked the RHCs to provide technical information, such as the present capabilities of the local exchange network and the list of network features that could be unbundled. They also asked for any existing ONA blueprints. The RHCs, by contrast, wanted industry participants to state what future enhanced services they planned to offer and what unbundled network functions these services would require. In short, each side wanted the other to provide its plans as the basis for development of an ONA. As a result of the dispute, the hoped-for exchange of information, which is crucial to ONA development, did not occur. Whether that exchange can or will take place seems to have become the central issue of debate facing the voluntary effort of the BOCs and other industry participants to develop ONA plans.

c. The second ONAF meeting ("ONAF2"), held in Los Angeles at the end of March 1987, provided further evidence that efforts to achieve uniformity among the seven RHCs are likely to prove difficult. Although a number of the RHCs have stated repeatedly that they share a general intent to design national standards and uniformity into their ONA plans, RHC presentations at the ONAF2 reveal that "uniformity" is, at present, mostly a theory.

d. Each of the RHCs gave presentations on their ONA plans during the ONAF2, and four of the seven RHCs proposed BSE concepts that were significantly different from each other.

i) US West, for example, divided BSEs into essential services (having no readily available alternative; to be offered under tariff) and non-essential services (similar capabilities can be offered by substitute services and can be offered competitively).

ii) Southwestern Bell proposed a similar division, although it grouped its elemental offerings into functional modules. It suggested offering Modular Service Elements, which would provide users with essential network interconnections, and Modular Service Options, which would be add-on functions. Southwestern Bell rejected the notion that the offering of individual network "primitives" would be useful.

iii) NYNEX diverged most from what the industry had expected BSEs to be—based on the FCC's *Computer III Phase I Order*—and proposed a set of five network access arrangements that it termed Open Network Serving Arrangements. The five options focus on the means by which users would be connected to the basic transmission network.

iv) Ameritech opted for a more "conventional" (or more expected) approach to BSEs. It provided an initial list of BSEs grouped into two categories—internal network functions and call information. Among the initial BSEs were automatic number identification, central office announcements, signalling to indicate answers and disconnects by called party, and provision of called party number.

4. Throughout the proceedings at the first ONAF and at ONAF2, industry participants and the RHCs underscored a number of basic issues requiring resolution, such as certain definitional questions. For example, as the proceedings during ONAF2 make clear, there is still no real consensus as to what constitutes a BSE. Nor is there agreement about the boundaries of an enhanced service, whose elements must be unbundled. In addition, it is not clear whether agreed-upon definitions would have to be applied on a uniform basis nationwide or only within a BOC's region. It is likely that the FCC will become involved in such basic definitional issues.

5. In addition to considering the design of future network architectures that will comply with ONA principles, the RHCs must grapple with how to bring their existing networks into compliance with ONA. Reconfiguring existing networks will require the RHCs to determine what "services" are now available and how much unbundling of those services can be managed. Participants in the ONAF asked, for example, whether the BOCs have the technical capabilities to unbundle switching and service concentration features. Such an unbundling process could affect the price charged for existing services. To the extent that the RHCs decide or are required to break down and price out their current networks, they will have to charge themselves for component features that they currently include as part of an overall service offering.

6. The lack of specificity in the FCC's ONA requirements has proved a source of both controversy and concern. One area of substantial concern (and disagreement) is the extent to which the ONA requirements will be used to break up carrier networks into many elemental functions.

a. The FCC has said that its complaint procedures may be used to challenge aspects of ONA plans that are believed to have anticompetitive effects. It remains to be seen whether these procedures will be used by competing service providers to unbundle basic networks to such an extent that ONA will become the vehicle for turning the BOCs into wholesale vendors of elemental signalling, switching, and transport capabilities.

b. AT&T's petition for reconsideration, which resulted in the FCC's decision to modify the ONA requirements applicable to AT&T, paid close attention to the question of whether unbundling requirements would harm AT&T. That petition argued that unbundling "would cripple AT&T's ability to compete effectively in the provision of basic services" by preventing it from being able "to differentiate its basic services from those of its competitors". AT&T Petition for Reconsideration 13–14 (August 4, 1986). According to AT&T, basic service providers such as MCI and US

Sprint could use ONA (or, possibly, CEI) to force AT&T to make available to them various network features that currently allow AT&T to offer certain exclusive basic services, such as call routing based on the time of day, call screening and blocking, and various signalling and support features. Because CEI must be made available to all users (not just enhanced service providers), and because ONA must consist of unbundled BSEs offered under tariff to the public, AT&T argued that competing basic service providers would benefit from these regulatory schemes both by using AT&T network capabilities to develop "'me too' services" and by making "unwarranted unbundling demands, in order to obtain an even greater competitive advantage or merely to delay the introduction of AT&T's new basic or enhanced service". *Id.* at 15.

   c. Although the RHCs would appear to face similar potentially dire consequences, they opposed AT&T's petition and, as described above, have begun the process of developing ONA plans. Of course, the RHCs now operate in less competitive markets than does AT&T, making the potential competitive threat of unbundling appear less severe, though no less objectionable in theory. The RHCs, unlike AT&T, also have a significant incentive for complying with the FCC's new regulatory scheme: the possibility of being released from the line-of-business restrictions of the MFJ.

   d. The RHCs and others also have pointed to paragraph 217 of the *Computer III Phase I Order* as a way of countering AT&T's claims. In that paragraph, the FCC recognized "the inefficiencies that may occur from unnecessarily unbundled or splintered services". The RHCs have claimed that this language makes clear the FCC's sensitivity to the possibility that CEI or ONA could be used to dismantle a carrier's network, and demonstrates that attempts by basic service providers to use CEI and ONA as means for competing unfairly will not be allowed to control these processes.

   e. It is not clear, however, how the FCC will resolve disputes over decisions to unbundle or not to unbundle certain network features. As noted above, the FCC's complaint procedures may be used to attack the propriety of an ONA offering; the FCC has not stated, however, what standards will be applied to any disagreement over unbundling.

   f. In its petition, AT&T, for example, pointed to paragraph 158 of the *Computer III Phase I Order*, which says that "[a]ll basic network capabilities utilized by the carrier's enhanced service offerings, including signalling, switching, billing, and network management, are subject to this unbundling requirement", to argue that, despite the FCC's good intentions, its decision may have a disastrously broad application. For this reason, AT&T argued, it should be permitted to make unbundling decisions in response to marketplace demands, not regulatory directives. AT&T has said that it should be left free to balance the advantages of making basic features available to users to help them offer in-demand enhanced services against the disadvantages of permitting competing basic service providers to use those features to offer basic services that previously have been offered only by AT&T.

       g. The FCC's decision in its *Phase I Reconsideration Order* to modify the ONA requirements applicable to AT&T clearly finds merit in AT&T's arguments. One might wonder, then, what the consequences of ONA might be for the RHCs as they are subjected to more competitive market situations.

    7. An initial question raised by CEI is whether the FCC has chosen a threshold standard that is rigorous enough to prompt the development of the CEI concept. CEI requires AT&T and the RHCs to provide "non-discriminatory" treatment (*i.e.*, treatment that is no better or worse than a carrier provides to itself and to its affiliates).

       a. It is not clear that this standard will maximize the development of new services and competition. Should a service provider be entitled to receive CEI with any facility of any carrier upon any "reasonable request"?

       b. ONA, which would make certain BSEs available regardless of the enhanced services activities of the carriers, may encourage the development of new enhanced services more successfully. (At least AT&T has suggested, however, that ONA requirements imposed by the FCC will have the effect of keeping it out of the enhanced services market, thereby slowing the development of that market.)

    8. Although the FCC's CEI requirements are far more explicit than those for ONA, there continue to be a number of issues that will have to be clarified in the course of applying the CEI standards to specific factual situations.

       a. How will the FCC handle requests for waivers of the CEI policy, and what impact might the grant or denial of these requests have on the market? The FCC has indicated that it expects waiver requests to be rare and to be made only when a carrier has an alternative interconnection arrangement that will closely approximate the results of the nine CEI parameters.

       b. Would the FCC grant a waiver for a CEI offering that could accommodate only a limited number of enhanced service providers, if capacity were made available on a first-come, first-served basis? The FCC and enhanced service providers might object if an RHC provided CEI to its own enhanced service operation in this situation. It might be argued that limited capacity should be allocated by lottery or auction to guard against the possibility that an RHC always would offer CEI to its own enhanced service operations in situations where only a limited number of service providers could be accommodated.

       c. Can a service provider, after reviewing proposed CEI specifications, demand modifications that allegedly would achieve greater "comparability" or that would allow its particular service to be offered? Who would decide the extent of a carrier's CEI obligations? It remains to be seen how disputes that arise during the "testing" phase of the CEI planning process, in which carriers and third-party service providers will be permitted to try out any proposed CEI arrangements before they are approved by the FCC, will be resolved.

9. Without some uniformity among carrier ONA plans, and with many intra- and inter-Local Access and Transport Area facilities not being subject to ONA requirements, it may be difficult for enhanced service providers to provide their services on a relatively uniform basis in different regions of the country or nationwide. Market demand may prompt carriers not covered by ONA requirements to make available certain of the BSEs needed to support enhanced services with significant user demand. Carriers not offering such BSEs should at least be able to transport the intelligence needed to support various enhanced service units, possibly minimizing the impact of not imposing ONA obligations on interexchange carriers. (The unavailability of BSEs in a particular local exchange area may leave customers in that area without the benefit of some or many enhanced services, or may require that such customers place toll calls to connect with a node capable of providing the necessary enhanced service features.)

a. A number of the RHCs have been developing as an ONA plan the concept of the Feature Node Service Interface ("FNSI"), in which the carrier deploys a relatively unsophisticated switch and locates enhanced service equipment off-site, in nodes, rather than as part of a single switch or a central switching facility. Yet, interest in FNSI varies from company to company; Ameritech appears to be the most ardent advocate of the concept. Thus, there is no assurance that FNSI will become a widespread approach to ONA.

b. Even if FNSI were to be widely adopted, co-ordination among various RHCs is likely to prove difficult because standards and interfaces are almost certain to vary from one supplier to the next.

10. AT&T and at least some RHCs believe that regulation of the network design process is a dangerous step away from the general trend toward deregulation and may be a permanent—rather than a transitory—addition of new regulatory requirements in the U.S. telecommunications market. Whether ONA is truly a step toward "reregulation" remains to be seen. AT&T's petition for reconsideration, discussed above in Section II.C.6, opposed ONA that was prescribed by regulation; it was less concerned with the development of ONA based upon market demand. A number of the RHCs seem to have adopted a similar stance; at the ONAF2 discussed above in Section II.C.3, they supported an approach under which market demand would be used to determine what BSEs should be offered.

11. Another difficult area concerns the future co-ordination of federal and state regulatory interests. The FCC's authority to assert the supremacy of federal power to prevent states from imposing regulatory requirements that are different from, or that conflict with, those set forth in the *Computer III* regulatory scheme may have been undercut by two recent federal court decisions—*Louisiana Public Service Comm'n v. FCC*, 476 U.S. 355 (1986) (reversing the FCC's decision to preempt state depreciation

rules for common carriers that were inconsistent with the federal rules) and *California Public Utility Comm'n v. FCC*, 798 F. 2d 1515 (D.C. Cir. 1986) (reversing the FCC's preemption of state entry restrictions on intrastate common carrier services offered over FM subcarrier frequencies).

  a. The decisions ultimately may be interpreted to allow a state's regulators to impose more or less stringent regulatory safeguards than those adopted by the FCC on the intrastate enhanced services of carriers within that state's jurisdiction. The California Public Utilities Commission made this argument in a petition for reconsideration of the *Computer III Phase I Order* that was rejected in the *Phase I Reconsideration Order*.

  b. In the wake of these recent decisions, one equally important, but separate, question is whether the FCC can still reasonably insist that all state regulation of entities offering enhanced services is preempted. If an enhanced service provider were to offer some basic service, in addition to its enhanced service offerings, it might be viewed by state regulatory officials as a "carrier" subject to state regulation with respect to all of its intrastate offerings.

D. Prospects

  1. ONA is almost certain to have some impact outside the United States; thus, it may be useful to consider how international interests can be taken into account during the planning process. Such planning may be too focused at an operational level to be handled effectively within the form of the Consultative Committee on International Telegraph and Telephone ("CCITT") of the International Telecommunication Union ("ITU"). It may be possible to encourage international participation in the ONAF; such participation might also be co-ordinated by specific groups, such as the Conférence Européenne des Postes et Télécommunications ("CEPT") or the International Telecommunications Users Group ("IN-TUG"). These issues are discussed more fully in Section XIII, below.

  2. Decisions by Judge Greene about the conditions under which the RHCs can involve themselves in the enhanced services market will have a substantial impact on the development of CEI and ONA, as well as on the evolution of specific enhanced services. The terms of the MFJ already may be hindering the development of CEI plans. Over the longer term, the potential for a jurisdictional conflict between Judge Greene and the FCC looms as a threat to the FCC's entire scheme of regulation under the *Computer III* decision.

  a. The RHCs may not be filing CEI plans in part because they believe that the MFJ prevents them from taking advantage of the benefits of CEI (*i.e.*, the ability to offer enhanced services on an unseparated basis). The question of whether the MFJ prohibits or restricts the RHCs from offering some or most enhanced services has never been put squarely before Judge Greene. Nevertheless, the RHCs apparently believe that many (if not all) enhanced services fall within the definition of "information services" contained in the MFJ and that, as a result, they are prohibited from offering such services.

b. In its April 1987 filing with Judge Greene, discussed below in Section II.D.8, the Department of Justice said explicitly that "[r]egardless of FCC approval, the BOCs could not actually provide enhanced services (except the types of protocol conversion services that are not deemed information services) until the [information services restriction in the] decree . . . is removed". *Response of the United States to Comments on its Report and Recommendations Concerning the Line-of-Business Restrictions Imposed on the Bell Operating Companies by the Modification of Final Judgment* at 83 (filed April 27, 1987) [hereinafter referred to as the "DoJ Response"].

c. It is not clear whether Judge Greene would find the non-structural safeguards contained in a CEI plan adequate to permit an RHC to provide an enhanced service. The nine CEI parameters (described above in Section II.B.7) might be viewed as a satisfactory way of ensuring that an RHC could not exert an anticompetitive influence on the enhanced (or "information") services market; in that event it would seem that a CEI plan could provide Judge Greene with a rationale for lifting the information services restriction of the MFJ, or otherwise waiving the prohibition with respect to particular enhanced service activities.

d. Although CEI might enable the RHCs to enter the enhanced services market consistent with the terms of the MFJ, the RHCs now appear to be focusing their attention on the complex task of developing ONA plans. Thus, CEI may not become an "interim" form of ONA. Such a rejection of CEI could leave the enhanced services market languishing until late 1989 or 1990, which is when ONA plans might first gain FCC approval and begin to be implemented. It also could make the ONA process more difficult: there would be no prior experience with CEI to serve as a backdrop for agency and industry discussions of what network unbundling is feasible, desirable, necessary, and efficient.

3. The ongoing review of the MFJ may stave off a potentially grave confrontation between the FCC and Judge Greene over the conditions under which the RHCs may participate in the enhanced services market. The likelihood of such a confrontation increased when the FCC adopted its *Computer III* decision because the decision reflects an approach to the regulation of RHC involvement in the enhanced services market that is strongly at odds with the approach taken by the court. In its three *Computer Inquiries*, the FCC gradually has moved toward permitting the dominant regulated carriers to straddle both sides of the "basic" and "enhanced" services fence. The courts that have wrestled with issues of market dominance in an antitrust context, by contrast, have opted to guard against potentially anticompetitive behavior by erecting a very high wall between these market sectors; the 1956 Consent Decree required AT&T to stay wholly within what has since become the "basic" services arena, and the

MFJ now erects a similar barrier around the telecommunications activities of the RHCs. With the adoption of non-structural safeguards in the *Computer III* decision, the regulatory and the judicial approaches to regulating the RHCs have become more distinct, and more potentially at odds with each other, than they were in the past. In approving the *Computer III* rules, some of the commissioners and members of the FCC staff noted that the MFJ was likely to pose at least some obstacle to full implementation of the rules.

  a. Whether a jurisdictional clash will develop is likely to depend on whether Judge Greene accepts or rejects the recommendations of the Justice Department that were filed with the court on February 2, 1987 (and modified in part on April 27, 1987), as part of the triennial review process required by the terms of the MFJ. *Report and Recommendations of the United States Concerning the Line of Business Restrictions Imposed on the Bell Operating Companies by the Modification of Final Judgment* at 134, *United States v. American Telephone & Telegraph Co.*, 552 F. Supp. 131 (D.D.C. 1982), *aff'd sub nom. Maryland v. United States*, 460 U.S. 1001 (1983) (No. 82-0192) [hereinafter referred to as the "DoJ Recommendations"], *modified in part*, DoJ Response. If the court accepted the Department's recommendation to eliminate the MFJ's information services prohibition, regulation of enhanced services would be left to the FCC, avoiding the potential for a clash between the agency and the court.

  b. The Department's filings with the court recommended removal of the MFJ's restrictions on BOC involvement in the information services and equipment manufacturing businesses. It also recommended removal of the restriction on non-telecommunications businesses, which has been subject to hundreds of waivers since the divestiture. Finally, it recommended retention of the restriction on RHC involvement in the long-distance telecommunications market, except with respect to cellular radio, paging, and other mobile services.

  c. The Justice Department originally proposed relaxing the long-distance prohibition and adopting a modified restriction that would have prohibited an RHC from providing long-distance services to, from, or within areas in which it is effectively a monopoly provider of local telephone service. This restriction could have been lifted in regions of the country where states removed regulations that essentially guaranteed the RHC a monopoly franchise for local exchange service. *See generally* DoJ Recommendations, at 59–104.

  d. After reviewing comments on its initial recommendations, the Justice Department decided that although "the conceptual and policy considerations underlying our original proposal were sound, the practical difficulties in implementing it would be likely to outweigh the potential benefits at this time". DoJ Response, at 24. The Department concluded that "it probably is not possible at this time to establish in a general, prospective order a clear and enforceable distinction between 'in-region' and 'out-of-region' services that would provide an effective alternative to case-by-case review under the waiver process". *Id.* at 27. In addition, it decided, "the comments . . . did not disclose any anticipated competitive benefits from BOC out-of-region interexchange services sufficient to outweigh the potential costs of attempting to modify the decree restrictions". *Id.* As a result, the Department modified its recommendation to advocate retention of the prohibition on RHC involvement in the long-distance market and reliance on the waiver process to permit market entry in specific cases where competitive conditions justify such entry.

   e. In recommending elimination of the information services restriction, the Justice Department concluded that the loss of efficiency resulting from the prohibition almost certainly outweighed any possible risks of anticompetitive behavior by the RHCs. Moreover, in the view of the Department, the court almost certainly would be unable to fashion a decree provision that would apply only to those information services in which the RHCs had the greatest incentive and ability to act anti-competitively (*i.e.*, "in-region" versus "out-of-region" services, or services that are dependent on RHC facilities versus those that are less dependent or independent). Thus, the Department concluded, the court was doomed to imposing an overly broad prohibition that would harm the enhanced services market more than it would benefit it. As a result, the Department urged removal of the restriction in favor of reliance on non-structural safeguards, including CEI, ONA, and cost accounting requirements administered by the FCC. DoJ Recommendations, at 137–47; DoJ Response, at 60–63.

   f. In advocating the elimination of the information services prohibition, the Justice Department expressed some concern about the court's continued involvement in an area that required it to make difficult boundary line judgments about services that could be characterized as basic, enhanced, or non-telecommunications (*e.g.*, information and transactional services). The Department's implicit concern was that the court would flounder in trying to apply increasingly fuzzy boundary lines and might bar the RHCs from providing certain services that could not be separated from the transmission network without great expense or inefficiency. In the Department's view, the FCC was much better equipped to make such complex technical boundary line decisions, although even the FCC has struggled with defining the boundary lines, as is evident from the fact that it has required three separate *Computer Inquiries* in fifteen years to clarify the basic/enhanced dichotomy.

   g. The Department also noted that the information services restriction, unlike the interexchange services ban, might not be well tailored to furthering the development of a competitive market. The restriction was based largely on speculation about market effects. (The interexchange services ban, by contrast, was at the heart of the competitive concerns that prompted the antitrust suit against AT&T in the first place.) The information services restriction also has tended to deprive consumers of certain services; the long-distance restriction has not impeded the development of a competitive interexchange services market. DoJ Recommendations, at 152–4.

4. The Department's recommendations are based largely on a comprehensive examination of the U.S. telecommunications industry prepared for the Justice Department by an independent consultant, Dr Peter W. Huber. U.S. Department of Justice, *The Geodesic Network: 1987 Report on Competition in the Telephone Industry* (Jan. 1987) (prepared by Dr Peter W. Huber) [hereinafter referred to as the "Huber Report"]. The Huber Report contains an interesting vision of the evolving U.S. telecommunications business; it suggests that the changing network infrastructure will be able to support competition even though it necessarily will involve significant vertical integration. Therefore, restrictions on an RHC's lines of business, such as those contained in the MFJ, not only are inefficient, but also are counterproductive.

a. As the title suggests, the Huber Report relies on geometric terms to describe the U.S. telecommunications network. The term "geodesic" is used to describe a network with a multitude of nodes and switches connecting relatively short transmission paths. Dr Huber contrasts this description with his vision of the U.S. network before about 1970. Until then, he contends, the network was pyramidal, with a large number of small and unsophisticated switches handing off traffic to an ever smaller number of increasingly more complex and intelligent nodes. At each switch, traffic was concentrated, and the more intelligent the switch, the smaller the number of connecting transmission lines that would be available. *See id.* at 1.2–1.6.

b. The change in the configuration resulted because technology has made switching and other forms of network intelligence less expensive than transmission—at least over the last mile, where twisted copper pairs remain the standard link. As a result, according to the Huber Report, it is cheaper to add additional switches than to install new, long wires between existing switches. The analogy may be seen in the computer and data processing industry; what was once an industry dependent upon telecommunications links between users and host computers has become a distributed array of minicomputers and microcomputers. Rather than pay communications charges to transport intelligence, users find it more cost-effective to acquire their own intelligence.

c. The Huber Report goes on to suggest that the distribution of processing capabilities throughout the network has created a far more complex structure that requires users to reassemble what once were integrated pieces. The industry realizes that users will place a value on that reassembly process, and so market participants seek to integrate vertically in order to offer users "one-stop shopping" (*e.g.*, IBM/Rolm/MCI, GTE/US Sprint/equipment divisions, Contel/Comsat/Contel, ASC/Contel Executone/Contel Computer Systems). *Id.* at Tables G.5a and G.6. The difference between the pre-divestiture and post-divestiture eras, however, the Huber

Report suggests, is that vertical integration no longer precludes horizontal competition. The proliferation of low-cost switching capabilities and the development of "open architecture" connections make it plausible to move traffic "horizontally" through the network (among competing firms performing the same functions), rather than just vertically (from one firm's local, to its long-distance, to its database operations). *Id.* at 1.09–1.10, 1.30–1.35. Thus, even with vertical integration, end users will have sufficient choice among offerings to ensure that competitive benefits are realized.

    d.   According to Dr Huber, technology is ensuring competition by moving network capabilities out of the hands of a few and into the hands of many—end users, basic service providers, and enhanced service providers. The obstacles to competition are policies that inhibit entry at all levels of the network so that alternatives can be constructed around and between the many dispersed nodes. Thus, limits on the construction or resale of local transmission lines negate the competitive possibilities introduced by PBXs, minicomputers, and microcomputers. More dramatically, says the Huber Report, rules and regulations that limit entry into market sectors—such as those contained in the MFJ—undercut the possibilities for competition by preventing a further dispersion of intelligence and the additional development of competitive service offerings based around existing nodes.

    e.   In the view presented by the Huber Report, the MFJ, like the Consent Decree that preceded it, is an ill-advised means for structuring the market. The 1956 Consent Decree, according to Dr Huber, handed AT&T a monopoly in one market in exchange for its agreement not to enter the computer processing market, which is the very market that, when developed, opened the door for competition with AT&T. The MFJ is similarly flawed, says Dr Huber; the RHCs are given a local service monopoly and are prevented from helping to develop equipment and information offerings that could lead the way to greater competition at the local level.

    f.   With respect to information services specifically, the Huber Report concludes that it is unlikely that an RHC could use its dominance in local transmission in one section of the U.S. to impede competition in what inevitably will be a national or global market for these services. Moreover, the Report contends, the RHCs might help develop intelligent network capabilities; the result could be additional dispersion of intelligence—consistent with the geodesic model—and an increase in competitive potential. Under this view, lifting the information services restriction would be pro-competitive.

    g.   The Huber Report also takes issue with the very notion of a basic/enhanced distinction as it applies to the evolving network. According to Dr Huber, the FCC's boundary line is nothing more than an articulation of what AT&T was and was not permitted to do at the time the 1956 Consent Decree was signed. What AT&T was permitted to do was defined as "basic", even though "[b]y standards prevailing in *1926*, of course, the 'basic' network is already permeated with electronic 'information services'". *Id.* at 1.28 [emphasis in original]. He contends that the "basic" network can perform code and protocol functions related to voice services and can store and retrieve information for voice service billing and for services tied to voice communications (*e.g.,* wrong number or disconnection messages); however, it cannot perform the same functions for "inter-machine" (*i.e.,* data) communications because such communications "were unknown in 1956". *Id.* Thus, Dr Huber concludes, the boundary line has no economic or technological basis; it is merely a "regulatory monument to the past". *Id.* (Dr Huber's observation, of course, highlights why the FCC has struggled to define particular services as either "basic" or "enhanced", particularly clause one enhanced services, which are so much a part of the functioning of the basic transmission network.)

h. The Huber Report condemns the basic/enhanced boundary line because of the way it has been used in the MFJ to prevent the development of an intelligent network. According to Dr Huber, such a preoccupation is wasteful. The evolving network necessarily will have to include certain processing, storage, and retrieval capabilities; however, the focus of technology is on distribution of network intelligence—into CPE, computers, and attachments to network switches (as contemplated by Ameritech's FNSI approach to ONA). Thus, according to the Huber Report, network operators, such as the RHCs, cannot monopolize the intelligence or the information services constructed from that intelligence. Continued regulatory vigilance is warranted to guard against "some anticompetitive mischief [by the RHCs] at the edges of the [information services] market". *Id.* at 1.30. However, users are not well served by efforts to segregate basic and enhanced functions, as the FCC has concluded in *Computer III*. According to Dr Huber, such segregation contradicts the evolutionary forces already at work on the telecommunications network.

5. The Huber Report is a fascinating study because it suggests that the MFJ has got things all wrong and that, perhaps, the FCC is walking down a more appropriate path (although using an admittedly imperfect industry "map", *i.e.,* the basic/enhanced dichotomy). Dr Huber would seem to be satisfied with using the basic/enhanced boundary line to trigger network access obligations and to require the RHCs to further disperse network intelligence; the approach supports what Dr Huber suggests is the inevitable development of the telecommunications sector. It also removes the anachronistic structural separation requirements that he sees as being contrary to the natural evolution of the market.

6. One question, however, is whether this vision of the marketplace, which involves a very forward-looking view of telecommunications in the U.S., can justify modification of the MFJ. Such modification requires, according to Section VIII(C) of the MFJ, a finding that there is "no substantial possibility" that the RHCs could use their "monopoly power to impede competition in the relevant market". It is not

clear that Dr Huber's vision, which forms the basis for the Justice Department recommendations, together with the Department's conclusions, will be found sufficient to make the showing necessary for Judge Greene to modify the MFJ according to its terms. With respect to information services at least, both Dr Huber and the Justice Department contend that FCC regulation will be sufficient to protect against anticompetitive practices by the RHCs. It is ironic that the MFJ was drafted in large part as a response to dissatisfaction with the FCC's ability to monitor competition in the interexchange market and a belief that a court exercising jurisdiction under the anti-trust laws could do better. Both the Department and Dr Huber are now looking to an untested regulatory regime—the product of the *Computer III* decision—as a superior alternative to court management of the telecommunications sector.

7. The more than 100 comments on the DoJ Recommendations that interested parties have filed with the court have varied widely. In general, however, the commenters supported only some of the initial Recommendations. A large number contended that the Department had not made the showing required for modification of the MFJ. *See, e.g., Comments of MCI* at 3, *United States v. American Telephone & Telegraph Co.*, 552 F. Supp. 131 (D.D.C. 1982), *aff'd mem, sub nom. Maryland v. United States*, 460 U.S. 1001 (1983) (No. 82-0192) ("Because the standard for lifting the restrictions—elimination of the Bell Company local bottlenecks—has not been met, the text, history, and purposes of the judgment demand that Bell Companies continue to be barred from competitive markets".). *But see Comments of the FCC* at 5–6 ("The Department correctly applied the standard that had been incorporated into the decree . . . [and] concluded that the increased competitiveness of those markets, improved regulatory tools, evolutions in technology, and actual experiences over the past five years, when considered together, clearly tilt the balance in favor of restricting the decree's flat prohibitions, ..."). Rather than attempt to summarize the voluminous comments, the discussion that follows briefly sets out a sample of the views expressed on the Department's recommendation that the information services ban be lifted to illustrate the range of opinions before the court.

a. The Computer and Communications Industry Association supported the Department's recommendation to lift the ban, provided that the RHCs are permitted to provide information services only in compliance with the FCC's *Computer III* rules. Those rules, it said, were sufficient to guard against anticompetitive conduct.

b. The Association of Data Processing Service Organizations (ADAPSO) criticized both the Department and Dr Huber for failing to demonstrate that the RHCs could not use their monopoly positions to impede competition in the information services market. Briefly, ADAPSO argued that (*i*) Dr Huber's geodesic network already existed in 1982, when the MFJ was entered: (*ii*) the fact that switching and intelligence capabilities are dispersed is irrelevant because the RHCs continue to have monopoly control over local transmission activities; (*iii*) the opportunity for cost shifting by the RHCs remains substantial; (*iv*) the FCC's regulatory safeguards are untested; and (*v*) the alleged loss of efficiency resulting from the information services ban is speculative. Thus, ADAPSO argues, either the ban should be retained or structural separation should be required.

   c. The FCC supported the Department's position, citing changes in technology, network configuration, and regulatory safeguards as justifying the modification of the MFJ.

   d. AT&T declined to take a position on the information services issue. It asserted that although the RHCs continue to have a monopoly position in local markets, that monopoly may or may not give them power to compete unfairly in the information services business. Claiming that its own lack of involvement in information services left it without any basis for supporting elimination or retention of the information services ban (the two "extreme" positions), AT&T suggested that the MFJ might be modified to allow the RHCs into the information services under certain conditions designed to protect competition. It said, for example, that the court might turn over to the FCC the task of monitoring and regulating RHC involvement in the offering of information services. (As discussed below in Section II.D.12, AT&T petitioned the court on December 9, 1986, to turn over to the FCC the job of screening all RHC waiver requests.)

   8. In its response to the comments, the Justice Department argued that RHC involvement in the information services market is unlikely to impede competition because (*i*) many information services are not dependent on local transmission facilities, (*ii*) the FCC's non-structural safeguards appear adequate to expose and guard against anticompetitive activities, and (*iii*) consumers are likely to suffer in the absence of RHC involvement in this market.

   a. The Justice Department said that if the information services restriction is not removed, the market is not likely to benefit from the development of ONA. Recognizing the "extensive and expensive network design changes" required by the *Computer III* rules, the Department concluded that "[c]ontinuing the decree prohibition . . . would significantly undercut the incentive the FCC has created [for the RHCs to develop ONA plans] and thus make successful development of ONA very unlikely". DoJ Response, at 74.

   b. The Department also concluded that the FCC was the most appropriate forum "to supervise the full transition to the information services age". *Id.* at 78. The Department was particularly supportive of the *Computer III* rules and the processes that the FCC has developed to ensure that there is broad participation in the review and approval of plans to comply with the various non-structural safeguards. *Id.* at 80, 88. Recognizing that the new rules have not been tested in the market, it said, nonetheless, that requiring the RHCs to obtain waivers from the court—in addition to those FCC approvals required by the *Computer III* rules—

would merely add unnecessary delay to the process of developing new information services. *Id.* at 86–87.

9. Judge Greene will review and evaluate the Department's recommendations, as set out in the DoJ Recommendations and the DoJ Response, in proceedings that are expected to last until the latter part of 1987.

10. If the MFJ's information services restriction is not relaxed, an appellate court decision that reversed an earlier decision by Judge Greene might figure in the debate over whether the RHCs, consistent with the MFJ, can provide enhanced services on an unseparated basis outside their monopoly service regions. *United States v. Western Electric Co., Inc.*, 797 F. 2d 1082 (D.C. Cir. 1986).

a. The Court of Appeals, in its decision, held that the MFJ should not be read as preventing an RHC from providing "exchange telecommunications and exchange access service[s]" outside the region in which it serves as the primary local telephone company. Judge Greene had held that such "extraterritorial" services could be provided only after a waiver had been obtained from his court. If the RHCs rely on this decision to enter enhanced service markets nationwide, they may face an argument from Judge Greene or the Justice Department that such enhanced services are not "exchange telecommunications and exchange access service[s]".

b. Many observers believe that Judge Greene will consider particular enhanced services either (*i*) "information services" that the MFJ explicitly prohibits the RHCs from offering unless they can demonstrate that there is "no substantial possibility that [the RHC] could use its monopoly power to impede competition in the relevant market" or (*ii*) other than "exchange telecommunications and exchange access service[s]" or "natural monopoly service[s] actually regulated by tariff" and, therefore, beyond the permitted lines of business of the RHCs, unless they are offered through a separate subsidiary pursuant to a waiver from Judge Greene's court. Any separate subsidiary requirement, of course, would be inconsistent with the regulatory scheme of the FCC's *Computer III* rules and could lead to a jurisdictional crisis.

11. The significance of these potential conflicts and a general dissatisfaction with the involvement of the court and the Department of Justice in the process of formulating U.S. telecommunications policy resulted in Congressional support for 1986 legislation that would have transferred the job of administering the MFJ's provisions from Judge Greene to the FCC. S. 2565, a bill that was introduced in the Senate by then-Majority Leader Robert Dole (R.-Kan.) and strongly backed by the Reagan Administration, would have adopted the MFJ's provisions as rules of the FCC. S. 2565, 99th Cong., 2d Sess. (1986). Some FCC Commissioners have voiced their opposition to some or all of the MFJ restrictions imposed on the RHCs; thus, it was widely believed that such legislation would have led to an FCC rulemaking proceeding that would have eliminated or relaxed many of these restrictions. Procedurally, it was

expected that, if the legislation had been adopted, Judge Greene would have vacated the MFJ as being unnecessary. The 99th Congress adjourned before any action had been taken on the bill. With the release of the Huber Report and the start of the court's process of reviewing the MFJ, it is expected that no new legislation will be acted upon before the review process is complete.

12. As noted above briefly, on December 9, 1986, after the 99th Congress had adjourned, AT&T submitted a motion to Judge Greene asking that the waiver screening function being performed by the Justice Department be transferred to the FCC. This request contended that the Justice Department had been so overwhelmed with waiver requests (which were being submitted at the rate of one per week) that its ability to act as the prosecutorial agency charged with enforcing the MFJ was being hampered. The RHCs criticized the proposal. They argued that it was part of an attempt by AT&T to introduce additional procedural steps into the waiver process in an effort to impede BOC efforts to diversify their businesses. The court opened the AT&T proposal up for comment on the same schedule as the DoJ Recommendations. Initial comments on AT&T's proposal were generally unfavorable.

13. The MFJ poses a much less significant obstacle to applying the *Computer III* rules to AT&T's enhanced service offerings. Under the MFJ, AT&T is prohibited only from offering "electronic publishing" services, which are services that provide information "originated, authored, compiled, collected, or edited" by AT&T or an affiliate. Inasmuch as few proposed enhanced services are likely to fall within this category, the MFJ is probably not a major barrier to applying the *Computer III* rules to AT&T. To date, little regulatory or judicial attention has been focused on this prohibition.

14. The practical significance of the basic/enhanced distinction may diminish as the FCC takes steps to reduce the regulation of specific basic services.

a. Since 1979, the FCC gradually has streamlined the regulatory requirements applicable to the basic service activities of particular groups of carriers. *Policy and Rules Concerning Rates and Facilities Authorizations for Competitive Carriers*, 85 F.C.C.2d 1 (1980) (First Report and Order); 91 F.C.C.2d 59 (1982) (Second Report and Order), *recon.* FCC No. 83–69 (released March 21, 1983); 48 *Fed. Reg.* 46791 (Oct. 15, 1983) (Third Report and Order); 95 F.C.C.2d 554 (1983) (Fourth Report and Order); 98 F.C.C.2d 1191 (1984) (Fifth Report and Order); 99 F.C.C.2d 1020 (1985) (Sixth Report and Order), *rev'd sub nom. MCI Communications Corp. v. FCC*, 765 F.2d 1186 (D.C. Cir. 1985). Carriers to which such streamlined regulation applies are known as "non-dominant" carriers.

b. In December 1986, the Commission proposed reducing the tariff regulation of particular *services*, even if they are offered by carriers now classified as dominant or not yet classified as non-dominant. *Decreased Regulation of Certain Basic Telecommunications Services*, FCC No. 86–421 (released Jan. 9, 1987) (Notice of Proposed Rulemaking) [hereinafter referred to as *Basic Services Deregulation*]. The FCC has proposed streamlining the regulation of defined service markets or submarkets in which it finds that no carriers have "market power", defined initially as the ability to set the price of a service. The Notice raises three basic issues requiring comment: (*i*) how should a service market or submarket be defined; (*ii*) how should market power be assessed; and (*iii*) should competitive safeguards such as CEI and cost allocation requirements be applied to the basic service offerings of dominant carriers that are given the benefit of streamlined regulation?

c. The FCC also has proposed streamlining the regulation of packet-switched services and of equipment and services provided under contracts awarded in a competitive bidding process. The focus of future proceedings in the docket—after the basic parameters outlined above have been established—would be to identify basic services that are offered on a competitive basis by dominant and non-dominant carriers and to determine whether streamlined regulation and certain competitive safeguards should be applied to them.

d. The FCC's proposal to streamline the regulation of packet services provides an example of the potential complexity of this endeavor. The FCC notes in its Notice that although most packet services that include protocol processing functions are considered enhanced services and are not subject to regulation, the FCC regulates the "basic" services portion of packet services provided by AT&T and the RHCs. These basic components are required to be offered under tariff; the RHCs also must comply with the requirements of specific waiver decisions to offer protocol conversion on a collocated basis. *See, e.g., Asynchronous/X.25 Waiver Order*. Thus, deregulation of packet services would affect primarily AT&T and the RHCs. *Basic Services Deregulation*, at para. 21.

e. Identifying appropriate markets and submarkets as candidates for the application of streamlined regulation clearly will be difficult. In the Notice of Proposed Rulemaking, for example, the FCC noted that packet services might consist of a variety of submarkets, such as one that distinguishes intraLATA and interLATA offerings (the latter being foreclosed to the BOCs). It also might include circuit-switched as well as packet-switched services that are competitive or substitutable. *Id.* at paras. 22–25.

f. The FCC also might face obstacles in its effort to streamline the regulation of certain basic services. For example, to the extent that it seeks to streamline the regulation of a BOC packet service offered on an intrastate basis, it may have problems pre-empting more stringent state regulations applied to the intrastate "basic" elements previously identified by the FCC. *See id.* at para. 21. It is not clear how the FCC would deal with this problem. Generally speaking, it asserts its authority to preempt inconsistent state regulation of packet services on the basis of its view that packet services involving protocol processing functions are enhanced services (because the enhanced elements "contaminate" the entire service) and that, under the *Computer II* and *Computer III* decisions, state regulation of enhanced service offerings are preempted. However, the FCC's division of the elements of a BOC packet offering—for purposes of applying the *Computer II* and *Computer III* rules—may open the door for state interference with the FCC's plans. The FCC's Notice in this proceeding is vague on this issue and says only that no preemption issues are raised because it intends to streamline only interstate tariff requirements applicable to basic services. *Id.* at para. 46.

g. As noted above, the FCC's Notice asks whether non-structural safeguards or cost-allocation requirements should be applied to streamlined services offered by dominant carriers. If these safeguards are made applicable to basic services considered appropriate for treatment under streamlined regulation, the FCC's decision to do so could be viewed, in practice, as moving away from using the basic/enhanced boundary line to determine what degree of regulation should be imposed on a particular service and toward the kind of marketplace evaluation that was initially proposed in the *Computer III* proceedings and rejected soundly by commenters.

h. Comments on the FCC's proposal have been generally negative. The deregulation proposal has been called too limited, too complex, or simply inappropriate by various parties.

i. FCC Commissioner Mimi Weyforth Dawson, in a separate statement, suggested a variation on the FCC's proposal that had been discussed previously by FCC Chairman (then Commissioner) Dennis Patrick. Under her approach, the FCC would avoid trying to define various service markets and submarkets. Rather, it would retain its view, espoused in the *Competitive Carrier* proceeding, that all services have broad supply and demand substitutability. It then would identify "those 'core services' that are substitutes and building blocks for all other services". Core services provided by dominant carriers would be fully regulated, and all non-core services would be subject to streamlined regulation, regardless of who provided them.

15. A remaining issue is whether the FCC will retain rate-of-return regulation for services that continue to be subject to full regulatory requirements. In late 1986, various Commissioners have criticized rate-of-return regulation as imposing various inefficiencies, including the distortion of investment incentives, the incurring of substantial administrative costs, and the discouragement of innovation and development. Certain carriers, industry groups, and other government agencies also have criticized rate-of-return regulation. Although the FCC has not yet instituted a formal proceeding to explore replacement of the rate-of-return scheme, several alternatives have been discussed, including, most commonly, the application of a price cap to an identified "basket" of core services, such as the U.K. Government has included in British Telecom's license to function as a Public Telecommunications Operator.

16. A Commission proposal to regulate "foreign-owned"

providers of enhanced services could have a significant impact on the regulation of enhanced services within the United States. As part of a proceeding initiated to develop a role for the FCC in telecommunications trade issues, the Commission has proposed that "foreign-owned" entities from "closed" telecommunications markets be required to obtain certification under the Communications Act before offering an enhanced service within the United States. *Regulatory Policies and International Telecommunications*, FCC No. 86-563 (released Jan. 30, 1987). Leaving aside questions about the appropriateness (and the legality) of making telecommunications policy decisions on the basis of trade considerations, adoption of the FCC's proposal could lead to increased regulation of enhanced services or a complete breakdown in the basic/enhanced distinction. Largely for many of the reasons set out below, the initial round of comments submitted to the FCC in this proceeding has been negative.

a. By imposing on enhanced services specific regulatory obligations, the FCC would involve itself in having to define the outer boundary of its enhanced service category. Because enhanced services are not regulated under the present regulatory scheme, the FCC has not had to distinguish carefully between an enhanced communications service that may be subject to its regulatory powers and a related non-communications activity that is not subject to those powers. Once regulatory requirements are imposed on enhanced services, however, the FCC will have to determine specifically the limits of its jurisdiction to avoid regulating services such as data processing, with respect to which it lacks regulatory authority.

b. The scope of the Commission's jurisdiction over enhanced services has never been precisely defined. The courts have affirmed the Commission's regulation of the enhanced service activities of common carriers otherwise subject to regulation under the Communications Act. *See, e.g., GTE Service Corp. v. FCC*, 474 F.2d 724, 731 (2d Cir. 1973) (affirming the maximum separation policy of *Computer I*). However, the FCC has never squarely faced, and the courts have never addressed, the question of whether enhanced service providers not otherwise subject to Commission jurisdiction could be regulated. In fact, the Commission explicitly avoided this issue in *Computer II*, saying it saw no reason "to enter at this time the jurisdictional thickets presented by . . . the activities of those who are neither licensed under Title III or [sic] certificated under Title II . . .". *Computer II*, 84 F.C.C.2d at 95-96 (Reconsideration Order).

c. The FCC is likely to find that attempts to establish a narrow definition of enhanced services subject to FCC jurisdiction are difficult, if not impossible. Such a task would return the FCC to the dilemmas posed by the *Computer I* regime, where it sought in vain to separate services that are "primarily communications" from those that are "primarily data processing". When it adopted the basic/enhanced dichotomy in the *Computer II* proceeding, it avoided the need to distinguish among activities outside the "basic" services category. The Commission recognized the difficulties of making such fine distinctions. To do so now, after technological developments have made the market far more complex than it was in the mid-1970s, almost certainly would result in lengthy regulatory proceedings that could cause significant delays in the introduction of enhanced and non-communications services. As the recent debate over the appropriate classification of protocol conversion offerings in the *Computer III* proceeding has demonstrated, the dividing line between regulatory categories is inherently difficult to define.

    d. If the Commission were to use this international regulation proceeding as a vehicle for imposing regulatory restraints on a broad array of "foreign-owned" service providers operating in the U.S., it would have to apply the enhanced services category broadly. This approach could cause a large number of activities to become potential targets for regulation, including many that are not now thought to be within the FCC's jurisdiction, such as electronic information or transactional services.

    e. Although only certain "foreign-owned" entities actually would be regulated, many market participants might object to the FCC's actions because of the potential precedential impact of its decision. Once a service was considered to be a "communications" activity subject to regulation, it would be subject to more restrictive treatment, both inside and outside the U.S. Companies with multinational operations might be particularly concerned about such a result. Although they might not be regulated in the U.S. (or not regulated very strictly), the classification of their activities as "communications" activities subject to regulation in the U.S. could be used against them in other countries where "non-basic" services are more closely regulated.

    f. By travelling down this path, the FCC could end up either undercutting its own stated goal of fostering competition in a deregulated environment or drawing such arbitrary distinctions between "enhanced" and "other" services that it would undermine the viability of the basic/enhanced distinction.

III. UNITED KINGDOM

A. Background

1. "Value-added services" were initially viewed as "add-ons" or attachments to public switched network services. These services might have included electronic mail and hybrid information services.

2. The proposed venture between British Telecommunications ("BT") and IBM required the government to address the question whether protocol conversion services could be offered using leased lines. Although the venture was rejected, the government decided that leased lines could be used for a protocol conversion service. In its June 1985 Consultative Document, the government proposed a new category of "managed data network services" ("MDNS").

3. The distinction between value-added and MDNS services proved confusing. Thus, in December 1985, the Department of Trade and Industry (the "DTI") abandoned the distinction in its Revised Government Proposals for the Future Licensing of Value Added and Data Services ("Revised Government Proposals").

4. In March 1986, in a ministerial statement, the government announced its plans for a new value-added and data network services Class Licence. The draft Class Licence for Value Added and Data Network Services was released by the DTI in July 1986. On April 30, 1987, the DTI released the Class Licence for the Running of Telecommunications Systems Providing Value Added and Data Services ("VADS Class Licence") and the Class Licence for PTO (Public Telecommunications Operator) Group Associates.

a. In very broadest outline, the VADS Licence is an echo of the Revised Government Proposals. There has been some improvement in the clarity of the language (as compared with the draft Class Licence of July 1986) and the DTI has issued an explanatory guide to the Licence. Department of Trade and Industry, "Explanatory Guide to the Telecommunications Class Licence for the Running of Systems for Value Added and Data Services" (1987).

b. The Licence will be issued to all operators of telecommunications systems, whether in-house, or connected to the public network; as noted above, PTO Group Associates will operate under a separate, but quite similar, Licence. It appears that the Licence will permit all value-added services and allow the provision of all basic conveyance services except live voice and telex in return for payment. "Major Service Providers" and providers of "Trilateral Services" for reward would have to abide by various restrictions, enumerated below, that largely deal with ensuring fair competition and Open Systems Interconnection ("OSI") standards. All other providers of value-added services would be subject to restrictions on linking sales, to a condition safeguarding customer privacy, and to numbering plan requirements.

B. Problems

1. At the outset it is important to emphasize the relative complexity of the VADS Class Licence. The Licence draws several clear lines of demarcation that trigger sets of regulatory conditions. In reality, these points of differentiation may not be so easy to ascertain and implement.

a. First, a telecommunications system can be run under the Licence if it is an "Applicable System", as defined in Annex A to the Licence. The principal regulatory constraint for qualifying as an Applicable System is focused on location: a telecommunication system can only be run in a single set of premises occupied by the licensee (with two exceptions, one for a single person located within the same building and one for a person or group in separate premises that are located within two hundred meters of each other).

      b. Thus, nodes linked by leased lines constitute separate, licensable Applicable Systems; in short, a licensed "system" is not a network. Licensees cannot, of course, provide their own lines, which would be viewed as an infringement on the licences granted to the PTOs.

    2. The Licence itself does not make a sharp demarcation between value-added services and "basic services". Schedule 3 of the Licence permits a licensee to offer any telecommunication service other than cable program services, land mobile radio services, and a service to others "the only substantial element of which is conveyance of live speech or Telex Messages". VADS Class Licence, Schedule 3, Para. 1(b)(iii).

    3. The Licence also prohibits "Simple Resale Service", both domestically and internationally. "Simple Resale" is "the conveyance and no more" of Messages between a licensee, the public switched network, and a connection between the licensee and a leased circuit (or another licensee connected to the public network).

    4. For domestic services, the VADS Class Licence uses the concept of "Trilateral Services", which (according to the Explanatory Notes accompanying the craft Class Licence) is to replace the definition of Basic Conveyance. For international services, the VADS Class Licence does define "basic conveyance" and "value-added services".

      a. In general, the VADS Class Licence (like its predecessor drafts) seems less concerned with definitions, where the intent would have been to remove certain "basic" conveyance services from the scope of licensee authorization. The principal intent of the Licence is to provide a liberalized arrangement for all services other than "basic" conveyance. In lieu of a definitional approach, the Licence proceeds from the premise that distinguishing what is permitted from that which is prohibited can be done on the basis of network configurations and is contingent on whether services are offered for consideration or not.

      b. Certain routing restrictions apply if, without consideration, a licensee is a customer of another licensee and receives traffic from that licensee, or a licensee conveys basic voice or telex traffic, as well as providing value-added or data services. Condition 3. In such cases, the Licence treats data traffic routed without consideration differently from basic voice or basic telex. That is, data traffic can be freely routed within a group's network, the licensee can have an unlimited number of leased lines connecting it to others—all provided that any individual message can only be routed over one such line. Condition 3.3. If the licensee wants to route over more than one line, it must be done for consideration, thereby converting the licensee into a Trilateral Service Provider subject to specific regulatory conditions of the Licence.

      c. The rules for conveying basic voice or basic telex traffic (or directory information services) without consideration are somewhat complicated, but turn on the number and type of leased circuits that can connect a group network to an Applicable System or to a licence under the Branch Systems General Licence. Essentially, such messages cannot be routed over two leased circuits so that the licensee is acting as a transiting system to entities outside its group. Condition 3.4–3.6. Beyond this rule, however, the Licence contains certain conditions on the type and use of leased circuits, particularly with respect to whether public switched network traffic is carried.

    d. (Annex B to the VADS Class Licence, for example, explains what messages can and cannot be conveyed by a licensee; thus, in lieu of describing the messages themselves—or the services provided by the licensee—the Annex focuses on the connections between the licensee's system and private circuits (whether bilateral—between two unaffiliated entities—or not), the public switched network, or a "Group Applicable System".)

    e. Where a licensee offers domestic Value Added and Data Network services (*i.e.* something more than live speech or telex as the "only substantial element" of the services) for consideration, there are no routing restrictions, except for the prohibition on simple resale.

    5. The licensing of international services is also divided between services offered for no consideration and services offered for consideration. In addition, Condition 4 of the VADS Class Licence, which pertains to international services, does define "Basic Conveyance" and "Value Added Service". (The Revised Government Proposals had predicated the regulatory regime, for both domestic and international services, on the boundary line drawn by such definitions. Revised Government Proposals, para. 7.)

    a. "Basic Conveyance" is defined as the conveyance of a message "without any additional services having been provided in respect of the Message; or any deliberate removal of or addition to the information content of the Message in the course of conveyance except such as to permit or facilitate its conveyance to, or presentation at, its destination in an accurate, reliable and economical manner". Condition 4.8, VADS Class Licence.

    b. Value-added service had been defined in the Revised Government Proposals as services "falling outside the definition" of "basic conveyance". Revised Government Proposals, para. 7.2.1. The VADS Class Licence, however, defines such a service as one that is "additional" to basic conveyance, "together with any conveyance of Messages which is necessarily ancillary or incidental to that service". Condition 4.8.

    c. For consideration, licensees can provide directory information services, value-added services, and other services provided to a closed user group or otherwise negotiated by bilateral arrangement. Condition 4.2. Read in conjunction with other provisions in the VADS Class Licence, an Applicable System can be used to provide basic data services to the members of a closed user group (defined as having common business interests).

d. Where no consideration is rendered to the licensee offering an international service, the VADS Class Licence sets out conditions (similar to those in Condition 3) specifying the number and use of international leased circuits. In this situation, Condition 4.4 of the VADS Class Licence prohibits licensees from conveying messages via a leased circuit or the public switched network and a foreign telecommunications system run by someone other than the licensee. Thus, a licensee can route international traffic from or to an entity outside its group and in another country, but not to anyone in the U.K. not a member of the group (an activity that must be undertaken for consideration as a Trilateral Service.)

6. As noted, the VADS Class Licence prohibits Simple Resale—the "conveyance and no more" of messages—and the splitting of large capacity circuits. Condition 2.1. Licensees that offer a service that "includes" live voice transmission must charge for the conveyance of such messages the lesser of (*i*) at least 25 per cent above the lowest charge that would have been charged by a PTO or (*ii*) the highest charge that would have been charged by a PTO. Condition 2.2. How such charging principles could be established by a licensee offering an integrated voice and data offering is not clear, because it is unlikely that the licensee could or would separate—and be able to compare with the comparable PTO tariff—the charge for the voice component of its service.

7. As mentioned above, the VADS Class Licence contains a series of conditions applicable to both Major Service Providers and providers of Trilateral Services offering two sets of services: (*i*) those provided for consideration to an entity outside their group or (*ii*) those provided to another member of the group who uses the service to provide a different licensable service for consideration outside the group. It is far from clear how the fair trading and OSI conditions might work or apply in practice.

8. The VADS Class Licence defines a "Major Service Provider" by reference to annual turnover: an enterprise with £1 million in annual turnover in providing services over any "Applicable Systems" or £50 million in group turnover. Schedule 1, Part 1, para. 1(m). Thus, if the monetary benchmarks are met, the turnover from value-added services need only be a small part of the total for the enterprise to be considered a Major Service Provider. A large company that might hope to offer limited value-added services to its customers, for example, might very well conclude that the regulatory conditions (including accounting oversight) triggered by its non-telecommunications turnover make it infeasible or uneconomic to offer such services.

9. One such condition is that all Major Service Providers and providers of Trilateral Services publish—by sending to the Office of Telecommunications ("Oftel") and placing in their own principal offices—tariffs for each service that they offer and their charges for connecting

apparatus. Condition 13. Furthermore, all such providers must register with Oftel. Condition 19.

10. Such providers are also prohibited from engaging in several practices that might impede the development of a competitive environment for value-added services. (The DTI has issued three "Proposed Modifications to the Conditions of the Licences" granted to the PTOs to ensure that rules on cross-subsidization and fair trading apply to the value-added and data services businesses of the PTOs.)

a. First, the VADS Class Licence bars predatory pricing arrangements; licensees cannot show "undue" preference or exercise "undue" discrimination against persons or classes. Condition 10. The provision, although it is rather general, can be read to adopt some of the "resale" aspects of the separate subsidiary requirements in the U.S. It seems that a licensee—or one member of a group—cannot offer "basic" or other services to other members of the group at a price or on terms and conditions more favorable than are offered to other, unaffiliated customers. Condition 10.2.

b. As a corollary proposition, licensees are prohibited from cross-subsidizing their telecommunications businesses with revenues from other sources. Condition 11. The VADS Class Licence requires that intra-group transfers are to be at "full cost". Condition 11.2. (See also Proposed Modifications of the Conditions of the Licence Granted to British Telecom, 26 February 1987, para. 2(c)(ii) ("full cost" cost transfer)). Similarly, separate accounting records are required for a licensee's telecommunications activities. Condition 12.

c. Furthermore, the VADS Class Licence prohibits business arrangements that would foster exclusive dealing arrangements with suppliers of apparatus and telecommunications services. Condition 14.

11. Major Service Providers are required to provide access in accordance with OSI standards. Conditions 9 and 17. The Revised Government Proposals had seemed to indicate a certain interest in permitting the continued use of proprietary standards. Revised Government Proposals, at para. 16.5.3.

a. The VADS Class Licence does permit the use of other standards so long as the licensee can ensure that the use of such standards is not an "undue or unfair inducement" to others who wish to use OSI standards instead of the proprietary standards. Condition 17.4. At the same time, the licensee using a proprietary standard must explain to Oftel why its services cannot conform to the OSI standard. Condition 17.3.

b. The VADS Class Licence is an improvement over the Revised Government Proposals in balancing the OSI standard and proprietary standards. The Proposals had required that OSI access should be "broadly comparable" to proprietary access. Revised Government Proposals, at para. 16.5.4.(iv). It was uncertain what that requirement meant or how it could be measured. The VADS Class Licence, however, leaves it to the licensee to select its standard, so long as its own choice does not preclude its customers from themselves exercising free choice. (It should be noted, however, that the DTI's "Explanatory Guide" to the Licence retains the language from the Proposals in suggesting that the licensee, in explaining to Oftel why it is providing services under a proprietary standard, must demonstrate that the OSI access is "broadly comparable" in performance and price. Explanatory Guide, at 29.) Given what might be detailed regulatory oversight by Oftel of licensees offering proprietary standard access, the amount of actual flexibility that they will have to do so is not known.

       c. Once OSI standards are specified by Oftel, the licensee has twelve months to adjust its network to provide services in conformity therewith. Condition 17.1.

       d. Major Service Providers must notify Oftel six months in advance of the effective date of any proposals to change the means of access to their services, whether by an OSI or by a proprietary standard. The standard for notification is relatively vague and broad, and, therefore, seemingly rather restrictive. The licensee need only notify the Director when it might "reasonably anticipate" that the changes would cause anyone connected to its system, connecting apparatus to its system, producing apparatus for its system, or providing a service via its system to modify, replace, or cease to produce telecommunications apparatus or a telecommunications service. Condition 18.1. This notification standard might unnecessarily require licensees to divulge proprietary information and, thereby, impair the overall competitiveness of the sector.

      12. The Revised Government Proposals had excluded telex services, except when provided by means of a PTO switched network, from the scope of "basic conveyance services". para. 7.1.(ii). As noted above, the VADS Class Licence has a more restrictive regime for in-house live speech and "Telex Messages" than for other (*i.e.*, data) services. Condition 3.3. In addition, the VADS Class Licence now defines "Telex", VADS Class Licence, Licence, para. 5(n), and thus clarifies some of the definitional ambiguity left by the Revised Government Proposals. Nevertheless, it is possible that the definition might permit other services, such as electronic mail, to be classified as "telex".

      13. Other than the discussion of OSI standards in the Revised Government Proposals and in the VADS Class Licence, there has not yet been a clear enunciation of British policy on the nexus between value-added services and ISDN. An articulated policy on this relationship is necessary because ISDN pricing and infrastructure will affect the development of national and international value-added services.

       a. At present, the British standards for ISDN—in bit rate, services, and signalling—are not completely aligned with those of the CCITT. In the U.K., Integrated Digital Access services ("IDA") will be based on a primary 64 Kbps channel and two 8 Kbps secondary channels, a configuration that does not conform to CCITT standards. Multiline IDA will be based on thirty 64 Kbps channels and a digital access signaling system in slot 16. BT also has its own version of signaling system D.7, which does not conform entirely with Mercury's signalling system.

b. Demands from customers are compelling implementation of ISDN services in the U.K. BT is hurrying to make digital capabilities available to its customers. Pilot services (which are not perceived as simply "trial") using System X switches are being initiated in the Manchester area. Remote access multiplexing will be available in sixty sites in 1986 and 180 sites in 1987.

c. Implementing the CCITT guidelines for transmission standards using the twisted pair of the British local network poses a long-term problem. Over certain distances it will be difficult to offer services in accordance with the 2B plus D standard. In implementing international ISDN services, therefore, the British are expecting the use of gateways to remove differences in operational standards between their network and those of other nations.

C. Prospects

1. Having now issued the VADS Class Licence, the DTI will need to continue to work together with Oftel to ensure that the various licenses and regulatory conditions that are being developed will create a coherent and unified framework for the provision of value-added and data services. The VADS Class Licence confers several significant monitoring functions on the Director of Oftel. In implementing the accounting, exclusive dealing, and OSI conditions of the Licence, Oftel will need to continue developing its expertise.

2. Oftel's relationship with the DTI remains good, but delicate; now that the VADS Class Licence has been released, it will be principally for Oftel to answer questions and monitor the successs of the Licence. How the two bodies will work together in the value-added sector, particularly on the international side, merits continued observation.

3. The VADS Class Licence, at least for certain offerings (principally domestic, not-for-consideration), looks at routing configurations and not at the content of messages. It remains to be seen how this approach will work in practice. Interpreting for licensees the categories of permitted and prohibited messages, which depend on how they are sent and the number and connection of leased circuits used, and ascertaining licensee compliance, may require a new layer of regulatory approval at Oftel. Moreover, by enlarging the scope of entities that are subject to the licensing regime, the VADS Class Licence may expose providers operating beyond the U.K. to heightened regulatory scrutiny internationally and in other countries.

4. Value-added service providers and users, along with Oftel, will focus substantial attention on the conditions relating to adherence to OSI standards. There will be ongoing inquiry into how such conditions can

be made meaningful and concrete, and how they will intersect with the development of ISDN in the U.K.

     5. It is not certain how the fair dealing provisions and the conditions on competition will apply to those value-added services offered by a Major Service Provider or the provider of a Trilateral Service subject to them. The relationship between the telecommunications regulators and the authorities responsible for enforcing competition laws in the U.K. is, as yet, unresolved.

     6. Also at the center of attention will be the arrangements for the provision of international services. Some providers of value-added services had been troubled by the volume-sensitive pricing scheme of Recommendation D.6 to which the Revised Government Proposals referred obliquely. The VADS Class Licence broadly authorizes the use of international private leased circuits to provide the services that are to be opened to competition.

     a. The VADS Class Licence explicitly permits international directory information or value-added services using leased circuits. Condition 4.2.

     b. Moreover, as noted above, Condition 4.2(iii)(b) of the VADS Class Licence implies that the British Government is not entirely adverse to reaching agreements on a bilateral basis with other administrations that might permit further liberalization. Thus, the government may be exploring alternative arrangements beyond those contained in Recommendation D.6.

     7. To the extent that the British continue their restrictions on non-PTO suppliers of value-added services, particularly those subject to the fair trading and other conditions in Part 3 of Schedule 1 of the Licence, their regulatory regime is increasingly coming to be compared with policies in Japan. The Japanese view their regulatory framework as significantly more "liberal" than that of their British counterparts. In addition, policies in the U.K., particularly on the international front, may become a focus for U.S. trade negotiators.

IV. JAPAN

A. Background

     1. The Japanese view their regulatory approach as avoiding the definitional pitfalls of *Computer II*. The split between the provision of "facilities" ("Type I" under the Telecommunications Business Law) and "services" ("Type II") is seen by the Japanese as "more advanced" than the approach adopted in the United States.

     2. Japanese regulatory policymakers may find avoiding service-based distinctions somewhat difficult.

a. The Telecommunications Business Law does not restrict Type II services exclusively to non-voice services; there may, however, be a *de facto* limitation to data services. At present, there are still restrictions in the tariffs of Nippon Telegraph and Telephone ("NTT") on voice resale of leased lines connected to the public switched network. The new Type I carriers, however, are permitted to resell NTT circuits to serve areas not served by their own facilities. Pressure to maintain restrictions on pure voice resale will continue until local rates are increased.

b. It is uncertain to what extent the Ministry of Posts and Telecommunications (the "MPT") has determined to lift restrictions on voice resale. Some observers view this as unlikely in the present environment, until local rates are increased; others believe that NTT is not adverse to voice resale, at least by Type II carriers. At present, leased lines can be used by Type II entities to provide voice grade services. As yet, however, there is no interconnection agreement between NTT and Type I or Type II carriers. Eventually, there may be flexibility in the use of leased circuits not dissimilar to that provided under the branch licence in the United Kingdom.

c. Another issue that must be addressed is the status of entities that attempt to resell leased circuits on the new Type I satellite-based carriers. Large users, for example, may make commitments to acquire such circuits and may wish to offer excess capacity to others. The MPT has yet to resolve the status of such satellite-based resellers, although classifying them as Type I carriers seems to be a disfavored option.

d. There are now over 200 Type II providers. Most of these offerings are remote access data processing. Other kinds of services have not developed to any significant extent.

e. One subsidiary of NTT, the Data Communications Bureau, is the most significant provider of Type II services. In total, NTT now has approximately sixty subsidiaries; one will address issues of standards and protocols for value-added services. In offering Type II services, NTT is anxious to avoid having to compete as a Type I entity, with accompanying tariff restrictions, against Type II entities, which are essentially unregulated.

f. Increasingly, policymakers are focusing on the dominance of the Data Communications Bureau. Some observers believe that NTT will divest this subsidiary in the next few years as part of an effort to maintain the distinction between facilities and services. An important structural factor is that Dr Hisashi Shinto, president of NTT, apparently believes that separation may be necessary to avoid regional separation of NTT itself. (The Second *Ad Hoc* Commission on Administrative Reform originally had recommended in the early 1980s that NTT be separated into regional companies.)

g. In 1986, the Keidanren issued a report on "Major Issues Under New Telecom Legislation". In commenting on the state of competition, the report emphasized the need for effective competitive safeguards and separation of the Data Communications Bureau subsidiary from NTT's basic services. The Keidanren recommendation is one for arm's-length separation, but not divestiture of this line of business. There is a consensus within the Keidanren that separation of remote access data processing services should be required; as to other services, such as packet-switching, there is no common view. At this point, it is not clear whether the MPT is eager to require such separations between NTT's main operations and its subsidiaries.

h. Many of the concerns about NTT's structure will be addressed in 1988, when the restructuring of NTT is due to be reviewed. Other review processes are being initiated, however. For example, during 1988, the Computer Communications Division of the Telecommunications Bureau of the MPT will be examining a wide-ranging set of policy issues; one area for examination is the arrangements for data connection between Type I and other service providers.

3. Another issue facing the MPT is the opening of competition in the international market—both in Type I and Type II services. There are two sets of issues: (*i*) whether new international carriers, possible alternatives to Kokusai Denshin Denwa, Ltd. ("KDD"), will be authorized and (*ii*) to what extent Type II entities will be permitted to operate internationally, if, by so doing, they might severely undercut KDD's role.

a. Regarding the question of Type I competition to KDD, there are now two major groups exploring the feasibility of filing an application with the MPT to compete with KDD. At present, however, there is no formal MPT process for authorizing international competition.

b. The first of these groups, International Telecom Japan, Inc. ("ITJ"), is a joint-venture company of seven private corporations—Mitsui & Co., Mitsubishi Corp, Sumitomo Corp., Matsushita Electric Industrial Co., Marubeni Corp., Nissho Iwai Corp., and The Bank of Tokyo, Ltd. The trading company members had wanted communications capacity to serve their own interests as well as to take the opportunity of liberalization in the telecommunications sector to develop a commercial alternative to KDD.

c. ITJ's strategy is to lease Intelsat satellite services from KDD or obtain indefeasible rights of users interests in submarine cables. This approach to the provision of international circuits is similar to the arrangements that the airlines established in creating the Société Internationale de Télécommunications Aéronautiques ("SITA"). In the case of ITJ, however, the entity would actually be an international carrier. The business plan calls for ITJ to build its own earth stations, one near Tokyo and one in Western Japan, along with other facilities. At present, it does not plan to construct fiber optic facilities; however, it has not ruled out the option of co-ownership if existing or planned capacity should prove insufficient. At this point, ITJ is still in the planning stage, although the present schedule calls for the launching of service sometime in 1989.

d. KDD has detailed two engineers to ITJ to serve as advisers, and several more are assisting in the feasibility study. Furthermore, given that ITJ plans to lease circuits from KDD, some observers and companies are skeptical of the possibility that ITJ would be a vigorous competitor to KDD. Nevertheless, because KDD is viewed in some circles as rather conservative in interpreting CCITT guidelines, ITJ could, in marshalling the forces of several of Japan's largest commercial enterprises, create pressure to liberalize arrangements for the use of circuits.

e. The other would-be international competitor is Kokusai Digital Tshushin Kikaku (International Digital Communications Planning) ("IDC"), a consortium of over twenty companies. C. Itoh & Co. and Cable & Wireless each have a 20 per cent stake in IDC; other shareholders include Toyota Motors, Pacific Telesis International, Merrill Lynch, NEC, Fujitsu, Nissan, Nippon Steel, Toshiba, Nomura Securities, and a group of Japanese banks (including the banking arms of Sumitomo Corp. and Mitsui & Co). In addition, NTT International appears to support the entry of this entity.

f. At present, IDC is engaged in a feasibility study. Its business plan is to begin with the provision of leased circuit services via Intelsat satellites and Pacific region cables; in 1989, switched services would be offered. IDC plans to construct a private transpacific fiber optic cable with Pacific Telecom Cable, Inc. and eventually to hook-up with other Pacific region cables; the U.S. Federal Communications Commission has issued a cable landing license to Pacific Telecom Cable. Given the international make-up of the IDC consortium, its communications expertise, the strength of its members in Japan, and its plans to use Cable & Wireless facilities worldwide, it is viewed as a potentially strong competitor to KDD.

g. In the context of supporting the third KDD, NTT's expanding international role is of some interest. NTT International, established in October 1985 as a subsidiary of NTT, designs, constructs, sells, and operates overseas telecommunications facilities and supplies engineering and consultation activities outside Japan. NTT views establishing itself as a player on the international scene as an important goal.

h. The MPT is cautious about the involvement of NTT in international activities and the scope of such participation is unclear. The MPT apparently has suggested that the participation of a domestic carrier in international ventures (and KDD's in domestic entities) could not exceed a certain percentage of the capital share of the total. Hence, continuing erosion of the insularity of the Japanese telecommunications market may be reflected in NTT's ability to become involved in international services. It is uncertain, however, whether NTT could, for example, supply end-to-end service internationally; this matter may well be worked out when a decision is made as to the extent of competition that will be permitted in international services.

i. There may be problems, say some observers, in the MPT's licensing of IDC. One concern may be the involvement of Cable & Wireless. Many Japanese users route international traffic through Hong

Kong or Singapore due to the rigid tariffing policies of KDD. The MPT's concerns, therefore, may reflect KDD's sensitivities. Moreover, in its efforts to obtain an interest in a domestic Type I carrier, Cable & Wireless appears to have created some friction. There have been significant concerns that Cable & Wireless might control IDC; some officials have pointed out that, if this were the case, Japan would be virtually the only country with an international telecommunications provider subject to "foreign control".

j. The international market is not large and the MPT, therefore, has been attempting to persuade ITJ and IDC to reorganize and combine their forces. ITJ, as well as IDC, have staunchly resisted this pressure heretofore, in a manner that is not characteristic of Japanese companies. In dealing with domestic Type I applicants, however, the MPT essentially decided to permit decisions on feasibility to be resolved by users—and a similar approach may eventually be taken with regard to international Type I carriers. Moreover, whereas the Ministry for International Trade and Industry ("MITI") was one of the leaders of the domestic liberalization of telecommunications, it is significantly less involved in these international issues.

k. A strikingly similar rationale lies behind both would-be competitors to KDD. The problems of users are international and assistance is needed in establishing circuits throughout the world. KDD is seen by many Japanese users as domestic; future international carriers actually should be international in scope and outlook. Cable & Wireless in particular is, for this reason, seen by many users as a company with a modern orientation.

l. Both IDC and ITJ, to the extent that user interests are represented among their shareholders, are likely to be sensitive to user needs. As entities involved in international financial transactions increase their demands for telecommunications capacity, they are coming to establish the parameters for international services. Like the maritime, and then airline, interests that first created significant demand for international circuits, the international financial markets require flexible arrangements for multiple voice circuits and arrangements that do not impede the efficiency or time sensitivity of international services.

m. User groups agree that demand should be taken into account in planning new services. The MPT may not be so involved in evaluating traffic demand as in assessing the need for new transoceanic fiber optic cables. Users believe, in any event, that such assessments should be made by the market and not by the MPT.

4. As far as Type II carriers are concerned, the MPT is facing the difficult problem of drafting regulations to implement a legal scheme for international Value Added Network Services (VANS). The general terms under which VANS will be offered internationally are contained in amendments to the Telecommunications Business Law adopted by the Diet in May 1987. The MPT's regulations, however, will need to resolve many

uncertainties that surround the international VANS business in Japan—even after adoption of the new legislation. In drafting these regulations, the MPT will continue to be concerned with the number and competitiveness of international Type II carriers. Further discussion on the Japanese approach to the development and regulation of international VANS is contained in Sections IV.C and XIV below.

B. Problems

1. There could be significant pricing consequences if the restrictions on voice resale are removed. If unrestricted resale were authorized, NTT would have substantial incentive to harmonize its public switched and leased line tariffs on a rapid basis. Such harmonization would accelerate price reductions for interexchange voice services. Downward pressure on NTT's interexchange rates could dampen the incentives for new Type I entrants to construct networks that would compete with NTT.

2. NTT is now in the process of proposing a major rebalancing of its rate structure. There has been considerable speculation that the MPT is urging NTT to be extremely cautious with respect to its pricing policies owing to their impact on the structure of competition.

   a. In the eyes of the MPT, competition in Type I services should not be based on price but on quality of service. The concept appears to be that the new common carriers will have prices lower than NTT, with the range of the NTT network and the quality of its service justifying higher pricing.

   b. For this reason, the MPT has determined that the new Type I carriers will essentially have similar rate structures. The policy behind the MPT scheme is apparently that differentiated pricing would weaken all the new common carriers, to the advantage of NTT.

   c. Some of the Type I entities, however, would like to see more competition among the carriers. Daini-Denden, for example, sees itself as being more cost-effective and efficient than its two major terrestrial competitors, which are affiliated with the Ministry of Construction (Teleway Japan) and with the Japanese National Railways (Japan Telecom). Furthermore, Daini-Denden also believes that it has substantial advantages over Tokyo Telecommunication Network ("TTNet"), which has just been granted a Type I license for the region around Tokyo that its 50 per cent shareholder, the Tokyo Electric Power Co., is licensed to serve.

   d. NTT's problem in proposing rate rebalancing is that there is no regulatory scheme for reviewing rate proposals. NTT has just begun to restructure its accounting scheme. Furthermore, there is no agreement on what principles should be applied to cost-based pricing, *i.e.*, whether marginal cost or average cost approaches are to be used. Consequently, NTT must expect an *ad hoc* response to its tariff offerings on a service-by-service basis.

e. It may be easier for NTT to adapt more generic accounting standards that identify costs for whole baskets of services such as interexchange, local service, and terminal equipment. With such standards, the MPT might focus less on individual prices for particular services.

f. NTT's concerns with its tariffs are not restricted to its offerings on the Tokyo-Osaka route. (Some 38 per cent of NTT's interexchange call revenues are from the Kanto, Chubu, and Kinki regions, though there is no precise breakdown on revenues from the Tokyo to Osaka route itself.) Although two of the terrestrial carriers have not yet begun service, Japan Telecom now offers leased line services that are priced approximately 24 per cent lower on the Tokyo-Osaka route than are those of NTT.

g. A significant percentage of NTT's revenues are from large business users in the Tokyo area—customers targeted by TTNet, which already has its own network of microwave and fiber optic facilities. TTNet's parent, Tokyo Electric, also has close relationships with major industrial customers and households, significant capital, and in-house telecommunications engineers, and its rates are controlled by MITI. TTNet's rates will be controlled, however, by MPT. Furthermore, although there is some conservatism in the MPT regarding alternative local exchange links, other Type I providers may also be exploring the possibility of establishing bypass facilities for building or complexes in which large users are located.

h. Given the potential for intense competition at the local level, NTT appears to have relatively little flexibility to cross-subsidize its interexchange offerings with local revenues. Similarly, although NTT is insisting that Type I carriers pay access charges to cover the losses for operating local services, such rate policies might create incentives for customers to leave the NTT network.

3. Uncertainties about the rate setting and review process have created important questions regarding the regulatory framework in which NTT and the other Type I and Type II providers are operating. Some observers believe that a more formal arrangement for oversight by the MPT is required—perhaps drawing from the British experience with Oftel—while others dissent from this view.

a. NTT may well conclude that it would be in its own interest to move toward a more formal set of regulatory procedures. Greater formality might reduce the potential for *ad hoc* rate determinations. New dispute resolution mechanisms, however, might also cause NTT to run the risk of losing certain regulatory positions that, without changes in the framework, it might be able to protect in the short term. Ultimately, a process that identified key transitional issues on a timely and effective basis might be better for NTT.

b. There is still some reluctance about a more formal regulatory procedure within the MPT, however. Greater regulatory formalism had been used in the early 1950s; those more formal procedures, however, were abandoned thereafter, once Japan had regained more political autonomy. Recommendations for different or more formal procedures are, therefore, likely to receive a mixed reaction—not altogether foreign, yet reminiscent of the occupation period.

c. Even if the MPT decides not to adopt a more formal regulatory process, there may be pressures to increase legal controls over the emergence of competition in the telecommunications sector. The Fair Trading Commission occasionally has taken an interest in intervening on telecommunications issues—access, competition between Type I carriers, and the provision of customer premises equipment. The Commission established an advisory committee on telecommunications, and issued a report early in 1986. Such intervention by the Commission is not viewed as necessary—and may be resisted—by the MPT.

d. Developing a more formal, arm's-length procedure would not be easy because policy is made through a complicated process of using ministry-appointed committees for consultation with the industry on important issues. Experts are asked to offer their views in these committees, but written comments are seldom supplied and considered in a formal sense. The possibilities for those outside the committee to supply their views are somewhat limited as well.

e. The process of building a consensus—of "nemawashi"—is ingrained in the Japanese administrative tradition. Although such consensus-building is often seen as impeding innovative changes in policy, the origin of nemawashi—which means pruning and cutting away old roots—refers to preparations for change. Hence, nothing is inherently incompatible about changing policy and continuing to rely on the Japanese administrative tradition.

4. The Japanese approach to ISDN is also in a state of some evolution. In June 1986, on the recommendation of the Data Communications Development Council, the MPT decided to hold up the implementation of Integrated Network Services ("INS", the Japanese version of ISDN) because the NTT technical standards were likely to diverge from the worldwide two B channels (128 Kbps) plus a D (16 Kbps) arrangements. (The NTT INS model interface is based on 64 Kbps plus 4 Kbps and a 16 Kbps plus 4 Kbps and was to be implemented on an experimental basis in three major cities—Tokyo, Osaka, and Nagoya—in late 1985. The INS "Y" interface was viewed as simple, economical, and more advanced than the CCITT standardization process, out of which had evolved the "I" interface.)

a. The decision to block NTT's offering of INS services was taken as a result of considerable pressure from Japanese equipment manufacturers. These manufacturers were concerned that equipment engineered for the Japanese market could not be marketed effectively elsewhere. NTT itself has no manufacturing capability; thus, such pressure reflected a new balance of forces in Japan. One consequence of the concern expressed by the manufacturing sector was that NTT was forced to face a postponement of its new digital services for almost two years. (The Japanese multiline standard will, like that of the U.S., be based on twenty-three B plus D, while the European standard is based on thirty B plus D.)

      b. Part of the review of ISDN will be an assessment of how to structure network access arrangements for value-added services. The MPT is likely to focus on issues that are not unlike those now being explored in the Supplemental Notice in the *Computer III* proceeding; in the United States, the FCC is examining the extent to which value-added entities should be afforded access to the signal capabilities of the D channel.

    5. In restructuring its relationship with its subsidiaries, NTT has already established several Type II subsidiaries to compete in the provision of value-added services. These include NTT PC Communications, Internet (jointly owned by NTT and several Japanese mainframe computer makers), and Nippon Information and Communications (jointly owned by NTT and IBM). Increasingly, the MPT will be confronted with the issues of what services can be offered by those subsidiaries and what will be the terms of their relationship.

      a. NTT has been offering services to its subsidiaries on a tariffed basis. If it were to offer services on a "resale" basis, it could, in services provided by its Type II subsidiaries, avoid the rate regulation that is applicable to Type I entities.

      b. If the MPT were to require a formal separation between parent and subsidiaries, it might have to address questions as to whether restrictions on the flow of information or the maintenance of common facilities would be necessary. What accounting and separation requirements should govern the parent-subsidiary relationship?

    6. As explained more fully in Section XI, the MPT will be required to determine the regulatory framework for the offering of services internationally by Type II entities.

    7. U.S. trade pressure has resulted in regulatory interpretations that have gone a long way toward eviscerating the distinction between General Type II and Special Type II service providers. (Special II Type entities use more than five hundred access lines calculated in terms of 1,200 bps per line.) General Type II entities have considerable flexibility in pricing; those classified as Special Type II do not, and must offer services on a non-discriminatory basis. It may be difficult for the MPT to handle the evolution of a carrier from the smaller, General Type II, to the larger, Special Type II, category. Once a Type II entity markets a service under the more flexible General framework, is it realistic to expect a transition to a more rigid scheme if the scale of the provider expands?

C. Prospects

    1. The MPT will need to resolve ambiguities that still surround the complex international aspects of changes in domestic telecommunications policy. The Ministry is currently grappling with issues affecting both Type I and Type II entities.

a. In reviewing the international side of Japanese telecommunications policy, the MPT has, as a threshold issue, to decide whether to admit one or more new Type I international carriers. If it decides to do so, it will need to draw up an application and approval process. There is still significant uncertainty whether ITJ and IDC will form a single entity, a prospect that looks less and less likely, or whether the MPT will permit both carriers to operate.

b. Second, the MPT will be confronted with the difficult issues of properly delineating the role of KDD in relation to new Type II providers of international services. On September 30, 1986, the International Type II Business Study Group, an advisory committee to the Director General of the Telecommunications Bureau, MPT, submitted its final report as part of a lengthy study process within the Ministry. The report recommended the adoption of Recognized Private Operating Agency status for international VANS providers. The legislative amendments adopted by the Diet in May 1987 have not resolved the question of whether international VANS operators will be required to obtain RPOA status; this issue and others will need to be addressed by the Ministry in its implementing regulations.

c. Under revisions to Article 58 of the Telecommunications Business Law, Special Type II entities will be able to enter into contracts with Type I entities to acquire "non-tariff-based" transmission services. It is expected that the Ministry will draft implementing regulations under which international VANS will be permitted (or required) to be designated as Special Type II entities to use such "non-tariff-based" services. Such contractual arrangements will be subject to MPT authorization.

d. Ongoing trade discussions between the U.S. and Japan are expected to address how this new arrangement will be implemented. One question is whether entities operating internationally will be permitted to obtain RPOA status and to use tariffed international leased lines as an alternative to using the "non-tariff-based" services (a term still undefined) to operate as a Special Type II entity, or whether such "non-tariff-based" services will be the only option for international VANS operators, whether or not they obtain RPOA status.

2. NTT is likely to continue to want to expand its international presence, and the MPT may need to detail or apply its guidelines preventing KDD and NTT from becoming too involved in the other's markets.

3. Trade pressure from the U.S. with respect to international value-added services is intense, though not necessarily as much so as was the case regarding the policies applicable to domestic VANs. Nevertheless, the issue of whether one or two international Type I entities will be authorized, and whether foreign ownership of such entities will be permitted, has grabbed the attention of trade policymakers in the U.S. In particular, the Congress and individuals in the Executive Branch are keenly interested in the process of extending the liberalization in Japanese policy to the international environment.

4. The parameters of competition domestically are still not yet entirely certain. As part of the ongoing process of reviewing the state of competition, the MPT established two new important study committees in mid-1986: the Committee on Data Communications with Computers and a committee on telecommunications infrastructure.

   a. Among the Type I carriers, it is unclear how vigorous competition will be. The MPT tariffing policy seems to ensure that most competition will be between NTT, on the one hand, and the new common carriers, on the other. The extent to which the new common carriers will be able to differentiate themselves is equally unknown.

   b. The strength and dominance of NTT is likely to mean that most of the new Type I entrants will serve niche markets, at least in the short run. There is considerable interest in the process of consolidation and merger in the interexchange market in the U.S. Many observers believe that a similar "shake-down" will occur in Japan.

   c. Any actual competition between NTT and new Type I entrants that does emerge will probably preclude the adoption of usage-sensitive pricing policies.

5. At present, of course, similar competitive constraints do not exist with respect to international circuits. Nevertheless, facilities-based competition using Japanese national satellite systems may be allowed to spill over into the regional and broader international arena. Thus, it is unlikely that KDD will be able to depart from its flat-rate pricing policies for existing customers; however, KDD would still be faced with having to differentiate between entities eligible for flat-rate prices and those that are not.

V. FRANCE

A. Background

1. Under the July 29, 1982, Law on Audiovisual Communication, France has adopted a liberal approach to the provision of value-added or information-based services—provided that the services of the public network are used. Electronic mailbox and message switching in connection with transactional services can be offered by third parties. Interactive services may be freely provided, subject to prior declaration.

2. The use of leased lines for providing value-added services is restricted. The rates for the Transpac public packet-switched services are distance-insensitive, and their pricing makes them attractive for value-added offerings.

3. The Direction Générale des Télécommunications ("DGT") has offered many new services through *filiales*—separate subsidiaries

organized as *sociétés d'économie mixte*. The *filiales* under Compagnie Générale des Communications ("COGECOM") include France Câbles et Radio, EGT (marketing peripheral equipment), Télésystèmes (establishment and operation of information networks, electronic mail systems), and Transpac (packet switching). The *filiales* obtain services from the DGT on a "resale" basis and, potentially, compete with the DGT's services.

4. The *filiales* also are used either to market directly such services as public domestic packet-switching or to support DGT marketing of services such as high-speed data services (Transfix, Transcom, Transdyn) using the digitized terrestrial network or the high-speed digital satellite capacity of Télécom-1 (which is considered to be the first step toward ISDN).

5. The boundary lines between the DGT and the *filiales* are not tight; nevertheless, the DGT uses the organizational structure of the subsidiaries as a way of establishing the line of demarcation between its monopoly and its competitive services. The DGT takes the position that the limits of its monopoly are defined by the first three OSI layers; however, it has made efforts to standardize above these layers. The DGT itself offers services such as teletex or videotex for terminals and hosts that private manufacturers may supply.

6. With the election of the Chirac Government in 1986, there are some pressures to loosen the ties between the *filiales* and the DGT—through privatization of some of the *filiales* in whole or in part. The DGT, however, is pressing for greater autonomy and for a different legal status; consequently, it is advocating integration of the *filiales* into a DGT that will be organized more entrepreneurially than at present.

7. The DGT has adopted a very aggressive pricing policy for international services. There is substantial movement toward cost-based pricing with, for example, decreases in transatlantic tariffs for voice services of 25 per cent in 1986, as well as decreases in the tariffs of analogue and digital leased lines. The DGT is unlikely to implement a usage-sensitive pricing structure if there is not agreement to do so among the other PTTs. It does not, however, see such agreement as probable, given the competitive market emerging from developments in the U.K. and the Netherlands.

8. Prices for business customers are being reduced. There is considerable caution about raising local rates. The DGT will have more flexibility to pursue this pricing strategy when its subsidies to the manufacturing industry are reduced. The DGT policy seems to be one of stimulating use of its services by businesses, while examining options to increase local rates in accordance with time-sensitive charging principles.

9. In the last year or so, the DGT has reduced interexchange rates by 5 per cent. At the same time, the calling period has been reduced from twenty minutes to six minutes, in an effort to bring the price of services more closely in line with costs. These steps are part of a long-range, ten-year plan to realign long-distance and local tariffs.

B. Problems

1. Transpac pricing structures make leased lines attractive only for limited value-added applications, *i.e.*, those requiring high traffic volume. Hence, opportunities for entry of new value-added service providers using leased lines may be somewhat limited and should be examined carefully by would-be entrants.

2. The DGT offers bearer services corresponding to the lower OSI protocol layers, with terminals and hosts connected to DGT facilities allowing higher-layer functionalities. Nevertheless, users may view the DGT's focus on "standardization" of higher-layer functionalities, and the evolution of a common environment for information-based services, as an obstacle to the development of new services—an obstacle greater than the limited availability of leased lines for value-added services.

3. One issue for the future is the place of the French development of ISDN in Europe. In France, the DGT's approach to ISDN will have an important bearing on its policy toward the future provision of value-added services. At present, the DGT is involved in a pilot program in Brittany to explore the technical feasibility of, and demand for, ISDN services; the ISDN test is to start in mid-1988 and will offer, among many other new services, audiographic and audio videotext services. The test area will involve the city of Rennes and remote concentrators for 300 subscribers will be connected to three exchanges; this pilot network will soon thereafter be extended to the Paris metropolitan area. The experiment will test various competing methods of connecting subscribers to E 10 switches. Analogue lines will be connected first; in 1988, digital lines will be utilized.

a. As far as the network in Brittany is concerned, these experimental ISDN services are currently targeted at mid-sized professional users and will be extended in the Paris network test to large volume users who may have new applications. The DGT will have to address the question of whether specialized leased line services could be required, regardless of how the demand for ISDN services develops.

b. High-speed digital facilities offered by the Télécom-1 satellite are already used in, for example, the existing Transdyn-ISDN service. The DGT, however, is assessing how to integrate further the provision of Télécom-1 services into ISDN planning. The service requirements of large users can be adequately met by existing specialized networks for voice services and they are sensitive about maintaining access to traditional private line and satellite services. They would like to have the option for direct access that bypasses significant parts of the switching hierarchy.

c. The pilot program in Britanny and in the Paris area is based on CCITT interfaces and protocols. (These elements would include the 2B plus D basic access, CCITT signalling standard number seven, common channel signalling, and use of the "S" interface, among others.) The Commission of the European Communities, however, has been concerned about the apparent lack of coherent European planning for ISDN; it has transmitted to CEPT the report of the Groupe d'Analyses et de Prévision ("GAP"), which urges greater convergence of standards within Europe.

    d. Many PTTs have had a mixed reaction to the GAP report. Some have stressed that they are working on ISDN development but that the demand for ISDN services does not exist as yet; they point out that the focus must be on narrowband ISDN services and, only subsequently, on broadband services. The Commission, however, is concerned that manufacturers will be uninterested in a new generation of ISDN-related equipment unless a large integrated market exists.

    4. In France, as elsewhere, there is some uncertainty about the future demand for ISDN services. Large users will continue to demand specialized facilities. One issue, therefore, is whether ISDN services at the start will be aimed at medium-sized users, although they have been targeted for the larger users as well. In addition, ISDN pricing for 64 Kbps channels initially may be set at 1.5 to 2 times the voice circuit rate, a pricing structure that may deter utilization; the DGT forecasts that, after a few years, ISDN pricing should decrease to be on a par with the voice tariff. Pricing, along with costs associated with equipment conversion, is causing users to become concerned that they may become subject to coercive pressures to migrate to ISDN services.

    a. If, however, prices for ISDN services are set too low, there will be incentives to bypass existing services, with their rate structures, by encouraging the multiplexing of multiple voice channels on a 64 Kbit/s line.

    b. For a variety of reasons, therefore, the development of ISDN services in France and elsewhere may be deliberate. This slow pace seems likely to affect the emergence of value-added services. Integrated digital networks, of course, afford different pricing schemes for "virtual" private line services. Such circuits are not permanently or physically maintained on a full-time basis; therefore, it would seem reasonable to base pricing on time of availability to the user.

    c. The trend toward new pricing structures is already apparent outside France—even in the U.S., where software defined networks ("SDNs") are offered and customers have the option for paying only for available facilities.

    d. Nevertheless, despite the likelihood of implementing new rate structures and arrangements for digital services, it seems unlikely in France and elsewhere that policymakers will be tempted to substitute usage-sensitive pricing for the traditional pricing schemes for leased circuits. This is because of the clear need for full-time circuits that are not necessarily integrated into ISDN configurations, and because users will bypass a market if it does not make such circuits available.

    e. Not only large users, however, but international value-added service providers as well, will seek out the most convenient pricing arrangements. Thus, it is not probable that French policymakers will be willing to risk the loss of such providers by adopting rate structures for ISDN services that are less accommodating than those of their European neighbors.

C. Prospects

1. Although the Chirac Government has proposed changes in structure, policy is likely to evolve slowly. One area for emphasis will be affording the DGT more independence from the general budget process: that is, reducing the present DGT subsidies that are mandated to further industrial policy goals.

2. As part of a comprehensive program to restructure French telecommunications, the government has announced a plan for the liberalization of a wide range of value-added services.

   a. One cornerstone of the plan is that service providers will be able to use leased lines to create networks. Two groups—IBM and Paribas, the banking organization, and Olivetti and Suez, the financial services concern—have been positioned to provide such services.

   b. The French are currently exploring the utility of a distinction between an "open" and a "closed" network. An "open" network would provide service to an unlimited set of third parties; a "closed" network provides service to a known set of individuals rather than to the public at large. Flat-rate pricing would be applied to "closed" leased line networks; volume-sensitive pricing principles may obtain for the "open" networks.

   c. In practice, of course, it may be difficult to differentiate among open and closed networks. For certain services not generally available to the public, the number of users might be "closed", though not identified. This might, for example, be the case for transactional or information services, where the user might have some relationship to the operator of the network.

3. Structural change is also an important component of the proposed program. In 1986, the government created an independent agency to regulate both broadcasting and telecommunications. Effectively, then, there will be a separation of the DGT's operational and regulatory roles. The result will be that the DGT might be providing services on a competitive basis with other service providers.

   a. On September 30, 1986, the government published the law "Rélative à la Liberté de Communication", by which it created the Commission Nationale des Communications et Libertés ("CNCL"). The CNCL, in the words of the law, is in part intended to regulate the telecommunications sector; it is also intended to ensure equality and to favor free competition and advance the pluralistic expression of opinion.

   b. The CNCL is an independent regulatory body of thirteen members. Two members are appointed by the Président de la République, two members by the Président de l'Assemblée Nationale, two members by the Président du Sénat, one member from the Conseil d'Etat, one member from La Cour de Cassation, one member from La Cour des Comptes, one member from L'Académie Française. Three other members, who are chosen by the first ten, are selected from among experts in the audiovisual, telecommunications, and printed press fields, respectively. One of the thirteen members is selected by the others as the CNCL President; Gabriel de Broglie, who was appointed by the Président du Sénat and has a background in broadcasting and audiovisual, is the first chairman of the CNCL. For this first term of the CNCL, seven members are serving nine-year terms, and the six others are serving five-year terms.

 c. The CNCL has broad powers over broadcasting and audiovisual services. In addition, under Article 10 of the law, it is to be consulted during an interim period (to the end of 1987), pursuant to articles L. 33 and L. 34 of the Code des Postes et Télécommunications to approve telecommunications networks and services. The CNCL is to consult with the Minister of the PTT concerning the establishment and use of all telecommunications networks and installations for third-party use, except those of the State. The DGT will continue to have authority to act on applications for any new value-added services.

 d. Due to the political situation (the pendency of the presidential elections in 1988), there has been some delay in enacting the legislation that was, by December 31, 1987, to have set forth the principles applicable to competition in the telecommunications sector. In the meantime, the CNCL is charged with providing the authorizations, pursuant to the code, for establishment and installation of all telecommunications networks, except those of the State.

 e. It is not clear how the CNCL is to exercise its interim authority. Under Article 10, it is only to consider the constraints on public service; it is given little direction about other licensing criteria. Certainly, the scope of private network services is not clearly defined. The distinction between value-added services and private services will presumably be worked out between the CNCL and the DGT.

 f. Furthermore, with respect to any pending applications, it is not certain what the respective roles of the DGT and the CNCL might be. The definition of value-added services that the DGT will adopt is also unclear. There is an early indication that the DGT does not consider Transpac services to be value-added, but that activities such as protocol conversion and electronic messaging would fall within the definition. The DGT is studying a proposal to create a more flexible regulatory environment in which leased lines could be supplied to a wider range of providers of value-added services.

 g. There does not appear to have been any progress on drafting a definitive law establishing the principles of competition in the telecommunications industry. The view of the Minister of the PTT and the government on this issue are still undefined. The government is interested, however, in widening competition among French companies, possibly in conjunction with foreign firms. One example of this development is the association between the Compagnie Générale d'Electricité ("CGE") and ITT Corp.

  f. As part of the long-range program, there may ultimately be some liberalization of the DGT's monopoly over the provision of the basic telephone service. At present, however, it is not contemplated that there will be competition in long-distance or local telephone services.

VI. THE NETHERLANDS

A. Background

  1. Several commissions have been examining the role and future of the Dutch PTT. The Swarttouw Commission report (March 1982), and the government response (January 1984) thereto, were followed by the Steenbergen Commission (work begun in October 1984).

  2. The report of the Steenbergen Commission (summer 1985) was reviewed by the Cabinet in mid-1986; the Cabinet adopted several of the Commission's key recommendations. The recommendations have now been considered and approved by the Dutch Parliament. The key provisions of the proposal under consideration are as follows:

  3. The PTT, which is now a government service, will be transformed into a limited liability company known as NV PTT. The government will own 100 per cent of the shares of NV PTT. The target date for the establishment of NV PTT is January 1, 1989.

  4. NV PTT will be a holding company with two subsidiaries for posts and for telecommunications. The financial administration for posts and telecommunications activities will be separated. Any decision as to a formal organizational split has been left to the future. Moreover, in light of a more general recommendation that governmental functions should be decentralized, the headquarters of the holding company will be moved to the north of the country, while the headquarters of the Telecommunications BV subsidiary will remain in The Hague. Thus, as a practical matter, geographical separation may enhance the managerial autonomy of the telecommunications executives.

  5. NV PTT will be obliged to supply leased lines for value-added services offered under licence by the Secretary of Transportation and Public Works. There will be special studies of the policies appropriate for such licences. The intention is to introduce such services prior to January 1, 1989.

  6. Several new regulatory procedures will be adopted:

    a. A special bureau will be created in the Ministry of Transport and Public Works to draft regulations and implement policy.

    b. "On the basis of existing legislation", a procedure for

appeals from Ministry decisions will be established and such appeals will be dealt with by a special advisory board.

c. Final appeal will be lodged with the Council of State.

d. An Advisory Council on Telecommunications Policy will be established to advise the government on technological developments and governmental policy.

7. The Cabinet decided not to separate rigidly the competitive and concessionary services within the Telecommunications BV—as the Steenbergen Commission had proposed. Instead, competitive services initially will be offered by a branch of the Telecommunications BV. (It is possible, however, that a structural separation between the competitive and concessionary services may be adopted in the early 1990s.) Several safeguards will control the relationship between the entity providing the concessionary services and the provider of commercial services, which will be subject to competition. These safeguards include:

a. Restricting information flows between the two branches.

b. The competitive branch will purchase capacity from Telecommunications BV on the basis of tariffs.

c. Accounting safeguards and procedures will be established.

B. Problems

1. The proposals under consideration will become effective in 1989. Nevertheless, there will be substantial pressure for earlier implementation of some of the measures toward liberalization. Arrangements will develop on an *ad hoc* basis.

2. Many user groups are frustrated by the lack of information about the transition arrangements and do not see any mechanism by which they might be able to influence the decisionmaking process.

3. The Dutch PTT is faced with a transition process that is quite complex. It must make difficult decisions about the proper scope of the basic—"concessionary"—services.

a. The PTT may follow closely the approach of the VADS Licence in the U.K., thereby leaving intact restrictions only on basic voice and telex services. Packet switching will probably be treated as a bearer service, so that it is not likely that it will, at least initially, be opened to competition.

b. Boundary line issues over services are likely to be addressed in an *ad hoc* fashion through the new regulatory procedures being adopted. The Dutch PTT seems prepared to relegate the task of refining the scope of "competitive" and "concessionary" services to this process.

4. One difficult area for the PTT is how to ensure an easy transition for services that are now "liberalized". Various electronic mailbox and other add-on services, when offered over the public network, have been authorized for many years. Similarly, the PTT has allowed substantial

leeway for two-party uses of leased line services. Whether any such services will be viewed as being subject to the new licensing procedures remains uncertain.

C. Prospects

1. There will be a substantial effort to devise procedures for consultation between the PTT and users. In 1987, the PTT must develop a plan for the transition. At the same time, it will need to determine how much, and in what fashion, public dialogue should ensue with respect to such a plan.
2. The PTT will probably follow closely the regulatory steps of Oftel and the DTI in the U.K. and the pricing policies of Cable & Wireless and BT.
3. The PTT is concerned about recent reductions in the price of international services and the impact of these reductions on revenues; local tariffs cannot be raised quickly enough to compensate for such lost revenues. Observers of the PTT, however, see an irreversible trend toward further cost-based pricing and believe that there is little likelihood that usage-based pricing will be implemented for services other than packet switching.
4. The government is unlikely to make significant increases in the charges for leased lines that are used to provide value-added services. One reason for this is that it has followed a *de facto* policy of encouraging the development of the information-based and transactional services dependent on these lines.
5. Based on the present situation, the Ministry of Finance and the PTT have worked out arrangements to ensure an acceptable level of financial contribution by the PTT to the government. The PTT is expected to earn risk-related rates of return that reflect the competitive state of international services. At the same time, NV PTT, as a limited liability company, will be able to obtain funds on capital markets. Consequently, the PTT will have added ability to invest in new facilities and services.

VII. FINLAND

A. Background

1. The basic legislation in Finland is antiquated—an 1886 czarist decree, a 1919 telegraphy statute, and a 1927 Radio Act. These statutory provisions have not been applied to new data services or even to the construction of a competitive facilities network for data services.
2. The Finnish industry structure is a public-private hybrid consisting of the Finnish PTT (offering international, interexchange, and local services in smaller and rural communities) and privately (co-

operatively) owned local exchange companies, that provide local service in Finland's largest cities—Helsinki, Tampere, and Turku.

3. For several years, the age of the Finnish legislation has led many in Finland to believe that new telecommunications legislation is needed. Such legislation has recently been the subject of debate in Finland.

a. In early summer 1986, the Finnish Cabinet approved for consideration by the Eduskunta, the Finnish Parliament, the Telecommunications Operating Act (the "Act"), which was intended to modernize the Finnish legal and regulatory scheme. The Eduskunta approved the Act on December 19, 1986, to become effective on March 1, 1987.

b. The Act addresses the provision of terminal equipment, of network facilities, and of value-added services. There had been some ambiguities in the explanatory language accompanying the text of the bill that was sent to the Eduskunta. The Eduskunta removed some of these ambiguities in language that it added to the bill.

c. The Act permits full competition in the field of equipment, while regulating network facilities. Competition in value-added services is permitted in principle; the Act appears to permit the provision of services that are not offered to the general public and are not provided over separate network facilities; there is, however, no definitional distinction in the legislation between network facilities and value-added services.

d. The legislative language appears to authorize resale of communications services without concession. The explanatory language accompanying the bill had stated that resale of dedicated circuits was prohibited and that only terminals and subscriber lines would be available for resale. The language added by the Eduskunta, however, permits resale in principle, with the caveat that resale must not affect the public telecommunications services offered by the telephone companies. Although it is not entirely clear what this proviso means, it is read to include the private companies as well as the PTT.

e. The Act does not modify existing industry relationships; however, it creates a formal regulatory structure within which the industry would develop. One essential element of the law is that it separates the operational and regulatory roles of the PTT; the Ministry of Transport and Communications, for example, is charged with licensing separate service providers and is given supervisory authority over compliance with the Act. Telecommunications Operating Act, Secs. 5 and 18.

f. The Act also explicitly authorizes the PTT to bypass the private telephone companies. This provision had been resisted by the companies. Nevertheless, even if the bypass provision had been eliminated, the possibility of limited bypass would have remained because radio frequencies would still be available for that purpose.

4. The PTT is integrated with the Ministry of Transport and Communications. Independently of the Telecommunications Act that has just been enacted, it is seeking more autonomy in the area of financing and is urging that it be granted public corporation status. In February 1985, the

Rekola Commission recommended that the PTT be given broader control of day-to-day activities and be overseen by a board of directors. In January 1986, a government commission recommended that changes be made in the organic legislation for the PTT; such changes would effectively turn the PTT into a public corporation by January 1, 1988.

     5. Competition in interexchange services is evolving with the entry of Datatie Oy (Dataway Ltd.). Datatie is a joint venture of the Helsinki Telephone Company and many private organizations including Kansallis-Osake-Pankki (KOP) and the Union Bank of Finland, Finland's two largest banks, as well as other private telephone companies and industrial organizations.

        a. The Datatie infrastructure has been completed between Helsinki, Turku, and Tampere; in the northwest of Finland, the data network reached the city of Vaasa in November 1986. The new carrier has not yet moved into eastern Finland, where the PTT operates many of the local telephone companies; in any event, data traffic to that region is limited and, at least in the first phase of the business, service there is not seen as economically viable.

        b. Datatie is unable to obtain the radio facilities necessary to extend its services to those private telephone companies that are separated from the Datatie network by territory served by the PTT. Datatie is also not able to obtain access to satellite services because they are also controlled by the PTT's licensing authority.

        c. Some data services are developing using Datatie facilities.

B. Problems

     1. As evidenced by disputes over the licensing of facilities to Datatie, there is uncertainty about the scope and terms of competition between the private telephone companies and the PTT. There has been something of a "telecommunications war" between the two groups over their respective roles in offering packet switching and other data services in each other's territory.

     2. The Ministry of Transport and Communications and the Ministry of Finance are reluctant to allow the PTT too much autonomy. Although the recommendation is pending to convert the PTT into a public corporation, there is no express linkage to telecommunications legislation that will address only the competitive relationship between the PTT and the private telephone companies.

C. Prospects

     1. Interexchange competition will help to create an environment that is more receptive to value-added services.

     2. Interexchange competition between Datatie and the PTT will preclude the adoption of usage-sensitive pricing. Indeed, tariffs for data

services decreased in 1986 due partly to such competition. Reflecting trends in international services, the PTT and users will press for cost-based pricing. The PTT, for example, has instituted a five-year program of annual 10 per cent reductions in long-distance charges.

  a. In 1986, the Ministry of Finance decided that the cut in long-distance rates should be limited to 6 per cent to protect the revenues flowing to the government. This decision imposes pressure on the Finnish PTT, which, along with its Scandinavian counterparts, perceives itself as suffering from the bypassing of its international facilities. Thus, the availability of the switching hubs of London and Amsterdam has affected not only administrations in Western Europe but in Northern Europe as well.

  b. Some Finnish observers believe that long-distance telephone rates can and should be reduced but that local rates will not need to be adjusted upward. Their view is that the private telephone companies have had to recover their costs without being able to subsidize their local services from other revenue sources.

 3. The impact of the Act is not yet clear. There are varying opinions about its effects.

  a. The PTT had argued that the Act was a necessary change and would not alter industry relationships substantially. Others, including many user organizations, were unclear about the boundary between resale and private network activities. For this reason, although Finnish user organizations supported the legislation when it was being debated, they did have significant reservations.

  b. There is also bound to be some uncertainty about the provision that resale must not affect the public services. If the ultimate interpretation of that language is restrictive, and many resale activities are not permitted, a shadow will be cast over the development of value-added services in Finland.

  c. Conflicts between the language of the text and the accompanying legislative history may heighten the competitive relationship between the PTT and the local telephone companies. Litigation is one possible outcome.

  d. The Act confers on the Ministry of Transportation and Communications the authority to review the charges of entities other than the PTT. Special authority has been given for the PTT's tariffs. There is still some uncertainty as to how the tariffing review function will develop in a coherent way, so as to encourage the flourishing of a competitive environment for value-added services.

 4. One strategy frequently discussed in Finland is trying to attract more information-based businesses to use the country as a hub for new services.

  a. Finland has basically vigorous information-based industries as well as strong capabilities in the area of remote access data processing. Finnish suppliers, however, have generally had a difficult time gaining access to the bigger European markets due to close relationships between some national manufacturers and PTTs. Some Finnish manufacturers believe that the only way for them to penetrate the European market significantly may be to ally their interests with those of larger European users or multinational corporations.

b. If Finland were to become a hub for new services, the Finnish PTT would need to take an active role in working out international interconnection agreements for VAN services operating through nodes in Finland.

VIII. CANADA

A. Background

1. In July 1984, the Canadian Radio-television and Telecommunications Commission ("CRTC") essentially adopted the definitional approach of *Computer II*. See Enhanced Services, Telecom Decision CRTC 84–18, July 12, 1984 (Decision 84–18).

2. The CRTC declined to impose a separate subsidiary requirement on Bell Canada. However, it directed the federally-regulated carriers to identify which of the services they provide should be considered as enhanced. These services were to be transferred to separate subsidiaries of the carrier entities.

a. Some of the federally-regulated carriers identified certain services as enhanced. Certain services, such as Datapac access arrangements, that had been described as basic were, argued some users, enhanced. To resolve controversy over how the distinction between "basic" and "enhanced" ought to be applied to actual services, the CRTC initiated a proceeding in late 1984. CRTC Telecom Public Notice 1984–72, Dec. 11, 1984.

b. The CRTC first concluded that the touchstone of the distinction was the "availability" rather than the actual use of the enhanced feature that is relevant for the purpose of classifying a service. See Identification of Enhanced Services, Telecom Decision CRTC 85–17, Aug. 13, 1985. Adopting a view espoused by the FCC, which focused on an application that acts upon the content, code or protocol of subscriber information, the CRTC also concluded that speed conversion alone does not constitute an enhancement to a basic service. In 1985, the CRTC ruled on a series of services in a decision that simultaneously confirmed that the essentials of the U.S. distinction were to be applied in Canada and that the CRTC was not reluctant to opine on the appropriate classification of particular offerings.

c. The CRTC, however, found that certain services, though enhanced, ought not to be subject to the costing requirements established in Decision 84–18. Services such as "911" emergency service and voice relay for the deaf, though they possess "enhanced" features, are likely to remain monopoly services. Thus, departing from the proposition that the definitional distinction triggers accounting consequences, the CRTC has exempted certain services on an evaluation of the likelihood that competition will develop in those services.

        d. Where memory and storage features are part of the service, but "serve only to facilitate the transmission of information", the service should be classified as "basic". *Id.* at 13. Where, however, the storage and retrieval functions are within the control of the subscriber and enable it to control the time of message delivery, the service should be regarded as "enhanced". *Id.* at 19.

    3. On the basis of Section 5(3) of the Bell Canada Special Act, which states that Bell Canada must act solely as a common carrier, Bell Canada is precluded from engaging in electronic publishing or from creating or distributing its own data bases.

    4. With respect to interexchange competition, in the Fall of 1985 the CRTC dismissed the application of CNCP to obtain interconnection for switched interexchange services. *See* Interexchange Competition and Related Issues, Telecom Decision CRTC 85–19, Aug. 29, 1985. The ground for dismissal was, according to the CRTC, that the CNCP business plan was flawed: if CNCP had to pay the high level of contribution to local rates that had been forecast, its proposal would have been uneconomic.

    5. CNCP did not appeal the denial of its application to the courts. After several months, however, it did apply to the CRTC for reconsideration. The CRTC has not yet decided to review the application for reconsideration. If there is "new evidence", and it is felt that it would be useful to open the application to public comment, the CRTC will establish a set of procedures.

    6. The CRTC has now issued two decisions substantially liberalizing the resale and sharing of services to provide a wide range of services.

        a. Essentially, all services other than Message Telephone Service (MTS) and Wide Area Telephone Service (WATS) can be resold or shared to provide all services (*i.e.*, including data, enhanced, and basic services) other than basic interexchange voice services that provide access to the public switched network, except that users may share MTS to provide MTS-like services. Tariff Revisions Related to Resale and Sharing, Telecom Decision CRTC 87–2, Feb. 12, 1987 (Decision 87–2). Primary exchange voice services—including shared tenant services and individual line, PBX trunk, and Centrex services—can be provided via sharing arrangements, except for public pay telephone service. Resale to Provide Primary Exchange Voice Services, Telecom Decision CRTC 87–1, Feb. 12, 1987.

        b. As part of the process authorizing resale, the CRTC has been endeavoring to rebalance rates to reduce cream-skimming. The proposal to rebalance rates was released for public comment in mid-1986. With its decision to adopt the facilities-based restrictions noted above, however, the CRTC has concluded that the impact of permitting sharing and resale of certain services would not be uneconomic or likely to erode the contribution of MTS/WATS.

    c. The CRTC decisions incorporate restrictions that essentially distinguish sharing from resale. Two companies will be permitted to share a leased circuit. In addition, a reseller could resell one hundred voice circuits to one hundred separate customers for their exclusive use, but would not be permitted to sell to five hundred customers. In other words, each circuit shall be dedicated to a user, each circuit shall terminate at user equipment (or at a Centrex facility dedicated to the user), and circuits that terminate at central offices and are used by resellers cannot pass through non-user-provided switches; sharing groups must obtain services directly from the carrier. Decision 87-2, Annex A, para. 2(5), at 32. In short, simultaneous "reselling" and "sharing" is not permitted.

    7. At present, there are few Canadian enhanced service providers (outside the licensed carriers) and few have sought to be licensed by the CRTC. The principal explanation for the dearth of value-added providers is that large users are able to solve their own needs for value-added services by using the services of the two national data and packet-switching networks of Telecom Canada and CNCP. In addition, enhanced service providers are unable to offer national service without securing the agreement of the exchange carriers to obtain local services.

    8. Teleglobe Canada was privatized in April 1987. A letter of intent had been signed in February with Memotec Data Inc. of Montreal. Bell Canada Enterprises, the holding company of Bell Canada, is purchasing one-third of the shares of Memotec.

    a. The impetus for privatization has been driven by an intention to regularize the regulatory status of Teleglobe Canada, to reduce rates and to limit the incentive for bypass through the U.S. With the privatization, these objectives will be met. First, the legislation privatizing Teleglobe made it subject to the jurisdiction of the CRTC. Bill C-38, Teleglobe Canada Reorganization and Divestiture, Sections 13-18, Second Session, 33rd Parl., 35-36 Eliz. II, 1986-87.

    b. At the same time, the Minister of State (Privatization) has forecast that international telephone rates will be reduced by 13 per cent in 1988. Minister of State, Privatization, "Teleglobe Canada to be Sold to Memotec Data Inc.", News Release, Feb. 11, 1987.

B. Problems

    1. It is unclear, as a matter of law, whether the CRTC is empowered to de-tariff Bell Canada services. There has been legislation that would give the CRTC the authority to forbear from regulation of carriers under its jurisdiction. The issue of forbearance was addressed explicitly in the bill privatizing Teleglobe Canada. The CRTC is expressly permitted to

forbear from regulating where activities of Teleglobe are subject to a degree of competition that obviates the need for regulation. Bill C–38, Section 15. This provision may be a foothold for further legislation that would permit the CRTC to extend its power to forbear to domestic carriers.

  2. The division of jurisdiction between the provinces and the federal government has made it uncertain whether enhanced services can be offered in provinces where carriers are not subject to federal jurisdiction, *i.e.*, outside Ontario, Quebec, and British Columbia.

  3. The rate rebalancing process, widely viewed as a predicate for any interexchange competition, is moving ahead slowly.

C. Prospects

  1. Litigation (the *Alberta Government Telephones* case now pending in the Canadian Supreme Court) and federal-provincial negotiations may result in a uniform approach to value-added services.

   a. Substantial progress has been made in these negotiations. A joint study has examined the issues of pricing and universal service. *See* Federal-Provincial Examination of Telecommunications Pricing and the Universal Availability of Affordable Telephone Service, Report (Oct. 1986). Although the Report does not expressly address value-added services, it does address the need to facilitate business communications and to encourage innovation in technology and services.

   b. The Report serves as background for what is described as an historic accord between the federal, provincial, and territorial Ministers responsible for communications. In Spring 1987, these Ministers met to adopt six principles that will constitute the basis for a coherent Canadian telecommunications policy. They signed a Memorandum of Understanding to support the consensus reached on interconnection policy and on sharing government responsibilities in the sector. Department of Communications, "News Release", April 3, 1987. The evolution of a national Canadian telecommunications policy will significantly facilitate the growth of value-added services.

  2. The CRTC continues to follow closely the path charted by the FCC in the *Computer II* decision. As part of its resale and sharing decisions, it has been looking at access arrangements. It is likely, therefore, that the CRTC will examine developments in the FCC's *Computer III* proceeding. Eventually, it will adopt a flexible approach to the provision of "enhanced services" by Bell Canada. That is, separation of facilities will not be required; instead, there will be a general condition that dealings be at arm's length.

  3. The decisions to liberalize resale and sharing for data and enhanced services are likely to create opportunities for new providers of value-added services. At the same time, the CRTC may be confronted with the need to render additional decisions on the regulatory status of services offered by carriers.

4. The CRTC will probably look at the FCC policies on "comparably efficient interconnection", *see* Section II.B, above. Moreover, debate in the U.S. over the MFJ provision barring the BOCs from offering "information services" might influence Canadian interpretations of the Bell Canada Special Act Section 5(3) restrictions on Bell Canada.

IX. ITALY

A. Background

1. Some value-added services have been provided by implementation of an entrepreneurial strategy that encourages joint ventures between Societa Torinese Esercizi Telefonici ("STET") and other Italian industrial interests. STET has been involved with a joint venture for travel services, *i.e.*, SIGMA. It has also entered into a joint venture with Montedison to form Televas. Another joint venture has been formed in the area of financial services.

2. The structural issues in Italian telecommunications are complicated by the fragmentation in the provision of service. For some time, there have been plans to privatize the State Agency for Telephone Services ("ASST"), which provides much of the long-distance service and regional international services, and transfer it to the STET group. One of the impetuses for restructuring is the separation of ASST's regulatory and operational responsibilities. Political issues, however, have delayed the long-awaited restructuring of the telecommunications sector.

B. Problems

1. The permissible scope of the joint-venture activities has not been completely defined.

2. There is no regulatory body or mechanism to define the scope of the ventures.

C. Prospects

1. The Italian approach is entrepreneurial. Decisions on what kinds of services are permitted are made on an *ad hoc* basis; the various public and quasi-public entities have substantial leeway to structure new service arrangements.

2. Rationalization of the backbone transmission facilities and the restructuring of ASST within STET is proving difficult to accomplish. This effort at resolving the structuring issues may work to deflect decisionmakers from addressing questions of how, and by whom, value-added services are to be provided.

X. SPAIN

A. Background

1. In March 1986, the government drafted new comprehensive legislation on telecommunications that would have established the framework in which different types of services were to be provided and to demarcate the roles of the public and private sectors. The bill met with substantial objection from several quarters and was never introduced for legislative consideration.

2. In March 1987, a bill on telecommunications was introduced in Parliament. The law creates two classes of services.

    a. Final Telecommunications Services are essentially end-to-end services such as telephony, telex, facsimile, and videotex. These are offered under monopoly to the public.

    b. Value-Added Services may be offered competitively. Article 20.1, Regulation of Telecommunications, No. 121/000029 (*Official Gazette*, March 21, 1987). They are defined as services that add other facilities to the support service (*i.e.*, the Carrier or Final Telecommunications Service) or satisfy such needs as accessing stored information, transmitting information or carrying out the processing, storage and recovery of information. *Id.*

    c. The bill establishes two classes of value-added services. The first, which consists of services using the tariffed public-switched network, is subject only to a notification regime. The second, which includes services that make use of leased lines, will be considered a public service requiring licensing. Where, however, the Value-Added Service does not serve third parties, the services will not be considered public and may be provided subject only to administrative authorization. Articles 21 and 22.

B. Problems

1. It appears that one reason for the opposition to the March 1986 draft was the imprecision in some of the categories that it would have established. Although many of these difficulties have been rectified in the 1987 proposal, some important points should be made about the latest version of the legislation.

    a. The latest proposal distinguishes between "Final Telecommunications Services", offered to the public in general, and "Carrier Services". Article 14. Carrier services are those that provide the capacity for the transmission of signals—essentially the infrastructure support for the Final Telecommunications Services and Value-Added Services. Carrier services are provided pursuant to a monopoly regime. Article 14.5. Nevertheless, the law appears to suggest that some non-monopoly carrier services may be authorized under license for the provision of value-added services, with such license being granted only if existing Carrier Services or Final Telecommunications Services are not adequate. Article 23.1.

        b. Telephone, mobile automatic telephone, mobile maritime, telegram, telex, teletex, mobile maritime radio telegraphy, telefax, bureaufax, datafax, videotex, and video telephone are "Final Telecommunications Services" that will be reserved to the State. Article 13. Final Telecommunications Services are defined as those that provide complete end-to-end service for communication, including terminal functions and, generally, requiring switching elements. However, any Final Telecommunications Services not expressly listed in the bill are presumably not included within the scope of the monopoly; these might have to be provided on a competitive basis. Article 22.

        c. With respect to the scope of the "Final Services" included within the monopoly, *e.g.*, "telex" and "telefax", there remain significant ambiguities in the March 1987 proposal. Similar ambiguities contributed, in part, to the withdrawal of the 1986 draft.

        2. In principle, the provision of value-added services is liberalized significantly. Article 23.3. However, certain limits are set out expressly in the proposal. First, a service will not be authorized if it is "equivalent" to a Final Telecommunications or Carrier Service already in operation. Article 24.2. Second, simple resale appears to be proscribed; the bill states that the Value-Added Service must offer characteristics that differentiate it from the underlying support service. Article 24.2.

        3. Both the 1986 and 1987 proposals empower the State to limit competition in "Value-Added Services" based on certain concerns. Competition may be limited where no private sector initiative exists for providing a particular service, where such limitation is necessary to further the public and social interest in the service, and where limitation is necessary to preserve economies of scale. Article 24.4. Thus, the criteria by which the State could determine that competition ought to be limited are not well defined and will be difficult to interpret.

        4. One problem with the March 1986 proposal was the failure to delineate clearly how a new regulatory mechanism might work. In the 1987 draft, substantial power is vested in the Ministry of Transport, Tourism, and Communications to ensure that fair competition in Value-Added Services develops, particularly with respect to the offerings of entities authorized to provide Carrier or Final Telecommunications Services. Article 24.5. To ensure that no unfair cross-subsidization occurs, the bill requires the separation of accounting between competitive and monopoly activities under the supervision of the Ministry.

C. Prospects

        1. The legislative framework under consideration is, in principle, rather liberal. Passage, perhaps in an amended version, is likely before the end of 1987. U.S. negotiators have had an exploratory round of meetings

with Spanish regulatory officials. As the new proposal is reviewed and, if it passes, implemented, the U.S. may continue to try to influence the course of Spanish policy.

2. Spain is likely to liberalize its approach to value-added services to attract international telecommunications business. At this point, the Spanish thinking, and the motivations underlying it, might profitably be compared with those of the Dutch.

XI. THE FEDERAL REPUBLIC OF GERMANY

A. Background

1. Issues of pricing policy that focus on the potential for arbitrage between public switched and private line services are of key importance in considering the provision of value-added services in the Federal Republic of Germany. The predominant concern is one of "cream skimming". Official policy of the Deutsche Bundespost is to implement the various proposals for rate harmonization—to strive for equivalency between public switched tariffs and leased line services by charging for leased lines in accordance with usage-sensitive principles. Such harmonization of tariffs has been viewed as a precondition for a total liberalization of value-added services.

2. Currently, the Bundespost provides a full range of services that are not separately denominated as value-added, informational, transactional, or basic. There are also several hundred private providers of value-added services that use Bundespost leased lines; some of these offer services to third parties. Such private suppliers are not, however, viewed as being in any sense in competition with the Bundespost. Once new usage-sensitive tariffs are in place, existing service-based—rather than facilities-based—competition will intensify.

3. In April 1986, the Ministry of Posts and Telecommunications released Draft Telecommunications Regulations (Entwurf der Telekommunikationsordnung or "TKO"); the TKO will be implemented in 1988. The TKO is an ambitious undertaking to develop a single, integrated regulatory scheme to lay the groundwork for an ISDN environment and to open further the market for value-added services. In preparation for ISDN, the TKO seeks to integrate existing, service-based tariffing and other regulations, to publish new tariffs for ISDN services (and integrate those with the restructured, but existing, tariffs), and to endeavor to reduce the restrictions on usage of Bundespost facilities in order to encourage the development of value-added services.

   a. Like the separate regulatory frameworks that it replaces, the TKO will govern the fees and conditions of use of telecommunications services. It establishes tariffs for uses of trunks and networks, and sets out conditions on privately-operated systems that are capable of performing switching, concentration, or dedicated one-way communications functions. TKO, at § 9. The TKO also permits branch lines not owned by the

Bundespost to be used for voice communications. TKO, § 12. Trunks can be interconnected to offer certain permitted services; to prevent the formation of resale networks, however, it will be forbidden to interconnect certain "universal trunks" and dial links. TKO, at §§ 9 and 13(2).

  b. The TKO focuses on types of systems and classifies them by their configuration, capabilities, and size. Fees are then imposed on each category. TKO, at §§ 98–135.

  c. The TKO attempts to harmonize leased line and switched tariffs in Chapter 8, which sets out the fees for leased line services. It establishes charging principles based on distance and connection or use time, imposing a minimum 80-hour charge on private lines, with additional charging on a time-sensitive basis.

  4. The TKO recognizes that flat prohibitions on third-party traffic can thwart the offering of value-added services that are not simple substitutes for public switched services. Seeking to eliminate tariff arbitrage, which could result from the distortions in the Bundespost's pricing structure, the Bundespost would approve value-added services without burdensome restrictions. The restrictions that remain, however, will be subject to reevaluation over the next few years.

  a. Given the difficulty of differentiating between enhanced services and simple resale, the TKO proposes a multi-part resolution of the problem. First, there will be no usage-based fees for traffic carried entirely on intracorporate networks.

  b. Second, time-sensitive tariffs will be applied to leased lines and dial links to minimize restrictions on the interconnection of leased line services and on the interconnection of leased line and switched services. The concept used is that of a "net tariff", to avoid undue increases in the pricing of both existing and future applications. The Bundespost's pricing schedule allows for an advantage from tariff arbitrage of up to 25 per cent (*i.e.*, the difference between comparable usage of switched and private line facilities).

  c. Third, in restating both the Bundespost's statutory responsibilities to carry out its public service functions and current regulations, the TKO prohibits network competition.

  d. Furthermore, certain types of interconnection—of telex with data trunks, for example—are prohibited to forestall bypass by concentrating traffic and sending it on high-speed and, when the costs of sending each message are aggregated, lower-priced links.

  e. Prohibited message-switching activity is defined as interconnection of dial trunks, if there is no operator intervention or operator processing of the message. Processing does not include changes in transmission rate, a change in coding, or the insertion of non-substantive message data. Sequential data bank retrieval is permitted, however. It is not clear how these restrictions will be enforced. The Bundespost believes that marketing activities of system operators will be necessary for resale services to be profitable, and, therefore, would be readily discovered.

B. Problems

1. Although the TKO is an attempt to implement usage-sensitive pricing in a coherent and well-considered way, its adoption might reduce some incentives for launching a new value-added service and could eliminate some of the benefits of such services. With respect to the latter, third-party services, which are permitted under the TKO (but are subject to usage-sensitive pricing), are important because they can result in agreements being reached on technical standards or in the development of new markets for the Bundespost.

2. Furthermore, usage-sensitive pricing is sharply at odds with trends elsewhere in pricing policy, *e.g.*, in the U.S., the U.K., France, the Netherlands, Finland, Japan, and Canada. Therefore, implementation of the TKO's usage-sensitive pricing might place Germany at a competitive disadvantage in providing international services.

3. The TKO does not address the issue of how to assure non-discriminatory treatment of value-added services offered by the Bundespost and those that are currently or might eventually be provided by third parties. This is so because the TKO, to the extent that it is a consolidation of existing regulations that govern the use of leased and switched services, views value-added service providers as the customers, not the competitors, of the Bundespost.

4. The TKO, therefore, is not targeted at developing a framework for competition between the Bundespost and other providers of value-added services. Several regulatory questions, having to do with the structure and fairness of any such competition, will need to be answered.

  a. Will, for example, the value-added services offered by the Bundespost also be based on the TKO's usage-sensitive tariffs? At present, for the few value-added services that it does offer, the Bundespost does not itself charge on a volume-sensitive basis.

  b. Would a policy of implementing the same tariffs for the Bundespost and its competitors necessitate the implementation of a Bundespost subsidiary for value-added services?

  c. If third parties are permitted to offer value-added services, will the operational and regulatory responsibilities of the Bundespost need to be separated?

C. Prospects

1. The development of the TKO and the implementation of usage-based pricing will be a major focal point in the coming years. What will be the impact of pricing trends elsewhere in Europe on pricing policies in Germany? There may be more attention paid to whether cost-based pricing might be introduced with respect to such new services as ISDN.

2. If competition between the Bundespost and private suppliers develops in the value-added sector, even greater attention will need to be paid to the tariff structure. There is currently some discussion within the Federal Republic as to whether the Bundespost would obtain a competitive advantage by not using a volume-sensitive internal tariff for its value-added services, and, if so, whether such cost allocation is unfair vis-à-vis would-be competitors.

3. In the near future, considerable attention will be paid to the management structure of the Bundespost. The release of the report of the Government Committee on Telecommunications (the Witte Commission), expected in 1987, will heighten public and political attention to the Bundespost's organization. The Bundespost may evolve along the lines of the DGT, with separate entities for new services, *i.e.*, terminal equipment and value-added services.

a. The Witte Commission reportedly will recommend that there be such a separation. The monopoly, facilities-based, operation would be known as "Telenetz" and the value-added part would be called "Teledienst". According to preliminary reports, both parts would be operated commercially.

b. There may be management-related benefits to such a separated structure. Indeed, a report by the U.S. firm of McKinsey & Co. prepared in connection with the work of the Witte Commission—and heavily criticized by the Bundespost—notes that some perceived inadequacies in the Bundespost's performance in marketing and innovation could be remedied by an organizational realignment. The Witte Commission reportedly came close to, but ultimately decided against, recommending that the government permit private, facilities-based, networks to operate in competition with the Bundespost. Instead, however, it reportedly will recommend a government review every three years, with the focus being on whether the Bundespost is leasing private lines at internationally competitive rates.

4. Beyond the Bundespost's management structure, however, renewed attention will undoubtedly be paid to the possible separation of its regulatory and operational functions—as has been the case in other countries, *i.e.*, France, Finland, and the Netherlands. One of the most important of the reported Witte Commission recommendations is that the Bundespost's telecommunications operations be separated from the Ministry. German policymakers will need to decide what kind of regulatory mechanisms might be appropriate to oversee the Bundespost's activities in the areas—those in which "Teledienst" operates—that are opened to competition. It is likely, though not certain, that the Ministry itself will retain the new "regulatory" functions; how regulation will develop and be exercised, consistent with the administrative tradition in Germany, is one of the critical issues that must be addressed in German telecommunications policy.

XI. AUSTRALIA

A. Background

1. As is the case in much of the industrialized world, policymakers in Australia are examining the structure and regulatory processes of both the domestic and international telecommunications environment. Indeed, on April 7, 1987, the Hon. Michael Duffy MP, Minister for Communications, acknowledged the debate on the appropriate regulatory regime for the provision of telecommunications services. Australia has had to confront a difficult array of circumstances in delivering telecommunications services: a small population that is concentrated in a relatively small part of the country, with the rest of the country sparsely populated; a country with a large land mass, nearly the size of Europe or the continental United States, but with a market only one-twentieth the size; pressures to keep local tariffs low and to ensure uniform, universal service; a location that is remote from much of the rest of the developed world; all combined with the desire to develop a viable local telecommunications industry, with a full range of design and manufacturing capabilities. Despite these hurdles, Australia has managed to develop a superb domestic and international telecommunications infrastructure, with one of the highest telephone densities in the world.

2. At the present time, however, a series of important issues are confronting the Department of Communications and the other players on the Australian telecommunications scene: the Commonwealth Government's Australian Telecommunications Commission ("Telecom Australia"), Overseas Telecommunications Commission (Australia) ("OTC(A)"), and AUSSAT Pty Ltd ("AUSSAT"); and State Government telecommunications systems, such as Q-Net, a private (basically leased line) network emerging in Queensland. As described in greater detail below, these issues are far-ranging, and include the following:

    a. Will service-based competition to Telecom Australia develop? How will the usage of facilities be liberalized? Key factors include political, cultural, and economic pressures to maintain universal service, the viability of continuing cross-subsidization between Telecom Australia services, new policies on sharing leased lines, and the niche that will be served by AUSSAT.

    b. Will there be facilities-based competition with either Telecom Australia or OTC(A), or both, and would such competition emerge as a result of the entrance of new entities or from a structural reorganization among existing organizations?

    c. What is the relationship between international and domestic services? There appears to be increasing pressure on the present line of demarcation between Telecom Australia and OTC(A) responsibilities.

d. How should regulatory oversight and responsibility be allocated? Should it reside in the facilities providers, in a body unaffiliated with any service provider (such as the Department of Communications), or in some hybrid arrangement?

e. What are the regional and international plans of OTC(A)?

3. When the Postmaster General's Department (Australian Post Office) was divided into three parts in July 1975, the Department of Communications, Australian Postal Commission (Australia Post), and Telecom Australia were created, with Telecom Australia established as a statutory authority under the Telecommunications Act 1975.

a. Telecom Australia has been created as an institution with legislation that regulates the Commission-Minister relationship. This arrangement insulates it from political expediency. The Commission is managed by commissioners appointed by the Governor General; six of these are part-time, one of whom is the Secretary to the Department of Communications, and a seventh is a full-time commissioner who is the Managing Director. It is organized regionally, with policy and national departments at the headquarters, with state administrations responsible for implementing national policy, and with district organizations charged with marketing, installation, and operation.

b. The Telecommunications Act 1975 confers a monopoly in certain services (particularly public switched telephone services) on Telecom Australia. No other person or organization can construct, maintain, or operate telecommunications installations within Australia unless authorized by Telecom Australia. The present government has reaffirmed that Telecom Australia is the national common carrier.

4. The Department of Communications is responsible for advising the Minister of Communications on policy matters. In addition to Telecom Australia, OTC(A), AUSSAT, Australia Post, and other communications-related instrumentalities all report to the Minister, and the Department is charged with co-ordinating advice on telecommunications policy to the Minister. The instrumentalities can formulate such advice in the first instance, though there is nothing preventing the Department from initiating independent advice to the Minister.

a. Initially, the Department may have been hampered in participating fully in the formulation of advice on telecommunications policy. As a result of the 1975 reorganization, virtually all of the telecommunications policy planning personnel were allocated to Telecom Australia. Since that time, the Department has increased its staff, and significant expertise in telecommunications policymaking now resides there.

b. Other government departments, particularly the Department of Industry, Technology and Commerce (and its Business Regulation Review Unit and Information and Services Industries branch), are paying considerable and increasing attention to matters concerning developments in the communications industry.

c. After consulting with Telecom Australia, the Minister for

Communications has some qualified power to give it written directions on the performance of its functions. The Minister has exercised his power of direction only once, with respect to Australia Post (and there is some debate over the extent to which that entity complied therewith), and, consequently, these powers are not seen as the primary means of making policy.

d. Telecom Australia is required to furnish an Annual Report of its operations and a balance sheet to the Minister, for presentation to Parliament; in addition, it produces an annual Services and Business Outlook to provide Parliament and the public with an outline of some of the issues it considers important for the coming year. Finally, it contributes to, and appears before, various Parliamentary Committees.

5. AUSSAT was formed in November 1981 as an incorporated entity to operate the Australian national satellite system. Telecom Australia holds 25 per cent of its shares, with 75 per cent held by the Minister for Communications on behalf of the Commonwealth. AUSSAT is managed by a board of nine directors. Its primary function originally was to provide broadcasting services to remote regions. Television and video applications represent more than 60 per cent of AUSSAT use. Now, however, AUSSAT is increasingly becoming involved in the provision of telecommunications, and particularly specialized business services, throughout Australia.

a. The Satellite Communications Act prohibits AUSSAT from providing public switched services in competition with Telecom Australia. Rather, AUSSAT leases satellite capacity to Telecom Australia, which it then resells to customers as a premium service. Together, as the Satellite Communications Act states (Section 7), AUSSAT and Telecom Australia provide "the national telecommunications network for Australia".

b. Telecom Australia has consistently maintained that it is more cost-effective to complete its basic network by terrestrial means, but it was nonetheless an early customer of AUSSAT satellite capacity. Importantly, AUSSAT offers private leased circuits to large users. Such satellite-based networks can be interconnected with the Telecom Australia public network, subject to their adhering to the terms and charges for interconnection as published by Telecom Australia.

c. AUSSAT may be a significant factor in the introduction of competition in existing services or of new services. As an incorporated company, it may have more flexibility than either Telecom Australia or OTC(A). Moreover, many of its top executives are entrepreneurially oriented and have backgrounds with OTC(A). They have brought a market-driven approach to the supply of new services. AUSSAT does operate under some constraints; it must have proper regard to public service terms and conditions for employees and its ability to expand its borrowing is restrained, due to its present, highly leveraged, condition.

d. AUSSAT services may also help erode some of the distinction between domestic and international services. The third AUSSAT satellite will have a beam with uplink and downlink capacity for the South West Pacific region, including New Zealand and the smaller islands of the region. In November 1986, AUSSAT signed an agreement to provide space facilities to the New Zealand Post Office, for it to provide domestic services.

6. OTC(A) was established as a Commonwealth business enterprise in 1946 by combining the international telecommunications functions of Cable & Wireless Ltd and Amalgamated Wireless Australia Ltd. It is a statutory authority, but, unlike Telecom Australia, no legislative monopoly is conferred on it. Although OTC(A), therefore, has no formal monopoly under the Overseas Telecommunications Commission Act, Section 60 does allow the Governor-General to proclaim that, after a specific date, an overseas service cannot "be conducted, controlled or managed otherwise than by or on behalf of the Commission (OTC(A))". To date, this power has never been exercised.

  a. Due principally to Australia's location, to the European ties of many Australians, and to the active marketing of, and low tariff policies for, international services, Australians are comparatively large users of international services; *per capita*, Australians make three times as many international calls as Americans and twice as many as the British. OTC(A) has had, therefore, to be an extremely active player in the development of the international telecommunications infrastructure. Indeed, OTC(A) is one of the largest owners of international facilities in the world. Australia is the sixth largest user of Intelsat, and OTC(A) is the world's third largest owner of submarine cable facilities, with substantial investments in the North Atlantic, including an interest in the new TAT-8 cable.

  b. Pressures to erode the line of demarcation between the jurisdiction of OTC(A) and Telecom Australia (and possibly AUSSAT) emerge from time to time. OTC(A) is offering a series of Intelsat Business Services (called SatNet in Australia) that are end-to-end services. As described below, some of these services may be interconnected with the Telecom Australia network, but interconnection may not be required for future IBS services with customer premises earth stations.

  c. For the non-IBS services, OTC(A) has had to co-ordinate its shared use policies with Telecom Australia. Telecom Australia, however, has taken a fairly restrictive view on shared use, based on its views of its role as a common carrier and its responsibilities. As discussed in greater detail below, such co-ordination is now more readily effectuated than it appears to have been in the past.

  d. With a decidedly entrepreneurial outlook OTC(A) is run not entirely unlike a private sector business. It has developed a set of five-year business plans that are aimed at satisfying its four key audiences: its customers, its correspondents, its domestic affiliates (Telecom Australia, AUSSAT, and Australia Post), and the government. These plans concentrate on its telephone, business information services, maritime group, and consultancies.

7. Until the process that culminated in the division of the Postmaster General's Department in the mid-1970s, national policymakers and politicians had paid some, but not much, attention to telecommunica-

tions policy. Since that time, however, there has been regular attention to telecommunications policy as part of an ongoing process of review in response to user needs. *See* Commission of Inquiry into the Australian Post Office ("Vernon Report") (April 1974); Committee of Inquiry into Telecommunications Services in Australia ("Davidson Report") (October 1982); H. Ergas, *Telecommunications and the Australian Economy* (1986). In 1984 and 1986, the Expenditure Committee of the House of Representatives published reports on the tariffs of Telecom Australia. There is now an infrastructure committee, comprising Commonwealth Government (Australian Labor Party) backbench members of the Parliament, that is attentive to telecommunications policy. The current policy review in Australia is, in sum, taking place in an environment where telecommunications could become a highly significant political issue.

    a. The Labor Party, however, with its strong ties to union interests, has expressed a commitment to the current ownership structure of the telecommunications sector. With the election held on July 11, 1987, and the strength of the Labor Party victory, it seems likely that this commitment will continue.

    b. One of the opposition parties, the Liberals, might be thought to advocate privatization and deregulation. In 1985, the Liberals were interested in the possibilities of privatization; subsequently, and as a result of electoral reversals, they have moved somewhat away from strong advocacy of that position, at least with respect to Telecom Australia. Moreover, the Liberals have been allied with the National Country Party, which is committed to development of, and low-cost service to, the rural areas. As a result, there is substantial commitment by the opposition to rural services and cross-subsidization, and, perhaps, to maintaining the *status quo*, at least with respect to domestic public switched services.

B. Problems

1. The two critical issues that face Australian policymakers are, first, the locus of regulatory policy and, second, how to structure the telecommunications sector to maximize efficiency and deliver new and existing services on an affordable and universal basis. These questions and others have been the subject of a series of studies, reports, and papers.

    a. The Vernon Report focused on the structure of the telecommunications sector. Among other conclusions, it recommended joining Telecom Australia and OTC(A). The Whitlam Government did follow through on that recommendation, but the Senate voted against it. Since that time, there has been no significant push for integration of the two entities—or the services that they provide. Today, some players are seeking to broaden the agenda for discussion, to develop competitive alternatives to these two providers.

b. The Davidson Report examined the provision and structure of the domestic telecommunications sector. It recommended that there should be some liberalization in telecommunications policies in the following areas: permitting the resale of capacity leased from Telecom Australia; reallocating responsibility for licensing independent networks from Telecom to the Minister; liberalizing policies with respect to the interconnection of leased and independent private networks; separating marketing of terminal equipment from the network operator; permitting free supply and maintenance by private enterprise of terminal equipment; and separating ownership of new information services from the provision of the public system carrying the service.

c. The Report further recommended that cross-subsidies should be reduced and that Telecom organizational arrangements should be modified to separate operational and regulatory responsibilities. Many of the recommendations dealing with management issues were accepted by Telecom Australia and implemented. Nevertheless, with the election of the Labor Government, and as a result of considerable political opposition, the key recommendations, covering network access and structural change, were rejected.

2. The present government needs to examine the array of questions arising from regulatory policies and structural arrangements in the telecommunications and other sectors.

a. As part of an extended review of government administration, for example, the government released a Policy Discussion Paper entitled "Statutory Authorities and Government Business Enterprises" in June 1986. This document, which contains proposed policy guidelines, seeks to increase both the performance and accountability of statutory authorities and government business enterprises, such as Telecom Australia and OTC(A). In balancing the need for entrepreneurial initiative within businesses and for government to ensure that important policy objectives are implemented, the Paper seeks to strike a middle course. Thus, it sets out to propose that existing direct controls over government business enterprises be reduced.

b. Nevertheless, the Labor Government is interested in efficiency, with both accountability and a commitment to economic and social growth. It proposes, therefore, that the statutory authorities under its control should prepare three-to-five-year strategic plans containing objectives and developments in key programs, with forecasts, staffing plans, and other matters bearing on performance. These plans would be provided to the particular Minister responsible for overseeing a specific enterprise. This Minister, with the Treasurer and Minister of Finance, and in consultation with the enterprise, would determine financial targets to be met by the enterprise.

c. Telecom Australia is keenly anxious for greater freedom of action and independence to act in an entrepreneurial fashion. Thus, though endorsing the avowed aim of achieving efficiency in the government business enterprises, it submitted comments in August 1986 that "deplored" what it saw as the proposed additional restraints on it and other statutory authorities and the proposal to place them under the control and direction of others in the government besides the responsible Minister. OTC(A) also vigorously objected to several suggestions in the proposed guidelines that government control be augmented.

d. In its comments, which were entitled "Managing Government Business Enterprises: Control and Accountability", Telecom Australia criticized several aspects of the proposed guidelines. First, it said that external approval of corporate and strategic plans was incompatible with the view that those who are responsible for implementing such plans should be held accountable for them. Currently, by contrast, Telecom Australia submits a one-to-three-year corporate plan to the Minister for his information. Second, there was no explicit statement in the proposed guidelines, argued Telecom Australia, as to which direct controls would be reduced.

e. Hence, the Telecom Australia submission was used as a means of articulating Telecom Australia's firmly held view that its demonstrably excellent record in financial management and service provision warrants a relaxation of existing controls. Specifically, Telecom Australia argues that two important predicates for efficiency are in place: there is now a clear government Charter for its enterprise, and there are adequate accountability mechanisms. What is lacking is the removal of constraints that impede efficiency; easing these constraints would imply less dependence on approval of the Loan Council for borrowings, vesting of staffing decisions in Telecom Australia, more discretion in contract approval, and greater autonomy in setting tariffs.

f. With respect to borrowing, in particular, Telecom Australia has felt somewhat constrained by the need to obtain the approval of the Treasurer and the Loan Council before it borrows on the Australian money market. The Loan Council determines the aggregate annual borrowing programs of the Commonwealth and State Governments and their authorities. The Treasurer approves borrowings within Commonwealth programs. At present, Telecom Australia finances its operational expenditures entirely from internal sources; its capital program is also largely self-financed (71 per cent in 1983–4; 65 per cent in 1984–5). Nevertheless, it does require access to public funds, borrowing, for example, A$640 million in 1986. However, the Commonwealth Government attempts to limit public sector borrowing to minimize the impact on private sector borrowing, and this limitation, as applied to Telecom Australia, may be quite significant with respect to the implementation of its plans.

g. Another constraint on Telecom Australia is its annual payment to the government. It owes A$4.5 billion, which is the amount of its indebtedness to the government at the time of the 1975 separation. Anually, it pays A$600 million as interest on this debt. The interest rates have been raised significantly over the years in line with market rates, with the effect of increasing the amount of these transfer payments to the government.

   h.   Telecom Australia pays no taxes, however. Nevertheless, in May 1987 the government announced that it had removed the sales tax exemption from certain Commonwealth commercial authorities, and that Commonwealth agencies other than Departments would be required to pay customs duty on their imports from July 1, 1987. The government estimates that revenues from these measures will total at least A$360 million in 1987-8, almost all of which will come from Telecom Australia (and Australia Post). Both instrumentalities have applied to the Prices Surveillance Authority for increases in basic tariffs to cover the level of the imposts.

   i.   The Minister for Communications, together with Telecom Australia and OTC(A), has challenged the premises of the proposed policy guidelines. Greater accountability for the government business enterprises is seen as an effort by the Ministry of Finance to raise more revenues from the statutory authorities, though such accountability ultimately would diminish their economic and managerial flexibility. Requiring Ministry of Finance approval of business plans has also been seen by some as a mechanism for determining where additional funds are located within a government business enterprise.

   3.   At present, and despite its claim that its managerial flexibility is considerably impaired by present constraints, Telecom Australia does have significant policymaking—regulatory—authority over the use of network facilities in Australia. Indeed, its authority extends in part to the activities of both OTC(A) and AUSSAT because their facilities must be interconnected to Telecom Australia's domestic services. In this capacity, Telecom Australia is, therefore, exercising both regulatory and operational responsibilities—for which it has been criticized by users and by some at the political level.

   a.   There is considerable pressure in Australia, therefore, to revisit the question of regulatory oversight. The options being considered are maintaining the *status quo*, setting up a separate regulatory body such as Oftel, or following another course that might separate regulatory authority within, or place it outside, Telecom Australia. In early 1987, there was significant internal activity within Telecom to remove the regulatory function from those parts of the organization associated with commercial activities; now, the Legal and Policy Branch, which manages all regulatory matters, reports separately to the chief executive level.

   b.   Prior to this internal restructuring, in 1985 and 1986, Telecom Australia's policymaking processes had become somewhat more structured than has historically been the case. Its Legal and Policy Branch has released policy statements on common carriage, common interest groups, and authorization of leased lines; on the endorsement and listing conditions for PABX systems; and on the interconnection of private networks with Telecom Australia networks.

c. The formulation process is relatively informal, with Telecom Australia drafting a policy, gathering comments from interested parties, and incorporating those comments into a final policy.

d. The current avenues for redress from Telecom Australia policies are relatively untested or are essentially not available with respect to substantive challenges. Telecom Australia does make information on its policies available to users; in addition, information including material relating to regulatory policies and practices can be obtained from Telecom Australia and under the Freedom of Information Act.

e. The present methods for procedural redress include an appeal to the Administrative Appeals Tribunal, which is a quasi-judicial entity that can, where the Telecommunications (General) by-laws permit, look to specific decisions within a policy, but not to the policy itself. The Tribunal does not take the lead in formulating telecommunications policy, but it does help to ensure impartial review of an individual decision made by Telecom Australia. Implicitly, therefore, the Tribunal might have a role in influencing Telecom Australia to formulate substantive policies where none might otherwise exist.

f. Another possible avenue of redress would be an appeal to the federal courts under the Administrative Decisions (Judicial Review) Act 1977; this has not yet been pursued. It is also possible that there might be some relief available from the Department of Communications or the Minister. Complaints that Telecom Australia is acting illegally, *e.g.*, in violation of the antitrust laws, might be heard in Federal Court; the *Tytel* case, discussed in the following paragraphs, is an example of such litigation.

g. Some business and other users, who find current arrangements constraining, are less satisfied with the dual regulatory and operational nature of Telecom Australia's responsibilities. Telecom's Viatel videotex service, for example, competes with other specialized information services, including those operated by AAP/Reuters, Elders, ICL, and others. These suppliers of value-added services complain that it is difficult to compete with Telecom Australia both because it sets the ground rules for such competition and because they consider that there is significant cross-subsidization of Telecom's "competitive" services. In addition, they have complained historically that Telecom Australia enjoys a tax-free status, though it pays tax where equipment is for sale to consumers. (The Treasurer's recent announcement that Telecom Australia would no longer be eligible for sales tax and custom duty exemptions has, to a certain extent, removed the ground for this complaint.) Provoking especially bitter reaction is the response of Telecom Australia to the marketplace failure of its several-thousand-dollar (Australian) Computerphone in the marketplace; it gave the equipment to its customers, something that the private sector could not afford to do.

h. The terminal equipment market is subject to competition, with thousands of items approved for supply by Telecom Australia, although Telecom Australia also supplies such equipment. Moreover, even though customers can purchase their own PABXs, Telecom Australia insists on maintaining that equipment. Although Telecom Australia is not uncomfortable in performing the roles prescribed by the statutes, some observers within the organization have offered the view that there is some uneasiness in its acting as both supplier and regulator.

i. The *Tytel* case was brought in Federal Court against Telecom Australia under Section 46 of the Trade Practices Act 1974. The allegation is that Telecom is using its monopoly powers to preserve its market position in the marketing of its Versatel premium telephone. In an interlocutory ruling for an interim order (an injunction), handed down in July 1986, the court concluded that Telecom Australia should be treated as a corporation and that the Trade Practices Act is applicable to it. The judge did not issue an interlocutory injunction restraining Telecom from marketing the Versatel; the court concluded, however, that the evidence could be read such that Telecom Australia had used its power to damage its competitors, Tytel and Tycom, or to deter them from competing with Telecom Australia, and that such matters might be better pursued at a full hearing of the claim.

j. *Tytel* raises issues that are at the heart of the controversy over the division of Telecom Australia's commercial and regulatory responsibilities: is Telecom exercising its administrative or its commercial powers in setting the prices, and regulating the competitive conditions, for the marketing of its product? Commentators have used the case to explore this difficult issue; for its part, Telecom Australia concedes that the sale of equipment was a "commercial practice". Some observers have said that the decision, though interlocutory, implicitly rejects the distinction between the exercise of commercial and administrative functions.

4. Telecom Australia is vested with substantial discretion to set tariffs and the charges for interconnection. The Department of Communications, with responsibility for advising the Minister, has no power *per se* to review tariffs. There is some pressure for greater review of, and political accountability for, Telecom Australia tariffs.

a. As noted earlier, however, Section 7 of the Telecommunications Act 1975 does appear to accord the Minister of Communications the power of direction with respect to the performance of Telecom Australia's functions. With respect to rentals or charges for standard telephone services or charges for domestic telephone calls, there is no power of direction, but the approval of the Minister is required and a review procedure is available. Telecommunications Act 1975, Sections 11 and 12. The power of direction has never been exercised with respect to Telecom Australia; in any event, there is legal advice to the effect that the power is limited.

b. Price increases for certain services are, however, subject to review by the Prices Surveillance Authority ("PSA"). These services are basic offerings—for access to telephone service, for voice calls, and for telegraph messages; interconnect and data service charges are not subject to review by the PSA. The PSA looks at both the level and structure of Telecom Australia pricing. It makes recommendations to the Minister and to the Treasurer on the impact of rate increases.

    c. The PSA is, however, viewed as a strong independent agency, with its current membership consisting of a professional economist (and Mayor of Waverley), a union representative, a businessman, and an economist. Its recommendations are given considerable weight in decisions to contain price increases. Rate increases in the domestic telecommunications sector, however, historically have been below increases in the consumer price index. Therefore, the PSA generally has not sought to recommend that Telecom Australia vary its rates from those proposed; however, in 1984, in the first reference to the PSA, the PSA would have sought to recommend a reduction in non-business charges had Telecom Australia not agreed to such a reduction itself.

    5. Relating to the issue of tariff structure and review is the issue of cross-subsidization. Implicit in most of the debate over the structure of the telecommunications sector in Australia is the notion that service should be available to the remote and relatively unpopulated areas of the country and that subsidies for such services should be internal. At the center of the discussions over the privatization of Telecom Australia—or in the introduction of competition in transport services—is the impact of cross-subsidization. In 1985, but not all that frequently before then, the government stated that cross-subsidization was an express policy.

    a. As part of its Inquiry in 1984, the PSA, however, asked Telecom Australia what its policy was on cross-subsidization. To respond to the PSA, Telecom Australia solicited from the Minister of Communications an explanation of the government's position. The fundamental policy of applying uniform standard charges to all customers for the provision and maintenance of service, and the endorsement thereby of cross-subsidization, was explicitly confirmed in a letter to Telecom Australia from the Minister in August 1984. In its commitment to the principle of uniform services at uniform prices, the government acknowledges that some cross-subsidization is necessary and supports Telecom Australia pricing as consistent with both law and public policy goals.

    b. In addition to the Minister's letter, the Minister of Communications had asked Telecom Australia to study the cross-subsidization of telephone services as part of the debate over privatization and deregulation. The study, released in August 1986, examined the cross-subsidization of non-metropolitan subscribers by metropolitan subscribers. It concluded that the cross-subsidization of rural, remote, and other non-metropolitan rentals and local calls in 1984–5 amounted to A$459 million, or an annual average of A$259 for the 1,560,000 services that are currently subsidized. Telecom Australia, *National, State and District Profitability Study 1984/85.*

    c. Beyond the subsidy of country subscribers by metropolitan subscribers, cross-subsidy takes on other forms in Telecom Australia.

These are relatively common forms of cross-subsidization in other industrialized countries. For example, by paying more for the same services, business subscribers subsidize residential subscribers; revenues from major capital city trunk routes subsidize country services; subscribers close to exchanges subsidize subscribers remote from exchanges; the tariff differential in the equivalent bandwidth for telephony and television usage means that telephony subsidizes television services; profitable services subsidize unprofitable services; and present services subsidize future services by funding capital programs.

d. The importance of maintaining the metropolitan-rural cross-subsidy in particular is emerging as a political point of some significance. The present Labor Government has stated that privatization, and concomitant profit orientation, might bring an end to cross-subsidization. The result, according to an October 1986 speech by the Minister for Finance, would be the end of telephone (or mail) service to one-third of the people and 95 per cent of the country. There is some dispute, however, over the impact of liberalization and whether the inevitable result of privatization would be a reduction in service, the magnitude of which is estimated by the opponents of any substantial change in the telecommunications sector.

e. The question of autonomy and accountability for Telecom Australia appears to be another element in the public debate over cross-subsidization. How should Telecom Australia be made more accountable—and to whom? As noted above, one reason for promulgating the proposed guidelines on business enterprises is to develop methods for increasing revenues—dividends to the government or taxes—from enterprises such as Telecom Australia. One reason for the protectiveness of the Minister of Communications, therefore, is that boosting payments to the government would impede the ability of Telecom Australia to finance itself internally and to continue its policy of cross-subsidization. Not surprisingly, the future of cross-subsidization is closely tied to, and is in some sense inconsistent with, a policy of increasing the fiscal accountability of Telecom Australia.

6. To increase efficiency, and maximize business opportunities, Telecom Australia is also looking at structural reorganization. The restructuring is to create a more business-oriented organization that would operate through a series of business divisions and subsidiaries that might be more insulated from the direct control of, and oversight of, the government; ultimate accountability might be ensured through the parent organization.

a. Most Telecom Australia employees are hired at public sector rates. Nevertheless, at present the level of staffing and personnel policies are not subject to direct control by other entities, though they are subject to government policies co-ordinated by the Department of Employment and Industrial Relations. Moreover, Telecom Australia also hires salesmen outside the civil service schedules and has created an incentive structure for some of these employees. Much as the French have done with the subsidiaries of the DGT, Telecom Australia is currently looking at the possibility of creating separate subsidiaries to hire additional employees outside the civil service scales. This restructuring is seen as a significant step to hiring high quality employees and to increasing its efficiency, should a more competitive structure emerge in Australia.

  b. One subsidiary already established by Telecom Australia is Telecom Australia International, Ltd. This company, established as a registered, limited liability company, markets Telecom Australia expertise through consultancy and other services abroad. A change in the law was required to create this subsidiary, but it is viewed as a precedent for other subsidiaries that might offer services on a competitive basis.

  c. Telecom Australia will argue against the application of constraints and controls to its subsidiaries. They will not be government business enterprises created pursuant to statute. Whether Telecom Australia will succeed in protecting such autonomy for its subsidiaries, and in transferring service offerings to them, is a political question of some significance.

  d. Another possible structural reorganization, currently the subject of an internal study, is to break Telecom Australia into three groups—serving big account customers; medium and small-sized businesses; and residential, remote, and rural customers. Each group would have its own needs and services, and its own managing director. One problem with this approach is how cost accounting would divide the costs for overhead functions such as research and engineering. Another problem is whether each of the ninety regions would be broken into three parts. It is not known, moreover, how services that are offered to two or more of the customer groups would be marketed and provided across the three divisions.

 7. One vehicle for introducing some limited competition into the telecommunications sector is AUSSAT. As noted already, the Satellite Communications Act specifies that AUSSAT cannot provide switched services, but does permit some limited competition with Telecom Australia. Telecom Australia views AUSSAT as a competitive source of private network long-distance transmission capacity. Telecom Australia, *Telecom—The Facts* 24 (1986). Several issues arise out of this competitive relationship between AUSSAT and Telecom Australia. Any differences are resolved in the first instance in the marketplace and by the two organizations. If there are disputes about AUSSAT's charter, the government would seek to resolve them. Nevertheless, no regulatory body—other than Telecom Australia—now exists to resolve any disputes.

  a. AUSSAT does not have to rely on Telecom Australia to provide the local loops for its services. It could provide direct point-to-multipoint services, so long as they are "private". The issue, however, is to what extent AUSSAT services can be used flexibly, yet not be considered to violate the statutory proscriptions on resale or the carriage of third-party traffic.

b. AUSSAT may permit a customer, or a set of customers (such as a group of banks), to share a leased circuit because they constitute a "common interest group" that would not be involved in the provision of a public, switched service. The AUSSAT policy on what constitutes a common interest group is not necessarily congruent with that of Telecom Australia, especially if no interconnection with Telecom Australia is required.

c. With respect to the interconnection of AUSSAT satellite networks with terrestrial facilities, however, Telecom Australia adopts a fairly strict construction of AUSSAT's organic Act. Telecom Australia might not permit an AUSSAT common interest group to interconnect with terrestrial facilities on the grounds that the AUSSAT customer is not a *bona fide* group or association formed for purposes other than sharing telecommunications facilities. There is an intention to resolve these differences in interpretation of common interest groups. Thus, by virtue of its control over interconnection arrangements (and with two Telecom directors on the AUSSAT board), Telecom Australia does have some power to influence AUSSAT's market position.

8. The development of AUSSAT has, in fact, made possible the creation of a private network operated by the State of Queensland. The emergence of Q-Net has raised a series of questions about the use and economics of private networks, the comparative advantages of satellite-based communications, and the overall impact of AUSSAT as a new common carrier in Australia.

a. As background, the Australian Constitution of 1901 vests the responsibilities for postal, telegraphic, and telephonic services with the Commonwealth. Constitution of the Commonwealth Act, Section 51, para. (V). This power is not exclusive, however, and the states may continue to exercise certain powers governed by Section 109, and court tests thereunder. Section 94 of the Telecommunications Act reflects an agreement reached at the Constitutional Conventions regarding telegraph and other signalling/communications systems of colonial railways and other transport facilities. The states now have significant telecommunications networks to carry out various functions within their province (including health, education, police, and power); these networks are largely based on lines leased from Telecom Australia and supplemented in some cases with the states' own facilities.

b. In 1985, the State of Queensland decided that it would develop the Q-Net pilot program and began formulating a ten-year telecommunications strategy plan for the state. Although Q-Net does use terrestrial lines leased from Telecom Australia, it is based on the principle that a satellite-based network, using AUSSAT facilities, could serve all government departments; there would be no need for each government department to have its own leased lines. The Queensland Government is supplementing the AUSSAT circuits with microwave facilities to complete the local end of the network. The first phase of Q-Net construction began in 1985, with the first communications on the network taking place in

December of that year. The Queensland Government has believed that its network is both cheaper and more efficient than Telecom Australia. However, in April 1987, it decided to sell off Q-Net and to call publicly for expressions of interest.

  c. Q-Net Services currently include the School of the Air trial, a family medicine program and an early literacy education program, as well as telecommunications services to remote areas. A second phase of the project, for 1986–7, was to extend voice capacity to ten locations. Among the planned uses of Q-Net are a state emergency service, services to Queensland Railways, transmission of drug information, and various health programs. In addition, Q-Net is planning, and has placed orders for earth stations for, a low-cost data network to serve the needs of government departments at various locations throughout the state.

  d. Both Western Australia and the State of Victoria have had an interest in Q-Net developments; Victoria is working with Telecom on a major terrestrial private network; committees to consider the establishment of state government-owned and operated private networks have been established in the other states. Such networks could serve areas at present under-served in Western Australia, for example, as well as the government's intrastate communications. It is reported that the government of the State of New South Wales investigated the establishment of a network such as Q-Net; various recommendations were made and a cost saving of approximately 20 per cent was forecast.

  e. Q-Net (and the other potential state networks) have an interest in connecting their networks with the Telecom Australia network in major towns and cities. They would be permitted to do so under the Telecom Australia interconnect policy of September 1, 1985. To preserve its role as the national carrier and in carrying out the policy on sharing of private networks, Telecom Australia, however, has taken the position that state businesses and commercial undertakings with separate legal identities do not have a single interest in common with the administrative organs of the state governments; they are not, in short, a single common interest group. The State of Queensland had contended that it was a common user group; it has now, however, reluctantly accepted the Telecom Australia position and formed some common interest groups within the state.

  f. Q-Net would like to provide telephone access from remote communities to the Telecom Australia network via a switch located in Brisbane. Telecom Australia argues vigorously, however, that only information relating to state government functions can be transmitted over Q-Net and that the transmission of non-government traffic is prohibited.

  g. In late 1986, for example, Q-Net and Telecom Australia came into conflict over service to the remote area of Mornington Island, which has a population of 1,100, most of whom are aborigines. The island is currently served by one public booth. Although a low-cost Q-Net earth station had been installed on the island, Telecom Australia regulations, which now prohibit the provision of "public services" over private facilities, prevented either individuals or the local government from using the service; Telecom Australia, in fact, installed its own earth station as part of its Iterra system, which is also not available for use by individuals. The debate, according to Telecom Australia, is not just whether Q-Net service to a particular area is more efficient or low-cost, but how Telecom can fulfill its responsibilities under the Rural and Remote Program to provide service to all Australians.

9. Beyond AUSSAT-based services, the monopoly posture of Telecom Australia has made it the target of businesses contemplating the launch of a facilities-based competitor to serve large users. In 1981, a consortium of large business interests, including IBM, banks, and Kerry Packer's group, set up Business Telecommunications Services to look at the question of providing low-cost facilities for companies of their size. Although this enterprise might have been viable in the business environment of a Liberal Government, the venture essentially collapsed when the Labor Party came to power.

10. The global trend toward easing restrictions on the use of network facilities is making its mark on Australian telecommunications. Telecom Australia policies on the provision of value-added services over leased lines are gradually becoming articulated, though there is some substantial aversion to enunciating a definitional distinction between basic and value-added service; indeed, a draft Value-Added Services Regulatory Policy was circulated by Telecom Australia on April 28, 1987 for public comment. In the past, the line of demarcation that has been preferred had been described as "rough and ready" and as pragmatic, as practical in both theory and application.

a. Telecom Australia's stance, in short, is to divide the world into three sectors: some services would be "open", others would be "common carriage", and the hard, in-between, services would be decided on a case-by-case basis. At one end of the spectrum, Telecom Australia is clear that it would permit leased line access to a value-added service on a point-to-point basis. At the other, there is a disinclination to permit a group of unaffiliated entities to create a "common interest group", the primary "common" interest of which is the sharing of carrier facilities. For the in-between cases, Telecom Australia will make leased lines available to *bona fide* common interest groups, either on an "in house" basis or leased to the groups themselves. Telecom itself is keenly interested in providing both common carrier services and services directly competitive with the private sector.

b. Business organizations, would-be suppliers of value-added services, and other users have called for a more precise delineation of the distinction between common carriage and enhanced or value-added services. The imprecision, they claim, works to their disadvantage and permits Telecom Australia to stifle the introduction of legitimate, and arguably competitive, services. Henry Ergas, in his influential study of the Australian telecommunications sector, points out that private sector involvement in the development of value-added networks should be promoted by developing a specific policy for VANs and that that policy should, among other things, clarify the distinction between enhanced and basic services. H. Ergas, *Telecommunications and the Australian Economy* 83 (1986).

11. Despite these calls for more precision in regulatory policy toward value-added networks, Telecom Australia has maintained that liberalization can be achieved—consistent with maintaining the viability of its network—through an approach that has been, until the release of the April 1987 policy, somewhat more *ad hoc*.

a. At present, there are very significant local calling areas (for example, in a thirty-mile radius around Melbourne) that are tariffed at a flat rate per call. These can create substantial incentives for local resale by affording users the capability of creating a leased line for what is effectively the price of a local call. Although it would not necessarily have been engaged in resale, one bank, for example, had developed plans for development of an electronic funds transfer network that were based on a single price for a local telephone call.

b. Within Telecom Australia there is some thought that if volume-sensitive pricing were adopted at the local level, greater user control over the local network would be encouraged, while, at the same time, its own resources would be allocated more efficiently. Telecom Australia is, therefore, contemplating the options for introducing local measured service. The risk in so doing, however, is that time-sensitive pricing can increase user incentives to bypass the local network. In addition, the introduction of local measured service could become a political issue that might increase pressures on Telecom Australia, or might force a broader review of its tariff structures.

12. Relations between Telecom Australia and OTC(A) improved significantly in 1985 and 1986. In the past, however, there have been some differences over the provision of overlapping services, and it is likely that those differences will be exacerbated as the boundary between international and domestic offerings erodes.

a. For some time, there had been some jurisdictional disagreement between Telecom Australia and OTC(A) over the provision of an electronic mail service. OTC(A) wanted its service, Minerva, to be available on a domestic basis. Telecom Australia already had such a service, Telememo. There is now a memorandum of agreement between the two organizations to provide the services jointly, and the two offerings have been merged.

b. Recognizing the primacy of OTC(A)'s role as the international carrier, Telecom Australia would be interested in expanding its interests internationally by entering into additional joint ventures with OTC(A). Telecom Australia is keenly aware of the need to ensure that both entities keep within their respective statutory spheres for carrier services. It is likely to resist what it sees as OTC(A)'s domestic incursions behind the international gateway. Tension is inherent in a regime that divides the provision of domestic and international services. Both Telecom Australia and OTC(A) see themselves as providing end-to-end service. OTC(A) is uncomfortable acting as a carrier's carrier, akin to the role historically played by Teleglobe Canada. In short, OTC(A) and Telecom Australia are already competing, to the extent that OTC(A) rejects the role that Telecom Australia might like to forge for itself—of offering services, setting up customers, and then arranging interconnection with OTC(A).

c. The early stages of this competitive struggle are being played out in the development of the SatNet services that OTC(A) is marketing to its Australian customers. Currently, Telecom Australia is not altogether bypassed in these offerings. The SatNet 1 major city services require a domestic, terrestrial link to the C-band dish. (Although AUSSAT could conceivably provide the link between the international earth station and the customer premises, the IBS service would then be provided in a less favorable, double-hop configuration.) More troubling for Telecom Australia, however, are the small station SatNet 3 services that could link the financial community with the Pacific Islands, rural areas, or the rest of the world—and for which no co-ordination with Telecom would be required.

d. Telecom Australia and OTC(A), recognizing the existence of these tensions, have taken steps to provide for the resolution of policy conflicts and the co-ordinated development of policy. With such co-ordination, questions about differences between Telecom Australia and OTC(A) over the definition of value-added services, and how they are to be provided, are being resolved in a more open approach than had historically been the case. The memorandum of agreement encourages the establishment of a joint offering to meet customer needs when the services involve both domestic and international users. OTC(A) may review some ideas about offering a new service and then explore with Telecom Australia whether an agreement can be reached on the provision of that service. Telecom Australia, for its part, is not concerned about an international VAN offering "competing" with OTC(A), so long as the authority of Telecom Australia to provide the domestic links and access to the international network remains inviolate.

e. Increasingly, OTC(A) is also co-ordinating with the Legal and Policy Branch of Telecom Australia on the use of private leased circuits. For international value-added services, it makes commercial sense for the two entities to adopt a joint, or co-ordinated, approach. In practice, however, because Telecom Australia provides the domestic access to international services, OTC(A) does not have much negotiating clout. OTC(A) is sensitive to the fact that an international user might need to deal with four separate organizations (domestic and international at each end of the circuit); thus, it attempts to co-ordinate with Telecom Australia to the greatest extent possible to minimize inconvenience to the customer.

13. In the international sector itself, OTC(A) is both very entrepreneurial and highly attentive to user needs and requirements. Its

principal objective is to have Australia become a hub for the Pacific Basin. Although Australia is at somewhat of a geographic disadvantage in this, OTC(A) makes much of the low cost of doing business and the English-speaking, stable, and free market nature of the Australian business environment.

    a. In terms of marketing, OTC(A) is quite attentive to the pricing of its services in relationship to other administrations in the region. For example, OTC(A)'s rate for telephone services to Japan is one-third of the KDD telephone rate to the United States. These pricing differentials can make the hubbing concept quite attractive to multinationals needing transpacific circuits. Indeed, OTC(A) has had considerable success in persuading many large U.S. and Japanese users to route their Pacific Basin communications through Australia; smaller circuits are then run from Australia to Japan, Southeast Asia and elsewhere.

    b. To foster development of its hubbing concept, OTC(A) is engaged in an active facilities planning and construction program. In August 1986, the Australia-Indonesia-Singapore cable first became operational. OTC(A) is participating in the planning of the world's largest fiber optic network, reaching from Australia up to Japan and across the Tasman Sea to New Zealand, Hawaii, and North America, with service to begin in 1993.

    c. OTC(A) is also paying close attention to the possible liberalization of the international telecommunications sector in Japan and to the market sector opportunities that may develop with the emergence of competition for KDD.

    d. OTC(A) is also attentive to the still amorphous plans being developed by the New Zealand administration to serve as a new Pacific hub. Australia, however, with its larger industrial base, already significant investment in international facilities, and a location closer to Southeast Asia, would seem well positioned to compete with New Zealand as the principal telecommunications hub of the Southwest Pacific region.

    e. OTC(A) has decided to interconnect with the new U.S.-based international carriers, but has approached the issue from a business-oriented perspective. It will not interconnect with all carriers: given some diseconomies in splitting a traffic stream, its principal criterion for determining whether to interconnect is dependent on the ability of the carrier seeking interconnection to establish a "reasonable market share" of traffic to Australia.

    14. OTC(A) operates as a commercial organization; thus, it maintains that it has positioned itself to adapt to whatever market and other changes, such as privatization, take place. Of considerable concern, however, are the current policy debates over the introduction and form of any competition in international services.

    a. OTC(A)'s present position is that its monopoly of facilities and basic services should be maintained, but that financial or other value-added international services should be opened to competition. Beyond that posture, however, it is not clear that OTC(A) has a well-articulated policy on what kinds of value-added services might be permitted. It has, however, extensively reviewed other countries' policies on value-added services and has formulated its policies in discussions with Telecom Australia and with its own customers.

      b. Some of OTC(A)'s biggest customers—banks, computer bureaus, and the travel industry—could become significant services competitors of OTC(A) if a liberalized policy toward the introduction of value-added services is adopted. Once a large network is in place, and given that international communications is an essential component of any Australian business network, there would be substantial, and attractive, incentives to message switch, *e.g.*, between large banking customers.

      c. A cornerstone of OTC(A) policy, therefore, is to concentrate its energies on satisfying customer applications; for this, it has employed a large sales force, is actively engaged in market research, and has actively supported user interests. These efforts have helped to generate excellent relationships between OTC(A) and the user community. The wisdom of this approach is that the customer is relieved of the need to become a "carrier" and, consequently, the political pressure for liberalization, competition, or privatization is alleviated.

      d. One option identified by OTC(A) is movement toward a volume-sensitive pricing approach as a means of liberalizing circuit usage. Some of OTC(A)'s exploratory thoughts along this line have been discussed with a couple of its customers. However, Telecom Australia's approach is not usage-sensitive; thus, OTC(A) would need to resolve possible differences in pricing structures before moving from flat-rate charging principles for any of its private lines that are interconnected to domestic networks.

      e. Beyond the possible introduction of usage-sensitive pricing for private line services, OTC(A) points to significant economic problems in maintaining time-based tariffs for a range of services. If the volume of telex traffic increases, for example, but users shift to higher capacity circuits as they are installed, or to services such as international facsimile, OTC(A)'s net revenues would decline.

C. Prospects

      1. It appears that current discussions in Australia are addressing the important issue of the appropriate locus of the telecommunications regulatory and policymaking apparatus. The present situation, according to the criticisms of users and other observers, has Telecom Australia effectively setting policy, and establishing the terms of interconnection of OTC(A) and AUSSAT facilities. This criticism is exacerbated by Telecom's dual commercial and regulatory roles. As noted above, however, Telecom Australia has taken certain steps toward internal restructuring to bifurcate its regulatory and operational roles.

      a. The *Tytel* case is only one, relatively early manifestation of this criticism. In the absence of a more formal separation of its roles, Telecom Australia may face increasingly vigorous litigants, with the risk that such litigation may force structural change.

   b. Telecom Australia may well take advantage of its planned corporate reorganization to effect further structural changes that might alleviate such risks and mitigate political and user pressures. If it were so inclined, it could view the restructuring as an opportunity to separate the provision of its basic transmission services from its competitive—value-added services and terminal equipment—offerings. It is at present upgrading its cost accounting system; this may be a predicate for separating costs on a service-by-service basis.

2. For those who have focused on the issue, it appears that there is still considerable uncertainty about whether regulatory activities should be relocated outside Telecom Australia—and, if so, how and where else. Any new center of policymaking or regulation should be separate and unbiased: it is difficult for one entity to be both umpire and player. Indeed, some users critical of Telecom Australia view such procedural and institutional changes as more important than specific shifts in substantive policies. In part, of course, they believe that an independent regulatory body would be more likely to generate policy outcomes that are more responsive to their perceived priorities.

   a. Some observers believe that one obvious candidate for the role of regulator is the Department of Communications. There is, however, some considerable reticence about the Department taking on the regulatory role; in any event, legislation would be required to give it the requisite competency to do so. Although there is agreement that the Department has an excellent, though small, staff, users and other observers question whether it could readily acquire the expertise needed to deal with the complex regulatory issues it would face. The Department is moving rapidly to reinvigorate its policy activities. Nevertheless, any shift of responsibilities for policymaking from Telecom Australia would require a simultaneous shift of expertise and institutional experience.

   b. Telecom Australia itself would, no doubt, be wary of turning over to the Department, or any other new entity for that matter, those individuals who have the greatest knowledge of its potential regulatory vulnerabilities. From the users' perspective, moreover, there would be a strong preference for a new, independent regulatory perspective rather than one that had descended from Telecom Australia.

   c. Another reason why there is some question about whether the Department is the appropriate entity to regulate the telecommunications sector is its political character. The Department does serve the Minister; thus, its political and policy responsibilities are, to a certain extent, intermingled at present. The concern is that the Department might be beholden to the political interests and perspectives of the Minister, and thus be less able to act with detachment or to develop long-range policies.

3. Although the statute vests regulatory authority in the Board of Commissioners of Telecom Australia, the Board, as distinct from a branch within Telecom Australia, could take the lead in initiating and formulating policy, and in gathering public comment. It might be well suited to do so, given that its membership comprises outside experts and union and management representatives. One threshold issue would be whether the representatives of Telecom management would have to be rescued from addressing policies that might affect Telecom Australia. Another question is the multiple membership of individuals on the Telecom Australia, OTC(A), and AUSSAT boards. Vesting the principal regulatory power in the Telecom Australia Board might create similar pressures for recusal—given the direct impact of several Telecom policies on the other bodies. A more pragmatic solution might be to separate the commissions from the authorities themselves, creating new entities that would be similar to the boards that oversee other sectors in Australia.

4. The fair and unbiased nature of the Australian Broadcasting Tribunal and the Trade Practices Commission may make them useful models for the creation of a new, independent organization to regulate the telecommunications sector. Ultimately, Australian policymakers may well conclude that an entity similar to Oftel, but with a more collegial structure and less legal autonomy, would be a suitable institution in a transitional period.

5. As Telecom Australia moves to liberalize use of its network facilities, its approach of dividing all services into three—"open", "closed", and "gray"—will leave many users of leased lines in some doubt. OTC(A)'s examination of volume-sensitive pricing as a complement to network liberalization parallels the adoption by the Deutsche Bundespost of such a scheme. Although users may not prefer that option either domestically or internationally, it is one way in which Telecom Australia could develop a more transparent policy with respect to value-added services.

6. Volume-sensitive pricing is seen by some (though not necessarily by OTC(A)) as an enlightened effort to permit OTC(A) to participate in the revenues from developing value-added and other leased-line dependent services. Government officials stress, however, that such participation is unprecedented for other providers of essential infrastructure services. Moreover, officials from other Cabinet offices express skepticism that OTC(A) profit participation in new ventures is a legitimate response to pressures to liberalize. They note that other infrastructure authorities do not exact any premiums for offering services.

7. Ongoing OTC(A) review of rate structures is critical not only to the provision of new services, but also to achieving its goal of having Australia serve as a hub in the Pacific. This attentiveness to Australia's geographic position and its regional role may ensure that OTC(A)'s practices with respect to the use of leased lines are competitive internationally. In other words, there may be disincentives for OTC(A) to move to a

volume-based structure if flat-rate tariffs prevail elsewhere—in Singapore, Tokyo, or Hong Kong.

a. Despite difficulties in competing with these other Western Pacific administrations, there are several factors that may favor OTC(A)'s initiatives. First, the economics of the high-capacity fiber links that are being planned to North America mean that enormous capacity will become available at very low incremental costs.

b. Second, the long routes in the Northern Pacific, and from Australia to Southeast Asia and Japan, are not necessarily fatal to OTC(A)'s plans. The cable links being used, or that will be used in the future, are relatively distance-insensitive and the facilities are both fast and efficient. In addition, Australia has the natural comparative advantages of a common culture and language with North America.

c. Finally, the liberalization of the Australian financial market has had an extraordinary impact on the international telecommunications sector. U.S., British, and Japanese banking entities are locating in Australia. At least one Australian bank, Westpac, is located in New York. These multinational banking entities want their branches to be connected, and are forcing up the demand for Australia-based international facilities. Incentives for increased efficiency by OTC(A), which is in competition with other regional administrations, will inevitably result from the greater demand for leased circuits by financial institutions.

8. Further pressure for liberalization of international services is also coming from New Zealand, where there have been some significant steps to liberalize the provision of services. Some compare the impact of the New Zealanders on Australian telecommunications policy with the impact of Ireland on the United Kingdom.

9. Although the domestic and international telecommunications sectors in Australia are served by different entities—as is the case in Japan and Canada—the line between the two is gradually blurring. One likely development is that Telecom Australia's regulatory and policymaking influence will change, in significant part as a function of international pressures on the Australian market.

a. Many officials, policymakers, users, and providers believe that telecommunications has historically not had a high profile in the government portfolio. Thus, to a certain extent, Telecom Australia has stepped into the regulatory vacuum. Australian policymakers, already highly sensitive to the exigencies of, and competition in, international trade, are becoming more so. Advisory groups and intragovernmental task forces are addressing trade-related and information-industry issues. These governmental activities are partly a result of the realization that the telecommunications sector is critical to trade, especially in light of Australia's highly export- and service-oriented economy. Thus, it is increasingly apparent that telecommunications policy should be given an ascendant place in the government's priorities.

b. Some observers believe, however, that Australia—like

most countries—is rather inward-looking and not particularly attentive to international pressures. These individuals have speculated that Australians do not think specifically in international terms. Nevertheless, the revolutionary changes and growth in the Australian banking sector are predicated on Australia's positioning itself in the international marketplace.

   c. Given, then, the importance of large Australian and foreign-based multinational users to the Australian economy, OTC(A) itself may become a vehicle for exerting pressure for change. In addition, various government departments, with portfolios in the trade area, may become more influential in the policymaking process.

  10. OTC(A)'s implementation of the various SatNet services will further erode the boundary between domestic and international services. SatNet 1 and SatNet 2 were inaugurated in 1986; with SatNet 3, small earth stations will be located on user premises.

   a. These dishes will be used for transmitting and receiving. Theoretically, at least, the same facilities—earth stations and international transponders—could be used for both regional and national services.

   b. Telecom Australia has interposed significant obstacles to OTC(A)'s integrating backwards to serve large customers with direct links from international earth stations. Pressures from users for such direct coaxial, fiber optic, or microwave links will, however, be hard to resist, especially in Sydney and Melbourne.

  11. Conversely, Telecom Australia may apply pressure to enter the international market, although perhaps not in full-fledged, facilities-based competition with OTC(A). The entrance of a competitor to OTC(A) does appear legally possible because OTC(A) has a *de facto* rather than a statutory monopoly. *See* Section XII.A.6. above. Nevertheless, the uncertainty of the monopoly power, since it has never been tested, might tend to inhibit the emergence of competition. If competition were to develop, however, it would be more likely to do so in services rather than facilities.

   a. In competing with another entity for international services, OTC(A) has the advantage of historic interconnection arrangements overseas and is, as noted, a heavy investor in international facilities. It would be quite difficult for a new entrant to replicate these arrangements.

   b. If Telecom Australia were to offer international (value-added, though perhaps not carrier) services, it, or another internationally-oriented entity collaborating with it, would have an advantage, of course, in controlling originating international traffic. Thus, it would be impossible to permit competition in the international sector unless there were a complex set of interconnection arrangements that guaranteed OTC(A) access to domestic traffic and a fair opportunity to compete with Telecom Australia.

   c. Another advantage accruing to Telecom Australia, if it were to seek to enter the international market in some way, would be its ability to offer nationwide access for international services. OTC(A) is only able to provide services from the gateway and would not be able to compete on an equivalent basis unless it were able to construct its own domestic facilities, use other carriers (such as AUSSAT), or obtain Telecom Australia services on a resale basis. The first option—constructing a network of domestic facilities—is not feasible or economic. The second option, use of AUSSAT facilities, would be problematic in light of the double hop that would be involved. The viability of the third option, resale of Telecom Australia facilities, is dependent on the terms and conditions of availability.

12. AUSSAT may well prove to be a significant lever in opening up the domestic market in Australia. It has already made its mark by becoming the dominant carrier in the market for television distribution services. AUSSAT is delivering regional and remote-area television services, as well as video entertainment services to hotels and clubs. Now, however, it is orienting itself to the supply of innovative business services.

    a. AUSSAT's entrepreneurial executives see business opportunities in some of the discontent with Telecom Australia. A considerable number of private business networks will be developed, particularly in a country the size of Australia, where satellite communications makes some sense. The point-to-multipoint capability of AUSSAT is attractive for banks and other large companies that may have branches or offices scattered across Australia.

    b. For most businesses, the initial interest has been in voice services. Businesses, however, are beginning to demand satellite networks that can carry data, including electronic mail. Although AUSSAT cannot provide public switched services, it can offer businesses private networks and obviate the need to deal with Telecom Australia.

    c. AUSSAT offers service to large users, who may have their own network of earth stations and transponders, and to others who might use the proposed capital city network, which relies on terrestrial links to customer premises. STARNET is an AUSSAT business communications service that operates on a star system basis, with a small, branch-based network of earth stations around the hub of a major city dish. This network would be directly connected to user terminals. Alternatively, the network might rely on communications directly between branches and a head office, and between branches. The present AUSSAT satellite is configured for data entry and interactive services directly on customer premises.

    d. The ultimate success of these new services depends on the ability of AUSSAT to aggregate usage, on the ability to share capacity and ground facilities. AUSSAT is confident that the services will be developed in this way, and use of Telecom Australia facilities will not be required in many instances. Beyond having to cope with the interconnection policies of Telecom Australia in those situations where Telecom facilities are required, the viability of AUSSAT services will depend on Telecom pricing policy, its approaches to rate of return, and the form and extent of cross-subsidies between services. For these last factors, AUSSAT's success may ultimately depend on independent regulation.

13. The development of Q-Net and other satellite-based

government (or private) networks will place considerable pressure on Telecom Australia to make its offerings available on a more flexible and cost-effective basis. As noted above, Telecom Australia's pricing flexibility in response to the development of a Q-Net-like system has already manifested itself.

    a. Policymakers in Australia will have to come to grips with the very significant competitive alternative afforded by AUSSAT. Q-Net and systems like it will continue to push and prod the regulatory boundaries on AUSSAT offerings. Ultimately, it is difficult to maintain and monitor prohibitions on interconnection of facilities to provide switched service.

    b. AUSSAT, however, enjoys a certain amount of political insulation in acting as a competitor, largely because of the important services that it provides. It offers connections for remote transmitters for telephony services, for example. Moreover, state government officials, notably including Queensland's former Minister for Industry, Small Business, and Technology, are protective of the AUSSAT services that could be supplied to develop alternative networks, whether owned by the government or by non-governmental entities providing services to the state governments.

14. The most important issues in Australian telecommunications policy do not appear to be structural, but concentrate on the locus of regulatory authority and invigorating service-based competition. Nevertheless, in terms of the structure of the telecommunications sector, several models for change are under discussion.

    a. One option would be to introduce competition in domestic services. This model principally focuses on the future role of AUSSAT. Some observers have floated the idea, however, that competition might include permitting OTC(A) to integrate backwards or permitting a new carrier to enter the market. Although not a likely step in the near future, privitization of Telecom Australia could be a complementary step to this action. The chief difficulty with competition and privatization, of course, would be the future of the policy of cross-subsidization (and of Telecom Australia's debt repayments to the government).

    b. Some attention, however, has been given to the possible privatization of Telecom Australia, AUSSAT and OTC(A). A report on Efficiency in Public Trading Enterprises prepared by the Economic Planning and Advisory Council recommends increasing competition, which it views as an option distinct from privatization. A further recommendation is the use of direct budget subsidies and levies on profitable areas as an alternative to cross-subsidy. This model is potentially workable, of course, particularly if any such facilities-based competition is introduced gradually and in a limited way. The British model is a useful illustration of how the Australians might maintain certain universal service requirements by imposing conditions on Telecom Australia.

    c. Any steps toward privatization of Telecom Australia are likely to be met with strong opposition by Telecom and its unions. Privatization is seen by the unions as weakening Telecom Australia's strength, with jobs flowing to the private, less-unionized, private sector.

d. If the Liberal/National Party alliance should win the next election, there will be serious thought given to the privatization of Telecom Australia. The former shadow Communications Minister, Ian Macphee, is on record as allowing the private sector to play a much larger role in the field of telecommunications.

15. A second option might be to introduce competition in international services. It would not seem that there is a great need for facilities-based competition to OTC(A). Rather, the critical issue would seem to be whether and how to open up the market for international services. If a duopoly were viewed as necessary in the context of Australian services, one possible approach might be to permit Telecom Australia to offer international services. As noted above, unless OTC(A) were afforded access to domestic services, and a rational system of allocating traffic from Telecom Australia to OTC(A) were developed, this model would forestall any emergence of effective competition in the international sector.

16. A third possible option would move toward consolidation rather than competition: the plan would be to merge Telecom Australia and OTC(A). There are several possible issues that would have to be addressed if this course were followed.

a. First, the Minister of Communications is on record as being satisfied with the independence of OTC(A) and maintaining two separate organizations for domestic and international services. By itself, of course, consolidation is not necessarily bad; many nations do not divide the domestic and international services.

b. Advocates of this view point out that such consolidation recognizes the difficulties in maintaining the line between the two sectors and, in a country such as Australia, the importance of integrated domestic/international offerings. In addition, they argue, a merger might result in strengthened resources for the international carrier, which could be of critical importance in competing with foreign administrations.

c. Nevertheless, by all accounts OTC(A) has done an excellent job in providing international services and representing Australian telecommunications internationally. It has good relations with its users. Given the high degree of satisfaction with OTC(A), there may not be many compelling reasons to link it to Telecom Australia at this time. More importantly, users want more choice in structuring services, not less, and this option, unless coupled with the introduction of a new carrier, could significantly curtail liberalizing initiatives.

17. A fourth option that has also been the subject of some discussion might be a co-operative effort between—or merger of—AUSSAT and OTC(A) to provide satellite-based domestic services that could be integrated with international offerings.

a. For international services, however, the double-hop problem for the domestic tail to large users with their own earth stations would be significant, unless interconnection with Telecom Australia is available.

b. Furthermore, the merger would require the institution of some regulatory arrangement for interconnecting the AUSSAT/OTC(A) services with Telecom Australia for the local loop. If the services were to be only private line, it is not clear what advantages would be achieved; thus, this option would necessitate the lifting of the prohibition on AUSSAT's providing public switched services. This step would permit the combined AUSSAT/OTC(A) to provide domestic services in competition with Telecom Australia, raising some of the issues of the first option. At the same time, Telecom Australia could argue that it should be permitted to integrate internationally, lest it lose all access to inward- and outward-bound international traffic.

18. A final, less satisfactory, option has also been floated as a possible alternative. This option would seek to realign international and domestic services on modal lines. AUSSAT might act as Intelsat correspondent and OTC(A), with its significant cable interests, could act in concert (or be merged) with Telecom Australia. This option would raise several issues for discussion.

a. First, this option would require a decisionmaker to work out the interconnection arrangements between the satellite carrier and the terrestrial network, which would in most cases be necessary to complete the local loop.

b. Moreover, cable and satellite arrangements are often complementary and not competitive. There are reasons why an international carrier might want to shift traffic among the modes.

c. From a domestic perspective, such an alignment also carries with it many of the problems raised by the first model—how to resolve universal service and cross-subsidization concerns. Internationally, it would seem to leave an entity that would be weaker, not stronger, in competing with other administrations.

19. Despite the options for structural modifications in Australia, the issues of the near term may not require such significant action. In the future, the changes in telecommunications policy that will be discussed and will be the subject of political and regulatory activity do not constitute major surgery.

a. Rather, the focus will be on where regulatory authority should be located, and what should be the relationship among the regulated and regulatory bodies. Another area for exploration is how to draw the boundary line between value-added and other information-based services, and how to facilitate and encourage their introduction.

b. Structurally, the focal point of attention will be in the domestic, rather than the international, arena. The principal issue is how far AUSSAT will go—should be permitted to go—as a competitor to Telecom Australia. The desirability and viability of the restrictions on the range of services AUSSAT can offer will remain under examination.

c. Internationally, although there is speculation about the role of OTC(A), the most significant questions for the future are of a more peripheral nature. There are, for example, still some questions to be worked out regarding the relationship between Telecom Australia and OTC(A) in the introduction of new international services. The two bodies will continue to work on harmonizing their approaches to value-added services. Similarly, as the relationship between OTC(A) and AUSSAT is, of course, of more recent vintage, it, too, will be worked out in the coming years.

d. The Australian telecommunications organizations deliver excellent service in a physical and economic context that is enormously challenging. Fine tuning and some structural adjustments in telecommunications policy, and not a radical restructuring of the sector, may well be an entirely appropriate course for the next few years.

XIII. THE CONVERGENCE OF NATIONAL APPROACHES

A. Facing Common Economic Pressures

1. In reviewing the preceding descriptions of the telecommunications sectors in some of the leading countries of the industrialized world, it is obvious that there are significant differences in regulatory approaches to the provision of services. Forces that are now seen as almost irrepressible are causing worldwide review and, in many countries, significant shifts in policy. These pressures were one of the principal topics discussed in Phase I of the Study of Telecommunications Structures. In short, movement from a regime where a single, monopolistic entity supplies telecommunications service is rampant.

a. One important consequence of this development is that nations are being confronted with difficult decisions about "who" can do "what". Liberalization in telecommunications terms does not mean that all new players are equal to the traditional supplier. Conversely, there may be limitations on the ability of the erstwhile monopolist to compete with new, private sector entities. The question at the heart of this paper is how to demarcate industry sectors—whether on technical, economic, or market-based criteria—and what sort of regulatory parameters should be formulated. To the extent that there is some convergence of approaches in this area, such confluence is discussed below in Section XIII.B.

b. National policymakers and administrations are also facing a mix of economic pressures on existing institutions and on long-standing policies of political and social origin. These economic pressures do not exist in isolation from national or foreign shifts in telecommunications policy. They are, rather, themselves both reactions to such changes and factors in compelling (or resisting) further changes.

2. In virtually every country in the industrialized world, one major source of economic pressure is network upgrade and installation. The emergence of new technologies—cable, broad band fiber optic, and satellites, among others—are straining the resources of governments, administrations, and the private sector.

a. In many countries, the costs of network improvements have been a fundamental component of infrastructure development. The massive expenditures to install a digital network in France, to extend and improve the network in Italy, and to fund satellite projects in several countries are all motivated, in part, by the view that the best service possible must be delivered to the greatest number. Geography or a dispersed population, as well as the universal service imperative, all drive infrastructure expenditures upward. As a result, of course, countries as different as Australia, France, Finland, and the U.S. have among the best telecommunications infrastructures in the world.

b. Other reasons for expending substantial resources on the network are political, ideological, or a product of industrial policies. The wiring with coaxial cable of the Federal Republic of Germany is often thought to be the result of a political decision—not necessarily driven by public demand or a national consensus. Similarly, the plans of the Commission of the European Communities for an overlay broad band network in Europe are motivated as much by a political reaction to trade-related issues—the need to keep up with developments in the U.S. and Japan—as they are by forecast demand.

c. The European development illustrates, however, what is perhaps the most compelling factor leading to investments in infrastructure: the role of competition. In the U.S., MCI and US Sprint are racing to complete transcontinental fiber optic networks; they are doing so not only because customers are demanding those facilities, but also because they believe that significant advantages in market position will accrue to the "winner". In the U.K., British Telecom is facing competition from the technologically advanced, though less universal, fiber optic network that Mercury has constructed. The structure of competition in Japan will not be predicated on price; rather, the new Type I carriers are forging competitive strategies on the basis of the new technologies in which they have invested—fiber optic links for the Tokyo-Osaka corridor and satellite-delivered business services to all of Japan.

d. As much as private sector competitors are investing in infrastructure to compete domestically, national administrations in Europe and around the world are attempting to position themselves competitively. As an economic matter, there are two inter-related ways of doing so: competitive pricing and advanced and available infrastructures.

e. Infrastructure investment by administrations can, therefore, be motivated by a commercial desire to be the first in a region. The French decision to launch Télécom-1 is a case in point. In Australia, the incentives for the significant investments made in domestic and international facilities are partly a product of regional competitiveness. Australians want to maintain their competitiveness in service-sector industries and they want to become a regional center for industry and finance in the Pacific Basin. To do so, they are installing terrestrial and satellite networks domestically, and are investing in submarine fiber optic cables to become a telecommunications—and, they hope, a business—hub for the Pacific.

3. To help recover the costs of these investments and to reduce costs elsewhere, administrations are adopting various strategies. One of the most common strategies is to increase network utilization to supplement revenues.

a. Some nations are attempting to increase usage by straightforward means; advertising, particularly of long-distance or international services, is common in the U.K., France, and the U.S. In the U.S., there have also been experiments with advertising to increase local calling.

b. Another method of increasing usage is to stimulate services operating over the network. In a strategy aimed primarily at residential subscribers, the French have been very successful in increasing usage of the Transpac packet-switched network by distributing Minitel terminals; from 1984 to 1985 the number of Minitels more than doubled and the use of the Transpac network grew by 45 per cent.

c. A more business-oriented strategy that is implicit in the moves of some administrations is liberalization of the use of the network. By permitting private sector entities to develop new services that depend on the network, and permitting their interconnection, utilization of the network increases. In the U.S., Canada, the U.K., France, and Japan, traffic volume has increased or will increase as deregulation and liberalization take hold.

4. Liberalization is also tied to difficult questions about the future of a cross-subsidized rate structure and to initiatives to rebalance rates. Facilities-based competition in the U.S. and in the U.K. is forcing prices closer to costs; this is particularly the case in the interexchange markets, where there is viable competition.

a. Many countries are reluctant to permit competition in facilities because it is viewed as encouraging some cream skimming—service to the more lucrative routes—unless universal service obligations are imposed on all entrants. In Canada and Australia, very real political concerns about cross-subsidization and the future of service to rural or remote areas are forestalling any movement to competition in public switched services.

b. Conversely, it may be difficult to hobble the dominant or formerly monopoly carrier with universal service obligations if it is to engage in price-related competition on the high-traffic routes. In the U.K., for example, British Telecom is subject to a set of conditions contained in its license, and it is expressly limited by a formula in implementing any rate increases. Policymakers must walk a fine line between giving competition a chance by encouraging the entry of new carriers and not imposing unduly onerous obligations on the traditional service providers.

c. Different approaches to making it economically possible for competition to develop are emerging worldwide. In Canada, rate rebalancing is the predicate for the introduction of competition in switched services. A series of studies over the last few years has focused on how this might be accomplished. Nevertheless, political exigencies—service to less populated areas is likely to be more expensive as internal cross-subsidies are ended—has made it difficult to rebalance rates. The Bundespost's rate structure has similar, complicating social and political components.

  d. In France, measured service has been introduced in an attempt to increase local revenues in order to defray the costs of the local network. Similar steps are being considered in Australia. In France, there is also a long-term plan to bring long-distance and local rates into alignment; the reduction in long-distance tariffs is coupled with a reduction in the calling period to which the tariff is applied.

  e. Subsidies that must be paid by the telecommunications administrations may also make it difficult to move prices closer to costs. The Bundespost's subsidy to the postal side, and payments to national treasuries by the Bundespost, the French DGT, the Dutch PTT, and Telecom Australia, are common problems that more entrepreneurially-oriented administrations and national policymakers are having to confront.

  5. Liberalization in use of the network may also lead to economic pressures from service-based competition with the provider of network facilities. The concern is not so much with intra-company use of leased lines, but with service providers linking lines to form value-added or other services. Although such innovation may be a welcome development for customers, PTTs are concerned that resale or leased lines to permit message-switching or other third-party traffic will inevitably follow. Thus, how to ensure that leased lines are available—and with what tariff structure—is a major concern of policymakers around the world.

  a. Some policymakers and administrations perceive that the economic pressures on the network provider resulting from liberalizing the usage of leased lines could be grave. This is the position taken in Germany, where "harmonization" of leased line and switched tariffs is taking place. The "first-best" solution from an economic standpoint would be to increase the prices of local calls; this is not feasible politically, however.

  b. The "second best" solution is to introduce volume-sensitive charging principles into leased-line tariffs. This the Bundespost did in the middle of 1986 when it adopted the TKO, which will be effective in 1988. The intention, of course, is to make pure resale economically unattractive. The difficulty with this course is that it moves the tariffing principle for leased circuits away from costs. Moreover, users may move traffic out of Germany, to the extent possible, to avoid the higher prices that will result from the new tariff structure.

  c. The German move has not been followed elsewhere, although it is being examined carefully within CEPT, in France, and in other major European countries. In nations, such as the U.K., where facilities-based competition has emerged, it is highly unlikely that volume-based pricing would survive.

  d. A final, regulatory approach to the problem of "cream-skimming" by customers of leased lines is proscribing "pure resale". Simple resale is prohibited in the U.K. and is barred in Japan by NTT tariffs. The effectiveness of this approach depends on how well regulators can monitor "pure resale" activities, and how they can be differentiated from other uses of underlying capacity in value-added services. Those administrations that view this regulatory solution as difficult to implement, therefore, view the Bundespost's approach with some degree of envy.

B. Regulatory and Technical Convergences

1. The regulatory models and approaches being vigorously pursued by national policymakers differ widely. Nevertheless, some common perspectives are emerging. It is improbable that a truly harmonized, uniform view will ever evolve. Regulators do face a common set of problems, however: how to differentiate between network and value-added services, and how to interconnect such services with the network. Thus, there can be no surprise that the approaches that are being considered and implemented do bear some similarity to one another.

2. The approach adopted in the U.S. and Canada, to distinguish between basic and enhanced services, has been somewhat difficult to apply to new services. Protocol processing services, for example, can be both integrated with and provided separately from underlying service. One regulatory question has centered on the comparative efficiencies of having carriers and enhanced service providers offer such services either separately from or with transmission services. Nevertheless, at least in the U.S., the enhanced services sector is flourishing, largely due to the relaxed regulatory environment in which such services operate. The critical regulatory issue is whether and on what terms the BOCs will be able to offer such services if and when the MFJ restrictions are relaxed.

3. The Japanese and others have criticized the 'basic'/'enhanced' dichotomy as troubling. First, it relies on criteria that are neither technical nor precise. Second, it can be difficult to determine the status of some services that arguably would be enhanced if they are bundled with basic offerings. The Japanese, therefore, have developed a "horizontal" distinction between "facilities" and "services". Type I entities provide network facilities; services dependent on those facilities can be provided by Type II companies.

a. The distinction between "facilities" and "services" is not without problems. With respect to domestic offerings, the issues raised by this distinction are discussed above in Section IV; different, and more difficult, problems are raised by applying the "horizontal" split to international services. *See* Section XIV.D, below.

b. Despite these problems, there appears to be an increasing interest in the Japanese scheme. The Commission of the European Communities has followed developments in Japan closely. Several countries, particularly those with a political and social reluctance to introduce facilities-based competition, admire the Japanese model as a way of maintaining a monopoly on facilities while liberalizing services. This is close to the approach being implemented in the Netherlands and may be attractive to the French, too.

    4. In the U.S., the concepts of CEI and ONA also seem to rely, at least in part, on the distinction between the provision of facilities and that of services. As described above in Section II.B, operators of networks must make certain BSEs available to service providers under an ONA plan; CEI, of course, only requires network providers to do so if they offer an enhanced service.

    a. The unbundling of network elements to permit providers of new services to build their own offerings is an innovative technological and regulatory approach that is attractive to some policymakers outside the U.S. The Commission of the European Communities, for example, is examining ONA and the evolution of other regulatory concepts in the U.S.

    b. It seems unlikely that ONA will be exported on a wholesale basis. First, other countries will wait to see how the U.S. market develops as ONA is actually implemented. Nevertheless, bilateral and multilateral discussions will focus on issues of interconnection. There will be pressure to make certain services or service features available outside the U.S.; in this way, then, the utility of the ONA concept will be explored internationally.

    c. In Europe, there is significant sensitivity to the entry of PTTs, such as the Bundespost, into the market for value-added services. ONA and CEI, if successful in the U.S., could be evidence that market structures can be developed to allow service providers to compete with the providers of the facilities, without risking that facilities providers will stifle competition. By unbundling service elements and making them available to all on a tariffed basis, a PTT could be allowed to compete on an equitable basis with the private sector.

    d. Although it is unlikely that many countries in Europe would embrace the regulatory supervision that may be required by ONA and CEI, they could try to import the concept of network unbundling as a way of fostering a co-operative relationship between carriers and service providers. The degree of unbundling actually done might be left to market forces, perhaps with some governmental oversight to guard against anticompetitive behavior.

    e. Users and service providers with international operations may attempt to export some of the features of ONA—assuming, of course, that ONA proves successful. They might seek to persuade PTTs and other carriers to make available to them certain unbundled network features that are used in the U.S. to offer or to take advantage of particular enhanced services. If certain carriers or PTTs were willing to offer such capabilities, market pressures could force other carriers to consider similar moves.

    5. Both ONA and the distinction between facilities and services are regulatory vehicles for enabling new or existing providers to

develop value-added or other services that depend on underlying network facilities. The preceding sections of this paper discuss in some detail the various national approaches to achieving this goal. One approach that may gain adherence internationally is that being considered in France.

   a. As described above in Section V.C, the French are contemplating a distinction between an "open" and a "closed" network. Use of network facilities to build "closed" networks would be permitted, while "open" networks, offering services to the public, would be viewed as siphoning traffic from the public switched network.

   b. This concept is somewhat analogous to a regulatory concept that has been applied by Telecom Australia, but is different in an important way. In Australia, closed user groups can lease lines in connection with the activities of a particular group, provided that the purpose of forming the group is not solely telecommunications-related.

   c. The emerging French concept differs from that of Telecom Australia in that it would permit relatively liberal use of leased lines by groups that exist as "groups" only to use telecommunications capacity. So long as the group is "closed" and the identities of the users known, flat-rate pricing would be available. This approach initially would appear to have some appeal because it is a distinction that is relatively simple to understand and because it might afford considerable flexibility to the providers of value-added services.

   d. The difficulties with the concept are that many new uses of leased lines involve floating groups of customers. When combined with financial information or transactional capabilities, leased lines might be offered to the customers of a bank, to brokers, to purchasers of commodities, or to investors. The point has been made, of course, that these services should not be treated as—or be subject to the same kind of telecommunications regulation as—value-added services.

   e. In any event, for these integrated offerings, it will be difficult to apply the distinction because it may be impractical or impossible to discover the identity of users. Thus, under the proposed approach, such offerings might be considered "open" and be tariffed on a volume-sensitive basis—an unfortunate and inappropriate result. Considerable thought, therefore, needs to be given to the "open"/"closed" conceptual framework.

C. New Regulatory and Industry Structures

   1. Changes in substantive telecommunications policies are forcing policymakers around the world to focus on the need for, and role of, regulatory authorities. Even in countries where services are supplied on a monopoly basis, the role of regulation is now viewed as an important adjunct of liberalizing services.

   a. As administrations, such as the Bundespost and Telecom Australia, desire to enter a market in which they are competing with private sector entities, vesting the joint responsibility for operating the network and regulating its usage is viewed as untenable. Efforts are being made to review the regulatory authority of PTTs and to assess how that function can be separated from the performance of network functions. In Germany, the governmental commission on the future of the Bundespost is assessing how the separation can be effected. In Australia, questions about whether the Department of Communications should assume regulatory responsibilities are the subject of vigorous debate.

b. Where new entities are being permitted to compete in a more direct way with the existing provider, new regulatory institutions are being established: Oftel in the U.K., the CNCL in France, and a regulatory process in the Netherlands. In Japan, the MPT is being forced to take a more active role in setting the ground rules for competition, including review of NTT tariffs and determining to what extent the new Type I entities can and should compete among each other and with NTT.

c. The development of a specific regulatory mechanism for a particular national environment can be difficult. New regulatory institutions may be created in a setting where regulation or transparency in decision-making may not be traditional. Such institutions can be short-staffed or low on expertise, at least at the outset. Money and resources must be allocated to the institutions if there is any hope of implementing effectively the political decision to liberalize.

d. Furthermore, the legislation creating the regulatory body must contain a general framework outlining the principles that the regulator is to follow in carrying out the political will. The regulator needs to gain credibility quickly with the entities that it is regulating, lest its authority not be respected. Comment procedures must be developed so that the public can have a say—and stake—in the decisions that are made. At the outset, then, institution-building can be a trying task.

2. Several factors are forcing the transition from the monopoly provision of telecommunications services worldwide to a more liberalized environment. Perhaps the presence of new technological capabilities and user pressures are among the most important of these. These same factors are leading to the erosion of another structural characteristic of at least some national telecommunications sectors; that is, the distinction between international and domestic services is blurring.

a. Historically, national and international services have been subject to separate regulatory treatments. In all countries this is because an international service must take account of at least two regulatory frameworks, one at each end of the circuit. National administrations have operated by consensus in the area, unwilling to impose their domestic regulatory schemes on sovereign states. Similarly, an additional and complicating factor in structuring international services is the involvement of an institution, such as Intelsat, not generally present in the domestic sector; these institutions are not subject to domestic control, of course, although they may well be influenced by domestic regulation.

b. In certain countries, however, there is yet another reason why domestic and international services are subject to disparate regulatory regimes. In these countries, much of that difference can be attributed to the very structure of the sector; one organization provides domestic services, another provides international services. The two entities may be wholly separate and unaffiliated, as is the case in Japan, Canada, Australia, Italy, Cameroon, and Indonesia, for example. Conversely, as is true in India, the international entity may be organizationally separate from, but affiliated with, the domestic supplier. In the countries with separate providers of international services, those entities operate through international gateways, which are the points at which they are given access to the domestic facilities of the other organization.

c. The separation of both the responsibility and the facilities for the provision of domestic and international services is undergoing significant stress. As commerce itself is increasingly international, businesses are becoming more international in their use of telecommunications services; in their view, there is and should be no difference between the domestic and international services that are available, except that international services extend beyond national borders.

d. To serve the needs of these multinational customers, the providers of international services—OTC (A) or the newly-privatized Teleglobe Canada, for example—want to offer end-to-end service. For the domestic segment, of course, they must rely on the domestic carrier, which sets the conditions and terms for interconnection. The international providers resist this exercise of authority over the structure of their service offerings and any decisions regarding to whom they will make circuits available.

e. Conversely, the domestic service providers want to market international services to their own customers. They are interested in extending their monopoly over domestic services to participate in the market for what can often be very lucrative international services. Many domestic providers have set up "international" divisions to explore business opportunities and ventures overseas. As they control the local access facilities and, by regulation, could even control dedicated links from customers to international gateways, the domestic providers can exercise significant clout over the structure and tariffing of international services.

f. These tensions are being confronted directly in the marketing of international satellite services. Satellite technology enables the international carrier to provide service directly to customer premises, bypassing the domestic carrier entirely. For large users, going directly to Intelsat or regional satellites might be an attractive option. They will want to deal with one entity, which may well be the international carrier.

g. The ability of international carriers to provide end-to-end services without relying on domestic services at all is forcing policymakers to review structural arrangements. Some of the options available have been noted above in the discussion on developments in Australia. *See* Section XII.

They might include permitting the international provider to integrate backward into the domestic market or, conversely, permitting the domestic provider to integrate forward beyond national borders.

h. Another hallmark of the steady erosion between the domestic and international sectors is the fact that deregulation or liberalization on the domestic side may spawn competition in international carriage. Users that are becoming accustomed to responsiveness on the part of domestic carriers operating in a competitive environment will press for similar flexibility in the provision of international services; this is likely to happen in Japan, for example. In short, it will be increasingly difficult to maintain the separation between the international and domestic sectors. Concurrently, therefore, policymakers will be forced to forge what can only be a single telecommunications policy, one that takes adequate account of pressures both international and domestic.

XIV. INTERNATIONAL VALUE-ADDED OR ENHANCED SERVICES: HOW TO DEVELOP ARRANGEMENTS FOR INTERCONNECTION

A. Overview of International Issues

1. A supplier of international enhanced or value-added services faces the difficult task of having to comply with varied national approaches to the provision and regulation of telecommunications facilities and services. These variations in national market structures and differences among regulatory environments complicate the international provision of service and the negotiation of interconnection agreements for the origination and termination of traffic and designating routing.

2. The D-Series Recommendations of the CCITT may pose further difficulties for international providers of value-added services. Variations in how these Recommendations are interpreted and applied can lead to regulatory inconsistencies that can interpose significant obstacles to the international offering of a service based on leased lines.

a. The D-Series Recommendations encourage administrations to make leased lines available. Nevertheless, the Recommendations, and their interpretation by administrations, emphasize that leased lines are to be used principally for non-public services.

b. The Recommendations, as interpreted by most administrations, are read as prohibiting resale and the offering of services that are viewed as infringing the function of an administration. Thus, the offering of third-party messaging-switching or telex services, howsoever those services might be defined, is often proscribed for value-added service providers.

3. In 1986–7, there have been several major regulatory developments that will complicate further the question of how suppliers of international value-added services will be able to structure their offerings.

Many, but by no means all, of these developments are emerging from the United States.

    a. The movement toward an ONA environment in the U.S. will provide opportunities for the enhanced service sector, but will provoke questions inside and outside the U.S. about the facilities that will be made available.

    b. The FCC's decision in May 1986 to permit value-added service suppliers to obtain Recognized Private Operating Agency ("RPOA") status and to purchase indefeasible rights of users ("IRUs") interests in transoceanic cables creates additional issues about how providers of international service are to be treated. Although the terms under which traditional telephone and telex services are provided may remain stable, there is considerable confusion over how value-added service providers will be able to structure their operating relationships in the new international environment.

    c. As discussed above in Section II.B.17, the FCC also will consider, as part of its Supplemental Notice in the *Computer III* proceeding, whether it should impose on the enhanced service operations of any dominant U.S. international carrier the non-structural safeguards imposed on the domestic operations of AT&T and the BOCs.

4. In Japan, the entry of new international service providers, both facilities- and service-based, raises unanswered questions about how the Type I/Type II dichotomy will be applied internationally. At present, new Type I carriers are not authorized to operate internationally, although, as discussed above in Section IV, two entities are poised for entry into the international market.

    a. Type II entities can operate through KDD's public switched facilities; KDD's position is that affording such providers access to leased lines would violate the CCITT Recommendations' prohibition on resale. Suppliers of value-added services might be given RPOA status, but difficult interconnection issues would still need to be resolved.

    b. The conservative position of KDD can cause some anomalous results. In the last couple of years, one lessee of lines from KDD, a supplier of an information and transactional service, was permitted to operate and market its service in Japan. The condition of its doing so, however, was that the service be legally packaged as, and considered to be, a service of KDD.

5. In the U.K., the Revised Government Proposals of late 1985 expressed support for the use by value-added service providers of international leased circuits to the extent permitted by the CCITT Recommendations. Revised Government Proposals, at paras. 30–33. The VADS Class Licence contains nothing that would suggest that the position of the government has changed.

    a. These proposals essentially reiterate, without adding to, the conditions stated in the CCITT Recommendations. Entities other than BT or Mercury may not be able to offer public services over leased lines because such offerings would be viewed as involving resale. "Non-public" services and services in which leased lines are used in accordance with the CCITT Recommendations would be permitted, contingent on obtaining the necessary interconnection agreements.

      b. As noted above in Section III, the Revised Government Proposals had stated that reference to CCITT Recommendation D.6 is appropriate for certain leased line services. The government has offered its assistance in the negotiation of interconnection agreements, with the DTI "prepared, when necessary and within the limits of the CCITT framework, to take up with particular administrations evidence of discrimination against UK operators[, recognizing] . . . that the agreement of sovereign national administrations cannot be guaranteed . . .". Revised Government Proposals, at para. 32. The VADS Class Licence suggests that some bilateral agreements may also be appropriate for establishing the regulatory parameters for value-added services.

      6. One problem with ascertaining the status of suppliers of value-added services that operate internationally is that they do not occupy a well-defined regulatory niche in international telecommunications. Carriers—usually national administrations—provide facilities and "public correspondence services". Thus, countries that have liberalized domestic value-added services, or are in the process of doing so, are still facing a series of issues on how to treat international value-added service providers.

      7. Differences in national regulatory regimes can make it quite difficult for the provision of services on an international basis. Adding to the complexity of providing service is the multiplicity of players in the international environment—new facilities-based competitors, new service providers, and new regulators. One of the most pressing problems facing policymakers, therefore, is how to structure international arrangements.

      a. Existing institutions may have insufficient expertise to address the regulatory environment in which these new services are developing. The providers of value-added or enhanced services are often in the business of supplying information, providing financial services, or providing transactional capabilities, and not in supplying telecommunications capacity to their customers.

      b. New mechanisms need to be created to facilitate accommodation among differing regulatory regimes and to remove obstacles to interconnection. The new vehicles for achieving interconnection will have to be less formal, less governmental, and less multilateral than the present arrangements for developing the existing international regulatory regime.

      c. Discussions between parties seeking and affording interconnection will have to proceed bilaterally and on a more commercial basis. At the same time, it will be increasingly important to bring together national and regional regulators to discuss similarities and differences in their own approaches, and how these approaches can be harmonized to provide a hospitable environment for new services. The model that could evolve may well be not unlike the fact-finding missions and bilateral negotiations that now take place under the aegis of trade officials.

B. The Impact of ONA on International Services

1. The movement toward the implementation of ONA in the U.S. by the BOCs and, possibly, AT&T will have a significant impact on the development of international value-added services. A PTT could acquire BSEs from a BOC or from AT&T and assemble its own enhanced service offering. This service could be transmitted between the U.S. and the PTT's country. In this event, one result of ONA might be the export of various enhanced service capabilities from the U.S. Thus, a major effect of ONA is that the unbundling envisioned by the FCC could be attractive to foreign entities seeking to provide international enhanced services, if not U.S. domestic services.

2. If foreign companies become involved in providing international enhanced services on an end-to-end basis, either on their own or through a joint venture, one question is whether the FCC would adopt an aggressive stance in regulating that offering.

a. Enhanced services are, of course, left unregulated by the FCC, although certain requirements were imposed on AT&T and the BOCs due to their market power. The FCC argues that it has jurisdiction to regulate enhanced services; thus, if a PTT offering an enhanced service had substantial market power, or if the FCC, for some other reason, wanted to regulate that PTT, it could probably exercise its regulatory authority over that PTT's enhanced service offerings.

b. In 1985, in deciding to apply a "streamlined" regulatory regime to many of the international basic service offerings of U.S. carriers, the FCC declined to afford similar flexibility to the basic offerings of "foreign-owned" carriers. *International Competitive Carrier Policies*, 102 F.C.C.2d 812 (1985), *recon. denied*, FCC No. 86-339 (released Aug. 7, 1986). Under the regulatory scheme established by the FCC, a carrier in which more than 15 per cent of the stock is owned by a "foreign telecommunications entity" is treated as a dominant carrier and is not permitted to operate under streamlined regulatory procedures. *Id.* at 842 and n.74. Dominant carriers must file tariffs supported by significant documentation, and the FCC must approve the establishment or discontinuance of particular service routes.

c. The regulatory disparity between domestic and foreign-owned carriers is predicated on the rationale that foreign carriers might take advantage of U.S. deregulation to arrange end-to-end services that would be given preferential treatment in the negotiation of correspondent agreements. The FCC requires all foreign-owned carriers to file quarterly reports showing the amounts of traffic being carried between the United States and each foreign destination.

d. The FCC also intends that this regulatory scheme should be a possible source of leverage for opening foreign markets to U.S. carriers. The FCC has broad regulatory authority over dominant carriers; thus, it could condition the authorization of a foreign-owned carrier on an agreement by that carrier's country to permit U.S. companies to carry traffic between the U.S. and that country.

e. For international enhanced services, the relevance of the scheme erected by the decision in *International Competitive Carrier Policies* is clear: the FCC could use the dominant classification of foreign-owned carriers as a readily available rationale for imposing a more rigid regulatory framework on their enhanced services. Such entities, for example, might be required to comply with some or all of the *Computer III* non-structural safeguards, although this result seems unlikely at present.

4. The outcome of the Supplemental Notice in *Computer III* may also be significant in a foreign entity's decision to enter the market for international enhanced services.

a. In the *Computer III* proceeding the FCC is still deciding how to classify certain protocol conversion services. If it ultimately decides that those services should be treated as "basic", the FCC could seek to regulate as dominant those foreign-owned carriers that offer services that are, or rely on, protocol conversion offerings.

b. Foreign companies may be less interested in using protocol conversion capabilities to develop integrated offerings if that step would subject them to the full exercise of regulatory authority. Such a regulatory disincentive could work to offset the interest of foreign companies in using network elements available in the U.S. to assemble new end-to-end international services.

5. Significant regulatory and trade-related issues also might be raised by the provision of services internationally that make use of BSEs. A PTT or other foreign-owned provider of international services could choose to transport internationally the intelligence contained in a BSE that it obtains under tariff from a U.S. carrier as part of its service. The PTT could either do so separately, by moving the raw network capability outside the U.S., or do so by using the BSE as a building block of an international enhanced service.

a. Notwithstanding the fact that such a network capability might be a building block for, and aggregated with, an enhanced service, the FCC could take the view that the purchase and movement of that network capability overseas should be regarded as the international provision of a basic service. For purely domestic services in the U.S., of course, the bundling of BSEs with information or data processing activities would be viewed as an enhanced service; such a service would not be subject to regulation if provided by a non-dominant carrier.

b. For international enhanced services provided by a PTT or foreign-owned entity, however, the regulatory posture of the FCC could be quite different. In applying its *Computer II* decision to international enhanced services, the FCC took the view that such services combined resale (of a basic service) with an enhancement. By that decision, of course, such services are not regulated.

    c. Nevertheless, by analogy with its different treatment of domestic and international enhanced services, the FCC could view an international enhanced service built on BSEs as the combination of a basic and an enhanced service. It might, therefore, argue that the international movement of a BSE, even if combined with enhancements, also constituted a basic service. And, on that ground, the FCC could attempt to exert jurisdiction over, and license, the international enhanced service provider; at the least, the FCC might take the position that the transport of the BSE overseas was a licensable activity.

    d. The FCC might treat the entity offering such a service as a dominant international carrier under its *International Competitive Carrier* policy. In particular, given the FCC's concern about ensuring fairness and opening foreign markets, it might use the threat of classifying such entity as dominant as leverage. That is, the FCC might view the use by a PTT or foreign-owned carrier of unbundled network capabilities in the U.S. as unfair if the country of such carrier were to refuse to make similar capabilities available to U.S.-based service providers. Consequently, if pushed, the FCC could use its power to regulate the carriage of a BSE by such carrier to attempt to obtain reciprocal rights for U.S. providers.

    6. If network elements are unbundled in the U.S. but not elsewhere, it would seem that there would be discontinuities between the capabilities available in the U.S. and in other countries. It is not clear whether the international offering of services developed by assembling BSEs would require foreign carriers to unbundle their own networks and separate out similar BSEs.

    a. AT&T has said that within the United States it could transport any service developed as a result of the implementation of ONA—whether it is exempted from having to adopt its own ONA or simply adopts a dissimilar ONA. A PTT could probably provide similar transmission capabilities. However, services that require subscriber interaction with a local network to generate necessary information would not be available to non-U.S. customers, unless either the PTT offered the necessary enhanced service capability in its own country or provided a mechanism for foreign customers to connect with a processing node in the United States.

    b. Thus, it could be difficult for the international providers of value-added services to realize fully the advantages of unbundling in the U.S. As noted above, if the PTT did not offer similar capabilities in its own country, the FCC might take the position that market access opportunities were unequal and use its authority to exercise regulatory authority over the PTT enhanced service provider operating to and in the U.S.

    c. If, however, the disparities in the available network functionalities of the U.S. and the other country were significant, both U.S.- and foreign-based service providers would exert pressure on foreign regulators to make comparable network elements available. Over time, therefore, the ONA environment in the U.S. is likely to generate substantial economic and political incentives for other nations to unbundle some of the basic elements of their networks.

C. RPOAs and IRUs in the United States

1. The United States has proceeded somewhat further in establishing a framework explicitly for providers of international enhanced or value-added services. In mid-1986, the FCC promulgated a set of rules that will permit enhanced service providers and other non-carriers to be designated as RPOAs and to purchase IRU ownership interests in transoceanic cables. *International Communications Policies Governing Designation of Recognized Private Operating Agencies, Grants of IRUs in International Facilities and Assignment of Data Network Identification Codes*, 104 F.C.C.2d 208 (1986) ("RPOA and IRU Order").

 a. The objectives of the FCC have been forthright: to remove barriers to entry and regulatory burdens in order to stimulate competition in enhanced services. *Id.* at 249. The cornerstone of the FCC's new policy is that certain enhanced service providers may, but are not required to, obtain RPOA status. Such providers may want to do so if they believe that designation as an RPOA will reassure PTTs that they will adhere to ITU regulations and that obtaining RPOA status will facilitate interconnection arrangements.

 b. In its RPOA and IRU Order, the FCC expressly reiterated concerns that the offering of enhanced services overseas via leased channels might be considered prohibited resale in some situations and thereby violative of Recommendation D.1. The FCC said that its decision was not intended to "erode, disregard or subvert the right of PTTs to limit or prohibit resale of their leased channels". *Id.* at n.132. Nevertheless, in the analysis contained in the order extending the *Computer II* dichotomy to the international arena, the FCC stated that resale is permitted—subject to CCITT Recommendations and operating arrangements. In the RPOA and IRU Order, it concluded that there is no prohibited resale whenever an enhanced service provider has an operating agreement with a PTT. *Id.* at 255.

2. The process of obtaining RPOA status is relatively straightforward. Enhanced service providers offering "public correspondence" service and agreeing to adhere to the ITU regulations are eligible to receive RPOA status from the U.S. Department of State.

 a. The FCC has chosen not to equate "public correspondence" with "common carriage"; "telecommunications" are apparently defined as a transmission without "change in the content". "Public correspondence" includes an offering to just one member of the public. Pure data processors do not offer "public correspondence" and are, therefore, not eligible for RPOA status. *Id.* at 246–48.

    b. It is not clear how the FCC would treat "hybrid" services that affect both the form and the content of a communication, such as a database service packaged with the capability to perform asynchronous-to-X.25 conversions.

3. Once an eligible service provider decides that RPOA status is desirable, the FCC has made it clear that such status should be relatively available.

    a. An application must be submitted and must include certain basic corporate information together with a certification that the applicant will comply with all ITU regulations. Membership in the CCITT will remain voluntary.

    b. The application also requires disclosure of any foreign ownership of 20 per cent or more of an applicant's stock. Such foreign entities are not barred from providing enhanced services in the United States. Rather, the information is intended to permit a review of the impact, and fairness, of allowing a foreign entity to operate in the U.S. if the country in which the said entity is based does not afford equivalent access to U.S.-based providers.

    c. There is some question whether this certification process, as applied to service providers in which there are foreign interests, could be used to exert pressure on foreign administrations to enter into interconnection agreements with U.S.-based providers.

4. Although the FCC believes that an enhanced services provider need not be a regulated or licensed carrier to obtain RPOA status, administrations may perceive RPOAs as regulated entities that have been selected to fill the role of a PTT. Thus, they do not view according entities RPOA status as an endorsement of expanded international competition. The FCC, however, has used the RPOA label to lend legitimacy to emerging competitive service providers. The result may be a dilution of the value of RPOA status for U.S. companies operating in the world market.

5. There has been considerable confusion regarding the application of the D-Series proscriptions on resale to enhanced service providers.

    a. The FCC decision notes that there is much less danger of the activities of an enhanced service provider being deemed to "infringe" the functions of an administration if it is viewed as an RPOA and has obtained an operating agreement. This view is consistent with the FCC's earlier decisions that the offering of an enhanced service, to the extent that it might be considered "resale", is governed by the CCITT Recommendations and the requirement that an operating agreement be obtained.

    b. The proscription on resale, however, may only have been intended to apply to users, and not to RPOAs or administrations. Carriers have leased lines and are permitted to provide enhanced services, to the extent that such services are viewed as "resale". There is some question, then, how the D-Series conditions could be viewed as applying at all to RPOA-enhanced service providers.

   c. Furthermore, the difficulty with the FCC's approach is that it apparently makes the assumption that the provision of an enhanced service is the resale of communications services such that the service might be viewed as message switching or other third-party carriage. In fact, services such as remote access data processing have never been viewed as "resale" *per se*. Moreover, many other enhanced services are information-based or transactional; such services are not "resale".

   d. With respect to such services, the FCC has left it unclear whether they are "public correspondence" services for which RPOA status may be obtained. The problem is, therefore, that by characterizing enhanced services as involving resale, the FCC may well have undercut its own objective—increasing the burden of persuasion for providers negotiating with administrations, *i.e.*, arguing that their offerings do not "infringe" on functions within the exclusive domain of administrations.

   6. Determining which RPOAs may participate in the facilities planning or settlements processes may also be problematic. Given the FCC's broad interpretation of RPOA status, it may be difficult to exclude certain RPOAs from these planning and management activities.

   7. The FCC's decision to permit enhanced service providers to acquire IRUs may present even more difficult issues because it may create entities that are "hybrids", from an international regulatory perspective.

   a. Under CCITT Recommendation D.1, the restriction on resale and the prohibition on infringing the functions of an administration are contingent on the leasing of lines from an administration by a "customer". These restrictions may not be applicable to enhanced service providers holding IRUs because such providers essentially own—not lease—circuits. On their own terms, then, the CCITT Recommendations might no longer serve as a barrier to IRU-based providers offering a range of services.

   b. Further questions are raised by the impact of allowing users to purchase IRUs and the extent to which the new policy actually may raise an added barrier for enhanced service providers. To avoid infringing the rights of PTT co-owners in a cable, and to recognize their half-interests in circuits, the FCC has stated that users may acquire the U.S. half-interest. To provide service, however, an enhanced service provider will have to purchase the other half of the circuit from the PTT and reach an operating agreement with the foreign administration.

   c. In its Notice of Proposed Rulemaking, the FCC had said that it would retain sufficient jurisdiction—under its ancillary powers—over the IRU owner to ensure compliance with domestic and international regulations. There is significant uncertainty, however, as to how ITU regulations might apply to holders of IRUs. As noted above, the D-Series Recommendations might not apply to IRU holders—and resale might be permitted, therefore—because they will no longer lease circuits from administrations. The terms of the operating agreements between enhanced service providers and administrations may still bar resale, despite the inapplicability of the CCITT Recommendations.

8. The ability and extent to which holders of IRUs will want, or are able, to participate in the facilities planning process are additional areas of uncertainty.

   a. The FCC has decided that IRU owners will not participate in the planning process and will not have a vote in decisions about the day-to-day operations of the cable. 104 F.C.C.2d at 257.

   b. It is not clear why IRU owners, who will have significant economic interests in the operation of their cable and in the state of facilities competition generally, should be excluded from either the planning process or management, except that the processes will be simplified by such exclusion. IRU owners, however, are required to make periodic maintenance payments to the group of entities that constructed the cable; this group will continue to make all decisions about the cable, even if all members of the group have sold IRUs for all of their assigned capacity. In such a situation, the separation of management power from economic interest might raise questions as to whether the cable is being managed to serve the interests of the IRU holders—those with the most at stake.

D. The Evolving Japanese Approach to VANs

1. Introduction

   a. In Japan, the question of whether Type II providers should be permitted to operate internationally and, if so, under what regulatory scheme, has been the subject of significant debate since the Telecommunications Business Law took effect in April 1985.

   b. In November 1985, an "International Type II Telecommunications Business Study Group" was established to study the issue; as discussed above in Section IV.C, its recommendations were submitted to the MPT at the end of September 1986. In March 1986, an advisory panel formed in October 1984 under the Communications Policy Bureau of the MPT released a report on "Japan's Role in Telecommunications".

   c. The report examined the alternatives by which international VANs could be established: (*i*) to urge a revision of CCITT Recommendations D.1 or D.6; (*ii*) to approve resale on a bilateral basis; and (*iii*) to designate international VAN operators as RPOAs, not as "customers" of leased lines. The panel concluded that VAN operators should be classified as carriers, or RPOAs. The Keidanren report on "Major Issues Under New Telecom Legislation" reached a similar result, *i.e.*, that Type II entities should be regarded as private operating agencies.

   d. Although the study group report of September 1986 agreed with both the advisory panel and the Keidanren that international

VANs should be classified as RPOAs, the MPT was still left with several options. One possibility was the adoption of more than one classification for international VANs.

2. The May 1987 Amendments to the Telecommunications Business Law

a. As a first step in the process of establishing a legal regime in Japan for the operation of international VANs, the Diet adopted amendments to the Telecommunications Business Law in May 1987. These amendments are general in nature and, most importantly, under Article 38 as revised, provide for Special Type II entities to enter into contracts with Type I carriers for "non-tariff-based" services.

b. Under a series of principles agreed to by U.S. and Japanese negotiators engaged in ongoing trade talks about international VANS, it is expected that the Ministry will set forth that international VAN providers can operate as Special Type II entities and can make use of these "non-tariff-based" services to provide international VANS consistently with the D-Series Recommendations. This operating arrangement has been developed to avoid a conflict with the D.1 Recommendation, which advocates limiting the use for third-party communications of international leased lines, which are tariffed offerings. It is asserted that the "non-tariff-based" services expected to be used to provide international VANS fall outside the scope of the D.1 Recommendation because they are not international leased lines.

c. Although the operating arrangement contemplated by Article 38 contains the potential for international VANs to escape the limitations of the D-Series Recommendations, international VANs would continue to be subject to international regulations, even under this operating configuration. Article 37 requires that Special Type II entities "sincerely fulfill the obligation imposed by treaties and other international agreements with respect to telecommunication business". It is not yet clear precisely what this requirement will mean in terms of subjecting international Special Type II entities to ITU regulations and CCITT recommendations.

d. It is clear, however, that the Japanese Government remains concerned about continuing to be perceived as acting in conformity with international telecommunications accords. Whether the phrase "other international agreements" will be read to encompass bilateral operating arrangements for international VAN operators—even if those agreements permit activities that might otherwise be prohibited by application of the CCITT Recommendations—is not yet certain.

e. The legislation leaves unresolved virtually all the details of how international VANs will be provided. As is typically the case in Japan, many of the details will be supplied by the Ministry's implementing regulations, which are in the process of being drafted. Several important issues will have to be resolved by the regulations or by other ministerial directives.

f. First, the terms on which Special Type II entities will be able to acquire "non-tariff-based" services will be crucial to the viability of international VANs if VAN operators are required to obtain services under contract from Type I entities as prescribed by amended Article 38.

i) At present, KDD is the only Type I entity from which such "non-tariff-based" services can be obtained. KDD has long advocated the imposition of volume-sensitive charging for the international VAN activities of third-party users. Although Japanese officials have assured U.S. trade negotiators that volume-sensitive pricing will not be the *quid pro quo* for operating internationally, there is not yet any clear legal impediment to KDD's insistence on such a pricing scheme.

ii) Under Article 38, service agreements between Type I and Special Type II entities must be authorized by the Ministry. It remains to be seen whether the Ministry will use that power to guard against the imposition of volume-sensitive pricing.

iii) Under Article 39, the Ministry may order interconnection between Type I and Special Type II entities. The Ministry might use this power to avoid volume-sensitive pricing requirements. Alternatively, it might use this power to require acceptance by an international Special Type II entity of a volume-sensitive pricing arrangement, at least in certain circumstances. It is worth noting that under Article 37 the Minister may issue an order if he determines, *inter alia*, that "a Type II telecommunications carrier's operations make it difficult for a Type I telecommunications carrier to financially maintain its telecommunications circuit facilities which have been designed to satisfy the demand . . .".

iv) Under Article 36(2), Type I entities are obliged not to "discriminate" against "a specified telecommunications carrier in interconnecting . . .". Japan has assured U.S. negotiators that the Ministry will use its powers under the Telecommunications Business Law to ensure that the prices of non-tariff-based services are reasonable and that contracts for such services are not otherwise discriminatory. It is not clear, however, whether the Ministry would find discrimination to exist if entities obtaining international leased lines were able to pay flat rates and entities required to use non-tariff-based services, *i.e.*, international VANs, were required to pay volume-sensitive charges.

v) More than anything else, the terms on which non-tariff-based services are made available may depend on the extent to which the MPT authorizes new Type I entities to compete with KDD.

g. Second, decisions will have to be made about whether the size of the international VAN market will be limited or otherwise controlled. The requirement that interconnection arrangements between Type I and Type II entities be authorized by the Ministry provides an opportunity for regulation of the international VAN market.

i) Article 38(3) obliges the Minister to authorize such interconnection arrangements "in so far as [they] promote the public interest". It is not clear what this provision means or how it is to be interpreted.

ii) In trade discussions with Japanese officials, the U.S. has been assured only that a shortage of Data Network Identification Codes ("DNICs") will not be a basis for limiting the number of international VANs. Thus, if international VANs are required to use "authorized" interconnection arrangements or otherwise to gain approval (perhaps because they will have to obtain RPOA status), the potential for regulation of the international VAN market would be present.

h. The Ministry also will have to decide whether international VANs will be required or permitted to obtain RPOA status. There has been some talk between U.S. and Japanese officials about leaving RPOA designation as an option. As discussed above, however, the government studies that preceded adoption of the recent legislative amendments almost uniformly favored the mandatory imposition of RPOA status on international VANs and, within the Ministry, there was sentiment in favor of this approach.

i) It is possible that international VANs would be permitted to operate as Special Type II entities with or without RPOA status; alternatively, RPOA status might be made mandatory.

ii) A remaining question is whether an RPOA could offer an international VAN service as a Special Type II entity using either authorized "non-tariff-based" services or using some other service arrangement, such as a leased line. Article 38 does not require that Special Type II entities obtain "non-tariff-based" services to operate; it merely permits this arrangement, subject to authorization by the Ministry.

i. The Ministry also may have to become involved in making distinctions among types of services. The Japanese have avoided such distinctions deliberately and, as noted above in Section IV.A, have criticized the regulatory approach of the U.S. (which distinguishes between basic and enhanced services) as being less advanced than the facilities/services distinction adopted in Japan.

j. Because most domestic VANs in Japan may now operate as General Type II entities—subject to virtually no regulation—many entities may have classified themselves as such, even though they are not really offering communications services that one would expect to be subject to telecommunications regulation. If these entities now seek to extend their services internationally, they could be required to become Special Type II entities.

i) As a result, they might be subject to treatment under international telecommunications policies that will unnecessarily restrict their businesses. To avoid such a result, there may be some need for the Ministry to distinguish between services that are properly classified as value-added communications offerings and those that are related non-communications activities.

ii) Some entities currently use international leased lines to provide something other than an international VAN service, such as data processing. It is not clear whether such an entity would be able to route future value-added traffic over those leased lines or whether it would be required to enter into new contractual arrangements for additional "non-tariff-based" services to handle such international VAN traffic—even if it has excess capacity on its leased lines.

iii) An entity operating an intracorporate VAN also might carry third-party value-added traffic internationally. The Ministry would have to decide whether, in that event, the service provider would be considered a Special Type II entity for all purposes.

iv) In short, it is likely that the Ministry will have to decide how to treat a "mixed" offering under the new international legal scheme.

k. Although not part of the amended legislation, the legal scheme eventually will have to draw distinctions between domestic and international VANs. As noted above in Section IV.B.7, the distinctions between Special and General Type II entities have largely been eviscerated, although Special Type I entities continue to be subject to certain additional obligations, such as interconnection and non-discrimination requirements.

i) Because the General Type II category has become so expansive, however, most domestic VANs operate as General Type II entities. Under the new legal regime, however, such entities would be required to become Special Type II entities to extend their services internationally.

ii) It is not clear whether a single entity could be a General Type II entity for domestic purposes and a Special Type II entity for international purposes. It is also unclear whether service providers would be reluctant to extend their services internationally if, as a result, they were required to become Special Type II entities for all purposes and to abide by the more rigid legal regime applicable to such status.

l. The Ministry will need to define what the interconnection and non-discrimination obligations imposed on Special Type II entities will mean for international VANs. Could these mean, for example, that international VANs will be subject to "common carrier-like" obligations (*i.e.*, publishing tariffs, offering service in a non-discriminatory fashion)?

m. The new legal scheme could have the effect of blurring distinctions among carriers, service providers, and users.

i) In Japan, a Type I entity "owns" a transmission facility. It is not clear whether possession of an IRU constitutes ownership of a facility. If it does, and if a user and a Type II carrier also may acquire IRUs (in the latter case, the IRU functioning as a "non-tariff-based service"), it is difficult to envision how one would distinguish—on a principled basis—among the various entities.

ii) If the legal distinctions begin to break down, there could be substantial problems in ensuring that entities providing comparable services are subject to similar legal and regulatory requirements.

iii) If an IRU is considered to be something other than a "leased line", an international VAN operator could have an incentive to acquire an IRU in an effort to escape the third-party service limitations of the D-Series Recommendations applicable to leased lines (assuming that a satisfactory correspondent arrangement could be found).

3. Continuing Problems and General Policy Considerations in Japan

a. Although the recent amendments to the Telecommunications Business Law stake out the future lines along which Japanese policies toward international VANS will evolve, the legislation does not resolve definitively all the policy issues addressed by the Advisory Panel Report. Open issues concern (*i*) the extent of reliance on the RPOA concept and the implications of imposing such status on an international VAN operator: (*ii*) how to distinguish a Type I entity and the provider of a Type II international VAN service; (*iii*) whether to impose a usage-based tariff under CCITT Recommendation D.6, or some *ad hoc* arrangement; (*iv*) how much to emphasize the role for unique bilateral arrangements with different countries; (*v*) how to rationalize such bilateral initiatives with Japan's sensitivity to the interests of administrations in the Third World; (*vi*) how to bridge major disparities between the U.S., the U.K., and Japan regarding VANS; and (*vii*) to what extent a new approach to value-added services could be used to avoid the restriction on resale. These issues are discussed briefly below.

b. The amendments leave unresolved the relationship of an international VAN and an RPOA. The MPT's primary inclination seems to follow the recommendations that it has received and adopt RPOA status for all international VAN operators. The MPT apparently disagrees with the FCC approach, *i.e.*, that RPOA status should be voluntary. Its position seems to be that the prevailing thinking apparently is that all entities operating internationally—both Type I and Type II—should be treated alike and that, therefore, RPOA status should be compulsory.

i) Imposing RPOA status on all VAN operators may have troubling implications because RPOAs typically have entered into correspondent and division-of-revenues agreements with partners on the other end of the international circuit. Such agreements are not typical, or warranted, in the case of remote access data processors or various types of information vendors, who ordinarily structure their arrangements on an end-to-end basis.

ii) The MPT appears to concede that such providers ought not to be treated as RPOAs. It is, nevertheless, not clear that adequate criteria can be developed to separate data processing or information providers from entities for which RPOA status may be more appropriate, especially as data processors and information providers diversify and offer new or "hybrid" services.

c. A further issue raised by the Japanese approach is the difficulty in distinguishing between the proposed new Type I entities that obtain circuits to provide international transmission capacity—as is contemplated by ITJ—and Special Type II entities that acquire circuits on a contract basis as an international VAN. As a practical matter, it may turn out to be difficult for the MPT to differentiate between the two unless it turns to a scheme premised on the classification of services. The MPT may have to base its distinction on differences in the types of facilities—and the rates for such facilities that are available to a Type I international entity and what the MPT refers to as a Type II international entity. Difficult issues of discrimination may be raised, at least to the extent that Type I and Special Type II entities offer similar services.

    d. One approach to the provision of international VANS that was studied by the MPT Advisory Panel was reliance on CCITT Recommendation D.6 as a basis for permitting the use of international leased lines.

    i) The principal difficulty with any option oriented toward D.6 is that it is not likely to be accepted by the U.S. KDD, the Deutsche Bundespost, British Telecom, and sometimes even the Department of Trade and Industry in the U.K. have suggested possible reliance on D.6. Nevertheless, as it becomes increasingly difficult to distinguish a private service and value-added offering, it is highly unlikely that large multinational users would ever accede to fundamental changes in the flat-rate pricing structure.

    ii) It is not clear that the MPT's proposed approach of relying on "non-tariff-based" services will avoid the practical problems raised by Recommendation D.6. The issue of volume-based tariffs may need to be addressed in the context of a non-tariff-based arrangement between international VANs operators and Type I entities.

    e. Another issue still to be faced by the Japanese is how much the new legal regime will be based on *ad hoc*, bilateral negotiations in accordance with Article 31 of the Convention of the International Telecommunications Union. The parties to such an agreement could take the position that their understanding supersedes CCITT Recommendations.

    i) In their proposed approach to dealing with international VANS, the Japanese appear to want to avoid the appearances of bypassing the D-Series Recommendations directly. In fact, however, that is precisely the practical effect of insisting on creating the concept of a "non-tariff-based" service—one that is exactly like a leased line service—and then insisting that the D-Series does not apply. In light of the lengths to which the Japanese have gone to avoid the appearance of superseding the D-Series through the "legal fiction" of a "non-tariff-based" service, it may be worthwhile to examine why the Japanese are so sensitive to new policies centered around bilateral negotiations.

    ii) Although bilateral arrangements might be quite easy to negotiate between the United States and Japan, the Japanese remain very concerned about the reactions of other nations to a bilateral U.S.-Japan agreement. Certainly, the Commission of the European Communities has expressed an interest in bilateral consultations with the Japanese; it is likely to feel excluded by negotiations in which the U.S. and Japan were the only participants.

iii) The general preference of the Japanese might well be for a solution to be reached in the CCITT forum. Many representatives to the CCITT, however, are not necessarily so interested in the development of value-added services. The Japanese "compromise" appears to be to devise a new concept which is somehow viewed as outside or perhaps inconsistent with the CCITT framework.

f. A Japanese concern emerging from the possible development of a bilateral framework for new international arrangements is keenly focused on relations between the industrialized and developing countries. In particular, the MPT is aware that the expansion of value-added services may not be seen as serving the developing world, and that separately negotiated bilateral arrangements may be perceived as insensitive to the international fora in which the needs of the Third World are addressed.

i) These concerns could be mitigated, however, by addressing the implications of new value-added services in consultations with administrations in the Third World. The risk that new international arrangements will be seen as increasing the disparity between the industrialized and developing countries might be mitigated by demonstrating that value-added services could be offered independently from transmission network facilities. New categories for service-based competitors might permit flexibility for private or foreign investment, while sovereign control could be maintained over backbone facilities.

ii) As to Japan's partners in the industrialized world, bilateral consultations are still very much in the process of being worked out. Among the issues central to these discussions will be the establishment of interconnection arrangements for new international VAN services. Concerns that bilateral arrangements were undermining the international scheme might be lessened by maintaining open lines of contact during discussions with the U.S. or the U.K.

iii) A significant impediment to the special round of talks likely to emerge among the U.S., the U.K., and Japan is the difference between the various national approaches to the regulation of value-added services. One example that seems significant to the Japanese is that the British include data processing carriers within value-added services, whereas, by contrast, such entities are excluded from the scope of Type II services by the Japanese.

g. Despite the approach adopted in the May 1987 amendments, the Japanese will still have to address the question of what types of services are considered to be resale. Japanese policymakers must determine under what circumstances a customer of a leased circuit must seek authorization as an operator of an international VAN.

i) In deciding on the threshold definition for an international VAN service, the Japanese might reasonably focus on the fundamental nature of the service being offered. For example, one of the principal criteria would be whether the primary purpose of the offering was to provide a communications service or some other offering—such as an information-based or transactional service—that has never been viewed as involving resale. Though the Japanese traditionally have shied away from a "hybrid service" test along the lines of *Computer I*, such a distinction might prove useful. Several difficulties would, however, remain.

ii) As noted above, one difficulty with this approach is that the FCC has taken the position that enhanced services might involve the resale of communications. *See* Section XIV.C.5 above. In so doing, the FCC has attempted to reassure European and other administrations that it would not unilaterally apply pressure to afford enhanced service vendors market access.

iii) Similarly, despite the difficulties in distinguishing among the providers of international services, the Japanese generally have been reluctant to establish categories other than that of the "Type II" entity. There does appear to be some willingness, however, to grapple with the problem of classifying services by type, to determine which service providers should be compelled to obtain RPOA status. In attempting to develop such criteria, Japan, and perhaps the U.S., may move toward a reappraisal of their domestic schemes for classifying services.

h. Such reappraisal would seem appropriate for many services that are classified as "value-added". Many of the new services are embedded in business operations—the purchase and sale of securities, the movement of money, transactions in commodities, and the flow of financial information. The development of these services, which combine some communications capabilities with a more general commercial offering, is discussed at some length in Chapter III of this book on transactional systems in the financial services sector.

i) When these services are used on an international basis, they should not be subject to telecommunications regulation—whether under the Type II scheme, as enhanced service providers, or as entities licensed under a class licence. The service being provided is not communications, but a financial or information service—or even a market—for which the "value-added" category is inappropriate.

ii) The current national and international regulatory frameworks, however, do not have a classification for such new services. Indeed, it is not easy to place bright lines on the spectrum ranging from entities that propose to lease international circuits to provide international capacity (as ITJ plans to do) to those providing protocol conversion services, to information providers, and to offerors of integrated transactional services. Nevertheless, at least for services at the financial/transactional end of the spectrum, a new classification might be useful. In lieu of such, however, providers of such services should simply be treated as customers for the purpose of enforcing the D-Series Recommendations.

E. A Process for Developing Arrangements for International Value-Added Services—Part I: The ITU

1. Traditionally, the structure of the international telecommunications environment was formed by monopoly providers on each end of a circuit who negotiated operating agreements for the provision of services. Today, the rapidly changing sectors of telecommunications and telecommunications-based services are populated by a diverse set of players who have not historically been part of that process, yet are growing in number. These entrants want a role in framing the international arena in which they operate.

    a. The issues of interconnection are complicated enough for pure telephony. In those countries where two or more providers of international public switched telephone services have been authorized, the agreements between monopoly service providers on both sides of a circuit must be modified to take account of the existence of multiple suppliers, the need for new traffic routing and interconnection configurations, and the potential for competition among suppliers with respect to the terms and conditions for dividing revenues. Thus, there now must be new arrangements for the new services.

    b. In the value-added and information services sector, discussions that might lead to new international agreements or other understandings are even more complex. The models being adopted by the U.S., the U.K., Japan, and other industrialized nations for liberalized service-based competition do not coincide. Devising interconnection arrangements among the value-added service providers in light of these regulatory inconsistencies or disparities will be an exceptionally important task for officials over the next several years.

    c. All these changes—the emergence of new services, new players, and new industry sectors—are, therefore, forcing policymakers to take a hard look at the mechanisms by which international interconnection arrangements for such new services can be worked out.

2. The first institution to which policymakers worldwide might look for assistance is the ITU. Nevertheless, the role and utility of the ITU in such a complicated environment, marked by the cross-currents of several industry sectors, is increasingly uncertain. Many of the regulatory issues raised by new interconnection relationships or by hybrid service offerings do not fit neatly within the service categories of telephony and telex, which have been the traditional subjects of ITU oversight and regulation.

3. As discussed throughout this Section XIV, it is not entirely clear how the CCITT D-Series Recommendations on leased-line usage will apply to new value-added service providers. The D-Series Recommendations may be inapplicable to enhanced service providers with RPOA status, or to service providers purchasing IRUs. Although the conditions contained in the D-Series might be written by the PTTs into operating agreements,

that development will only underscore the extent to which a uniform global regulatory regime is being transformed into one marked by a series of bilateral relationships. In this environment, the role of the ITU may need to be re-examined.

4. Furthermore, and as detailed in Chapter III, the new value-added services are often as much "banking", "securities", or "commodities transactions" as they are telecommunications. Fueled by the internationalization and globalization of financial markets, institutional trading networks and electronic markets for securities, commodities, and foreign exchange are developing around the world.

a. To treat such information or transactional services as within the ambit of telecommunications regulation is perceived by service providers and users as mischaracterizing the offering. Although buyers and sellers can be linked together, it would be inappropriate to describe the services as engaged in message-switching activities. As noted above in Section XIV.D.3.g, it is inaccurate to categorize such services as value-added: such services are not communications, but financial services.

b. Howsoever such services might be classified by national regulators, it is clear that, in any event, they often have important non-telecommunications components. How they are regulated will require a broader understanding of service sectors outside telecommunications.

c. The ITU's expertise, however, is in the field of telecommunications. ITU decisions are reached by engineers and telecommunications officials from the Members. The ITU does not have the institutional reservoir of experience in areas such as banking, securities, and commodities trading, that lie wholly outside the telecommunications sector. Yet it may be necessary to develop expertise in those fields to fathom whether there is a need for regulation. Thus, questions are being raised as to whether the ITU is the appropriate forum for addressing the propriety of treating new services as if they might involve "resale", "message switching", or some other "telecommunications" function.

5. More specifically, questions have been raised about the preparations for the World Administrative Telegraph and Telephone Conference, which will be held in Melbourne, Australia at the end of 1988 ("WATTC-88"). WATTC-88 is an outgrowth of the 1982 Nairobi Plenipotentiary Conference of the ITU, at which it was proposed that the ITU's telephone and telegraph regulations that have been applicable to carriers should be completely overhauled. Resolution Number 10 of the Plenipotentiary Conference considered it advisable to establish, to the extent necessary, "a broad international regulatory framework for all existing and foreseen new telecommunication services". That Resolution lays the foundation for the ongoing WATTC preparatory work and for the Conference itself.

a. The charge of the WATTC is to develop an integrated set of "telecommunications" regulations to which all service providers would be subject. At the end of April 1987, the Preparatory Committee for the

Conference ("PC-WATTC") completed its work in drafting a set of proposed regulations that seeks to expand the scope of the regulations. Both during the process of formulating the draft regulations, and now with the draft itself, significant controversy has surrounded the objectives and methods of the WATTC process.

b. The proposed regulations would, if adopted at WATTC-88, no longer be restricted to providers that offer services to the public; rather, all providers of services might be required to adhere to the ITU regulations. Intra-corporate users and value-added service providers are extremely concerned about the possibility that the ITU might adopt a new uniform regulatory regime when countries are, as the preceding Sections suggest, moving to liberalize value-added services.

c. At the heart of the controversy over the WATTC is the question of whether the regulations should be all-encompassing or minimalist in scope. That is, many countries believe that it is now appropriate to develop a unified set of regulations—to create a "level playing field"—for all carriers, value-added service providers, and intra-corporate users. By contrast, the U.S. and a few other countries in the process of liberalizing take the view that regulation should not be imposed if there is no perceived need for such regulation. They argue that, in the absence of a showing that regulation is required to regularize the environment, the WATTC should be reluctant to embrace a new framework. (In Nairobi, by way of illustration, the U.S. had argued that it would be premature to convene a WATTC.)

d. Moreover, the draft developed by the Preparatory Committee seeks to define, for the first time, what is "telecommunication" and a "telecommunication service". Although historically there has been an international consensus on telephony and telex services, there is none such for "telecommunication". Given the PC-WATTC proposed definition, users and service providers have several sets of concerns. First, given the flux in the international and national telecommunications environments, it may not be appropriate to adopt a definition that will, by the very nature of the ITU process, be static. Second, in light of the importance of definitions to national decisions on how to structure the telecommunications sector, there is some unease about a single, global definition.

e. Aside from their concern about the fact that the WATTC is seeking to establish a single definition, providers of value-added services believe that the definition proposed is far too broad, encompassing many services (*e.g.*, protocol conversion) that are not "telecommunication". There is a genuine fear that the provision of information or transactional services might be viewed as "telecommunication" and that administrations might therefore argue that the CCITT Recommendation prohibiting the use of leased lines to "infringe" the functions of an administration is being violated.

6. Many telecommunications administrations and carriers, however, are focusing on the growing overlap of new and traditional

services. In particular, they view functionally similar services as being offered to the public on the basis of inconsistent regulatory schemes and obligations.

    a. The more traditional PTTs are concerned with the unfairness of what appears to be a regulatory disparity between the treatment of telecommunications administrations and that of the providers of information-based, transactional, or other value-added services, which are essentially free of regulation.

    b. The thrust of many administrations before the CCITT is, therefore, to impose regulatory burdens on new services by non-carriers equivalent to those applicable to carrier-provided services. An important policy question is whether "new" services should be based on traditional legal and regulatory approaches or whether carrier-offered equivalent services can be provided under a less restrictive legal regime.

    7. In light of the significant changes in telecommunications, questions have been raised about the scope of the ITU's judisdiction and its continuing usefulness. These questions are implicitly being posed at the PC-WATTC, in negotiations for operating agreements, in bilateral trade negotiations, and in domestic national telecommunications policymaking entities. The role of the ITU may be an appropriate subject for further examination.

    a. In particular, it may be useful to examine whether the ITU can be effective as a multilateral forum for working out agreements for the provision of new value-added or enhanced services. This forum would wrestle with two aspects of establishing operating agreements: (i) the establishment of technical interfaces and operating accords, and (ii) the resolution of differences in the scope of services that can be offered in various countries.

    b. It may be necessary for the ITU to proceed on the premise that there is neither a single set of technical interfaces nor one of service definitions but that a variety of arrangements will have to be worked out over time.

F. A Process for Developing Arrangements for International Value-Added Services–Part II: A New Bilateralism

    1. Many of the new players in the international telecommunications sector view the ITU processes as too formal and too inflexible, focused to a great extent on technical matters, and incapable of developing the expertise necessary to wrestle with the regulatory issues raised by the new value-added, information, and electronic financial and transactional services. Such institutions are seen as being ponderous, largely as a result of the multiple interests that are represented, moving far too slowly to address the immediate questions presented by the new capabilities of technology, overly encumbered with political agendas, and diverted by more theoretical than real-world practical concerns. This perception may be shared by many

of the nations that are liberalizing their telecommunications sectors rapidly.

2. For both these new players and representatives of regulatory entities with liberalized policies, bilateral discussions are increasingly being thought of as the mechanism for structuring international service arrangements and for solving problems or disputes over regulatory differences or interconnection. Bilateral discussions are seen as a flexible and innovative way of establishing both general principles and resolving specific issues of disagreement or concern.

a. The international infrastructure has become much more complicated, and the various interests both more diffuse and more competitive. Administrations and private carriers are being pressed by business realities and budgetary constraints, which are being compounded by the demands of investing in costly new infrastructure technology such as broad band and satellite-based facilities. The suppliers of value-added services are threatening to compete in some sectors with the erstwhile monopolies; in the meantime, these very suppliers are themselves engaged in high-priced, risky start-up activities.

b. As noted above in Section XIII, and as explained in Section II of Chapter IV on "The Future of European Telecommunications Policy", administrations and other network providers are looking to bolster network utilization as a way of increasing revenues necessary to cope with the demands of investing in the infrastructure and social or other costs imposed on the telecommunications sector. One important way of boosting usage is to stimulate services. Thus, it is every bit in the financial interest of administrations and the providers of those new services to work together—for the sake of mutual commercial advancement—to make it possible for new international services to be interconnected and to flourish.

c. The telecommunications and related sectors are moving, therefore, from a regime characterized by government-to-government negotiation or one structured by agreements among state or private monopoly carriers. As liberalizing policies are adopted, that model is rapidly being replaced by another environment, one more typical of a business sector. In short, organizations providing telecommunications and related services are increasingly being driven by commercial and competitive concerns.

d. The more formal process of governmental-level discussions and the process of concluding operating agreements, of obtaining interconnection for services, and of developing worldwide standards on a multilateral basis was entirely appropriate for the era of monopolies. That age is now passing, however. The present transitional and future periods are, and will be, marked by competition. In other sectors, in which state monopolies do not dominate, businesses conduct their affairs bilaterally; inevitably, then, it is that model which will supplant the ITU and other more traditional mechanisms.

3. If a principal objective of administrations and regulators is stimulating usage of the network, the primary goal of bilateral discussions

should be to reach agreements to lighten the regulatory requirements imposed on facilities.

    a. The international telecommunications environment is, however, enormously complex, with its welter of inconsistent regulatory frameworks. Harmonization of national regulatory approaches will therefore certainly be difficult. Nevertheless, in order to maximize the possibilities for interconnection by new service providers, participants in a bilateral discussion should agree on a central principle: minimalism in regulation.

    b. To be more specific, one approach might borrow from an important concept implicit in the competition provisions of the Treaty of Rome. As described in Section VI of Chapter IV on European telecommunications policy, if one country imposes a set of regulations on a domestic service provider, there should be no need for a second country, in which that service provider seeks to operate, to impose a "substantially similar" set of regulations on that provider. Compliance with the regulations of the service provider's home country, in other words, should satisfy the concerns of the foreign nation, unless there were a strong national interest in subjecting that provider to a duplicative or different set of rules.

    c. Similarly, bilateral discussions over the international provision of value-added services should focus on whether and when there might be a need to impose a second, possibly inconsistent, set of regulations on the provider. If the country in which the provider is established imposes rules that satisfy the national interest of the foreign country, there should be no need to subject the provider to the rules of the foreign country, should it want to offer services there. Obviously, this approach would minimize possible unwarranted regulatory obstacles to the offering of an international value-added service—a goal that is in the interest of both network providers and the service sector.

    d. In addition to reaching general agreement on a set of principles for the establishment of value-added services, these discussions would be useful for several other reasons. Bilateral consultations could be used to exchange information. Little practical or operationally useful information flows from the multilateral institutions. One of the most critical functions of a bilateral discussion, therefore, would be to make more informal existing channels by which issues of common interest can be discussed.

    e. Perhaps most importantly, bilateral discussions should be used to resolve specific disputes over the interconnection of different types of value-added, informational, or transactional services. It would be useful to structure the discussions so that experts in financial matters, for example, would be present from both countries, as would be telecommunications officials and the party seeking to establish the service.

    4. In addition to the importance of agreeing on substantive objectives for such bilateral discussions, another key issue for resolution is establishing who should participate in them.

a. Historically, bilateral negotiations in international trade in services have been at a government-to-government level, with limited, if any, involvement by the private sector. As befits the more business-like and less rigid nature of the discussions, however, the private sector ought to participate jointly, with the assistance of public sector trade and telecommunications officials. These discussions should be held at the working level.

b. On each side of, and across, the negotiating table the business people from both the administrations and the service providers must talk with those responsible for making—and ultimately implementing—policy. Too often regulators from the telecommunications or securities sectors, for example, might be working at cross-purposes, or in isolation. These discussions should be used as an opportunity to provoke a dialogue among the various interests that would be charged with supervising the implementation of any interconnection arrangement.

c. The involvement of government officials is critical, of course, to the success of any international negotiations over regulatory policy, particularly where one or more of the parties involved may be governmental or government-affiliated entities. Trade officials should take the lead in initiating and then facilitating discourse, but the involvement of telecommunications regulators and representatives of other fields—depending on the types of services that might be at issue—would be indispensable.

d. Although telecommunications (and securities or financial) regulators may not be accustomed to bilateral, trade-like discussions, their presence is necessary for two important reasons. First, the discussions will focus on a sector or sectors where trade officials may be less experienced. During the course of the negotiations, which might become quite specific, it will be important for the trade officials to call on the expertise of the regulators into whose jurisdiction the services that are to be provided might fall.

e. Second, once the negotiations are concluded, telecommunications officials and other regulators will be charged with the task of implementing any agreement reached and overseeing adherence to its terms. If a domestic service provider believes that a foreign country is not complying with the terms of the agreement that had been reached—interconnection is being delayed unjustifiably, for example—it is important that there be available a regulator to whom complaints can be directed.

f. A very direct, hard-nosed trade approach to international negotiations cannot continue forever. At some point, objectives must be achieved—or abandoned—and regulators responsible for implementation will, of necessity, replace their peers from the ministries and departments of trade and commerce. Consequently, those regulators ought to be involved in the opening stages of the trade negotiations themselves.

5. At the outset, it appears that bilateral discussions most probably will be initiated between countries that have decided to liberalize the provision of telecommunications or value-added services. As Section

XIII explains, national approaches to telecommunications policy, though different, are converging on some key points. Thus, bilateral discussions might well be useful, both to resolve disputes among countries that otherwise might have much in common and, as a matter of precedent, to develop a set of public guidelines for other countries that may not be as far along in their review of telecommunications policies. Additional rounds of talks between the U.S. and Japan now seem possible.

a. If bilateral discussions are first undertaken between countries such as the U.S. and Japan, where liberalization is taking place, the consultations would have the strong advantage of proceeding from a certain commonality of purpose. They would permit negotiators to obtain relatively quick responses from their counterparts, to establish a framework for face-to-face discussions, and to enable negotiators to focus on a particularized set of issues. If discussions are restricted to countries with common outlooks, they would exclude other administrations that may be in the process of considering whether or how to create flexibility for the provision of value-added services.

b. Others believe that bilateral discussions will first focus on markets where a country with a more liberalized policy has the most to gain. Efforts may be made to persuade a country possessed of a more rigid framework to accommodate pressures for facilitating the interconnection of international value-added services. Discussions between the U.S. and the Federal Republic of Germany, for example, might fall into this category.

c. As a political and diplomatic matter, a wholly bilateral approach is not devoid of difficulties. If the U.S. were to conduct discussions with the U.K., there might be significant pressures applied on both parties to involve representatives from the Commission of the European Communities, at least as observers. The Commission, moreover, as noted above, is supportive of U.S.-Japan talks, provided that it, too, is able to participate in some bilateral discussions.

d. As also noted in connection with the discussion of the approach of Japan to bilateral discussions, there may also be sensitivity on the part of some administrations to the reaction of others that they are being excluded. Indeed, potentially adverse reactions by the excluded parties, especially those in the Third World, may preclude any bilateral discussions from reaching a definitive or successful conclusion.

6. Another problematic area for policymakers is how to balance the new bilateralism with developments in multilateral fora. From the standpoint of those working to implement a bilateral regime, the multilateral institutions, as is suggested above, are seen as being insufficiently responsive to their concerns.

a. The ITU is concerned with the possibility of increased levels of bilateral discussions among administrations that have adopted liberal approaches to the provision of value-added services. More particularly, of course, the ITU is unsure how agreements reached bilaterally will affect the consensus represented by CCITT meetings, regulations, and recommendations. In fact, bilateral processes may supplant the need for WATTC or other similar conferences at which the objective of global agreement is unattainable.

    b. Such bilateral discussions are, however, likely to coexist with any multilateral forum for dealing with such interconnection agreements. The question for the ITU is whether it can enhance its effectiveness in the future both by acquiescing in the inevitability of bilateral talks and by becoming a forum in which there is greater awareness of the increasingly trade-oriented nature of the international telecommunications environment.

    7. Not only must bilateral discussions take the ITU into account, and vice versa, but the new round of the General Agreement on Tariffs and Trade ("GATT") will further complicate the relationship between the various organs charged with resolving differences in approach to telecommunications policy.

    a. At this point, it is possible to make a guess, but not to do much more, with respect to what specific principles in telecommunications and services will be discussed within the GATT framework of the Uruguay round. The U.S., for example, began articulating its goals in trade in telecommunications services throughout 1986. One vehicle for doing this was the preparation of a paper for consultations between the U.S. and Israel on how the Declaration on Trade in Services of the U.S.-Israel Free Trade Area agreement would apply in the telecommunications sector. These principles are likely to include non-discrimination in the entry and provision of services, market access for enhanced services, and protection for the pricing structure and availability of leased lines.

    b. Despite the lack of certitude about what will be discussed in the new GATT round, one thing is certain: the discussions are meant to be broadly multilateral. The aim is to obtain the same kind of consensus that, as the PC-WATTC planners are coming to conclude, may well be difficult, if not impossible, to achieve in the WATTC itself. As the traditional consensus in the field of international telecommunications continues to erode, however, it may be increasingly difficult to reach a multilateral accord on substantive standards for market access for existing and new service providers. Bilateral discussions may be the only feasible way of resolving matters of dispute between the nationals of two countries.

    c. The opening of the GATT round will create a delicate problem for policymakers, who will have to decide to what extent bilateral talks can continue separately or must be folded into the multilateral discussion.

    d. Similarly, the inclusion of telecommunications trade on the agenda of the new GATT round raises questions about how to co-ordinate the GATT and CCITT mechanisms. If the implementation of value-added services, for example, is to be addressed in GATT, there may be increased pressures on the CCITT to modify or quicken the pace of its own agenda. Consequently, the vigor of policymakers in pursuing telecommunications and other services within the GATT may have an as yet unexamined impact on other specialized fora that traditionally have dealt with trade in services issues.

8. One new form of "multilateralism" might be a useful adjunct to the bilateral discussions that may increasingly come to characterize the international telecommunications sector. As discussed above, it will be critical that representatives of substantive regulatory and policy organs, along with the private sector, be present at any bilateral discussions.

a. One significant reason for having regulators from both sides participate, of course, is to have them exchange views on a particular regulatory approach. They may, for example, need to discuss how to implement changes that might be necessary to accommodate a particular would-be supplier of value-added services.

b. Outside the specific context of a bilateral discussion, however, regulators from around the world could benefit tremendously from the opportunity to exchange ideas and to harmonize approaches in a more informal process of consultation. The existing multilateral institutions represent governments—the ITU Plenipotentiary or the Intelsat Assembly of Parties—and administrations—CEPT, the Intelsat Board of Governors, and CCITT, in which the driving force is the national carriers.

c. There is no comparable organization for national regulators, however. Focusing only on the countries surveyed in this paper, these currently would include representatives from the FCC, from the CRTC, from the Japanese MPT, from Oftel, from the French CNCL, and perhaps from the Australian Department of Communications. As noted in Section XIII.B, above, however, one of the more significant global trends is the separation of operational and regulatory functions within a national administration. Thus, it is certain that the number of national officials charged with supervisory or other regulatory authority will increase dramatically over the next decade.

d. These officials have no mechanism for exchanging information about different models and approaches. Whether at a conference or in more informal working group meetings, they might usefully share perspectives on common pressures and concerns, and on how they cope with the complex mix of national forces.

e. Issues such as slowing the rise in rates for services, cross-subsidization, managing competition in services, setting conditions on the dominant carrier, and, of course, the regulatory regime for value-added and financial or transactional services could profitably be discussed outside a bilateral context and in a broader framework. Then, of course, should the time come for a particular set of bilateral discussions, the regulatory participants would already be aware of specific national positions, the array of pressures that are making it difficult to accommodate the party seeking (or refusing) interconnection, and the personalities of the individuals with whom they will be negotiating.

9. The process for developing international arrangements for value-added services should, therefore, be multidimensional. To the extent

that it is bilateral, it should be *ad hoc* and flexible. As between countries with dissimilar regulatory regimes, the discussions should be focused on achieving a consensus on general objectives as well as on specific problems. For countries with more in common, the focus should be on resolving particular complaints and disputes. There is still a critical role for multilateralism, however. By bringing together a broader group of people on a more forward-looking basis, a multilateral institution could begin to lay the groundwork for resolving the constellation of common issues and problems raised by the introduction of value-added services internationally.

CHAPTER III
TELECOMMUNICATIONS AND TRANSACTIONAL SERVICES: A CASE STUDY OF EMERGING STRUCTURAL AND REGULATORY ISSUES IN THE FINANCIAL SECTOR

TABLE OF CONTENTS

	Page
I. Overview	185
A. Growth of Electronic Transactions	185
B. Electronic Financial Services	187
II. Contours of the Market: Participants and Services	190
A. The Growing Potential for Electronic Services	191
B. Transactional and Trading Systems: Some Basic Features	195
C. Stages of Electronic Service Development	200
D. Participants in the Electronic Services Market	201
E. Examples of Electronic Financial Services	207
1. Transactional Services	208
2. Trading Services	210
a. Financial Management Systems	210
b. Inter-Exchange Links	211
c. Off-Market Systems and Automated Trading Networks	213
d. Market Support Functions	217
F. SITA: Case Example of a Developed Market System	219
III. Moving Toward International Services and Links	222
A. Introduction	222
B. Illustrative National Concerns	225
1. Introduction	225
2. Fitting Electronic Trading Systems Within the Confines of Existing Securities Market Functions	226
3. Segregating Banking and Securities Businesses	227
4. The Scope of Other Permissible Information Services Activities for U.S. Bank Holding Companies	231
5. Problems of Fitting Electronic Services Within Established Institutional Roles	233

Page

    C. The Development of Global Markets 237
        1. Introduction 237
        2. International Trading in Europe 241
        3. Multi-Exchange Pricing Information 242
        4. Multi-Exchange Execution Systems 245
        5. Settlement and Clearance Systems 250
    D. Additional Issues of Concern Among Financial Services
        Regulators 252
    E. The Impact of International Telecommunications Policies ... 259
        1. Introduction 259
        2. The D-Series Recommendations 259
    F. Summary 263

IV. Redefining the Relationship Between Telecommunications and
     Electronic Markets 265

CHAPTER III
TELECOMMUNICATIONS AND TRANSACTIONAL SERVICES: A CASE STUDY OF EMERGING STRUCTURAL AND REGULATORY ISSUES IN THE FINANCIAL SECTOR

I. OVERVIEW

A. Growth of Electronic Transactions

1. Businesses are increasingly using telecommunications services to complete a wide variety of transactions. Transmission, switching, and processing networks provide the capability to carry out transactions within a single business or among offices or affiliates of a large corporation. Such facilities are also increasingly being used to link closely related members of a particular industry and affiliated businesses in different or related sectors that are bound together by common "transactional ties". Through these innovative systems, new and more convenient services can be offered.

2. These electronic networks are intended to increase the efficiency of transactions by reducing the amount of time and the number of independent steps it takes to complete, verify, and settle a transaction. Through electronic systems, transactions are integrated with the payment and record-keeping activities that necessarily accompany—and support—them. The same information that is carried over a network to trigger a transaction can serve to initiate payment, verification, and settlement procedures.

3. Because electronic records, rather than paper exchanges, can be used to effect a transaction, the various parts of a deal can be streamlined and simplified. Transactional networks among industry participants can be used to track individual deals and compile aggregate transactional figures; these compilations can then serve as the basis for a periodic netting of disparate positions. As a result, each transaction need not be followed by complex settlement procedures; settlement can be postponed and carried out on a net basis.

4. The development of transactional networks and systems raises many complex legal and regulatory issues. As electronic services

permit participants to alter their relationships, their business practices, or the products that they buy and sell, existing legal norms necessarily will become outdated. As one would expect, technology quickly outstrips the capability of any legal system to adapt to change; therefore, a disjunction between the market structure envisioned by lawmakers and the one actually in existence is inevitable. Because no legal system can ever hope to catch up, the challenge faced by lawmakers and policymakers is to search for a more flexible framework that will not allow laws and regulations to frustrate adaptation and change within markets.

5. As markets and business relationships become increasingly international in scope, individual nations with less flexible legal environments face the risk that businesses will gravitate toward markets with more flexible—and accommodating—systems.

6. Electronic market services present a challenge—and an opportunity—for the telecommunications industry.

a. The challenge is to adapt telecommunications facilities and services to fit the demands of particular industry structures. The contours of electronic markets necessarily will be dictated by the business practices—and the legal structures—of each industry sector. If carriers and service providers attempt to force businesses to configure their systems to fit the shape of existing telecommunications services and practices, the potential for collaboration between the communications and the non-communications sectors will be reduced. The business community has made it clear that electronic networks that are designed to function as the circulatory systems of individual companies or entire market sectors must be subject to the control and supervision of the businesses being served.

b. There is a clear opportunity for telecommunications providers. As electronic networks over which transactions can be conducted develop, the demand for telecommunication facilities and services should increase dramatically.

c. However, carriers, service providers, and telecommunications regulators may have to alter their perspectives on the telecommunications business. They may have to view the telecommunications industry less as a separate sector and more as an input into, or a "factor of production" for, other businesses. The maintenance of rigid controls over the use of communications facilities and services almost certainly will slow the growth of transactional systems, which ultimately will harm both the telecommunications industry and the businesses that are increasingly dependent on telecommunications.

7. The subject of electronic transactional systems is, of course, a vast one. It is far beyond the scope of any one paper. Consequently, this paper focuses on electronic systems in the financial services industry, in which there has been a growing dependence on telecommunications. By focusing on a single market sector—albeit a broad and active one—it is hoped that some of the trends in the development of electronic services and some of the obstacles to their emergence can be highlighted.

B. Electronic Financial Services

1. Financial institutions are rapidly increasing their use of telecommunications services, to streamline their internal operations, to expand their trading activities, and to improve service to their customers. As the telecommunications and financial services businesses develop increasingly close alliances, new market opportunities—and threats—are emerging within each service sector.

   a. The growing demand in the financial services sector for high-speed transmission capabilities and sophisticated value-added services presents telecommunications carriers and service providers with an expanding range of market opportunities. It also generates pressures for the creation of elaborate linkages among national and international networks—including connection among private networks and between private and public networks—that often conflict with national and international circuit-use policies.

   b. The linkage of markets and of market participants made possible by telecommunications networks is creating more liquid and more extensive trading centers. It is also supporting the introduction of new market relationships and new financial products. At the same time, these increasingly interconnected networks are exerting pressures on once distinct institutions and markets: regional exchanges are being brought into the stream of national trading, national exchanges are being subjected to global market pressures, and often legally segregated banking and securities operations are being forced to grapple with increasingly competitive relationships.

   c. The pace of change in both markets is particularly rapid because the telecommunications and the financial services sectors are being generally deregulated—at both the national and the international levels. Deregulation has encouraged and accommodated new developments within the individual market sectors, although there still are many obstacles to the development of products and services envisioned by members of both industries.

2. The blending of telecommunications and financial services also presents a series of new "cross-sectoral" concerns. Lawmakers and regulators in the telecommunications and financial services fields historically have operated in relative isolation from each other. The integration of telecommunications and financial services products is straining traditional regulatory practices in both sectors. A significant question is whether outmoded legal and regulatory schemes will significantly impede this process of integration.

   a. The combination of telecommunications and financial services businesses changes the boundary lines of the industries. For example, when a bank offers an on-line transactional service to its customers, there may be some debate as to whether it is providing a regulated banking service, a telecommunications service that might be regulated (depending on the jurisdiction in which it is offered), an unregulated information processing service, or some hybrid service that has never been the subject of regulation.

    b.   Integration of the industries also results in the creation of new entities that may fit only awkwardly within existing legal and regulatory structures. For example, a telecommunications carrier which operates a processing center that serves as the focal point for a bond-trading network might be a regulated carrier, a regulated or unregulated value-added service provider, a regulated securities exchange or other transactional market, or some unidentified new entity.

3.   This paper focuses on some of the difficult issues presented by the integration of financial and telecommunications services.

    a.   For example, communications networks used to offer financial services should perhaps not be considered to be offering "communications" services. In the case of remote access data processing, for example, it is generally accepted that the use by a data processor's customers of leased lines does not involve the data processor in the business of reselling leased circuits; those circuits are viewed as necessary components of a non-communications business activity. The same point could be made regarding the use of leased lines as part of an electronic market that permits on-line trading of securities or commercial paper. The primary purpose for the use of the lines is the offering of a financial market service, not the resale of communications facilities or services.

    b.   Such a revisionist view of electronic network activities might encourage various telecommunications service providers to conclude that national and international restrictions on the resale and sharing of leased lines should not be applied to evolving financial services.

    i)   At the international level, for example, the process of aggregating buyers and sellers electronically is likely to require the interconnection of separate private networks operated by an array of multinational companies. To connect the maximum number of buyers and sellers into new electronic markets as a way of promoting the effectiveness of those markets, the networks must be accessible through the public switched network—usually at both ends of the leased lines. Such configurations, however, might be viewed by some national administrations as being inconsistent with the D-Series Recommendations of the Consultative Committee on International Telegraph and Telephone (the "CCITT") regarding the use of international leased circuits. For example, access to private networks via the public switched network is discouraged, in part, because such access permits users to bypass international public switched long-distance circuits.

    ii)   If these activities are not viewed as circuit resale or are considered to be outside the scope of "communications" services generally, regulatory restrictions applicable to communications circuit resale would be inapplicable.

c. At the national level, the services also raise a variety of traditional communications policy issues:

i) Under the terms of the value-added services license in the United Kingdom, are transactional services properly classified as value-added communications offerings?

ii) Should prohibitions on rate discrimination applicable to carriers be applied to electronic financial networks that are not intended to provide communications services to the public?

iii) Is it appropriate to apply standards developed for the purpose of promoting national networking policies to financial service networks that integrate the interests of banking and securities industry participants that are expert in and have primary responsibility for the development of operational procedures for their own industries?

iv) In the emerging regulatory setting in France, should electronic financial services be viewed as private or as value-added networks? Should the distinction between a private and a value-added network focus on the fact that a third party might use the service or that the primary purpose of circuit use is to conduct a business activity unrelated to communications?

v) Under the Japanese regulatory scheme, which adopts a very liberal approach toward the regulation of Type II activities, it is not significant whether a provider of an electronic network service is treated as a Type II entity or simply is not considered to be involved in offering telecommunications services subject to regulation. The national classification may, however, have substantial significance for a financial service that is to be offered internationally.

4. Regulators of the banking and securities markets will face similarly difficult issues of market access and structure.

a. Officials at the Ministry of Finance (the "MOF") in Japan, for example, were reluctant initially to allow Reuters to market its dealing service due to the potential impact of the service on Japanese brokers.

b. New electronic systems pose potentially serious challenges to stock exchanges or brokers. Electronic networks allow stocks and other financial instruments to be traded directly: markets can be decentralized, involving disparate participants linked electronically. Individual holders of large portfolios can periodically review price data, compare respective desires to buy or sell particular securities, and effect transactions directly. New electronic systems also permit a wider array of players to be involved in marketing securities and other financial instruments directly, in competition with existing brokerage and banking structures.

c. These systems can be both a threat to, and an opportunity for, existing markets and exchanges. The development of electronic trading capabilities—particularly for international trading—could be used by large financial institutions to expand the scope of off-exchange dealings and diminish the need for and usefulness of national exchanges. At the same time, exchanges might use electronic links as a way of establishing sophisticated multi-market trading systems that might include institutional systems, through a series of gateway links, or that might attract off-market traders back into organized markets.

    d. The degree of integration that will be permitted, both nationally and internationally, will depend in part on the extent to which technological linkages are accompanied by legal and regulatory changes that allow markets and institutions to function in flexible and harmonious ways.

  5. The pressures of changing market structures are certain to produce legal and regulatory changes. A question is how these changes will fit with the needs of emerging markets.

    a. Regulatory schemes have evolved in a number of countries to meet the needs of new market conditions. For example, several years ago specialized private network configurations were viewed as anomalous. In one case, however, arrangements were made to accommodate the diverse communications requirements of the airline industry. Over time, those arrangements have been modified to permit the network to become a transactional system both for the airlines themselves and for the various transactional needs of their passengers.

    b. This airline system, which has developed broadly and provides a good example of the potential for electronic linkages to meet the intertwined needs of related sectoral businesses, is discussed below, even though it is not part of the financial services industry. The discussion illustrates some of the possibilities of using telecommunications capabilities to meet specialized business needs.

    c. Regulatory "accommodations" are not always optimal, however. For example, another specialized network was developed for the banking sector; but a different set of tariff arrangements was adopted under the D.6 Recommendation of the CCITT. Leased circuits were made available, but charges were imposed on a usage-sensitive, rather than a flat-rate, basis. This pricing scheme has caused other potential international network operators to avoid the "shelter" of D.6 at virtually all costs.

  6. This paper is intended to provide an initial and very broad examination of an extremely complex topic. It is not a comprehensive compilation of the myriad legal and regulatory issues that will have to be faced as electronic financial networks are developed. The discussion that follows attempts, instead, to provide a general description and analysis of some of the major trends in the development of, and the possible future directions for, electronic transactional systems.

II. CONTOURS OF THE MARKET: PARTICIPANTS AND SERVICES

To assess the need for evolution in both national and international telecommunications policies—to permit greater exploitation of telecommunications by financial markets and institutions—it is necessary to assess the pressures and the trends in financial markets that are generating the demand for electronic services. Sections II and III of this paper are intended to describe generally the changing contours of financial markets and the pressures producing the demand for telecommunications services. Section II serves more as an overview of the financial services market. Section III focuses specifically on issues raised at the international level as national markets and institutions seek greater transborder integration or linkage.

A. The Growing Potential for Electronic Services

1. The growing use of and dependence on telecommunications by the financial services industry result from a variety of market developments.

a. In part, the liberalization of rules in many national financial markets has encouraged financial institutions to seek new opportunities and to provide new products. Telecommunications services, which permit the formation of sophisticated networks, the offering of distributed processing and transactional capabilities to customers on a twenty-four hour basis, and the accumulation of vast amounts of market information from different sources, have encouraged financial institutions to respond creatively—and often aggressively—to the new market opportunities.

b. The introduction of electronic transactional systems into the financial services industry has also come in response to customer demand. Capital markets have taken on a global scale: investment capital is being raised from sources around the world, and investments by a company based in one country are becoming more dispersed throughout the world's financial centers. Bankers and brokers thus require current (and constant) information on conditions in foreign capital markets. Corporate money managers also need more timely global financial information to manage diversified worldwide investment portfolios and to guard against the risk that delays in the receipt of information could have severe foreign-exchange or arbitrage consequences.

c. With the gradual increase in the foreign listing of stocks and the multi-market offering of various debt instruments, brokers and dealers have had to seek the ability to track conditions on various exchanges and in numerous capital markets and to trade in any one of a number of locations. Banks and other financial institutions, dissatisfied with regulatory and technological limits to international trading on many of the world's organized exchanges, have set up sophisticated dealing rooms that permit them to deal directly in a wide variety of financial instruments throughout the world.

d. To keep pace with increased trading, national settlement and clearing systems have had to move toward automation and, in some cases, electronic interconnection to foster the early stages of multinational settlement and clearance processes. The "back room" activities of institutional dealing rooms have been particularly pressured by the activity of traders; the move from paper records to electronic records has been a necessary part of the development of these sophisticated trading operations.

2. Changes in market practices, such as the increased ability of large corporations to obtain money directly from capital markets through the issuance of commercial paper and the development of new financial instruments that require the aggregation of buyers and sellers to produce a market in which trading can occur, have forced financial institutions to rethink their roles and to concentrate on responding to user demands for new kinds of products and services.

a. The growth of the commercial paper market, which permits corporations to raise funds directly rather than through a bank, has forced banks to shift their attention from the business of making loans to the business of "facilitating deals".

b. The banks have been able to develop a role in this transactional business owing to information to which they have historically had access and to their involvement in the settlements process, which is needed to complete transactions.

3. In some cases, improved telecommunications capabilities breed the development of new financial instruments because they give investors and traders the ability to compare different flows of information. Opportunities for arbitrage are produced, for example, by differentials between interest-rate quotations and stock-market indices. As a result of this trend, those institutions that collect and collate various data streams and provide access to the information in a raw form that can be processed by the powerful computers of a financial institution possess the building blocks of new financial markets.

4. As new financial markets evolve as the result of changing national and regional economic conditions, the movement away from focusing all trading activity on the floors of organized exchanges is likely to intensify. Such new markets may provide further business opportunities for institutional dealing rooms, representing new links in a growing electronic financial services network. Alternatively, the development of new organized markets or exchanges can intensify the pressures on information reporting systems and settlement and clearance processes to use telecommunications services.

a. As financial activity spreads out to a greater number of points, telecommunications becomes a key part of any effort to provide financial institutions with comprehensive and timely information from disparate markets or with instantaneous dealing capability requiring the support of automated and integrated settlement and clearing systems.

b. In France, for example, the government has taken steps to develop new markets for investment, such as the futures exchange—the MATIF (Marché à Terme d'Instruments Financiers). Other financial market innovations include the SICAV, a share investment arrangement, and the *certificat d'investissement*, which is intended to encourage private shareholding in state-controlled companies.

5. The larger exchanges are wary about these developments because they produce competitive pressures on existing commission rates and trading practices. Officials at the London Stock Exchange, for example, at one time had advocated rules that would have had the result of limiting the immediate competitive potential of off-market trading systems expected to develop in the wake of Big Bang. In the United States in mid-1986, the Securities and Exchange Commission (the "SEC") gave its staff authority to develop a comprehensive regulatory approach to off-market trading systems. The staff, in making its proposal, suggested that such regulation was necessary to create a more "level playing field" for exchanges and off-market systems. A question is whether the staff can fulfill its promise to devise a regulatory scheme that will achieve this purpose without frustrating innovation.

6. In addition to the potential challenge of new off-market systems, the exchanges face competition among themselves as electronic extensions of their trading activities beyond the boundaries of established markets place these historically separate trading floors in competition with each other. Deregulation in one market—in London, for example—could have far-reaching implications for other exchanges if brokers and dealers effecting transactions in foreign stocks increasingly are able to use electronic systems to move their business to a foreign exchange with more liberal trading rules.

7. The internationalization of national financial markets is similar, in this respect, to the export of liberalized telecommunications regimes. Financial market links, like international communications facilities, make it difficult to keep national developments within national borders. Financial market liberalization within one country may exert pressures on neighboring countries to adopt similar liberalizing measures as a way of remaining competitive as centers of financial activity. Telecommunications links between markets may increase the ability of users to "bypass" restrictive financial centers, thereby emphasizing the interrelationship of national markets.

a. Big Bang in London has been characterized as that city's bid to capture a significant amount of international market activity and to revitalize U.K. firms so that they can compete aggressively in the complex new international capital markets. As the London Stock Exchange opens its doors to foreign trading houses and to increased competition among brokerage businesses, and as a web of participants explore new electronic systems that are expected to increase the efficiency and scope of trading activities in London, the potential for national changes to have broad effects on other major global financial centers is substantial.

b. In France also, steps are being taken to respond to market liberalization and the trend toward global trading. The trading hours of the Bourse are being expanded to add a morning session. In addition, new technology may produce shifts in the role of *agents de change*, causing new patterns in trading that will focus on matching orders to buy and sell, rather than simply on finding the best available price for a sale. An additional result of various policy shifts will be to provide banks and agents with greater flexibility to set up independent market-making mechanisms on an off-exchange basis. Historically in France strict regulations have prevented these potential market-makers from taking substantial positions in securities; as a result, a broker in London is currently the only true market-maker in French securities. This broker has received business even though securities traded in this manner often had to be traded at a premium price. Overall, the changes may result in significant consolidations and a broad restructuring of the Paris stock exchange.

    c. This trend toward competition among exchanges, and the simultaneous effort to ease traditional regulatory restrictions on trading, concerns securities regulators in the United States, who often have maintained tighter control over trading activities than have their European counterparts. To the extent that the capital formation process becomes more mobile, however, it will be increasingly difficult to maintain strict national regulatory practices in isolation from international influences. In this respect, securities regulators in the U.S. view the effects of international competition in the financial markets with some of the same skepticism that European telecommunications regulators—as advocates of stricter regulatory practices in the telecommunications field—have viewed telecommunications deregulation in the United States.

    8. Having observed these market developments, one keen French commentator has identified two important results of the widespread movement toward electronic transactions and the automation of markets. He has pointed to the "marchéization" of data networks that use international circuits and has noted the tendency toward the dematerialization of transactions, as the allocation and transfer of funds increasingly have been accomplished by organizing and managing a flow of information stored as electronic pulses. N. Dinçbudak, *Contribution au Colloque sur la Monétique* 9–11 (1986).

    9. Continued change in financial markets is likely to increase the pressures on telecommunications carriers and service providers to devote their attention to developing value-added services that can be provided in conjunction with, or under contract to, a financial institution. Such a "grafting" of telecommunications functions onto the activities of financial institutions and markets highlights the degree to which telecommunications facilities and services may, in particular instances, be considered more as adjuncts to an industry sector than as components of a separately regulated and necessarily distinct activity known as telecommunications.

    a. The substantive expertise about the needs of, and successful strategies for, competing in a particular industry are not part of the assets of a carrier. Thus, the development of more generic value-added communications services and networks, which can be used by industry participants to provide electronic services being developed by them, appears to be the area of growth that is most attractive to carriers.

        b. High capacity systems using cost-efficient technologies, the structuring of gateways, and the development of protocol conversion capabilities that will maximize the number and variety of potential users are products that financial institutions are seeking from carriers in their efforts to offer evolving services.

    10. The trend in the relationship between the financial services and the telecommunications industry is to integrate telecommunications capabilities into the structures of the financial markets, rather than to configure financial markets in ways that correspond to the layout of transmission and switching networks. Financial markets have changed in response to market demands, the satisfaction of which has been made possible by the use of telecommunications capabilities; financial markets have not changed due to some abstract desire to align market structures with the emerging contours of communications networks. This trend may suggest the path down which telecommunications regulators (and providers) should be walking if their goal is to promote the use of the telecommunications infrastructure.

B. Transactional and Trading Systems: Some Basic Features

    1. Electronic services in the financial market can be separated into two broad categories.

        a. The first consists of banking and related services that provide users with specific transactional capabilities, such as the ability to make deposits and withdrawals, point-of-sale debiting, credit card verification, and account management. These services can range from single home electronic banking networks or automated teller machines ("ATMs"), which are designed principally for consumers, to more complex electronic banking systems and information/transactional networks that fill the needs of business customers.

        b. The second category consists of trading services and centers on market and exchange functions, including price and quote systems, execution and dealing networks, and clearance and settlement functions. These services are designed principally for financial institutions and industry participants, and they can be used both in conjunction with established trading mechanisms, such as formal exchanges or organized off-exchange networks, and to connect market participants with each other so that direct dealing in financial instruments is possible outside any formal market setting.

    2. These services are likely to develop along somewhat different paths because they will serve very different customer bases.

        a. Trading services are intended solely for sophisticated business users and industry specialists, such as brokers and dealers. Thus, they are being and will continue to be developed to respond to broad trends in the business community, including industry's need for access to various capital markets, the need of financial institutions to enter into more aggressive trading and dealing functions on an international scale, and the need of established exchanges to automate their operations and consider inter-exchange linkages as a way of reacting to the pressures of the increasingly integrated global market.

    b. Transactional services, which will appeal to both business and consumer users, will evolve more in line with the perceived and actual needs of small business users and individual consumers. To a certain extent, the demands of these groups will have to be aggregated and weighed by service providers. For example, consumers may exert significant influence on the characteristics of point-of-sale, ATM, and home banking services, although the demands of merchants and other small business users are likely to be important, particularly where these users will be the most profitable group of users for a particular service. Many of the features already available on home banking networks in the United States demonstrate the attentiveness of banks to the demands of small business users, who want more than simple (and relatively unprofitable) consumer banking features.

    c. For services such as ATMs that are specifically intended to appeal to a consumer market, technology, rather than demand, may play a more important role in guiding at least the early development of new services. As is generally true in the consumer products and services market, there is a fringe group of customers seeking "cutting-edge" services that exploit the advantages of new technology; however, this "adventurous" group tends to be rather small. Financial institutions, however, may look to these new services as a way of developing a distinctive market identity that could generate institutional loyalty among consumers (e.g., a particular bank might become associated with consumer convenience owing to its rapid and widespread use of home banking services and ATMs).

    d. Developments in the consumer market will also tend to focus on particularly local service configurations, reflecting primarily two factors: (*i*) because most individuals obtain services from a defined community area, they will require electronic financial services within that area and (*ii*) a major selling point of these consumer services is convenience, which requires a reduction in the travel time required for customers to reach a financial institution (either with at-home services or neighborhood "electronic offices"). There will, however, be national and international extensions of these consumer services; however, much of the early attention to transborder networking is likely to focus on the business community.

    3. There are many complex factors that will control the extent to which electronic financial services can develop outside of national market structures. To the extent that such services seek to connect heavily regulated national activities in markets where the regulations are significantly different, many obstacles will exist. Telecommunications policies that are applied to restrict the ability of service providers to create multinational

networks capable of serving a broad spectrum of end users will slow the development of these services.

    a. Trading services, for example, will develop on a multinational basis at different paces. Systems that are not tied to existing national exchanges are already operating, whereas systems designed to link national or regional exchanges are developing slowly. Such organized exchanges are characterized by elaborate sets of disparate national regulations and customs, and because some degree of harmonization or some willingness to operate in à more flexible manner is a prerequisite to the successful linkage of organized national and regional trading markets, trading services that link the exchanges face many obstacles.

    b. Credit card verification systems, which serve the interests of both consumer and business users, have already begun to develop internationally.

    c. International ATM networks will be relatively slow to develop, not due to a lack of demand on the part of the consumers whom these services would benefit, but due to the elaborate and differing national regulations that are applicable to retail banking operations.

    d. The development of multinational ATM networks illustrates some of the regulatory obstacles to the development of transborder transactional systems. A number of European-based credit and cash cards can be used anywhere within the European Community. The European Commission has taken a keen interest in exploring how a network of ATM terminals can be established to permit the use of national credit cards on a transborder basis. Establishing such a network of terminals could run into conflict with telecommunications policies.

    i) Unless the cards themselves can be fully standardized, the terminals will have to be capable of dealing with a number of different protocols and coding systems. In this event, the multinational use of transaction cards will involve an ATM network in which different companies will be using the same machines, on a sharing basis; the shared network could involve the use of a series of central switches to route data from the shared machines onto the separate private line networks of individual credit card companies. This network also might involve verification of the credit information through an interconnected, but unaffiliated, third-party clearing organization. In fact, the entire network might be run by a distinct operating entity; in some cases, that entity may be a co-operative venture of participating financial institutions; in other cases, it may be an unaffiliated third party.

    ii) The liberal telecommunications environment in the U.S. has fostered the growth of such shared networks within national borders; in fact, banking regulations that restrict branching proved a far greater obstacle to the development of these networks in the U.S. in the early stages. In Europe, however, these shared networks are only now beginning to emerge. As the networks develop, they will exert pressure on PTTs that want to leave intact restrictions on the shared use or resale of circuits. If efforts to liberalize access to leased lines focus on the application of new volume-sensitive tariffs to the lines, the pace at which these networks are introduced could be slowed significantly.

iii) In addition, regulatory conflicts between the telecommunications and financial services industries could hamper the growth of these networks. Telecommunications policies that may favor the use of a co-operatively-owned association to provide a shared ATM network may conflict with banking rules regarding permissible branching or banking activities.

4. A feature of emerging services that is common to both trading and transactional services is that they can reduce the expense, delay, and inaccuracy of paper transactions. The need to accept customer payments on a contingent basis, pending verification of available funds, is decreased as a result of the ability to conduct on-line verifications or to complete electronic funds transfers instantaneously; this result will reduce a financial institution's exposure to bad debt losses or other uncollectable commitments.

a. The dematerialization of transactions made possible by electronic services can be particularly useful for trading activities, because it replaces stock certificates or other paper evidences of ownership with a system of record entries. This process can simplify settlement procedures, thereby clearing the way for more rapid and constant transactions.

b. Dematerialization also has its dangers, because it makes transactional and payment systems dependent on electronic networks that could fail and that could camouflage fraudulent activities. In addition to being vulnerable to system failure, these electronic networks often do not produce a "paper trail" or some other form of tangible evidence of possession; as a result, disputes can be more difficult to resolve.

c. The consequences of failure of a central transactional system have become an acute concern as these systems have enabled high-volume, high-speed operations to develop which are completely dependent on computer and telecommunications links.

i) In November 1985, for example, a computer problem at the Bank of New York prevented that institution from settling transactions, forcing it into an overdraft position of nearly $30 billion by the end of a single day. The bank had to obtain an overnight bridging loan in excess of $23 billion from the Federal Reserve, which cost the bank almost $5 million, or approximately 7 per cent of its earnings for the first nine months of 1985. The software bug that caused the bank's one-day near-disaster also damaged its database and made subsequent account information recovery efforts more difficult.

ii) Financial institutions are concerned about "hackers", who might use their own computers to gain unauthorized access to an electronic transactional network and possibly wreak havoc with the database. Thus, financial institutions typically have installed elaborate encryption and security systems to protect against unauthorized uses.

However, programmers are capable of creating chaos in a transactional system by inserting intentional latent errors or by leaving themselves a way of gaining access to the system without going through the proper channels.

iii) More than hackers, financial institutions are concerned about system errors, user errors, losses of confidentiality, and system failures. A recent report by a major accounting firm found that within 30 U.S. financial institutions, there were 559 instances of potential exposure to loss caused by computer activities. Of these, 206 were considered potential causes of "material financial loss", and an additional 264 were viewed as possible sources of "substantial financial loss". The errors involved can be as simple as the one that brought the London Exchange's new on-line system to a halt on the first day after Big Bang: system designers simply underestimated the demand for the computer's services.

iv) Tracking down errors (and, of course, frauds that are deliberately concealed) involves costly and time-consuming auditing activities that must reconstruct what is often a complex web of electronic steps. System failures, caused by both hardware and software problems, as well as by a loss of electric power, are of even greater concern. As the Bank of New York incident demonstrated, an interruption of service can prove extremely costly. In addition, some observers have predicted that a more lengthy system failure could have irreversible consequences: the system might never be able to catch up on backlogged transactions, and market participants would lose confidence in the settlement process.

v) As a result, major clearinghouses in the United States, for example, have constructed elaborate back-up systems that are designed to be able to take over if the primary transactional system fails. In 1988, CHIPS, discussed below in Section II.E.2, plans to move from a back-up operation to an on-line standby system; the standby system will receive all data that the primary system receives and, in the case of a primary system failure, would be ready to go into operation immediately. A representative of the Federal Reserve Bank of New York stressed the need for such back-up systems in 1985, telling a congressional hearing that few banks could recover from a major computer failure within 24 hours.

d. Speed of execution made possible by electronic systems can be a two-edged sword. Although it has helped new markets to develop and has made possible the offering of new financial instruments and services, it has introduced an element of fluidity into the transactional network that, if not carefully controlled, could lead to a disastrous result.

i) Increasingly active markets have required that payment systems function essentially as credit systems, with bank participants building daylight overdrafts that are settled at the close of each business day. The Federal Reserve Bank of New York estimates that such overdrafts amount to as much as $75 billion each day. Unless an electronic system has appropriate controls to guard against the use of excessive credit by a single institution, there is a risk that a system participant will be unable to settle its transactions at the end of the day. Due to the speed with which transactions can be conducted electronically, the credit exposure of a system participant can grow quickly and get out of hand before the potential problem is identified—in the absence of proper controls.

ii) Banking regulators and clearing institutions in the United States have said that the failure of a single bank to settle could set off a chain reaction that could produce a system-wide failure. As a result, regulators are exploring "caps" on credit allowances and changes in settlement procedures as ways of guarding against the possibility of systemic failure.

C. Stages of Electronic Service Development

1. The development of electronic financial services can be divided into four stages, beginning with the offering to third parties by a financial institution of services previously used by it for internal purposes, such as data processing and various information management activities, including account balances and activity, and culminating with the provision of sophisticated financial management systems that offer information from a wide variety of sources on a real-time basis and permit users to complete transactions through the system.

2. In stage one, financial institutions provide information services, merely transmitting electronically information that had been available on paper (*e.g.*, account balances, interest rates on various instruments, stock prices, and other security price quotes).

3. In stage two, information services are coupled with transaction initiation capabilities, often from a " dumb" terminal. Electronic funds transfers (including ATMs) are part of this level of service, which also includes home banking and shopping and point-of-sale services.

4. The move to a fully interactive transactional system represents the third stage of development. In this type of system, a sophisticated communications system is required to link various "smart" terminals for the purpose of executing and completing such transactions as the issuance of a letter of credit or the making of various investment decisions.

5. Stage four involves the enhancement of a stage three electronic system. The fully interactive system is upgraded by the addition of real-time information capabilities so that corporate money managers and other investment decisionmakers can move funds and make investments on the basis of up-to-the-minute information from as wide a variety of sources as possible. The "goal" of such a system is the creation of a unified global market in which location, time differences, and currency differences would not represent barriers to immediate participation in any capital market. A significant obstacle to this stage of development is the lack of real-time information from most sources. Many transactions still require lag time, particularly to complete the settlements process.

6. The U.S. banks are currently further along in the development of stage four type services, which require real-time capabilities, due to the demand for their participation in the global trading market. Because the U.S. dollar continues to be the predominant currency for international trading, settlement through the New York Bank Clearinghouse, which requires participants to obtain the services of a U.S. bank, has focused substantial customer attention on the U.S. bank market. These customers have sought the capability to have continued access to updated information, and the U.S. banks, in competition for this lucrative business, have begun to respond.

7. European resistance to this real-time information developed partially out of a view that it would permit customers to maintain zero-balance accounts, which would reduce the profitability of account maintenance by banks. However, customers have demanded the ability to move funds instantaneously and have reacted to the resistance of some banks by taking their business elsewhere. Customer pressure, therefore, is forcing European banks to move in this direction.

8. Exchanges are in the relatively early stages of development with respect to systems designed to provide inter-exchange links. As discussed more fully in Section III below, the difficulties of co-ordinating disparate national pricing, trading, settlement, and clearance schemes—as well as various rules relating to the eligibility of entities to participate in exchange activities and of particular financial instruments to be traded on exchanges—stand in the way of the creation of more advanced services. Even within the United States, the disparity of rules from one exchange to the next makes exchange linkage a slow and tedious business.

D. Participants in the Electronic Services Market

1. Electronic services in financial markets involve a number of participating entities, which can be classified broadly as follows:

   a. *Banks.* As the repositories of vast amounts of financial information and the institutions that historically have had access to the settlements process, banks are well positioned to serve as the providers of new electronic services. The development of internal data and information processing systems for external use has provided banks with a starting point for new service offerings. The ability of businesses to raise capital directly, rather than to require bank loans, also provides banks with an incentive to seek new market roles that may involve the use of telecommunications capabilities.

   b. *Telecommunications Companies.* Telecommunications companies can benefit from the developing electronic service market by devising and offering high-capacity transmission and switching systems that can be used by banks, exchanges, large corporations, and other financial institutions seeking to offer or to create such new electronic market services.

In some cases, a carrier or other service provider may be able to function as a system operator or may participate in a joint venture in which it will contribute the technological expertise. Concerns about security and the management of sensitive financial data may cause certain financial institutions to resist contracting network operations out to a carrier, in which case the carrier's task will be to supply raw transmission capacity and possibly certain support software.

   c. *Exchanges.* Electronic systems enable exchanges to process their transactions more quickly and efficiently, allowing them to handle a larger daily volume of trades. Although banks and other financial institutions may use electronic services to establish direct trading links in the international market as a way of bypassing the limited scope of trading on any particular exchange, exchanges can use electronic services to combat the movement of traders away from established trading floors. Inter-exchange links might be a catalyst for the development of multinational trading schemes built upon the structures of organized exchanges. Such links can also be used to permit traders on one exchange to take advantage of trading conditions in a particular stock or commodity on another exchange. Securities, commodities, options, currencies, or futures not listed on a specific exchange could also be made available on the floor of that exchange through an inter-exchange link. Of course, the development of electronic trading networks also holds the potential to divert substantial amounts of trading activity off exchange floors and onto wholly electronic networks, making these services both a threat and an opportunity for exchanges.

   d. *Brokers and Dealers.* In response to customer demands for access to global markets so that the price of a particular stock or other financial instrument can be compared in a number of locations, brokers and dealers have sought increased availability of worldwide trading information. Direct dealing over complex international electronic networks has evolved to create vigorous trading systems outside the workings of organized exchanges or other marketplaces. The availability of electronic networks has also generated additional demands; arbitrage markets develop owing to the ability of certain traders to gain access to information about the price or availability of a particular item in different markets. As market linkages grow and as the dissemination of information to all participants becomes more equal, these markets will diminish; until then, however, the unequal distribution of electronic quotation and trading capabilities will foster market activity.

   e. *Information Companies.* A logical extension of the business of any company that has amassed vast databases—possibly as part of a publishing business—is to make that information available on line, on a real-time basis. In certain instances, financial institutions such as brokerage houses or banks may be acting as providers of financial information, rather than as transactional agents. The addition of computer processing capabilities that permit manipulation or analysis of data is a valuable addition to the raw database. Transactional capability, which typically will require the participation of some financial institution, may provide the system with the greatest flexibility (and the most demand).

  f. *Settlement and Clearance Systems.* Transactional systems require the participation of entities capable of providing clearance and settlement services; as markets have moved away from the practice of actually attempting to transfer paper certificates among buyers and sellers, particularly in international transactions, depositary institutions have become necessary. At the national level, all these functions have been or are being computerized, to permit them to handle the increased volume of trading that now typically occurs in national securities markets. The linkage of national clearing, settlement, and depositary systems through telecommunications networks stands as a major prerequisite to the emergence of integrated multinational market systems. Unless transborder transactions can be settled and cleared in a rapid and efficient manner, international markets will be unable to operate. Such linkages involve numerous obstacles, however, due to disparate national rules about membership and participation in particular systems and the ability of systems to handle currency exchanges and to accept particular forms of settlement. The development of these systems will be essential parts of the movement toward a paperless transactional market.

 2. As electronic services develop, these entities increasingly are able to perform new functions and possibly to operate in newly competitive ways.

  a. Banks already are moving into some of the business areas historically occupied by securities brokers and dealers.

  b. Brokers and dealers, in co-operation with each other, are able to perform some or all of the functions of an exchange.

  c. Information publishers are increasingly able to act like investment advisers—subject to concerns about regulation of such advisers under federal laws in the United States—or like financial institutions—providing information about stocks, bonds, options, commodities, and various commercial instruments that historically would have been provided by a banker, broker, or other financial adviser.

  d. Corporations, through the acquisition of a bank or other financial institution, may be able to provide their own clearing and settlement services. At least one large U.S. corporation, Chrysler, already has acquired a bank that permits it to bypass other financial institutions in certain transactions. Corporations also may be able to enter this process by adopting the "language" of financial institutions, which will enable them to conduct transactions in a more expeditious fashion. For example, SWIFT may be viewed as a "standards organization" that prescribes for banks a common language with which to conduct transactions. Although it also is an association of banks (with a limited number of non-bank participants) that provides for electronic transactions among its members, its system of protocols might be readily adopted by non-banks and could allow them to communicate with banks in "SWIFT language". Such communications, over whatever medium, might enable non-banks to avoid the need for using a bank as an intermediary.

e. Various financial institutions already are performing communications functions in support of their electronic services. The breadth of such functions is limited by communications laws in certain countries and, more broadly, by international policies regarding the use of leased lines for the transmission of third-party communications.

3. Telecommunications service providers and carriers have been less active in moving into the financial services markets.

a. In the United States, AT&T and the Bell Operating Companies (the "BOCs") are subject to restrictions on their involvement in "electronic publishing" and the offering of "information services", respectively, as a result of the Modified Final Judgment (the "MFJ") in the AT&T antitrust suit; thus, these companies have been effectively barred from providing most or all financial information services. For the present, at least, the BOCs also are subject to the MFJ's line-of-business restrictions, which probably would require the BOCs to seek a waiver of these restrictions from the court that approved the MFJ before offering an electronic financial service; a condition of such a waiver is that the service covered by the waiver be provided only through a separate subsidiary.

b. It is not yet clear whether these restrictions will continue to apply. As discussed more fully in Chapter II on "Boundary Lines", the Department of Justice has recommended to Judge Greene that most of the MFJ's line-of-business restrictions, including the information services restriction, be removed. A decision is not expected until the Fall of 1987. As U.S. communications policy is sorted out, however, it is likely that the BOCs and AT&T will be given increased freedom to enter new markets such as those for the provision of electronic financial services.

c. Although U.S. carriers and service providers other than AT&T and the BOCs and carriers and service providers in other countries are not subject to restrictions similar to those contained in the MFJ, there has been a tendency for telecommunications companies not to enter the financial service markets directly. Instead, these companies have used joint ventures or other less contractual arrangements in which financial institutions provide the network information or the transactional services. Even in the consumer markets, which have been served in Europe by videotex services often operated by the PTTs, there has been a reliance on third-party service providers to offer electronic financial services.

4. As traditional sectoral roles blur, and as financial institutions enter new markets and undertake new activities—both domestically and internationally—pressure increases for change in the structure of regulation.

a. In Japan, for example, new activity in a financial sector that has been viewed as relatively conservative is forcing policymakers to confront the need for regulatory change. Banks are facing competition from an increasingly sophisticated retail sector, which has been developing point-of-sale systems and electronic methods of settling transactions. As various businesses, encouraged by the Ministry of International Trade and Industry ("MITI"), have increased their use of new information technologies, pressure has mounted among banks to respond. This pressure, ultimately, may force regulators of the banking industry to permit or to encourage banks to move aggressively into the electronic transaction business on a distributed network basis.

b. The increased international influence of Japanese financial institutions, in part due to the favorable trade balance now enjoyed by Japan, also is likely to produce a greater demand for new electronic services from customers seeking to effect transactions through a Japanese bank. If these institutions are prevented from responding to the demand due to restrictions contained in laws such as the one that, like the Glass-Steagall Act in the United States, restricts Japanese banks to banking activities, they are likely to move into foreign markets with more relaxed regulatory climates. Such a move is likely to cause policymakers in Japan to review the existing laws and consider the adverse implications of a failure to change.

5. Changes in the relationships of market participants and in the functions that such participants perform may lead to delays in the implementation of new services, as regulators and policymakers attempt to judge the impact of proposed changes on existing market structures. Regulators may oppose a particular service configuration and attempt to decide how a new service could best fit within an existing market structure.

a. In Japan, for example, Reuters has attempted for almost five years to be permitted to offer its dealing services. It faced regulatory obstacles in both the communications and financial fields. The Ministry of Posts and Telecommunications (the "MPT") was required to determine whether the service should be classified as one eligible for the use of ordinary leased lines or as a "carrier-like" service required to use KDD's Venus-P service, to which tariffs with usage-sensitive charges would apply. Pending a more definitive solution of the MPT's policy toward new international service arrangements, the dealing service has been permitted to be offered to customers in Japan in collaboration with KDD.

b. The dealing service also faced resistance from the Ministry of Finance (the "MOF"), which was reluctant to approve an electronic market system that could have a potential adverse economic impact on foreign-exchange traders. (The traders were reluctant to compete with an electronic system.) These fears contrasted with the view of many observers, who believe that electronic systems will not become a direct substitute for brokerage systems that guarantee customers a greater degree of anonymity—often a critically important factor in a foreign-exchange trade. Ultimately, the resistance of some foreign-exchange brokers was overcome by the desire of many large banking institutions to have access to electronic trading capability. These banks have important influence within the MOF, and that influence finally prevailed.

c. The MOF has been similarly cautious about the authorization of other electronic trading systems. Some ministerial guidance has been issued regarding the implementation of such systems. However, the Ministry has tended to approach issues presented by new electronic systems primarily in an *ad hoc* fashion.

    d. The MOF's relatively traditional and conservative approach stands in contrast to the approaches of other ministries. Both MITI and the MPT sponsored long-range studies of future industry and regulatory developments in the telecommunications sector as a way of previewing the changes likely to come about from advances in technology and market demands for new services. The MOF does not appear to have initiated a comparable review of the financial industry, despite the fact that new electronic systems will have an important impact on the future of the banking and securities industries in Japan.

    6. Regulators may be particularly cautious in their oversight of new markets made possible by electronic networks capable of aggregating disparate users or of permitting market participants to bypass traditional transactional systems. Such new markets raise particularly difficult legal and regulatory problems because they integrate many functions: dissemination of information, initiation and completion of transactions, and various payment and settlement functions.

    a. The MOF in Japan has permitted Nikkei Quick to obtain a high-speed feed of quotations from the Tokyo Stock Exchange and to make this data stream available to customers. Other entities, however, have been able to obtain only low-speed quotation services, which are not suitable for the development of an off-market system. And even Quick, which has the necessary data to offer an on-line transactional service, has not been permitted to combine its information feed with the capability for its customers to execute transactions. Such transactions must be initiated by telephone. The MOF has been very cautious about allowing such an off-market system to develop.

    b. The issue of off-market electronic systems generally in Japan is a difficult one. Presently, large holders of securities can enter into bilateral transactions, and a major concern of the MOF seems to be whether an institution that conducts such bilateral trading on a regular basis is engaged in the business of trading securities, functioning as a broker-dealer—if it regularly trades with the same "partner"—or as some type of market or exchange. According to some Japanese observers, any step toward the creation of a centralized electronic market—or even an interlocking set of inquiry and response arrangements among institutions with large portfolios—would require prior administrative approval. Such approval might well be difficult to obtain, even though the trading arrangement may ultimately be in the interest of large insurance companies and banks, who may be able to realize efficiencies through private trading systems that they manage directly. A question for the future is whether large financial institutions that have significant trading positions can persuade their backers in the MOF to permit more liberal arrangements.

c. Some observers believe that Japanese financial officials will be observing closely the developments in London as Big Bang continues to open the securities market in the United Kingdom to a new era of market configurations. For example, the evolution of relationships between information vendors and the London Stock Exchange—either on a co-operative or competitive basis—may have a substantial impact on the future industry structure in Tokyo.

d. The MOF may adopt a less stringent approach toward electronic trading systems for instruments other than securities. Foreign-exchange, commodities, and futures trading may be opened more quickly to innovative market relationships because the vested interests of the brokerage community may be less significant in these areas. In particular, there may be a willingness to allow electronic capabilities for trading on foreign markets or in new financial instruments. The Ministry, no doubt, is aware that such a policy would create incentives for financial institutions to base their operations in Japan, rather than in other major financial markets that may be seeking to lure new trading capabilities.

7. The sorting out of national responses to changes in market structures that result from the development of electronic services will be a particularly critical aspect of the process of constructing international information and transactional services. This process is examined below in Section III.

E. Examples of Electronic Financial Services

Set out below are a number of the electronic systems now offered or being developed by various financial institutions and other related service providers (including vendors of database services). This compilation is intended to provide an overview of the range of new services that are altering the traditional contours of national and international financial markets.

The services have been divided into transactional and trading services, which are the two broad categories described above in Section II.B. Trading services have been further subdivided into four sections according to the characteristics and functions of the services described. These sections include financial management systems, which are comprehensive corporate-support networks that provide market participants with a broad range of financial market information (an increasing amount of which is real-time information); inter-exchange links, which are systems that enable organized exchanges to disseminate price information among disparate trading floors and that more recently have been used to permit inter-exchange trading; off-market systems and automated trading systems, which are on-line networks used either by an exchange or by some non-exchange organization to create an electronic marketplace for trading; and market support functions, which include clearing and settlement operations.

It should be noted that clearance and settlement systems are grouped with other trading systems below, although they will be instrumental to the operation of both types of services. This grouping was made because many of the most complex clearance and settlement problems relate to securities markets and efforts to construct inter-exchange links, particularly across national boundaries.

1. Transactional Services

a. Chase Manhattan Bank operates Chase Bank by Television, a home banking program that requires use of a television set, a telephone line, and a computer keyboard. Using the system, which enables customers to have access to the Chase computers through the public switched telephone network on a dial-up basis, customers can use either a bank card (that often is used for transactions on ATMs) or a credit card as identification for gaining access to current-account balances and check-clearing information.

b. Citibank has added an on-line brokerage service to its Direct Access home video banking system. Subscribers can enter orders over the Direct Access network, and the orders will be executed by a Citicorp brokerage unit. This system is similar to capabilities offered in connection with certain Citibank asset management accounts, which allow customers to enter on-line orders that are executed by a discount brokerage firm. Direct Access customers also can monitor and manage their individual retirement accounts and Simplified Employee Plans.

c. Pronto, Chemical Bank's video banking service, has added transactional capabilities to its system. Customers who select brokerage services will be routed to an affiliated service by means of a network gateway so they can retrieve price quotes, check their portfolios, obtain research information, and enter orders, which will be handled by a discount brokerage firm.

d. MasterCard and Visa have completed a proposal for a nationwide debit-card system in the United States called Entree that the companies hope will establish a uniform system for making point-of-sale electronic payments. The service would handle electronic, non-credit transactions at the point-of-sale. The network would involve only banks.

e. The Royal Bank of Canada has entered into a partnership arrangement with the Denver-based Plus system of shared ATMs to arrange for intercontinental sharing agreements with banks in the United Kingdom. Plus (and its chief rival, Cirrus) offer licenses to banks; licensees have the right to provide Plus network services within a defined geographic area. A competing bank must negotiate with the primary licensee to obtain a secondary license to offer network services over its ATMs. The Royal Bank will co-ordinate all data transmission between North America and the system's ATMs in the U.K. and also will process all foreign-exchange transactions involving Canadian, U.S., and British currency.

f. An electronic "sales representative", which links a video screen to an ATM network, is being developed to assist bank customers in opening accounts, applying for loans, and obtaining financial counselling services. The service integrates video disc technology with microprocessors to create a two-way system in which the video image will "respond" to customer information input through the ATM network. The "sales representative" also is linked to a bank's mainframe computer, so that it can provide customer account information as well.

g. A number of banks offer microcomputer systems that allow corporate customers to determine balances, cleared checks, and returned items on their corporate checking, loan, and investment accounts. They also can transfer funds among these accounts and, using the automated clearinghouse system, transfer funds to and from accounts with other financial institutions. There are plans to add a "check-writing" feature to certain of these systems.

h. In Australia, the banks have developed extensive electronic networks that are used for internal purposes and to support ATM and point-of-sale operations for customers. Australian banks use private networks to support their competitive point-of-sale systems; the networks tie together bank branches and participating retailers. Telecom Australia is now installing a dedicated point-of-sale network as an overlay to the public packet network. This overlay network will be accessible to multiple users and will be designed so that specific users can be included or excluded.

i) ANZ Bank operates the ANZPAK network, which provides both voice and data services over what is expected to be Australia's largest packet-switched network, linking all 1,200 of the bank's branches. Initial operations will depend upon lines leased from Telecom Australia; however, other options, including the use of domestic satellite links supplied by AUSSAT, are being considered.

ii) Westpac Bank has more than 1,100 terminals linked to its network, which supports both ATMs and point-of-sale terminals.

iii) National Australia Bank has 700 terminals connected through its network, and it expects to support approximately 5,000 point-of-sale terminals by 1990.

iv) It is expected that nationwide there will be approximately 60,000 terminals by 1990, up from approximately 5,000 in 1985. The range of services available through such terminals is likely to expand as smartcards are introduced in place of the magnetic stripe cards now in use.

i. Smartcards could have an impact on the structure of transactional networks because they will permit certain processing operations to be removed from the network and concentrated in the chip embedded in each user's card. There are three basic types of smartcards with various amounts of processing capabilities.

i) Wired logic cards contain 4.5 kilobytes of memory and a hard-wired processor that controls access to the memory. The hard-wired processor is not programmable; it is designed to check the validity of used identification codes and to block unauthorized access—functions that currently are performed by the network.

ii) Microprocessor cards are programmable, permitting them to be used for a wide variety of functions, including interactive operations either with a central computer (on-line) or with an individual terminal (off-line).

iii) Supersmart cards have a high-power microprocessor, a memory chip, a calculator-style keyboard that can be used to select functions, and a small display. Supersmart card proponents claim that they could replace terminals in many instances. Because these cards can function as distributed processing centers, they also could have a substantial impact on network use. In Australia, for example, it is thought that the volume of validation and account messages carried by the network and displayed over dumb terminals could be reduced. These short messages could be generated by the supersmart card on the basis of information contained within the card's own processor. Central network computers could be shifted to batch updating after normal business hours; the status of transactions during the day would be handled by processors in individual cards. The change would substantially alter the use of Telecom Australia circuits.

2. Trading Services

a. Financial Management Systems

i) The Royal Bank of Canada and the Bank of Nova Scotia are among the financial institutions working with real-time, 24-hour financial management systems designed to provide institutional money managers with constantly updated information about a variety of global markets. Some transactional capabilities may be included as part of the integrated system.

ii) Many larger banks such as NatWest have been operating cash management systems in collaboration with remote access data processing companies such as GEISCO. Gradually, these systems are being brought in-house as the number of customers increases.

iii) The Society for Worldwide Interbank Financial Telecommunication ("SWIFT") has long operated an inter-bank funds clearing system that is described below. In 1986, the board of SWIFT decided to establish a new subsidiary, SWIFT Communications Services, which will offer specialized banking services such as cash management, documentary credits, and transactional services for travellers checks, gold, and other precious metals. Another project that has been launched is an ECU netting system operated in collaboration with the Bank for International Settlements. Many within SWIFT have been concerned that these new services could jeopardize some of the organization's core activities. Others may be sensitive to the possibility that new services and activities might conflict with the specialized individual offerings of many of SWIFT's members.

iv) Telerate offers Teletrac, a trading and analytical service for dealers, institutional sales representatives, and analysts in the foreign-exchange and money markets. The software runs on a microcomputer and provides 24-hour, real-time coverage of world cash, futures, and options markets together with the analytical and decisionmaking functions. Market information is provided by satellite transmission to a special receiving antenna or over leased telephone lines.

v) Various companies, including Quotron, Reuters, and Telerate, market a broad array of financial information over various electronic networks. These financial information systems use phone lines, cable television system lines, and various broadcast frequencies, including satellite sidebands and FM radio and television subcarrier signals, to transmit data to their customers. The providers often analyze and edit data and monitor major news events and price movements. The services are marketed primarily to retail brokerage firms, although individual investors are being targeted.

b. Inter-Exchange Links

i) Since late 1985, the American Stock Exchange and the Toronto Stock Exchange have maintained a computer link that has permitted trading on either exchange of a common list of Canadian and U.S. stocks. Trading, which continues on a pilot basis, includes seven dually listed stocks; plans call for trading to be expanded over time to include all dually listed issues. The Toronto exchange has since established similar links with the Midwest Stock Exchange in Chicago and the Paris Bourse.

ii) Options markets in Amsterdam, Montreal, Sydney, and Boston also are interconnected.

iii) The initial stages of an Inter Bourse Data Information System ("IDIS") connecting European Community exchanges was approved in 1983 and is being used to provide historical quotations over the public telecommunications network for the stocks of a number of major companies whose stocks are traded on different European markets. It is expected that the prices of as many as 400 securities will be exchanged over the IDIS network.

iv) The National Association of Securities Dealers (the "NASD"), which operates the NASDAQ over-the-counter electronic market described below and is the U.S. self-regulatory agency responsible for regulating the U.S. over-the-counter markets, and the London Stock Exchange, which operates the London Stock Exchange Automated Quotation System ("SEAQ"), are testing an electronic quotation-sharing system known as the "London Bridge" that will be used to offer customers quotations on 600 U.S. and U.K. stocks. The quoted stocks will include the largest NASDAQ issues, certain non-U.K. securities traded on NASDAQ in the form of American Depositary Receipts ("ADRs"), issues traded on the London exchange, the 100 issues included in the Financial Times-Stock

Exchange Index, and certain of the international issues included in SEAQ. Within two years, the system partners expect that the link will allow traders in the U.S. and the U.K. to initiate, negotiate, and clear trades using computers. Until this time, traders will be required to monitor stock quotations on their computer screens and complete trades by telephone. Clearing services will be provided by a newly formed entity, International Securities Clearing Corp., which would be a subsidiary of the National Securities Clearing Corp. and would be formed to develop a linkage with the London Exchange's TALISMAN clearing system.

v) The Italian exchanges expect to be interconnected electronically in the near future, reducing the potential for arbitrage among the exchanges. The individual exchanges have been invigorated by the development of new pension funds, which have brought into the market capital from individual investors throughout Italy, where the savings rate is the second highest in the world (Japan's being the highest). These pension funds attracted 900,000 new investors in 1985. The move by IRI, the state holding company, to sell off minority interests in certain state-controlled companies, also is generating new activity on the stock exchanges, as are other moves by the government to de-nationalize certain companies. This increased activity, which has produced a greater volume of transactions requiring fast and accurate settlement procedures, has highlighted the fact that exchange procedures in Italy are still quite outmoded: reliance is still placed upon the French auction system and an ancient clearing system. The government's plan to permit foreign banks into Italy in January 1988 should have a substantial impact on the structure of the Italian financial community; although there is some concern about how new competition will affect Italy's domestic banking industry, it is likely that financial activity within Italy will increase greatly, possibly generating both additional funds for, and additional interest in, Italian capital markets.

vi) In the Federal Republic of Germany, an effort is under way to link together the eight German exchanges in Frankfurt, Düsseldorf, Bremen, Münich, Berlin, Stuttgart, Hannover, and Hamburg. The plan is not without significant obstacles: for example, the two largest exchanges—in Frankfurt and Düsseldorf—now focus their operations on incompatible computer software. At the same time that this linkage is being pursued, other steps are being considered to increase activity in the securities markets. The hours of operation for the exchanges are being extended, and steps are being taken to develop a "second" market for start-up companies that would have less stringent disclosure requirements. The German central bank, the Bundesbank, also has been taking steps to open up the German capital market in response to pressure from the international financial community. Various zero coupon bonds, floating rate bonds, and dual currency bonds, as well as currency swaps (which have been initiated elsewhere in Europe), have, since 1985, been authorized to be marketed.

vii) NASDAQ is connected to the U.S. National Market System to permit NASDAQ users to receive aggregate last-sale information on more than 2,000 issues traded on one or more of several U.S. exchanges.

viii) Other planned linkages include a proposal by the Philadelphia Stock Exchange and the London Stock Exchange to permit the dissemination of quotations for certain option contracts on six foreign currencies. The quotations would be disseminated on the floor of each exchange; no electronic trading is contemplated. The New York Stock Exchange is considering potential joint ventures with the London and Amsterdam exchanges that would involve both trading and market data exchanges. The American Stock Exchange is reviewing a possible link with the European Options Exchange in Amsterdam that would allow inter-exchange option trading.

ix) Efforts by exchanges to link themselves together are taking place at the same time as many brokerage firms are seeking to forge their own multi-exchange links. These firms, in response to customer demands for increased ability to participate in trading on a variety of world markets, have been working to enhance their access to information from overseas exchanges. In Japan, for example, a number of brokerage firms have ordered groups of voice-grade telephone circuits to link trading floors in New York with their trading rooms in Tokyo. These firms have opted for voice links, rather than data channels, because they are concerned that data systems would involve unacceptable delays as operators took time to enter pricing information into the systems. To gain the advantage of instantaneous access to the most current market pricing, these brokers have requested the installation of an unprecedented number of voice-grade circuits. Although these facility requests have been made for reasons unrelated to the business of telecommunications, they have unsettled KDD, the Japanese international carrier, which is concerned that the brokerage firms may intend to arbitrage or resell the circuits.

c. Off-Market Systems and Automated Trading Networks

i) The Computer Assisted Trading System ("CATS") is a computerized trading system developed by the Toronto Stock Exchange in 1977 that now accounts for 20 per cent of the daily trading volume on the exchange. Unlike NASDAQ, it is capable of aggregating orders into a single transaction, which permits it to handle an increased volume of transactions.

ii) The Paris Bourse introduced a version of CATS in 1986 known as the Cotation Assistée en Continue ("CAC"). It is expected that CAC will provide continuous quotations for as many as 200 stocks by the end of 1987. The system is designed to permit continuous trading of stocks in accordance with the auction principle used on the Paris Bourse, as compared with the competing market-maker system used by NASDAQ and other exchanges. At present, the only automated part of the transactional scheme is the connection between brokers and the so-called "quotation book", which is an electronic receptacle for buy/sell orders that provides users of the system with a continuous picture of the demand and supply for any particular security on the system. Executed orders are flashed over the system and removed from the quotation book to keep it current. Plans are being made to computerize the order-taking function of brokers, possibly allowing interconnection with France's Minitel system to permit on-line order routing and confirmation. It is not known whether linkages with the fully automated French clearing system, the Société Interprofessionnelle pour la Compensation des Valeurs Mobilières ("SICOVAM") will be developed in the future.

iii) The Computer-assisted Order Routing and Execution System ("CORES") that is being operated in Japan is a system similar to CATS. Another similar system is being considered by the Zürich exchange.

iv) NASDAQ, the National Association of Securities Dealers Automated Quotation System, is an over-the-counter electronic securities market run by the NASD that ties together 550 U.S. securities dealers and is the third-largest equity market in the world, behind the New York and Tokyo Stock Exchanges. More than 5,000 issues were being traded over NASDAQ in 1986, which uses a multiple market-maker system that permits dealers to compare continuous ask and bid prices from all market-makers for any security on the system. Except for those transactions that can be executed on-line over NASDAQ's Small Order Execution System (limited to trades involving 1,000 shares or less), most trades continue to be made by telephone or other separate communications link. NASDAQ is linked to clearing, settlement, and depositary services, and an on-line system for comparing the results of all trading between two parties is provided to assist users in checking clearance and settlement progress. The system contains various automated surveillance features that permit NASD authorities to keep close watches on system activity that exceeds pre-set parameters. Periodic system reports also permit early identification of market irregularities, including stock manipulation or insider trading.

v) The NASD had agreed with the Association of International Bond Dealers (the "AIBD") to create an international computer trading system for Eurobonds that will be linked to NASDAQ. (The AIBD represents more than 800 Eurobond dealers, primarily in Europe.) Initially, the system was to have provided users with electronic quotations, trade information, automatic confirmations of transactions, and electronic links to clearinghouses. Transactions in the $2.2 trillion Eurobond market would have been conducted by telephone, although the potential for offering on-line transactional capabilities was being discussed. Until the project was suspended, the system was seen as a way of increasing the worldwide visibility of the market and improving the efficiency of what is now a paper-and-telephone system.

vi) Central to London's Big Bang has been SEAQ, the automated system that is modeled on the NASDAQ system in the U.S. Operation of the system depends on which of four groupings in which a stock is included. The 60 or so most active stocks are in the alpha group; the next 500 most active are beta stocks; the least active stocks are gamma and delta. Information on non-U.K. issues (mostly South African and Australian securities) are handled separately through SEAQ International. Thirty-five registered market-makers are required to display firm bid and offer quotes for alpha and beta stocks in minimum 1,000-share units. (Fewer than half of the market-makers typically supply quotes for any one alpha issue; fewer than ten will deal in a single beta stock.) Alpha stock trades must be reported to SEAQ within five minutes to permit continuous display of pricing information; beta stock trades must be reported the following day. Gamma and delta stock price information is even less up-to-date. The system has permitted trading activity to move off the exchange floor, although all activity is still routed through and controlled by the exchange. The use of the market-maker system, which also is used by NASDAQ, has simplified the linkage between NASDAQ and SEAQ—the so-called London Bridge discussed above.

vii) Instinet provides system users in the United States with the ability to monitor market conditions, execute large block trades on line, and settle transactions. Trading information is made available from the seven U.S. stock exchanges and NASDAQ, as well as from more than 150 national and regional broker-dealers, market-makers, and subscribing institutional traders. The system also permits subscribers to negotiate trades on line and—of particular value to active traders of large blocks of stock—anonymously. It removes from the trading process a variety of intermediaries in an effort to speed up the process of order execution and to reduce the risk of errors. Instinet has pursued expansion into the international market principally through ties with Reuters. This business link has allowed U.S. subscribers to gain access to overseas exchanges and institutional traders; it also has provided certain overseas entities with access to the electronic U.S. market made available by Instinet. The internationalization of the system is likely to continue as business ties between Instinet and Reuters—which have been developing since late 1985—are strengthened. In December 1986, Reuters completed a cash tender offer that increased its beneficial ownership of Instinet's outstanding capital stock to approximately 49 per cent; subject to the approval of Instinet stockholders, Instinet will be merged into a subsidiary of Reuters.

viii) Reuters operates a worldwide dealing system that permits dealers in various countries to negotiate and execute trades in foreign exchange, bullion, and bonds. As is true of the Instinet system, electronic transactions are confirmed by "hard copy" printouts.

ix) The Intermarket Trading System ("ITS") in the U.S. links six of the seven U.S. stock exchanges and NASDAQ to permit trading in a number of multiply-quoted securities. The telecommunications network permits specialists on one exchange to seek a better price for a security than is available on their own exchange by entering a "commitment to trade" into the system, which specifies the price, quantity, and duration of commitment for a particular security. If that commitment is accepted on another exchange, acceptance is communicated by the transmission of an execution message. ITS does not provide quotations; instead, it relies on ITS users to survey the reported commitments and to respond to these commitments as a way of aggregating the trading activity in separate markets.

x) As major corporations have discovered that they can raise funds more cheaply through the bond market than through the banking system, the marketing of commercial paper has extended into Europe; in part, the success of this financial market ultimately will depend on the development of interconnected electronic financial networks. The process of marketing commercial paper depends heavily on prompt and accurate settlement and clearing systems; in fact, many observers believe that the risk of failed transactions is increased by an inability to link together various clearing systems. The success of the market also requires the development of a broader potential group of investors, which is most easily accomplished electronically through an on-line system that provides interested parties with convenient and timely data on available issues from a variety of world markets. The potentially vast size of this market may increase the likelihood that necessary electronic systems will develop; the Eurobond market, which turned over approximately $45 billion per week in 1986, already dwarfs the operations of the London Stock Exchange.

xi) The development of a market for interest-rate and currency swaps has complemented the emergence of a brisk commercial paper market. Although often highly complex, these transactions, in their simplest form, permit a borrower to exchange liabilities with floating interest rates for fixed-rate obligations—or vice versa. Many brokers with positions in interest-rate swaps—including the new International Swap Dealers Association—are exploring the possibility of enhancing the liquidity of their positions by increasing the opportunities for trading. Such liquidity may depend on the development of an electronic-based market that can aggregate a large number of entities from around the world with interests in swaps; without this kind of linkage, it may be extremely difficult to develop a swap "market".

xii) The Amsterdam Stock Exchange has responded to competition from the London exchange, in part, by encouraging the development of trading in overseas issues. The exchange has, for example, taken a number of steps to encourage trading in U.S. and Japanese shares. U.S. shares are traded through the American Shares Amsterdam System, and certain Japanese stocks are traded (in yen) before or after business hours in Tokyo with the involvement of several large Japanese securities firms. In the trading of domestic issues, attempts by regulators to keep market-makers on the stock exchange floor have produced dissatisfaction among some large traders. As a result, exchange officials have refocused their attention on efforts to create an electronic off-market system that will prevent these traders from taking their business to other markets, such as London.

xiii) The Amsterdam exchange also is seeking a broader role for its so-called "Parallel Market" to attract newer or smaller companies seeking venture capital funds. A number of banks and venture capital firms are now studying the feasibility of a European-wide system similar to NASDAQ that would be used to market interests in new companies, with prices quoted in ECUs. This kind of service would circulate price information through existing financial information vendors, such as Reuters or other similar companies. The potential for this system illustrates how new electronic systems may create new sources of capital for companies that might not be able to raise funds through existing stock exchanges.

xiv) In 1984, an electronic network called Intex was created for transactions involving gold contracts. The network is located in Bermuda and is developed around a central computer that links dealers together.

d. Market Support Functions

i) Clearing and settlement functions are provided by a large number of organizations worldwide, and details about the degree to which these operations are taking advantage of telecommunications capabilities are uneven. Certain international linkages among clearinghouses have already been described above and will not be repeated in this section.

ii) In Europe, clearing, settlement, and depositary functions are in various stages of automation, and institutions have entered into an array of bilateral and multilateral links. Among the most aggressive in terms of automation is the Danish depositary, Vaerdipapircentralen, which handles operations for the large Danish bond market. Established in 1980, it has committed itself to a policy of dematerialization, which includes the abolition of certificates and a reliance on computerized transfer systems. The Belgian securities depositary and transfer organization, the Caisse Interprofessionnelle de Dépôts et de Virements de Titres ("CIK") has established linkages with two of the German security-clearing associations, the Düsseldorf and the Frankfurt Kassenverein, that permit settlement of transactions in jointly quoted Belgian and German stocks. Because German law forbids the German associations from being members in CIK, however, the link is unidirectional: CIK is a member of the two Kassenverein and acts as a settlement representative for its members. SICOVAM, the French depositary, has sought aggressive links with CIK, the Dutch depositary, and TALISMAN in London. Lengthy negotiations with the Kassenverein had not resulted in any links by mid-1986. It remains to be seen whether the development of the IDIS network will produce a European settlements network that will permit the transmission of standardized settlement messages to linked national organizations. The development of a centralized European settlement organization would appear to be rather remote.

iii) Eurobond clearance and settlement operations are centered in Luxembourg and Brussels, where the two international bond organizations, CEDEL and EUROCLEAR, operate. CEDEL is a cooperative association of banks and financial institutions with its headquarters in Luxembourg that handles securities and precious metals transactions for participants in more than 50 countries. Computerized networking permits ownership transfer and same-day funds clearance to be performed. Participants are able to maintain deposit balances in their native currencies. CEDEL uses a variety of transmission networks to perform its activities, including Chemlink, GE Mark III, SWIFT, and *ad hoc* computer-to-computer linkages. EUROCLEAR, based in Brussels, began as a settlement service of the Brussels office of Morgan Guaranty Trust Company in 1968. It is now owned by a company whose shares are held by banks, brokers, and investment companies worldwide. Same-day transfer and payment, in a variety of currencies, are available; like CEDEL, certificates are retained by a network of depositary organizations around the world. Communications are routed principally over the GE Mark III network, although participants can choose their own form of communications and transmission routes.

iv) For inter-bank communications, SWIFT, established in 1973, serves as a hub of international settlement and clearance activity. Unlike CEDEL and EUROCLEAR, which are actually independent settlement organizations, SWIFT is simply a networking system that enables member banks to process a variety of transactions, including bank transfers, inter-bank securities trades, foreign-exchange activities, and various credit transactions. In 1987, SWIFT is expected to complete the much-delayed conversion from its old store-and-forward configuration ("SWIFT I") to a more interactive system with greater transaction processing capabilities and upgraded transmission features ("SWIFT II"). A debate that continues within SWIFT is the degree to which this inter-bank association should permit the participation of large securities houses as SWIFT feels increasing pressure to participate more broadly in the securities markets.

v) The Clearing House Interbank Payment System ("CHIPS") is an automated network set up by the twelve member banks of the New York Clearing House and serves as the principal means for settling international dollar transactions. Established in the early 1970s, the system has undergone a shift in focus. Originally most of the CHIPS transactions consisted of trade payments; today, the bulk of the transactions are related to foreign-exchange and Eurodollar transactions. CHIPS operates alongside FedWire, a clearing system operated by the Federal Reserve Board.

vi) The Clearing House Automated Payment System ("CHAPS") is a U.K. clearance and settlement system involving eleven banks in London and Scotland. Plans for Citibank to become a member of CHAPS are proceeding with the development of software that will allow for an interface between Citibank's internal network and CHAPS. London's Big Bang is dependent in part upon the services that can be provided through CHAPS, which permits payment functions to be automated along with the rest of the transaction process.

vii) Organizational linkages to support US.-Canadian exchange links include an arrangement between the National Securities Clearing Corporation and the Canadian Depositary for Securities, that is used to process over-the-counter transactions between U.S. and Canadian dealers as well as those that occur in the Boston Stock Exchange/Montreal Exchange and American Stock Exchange/Toronto Stock Exchange links. The Midwest Securities Trust Company and the Midwest Clearing Corp. have linked with the Canadian Depositary to settle trades completed over the link between the Midwest Stock Exchange and the Toronto Stock Exchange.

F. SITA: Case Example of a Developed Market System

1. In 1949, the world's major airlines created a non-profit co-operative organization to provide them with communications capabilities. This organization, the Société Internationale de Télécommunications Aéronautiques ("SITA"), has grown to include more than 300 airlines in 170 countries and now provides a complex and comprehensive telecommunications system that includes various data processing services.

    a. Initially, individual airlines pooled their private radio and cable circuits through SITA, for the benefit of all airlines.

    b. Over time, many of the airlines transferred administrative and operational responsibilities to SITA. Certain airlines, however, continue to operate complementary—and sometimes duplicative—systems of their own, although these systems usually are confined to national markets. Seventy-four individual airline systems housing 150 airlines are connected with the SITA network.

    c. SITA evolved, in large part, due to of the inability of an international telecommunications network established by agreement of the members of the International Civil Aviation Organization (the "ICAO") in 1945 to handle all the communications needs of the industry. The ICAO network continues to function as the main pipeline for international traffic control communications, although SITA supplements ICAO's traffic control functions in areas where the ICAO network is underdeveloped (particularly in less developed regions of the world).

2. In addition to telecommunications services, SITA offers data processing services to its members on a co-operative basis. Two main data processing centers, in Atlanta and London, offer thirteen services to network users, including flight plan generation, meteorological information, passenger reservation capabilities for small and medium-sized airlines, hotel reservation, and fare quotation and pricing.

3. Newer services include an air-to-ground digital communications system supported by a network of interconnected VHF stations operated by SITA, and a system emulation application that allows airlines to install a SITA-supplied terminal that is capable of being operated with

various individual airline systems (thereby eliminating the need for multiple dedicated terminal installations).

4. This dispersed industry is connected through more than 200 telecommunications centers and a vast array of wide-band (56 Kbps over satellite and terrestrial links), medium-speed (9.6–14.4 Kbps), and low-speed (50–300 baud) circuits that support both video display terminals and older teletype machines.

5. This elaborate network evolved over a lengthy period of time, in part with the help and support of telecommunications administrations that have permitted SITA to function as a single user of leased circuits, thereby eliminating potential conflicts with national and international restrictions on non-carrier provision of third-party message switching and the resale and shared use of leased lines. This issue is discussed more fully below in Section III.E.

a. From 1949 to 1966, SITA used store-and-forward technology and electromechanical switching equipment to connect its network participants. In 1966, a transition to a network that would provide continuous communications began with the introduction of computerized switching and the eventual deployment of packet-switching service. In 1971, Type A Service, which allows members to use computer terminals for communication, was introduced; older teletype and telex messages continued to be carried as Type B service. Until 1982, the backbone network consisted of nine major nodes around the world that performed essential routing functions.

b. At the end of the 1970s, SITA began to replace this network architecture with a new design that separates data transport, message switching, and network control functions.

i) Data transport is handled by a packet-switched network in which wide-band and medium-speed circuits are connected by distributed minicomputer nodes. The data network now handles all Type A Service traffic, as well as certain other data functions.

ii) Network control functions are handled by a network of regional control systems linked to the main control system in Paris. Functions such as supervision of network access, traffic monitoring, billing, and database management are handled by these systems.

iii) A user interface system to permit greater variety of terminals to use the SITA network was first introduced in 1986. The system supports the use of IBM's System Network Architecture ("SNA"), as well as previously used protocols.

iv) Message storage and handling is also being converted to an updated system that is expected to support new networking capabilities. System centers are in Tokyo and Atlanta.

6. SITA represents an effort to address the particular intra-industry communications needs of a global market sector. Airlines cannot, of course, operate in isolation. Passenger routing often requires the use of many different carriers, and there must be some ability for airline users to

plan all of their transportation needs from a single point. Thus, inter-airline communication is essential. Such communication requires not only the establishment of a transmission network, but also the creation of a central mechanism for connecting the data processing systems of individual airlines, so that flight information and seat availability data, for example, can be exchanged and updated by multiple users.

7. The SITA network also includes a variety of related users other than airlines, but only through indirect links. Car rental agencies, aircraft equipment manufacturers and suppliers, and customs and other airport authorities are all part of the travel marketplace, and there is increasing pressure within this market to permit these affiliated organizations to be connected directly into the SITA network. At present, connections between airlines and non-airline market participants are made off-network, with communications being relayed to the office of an airline or by a travel agent, who serves as a representative for the airlines, and then fed into the SITA network from there.

8. An obvious disadvantage of this arrangement is that it fails to take advantage of the efficiencies of direct electronic connections. Requests for travel arrangements cannot be made, processed, and confirmed in a rapid series of on-line steps; instead, less direct communications must occur through intermediaries, increasing delays and the risk of miscommunication. These arrangements also lack the capability for participants to have their transactions aggregated so that periodic net settlements can be used and continuous on-line monitoring of the relative positions of participants can be provided.

9. There is some question as to whether national telecommunications administrations will permit non-airline users to be linked directly into the SITA network. Such connections may be viewed as extending beyond the scope of a private network being used by a single "customer" (*i.e.*, the airline industry); they may be viewed as involving third-party message switching, which is the monopoly business of many national carriers. Even SITA's status as a single "customer" is coming under increasing scrutiny by telecommunications authorities; as discussed below in Section III.E, restrictions on third-party message switching and the resale and shared use of leased lines might be used as a rationale for imposing volume-sensitive tariffs on the circuits leased by SITA. Such tariffs would increase the usage charge being paid by SITA for transmission facilities (which are now leased under flat-rate tariffs), and the net effect could be to make the network less viable, thereby ultimately reducing the traffic carried over it or breaking the network apart completely.

10. The SITA network illustrates the usefulness of telecommunications capabilities that are made available to an industry sector for configuration in ways that suit the needs of that industry. The potential expansion of the network—and the obstacles to that expansion—highlight the dilemma for telecommunications policymakers. The application of traditional policies, such as limits on third-party circuit use, that are

designed to protect the monopoly activities of national carriers could well thwart the development of extensive electronic markets. The result could be a net loss of traffic for carriers. Efforts to accommodate the broad communications needs of industry groups should foster the development of elaborate markets with substantial telecommunications requirements. This approach may well prove more useful than the imposition of policies intended to force users to structure their transactional arrangements to comply with present network-use rules and patterns that carriers may favor because they perceive a need to protect their historic functions.

III. MOVING TOWARD INTERNATIONAL SERVICES AND LINKS

A. Introduction

1. At the national level, the development of electronic financial services raises many intricate securities and banking law questions, relating to the structure of markets and the proper role of particular institutions. A comprehensive examination of these questions is beyond the scope of this paper. Section III.B below, however, contains a brief review of some of the basic structural dilemmas that have been faced in the United States as new electronic services have been introduced. Policymakers around the world are confronting, and will continue to face, many of these same issues, although each country's resolution of these issues will reflect specific national policy objectives.

    a. Decisions will have to be made about how certain basic legal and regulatory objectives that underlie present financial market rules could be applied—if at all—to electronic services. In some cases decisions will be made by governmental authorities; in other cases, self-regulating organizations, such as exchanges, may be given the job of ensuring that national policies are carried out by new service offerings.

    b. Among the broad issues that are likely to be raised by many electronic services are (i) protecting customers from overreaching by financial institutions and by persons who are supposed to act in the role of agent or fiduciary, (ii) preserving the fairness and viability of various transactional markets, and (iii) maintaining the integrity of financial institutions, which is viewed as necessary to preserve user confidence in the marketplace and the banking industry.

2. Worldwide, the authorities responsible for the legal regimes applicable to financial markets are scrambling to decide how the opportunities presented by new services should be allocated among participants in the financial community. Legal and regulatory adjustments are also necessary to guard against the possibility that outmoded regulations will cause national markets to lose out on the business generated by new networks and markets.

a. In countries such as the United States, where broad legislation is supplemented by a large number of specific regulations and by state commercial codes, time is required to adjust regulations and change state laws—even if such change does not require the time-consuming process of amending the overall legislative scheme.

b. In other countries, such as the United Kingdom, where the financial markets are regulated largely by interpretation of the courts and application of older statutes, new developments may not be addressed for years, unless a major legislative overhaul is adopted or a dispute that produces a court decision resolves an open question.

c. In Japan, where banking and financial institutions tend to be rather reserved in their dealings with governmental officials, there may be a lack of dialogue between policymakers and industry decisionmakers that will produce a regulatory crisis. As a result, government officials may not be able to anticipate the kind of regulatory adjustment that would be required to respond to rapid changes in the boundaries of financial services and markets. The major financial institutions also may not be prepared for the chaos that could result from the disjunction of regulation and market conditions.

3. In practice, many of the ambiguities may be handled by private contractual arrangements or settled by institutional practices, such as those of clearinghouses, central banks, or exchanges. Of course, a claim that such agreements or practices violate the letter or spirit of the most directly applicable law may result in a court or a legislative decision that has a more profound or far-reaching impact. Ultimately, new rules will emerge to cope with the particular features of emerging electronic financial systems.

4. Telecommunications policy issues also will have to be examined as these services are introduced. Perhaps most critical to this examination will be the need to decide whether these services are properly classified as "communications", subject to regulations developed to control the business of message transmission. Electronic financial services might be viewed more as adjuncts to the financial services sector than as extensions of the business of providing value-added telecommunications services.

5. Decisions about the classification of electronic services for telecommunications policy purposes are likely to have substantial effects when these services are moved from national to international markets. To the extent that these services are viewed as being within the realm of "communications" activities at the national level, they are likely to be subject to leased circuit use restrictions and tariffing principles that could hinder their international development, even if they are left essentially unregulated in certain national markets.

6. The classification of a particular service in one country may well determine whether a foreign telecommunications administration views that service as a threat to or an infringement of its monopoly authority.

7. National regulatory and market structure decisions are of particular concern when the services and markets subject to those rules and

regulations are to be linked on a multinational basis. An unregulated value-added service in one country may be viewed by another country as a communications service subject to restrictive regulations designed to protect the business of a national monopoly carrier. An unregulated trading network in one country may be viewed by another country as an exchange operation subject to extensive regulations designed to protect the business of a national exchange or series of exchanges. Entities that are eligible to participate in one country's brokerage business or settlements process may be ineligible to participate in similar activities in another country.

8. Obstacles to international connections stand in opposition to some of the powerful forces within financial markets that are seeking to establish global trading links and transactional networks. Legal and regulatory discontinuities that frustrate interconnection either will have to give way to more flexible and compatible schemes or risk forcing financial institutions to assume new and still unregulated incarnations. In Europe, for example, regulations that stand in the way of inter-exchange linkages through which international trading could take place have prompted financial institutions to conduct almost all of their international trading outside of established exchanges; the trading arrangements, in many cases, are left essentially free of financial market regulations.

9. In some cases, multinational electronic services may be able to operate within the interstices of regulatory regimes; complex dealing rooms may provide a proper setting for elaborate, essentially unregulated, trading networks. In other cases, services will be more difficult to establish outside or despite regulatory schemes; transborder ATM networks or international exchange linkages, for example, are certain to pose difficult legal and regulatory problems that will have to be resolved before the services can be operated.

10. Telecommunications policies are likely to be an even greater obstacle. Even those services that can function without the benefit of broad changes in financial services rules will require extensive transmission and switching links that are certain to arouse the interest of national administrations and carriers. Particularly in the international market, as "private" networks link an increasingly large or diverse group of participants, questions may be raised about the propriety of services that are perceived as providing third-party message switching outside the PTTs' switched networks. At the very least, efforts may be made to impose volume-sensitive or other tariffs on such networks that will make them a less attractive alternative to the public switched network. Such efforts could frustrate the development of new services by making them uneconomical.

11. Regulators and policymakers face the challenge of trying to develop flexible regulatory schemes that would allow new services to be pieced together internationally with less difficulty than might be encountered if rigid national legal regimes had to be harmonized or "forced" together. Encouraging the development of these services could have the benefit of bringing them within the ambit of recognized national entities,

such as exchanges, and promoting the growth of new sources of traffic for existing telecommunications networks.

B. Illustrative National Concerns

1. Introduction

a. As electronic services alter the overall structure of, and the relationships within, traditional national financial services markets, rules adopted to manage those markets are likely to become inappropriate. The problems of defining new market structures will differ from one country to the next, depending on the way in which markets originally were organized and the manner in which law and policy changes are made. For example, extensive disclosure requirements developed to apply to defined national securities markets in the U.S. present a legal impediment to the development of international trading markets that could be difficult to overcome. Restrictive exchange membership rules and fixed commission schemes on European exchanges may stand in the way of efforts to broaden market participation as telecommunications links make the aggregation of disparate buyers and sellers more feasible.

b. The discussion that follows is intended to illustrate some of the problems that arise as electronic services alter the functioning of financial markets. The discussion focuses on problems faced in the U.S. due to the tendency of electronic services to permit or to require entities to cross established boundary lines that have been used by regulators to segregate various activities and entities.

c. The problems examined below, although not of universal application, are intended to give some meaning to the argument that the internationalization of financial markets through electronic linkages will require some revision—and, perhaps, harmonization—of national rules and market structures. These international links, and the opportunities and difficulties that they present, are discussed below in Section III.C.

d. The boundary lines considered in this section may be thought of as definitions intended to group together financial market participants and services having a set of common characteristics. Regulators in the U.S. use these boundary lines to prevent entities from becoming involved in activities that are viewed as being inconsistent with the roles and obligations imposed on different types of financial institutions. For example, a financial institution that is relied upon by users for its stability and security may be prevented from acquiring high-risk businesses or engaging directly in high-risk activities.

e. In practice, these boundary lines may become obstacles to the integration of various electronic activities or to changes in the identity of certain market participants that evolving market conditions and new technological capabilities make possible—or even demand.

2. Fitting Electronic Trading Systems Within the Confines of Existing Securities Market Functions

a. In the United States, the securities and commodities laws contain a number of different categories of entities, and regulations are developed in accordance with the roles that such entities are intended to play in particular markets. Among the most common entities are (*i*) Exchanges or Commodities Boards, (*ii*) Brokers and Dealers, (*iii*) Investment Advisers, (*iv*) Investment Companies, (*v*) Securities Information Processors, (*vi*) Clearing and Transfer Agents, and (*vii*) Commodity Pool Operators. It is likely that in attempting to classify providers of electronic services, legislative or regulatory bodies will seek to fit new entities within existing categories. If new regulatory categories are developed, they are likely to be derivative of established categories.

b. The category of Securities Information Processor ("SIP"), for example, may be viewed as a creation of Congress, developed to respond to the increased availability of market information and to distinguish between providers that directly advise customers as to the relative advantages or disadvantages of a particular investment—known as Investment Advisers—and those that merely disseminate information. In this regard, the Securities Information Processor may be considered a definition "derived" from the category of an Investment Adviser.

c. As one would expect, the regulatory categories have fluid boundaries so that an electronic service provider may, by adding or subtracting certain features to or from its system, alter the way in which it will be classified for regulatory purposes. The reason for the change is that different market functions raise different regulatory concerns, and the scheme of regulation that has been developed addresses those concerns according to the "pigeonhole" into which a service provider fits.

i) For example, a service provider that offers only securities information might be considered a SIP, whereas a service provider that couples this information with transactional capabilities may be considered something else—possibly a broker.

ii) The SEC has limited its regulation of SIPs to only those entities that have a monopolistic relationship with a particular exchange. Through this limitation, the SEC has suggested that an entity providing only market information does not have to be regulated unless it has the ability to influence a market by deciding who can receive the distributed information. Of course, only a monopoly supplier can enforce this kind of selective distribution.

iii) The SEC has not regulated as a SIP an information provider that also offers transactional capabilities, although such regulation would appear feasible within the current statutory framework. This limitation may be due to the fact that the SEC's view of the need for SIP regulation is relatively narrow, focusing on the concerns about the adverse competitive consequences noted above. Once an information provider becomes involved in transactional functions, a new set of concerns are raised, such as the security of that entity's assets (because it is functioning in a fiduciary capacity, to a certain extent). As a result, a new set of regulatory policies may be considered applicable—possibly those applied to brokers.

 d. The use of telecommunications technologies to link market participants also raises the possibility that a new service will be viewed for regulatory purposes as a market or an exchange. For example, the interconnection of disparate securities buyers and sellers, and the inclusion in the network of a bank acting as settlement agent, might be considered the formation of an exchange. If the network linked dealers together, as does NASDAQ, it might be considered an over-the-counter market.

 e. In Japan, for example, Article 191 of the Securities and Exchange Law of 1948 prohibits anyone from providing facilities similar to those provided by a securities market or exchange. The law defines an exchange as an entity formed for the purpose of providing a market necessary to effect securities transactions. Exchanges must be licensed by the MOF under Article 81 of the 1948 law. Because there are many restrictions in Japan on the degree of permissible off-exchange securities trading, it is likely that an electronic trading network would face some delays in obtaining a license. Reuters' five-year effort to gain MOF approval for its dealing service illustrates the uncertainties that surround the application of old laws to new market arrangements. Moreover, it seems unlikely that an electronic trading system could be operated without either being licensed as an exchange or otherwise gaining Ministry approval. As additional electronic systems are developed, the MOF may try to use its licensing power to limit the number of exchanges in Japan or otherwise to impose conditions on electronic systems.

3. Segregating Banking and Securities Businesses

 a. In the banking industry, similar definitional issues arise out of concerns about a bank's security if it becomes involved in risky activities, such as promoting and investing in securities. These concerns arose in the wake of the failure of the Bank of the United States in 1930 and due to damage caused to U.S. banks by the 1929 stock market crash, both of which were attributed largely to bank involvement in securities business and bank investment in stocks. The banking laws impose regulatory limits on the functions that a bank or a bank holding company may perform. As a result, electronic services that a bank may want to offer as an extension or expansion of its financial services business may involve it in activities that are not permissible areas for bank involvement.

 i) In the United States, for example, the Glass-Steagall Act has largely required the separation of banking and securities functions since its adoption in 1933. This law restricts banks from becoming involved in the securities business either directly or through affiliation with a business "principally engaged" in prohibited activities. Section 20 of the Glass-

Steagall Act, 12 U.S.C. § 377, prohibits a "member bank" (a national bank or a state-chartered bank that is a member of the Federal Reserve System) from being affiliated with a corporation "engaged principally in the issue, flotation, underwriting, public sale, or distribution at wholesale or retail or through syndicate participation of stocks, bonds, debentures, notes, or other securities . . .". Under Section 16, a member bank generally may not purchase securities for its own account or "underwrite any issue of securities or stock". 12 U.S.C. §. 24 (seventh). The activities of member and non-member banks are subject to Section 21 of the Glass-Steagall Act, 12 U.S.C. §. 378, which makes it illegal for any organization to be involved simultaneously in the securities business and in the business of receiving demand deposits. The prohibitions are subject to explicit exceptions for certain securities issued by federal, state, and local governments and government agencies. 12 U.S.C. §§. 24 (seventh) and 335.

ii) In addition to seeking to preserve the financial integrity of banking institutions (and thereby the funds of depositors), the prohibitions are designed to guard against the possibility that a bank would "favor" the securities of a company to which it has made certain loans, lend its reputation for prudence to efforts to promote securities (necessarily undercutting that reputation because of the risky nature of the investment banking business), or use information gathered in its role as a lender to guide its securities investments and brokerage decisions. In short, Congress believed that the demands and motivations of investment banking were inconsistent with those of commercial banking.

iii) In addition to exceptions for certain government securities, federal law permits member banks to participate in specific limited ways in the securities business. For example, member banks are permitted to engage in "discount brokerage". This business involves the bank in effecting securities transactions but does not involve it in advising brokerage clients about the wisdom or folly of particular investment decisions. In short, the bank is permitted to conduct the transaction (as an agent) but is not supposed to provide counselling or advisory services in conjunction with its brokerage activities (thereby guarding against the use of information gained from commercial banking activities in the course of making investment recommendations).

iv) An electronic service offering might test the outer limits of this regulatory division. A service that packages software capable of being used by a customer to analyze an investment decision with an on-line service that allows the customer to act on that "investment advice" by placing an electronic order with a bank's discount brokerage house may come close to being full-service brokerage that a bank may not provide. A decision might turn on whether the analytical software was being supplied by the bank as a component in an overall service or whether it was being made available through the bank, but clearly was being provided by an unrelated third party.

v) Decisions about whether a member bank is involved in

a prohibited securities industry activity will require determinations under Sections 16 and 21 of the Glass-Steagall Act about whether the bank is engaged in a prohibited business, such as "underwriting", and whether it is handling a "security". See, e.g., *Investment Company Institute v. Camp*, 401 U.S. 617 (1971) (holding that a bank's operation of an investment fund constituted impermissible "underwriting, issuing, selling, and distributing of securities").

vi) With respect to bank holding companies, decisions about the extent to which non-banking subsidiaries can become involved in "securities businesses" is somewhat more complex. A determination must be made under Section 20 of the Glass-Steagall Act that the non-banking subsidiary is not "principally engaged" in a prohibited securities activity, and the subsidiary's activity must be found to be "closely related to banking" under Section 4(c)(8) of the Bank Holding Company Act, 12 U.S.C. § 1843(c)(8). See, e.g., *Securities Industry Ass'n v. Bd. of Governors of the Federal Reserve System*, 408 U.S. 207 (1984) (affirming the Fed's decision that a bank holding company's acquisition of a discount brokerage firm does not constitute the acquisition of a business principally engaged in a prohibited securities industry activity and that discount brokerage is "closely related to banking").

vii) Early in 1987, the Federal Reserve Board issued a series of decisions permitting a number of bank holding companies to engage in limited underwriting activities through non-bank subsidiaries. In each case, the Fed has made it clear that non-bank subsidiaries must be engaged in securities industry activities otherwise prohibited by the Glass-Steagall Act to only a limited extent (generally limiting the activity to 5 per cent of the subsidiary's gross revenues and limiting the subsidiary to a 5 per cent share of the relevant market) and has set out a variety of conditions to protect the integrity of commercial banking functions, to guard against conflicts of interest, and to avoid other potentially adverse effects.

b. The Securities and Exchange Law of 1948 prescribes a separation of banking and securities functions in Japan. As in the U.S., however, there are certain securities trading functions, such as dealing in government bonds, that are permitted upon receipt of approval from the MOF.

i) The Japanese law is designed primarily to promote the development of a robust brokerage industry that is insulated from the control of Japan's banks, and only secondarily to prevent banks from becoming involved in high-risk securities transactions. Thus, the law may be more likely to succumb to international pressures that favor at least some integration of commercial and investment banking functions. For example, it appears that Japanese banks may engage in certain aspects of the "securities business", as defined by Japanese law, in foreign markets where banks typically engage in underwriting, brokerage, and dealing functions, without violating Article 65 of the 1948 law—the provision that requires separation of banking and securities business. This situation permits

Japanese banks to be competitive in foreign markets, where there is no need to protect the viability of a separate Japanese brokerage industry.

ii) Recently, Japanese banks have been working to erode the business separation by seeking permission to provide discount brokerage services (open only to trust banks, and not to city banks) and to operate in the growing secondary market in foreign bonds. As might be expected, these initiatives have been vigorously opposed by the Japanese securities industry.

iii) Under Japanese law, foreign companies seeking permission to engage in the securities business in Japan must be engaged primarily in the securities business. This provision is intended to preserve the banking/securities separation in Japan by guarding against the likelihood that large German or Swiss banks with active securities trading operations would attempt to enter the Japanese market; such banks not only might be formidable competitors in the brokerage and dealing markets, but also could use their "integrated" service offerings as an advantage in competing with Japanese banks.

iv) For foreign relations reasons, however, this prohibition was loosened by a 1971 Cabinet Order that permits foreign banks to seek Ministry approval to enter the Japanese securities business, provided that those banks do not engage in commercial banking operations within Japan and that they maintain their securities operations as part of a separate business. Under Ministry guidelines, a foreign bank can hold no more than 50 per cent of the securities affiliate seeking to enter the Japanese market.

v) It does not appear that this step has provided foreign banks with a real practical market entry opportunity or has had a detrimental impact on Japanese brokers and banks. For example, in mid-1986 the Ministry approved the first entry by a securities affiliate of a U.K. bank; that approval came just days before the Bank of England granted the first license to a Japanese securities firm seeking to enter the British securities market. The Japanese bid for entry had been held up since 1980, with the U.K. authorities insisting on reciprocal market entry opportunities. Three other applications by the major Japanese securities houses have remained on hold since 1980. The admission of the affiliate of the National Westminster Bank was followed by a decision to allow an affiliate of the French Société Générale to enter the Japanese securities business.

vi) The situation increasingly has assumed the tone of a trade negotiation. A request by the U.S. authorities for permission for the European securities affiliates of U.S. banks to enter the Japanese market has met with some skepticism in Japan. The Ministry argued that Japanese banks are not permitted to establish securities affiliates in the U.S. due to the prohibitions contained in the Glass-Steagall Act.

vii) Despite the attention to reciprocity issues, Ministry officials contend that a widespread influx of the securities affiliates of foreign banks could provide Japanese banks with an opportunity to enter the Japanese securities market through the back door. A number of Japanese banks already have entered into discussions among themselves about the possibility of seeking approval for the entry of their overseas securities affiliates into the Japanese securities business. Any such move is likely to be undertaken cautiously due to fears among some banks that large Japanese securities firms will respond by seeking to have their overseas banking affiliates allowed into the banking business in Japan.

4. The Scope of Other Permissible Information Services Activities for U.S. Bank Holding Companies

a. In general, a bank holding company cannot own a telecommunications business other than one involved in the transmission of data relating to the banking industry. Federal Reserve Board regulations currently permit bank holding companies to be involved in the business of transmitting only "financial, banking or economic data". 12 C.F.R § 225.25(b)(7) (1986) (part of Regulation Y).

b. This restriction, like similar restrictions on banks, is intended to guard against the perceived risks of diversification, including the risk that certain activities could jeopardize a bank's solvency. Thus, as noted briefly in Section III.B.3, Section 4(c)(8) of the Bank Holding Company Act permits the non-bank subsidiaries of bank holding companies to be involved in only those non-bank activities that are "so closely related to banking or managing or controlling banks as to be a proper incident thereto". 12 U.S.C. § 1843(c)(8). Courts have articulated this standard more fully, such that non-bank subsidiaries can provide services if: (*i*) banks generally have in fact provided the proposed services; (*ii*) banks generally provide services that are operationally or functionally so similar to the proposed services as to equip them particularly well to provide the proposed service; or (*iii*) banks generally provide services that are so integrally related to the proposed services as to require their provision in a specialized form. *National Courier Ass'n v. Board of Governors of the Federal Reserve System*, 516 F.2d 1229, 1237 (D.C. Cir. 1975).

c. This standard has been applied to the telecommunications field specifically to permit bank holding companies to become involved in data processing or information distribution activities (through their non-bank subsidiaries) if the data involved are of a type ordinarily produced by banks. *Order Approving Engaging in Data Processing and Data Transmission Activities*, 68 Fed. Res. Bull. 505 (1982), *aff'd sub nom. Association of Data Processing Service Organizations, Inc. v. Board of Governors of the Fed. Res. Sys*, 1745 F.2d 677 (D.C. 1984) (*ADAPSO*).

d. Activities incidental to those closely related to banking also are permitted. See *ADAPSO*, 745 F.2d at 695. Thus, otherwise prohibited activities can be engaged in if they are necessary to the performance of tasks that are closely related to banking. The explicit limitation on such incidental activity, however, is that it is allowed only to the extent that it is absolutely required. For example, a bank holding company probably could acquire a value-added service provider that would operate an electronic banking service. If the service provider also was offering other unrelated value-added services, however, and if the amount of business generated by these unrelated services far exceeded its electronic banking activity, the acquisition might be prohibited.

  e. As financial institutions become more deeply involved in the provision of electronic financial services, regulators will be faced with difficult questions about which activities are necessary to carry out banking activities, activities closely related to banking, and necessary incidental activities. Could a bank holding company, for example, acquire a telecommunications network company that offers an electronic market service in which the holding company's bank subsidiary serves as one of the banks providing settlement services?

  f. These rules were applied by the Federal Reserve Board in approving Citicorp's 1986 acquisition of Quotron. *Application Approving Acquisition of Quotron Systems, Inc.*, 72 Fed. Res. Bull. 497 (1986). The decision essentially concluded that most of Quotron's businesses amounted to permissible data processing services and certain other related—and permissible—activities. However, the Board required Citicorp to divest certain Quotron operations, and it imposed conditions on some of the acquired activities as a way of trying to maintain a close nexus between Quotron's business and the scope of permissible activities for a bank holding company.

  i) The Board considered Quotron to be offering essentially four types of services: two database or informational services; a series of "office services" such as spreadsheet, electronic mail, and book-keeping functions; and the design, assembly, and leasing of computer hardware to support the other three services.

  ii) With respect to the information services offerings, the Board found that these were essentially the transmission of "financial, banking or economic data" that a bank holding company could permissibly provide under the terms of Regulation Y. The Board, however, required that after Citicorp had acquired Quotron, Quotron would have to stop offering certain travel-related database services made available through third-party arrangements; these services clearly were not within the scope of data processing activities permitted by Regulation Y.

  iii) With respect to the "office services", the Board said that these could be provided to the extent that they were "limited [by Citicorp] to processing only those data provided by Quotron [*e.g.*, "financial, banking or economic data"] or contained in the customers' own data bases . . .".

  iv) The Board permitted the continued leasing of hardware because that hardware was "special-purpose" hardware and generally could be used only for services provided by Quotron; this activity was consistent with 12 C.F.R. § 225.24(b)(7)(iii) (1986). However, because the hardware also could be used by customers to have access to unrelated on-line information, the Board decided that Quotron hardware could not amount to more than 30 per cent of the cost of any packaged offering. In this way, the Board sought to minimize the likelihood that a significant economic interest in a business unrelated to banking activities would develop.

v) The Board did not allow the acquisition of Quotron's hardware design and assembly activities. The Board applied the *National Courier* case discussed above and concluded that the design and assembly of the hardware was not "necessary" to the provision of permissible data processing services. The Board noted that Quotron's competitors often purchased complete hardware systems from third-party vendors and that hardware of the type used by Quotron was available from outside sources.

5. Problems of Fitting Electronic Services Within Established Institutional Roles

a. Some of the potential problems of applying the definition-based scheme of regulation to new electronic offerings may be demonstrated more concretely by considering a hypothetical example of an electronic offering. Suppose that the Security Company offers a network service that permits pension fund managers, bank trust departments, and other institutional investors to communicate anonymous quotations for the sale and purchase of stocks listed on the New York Stock Exchange and the American Stock Exchange. Network users may "lock in" trades by transmitting their identification code and the network code for acceptance of the bid or of the ask quote.

i) In the United States, there are a number of definitional problems raised by this service. The network operator might be classified as a "securities exchange", which is defined as "any organization . . . or group of persons . . . which constitutes, maintains or provides a market place or facilities for bringing together purchasers and sellers of securities or for otherwise performing with respect to securities the functions commonly performed by a stock exchange as that term is generally understood, and includes the market place and the market facilities maintained by such exchange". 15 U.S.C. § 78c(a)(1).

ii) This definition, which was adopted by Congress in 1934, was intended to apply to something that had a physical situs and involved face-to-face dealing. Although the electronic network certainly lacks these features, it is not clear that the difference should be determinative. Yet, one may question whether a statute certainly not intended to apply to an electronic trading network should be "extended" readily; perhaps congressional or administrative action should be required before such an application is made.

iii) If the definition of a "securities exchange" is to be expanded to include this kind of computerized trading network, one might ask whether it also should include conference call capabilities of a telephone company that may be used by investors to effect securities trades. In this instance, the telephone network—at the time it is used to effect the securities trades—is difficult to distinguish from the dedicated network. An important difference, however, is that the public telephone network is used for many other purposes; in fact, only a very small percentage of the network's traffic probably concerns securities exchanges. This suggests that there may be a reason for confining the scope of the "securities exchange" definition to electronic services that are used exclusively, or principally, to effect stock trades.

iv) How, then, should we classify a private line leased for the purpose of conducting stock transactions, either by data exchange or by voice communication?

v) How might we classify an electronic network that offers multiple on-line services, one of which is a stock trading service?

vi) Under the Securities Exchange Act of 1934, a "securities exchange" is a self-regulating body that the government has endowed with powers to police its own operations and the activities of its participants. Suppose, then, that an electronic trading network is open only to registered brokers and dealers who already are subject to SEC oversight. It is possible that, in this case, it would not be seen as important to create an additional self-regulatory body out of the trading network.

vii) The network operator also might fall within the definition of a "broker": "any person engaged in the business of effecting transactions in securities for the account of others, [not including a bank]". 15 U.S.C. § 78c(a)(4).

viii) The difficulty with such a classification is that the network, as described, is more of a passive conduit than an active participant in the effectuation of transactions. If the network were to provide a gateway service for banks and clearing houses, so that transactions could be paid for and settled over the network, the outcome might be different.

ix) It is not clear, however, that the provision of gateway services that can be used to complete transactions constitutes the effectuation of such transactions by the network operator "for the account of others". Even in this situation, the network operator arguably is only bringing parties together, not actively completing transactions. It may be that a network operator would have to store transactional data in a central computer and then act as the processor of transactions "for the account" of network users to be considered a broker.

x) The network operator also might be considered a SIP, which is defined as "any person engaged in the business of (*i*) collecting, processing or preparing for distribution or publication, or assisting, participating in, or coordinating the distribution or publication of, information with respect to transactions in or quotations for any security or (*ii*) distributing or publishing (whether by means of a ticker tape, a communications network, a terminal display device, or otherwise) on a current and continuing basis, information with respect to such transactions or quotations". 15 U.S.C. § 78c(1)(22)(A).

xi) The problem with this definition is that the network operator is not really a pure provider of information; it is a provider of a communications service that allows for the on-network use of the information. It is more than a SIP, but perhaps not so much more that it rises to the level of being a broker or an exchange.

xii) This definitional "gap" may explain why the SEC has not chosen to regulate as a SIP an entity that provides information services and some transactional capabilities. A question is whether some new definition will be developed to encompass an electronic trading or dealing network.

b. Suppose that the network service described above is developed by one of the regional stock exchanges (not the New York or American Exchanges). The network allows for trading of securities listed on the New York or American Exchanges, and it is open to any registered broker-dealer. Trades can be effected completely by electronic communication, and there is no requirement that the electronic network broker or dealer should maintain a presence on the floor of the exchange that offers the electronic service. The rules of the New York and American Exchanges prohibit their members from effecting trades in listed securities for their own account unless the transaction takes place on that exchange or on the floor of a regional exchange.

i) One question raised in the United States is whether the computer network that is offered by the regional exchange should be considered an exchange facility or an "off-exchange" market.

ii) A second question is whether there should or can continue to be a rigid separation between organized exchanges.

c. The second question suggests the most far-reaching implications of the emerging electronic marketplace. Whereas exchange floors have long been the focal points for trading activity among a number of participants, with the establishment of elaborate communications networks and the inclusion in those networks of switches and processors that permit the collection of information, gateways among various market participants, and the ability to deal that was once possible only in face-to-face settings, the networks hold the potential to become the new centers of market activity. Institutional dealing rooms, as much as or more than exchange floors, can be hubs of activity, particularly for international trading that is less organized within formal exchange structures.

d. To the degree that exchanges use telecommunications to link their trading floors and thereby broaden the base of activity possible within the exchange, migration away from exchanges may be limited. The tension between new network arrangements and existing trading structures, however, is certain to be a central feature of the development phase of electronic financial services. It remains to be seen whether policymakers will attempt to bring new networking arrangements within the scope of regulatory schemes developed for existing exchanges. As discussed below in Section III.C, any such effort will be particularly difficult as networks cross national boundaries, because such arrangements will involve differing market structures and possibly incompatible regulatory regimes.

  e. In 1985, the SEC instituted a proceeding to examine some of the potential problems that could arise in applying U.S. regulations to multinational markets and systems designed to exploit those markets. *Request for Comments on Issues Concerning Internationalization of the World Securities Markets*, No. 34–21958 (released April 18, 1985).

  i) The SEC's release discusses three broad areas of concern: regulatory provisions that may be appropriate to manage increased international trading in securities, restrictions that should apply to the participation of various persons in a multinational distribution of securities, and potential problems in enforcing various rules internationally.

  ii) In the area of international trading rules, the release questions whether systems should be developed to provide a consolidated reporting and quotation system for securities "traded globally on an active basis". In the area of reporting, the SEC noted that a lack of uniformity in reporting requirements around the world could pose a substantial obstacle to the development of such a consolidated system. With regard to quotations, the SEC's inquiry focused on whether there would be enough simultaneous global trading to justify a consolidated quotation system. The SEC questioned whether information provided for debt securities—consisting principally of "indications of interest", rather than bids or offers—would be sufficient to support the dramatic increase in activity in the debt market expected to occur worldwide.

  iii) The anticipated growth of multiple listings of securities and inter-market links prompted the SEC to ask whether market observers expect pricing disparities to develop between exchanges and whether arbitrage activities would be sufficient to correct such disparities. If arbitrage could not be relied upon as a correcting mechanism, the SEC suggested, it might be appropriate to consider mechanisms in inter-market links that would permit orders to be routed automatically to the market with the best available price.

  iv) Noting that co-ordinated action among national clearing and settlement organizations would be essential to any pervasive international trading system, the SEC questioned whether such co-ordination would be best pursued on an *ad hoc* basis or whether major markets should consider participating in the formation of a new international entity that would serve as a clearinghouse or depositary for international trades. The release also asked whether an approval process for the participation of foreign clearing agencies in links with U.S. exchanges should be developed, possibly including a requirement that such entities register as clearing agencies under the Securities Exchange Act of 1934.

  v) The release also discussed trade-in-services-type issues, requesting comments on what actions, if any, might be taken to reduce perceived barriers to the entry of U.S. broker-dealers into foreign securities markets. Such perceived barriers include disparities in national broker-dealer regulatory schemes that may make it difficult or impossible for a broker-dealer in one country to qualify as a broker-dealer in another country; the SEC asked for comment on how such legal obstacles might be addressed.

vi) With regard to concerns about the participation of various persons and entities in multinational securities distributions and miscellaneous international enforcement problems, the SEC focused on questions about how U.S. methods for protecting investors and maintaining investor confidence in the integrity of markets and market participants could be applied outside the United States. The SEC questioned whether formal or informal agreements with other national exchanges or regulatory authorities (some of which already exist for operating inter-market links) would be adequate.

f. The SEC's inquiry makes it clear that the policy issues to be resolved become far more complex when electronic services cross national borders. The discussion that follows seeks to sketch out in some detail the broader dimensions of these issues. Rather than analyze specific national regulatory and legal obstacles to market integration through the development of elaborate telecommunications networks, the discussion attempts to highlight the substantial structural and legal changes that may be involved in any effort to develop international service offerings for the financial community. Both financial services and telecommunications issues are considered. The focus of the discussion is the potential for electronic linkage of European financial markets being pursued by various exchange authorities in Europe and being studied carefully by the European Commission.

C. The Development of Global Markets

1. Introduction

a. The amount of international securities trading has been rising rapidly in recent years. In 1984, for example, one study identified 236 issuers that had active daily trading in their stocks outside their home markets; of these 236 issuers, more than half were U.S. and Japanese companies. The volume of trading in foreign stocks within the U.S. alone rocketed from $2.03 billion in 1970 to $30 billion in 1983. Despite this increase in the international equities market, most attention is being focused on the active international debt markets, where trading volumes and offering amounts are substantially higher.

i) Perhaps the greatest activity has been in the Eurobond market, where total issues almost doubled between 1981 and 1983, from $26.5 billion to $45 billion.

ii) Additional pressures for multinational trading systems are being exerted by active foreign-exchange markets. In London, approximately $90 billion of exchange transactions are effectuated daily, primarily in dollars, Deutschmarks, yen, and pounds sterling. U.S. Treasury bonds are also heavily traded in London, with a daily volume of approximately $100 billion.

iii) Other requirements for global trading are being generated by burgeoning markets for various types of secured paper, such as mortgage-backed bonds. The growing securitization of the capital markets has a variety of causes. In part, banks have sought to guard against the risks of lending by developing instruments such as bonds that can be sold to third parties to distribute the burdens of lending transactions. Corporations have also found that the issuance of commercial paper may be cheaper than seeking bank loans. Investors have favored bonds, rather than bank deposits, as a way of earning higher yields on their investments.

iv) In part due to this trend toward securitization, the level of international loans has fallen by a quarter, from $100 billion to $75 billion in recent years, whereas the issuance of bonds and notes has quadrupled from $50 billion to $200 billion. The result is that banks increasingly are looking toward the securities markets as sources of business. Their involvement in these markets, however, concerns regulators in certain countries, such as the U.S. and Japan, who have tried to maintain a substantial separation between historically distinct banking and securities trading functions, despite erosions of the dividing line in both countries, as discussed above in Section III.B.3.

b. In response to this activity, financial markets around the world are examining the need for change and are studying ways of accommodating the demands of transborder trading activity. One clear example of the interest in developing market linkages—and of the many obstacles to making those linkages work—is in Europe, where the financial markets are undergoing a transformation for a number of reasons. The changes and the obstacles to change in Europe will be examined closely in this Section.

c. Deregulation in certain national financial markets is exerting transborder influences. Most notably, major European exchanges are feeling pressure to react to the changes brought about in the London Stock Exchange by Big Bang in October 1986. Big Bang involved the end of fixed commissions on securities trades and the elimination of the barrier between brokers (which take order for trades) and market-makers. The end of the commission system (under which the exchange fixed minimum fee levels) is certain to produce a new wave of competition—and diversification of activities—as happened in the U.S. after commission rates were unfixed. Brokers sought out new markets for the trading of financial instruments after the profitability of securities trading declined; also, discount brokerage services emerged to compete for certain segments of the market. Perhaps more importantly, with the end of the separation between market-makers (or jobbers) and brokers, these functions will be combined within single huge, integrated financial institutions, on a scale approaching that of large financial institutions in the United States. A number of mergers already have occurred to combine these functions.

d. The competitive effects of Big Bang have been augmented by the decision of the U.K. Government to permit major British and foreign banks to assume roles as new market-makers both in the equities market and in the market for British government bonds (gilt-edged paper, or "gilts"). For example, Barclays Bank has acquired Akroyd and Smithers, one of the two former primary jobbers in the gilts markets, and the Union Bank of Switzerland has entered into an alliance with an old gilts jobber, Phillips and Drew. Baring Brothers, a London merchant bank, and Lloyds Bank also have moved into market-maker roles. These banks previously had been excluded from participating in dealing capacities by exchange rules. It remains to be seen whether the decision to admit these firms to the exchange will affect the amount of business that they historically have conducted outside the official exchange.

e. As noted above in Section II.D, London also has taken a major step to move the center of trading activity from the exchange floor to the dealing rooms of major securities firms, with the development of the SEAQ system. It remains to be seen, however, whether, in the wake of Big Bang, trading on the London Stock Exchange will come to mirror the NASDAQ system in the United States.

f. Together with these market changes, the government is altering the regulatory scheme for the exchange. The Securities Association was formed as a new comprehensive self-regulatory organization in late 1986 through the merger of the London Stock Exchange and the International Securities Regulatory Organization, which was created in 1985 to oversee the activities of the major international securities houses in international securities dealings. The Securities Association and other self-regulatory bodies have been placed under the supervision of the Securities Investment Board (the "SIB"), also a self-regulatory body. Under the Financial Services Act of 1986, the SIB was to become a "designated agency" in mid-1987. As a result, the SIB is able to exercise authority delegated to it by the Secretary of State for Trade. Since June 4, 1987, the SIB has begun to function as the central component of a new self-regulating marketplace.

g. These major regulatory changes are intended to establish London in a preeminent position as a trading center for international equities and other financial instruments including Eurobonds. Such financial instruments are now substantially traded in unregulated markets, largely through relationships among large financial institutions. The various features of Big Bang and associated changes are evidence of a clear decision by the U.K. authorities to attempt to focus domestic and international trading activities within the revised structure of the organized London exchange. Such a plan has been pursued by altering the contours and conditions of the exchange to make it attractive to a wider array of participants and activities, rather than by adopting new rules that are intended to restrict the extent to which trading operations can occur outside the exchange.

h. Other European financial centers, by contrast, have been

less aggressive in revising the structure of their organized markets, although the actions in London are beginning to draw responses throughout the Continent. Continental exchanges traditionally have been hampered by more rigid exchange controls and regulatory practices than were present in London or in the United States. Nevertheless, efforts are now underway to revitalize the European markets. Among the changes being supported are the development and installation of more sophisticated communications and processing systems to support information dissemination, dealing, and clearance and settlement activities.

i. As market changes within Europe invigorate international trading operations and attract greater activity in foreign securities dealing, European banking and financial institutions will become increasingly involved in competitive rivalries with their counterparts from the U.S. and Japan. Financial institutions from the U.S. and Japan have for some time been actively expanding the scope and scale of their international operations. Not surprisingly, these operations have increasingly been dependent on a web of international telecommunications and data processing facilities that integrate numerous streams of financial and economic data into a complex system for executing financial transactions on the most advantageous basis in any financial market around the world. This rivalry has focused increased attention on the mechanisms and capabilities by which European financial institutions—particularly European exchanges—will be able to obtain access to similar financial data and execute and settle transactions in global markets.

j. As much as such international trading capability depends upon the exploitation of extensive and well-developed telecommunications facilities, it also requires the creation of flexible arrangements among exchanges and other financial institutions throughout Europe to permit the sharing of information and the execution and settlement of transactions in different markets. Such arrangements will require adjustments in regulations applicable to telecommunications activities as well as in rules that control banking and securities markets and in general competitive conditions.

k. It is critical for telecommunications policymakers to understand this process of restructuring within the financial markets. Carriers and administrations have the opportunity to serve as catalysts in the development of new markets and new alliances among institutions that could promote more widespread market changes and—ultimately—a significant new demand for the use of sophisticated telecommunications facilities and services.

i) The development of new telecommunications and data processing services that can be used to build new transactional networks is likely to prove an effective way of confronting—and overcoming—non-telecommunications regulatory barriers to the restructuring of financial markets. By facilitating the flow of information and the execution of cross-market transactions, these new telecommunications capabilities can encourage the emergence of new arrangements for conducting transactions outside of traditional market structures.

ii) These arrangements are likely to exert competitive pressures on existing institutions (both within a particular country and in those countries that are geographically or economically "related"). Such pressures ultimately may force the modernization of existing modes of doing business within European financial markets (including the alteration of regulatory schemes). The pressure will be most acute in those markets that fall far out of step with practices in other major financial markets which respond quickly and aggressively to the changing environment.

iii) Open and flexible telecommunications policies can provide the impetus to accelerate the process of structural adjustment in European and other financial markets.

2. International Trading in Europe

a. The level of international securities dealing within Europe, although difficult to quantify because much of it occurs outside of organized markets, is substantial. Some observers believe that the total volume of international dealing is equivalent to the whole of the trading on the Amsterdam Stock Exchange. The volume of international trading is three to four times greater than the aggregate amount of trading in foreign securities on domestic European exchanges.

b. Officials of the established European exchanges are concerned about the tendency of the international securities market to be concentrated outside exchange floors. In an effort to offset the trend away from exchanges, increasing attention has been focused on steps to link the floors of the major European exchanges and to develop a more integrated European capital market. This topic is discussed extensively in M. Hall and M. G. Duncan, *Proposal for a European Equities Market Through Linkage of the Community Stock Exchanges,* XV/299/85-E (June 6, 1985) (Report to the Commission of the European Communities and the Committee of Stock Exchanges of the EEC), which has been substantially relied upon here as a source of information concerning the characteristics of trading practices and of national markets. *See also* Commission of the European Communities, *Completing the Internal Market* (June 1985) (White Paper from the Commission to the European Council). Such linkages are intended to assure the integrity of national regulatory schemes; off-market international trading has tended to take place outside of any formal regulatory regime, and it is unclear, in some cases, what regulations might be applied to these trading activities.

c. The process of bringing international trading activities onto exchange floors—or within automated exchange systems such as SEAQ—will require substantial regulatory revision. Observers stress the need for major changes in four areas: (*i*) existing price quotation schemes, (*ii*) trading practices, (*iii*) membership rules on the exchanges, and (*iv*) the development of highly automated and carefully linked systems for the settlement of transactions.

d. Regulatory changes—perhaps leading to a significant degree of harmonization of market practices across national boundaries—may be an inevitable consequence of the closer integration of national financial markets. The emergence of a more unified regulatory scheme, or of a more flexible one that can accommodate particular national differences, appears to be an absolute prerequisite to the establishment of more formal international trading arrangements.

e. Linkages will require that individual exchanges move toward similar trading conditions for instruments acceptable for delivery and settlement in all markets. Movement toward common systems of generating market prices and toward similar membership rules for particular market participants would promote the emergence of a unified market.

3. Multi-Exchange Pricing Information

a. The development of integrated markets depends first upon the establishment of information systems to disseminate pricing information to and from various European exchanges and the major exchanges of the United States and Japan. Although the exchanges all generate these data, and although many of them have automated systems for tracking, compiling, and distributing the data, the information cannot necessarily be shared between exchanges. As a result, any trading system designed to function on the basis of price information assembled from a variety of sources—allowing buyers and sellers to view the complete array of available transactions—may be difficult to implement. (A system that would electronically process data being received from various exchanges and produce continuous integrated pricing information at a European level would be even more difficult to imagine and, therefore, is not considered below.)

i) Differences in the "meaning" of particular price information provided by different exchanges make comparability difficult and limit the usefulness of a system that displays multi-market price information. There is, for example, a fundamental difference between delayed or historical information about pricing and continuous current pricing information. Some exchanges rely on more constantly updated price information than do others. Historical information is not particularly useful to market participants making trading decisions on the basis of last-sale quotes. Even current market data differ from one system to the next, making it difficult to compare information.

ii) Within Europe, few exchanges provide continuous pricing information derived from market-makers. Instead, as in the case of the major French and German exchanges, official prices determined by some price-setting mechanism are used. In France, bids for blocks of stock are relayed through *agents de change* and are posted in an official book of quotations. On the basis of these quotations, offers to purchase are matched with bids. Although the Paris Bourse is moving in the direction of automating the bid and offer system, thereby edging toward a more continuous pricing scheme, the system still differs substantially from the pricing scheme underlying NASDAQ or available for alpha stocks on London's SEAQ system. In Germany, specified brokers fix the official prices of German stocks traded on the exchanges; the official price is supposed to be the one at which the greatest number of trades can be executed. However, the large banks engage in off-market transactions at prices that are not negotiated in accordance with the official market price. These transactions involve the banks in dealings in international securities, which take place almost completely in the off-exchange trading environment, and in arbitrage-like trading in domestic stocks that tends to promote some linkage among the German regional exchanges. Many observers believe that there might be legal complications if such off-market transactions were reported along with official market quotations.

iii) Market-makers, which have the capacity to execute large transactions and, therefore, to preserve the liquidity of the market, provide a useful function in a trading system designed to operate on a continuous price basis. Although London is alone among the European exchanges in having a fully developed market-making system, banks and securities houses throughout the other European countries typically perform market-making functions due to their large positions in particular securities. These functions, however, often are performed in trades that take place off exchange floors; thus, substantial changes in the structure of securities trading on the Continent would be required to move toward any unified system of market-making. Experts consider such a system to be a superior way of promoting a market with continuous pricing.

b. A pricing system that could support a multinational, multi-exchange trading network would have to be based upon comparable pricing information from source exchanges and would have to collect information on all significant trading activity. As a result, typically significant activity that occurs off-exchange in Germany or Paris would have to be brought into the information collection and distribution system. Without such information, quotations from exchanges alone probably would not form a reliable basis for execution of a transaction at the best available price.

c. At present, the largest multinational brokers base their transactions on a complex array of pricing information that is compiled in their dealing rooms. Seldom are decisions made based on reliance upon a single source of information.

d. Any effort to create an all-encompassing quotation system should be tempered by the realization that large securities firms almost certainly will augment whatever data are provided by such a comprehensive system. This is likely to be particularly true with a system that collects pricing information from multiple exchanges, because the information will be of more historical than continuous value. To the extent that exchange and off-exchange activity is not captured, current pricing information will vary from the information carried by the system. Most sophisticated securities firms would have the expertise and capability to integrate and process various available streams of information. The availability of highly sophisticated pricing information from the U.S. and other major non-European markets, however, would establish a level of minimum acceptability for any such system.

e. One valuable aspect of an effort to establish such a system is that it may well promote discussions among exchange authorities and major market participants about the process of harmonizing pricing procedures among different exchanges. As suggested above, telecommunications carriers and service providers that back the development of such a system could serve as facilitators of the emergence of market conditions that will support a more extensive and co-ordinated global trading network. The result would benefit both the financial services and the telecommunications industries.

i) The effort to establish the IDIS network is one such European initiative that may be viewed as a step toward encouraging the creation of conditions conducive to the development of a European-wide international securities market. However, many observers see major drawbacks in the plans for the IDIS system that could render it less effective and useful than currently available commercial information systems.

ii) There are, for example, important questions about which entities will be able to obtain access to the IDIS information stream and which entities will be able to originate data into the system.

iii) IDIS also may suffer because it is a system being backed and promoted by the exchanges. As a result, its services will be dependent upon widely differing views among national exchange officials about which entities may or should participate in an exchange-based information service. The system could be used as a vehicle for advancing a particular national exchange philosophy. Divisions among European exchanges—between the broker-dominated exchanges (such as in France and Italy) and the bank-dominated exchanges (such as in the Federal Republic of Germany and, to a lesser extent, the Netherlands)—may become the focal point of discussions about the structure of the IDIS network.

iv) Many observers view the IDIS system as being fundamentally flawed from the outset. The question is whether it will promote a serious dialogue on fundamental issues of the regulation of stock exchange activities at the national level.

f. If an individual system is viewed as being too complex to manage, there may be considerable value in supporting telecommunications policies that would encourage the linkage of individual networks so that financial institutions could be assured of having access to a substantial number of different information services that, in the aggregate, would constitute the basis for international transactional decisions. Such a situation would require the creation of gateways and sophisticated interactive capabilities so that traders could query databases or negotiate on-line with entities that have substantial positions in a particular security (*i.e.*, electronic market-makers).

g. These objectives might be accomplished through the augmentation of public switched networks, including high-speed data networks and packet-switched services. They also might be promoted by allowing a greater degree of interconnection among international private networks, or between private networks and the public switched network, than is permitted by CCITT Recommendations or is typically allowed by the policies of many European PTTs. These issues are discussed below in Section III.E.

4. Multi-Exchange Execution Systems

a. Establishing a unified system for executing orders on a number of European exchanges could be difficult due to the different structures of the various exchanges. Not only are brokerage arrangements different, but the extent of off-exchange activity varies widely, although in many cases it is significant and informally structured. As a result, a multi-market trading system would have to account for and seek to concentrate these disparate trading patterns.

b. A multi-exchange execution system would involve not only alignment of trading practices, but also co-ordination of exchange membership rules. Exchange participants that are vital to the functioning of a particular national market might not be permitted to function in a similar capacity on the exchange of another country. In addition, an exchange might object to having itself linked to another market if the linkage would allow entities not permitted to operate on the floor of the first exchange to gain access to that exchange's trading activity. The electronic network, in this instance, would become a back-door membership opportunity for certain financial institutions, such as large banks.

c. Membership and dealing configurations vary widely from one exchange to the next. A number of experts argue that some European-wide movement toward a system of specialists or market-makers, who can maintain positions in specific stocks, is essential to the formation of a unified market. Although such a result is possible, it would require many national changes. Few of the exchanges in Europe operate in this manner, and many restrict the ability of floor dealers to maintain substantial positions in traded securities. Decisions about dealing arrangements will have to be made along with decisions about membership issues—principally involving the degree of involvement of banks and the relationship of banks to the dealing operations within the exchanges.

i) In France, for example, there are really two transactional arrangements: one for deals involving French securities, and another for foreign security deals. *Agents de change* have a monopoly with respect to exchange-floor brokerage functions and must be involved in all deals for

French securities. Nonetheless, French banks play a significant role in effecting large transactions because brokerage firms have only a limited number of *agents de change* and are generally quite undercapitalized. As a result, except in the newly emerging Second Market, French brokers are not able to maintain significant positions in securities they trade and, thus, are viewed as having limited capability to arrange large transactions. The banks, by contrast, have substantial equity interests in major French corporations. One bank reportedly holds between 3 and 5 per cent of the equity of all publicly-held French companies. Because transactions in French securities must be arranged through *agents de change*, however, bank participation in such deals must be effected through the *agents*. In transactions involving foreign securities, where there is no requirement that an *agent de change* be involved, French banks and large institutional investors actively deal on an independent basis.

ii) In the Federal Republic of Germany, the brokerage business is dominated by large and well-financed German banks, including the three largest German banks—Dresdner, Commerzbank and the Deutsche Bank. Domestic transactions must be executed on one of the eight regional stock exchanges in accordance with an official price established by the *Kursmacher*. Despite these requirements, there is significant off-market trading, principally among the German banks. In addition, the large banks engage in international securities transactions outside the official market, both during and outside of official trading hours.

iii) In Italy, brokerage functions on the exchanges have been given to a specified number of agents, designated by law and appointed by government officials. These brokers have severely limited capital resources. As a result, there is significant off-exchange trading activity, particularly among the large banks. Until recently, the securities markets in Italy have been severely handicapped by these restrictive practices and by stringent foreign-exchange controls and limitations on the scope of equity investments by major financial institutions. Thus, it would be difficult to arrange for an interconnected European securities market structured around the official representatives in the Italian Stock Exchange. As discussed above in Section II.E, it remains to be seen how the entry of foreign banks into Italy in January 1988 will affect Italian financial markets. The increased availability of investment capital (through pension funds) and the denationalization of certain large companies, which has created new interest in the private equities market, also could exert pressure on the exchanges in Italy to upgrade their operations and seek a more fluid market environment, perhaps involving some inter-exchange linkage.

iv) In the Netherlands, both banks and brokers are active participants in the stock exchange. Thus, the Netherlands appears to have a structure between the broker-dominated and bank-dominated European market configurations. Banks maintain active trading positions in securities on the Amsterdam exchange as well as on the London exchange. Brokers tend to be better capitalized and more entrepreneurial than elsewhere in

Europe. Under Dutch law, the *hoekman* plays a central role as a market-maker in various securities. His role is sometimes compared with that of a specialist on the U.S. exchanges or a jobber in the now restructured London exchange. Because of the hybrid—and flexible—character of the Dutch exchange, it could be relatively easy to integrate into the European-wide securities market.

    d. The operation of active secondary markets that involve banks not permitted to function as exchange members (as in Italy or France) represents a significant obstacle to the development of market linkages. A multinational trading system based on the structure of existing national exchanges would exclude these important and influential financial institutions—as well as their large volume of off-market trading—from the system.

    e. In addition, moving secondary market activities onto the exchanges as part of a widespread consolidation effort could run up against a number of legal and structural obstacles. In Germany, for example, the off-market trading of the large banks is vital to the overall national structure of the German capital market, because it provides a system for adjusting variations among the official prices of particular stocks on the eight regional exchanges and also gives the German banks a free and vigorous role in international trading activity. Observers question whether this off-exchange trading could be brought within the restrictive structure of the German exchanges—for legal and policy reasons.

    f. It is likely that a central obstacle to the development of effective market linkages would be obtaining some agreement among participating countries about the appropriate role for commercial banks in trading activities. This process is certain to require the development of some acceptable way of separating dealing and commercial banking functions.

    i) As noted above in Section III.B, the efforts of large banks to enter the securities markets of other countries through foreign affiliates may be one way in which the role of banks in the securities business will be sorted out. The opening of the London market has created opportunities for commercial banks from the U.S. and Japan to enter the securities business; in their own countries, they have been barred from such diversification by the Glass-Steagall Act (U.S.) and Section 65 of the Securities and Exchange Law of 1948 (Japan), although there are signs of erosion at the edges of the separation requirements, with the banks moving into the discount brokerage business. In addition, officials in the U.S. are devoting increasing attention to the restrictions placed on bank involvement in various businesses, such as securities dealing. There is some concern among government officials that, unless some or all of these restrictions are modified or relaxed, U.S. banks will be deprived of lucrative opportunities and, therefore, will be less successful in the changing financial services market.

    ii) As mentioned earlier, these market entry opportunities have increasingly been addressed in bilateral trade negotiations. Officials in one country are conditioning their approval of a request by a foreign bank to enter the domestic securities business on the agreement of authorities in that foreign bank's home country to provide reciprocal opportunities in their own securities markets. Consequently, trade concerns, as much as national banking policies, may have an impact on market structure decisions.

iii) Changes in market entry rules will have to be accompanied by decisions about what form of separation—if any—is needed to preserve the overlapping and often inconsistent functions demanded by securities dealing and credit operations. In the U.K., for example, where the banks play an important role in the securities markets, a system of so-called Chinese Walls has been erected between the different sectors of financial conglomerates to guard against potential conflicts of interest. Despite these efforts at separation, questions remain about how relationships among persons performing different market functions within a single institution should be structured. There are also difficult questions about access to inside information and the availability of research information within the newly formed financial conglomerates. Consequently, trade concerns, as much as national banking policies, may have an impact on market structure decisions.

iv) Similar debates continue to take place within the U.S. and Japan, which have struggled for years with the task of deciding how banking and securities functions should be allocated among financial institutions.

g. Because broad changes in market structure may be difficult or time-consuming to work out, it may be quite important—particularly in the near future—to encourage the development of a web of interconnected electronic dealing systems. Such systems could include existing off-market trading practices that are prevalent in parts of Europe, particularly in the Federal Republic of Germany, France and Italy.

i) One question is whether this interconnection would have an impact on the status of off-exchange activity. Off-market trading typically is not subject to regulation in Europe; however, it is not clear how national authorities would respond to more organized and widespread computerized dealing systems. One possibility is that an effort to organize and computerize these operations would subject them to regulation as exchanges—or to prohibition due to pre-approval requirements applicable to entities functioning like exchanges.

ii) It also is possible that efforts to interconnect various trading networks would result in the creation of more advanced trading systems that would tend to precipitate changes in the trading procedures and practices of the national exchanges. Faced with a breakdown of existing market systems due to the exacerbation of tensions between exchange and off-exchange trading, exchange authorities might seek to move toward building a more formal—and co-operative—relationship between the markets.

h. Although there is some potential for integration of

separate markets, it may well be that the focus of attention should be on providing telecommunications support for existing markets as a basis for building technological links among those markets. With the technology in place, and with the potential for integration looming large, market participants could turn their attention toward the need for further regulatory revisions that would enable market linkages to function effectively.

i. To the extent that national or regional telecommunications policies are used to support the development of networks that can accommodate the functions of separate markets and provide interfaces between those markets, the policies could have the effect of accelerating the adaptation of divergent regulations. The result could be the creation of conditions conducive to the development of a more efficient, unified multinational capital market. It is essential in this situation that financial institutions, including participants with very diverse roles, such as banks, securities houses, and institutional investors, should be able to establish their own transactional systems designed to meet their own market needs. The limitations of existing exchanges demonstrate the many potential shortcomings of a system devised under the auspices of the institutions that traditionally have overseen the national securities markets in Europe.

j. From this perspective, telecommunications links should be viewed more as a source of pressure for change in the operation of existing markets than as a means of solidifying the current practices of those markets. To some extent, of course, electronic networks and systems will assist markets by enabling them to handle a wider array of transactions more quickly, more efficiently, and, possibly, on a more decentralized basis. More importantly, however, these links may be considered as opportunities for the expansion of alternative markets. Exchange authorities will have the choice of either seeking to limit the growth of those markets through the imposition of new restrictive rules or attempting to bring those markets together—perhaps under the umbrella of a new and more diversified exchange entity.

k. Off-exchange markets serve important functions in many countries, and their existence in some countries will make efforts to curtail or end them in other countries relatively ineffective—particularly as telecommunications capabilities expand the reach of those markets. Thus, authorities will have to face the task of adjusting market structures to accommodate multiple trading fora.

i) Secondary markets are particularly important for the trading of newer, less-established issues. In London, for example, there will be no fewer than three fora for trading in such securities: the Unlisted Securities Market, the Third Market (a lightly-regulated version of the over-the-counter market), and a new exchange, the London Securities Exchange. In addition, significant trading in new issues is likely to continue to be conducted through informal dealings by telephone.

ii) As is already the case in many national markets, off-exchange dealing arrangements are often instrumental to the establishment of markets for trading in foreign securities. These trading relationships, which have been built upon the direct dealings of large financial institutions, have developed as a way of overcoming the obstacles to international trading that exist on organized exchanges. Listing requirements, clearance and settlement obstacles, and pricing difficulties stand in the way of bringing active international trading onto the exchanges. Telecommunications capabilities, which have allowed institutions to link sophisticated data networks and have lessened dependence on telephone and telex links as the basic tools for direct international dealing, are strengthening these markets and making them powerful centers of activity that may have to be addressed directly by government efforts to revise national market structures.

5. Settlement and Clearance Systems

a. An additional essential element of a unified multinational trading market is the need for new arrangements for the settlement of securities transactions and for the transfer of share certificates.

b. In general, settlement, clearance, and depositary institutions are organized to handle domestic securities transactions and are designed to work in conjunction with national exchanges. These institutions have specific criteria for determining which entities may participate in their operations. They also have established procedures for handling transactions that are not typically applicable to international transactions, particularly those that are arranged through off-market negotiations. For example, according to Hall and Duncan, quoted above, a transaction that took two weeks to settle in London before Big Bang could be settled in two days in the Federal Republic of Germany and three days in Japan.

c. As described above in Section II.E, some bilateral settlement arrangements have been worked out between the various national settlement and clearance organizations, such as SICOVAM in France and CIK in Belgium. These arrangements are intended to handle a limited number of multinational transactions—typically those that deal with a small number of multiple-listed securities.

d. These bilateral arrangements may be contrasted with the much broader arrangement applicable to the settlement of Eurobond transactions and certain other trades in foreign bonds or commercial paper. With respect to these transactions there are three major European-wide settlement services.

i) EUROCLEAR and CEDEL, which are described above in Section II.E, provide clearing and settlement services for a large volume of transactions—particularly Eurobond transactions—for participating organizations from around the world. Unlike most of the national clearing systems, which are dependent upon telex messages for communications among participants, both services are essentially computerized. Moreover, unlike the national clearing systems, these private associations have far fewer restrictions on membership.

ii) SWIFT, which has focused almost exclusively on the business of inter-bank transfers and the confirmation of foreign-exchange transactions and various credit instruments, has recently begun to investigate its possible future role in clearing securities. However, as described in Section III.C.4 above, there is significant debate over the role of banks in the securities markets. Thus, any movement by SWIFT into the securities markets can be expected to be slow. Some national telecommunications administrations have also questioned the extent to which SWIFT should be permitted to serve an even wider base of users than it already serves. Because SWIFT's international transmission network continues to operate at the pleasure of the national administrations, it is unlikely that SWIFT would move aggressively to expand its base of users and risk being considered a direct competitor of the European PTTs in the business of third-party message switching.

e. A central policy question is whether movement toward multinational market linkage would be best served by efforts to develop a new, centralized clearing and settlement organization or by attempts to forge more widespread and efficient links among existing national organizations.

i) Some observers doubt that a successful arrangement can be built on an elaborate network of bilateral links, although these observers readily admit the difficulties that are likely to be faced by a more comprehensive approach leading toward the establishment of a multinational settlement organization and central depositary.

ii) One alternative would be to seek the establishment of an organization such as SWIFT that is designed to promote the development of common systems and protocols that could be used as the basis for harmonizing many of the activities of national settlement operations. Telecommunications links would, of course, be the central component of this organization; they would—as in the case of SWIFT—be operated and managed centrally. These links could form the basis of a needed information exchange network that would permit clearing agencies to assess market conditions and trading activities and so judge their exposures. With the infrastructure in place, the respective national members might be more likely to seek adjustments in their individual procedures. The central linkage organization could serve as the catalyst for such changes. To the extent that a particular market lacked continuous or relatively rapid exchange reporting capabilities, it might be encouraged to develop these capabilities if it were being perceived—both within and outside its market—as the obstacle to a more successful multinational linkage.

iii) One difficulty in developing multinational clearing and settlement systems is that they must accommodate differences among national exchanges with respect to the manner in which transactions are completed and the timing within which settlement must be effected. Harmonization of such features of national trading systems is, of course, a difficult and time-consuming task. To the extent that a central organization can provide financing and foreign-exchange services in connection with the settlement process—as do EUROCLEAR and CEDEL—these national differences may be less of an obstacle. These functions, however, expose the settlement organization to certain financial risks that are arguably inconsistent with its primary role as a protector of investors' interests. Consequently, national differences are likely to stand as a barrier to the emergence of a multinational settlement process.

  f. The task of ensuring the transfer of ownership—which often requires the delivery of paper certificates—is part of the settlement process that poses additional challenges to a multinational market initiative.

  i) Depositaries are institutions deeply rooted in local legal requirements and commercial practices. National depositaries have elaborate membership restrictions and are qualified to act as nominees for only certain classes of entities. Consequently, the development of a multinational system involves significant obstacles, such as agreement upon mutually acceptable membership criteria or upon an "open" membership structure. This obstacle could be overcome if some central organization were established in which national depositary institutions would participate; national institutions would retain their own local legal standards, but they would function as the members of, and participants in, this less structured multinational organization.

  ii) The process also can be simplified by dematerializing the transactional system and retaining paper certificates within their country of origin. Reliance would be placed on a trade in depositary certificates, such as American Depositary Receipts ("ADRs"), which are used in the United States for trading in foreign securities. This approach would overcome the problem of national laws that permit depositary institutions to hold only domestic securities. It also could resolve problems that result from national rules requiring the delivery of a physical certificate to consummate a transaction. Depositary receipts may be constructed in such a form as would make them acceptable for delivery and use in a variety of markets.

  iii) In the U.K., a new system known as Taurus is being devised by the Stock Exchange. This system will allow securities to be held in certificate list form in accounts maintained by the Stock Exchange. The system will generate information that will be used to change the registered ownership of stock certificates of publicly-traded companies. Transfers will be made directly by links between the Taurus system and the data-processing systems of the largest British registrar organizations, including Lloyds Bank and the National Westminster Bank.

D. Additional Issues of Concern Among Financial Services Regulators

  1. The discussion in Section III.C has sketched broadly many of the structural differences in the European capital markets that present potential obstacles to the establishment of international electronic trans-

actional systems. These market conditions are the product of complex and voluminous laws and regulations, and some of those laws and regulations have been noted—in Sections III.B and III.C—to illustrate the ways in which national financial regulations can impede market integration unless flexibility is introduced and co-operation among national authorities is fostered.

2. As has been noted previously, a comprehensive examination of all the potential legal and regulatory hurdles to the establishment of international transactional systems is beyond the scope of this paper. The intention of the present discussion is to illustrate generally the conditions that are both leading toward, and standing in the way of, market integration. The following discussion is provided to augment the material presented thus far in Section III and to raise some additional legal and regulatory issues relating to the establishment of international trading markets built through elaborate electronic links.

3. As Hall and Duncan, quoted above, point out, an immediate concern in such electronic markets, which will involve elaborate links of information streams, is who will decide how to segregate information into blocks so that system users performing different functions will have access to only that information that is necessary for the performance of their tasks. Systems almost certainly will need to be constructed in "levels", as has been done in the SEAQ and NASDAQ systems, for example; mechanisms for blocking will have to be devised. Trading information and messages used by clearing organizations would not be routed to individual dealers, and data collected for market-makers might be limited to their terminals. Although the design of the mechanisms by which these functions will be effected may be left to telecommunications companies, the structure of the levels and the "location" of blocks will need to be worked out by financial market regulators and participants.

4. Market supervision also will have to be handled by some entity or group of entities. Although there are many potential candidates, including individual exchanges or existing national regulatory bodies or other government units, the actual scheme of supervisory activities is likely to be extraordinarily complex due to the diversity of participants and market functions that will be involved.

a. If multinational organizations are developed, such as central clearing organizations or data collection units, they might be viewed as logical choices to function as self-regulatory organizations charged with policing the activities of their participants. But what country's laws would be applied and what authority would be used to exercise that authority? The need for multinational treaties or other complex agreements could frustrate the entire process—or at least impose substantial delays.

b. National exchanges might be given—or left with—self-regulatory powers. It is not clear, however, that a disparate group of self-regulatory entities, each of which is likely to have a varying amount of power, would provide an effective means of supervising a multinational market. If this approach were to be used, arrangements would have to be made among participating exchanges to co-operate in investigatory and prosecutorial activities because of the cross-exchange nature of likely trading patterns.

    c. The scheme of market supervision also would have to be reviewed to determine how differing national laws would be applied to international transactions. For example, would U.S. insider trading laws apply to (*i*) only transactions originated within the U.S., (*ii*) transactions originated anywhere in the world if U.S. securities are involved, or (*iii*) only transactions effected by or through a U.S. entity? Suppose the transaction involved West German stock that was purchased by an affiliate of a U.S. broker through a terminal located in Tokyo? What if the deal involved the stock of a U.S. company acquired by a French bank through its affiliate in Australia?

    d. Decisions also would have to be made about the adoption of special rules relating to the use and operation of the system itself, such as what penalties would be imposed for the unauthorized use of system information, or for the failure to report market activity in a timely fashion, or for the transmission of false or misleading messages. Although these kinds of issues are routinely handled at the national level for both electronic and face-to-face market activities, they could present a greater legal problem in the context of an international system. It is not clear that existing national rules for market conduct would be adequate. Moreover, if national rules were to be relied upon, to whom and in what fashion would they be applied?

    5. In its interim report on the internationalization of securities markets, the SEC considered a variety of regulatory issues, including the applicability of national disclosure and registration requirements and methods of enforcing national rules for market conduct. Securities and Exchange Commission, *Report to the House Committee on Energy and Commerce on the Internationalization of the Securities Market—Interim Progress Report* (Oct. 9, 1986) (the "1986 Interim Report"). The SEC's initial views appear to be indicative of the concerns of national authorities about the development of international trading systems.

    a. In theory, the various requirements of the Securities Act of 1933 and the Securities Exchange Act of 1934, the principal U.S. laws on securities trading, apply equally to domestic and foreign issuers selling or offering to sell their securities in the U.S. to the public. These laws impose on issuers various registration requirements, as well as periodic reporting, proxy, and insider trading disclosure rules.

    b. In practice, the SEC has tried to adjust the way in which its disclosure requirements apply to foreign issuers to account for legal and accounting differences among countries. By providing separate registration and reporting forms for foreign issuers, the SEC has relaxed disclosure standards with respect to proxy materials and insider reporting. Other rules that require the disclosure of management remuneration and information on transactions with management are applicable only if such disclosures are required by applicable foreign laws. Accounting requirements are also flexible. Foreign issuers are not required to meet U.S. Generally Accepted Accounting Principles ("GAAP"), provided that the issuer supplies the SEC—and investors—with a reconciliation of variations between its own accounting methods and GAAP.

        c. The SEC explored disclosure issues in depth in a 1985 release that requested public comment on the need to harmonize national prospectus disclosure standards and securities distribution systems. *Facilitation of Multinational Securities Offerings,* 50 Fed. Reg. 9281 (March 7, 1985) (SEC No. 33–6568).

        i) The release proposed two possible ways of addressing the problem of varying national disclosure requirements. One proposal would involve an effort among government authorities to reach a reciprocal arrangement whereby a prospectus meeting minimum standards in the issuer's country would be accepted for offerings in all participating countries. Comments filed in response to the release generally favored this proposal, although many commenters suggested that reciprocal treatment might be limited initially to certain high-grade securities. The release also considered a proposal for the development of a common prospectus meeting disclosure standards agreed upon by a number of countries. Commenters contended that the reciprocal approach would be more easily implemented and would respect the different customs, business practices, fairness, and disclosure traditions in each country.

        ii) As a way of deciding more precisely what regulatory action would be appropriate, the SEC is preparing a comparative study of national laws regulating disclosure and distribution standards in the U.S. and other major industrialized countries. The SEC is also drafting a comparison of accounting and auditing requirements in the United States, Canada, the United Kingdom, other Member States of the European Economic Community, and Japan.

        iii) Some commenters cautioned that there were variations in national regulations regarding the method of distributing registration and reporting information to investors and the timing for effectiveness of such information. Some commenters suggested that timing problems might be alleviated if there was agreement to rely solely on review by authorities in the issuer's home market and to allow that process to control the progress of an offering. As a result, there would be one, rather than several, effective dates. Such a method would avoid the problem of having an effective date in one country precede effectiveness in another, which could result in "gun-jumping" problems for U.S. companies, which are subject to strict rules regarding the release of pre-effective publicity.

        d. In the 1986 Interim Report, the SEC devoted substantial attention to the difficulties it faced in trying to enforce U.S. securities laws in an international market. Typically, the SEC confronts these problems while attempting to gather evidence located abroad as part of an investigation of alleged market abuses.

e. Two broad categories of foreign laws can frustrate the acquisition of evidence. Foreign companies that are the subject of an SEC investigation can assert the protection of their countries' secrecy laws, which often guard against compelled disclosure of confidential financial records. Although the protections of secrecy laws may be waived by a foreign entity participating in a U.S. trading market, the second category of possible legal obstacles to SEC investigations—blocking laws—may not be waived by the individual. Blocking laws can be asserted to prohibit the disclosure, copying, inspection, or removal of documents located outside the U.S. These laws may prohibit the disclosure of evidence requested as part of a foreign discovery request. Unlike secrecy laws, blocking laws are intended to assert the sovereignty of the foreign state in which the evidence is located—rather than the privacy interests of the foreign market participant—and, therefore, can be waived only by a foreign government.

f. The SEC has approached the problem of enforcement in the international market in two ways. It has proposed unilateral action in the form of a waiver-by-conduct rule, and it has sought bilateral and multilateral agreements among countries involved in the global trading markets.

i) Under a proposed waiver-by-conduct rule, foreign investors who trade in a U.S. market would be considered to have waived the protections of any applicable foreign secrecy laws. This waiver would be effective simultaneously with the start of trading in a U.S. market by a foreign person or entity. It would amount to an "implied consent" on the part of the non-U.S. trader to disclose information and evidence relevant to any U.S. regulatory investigation involving that trader. The waiver-by-conduct proposal would not apply to blocking laws, because, as discussed above, only a foreign state can waive application of its blocking laws.

ii) The waiver-by-conduct proposal has met with heavy criticism. It was viewed by some as a futile attempt to extend U.S. laws beyond national borders that would be perceived as an encroachment on the sovereignty of other nations. This attempt to extend U.S. securities laws might be expected to provoke foreign retaliation—rather than multinational co-operation. Other countries might attempt to adopt new legislative protections that would impede the enforcement of any implied waiver.

iii) The SEC's efforts are not without precedent, however. For example, the Commodities Futures Trading Commission (the "CFTC") has relied on a waiver-by-conduct theory in order to enforce its special call provisions and to adopt market surveillance rules directed at non-U.S. participants in the commodities and futures markets. These rules represent, in part, the response of the CFTC to delays in information gathering that result from foreign blocking and secrecy laws. The CFTC's waiver-by-conduct provisions have met with foreign resistance, however, because they essentially require a waiver of foreign bank secrecy laws as a condition for access to U.S. markets. The Swiss banks, for example, so objected to the CFTC's rules that they stopped trading on behalf of their clients in markets subject to the CFTC's supervision. If U.S. securities markets were to become subject to similar regulations, they could lose market participants to other exchanges, particularly if telecommunications links make multi-market trading more common.

iv) Although the waiver-by-conduct proposal may have a limited future, the SEC is reportedly attempting to include a form of implied consent in certain agreements relating to multinational markets.

g. As an alternative to rules that require market participants to abide by U.S. rules as a condition of entry into U.S. markets, the SEC has looked to the execution of bilateral and multilateral agreements as a way of establishing market rules that have the support of both U.S. and non-U.S. authorities.

i) The SEC has entered into bilateral arrangements with the U.K. and Japan. A memorandum of understanding with the U.K. Department of Trade and Industry marks the first co-operative securities market supervision arrangement between U.S. and U.K. authorities. The memorandum is intended to foster mutual assistance in investigations of insider trading and market manipulation. The memorandum also makes assistance available in the surveillance of investment businesses and brokerage firms. In keeping with its role as a first step toward broad bilateral initiatives in securities and commodities regulation, the memorandum states that negotiations regarding a formal treaty will begin in 1987.

ii) A similar memorandum with Japan offers a more *ad hoc* approach to bilateral securities law enforcement efforts. Signed in May 1986 with the Securities Bureau of the Ministry of Finance, this memorandum provides that U.S. and Japanese regulators will co-operate on requests for market surveillance and investigations on a case-by-case basis.

iii) Since 1982, the SEC has had a memorandum of understanding with the Swiss Government. The agreement was needed because insider trading is not a crime in Switzerland and, therefore, other mutual assistance treaties applicable to criminal actions were of no help. The memorandum led to a separate private agreement with Swiss bankers that allows banks to disclose certain information to the SEC without violating Swiss secrecy laws. In 1986, the memorandum was used for the first time to obtain information in a civil suit.

iv) Although the SEC has some bilateral agreements on which to rely, it continues to require that markets subject to its authority develop surveillance and information-sharing agreements. For example, prior to approving the linkage between the American and Toronto Stock Exchanges, the SEC required that agreements between the two exchanges be reached to govern surveillance and investigations; it also required the exchanges to obtain a co-operative commitment from the Ontario Securities Commission. Similar agreements have been or are being developed in the context of other U.S.-Canada market links.

v) A drawback of reliance upon bilateral agreements is that inconsistent applications of national securities laws can result. For example, violations of U.S. laws may go unpunished under the terms of the U.S.-Japan agreement, whereas the same conduct may be subject to punishment under the U.S.-U.K. agreement.

vi) Such inconsistency from one market link to the next can be minimized by the use of multilateral agreements. The SEC has used one multilateral agreement in past enforcement actions, although this agreement was not developed specifically for application to the securities market. In two instances, the SEC relied upon the Hague Convention on the Taking of Evidence Abroad to pursue international investigations. However, the process of acquiring information under that agreement has proved costly and time-consuming. As a result, the SEC argued in a 1986 case before the U.S. Supreme Court that U.S. courts should not be required to look to the Hague Convention in all instances where a discovery request is met with the assertion of a foreign secrecy or blocking law. Bilateral and multilateral agreements, the SEC said, should be given weight, and the U.S. courts should not defer significantly to conclusory secrecy claims or to blocking laws adopted solely to frustrate U.S. enforcement efforts. Of course, the approach of the U.S. courts is of only limited relevance; although the courts can support U.S. enforcement efforts, they cannot control the responses of non-U.S. authorities.

vii) In an effort to develop a more workable multilateral agreement, the SEC has participated in discussions within the International Organization of Securities Commissions and the Organization for Economic Co-operation and Development (the "OECD") about multinational enforcement needs and obstacles. Pursuant to an SEC proposal, the OECD has begun a survey of member countries to assess the interest of members in pursuing mutual assistance and co-operation efforts in the international trading area. Other members have offered alternative proposals, including one to establish a centralized regulatory forum in which future multilateral accords could be negotiated.

viii) A drawback of multilateral initiatives is that there really is no comprehensive multinational forum. The International Organization of Securities Commissions is the closest thing there is to such a forum, but it lacks the kind of established role that is enjoyed by the Cooke Committee of the Bank for International Settlements, which brings together the world's central banks with a series of supervisory agreements. It remains to be seen if the development of more active international securities markets will produce support for a similar organization.

6. The foregoing discussion has suggested just a few of the many complex and still-emerging legal and regulatory problems that will have to be faced as international markets and multi-market links are developed. As the discussion makes clear, co-operative efforts will be needed to identify and to attempt to resolve the obstacles. Such efforts will have to accompany the planning of technological links and electronic systems to permit market integration and transborder dealing. A brief discussion of the obstacles presented by international telecommunications policies is set forth in the next section of the paper.

E. The Impact of International Telecommunications Policies

1. Introduction

a. The offering of multinational dealing services is likely to create friction with current international telecommunications policies due to the manner in which such services would have to be configured. As noted previously, significant progress toward the integration of different national markets is likely to require the interconnection of private line networks and the sharing and resale of leased circuits. In addition, because efficient market activity requires the involvement of a broad array of financial institutions and market organizations, network development is likely to require some flow of information between public switched and private networks, particularly to provide users with dial-up access to systems.

b. Among the potential telecommunications policy obstacles to the development of these systems are the D-Series Recommendations of the CCITT, which are interpreted by most national administrations to prohibit the resale of international leased lines and the offering of services that are viewed as infringing on the business of an administration. The Recommendations have been applied by most administrations to limit the use of international leased lines essentially to activities that are readily distinguishable from public telecommunications services.

c. The application of the D-Series Recommendations to electronic transactional services raises a question about whether these services should be subject to the Recommendations at all. As discussed in Chapter II on "Boundary Lines", national policymakers in many countries continue to debate how best to fit value-added services provided to the public into the regulatory scheme for international telecommunications. Fitting transactional systems and similar specialized services into this scheme is an even more difficult task, and it may be that policymakers will conclude that such systems are sufficiently distinct from telecommunications activities to be best left free of telecommunications regulations. Whatever the conclusion, it will be important for regulators to focus on the distinctions between "public correspondence" services, other communications services, and specialized communications-related offerings, such as transactional and information services.

d. The following discussion highlights the most important of the D-Series Recommendations as a means of illustrating the ways in which they may conflict with the development of electronic transactional networks.

2. The D-Series Recommendations

a. Recommendation D.1 sets forth general principles. It explains that when administrations make available to a customer International Private Leased Circuits ("IPLCs"), they should take into account not only the Recommendations, but also any terms and conditions worked out by the administrations offering the circuits and the need to meet the requirements of customers. Recommendation D.1.1.1.

i) This provision allows for some flexibility on an administration-by-administration basis. Within the framework established by the other Recommendations, this flexibility could be used to promote the development of bilateral agreements that authorize market linkages intended to encourage financial institutions to engage in more organized international trading systems—as opposed to less centralized dealing-room links.

ii) A question is the extent to which administrations will be willing to take an aggressive view of transactional systems. Under such a view, these systems could well be considered the business of the customer of an international leased line and, therefore, consistent with the terms of the D-Series Recommendations.

b. Two of the D-Series Recommendations govern the scope of IPLC use.

i) Recommendation D.1.1.7 states that IPLCs "may be used only to exchange communications relating to the business of the customer. When the circuit is used to route communications from (to) one or more users other than the customer, these communications must be concerned exclusively with the activity for which the circuit is leased".

ii) The phrase "relating to the business of the customer" means that services that "relate to" the financial business of a provider of an electronic financial service may be provided over IPLCs. The breadth that administrations give to this phrase may determine whether links among quotation systems, dealing networks set up between market-makers or specialists, and clearing and settlement systems will be permitted.

iii) The phrase "communications must be concerned exclusively with the activity for which the circuit is leased" suggests that when users (*i.e.*, individuals having access to the IPLC) use a particular service to transmit some "communication", they must do so for purposes that fall within the terms of their relationship with the service provider. If administrations view that relationship narrowly, perhaps interpreting an electronic exchange system as being intended to accomplish the business of trading, but not of clearance or settlement, this phrase could be used to block the development of comprehensive networks. Of course, a broad view of this concept might permit the configuration of very diverse systems.

iv) Recommendation D.1.1.10 vests broad discretion in administrations to ensure that, among other things, a customer does not use an IPLC in a way that "would be regarded as an infringement of the functions of an Administration in providing telecommunications services to others". To prevent users from siphoning revenues from the public switched telephone network, an administration can rely on this Recommendation to refuse to supply an IPLC when it believes that a proposed service would be akin to message switching or any other service (including value-added services) offered by the administration.

v) The way in which administrations apply D.1.1.10 to

financial services networks could be a key to determining the true viability of these networks. To the extent that broad, multi-user systems are viewed as competitors of the public networks, the administrations can rely on this Recommendation to block their development. However, as discussed earlier in this paper, administrations ultimately may benefit more by viewing such systems as extensions of the financial services industry, rather than as new telecommunications offerings. If multinational financial markets are supported by carriers, through decisions to make available flexible transmission and switching configurations free from such burdensome communications-based rules as volume-sensitive tariffs and non-discrimination requirements, these electronic markets may develop more quickly and ultimately provide administrations with substantial new volumes of traffic. This same point applies to the interpretation given to Recommendations D.1.5 and D.1.7, which are discussed below.

c. The CCITT Recommendations bar the "resale" of IPLCs. "Customers" can "derive telecommunications channels" from a circuit and "extend" them "by means of other circuits leased by the same customer", but they cannot "sublease" such circuits. Recommendation D.1.1.8. The Recommendations also authorize administrations to "take all steps, appropriate in the circumstances, to ensure that the provisions governing the lease of international circuits are respected". Recommendation D.1.1.11.

d. Recommendation D.1.5. governs the provision of private leased circuit *networks* by an administration. All of the restrictions applicable to IPLCs apply to private line networks. Recommendation D.1.5.9.

i) This Recommendation begins, for example, by restating that circuit and message switching and transmission are the "exclusive function" of administrations. Recommendation D.1.5.1. There is a requirement that the equipment, configurations, and the scope of usage of the private network be reported to an administration. Note to Recommendation D.1.5.4.

ii) The Recommendation bars the interconnection of two or more private leased circuit networks unless the involved administrations agree. Recommendation D.1.5.6.

iii) Authorization for interconnection of the public switched network and leased line networks is completely within the discretion of each administration. Recommendations D.1.6.1.1. and D.1.6.1.2. Access must be on the customer's premises. Recommendation D.1.6.1.3a). Information "exchanges" over a private leased circuit must relate "solely to the activities for which the circuit has been leased", a principle like that contained in Recommendation D.1.1.7. Recommendation D.1.6.1.3b).

iv) One additional principle is that access to the public telephone network may not be allowed simultaneously at both ends of a circuit. Such access also "is strictly limited to subscribers of the national public network in the country where the circuit terminates". Recommendation D.1.6.3.1. This provision is intended to avoid bypass of the international public network; it may have the effect of barring two users from using the same service at the same time, an effect that would have a particularly severe impact on electronic transactional and market services.

    e. Recommendation D.1.7 focuses on the use of IPLCs in conjunction with data processing centers and operations. Underlying this Recommendation is the principle that the transmission of "intelligence" (not merely "information") between users, accompanied by processing, is not mere message switching. Recommendation D.1.7.3 d), however, prohibits the customer from operating "in the manner of an Administration by providing telecommunications services to others".

    f. Finally, Recommendation D.6 sets forth the general principles for the provision of facilities to organizations formed to meet the specialized international communication needs of their members.

    i) Developed for SWIFT, Recommendation D.6 applies in "exceptional circumstances" where administrations cannot supply services through public or specialized networks.

    ii) Recommendation D.6.2.1 sets forth the conditions governing the provision of such facilities. In general, large users are inclined to avoid whatever regulatory shelter Recommendation D.6 may provide because the tariff principles contained in the Recommendation are volume-based and permit no negotiation with an administration. Recommendation D.6.3.

    iii) It is not likely that D.6 would provide national exchanges with an attractive avenue for pursuing the development of international links.

    iv) The existence of the volume-sensitive tariffing principle set out in D.6 does not necessarily mean that large multi-member user groups will be subjected uniformly to this charging scheme. SITA, the non-profit co-operative association of airlines discussed above in Section II.F, has, for years, been classified by the PTTs as a single user; thus, leased circuits have been made available to it on a flat-rate basis. This charging arrangement originated before the adoption of Recommendation D.6 in 1980.

    v) Recently, as SITA has sought to include in its network entities involved in the travel industry and closely related to the business of the airlines, including car rental agencies and airport and customs authorities, and as the number of users, scope of participants, and volume of network traffic have increased, there have been discussions among administrations about applying the volume-sensitive charging scheme of Recommendation D.6 to the SITA network facilities. SITA has argued against a change in its tariff treatment. Part of this argument depends on a notion of reliance: SITA views itself as a unique organization that has developed with the encouragement of telecommunications policies that have made the construction of an elaborate electronic communications system affordable and economical. This system now plays a substantial role in ensuring the continued safety and reliability of air travel; any change in charging principles that made SITA's operation less viable would deprive the airlines of this important system. In addition, SITA contends, volume-sensitive charging would alter the global character of the system by forcing airlines in smaller countries off the network due to the increased cost of using the system.

vi) The way in which telecommunications authorities have classified SITA to permit and encourage the development of a global network is evidence of the degree to which a flexible application of international policies can be used to foster the growth of an electronic market system. The possibility that these same policies could be used to change the basis on which that system is operated highlights the choice faced by administrations. The imposition of charging and use restrictions designed to "protect" monopoly network functions (such as third-party message switching) could have the longer-range consequence of discouraging the development of systems that would route substantial amounts of traffic over network facilities and would increase the dependence of industry sectors on the telecommunications business.

F. Summary

1. International securities transactions involve a complex set of activities that require co-operation among a diverse group of participants located in a number of countries and operating under disparate national market systems. A typical international securities transaction requires (a) collection and analysis of all available pricing information, (b) addition of information with respect to foreign-exchange and interest rates that might affect the ultimate price in the delivery of the security, (c) initiation of a transaction through a market-maker, specialist, or other dealer in a particular market—possibly requiring the involvement of additional parties because of the limits on the position that a national dealer may maintain in a particular security, (d) confirmation of the transaction, (e) arrangement of payment for and delivery of the securities, (f) notification of the customer that the transaction has been entered into, and (g) delivery of the securities or other evidence of ownership/transfer to the buyer or other custodial institution or agent, together with verification and recordation of the transaction.

2. A goal of developing multinational market systems is to provide a facility for the integration of these many activities. Although one would expect that the many parts of a transaction could not be handled by a single system—particularly as the breadth and variety of the market was expanded—an important purpose of linkage across national borders would be to promote the development of harmonious market functions. By establishing structures for linkage, including both technological and organizational features, pressures would be placed on national markets to

co-operate with each other so that the linkages could be used by powerful financial institutions to conduct trading activities.

3. The need for flexibility in both technological and organizational links cannot be understated. As historic distinctions between the banking and securities businesses continue to erode, electronic transactional systems will be complex webs of connections among private networks for specialized user groups. Previously separate banking and securities functions will become increasingly connected; the dealing networks established by banks, for example, may be linked to information and order execution systems set up for brokers and dealers. Clearing organizations once developed for a certain set of institutions or transactions may need to be opened to new participants and made suitable for supporting less formal markets.

4. The specialized nature and market-intensive demands of transactional systems suggest that broad discretion needs to be left to entities other than the PTTs to establish the protocols and infrastructures for such systems.

a. An attempt to integrate distinct markets too closely could be counter-productive. Telecommunications companies could not be expected to assess correctly, for example, the subtleties of the relationship between the off-exchange trading of large German banks, the activities of the German regional exchanges, and the international securities markets. However, intermediaries should not be precluded from establishing capabilities that will encourage the connection of diverse but essential participants in a complex transactional network.

b. A failure to provide for numerous attractive and complex links could make market integration less efficient and ultimately less likely. Unless national clearing systems are given the opportunity to communicate with each other in an efficient and instantaneous manner, and unless pricing systems provide for a maximum degree of data collection from different trading centers (including direct dealing arrangements among banks and securities houses), market opportunities will not be presented and pressures will not be imposed on financial market authorities to adopt rules and regulations that will permit integration to occur. As a result, it is important that telecommunications authorities should not impede or inhibit the connection of different networks by imposing special tariffs on "bridges" between such networks. Volume-sensitive pricing that attempts to charge for all of the traffic that flows over the "bridge" could make those bridges so costly that they will not be used. In that event, communications policies would become a source of disaggregation, and carriers could lose out on the vast volume of traffic that ultimately might be carried over facilities linked to form a complex multinational trading system.

5. Pressure for the development of broad electronic market systems will come from the consumer services market as well, although, as this Chapter has stressed, more attention and activity is likely to be focused on trading markets and related business services. The consumer market,

however, is an important contributor to the mix of factors shaping the development of electronic financial services.

      a. The potential for conflict between the financial services and telecommunications sectors may well develop most quickly within Europe. European banks and financial services companies are growing more restive about their ability to complete with powerful U.S. and Japanese banks in offering consumer-oriented electronic financial services.

      b. U.S. and Japanese banks have been able to develop and promote their services in relatively open and deregulated domestic markets. By contrast, European banks have faced a relatively rigid telecommunications environment that has generally discouraged innovation within the financial community. As competitive pressures increase, these European institutions will undoubtedly be clamoring for more flexibility to use private lines, to share them with related companies, to interconnect different private line networks, and to obtain access to leased lines without paying volume-related surcharges.

    6. The degree of conflict among the financial services and telecommunications sectors may well depend upon the willingness of the telecommunications industry—and its regulators—to adjust their perspectives on evolving electronic market services.

      a. Interconnected transactional networks should not be viewed as potential replacements for, or alternatives to, existing public-switched services offered by the PTTs. Although new systems may well eliminate the need for much traditional telex traffic, these same transactional systems will demand complex and sophisticated transmission and switching services that will represent new sources of traffic for carriers. Less efficient services, such as telex, are destined to play a smaller role in the financial markets because they are inappropriate vehicles for the kinds of communications being demanded by increasingly diverse and active financial institutions.

      b. The issue is not whether these old modes of communication can be preserved, but whether new modes can be used to generate far greater amounts of traffic for telecommunications networks. A flexible approach by the PTTs to new market services is likely to stimulate increased transactions in the securities market and—ultimately—greater use of the telecommunications networks.

IV. REDEFINING THE RELATIONSHIP BETWEEN TELECOMMUNICATIONS AND ELECTRONIC MARKETS

    A. The development of electronic market services implicates a broad and complex array of national and international laws and policies. This paper has sought to document some of the important issues in the context of a single market sector—financial services. In an effort to distill some of these issues, the following discussion highlights several aspects of electronic market services that may be unique and that should be a focus of attention for telecommunications service providers and regulators.

B. First, electronic market services inevitably will seek to integrate the activities of a diverse set of market participants. These services are not typically intended to serve the general public; rather, they are designed to facilitate a complex set of business relationships that are integral to a particular transactional system. Entities participating in a particular system will not always be from the same "business sector", although there almost always will be ongoing business or contractual ties among the participants.

1. To the extent that restrictions on the interconnection of leased lines attempt to limit such activities to defined groups, such as a single business sector, the rules are likely to be more restrictive than is feasible if an electronic transactional system is to work efficiently. Moreover, the boundary lines of a specific "business sector" ultimately are subjective. An electronic system could be characterized broadly as involving players in the financial services industry; the same network could be described as involving entities in the banking business, the brokerage business, and the settlement and clearance business. Telecommunications authorities seeking to limit the scope of permissible leased-line use might opt for the latter description, whereas more liberal regulators might be comfortable with the former.

2. The possible breadth of participants in a single transactional system is illustrated by the wide array of business contacts that are critical to the functioning of the airline industry and the entity that serves its needs, SITA, which is discussed above in Section II.F. The airlines have ongoing ties with credit-card companies to verify credit purchases of tickets; with travel agents, who make bookings related to airline travel and other transportation or lodging accommodations; with aircraft manufacturers and suppliers; and with airport and customs authorities. In addition, due to consumer demand for the ability to plan all aspects of travel through a central point, airlines have sought to establish ties with such travel industry participants as car-rental agencies and hotels. The airline industry views all these activities as being central to its business and, therefore, is seeking to improve the efficiency and effectiveness of SITA by bringing a broader array of travel industry members into its electronic market. An electronic system that will serve an industry's needs must be flexible enough to adapt to the changing perspectives of that industry regarding the scope and purpose of its activities.

3. Ultimately, it is difficult to focus on industry groupings as a basis for determining the scope of permissible uses of private lines. Reliance on such industry characterizations is not likely to be productive because market sectors, such as the financial services sector, will continue to experience radical changes in their structure and in the relationships among the various players in a market sector. The important point to keep in mind is that the use of a transactional system by a broad array of entities is not intended as a substitute for public-switched telecommunications services; it

reflects an effort by businesses to replicate and improve their activities with the help of telecommunications capabilities.

4. Many of the new services are not intended to compete with the offerings of telecommunications service providers. In fact, they often create new business opportunities for the telecommunications industry. Consequently, the providers of these new specialized services believe that the regulatory regime applied to value-added services (which market their capabilities generally to anyone seeking a specific electronic capability) should not apply to systems that are designed to support the specific activities of a particular set of businesses.

C. Second, specialized service providers offering financial or transactional services often must establish a single price for their services; they are unable to separate the pricing of the communications capabilities from other elements of their services. As a result, regulations barring rate discrimination or setting rate levels for specialized services ultimately will affect the price of activities far removed from the telecommunications field. Electronic settlement and clearance functions, for example, should be priced according to the cost of offering financial services; whereas the cost of telecommunications elements constitutes a portion of the total cost of providing service, the price of that service should not necessarily be based on regulatory philosophies applicable to regulated carriers in the telecommunications industry.

D. Third, the imposition of technical standards on providers of specialized services may have a disruptive impact on businesses that are dependent on telecommunications but that must set the rules and protocols for their dealing systems in accordance with the standards of their own industry, not those of the telecommunications industry. Some national regulators—even in countries that usually are viewed as having very liberal policies—have insisted on setting certain specifications for value-added service providers. However, interconnection requirements or decisions about protocols affect the way in which an industry such as the financial services sector will be able to conduct electronic transactions. Standards generally are established within an industry grouping—by associations or regulatory bodies with a mandate to assure the effective performance of an industry sector other than the telecommunications field. Telecommunications authorities will need to be sensitive to the fact that technical standards applicable to transactional systems are likely to affect or conflict with the standards set in accordance with another industry's business practices.

E. Fourth, attention should be focused on the extent to which the layering of numerous telecommunications "rules of conduct" on market systems designed to facilitate transactions in specific business sectors could impede the international development of these systems. As stressed throughout this paper, there are many obstacles to the successful establishment of transborder electronic market services; the task of grappling with divergent national telecommunications regulations could well be the straw that breaks the camel's back. (The many telecommunications policy obstacles to establishing international value-added networks is discussed in Chapter II on "Boundary Lines".) As discussed in Chapter IV on "European Telecommunications Policy", the European Commission has discouraged the imposition of duplicative layers of regulation—one layer from the service provider's country of origin and the other from the country in which services are to be provided—in an effort to promote the development of a pan-European market for services. It may well be essential to consider that telecommunications regulations for transaction-oriented services are only one of possibly several tiers of regulation.

F. Fifth, as discussed above in Section III.E, it is important for telecommunications policymakers to focus on the unique nature of transactional services and the inappropriateness of grouping them with generic telecommunications services offered to the public.

1. As noted in Chapter II on "Boundary Lines", it has become increasingly difficult to differentiate between an international carrier and an international value-added service provider; the Japanese are now wrestling with this distinction. It may be useful to distinguish between these two types of entities and providers of electronic transactional services (and similar offerings).

2. In the absence of a regulatory classification differentiating between specialized service providers and these other entities, entry limitations imposed on carriers or value-added service providers serving the public could have serious and undesirable ramifications for the financial services industry and related sectors. For example, in Japan, there is no inclination among government officials to adopt a very open entry policy with respect to international carriers. Moreover, it appears that operators of international value-added networks will be required to have their operating arrangements authorized. This authorization process could be used to limit the participation of Type II service providers in the international market. The evolving situation in Japan with respect to international facilities and services is described more fully in Chapter II.

3. Any application of these restrictions could impede competition and international trade in the financial markets and in other sectors unrelated to the telecommunications field.

4. Thus, it may be important, as has been suggested elsewhere in this paper, to adopt new classifications for providers of transactional services in the international arena. Such a classification scheme would distinguish between the involvement of various market participants in a transactional network and the activities of entities engaged in the "simple resale" of communications capabilities. An international effort to interpret the provisions of CCITT Recommendation D.1 as being applicable only to such "simple resale" might be an important step toward promoting the development of new transactional services internationally.

G. Finally, the supervision of international electronic market systems should not be left to multinational fora that focus primarily on telecommunications issues. One forum cannot possibly grapple with the many perspectives that are likely to affect the development of such systems. As noted earlier in this paper, new transactional systems almost certainly will be a major topic of discussion in talks intended to establish a new trading framework for services. They will be the subject of bilateral and multilateral trade negotiations. For this reason, particularly, it is unrealistic to believe that the ITU—through the CCITT—can or should be the primary forum for establishing future international electronic market arrangements.

H. There is a risk that telecommunications regulations will be used—intentionally or unintentionally—to impede the emergence of new electronic market services. This result would be contrary to the interests of telecommunications providers faced with shrinking margins and increased investment demands. Telecommunications carriers are likely to profit more by allowing new services to develop than by exacting special tariff charges on new "electronic bridges" among players in a market or entities with regular transactional relationships. The key for telecommunications providers may be to remove barriers to these linkages and to promote the restructuring of other industry sectors by electronic means so that telecommunications transport services can become the most critical "commodity" in the emerging service-based economy.

CHAPTER IV
THE FUTURE OF EUROPEAN TELECOMMUNICATIONS POLICY

TABLE OF CONTENTS

Page

I. Introduction... 273
    A. Overview: The Context 273
    B. Europe: What Are the Issues for Discussion?................ 274

II. The Economic Environment—Pricing Trends..................... 274
    A. Response to Economic Pressures: Some General Trends 274
    B. New PTT Investment Policies: One Set of Responses to Economic Pressures 277

III. Emergence of a New Facilities Infrastructure 283
    A. Infrastructure for Satellite Services............................. 283
    B. The European Approach to ISDN 293

IV. Structure of European Competitive Relationships 298
    A. Introduction 298
    B. Facilities-Based Competition..................................... 298
    C. Satellite-Based Competition 299
    D. Service-Based Competition 300
    E. Increased Competitive Pressure 301

V. Role of Service-Based Competition in Achieving Market Integration in Europe 302
    A. Service Providers Urging Common Interfaces and Regulatory Policies.. 302
    B. A Unified Infrastructure 303
    C. Integration From "Demand" Side.............................. 303

VI. Role of Competition Policy and *British Telecom* Decision in Market Integration... 304
    A. Competition Policy 304
    B. Importance of the *British Telecom* Decision: Introduction 305
    C. Application of Article 86 to PTTs: Prohibiting Abuse of Dominant Position 306
    D. Use of Article 85 to Review and Regulate Agreements Among PTTs 310
    E. Use of Treaty Provisions on Free Flow of Services 313
    F. Some Concluding Observations on the Task Facing the Commission 317

			Page
VII.	Evolution of Regulatory Mechanisms		318
	A.	European Regulatory Processes	318
	B.	Relevance of Regulatory Mechanisms	320
VIII.	The Commission's Role in Integrating the European Telecommunications Market		321
	A.	Introduction: Shift in Commission's Focus	321
	B.	New Policy Initiatives: Commission Proposals to Classify Services	323
	C.	Some Suggestions for an Alternative Procedural Approach	329
	D.	A Consultative Process Within Europe	333
	E.	The Commission's Role in the International Context	336

CHAPTER IV
THE FUTURE OF EUROPEAN TELECOMMUNICATIONS POLICY

I. INTRODUCTION

A. Overview: The Context

1. This paper is an effort to explore in greater depth some of the European issues that were raised in the Synthesis of Phase I of the Study of Telecommunications Structures. What was suggestive and discursive in Phase I has been expanded significantly. Nevertheless, the rapid changes in Europe and the consequent emergence of new issues make this paper more of a dynamic snapshot than a definitive statement of the ultimate direction of European telecommunications policy.

2. The understanding and formulation of European telecommunications policy is a complex and daunting task. The multiplicity of nations, structural approaches, technologies, industrial policies, and economic and political pressures make the development of European policy overwhelmingly difficult. Beyond any national efforts to reconcile the welter of individual national approaches, however, European policymakers are attempting to mobilize at a regional level: the Commission of the European Communities ("Commission") is beginning to examine how a European-wide policy can be developed and implemented.

3. Further complications are presented, of course, by the fact that European policy cannot be developed in isolation from international pressures. Keenly sensitive to trade imbalances, policymakers across Europe are looking to competitive pressures from North America and Japan. This competition has two important aspects. First, there is competition in telecommunications goods and services themselves. Existing barriers to the provision of telecommunications goods and services on an international basis are the subject of significant pressures, and are gradually, in some cases swiftly, being torn down.

4. Second, international competition is fierce across the entire spectrum of goods and services. Certain sectors, such as banking, are obviously telecommunications-dependent. Beyond these sectors, however, it is increasingly clear that one of the most important factors worldwide in

the production and distribution of goods, and the provision of services, is a readily available and efficient supply of telecommunications facilities and services. Thus, one of the most significant factors in what is a far-reaching re-examination of telecommunications policy across Europe is the perceived urgency of enhancing the region's competitive posture.

B. Europe: What Are the Issues for Discussion?

1. There are several issues that bear on the development of European telecommunications policy. Some of them are themselves the subject of discussion among policymakers. Others are factors that affect, or are a product of, national and Commission policymaking. The issues in this paper are grouped as follows:

2. The economic environment in which services are developed. A particular focus is the financial pressures on PTTs that are a consequence of pricing changes in international services, and their various investment policies.

3. The emergence of a new facilities infrastructure, including satellite and broadband ISDN services. This development raises issues concerning the evolution of an efficient and integrated network and how it can best be made available to users.

4. The extent and structure of co-operation, and competition, within and between countries in Europe. Competition can take place in several ways—in terrestrial facilities, in the emergence of satellites, and in the development of national and European-wide services.

5. The role of service-based competition in achieving market integration within Europe.

6. The role of competition policy, and the implications of the *British Telecom* case, in structuring the facilities and services sectors.

7. The evolution of regulatory institutions within Europe that both implement changed policies and deal with pressures for market access.

8. An assessment of the role of the Commission, in conjunction with other European institutions, in establishing European telecommunications policy.

II. THE ECONOMIC ENVIRONMENT—PRICING TRENDS

A. Response to Economic Pressures: Some General Trends

1. Trends and developments in the international market are exerting similar economic pressures on virtually every administration in Europe. Many PTTs are responding to those pressures by lowering the prices of international and, to a certain extent, interexchange services to meet the competition from other administrations. There remains, however, significant reluctance to take the corollary, necessary step of increasing local rates and bringing them closer to costs.

2. In the United Kingdom, competition between British Telecom and Mercury has had the decided result of lowering the pricing of interexchange services. Moreover, unlike most of the rest of Europe, there have even been some increases in local rates. Such rate increases, of course, are not unconstrained and are subject to a cap determined by an index keyed to inflation.

3. On the Continent, PTT responses have been somewhat sporadic, varying in degree from country to country. Essentially, however, pricing responses have been confined to international tariffs.

    a. Change in France, however, has been marked, with significant pricing responses to developments in the U.K. and in the Netherlands. International tariffs have been lowered significantly. Local rate structures are being closely examined and local measured service is being introduced gradually.

    b. Historically, the Direction Générale des Télécommunications ("DGT") has provided financial support (*prélèvements*) to various manufacturing interests and to support French industrial policy. The realignment of the French industrial sector following the election of the Chirac Government, however, has effectively reduced the level of such support. Consequently, the DGT will have substantially enhanced flexibility to lower rates to business customers without significantly increasing local charges.

    c. In the Netherlands, pricing policy seems to be following British developments. Initial efforts may be focused on international services, which is where Dutch tariff policy is likely to have the largest impact on the rest of Europe.

4. Competition poses a threat to PTTs that are used to a stable, economically secure environment. The current era, marked by significant pricing competition, is less tranquil than before liberalization and privatization in the U.K. Throughout Europe, therefore, administrations, politicians, and large users are asking whether it is possible or desirable to co-ordinate pricing. Co-ordination, however, may now be an impossibility because of the presence of facilities-based competition in the U.K.

    a. From the standpoint of users, the desirability of some European-wide co-ordination in the levels of tariffs, if not their structure, is often raised in the context of comparing European tariffs with those of the United States. Some European industrialists have taken the view that gross and unjustified differentials between nations in the pricing of leased lines, for example, inject an unnecessarily complicating factor in making business decisions about traffic flow or the location of plants or offices.

    b. Conversely, one matter of great sensitivity for business users, in particular, is whether the European-wide movement toward an Integrated Services Digital Network ("ISDN") environment will result in co-ordinated pricing. If telephone rates are kept at the same levels, given the necessary infrastructure investments accompanying the introduction of ISDN, there may be pressure to increase prices for business services.

c. Administrations, however, are interested in standardizing tariffing principles, particularly for leased lines. Discussions on the possible movement to usage-sensitive pricing of leased lines are taking place within the Conférence Européene des Postes et Télécommunications ("CEPT"), the European organization of PTTs. These talks are undoubtedly being stimulated by the adoption of volume-sensitive tariffing for leased lines in the Federal Republic of Germany.

5. One European-wide, if not international, trend does seem to be movement toward the implementation of cost-based pricing policies for certain, largely international, services. Local services, however, are anything but immune from pressures for moving pricing closer to costs.

a. Rate rebalancing inevitably shifts the burden imposed on the different players in the telecommunications environment. In general, the less competitive part of the network—usually local services—end up carrying a larger burden than they had prior to tariff realignment.

b. Most administrations, and national policymakers, recognize that rebalancing rates does have real, significant political and social effects. In the U.K., for example, social objectives are of considerable importance. These are recognized and implemented in the licence conditions imposed on British Telecom.

c. Regulatory mechanisms or political supervision also can play a role in ensuring that repricing does not ignore non-economic goals. In the Federal Republic of Germany, pricing structures are based on national political decisions and are overseen by the Administrative Council of the Deutsche Bundespost ("Bundespost"). Consequently, tariffs historically have been set in relative isolation from international trends.

d. The Telekommunikationsordnung ("TKO") of mid-1986, for example, introduced usage-sensitive pricing for leased lines effective in 1988—a move not yet followed elsewhere in Europe. Cost-based, non-usage-sensitive, pricing for leased lines is viewed as not feasible within the next decade. Thus, usage-sensitive pricing policies are sometimes viewed as a solution that is "second-best" to genuine rate harmonization of switched and leased-line tariffs. The only avenue for significant liberalization of the conditions on leased-line usage, therefore, is a volume-sensitive tariff structure.

e. The impact of international developments is, nevertheless, felt in Germany. For example, the tariff structure for telex was based on low rental charges for terminal equipment—to encourage participation in the network—and higher call charges—to generate a profit. This policy had been relatively successful—with very high subscriber penetration. The *British Telecom* case, however, is read as permitting telex refile, allowing users to arbitrage the pricing of international telex services. As a result, the Bundespost had to restructure its telex tariffs to reduce the incentives to bypass German services.

f. In Germany, it is uncertain what impact a broader trend in Europe toward cost-based pricing may have on current usage-sensitive pricing. It may be difficult to achieve cost-based pricing in the current German political climate. A more cost-based pricing structure, however, may become feasible for ISDN services targeted at large users. Moreover, the government commission currently assessing the future of the Bundespost is also addressing pricing issues in light of international developments.

6. One issue for the future is the impact of international pricing pressures on the tariff structure for domestic ISDN services. As described below in Section III.B, the European Commission is looking at ISDN pricing in connection with its initiatives to promote public infrastructure development.

B. New PTT Investment Policies: One Set of Responses to Economic Pressures

1. The new environment confronting European PTTs is increasingly one of considerable complexity. Traditional pricing arrangements are under considerable stress as a result of the increasing rivalry in the relationship among the European PTTs and the impact of deregulation in the United States.

a. By moving toward cost-based pricing for infrastructure services, PTTs are concerned that they may have a more difficult time generating capital internally for investment. This is not, however, necessarily the case. It is quite possible, for example, that a more equitable distribution of cost burdens can actually increase use of the network and result in increased revenues.

b. The importance for the PTTs of being able to make the necessary investments cannot be overstated. For example, in order to generate an appropriate return for investors, European facilities suppliers such as British Telecom must offer new services. To do so, however, they must make significant infrastructure investments.

c. The carriers are wary of such investments if, in a liberalized environment, they are likely to redound to the ultimate benefit of users or third-party service providers. British Telecom and other facilities-providers, in offering services, are concerned that there may ultimately be a disincentive to invest at all in new facilities. That is, if the carrier can gain no advantage from the investment and is forced to act as a "wholesaler" for unaffiliated competitors, there is no point in investing at all.

d. The PTTs are boxed in financially. They are under pressure to upgrade their infrastructure and to establish narrow band ISDN networks. At the same time, they must maintain a sophisticated array of terminal equipment and switching equipment to remain competitive.

2. In confronting the various pressures brought about by change—and the dilemmas that result therefrom—European PTTs have a range of options. To survive in the new environment, PTTs will have to behave more like private sector entities. They will need to undertake significant business planning, develop marketing skills, and take advantage of the wide spectrum of financing sources that are available. In this last, in developing the financial capacity to make essential infrastructure and other investments, they can (*i*) increase revenues by raising tariffs; (*ii*) stimulate network use, or offer new services; (*iii*) cut operating costs; (*iv*) obtain greater flexibility in using external financing, and improve the range of sources that are available; (*v*) reduce general obligations to fund government budgets; and (*vi*) improve cash flow through increased depreciation of the existing infrastructure.

3. The first option—raising tariffs—may be difficult. Especially for international and interexchange services, as to which large users are quite price-sensitive, the flexibility of the PTTs to increase prices may be quite limited.

   a. Indeed, external pressures have already made it difficult to avoid a reduction, let alone an increase, in tariffs for international services. Such reductions are creating pressures for offsetting changes elsewhere just to maintain the *status quo*. International revenues may not be the largest portion of revenue streams for European PTTs, but they are still significant for almost all of them.

   b. For example, although figures are not generally available for most European PTTs, international services amounted to £1.428 billion, or 19 per cent of British Telecom's overall revenues of £7.653 billion in 1985; however, they amounted to a full £450 million or 30 per cent of the carrier's £1.48 billion in overall profits. For the year ending March 1986, British Telecom's international services also amounted to 19 per cent of total revenues (£1.58 billion in international revenues, £8.388 billion in total revenues), but dropped to 27 per cent of total profits (£488 million profits for international services, £1.8 billion overall). *British Telecom's Reports and Accounts.*

   c. Any offsetting increases in interexchange services, however, may create substantial incentives for large users to relocate network operating centers outside the country. They may also result in protests from powerful industry groups. Turning to local tariffs, it is, of course, exceptionally difficult to implement increases without unleashing strong political forces.

   d. The problem of adjusting tariff structures to compensate for any reductions in international revenues, or to increase revenues overall, varies widely from country to country. The range of differences and the relative magnitude of this difficulty are suggested by a summary comparison of the sources of revenues of some of the major European PTTs.

   e. Revenues from local services contributed the lowest percentage of revenues overall in France (16 per cent of the total). C. Pautrat and B. Hurez, "Place de la tarification dans la stratégie des Télécommunications", *Le Bulletin de l'IDATE*, 9, 19 (Feb. 1986). In Germany, 22 per cent of the revenues were from local services, followed by Italy, with 26 per cent, and then by the U.K., with 34 per cent. Conversely, in France, for example, inter-urban traffic, consisting of 15 per cent of the entire traffic flow, contributed a full 66 per cent of the revenues of the DGT, *id.*, while trunk traffic supplied 28 per cent of the revenues of the Bundespost. The differences, of course, are largely a function of geography, demographics, and the relative centralization or dispersion of population and industrial centers throughout these countries. Nevertheless, or due to these extrinsic factors, these figures, crude as they are, do suggest the problem facing the Bundespost: it is heavily dependent on interexchange revenues and has apparently had the most difficulty in raising local rates and revenues to their appropriate levels.

    f. As described below in Section II.B.4, PTTs may initiate new services to stimulate revenues. At the outset, however, it may be necessary to establish concessionary or reduced rates—and not recover costs—to do so. Observers have suggested, for example, that new ISDN services cannot be launched successfully without heavy subsidies at the outset. Although there is no ready vehicle for bearing such costs, some of the PTTs might be motivated to explore the feasibility of implementing usage-sensitive tariffs for leased lines.

    g. PTTs might look beyond telecommunications services to increase revenues. Several are active in supplying customer premises equipment. Nevertheless, in most countries in Europe the PTT does not have a monopoly on the supply of equipment beyond the main station. The heavy competition in the supply of equipment means that price-cutting is commonplace. Thus, the PTTs ought not to expect to earn substantial revenues from the equipment market.

   4. Although it may not be second nature to organizations accustomed to a stable environment, the PTTs can devote substantial resources to the marketing of their services—essentially the tactic at the heart of the second option. Increasing use of network facilities is perhaps the most cost-effective way of boosting revenues.

    a. Traditional telephone and telex traffic, however, has reached a point of saturation—a plateau—in some of the larger European countries. The major PTTs are approaching telephone densities of forty lines per hundred persons, approximately the current levels in the U.S. (At the end of 1984, France had 40.17 lines per hundred, Germany had 40.27, the U.K. had 37.07, and the Netherlands had 39.04. ITU, *Yearbook of Common Carrier Telecommunication Statistics*, 13th ed. (1986) ["*ITU 1986 Yearbook*"].) These levels have yet to be reached in Italy (28.93 lines per hundred) and some of the newer members of the Community (Spain having 23.14 per hundred, for example). *Id.* Nevertheless, penetration does begin to level off sharply when the rate is as high as it is in some of the major nations.

b. PTTs seeking new areas for growth are noting that new data services may be marketed to businesses with somewhat greater success. More importantly, liberalization of usage, to include permitting the development of VANS, would certainly increase usage of network facilities.

c. Thus, although new services can be developed, the risks of such entrepreneurship could be significant. Both the Bundespost and the DGT, for example, are playing significant roles in the implementation of cable television services in their respective countries. Substantial funds have been committed to these projects; in the case of Germany, the funding has been allocated by the political process. Nevertheless, as a result of both political uncertainties at the local level and the forecasted economic viability of the medium, the DGT is at present taking a far more skeptical look at its involvement in the installation of the cable infrastructure.

d. As noted in Section V below, there are ways in which the PTTs can reduce the risks of acting as entrepreneurs. Entering into a joint venture with an outside organization, whether private or public, is one method of allocating risk. In the provision of value-added services, for example, a PTT could provide the basic infrastructure while the private sector provides the "value". This model has been used in Italy, where Televas, a venture of STET and Montedison, now supplies data entry services.

e. In developing new services, another approach might be to examine the use of facilities, such as satellites, for ISDN services. Satellites are being launched without substantial initial capital risks by PTTs, with much of the development cost borne by the European Space Agency or by national space technology administrations. Satellites might permit the development of new markets, while minimizing risks to PTTs. The use of satellites for new services is addressed in greater detail in Section III.A, below.

5. There is a wide variety of possibilities available to PTTs under the third option—cutting the costs of operations. Several European telecommunications entities already have begun to address the necessity for making significant reductions in operating costs.

a. In 1984, British Telecom's operational and other expenditures (not including depreciation, interest, and taxes) were 67 per cent of total income. *ITU 1986 Yearbook*, at 287. After privatization, BT's objective was to reduce operating costs to approximately 50 per cent of revenues. In Germany, it seems unlikely that the Bundespost will be able to shed its various obligations to support postal services or universal service. Nevertheless, the Bundespost has adopted a more corporate-like institutional structure to squeeze out greater efficiencies. As a result, the operational/other expenditures of the Bundespost are only 40 per cent of its total income. *Id.* at 39.

b. French policymakers have used the *filiales* of the DGT as a competitive spur. (The comparable percentage of operational/other expenditures to total income for the DGT is 49 per cent. *Id.* at 149.) Now, under the Chirac Government, policymakers want broader flexibility to manage the DGT on a business-like basis. Within the DGT, there is greater impetus for reducing its obligations to support government fiscal policies. Efforts are being made to increase the DGT's autonomy and to base its plans on a *charte de gestion* to which the government will strictly adhere.

    c. Another method of reducing costs is to increase employee productivity, reduce the size of the labor force, and minimize management-labor strife. Almost everywhere in Europe PTTs have addressed the relationship between labor and management in an effort to meet the competitive challenge. These difficult issues have been confronted in direct, and often uncomfortable, ways in the privatization of British Telecom, which, as of 1984, had 11.24 staff persons per 1,000 main lines (as compared with 8.44 in Germany and 7.56 in France). *Id.* at 286, 38, and 148. The issue of staffing is being addressed in the restructuring of the Dutch PTT, though the ratio of staff per main lines in the Netherlands was only 4.92:1,000 in 1984. *Id.* at 264. In Italy, too, the role of the unions has had an impact in the eventual restructuring, streamlining, and consolidation of the telecommunications sector.

    d. PTTs also may begin to focus on their procurement of equipment, where open and more competitive procedures could reduce costs significantly. Several of the PTTs have only one or two suppliers of equipment because of direct or indirect affiliations with the manufacturers. The decision by the Chirac Government to end the subsidies to the French manufacturers of telecommunications equipment has somewhat relieved the DGT and is likely to bring down its equipment costs. The consolidations and mergers among the European manufacturers may leave the PTTs with a freer hand to select the best bargains among European suppliers.

    e. Many observers believe that the introduction of ISDN services will also cut costs by increasing the efficiency of PTT operations and by reducing maintenance expenses. To achieve these efficiencies, however, substantial investments must first be undertaken—the very investments for which some of these financing options might profitably be pursued.

    6. The fourth option—improving the efficiency and range of external funding sources—is of considerable concern to the PTTs. Many PTTs are able to finance only about 70–80 per cent of their investment requirements through cash flow. The amount of internally recovered investment capital is, moreover, holding steady or perhaps declining.

    a. The amount of internally generated funds vary substantially from country to country. As of the end of 1984, British Telecom's internal recovery was in excess of 130 per cent, but is likely to decline due to expenses involved in installing System X. The rates of self-financing of the DGT and the Bundespost, as of the end of 1984, are slightly in excess of 80 per cent. *1984 Annual Reports* of British Telecom, DGT and the Bundespost. (In Italy, the rate was 58 per cent. 1985/1994 Telecommunications Plan.) These rates are a function, at least in part, of the declining cost of servicing dollar-denominated debt over the past few years.

b. The major European PTTs have cumulative annual investment requirements averaging around $2 billion per year; with the addition of the other European PTTs, the total expected annual investment is of the order of $12 billion per year. Thus, the 6–7 billion ECU additional investment in ISDN in the period 1986–93 amounts to an increase of slightly less than 10 per cent per year in annual investment requirements.

c. The cost of obtaining external financing is high. Many PTTs are heavily in debt. For example, the debt/asset ratios for France, Germany, and the U.K. in 1984 were 60 per cent, 45.6 per cent, and 30.3 per cent respectively. (Looked at another way, debt service as a percentage of total revenues was 17.5 per cent in France, 7.4 per cent in Germany, 21 per cent in Italy and 5.1 per cent in the U.K.) 1984 *Annual Reports.* Moreover, much of the borrowing has been in dollar denominations, which tend to be subject to significant government controls. The burden of this debt has eased a little in 1985 and 1986 due to the increased strength of the European currencies. Thus, in 1985, the DGT debt/asset ratio improved to 54.7 per cent and the debt service/revenues percentage declined to 15.2 per cent. 1985 *Annual Report of the DGT,* at 16. In Italy, a recapitalization also contributed to lightening the debt load.

d. Obtaining financing through external borrowing may run into additional obstacles imposed by ministers of finance. If PTTs use the government's borrowing authority, ministers of finance may exact their "pound of flesh"—by forcing the administration to make contributions to the state treasury.

7. These contributions can be substantial; thus, the fifth (and overtly political) option for obtaining greater financing autonomy is to reduce the amount of payments by the PTTs to their national governments. The Bundespost pays about DM 4 billion into the national treasury. The DGT pays around FF 12 billion. It is difficult to achieve indpendence in financing while having to pay such subsidies to national governments.

8. The sixth option, increasing depreciation charges, is a route that most PTTs would like to take. If an administration were, however, nominally to move to a cost-based pricing structure, such a shift would exert an upward pressure on prices. Thus, suggesting any changes in depreciation schedules is likely to become a politically charged issue.

9. In short, there are limitations to most of the ways in which PTTs can raise the capital that they may require. Internal financing is constrained by difficulties in increasing prices. External financing subjects the PTT to a spectrum of restraints. Nevertheless, administrations in Europe will have to become more entrepreneurial with respect to their financing needs—and pursue a mix of strategies—if they are to satisfy user demands and flourish in the new environment.

III. EMERGENCE OF A NEW FACILITIES INFRASTRUCTURE

A. Infrastructure for Satellite Services

1. The implementation of new satellite facilities in Europe is a bit of a technological "wild card". Satellites will change the mix of pressures that are forcing PTTs and governments to reexamine telecommunications policy. These pressures come from various directions and are the product of a variety of institutional initiatives inside Europe.

   a. The investment plans and marketing strategies of the national PTTs are the critical elements in any European satellite policy. Changes in the regulatory environment may, moreover, create significant incentives for these PTTs to explore new uses of satellite-based services.

   b. These policies are reflected in CEPT, and in the approaches taken by the various CEPT committees that are examining the role of satellites in Europe. Ultimately, these views will become embedded in the policies of Eutelsat, the consortium of which all the CEPT administrations are members—twenty-six in all. The views developing within the specialized CEPT committees will need to be accepted by the PTTs, as well as by Eutelsat, whose very survival, of course, depends upon the increased use of satellites.

   c. The development of satellite services in Europe will inevitably be affected by the plans of the Commission in the ISDN area and by the implementation of broadband and narrowband ISDN networks. In addition, the European Space Agency ("ESA") and national satellite manufacturers are vigorously attempting to explore and stimulate new uses for satellite services in Europe.

2. These entities hold a variety of interests, some of which conflict. In 1985 and 1986, these differences were focused in discussions between CEPT and ESA. CEPT has a Coordination Committee for Satellite Telecommunications ("CCTS") that has been examining the future uses of satellites.

   a. To facilitate the exchange of information between ESA and CEPT, the CCTS decided to establish an *Ad Hoc* Action Group on Satellite Telecommunications Policy ("PTC SAT"). This group was supported by experts from the Groupe Satellite Européen de Télécommunications ("SET") of CEPT.

   b. For fifteen months during 1985, discussions took place with CEPT. ESA made a series of presentations and held discussions with PTC SAT and the SET experts. In May 1986, the CCTS released a provocative report on the future of satellites in Europe. CCTS, *Report of the CCTS on its Review of the European Space Agency's Future Telecommunications Programme*, Doc. T/CCTS(86) 11 (1986) ["*CCTS Report*"]. This report has been the subject of active discussion during the rest of 1986. These discussions will be of considerable assistance in co-ordinating CEPT telecommunications planning and ESA programs.

3. Such co-ordination is necessary because planning for satellites in Europe has been somewhat more helter-skelter, and significantly less market-oriented toward user needs, than is seen as desirable.
   a. Satellites are being planned and will be launched in the coming decade, and there will be anything but a shortage of satellite facilities. Indeed, some observers predict that there will be more than 100 transponders available in Europe by 1990; if proposed private satellites are launched, the total may approach 150.
   b. It will be necessary for the PTTs to develop a mechanism to take account of customer demands for service and market forecasts in planning satellite services. A brief review of European satellite projects is important for an understanding of the realities to be faced in developing a European satellite policy.
4. In France, Télécom-1 was launched in mid-1984. It provides high-speed digital links for broad band and wide area digital services, and videoconferencing. Télécom-1 is used to connect France's overseas departments in the Caribbean and off the coast of Eastern Canada with metropolitan France. Most of its usage at the present time is, however, for video links and corporate communications. There are already approximately thirty earth stations operating in France. The digital satellite is viewed as an integral component of the ISDN that will be implemented in France.
5. The Bundespost's Deutsche Fernmeldesatellit ("DFS") or Kopernikus was ordered in December 1983. The two-satellite system will be used for telephone, data, and videoconferencing, and for television distribution. The first Kopernikus satellite was scheduled to be operational in mid-1988. German media policy, especially regarding private broadcasting, has been the subject of considerable debate between the Bundespost and the *Laender*. Given that DFS will have television distribution capabilities, it is possible that discussions among the governments of the Federal Republic will lead to delay beyond that date.
6. The Italsat telecommunications satellite is scheduled to be launched in 1989. The Italians are forecasting the use of new services and are attempting to integrate the satellite closely into their terrestrial network and ISDN plans. The Italian Sarit project contemplates four satellites for the 1990s; these will both provide DBS channels and boost telecommunications capabilities.
7. There are plans for the Nordic communications satellite, Tele-X, to be launched in 1988. It is intended to provide DBS capabilities and new data and video services for the business community in Denmark, Finland, Norway, and Sweden.
   a. The Tele-X satellite is larger and of significantly greater power than existing or planned business communications satellites. The Tele-X concept, then, is to introduce business services with small and low-cost earth stations, minimizing fixed charges and facilitating installation at customer premises.

Chapter IV The future of European telecommunications policy   285

b. In early 1985, the Swedish Space Corporation undertook a market and applications study of the demand for the proposed Tele-X services in the Nordic countries. This study was extended, through desk research, and under a contract from ESA, to the rest of Europe. The study concluded that there would be significant demand in the 1990s, especially by manufacturing companies, for 2 Mbps data traffic in both the Nordic and greater European regions.

8. There are at least two private, European entities with advanced business plans to supply satellite services in Europe. The probability of their succeeding is largely dependent on the regulatory response by the PTTs, by Eutelsat, and by Intelsat.

a. One such would-be entrant, the Société Européene des Satellites ("SES") is based in Luxembourg. Its ASTRA satellite is medium-powered and will offer television services directly to consumers. The planned launch date is February 1988.

b. The other, Atlantic Satellites, is based in Ireland and is 80 per cent owned by Hughes Communications. Currently scheduled for launch in 1989, its principal purpose is to provide DBS services to the Irish and U.K. markets, and to provide very small aperture terminal ("VSAT") services in Europe. Nevertheless, it seems likely that the economic viability of Atlantic Satellites will largely depend on the likelihood that it can offer transatlantic services.

9. Beyond national satellite systems, Eutelsat already has a mature satellite system in operation. Eutelsat's ECS satellite was developed by ESA under contract and the first satellite in the system was launched in 1983. Eutelsat now distributes thirteen television services to over twenty countries. Nine television channels will be added to Eutelsat's distribution capability with the launch of the Eutelsat I-F4 satellite in 1987.

a. In May 1986, Eutelsat placed a contract for its second generation of satellites, to be launched from 1989 onwards. These satellites have higher power and larger capacity, enhancing their versatility and their economic attractiveness.

b. For reasons that will be described below and were the subject of examination in Phase I of the Study of Telecommunications Structures, Eutelsat has been much more successful at delivering television services than it has in offering telecommunications services. Indeed, telephony service via Eutelsat is only in its earliest stages. Questions are being raised about the economic viability of satellites in an environment in which fiber optic cables are being installed.

10. ESA itself is in the midst of three important programs intended to spur the development of new and creative satellite services in Europe. The use of satellites for non-television services in Europe has been considerably lower than anticipated and observers foresee the demand for television distribution capability slowing over the next decade. There are also problems with using satellites in network-oriented systems. Thus, ESA is becoming increasingly interested in exploring a user-oriented approach: to

discover some other uses of satellites that might be technologically and economically viable with customer-premises earth terminals.

a. The Olympus project is a large, multipurpose satellite platform, principally offering DBS technology for pan-European services. One of the two high-power channels will cover Italy, with the other covering the rest of Europe. ESA has concluded agreements with Radiotelevisione Italiana ("RAI") and the European Broadcasting Union ("EBU") regarding the DBS channels. These DBS channels, outside the prime broadcast hours, could also be used to distribute data, and encourage the development of tel-education, industrial training material and business communications in general. Four medium-power channels will provide specialized services to Europe, perhaps to be used as a switching platform to interconnect local area networks. A third payload will permit experiments, particularly in wideband services, via two steerable pencil-beam antennae. The target launch date is the middle of 1987.

b. The APOLLO project is funded jointly by ESA and the Commission. It is a pilot project for the delivery of electronic mail by satellite, integrated with the Eutelsat Satellite Multiservices System ("SMS"). A specialized application is the delivery of documents from central archives to users such as libraries; thus, the British Library and the Commission itself have shown interest in the APOLLO program. Other applications might include remote newspaper printing, and the one-way transmission of computer files or video images. CEPT administrations may participate in the field tests.

c. ESA is also interested in the mobile service applications of satellites for users travelling in land vehicles, small boats, and airplanes. These applications would require large investments; ESA therefore proposes to take advantage of spare capacity on Inmarsat (International Maritime Satellite Organization) satellites to test the market. This project, known as PROSAT, is being carried out in two phases. The first, now completed, investigated propagation throughout Europe. The PRODAT system is now under development; it will allow mobile stations to exchange data with a base station. The second phase of the PROSAT project is the demonstration of the PRODAT system, expected to start at the end of 1987.

11. Often the debate over the possible uses for satellites in Europe appears to start from the premise that national and regional satellite programs will be initiated as part of an industrial or political policy—with only subsequent attention being given to new applications. The ESA more generally has been effective in pressing for a different approach: looking at which new business services might represent a growth market in Europe and how satellites can deliver these services efficiently and practically. To a certain extent, the Tele-X studies and business forecasts share this perspective with ESA.

12. From the standpoint of CEPT, one of the critical issues for examination is whether the utility of satellites should be analyzed primarily in light of their practical utility in the supply of point-to-point services.

Many observers, and ESA in particular, have urged that a comparison between satellite and terrestrial services ought not to be made simply on the basis of the length of required point-to-point links. They stress that the capabilities and strengths of satellites should not be measured by comparing the technology with a "cable in the sky".

a. Indeed, one significant advantage of satellite systems is that the route costs and performance are distance-insensitive. However, satellites may be used more efficiently if capacity is treated as dynamic, rather than being assigned to serve specific links in a network. Thus, several factors are critical in determining the appropriate role for European satellite services.

b. ESA and others have stressed that satellites might be exceptionally useful in complementing the installation of high capacity digital links throughout Europe. *See* ESA, "The Role of Satellites in Integrated Broadband Communications", RACE Definition Phase (Nov. 1986). For example, one PTT study of the future of telecommunications services in Europe suggested that an overlay broad band infrastructure would connect the sixty most important urban areas, where there is significant potential demand. Consultancy Group, "Telecommunications Infrastructure in the Community", Contract No. AH/83/734 for the Commission (Sept. 1984). But these areas would exclude over 80 per cent of the Community's population, and leave two entire countries and most of three others outside the network.

c. A satellite-based integrated broad band network has several advantages. First, once the basic elements are put in place—the satellite launched and central switching and control centers operational—new points on the network can be deployed in a relatively rapid fashion. Services can be marketed and made operational while terrestrial links are being installed or await the development of demand along particular routes. Second, there are essentially no geographic limitations on the service, with services being provided economically via small earth stations.

d. Satellites offer particular advantages for business-oriented networks that may have widely varying interconnection requirements. Several, but by no means all, of the services now emerging rely on very small aperture terminal ("VSAT") networks. Some collect data from a wide number of points; these would include retail outlets supplying inventory information for distributors or point-of-sale information for credit or debit card services. Other services to the financial community distribute information to different locations dispersed throughout a particular country or throughout Europe; these might include the distribution of financial information, commodity data, and stock market transactions.

e. Other new services might use satellites for the one-way distribution of data to very low-cost earth stations. They might deliver software, news information, or photographs for newspapers. Some of these proposed services will use the signals of DBS facilities. Regulatory problems interposed by broadcast organizations and by the PTTs—regarding access to both space segment and earth stations—have made implementation of these proposals more difficult in Europe than in the U.S.

      f. Other satellite-based business applications include videoconferencing. Although these services would be prohibitively expensive if offered over terrestrial networks, small earth stations located on user premises might make them economically feasible.

13. These services seem promising, but have not taken off as quickly in Europe as some had hoped. Perhaps the most significant factor in any delay, beyond the slow development of the satellite infrastructure itself, are the obstacles erected by the PTTs.

      a. First, there is hardly unanimity among the PTTs on the relative priority of developing satellite capacity. Despite the CEPT consultative mechanism, the PTTs are not entirely in accord with respect to the need for and future role of satellite services. Different transmission media have different uses—and the needs of a country such as Germany or France may be distinct from those of smaller nations, such as Switzerland, or nations at the periphery of the satellite footprint.

      b. Second, as noted above, the cost principles of satellite services are different from those for terrestrial facilities. The PTTs are concerned that satellite pricing may pose a threat to the traditional, distance-sensitive pricing structures for terrestrial services.

      c. Third, the PTTs will have to make substantial investments in infrastructure over the coming years. They are concerned about the realistic balance that they can achieve between expenditures on new, high-capacity terrestrial facilities and those on the research and operational elements of satellite systems. Excessive investment in satellite links could jeopardize the prospects for efficient use of terrestrial links.

      d. The PTTs should be focusing on the extent to which satellite facilities are likely to complement, not supplant or dominate, terrestrial capabilities. Satellite and terrestrial facilities may be competitive at some point. At present, terrestrial networks are, of course, capable of offering interactive data retrieval services, for example. Satellites, however, may be better able to meet demands for large, dynamic networks priced attractively.

14. One of the more significant steps in Europe in acknowledging the flexibility and capabilities of satellites has been the dialogue between the ESA and the CCTS, and the resulting CCTS report. This report, in general, supports an expanded use of satellites, particularly in the context of incorporating satellite technology into the European switched network and, possibly, into the ISDN. *CCTS Report*, at paras. 2.1.1.4 and 2.1.5.1, at 5, 8.

      a. In addition, the CCTS explicitly recognized the "inherent benefits" of satellites for specialized point-to-multipoint services and thin-route and other remote-area services. *Id.* at para. 2.1.3.1, at 7. It also recognized the types of business services, some of which are noted above, for which European satellites might be particularly appropriate. *Id.* at para. 2.3, at 10–11.

        b. Although the CCTS appears well-informed, from the standpoint of those advocating the development of satellite technology in Europe, the key question is how to integrate its views into the planning process of CEPT and of individual PTTs. The concern of ESA and others, of course, is that planners within national administrations will continue to focus on terrestrial networks and overlook some of the advantages that have been the subject of the CCTS/ESA discussions.

    15. The PTTs are having a difficult time making decisions about how to strike the balance between investing in terrestrial and satellite networks. One crucial element in the decisionmaking process is the relationship between the research and development plans of ESA and the implementation of those plans by Eutelsat and entities such as CEPT.

        a. Many PTTs would prefer to see the development activities of ESA confined, to the greatest extent possible, to laboratory settings rather than highly visible and pace-setting in-orbit demonstrations. There is a great deal of institutional reluctance on the part of CEPT administrations to even the suggestion by ESA as to how operational capacity might be provided. *See, e.g., CCTS Report*, para. 4.3.1.3, at 22.

        b. ESA has undertaken research on advanced satellite switching capabilities, with onboard processing facilities. ESA is also actively developing intersatellite links; the use of direct connections between satellites in space would increase interconnectivity between satellites belonging to the same or different networks and reduce investment costs through greater flexibility in placing satellites in the geostationary orbit.

        c. Many of the PTTs do, therefore, favor a more conservative approach to research and development. Nevertheless, even within Europe they face an environment of great complexity. In Northern Europe, for example, the Tele-X system will take the lead in multipoint data distribution to low-cost earth stations. Although the Tele-X beams do not cover most of Europe, the presence of these services will stimulate the interest of European business users. European users also are now well aware of the widespread and rapid installation of VSAT services in the U.S., which will soon be mirrored in Japan; both these developments are likely to increase pressures on the PTTs. PTTs, however, have been slow to embrace the development of private, satellite-based networks that may be beyond their direct control.

        d. ESA technologies, therefore, will undoubtedly raise difficult policy questions affecting the future respective roles of the PTTs, Intelsat, and Eutelsat. Users are increasingly turning to ESA and, to a slightly lesser extent, Eutelsat, because they represent counterpoints to the PTTs. ESA has had an instrumental role in encouraging use of satellite services and is now working with user organizations to devise development plans for multipoint services.

e. Some leeway should be afforded to ESA in carrying out innovative development strategies. If policy issues become difficult to resolve, and there is a failure to permit a central body such as ESA to undertake research, European prospects in technology may be crippled. In the U.S. and Japan, expenditures on development are far less fettered by regulation or policy issues; manufacturers can pursue their development strategies without excessive concern about the potential impact on telecommunications policies. In the future, one development that merits careful attention is the interrelationship among PTTs, users, CEPT, ESA, and Eutelsat in exploring new uses for satellite capabilities.

16. What, then, of the role of Eutelsat, the preeminent European organization devoted to the development of a market for European satellite services? The Eutelsat experience, at least with respect to business communications and other telecommunications services, has been less than entirely satisfactory.

a. For Eutelsat services, users must enter into arrangements with each of the PTTs responsible for the territories in which satellite services are offered. There is no central organization either for marketing or for developing new satellite services. The sheer multiplicity of arrangements, and the efforts devoted to them, are viewed as having hindered usage of satellite services. Users would like to have the same service throughout Europe, but the disparate national marketing arrangements now in place make this difficult.

b. Some users would prefer to have Eutelsat exercise responsibility for the direct marketing of satellite services. This is not likely to occur, however. That is, given the wide range of views that the PTTs hold with respect to satellite services, it is improbable that Eutelsat, or any other new organization, would be allotted any centralized, or co-ordinative, responsibility.

17. Even though Eutelsat is not able to act as a European marketer of its own European services, individual PTTs are seizing the initiative and are marketing their national satellite services on a European-wide basis. This is particularly true of the DGT, which now has two operational Télécom-1 satellites and is also beginning to explore how it might market them internationally.

a. Through its France Câbles et Radio subsidiary, the DGT is involved in a joint venture with Agence France Presse. This entity, called Polycom, is involved in data broadcasting. At present, field trials have begun on Télécom-1 with ten earth stations; operational capability in France is expected by early 1987. Polycom's longer-range plans, however, are to market data services throughout Europe. To that end, it intends to inaugurate commercial service on a Eutelsat satellite in the first months of 1987. Polycom is studying how best to offer services on the most cost-efficient basis using available distribution systems. Thus, as VSAT services become less expensive in Europe, Polycom intends to combine its broadcasting capability with data packet networks.

b. Télécom-1 has already leased some of its capacity to the Bundespost. In addition, the DGT has reached agreements with both British Telecom and Cable & Wireless to market Télécom-1 capacity in the U.K. In addition to London, there are Télécom-1 earth stations in Belgium and Dublin, with others on order or being considered. These developments show quite dramatically that the emergence of facilities-based competition in one country—the U.K.—will launch the more competitive provision of network services in Europe as a whole.

c. The launch of the Kopernikus satellite by the Bundespost may also encourage transborder marketing of communications services. Some of the capacity of the system has been set aside for business services, some of which may link businesses in Austria, Switzerland, or other German-speaking areas.

18. In addition to European-wide initiatives being taken by national administrations, ESA programs might also have a significant role in encouraging the development of European-wide services. ESA's Olympus satellite, as noted above, will be used for some business capabilities. Other ESA programs will have significant regional, if not international, ramifications.

a. Although some of the capacity on Olympus has been reserved for Italy, the ESA's planning activities may result in a broader proposal, for services that might link several countries. Another component of the Olympus program, or perhaps of other ESA projects, may be experimentation with onboard processing capability. Such capability would, among other features, permit the conversion of transmission speeds by the satellite itself. This capability might facilitate the development of transnational satellite-based networks that do not depend on two separate links.

b. The steerable "pencil" beams on the Olympus satellite will be able to deliver a strong downlink signal to different geographic regions. These links can then be reoriented to serve other areas. One obvious application for such a capability would be transatlantic connections between a European satellite system and North American networks. Any decisions involving the use of this capability would have to be closely co-ordinated with Intelsat as well as CEPT.

c. Similarly, the technology for intersatellite links that is being developed by ESA, NASA, and Intelsat enhances the likelihood that regional satellite systems in one part of the world could be tied together with similar systems elsewhere. This technology, however, will provoke some difficult questions about the roles of Eutelsat, Intelsat, and regional satellite consortia.

19. The role of the Commission in developing a satellite telecommunications policy is sensitive. As a practical matter, the Commission must act as a buffer between satellite manufacturers, national advocates of industrial policies, PTTs, and users.

a. These interests are pulling the Commission in different

directions. The PTTs are wary about over-investment and the disruptive consequences of new technologies that could unsettle historic rate structures. Users are anxious to encourage technologies that will reduce the cost of services and make European multinationals more competitive with their U.S. and Japanese counterparts. Manufacturers and ESA want the broadest latitude to explore new market opportunities and for research and development.

b. The interesting problem for the Commission is how it will be able to integrate its approach toward satellites with its existing initiatives to encourage value-added services and in the area of ISDN development. The position of ESA with respect to broad band communications and satellites is discussed above in Section III.A.12. The initiatives of the Commission regarding ISDN are described below in Section III.B, and its developing policies on encouraging service-based competition are discussed in Section VIII.B, below.

c. It is not clear to what extent the Commission's promotion of narrow band and broad band ISDN services in Europe has taken account of satellite technology. ISDN services are developing across Europe in a very uneven way. The Commission's efforts at standardization are, at best, likely to be successful at developing a coherent approach to network planning only over the longer term; agreement may be reached early on regarding 64 Kbps services, but may be more difficult with respect to broad band services.

d. Furthermore, agreement will be required among administrations on how to structure international gateways. ESA, Eutelsat, and Intelsat point out that regional and international services in an ISDN environment will need gateways to be closer to the user. Thus, ISDN planning must anticipate the need for making connections at points other than a single international gateway.

e. Consequently, in stimulating new digital networks, the Commission might ultimately conclude that it should encourage the development of advanced satellite services, which would feature interconnection beyond points deep in the network rather than only between the international gateways, as at present. Another factor leading the Commission to support satellite-based networks is driven by industrial policy: if Europe cannot be an effective test market for satellite services and aerospace technologies being developed by European manufacturers, then their role in global markets may well be diminished, if not stifled altogether.

20. Moreover, in addressing the oft-stated concerns of some of the PTTs that satellites may be disruptive of terrestrial arrangements, the Commission might well conclude that satellite-based services offer significant new capabilities. Thus, it could reason, satellites do not simply threaten to duplicate terrestrial networks. Rather, they represent the potential for limited inter-modal competition; such competition could have a catalyzing effect on both the rate and service policies of the PTTs.

a. In this regard, the Commission might have an interest in

examining the parallels between the role of satellite services in Australia and the potential for a competitive relationship between satellites and terrestrial networks in Europe. Australian satellite services are described at length in Chapter II on "Boundary Lines". In brief, however, the services provided by AUSSAT are not viewed as eroding the core services provided by Telecom Australia; rather, they assure service to remote areas and are viewed as prodding Telecom into being more responsive to the needs of the business community. In addition, AUSSAT, by offering services to various state governments and large users, has pressured Telecom to move the prices of services toward costs.

b. Similarly, the Commission has looked at ways of stimulating the PTTs, the providers of terrestrial services, into becoming more responsive to users. It is also endeavoring, in a not entirely focused way, to address the question of how to price services. It is sensitive to how it might rationalize the pricing of services to facilitate service-based competition. Satellite services to meet new user needs may be one way of pressing the PTTs to price services in relation to cost.

21. The Commission is also interested in how it can expedite the process of liberalizing value-added services throughout Europe. As noted above, there are no institutions currently able to market satellite services to users on a European-wide basis.

a. The Commission, however, could take steps to press for more flexibility by third parties to market on a resale basis some of the capacity available on Eutelsat and other satellite systems in Europe. The services could only be used for services other than switched voice, of course.

b. Within individual countries, service liberalization might increase the prospects for use of satellite links for value-added services. The Commission might urge that administrations permit satellite links to be used on a cross-border basis for such services.

c. The Commission should consider whether it might include initiatives on satellite services in its policy statement. It might, for example, encourage PTTs to make satellite bandwidth available on a more flexible basis than has been the case in the past. Such flexibility might stimulate the use of entire transponders for the offering of value-added services on a European-wide basis. In this way, satellite-based services could generate pressure for national administrations to integrate the costs of their infrastructure and their rates more closely.

B. The European Approach to ISDN

1. Just as satellite services are developing in Europe, and are the subject of considerable examination and exploration by a range of institutions, so, too, is there significant movement toward an ISDN environment. One of the most critical aspects of the work in Europe is the role of the Commission and other Community institutions. Over the past

two years, the Commission has devoted considerable attention to the development of advanced integrated digital networks.

    a. In December 1986, the Council of Ministers accepted, subject to certain minor amendments, a draft recommendation from the Commission concerning the co-ordinated introduction of ISDN services in Europe. *See* "Proposal for a Council Recommendation on the Coordinated Introduction of the Integrated Services Digital Network (ISDN) in the European Community", COM(86) 205 final (May 20, 1986). This recommendation was the culmination of a process of consultation with the Senior Officials Group Telecommunications ("SOGT") and with the Group d'Analyses et de Prévisions ("GAP") that had been initiated by a December 1984 Recommendation of the Council.

    b. In November 1986, the proposed Recommendation had been reviewed and supported by the Industry Council of the Commission, which consists of representatives of the Ministries of Industry of the Member States. In December, prior to consideration by the Council, the European Parliament passed a resolution recommending acceptance of the proposal.

    c. The Annex to the Recommendation, as adopted by the Council, contained detailed recommendations on co-ordinating the introduction of ISDN. It includes defining the interface between public and private networks (identified to be at the S or T interface); the services initially defined; issues relating to numbering, addressing, and signalling; interworking between national ISDN trials; and tariffing considerations.

    d. The Recommendation endorsed a level of investment of between 6 and 7 billion ECU up to the end of 1993, in addition to investment in digitizing the network. This level of investment is thought to be necessary to achieve a critical mass of penetration of about 5 per cent of the 1983 telephone subscriber population in each country. Until that level is achieved, the Recommendation indicates that a demand-driven policy of developing new services cannot be realistically followed.

    e. Through its ISDN activities, the Commission hopes to stimulate a new market for terminal and telematic equipment. Its initiative is intended to encourage the development of more robust economies of scale and enhanced strength for European manufacturers in the face of competition from the U.S. and Japan.

    f. A major focus of the effort, therefore, is to achieve agreement on interfaces for terminal equipment and between public and private networks. Another target is to facilitate co-ordination among national ISDN planning and to develop common definitions of new services. The Commission is also endeavoring to achieve specification of the ISDN user part ("ISUP") protocol—part of the No. 7 signalling system that permits communications over ISDN networks.

    2. More attention in Europe has been focused on narrow band integrated networks, where services are being installed on a national basis. Often these plans, if not the various motivations for ISDN itself, vary

significantly from country to country. They are explored in greater depth in Chapter II on "Boundary Lines", which contains discussions of national ISDN plans.

a. In confronting the national plans, the Commission is hoping to achieve standardization of equipment interfaces. Its goal is to create, at the least, a unified market for ISDN-related terminal and switching equipment. With a single, European-wide market, it is thought that common integrated circuits can be produced in significant volume. Keyed to the Community's information technology program, the hope would be to maintain the global competitiveness of Europe's integrated circuit industry.

b. Disparate ISDN plans also might create several problems that the Commission is trying to anticipate. One such problem is the need to modify various numbering plans. Another, especially during the early years of ISDN development, is the co-existence of customers who are still served by analogue, as well as digital, switches. It may, therefore, be necessary to serve some customers of the ISDN with digital switches located in another area.

3. Leaving aside these operational issues, however, the Commission's principal role in the work on ISDN has been to influence the philosophy underlying the introduction of ISDN facilities. Many people in the Commission believe that narrow band ISDN networks offer an opportunity to provide a set of capabilities, and that these technological capabilities should be made available to the public.

a. Adherents of this view believe, then, that it would be unwise and shortsighted to treat the development of ISDN as merely providing large, corporate users with another set of capabilities. Accordingly, they argue that the new network should be designed and financed in the expectation that it will serve and be used by a significant number of residential customers.

b. This perspective on narrow band ISDN has rather broad policy implications. Arguably, the network should not be planned on the basis of current projections of demand for new services. Any such projections are seen as inherently unreliable because residential customers are unable to visualize the utility of various in-home data and telephony services.

c. According to those who contend that demand forecasts should not necessarily be determinative with regard to the wisdom of investing in an ISDN infrastructure, the public will not be able to perceive the advantages accruing from the installation of digital links. An ISDN, for example, would permit the operation on a single line of a telephone set and a home data terminal. Other types of ancillary telephony services, such as calling party identification, call forwarding, and call holding, can also be part of the service package. Thus, the view of those championing a "public" ISDN is that services—and the consumer demand for such services—will follow from the installation of the infrastructure.

d. Finally, it is probably inaccurate, in any event, to describe narrow band ISDN facilities as providing a whole set of new network capabilities that can be used at the outset. Such facilities are installed incrementally. Existing interexchange links are upgraded and digitized; switching facilities are converted. Eventually, but most significantly, steps are taken to establish digital capability on local loops; local cable need not be replaced, but only the scheme of repeaters and of line and switch terminations. To some degree, local connections can be upgraded and digitized by installing special loops or, for the largest customers, microwave facilities that connect user premises directly.

4. Most observers, however, believe that decisions about the installation of an ISDN must be based on realistic estimates of the demand for, and economic benefits flowing from, new services. The sheer magnitude of the investments at stake makes it difficult to assume that narrow band networks can be installed entirely on the basis of a supply-driven approach. Further complicating the problem is the fact that this investment must be made before the full scope of demand for new services can be known.

5. Considerations of industrial policy are also important determinants in deciding to invest in the infrastructure. In this connection, for example, an ISDN network is seen as possibly creating new domestic or European demand for home terminals and switching equipment. ISDN field trials currently under way throughout most of Europe are not usually designed to assist in appraising the potential market. Rather, like the DGT trials in Brittany, the objective is to assess the various approaches to connecting ISDN equipment to digital exchanges and to the interworking of analogue and digital services. For this reason, there is some skepticism about the ultimate utility of these trials in estimating demand.

6. Various assessments have been made about the potential market for ISDN services. Many informed observers are, however, highly skeptical of the demand forecasts.

a. Although there may be a residential market for ISDN services, the nature of the demand for enhanced telephony by residential subscribers is unproven. Early evidence from the U.S. and other markets is often cited to support this view.

b. Large users, who are supposedly the primary targets of the new capabilities, stress that they do not necessarily require integrated services because they now maintain high capacity systems to connect their major facilities. They emphasize emphatically and often that they are far more interested in maintaining private, leased circuits than in new integrated services. Many would like direct, satellite-based connections to their premises throughout Europe. In discussions about the implementation of ISDN, they state that ISDN is acceptable, and may even be an improvement, so long as leased lines, or their equivalents, continue to be available.

c. One oft-expressed concern of the large users is that they will be forced to migrate from existing network facilities and terminal equipment to an ISDN environment. Although they do not object, in principle, to digitization or network upgrading, they do not want higher prices for the new facilities. Nor do they want to bear higher network costs that might be distributed throughout the rate base of a provider.

   d. Users also have strong reservations about whether investment decisions are being carefully based on an appraisal of potential demand. If large users are skeptical of their use of ISDN facilities, what is left as the customer base are small- to medium-sized businesses, the market segment that the French trial is now evaluating.

7. Another difficulty in moving to ISDN services is how they should be priced, given the different sectors at which they are targeted. Some observers believe that the pricing of services for residential customers cannot be significantly above existing levels. They see the ceiling on ISDN pricing as a multiple of two or three times that at present. If prices are set too low, however, business users will have an incentive to bypass services by, for example, multiplexing a 64 Kbps circuit into several different access lines. Should this occur, network upgrading could mean significant revenue losses from the most affluent business customers.

8. The Commission's approach is supply-driven: a unified infrastructure of facilities will generate new, European markets for terminal and switching equipment, as well as for information services. Given the magnitude of the investments that are being and must be made, and in light of the uncertainty of demand, this approach is not without substantial risk. Indeed, many user groups have criticized the approach as insufficiently insensitive to demand. Most PTTs—and this is particularly the case for newly privatized entities such as British Telecom—must justify their construction and marketing activities.

9. One way of minimizing risks in the implementation of an ISDN infrastructure would be to rely to a greater extent on satellite technology. This approach has been discussed above in Section III.A.12. Satellites have, of course, some operational drawbacks, particularly for telephony services. They also have capabilities that may lend themselves well to the emergence of new multipoint distribution services.

10. An alternative approach would be to rely on stimulating demand for services by permitting more flexibility in the use of the infrastructure, an option discussed below in Section V. With usage of the infrastructure stimulated, revenue flows would be available to offset the substantial investments required.

   a. As discussed in Section II of Chapter II on "Boundary Lines", the thrust of regulatory policy in the United States has been to make available network capabilities in a scheme of open network architecture. Such an approach has two elements. First, the interexchange network capabilities offered to users must be identified carefully; this is particularly the case for the structure of rates applicable to services. Second, by unbundling local exchange network capabilities, these capabilities may be combined into new services. The result is likely to be the development of services that may well result in higher network utilization, minimizing the risk that there will be weak demand for ISDN services.

b. Thus, one strategy for developing ISDN services is to develop specific services on a more piecemeal basis, one more dependent on demand for services than on the supply of facilities. The PTT itself would not be precluded from offering any integrated service. Nevertheless, it might be encouraged to "de-integrate" such services and to offer the resulting building blocks to the promoters of new services, thereby supplementing its revenues.

IV. STRUCTURE OF EUROPEAN COMPETITIVE RELATIONSHIPS

A. Introduction

1. This section of the paper is intended to serve as a transition, to set forth a typology for the kinds of competition that do exist in Europe. It is generally thought that the existence of monopolistic PTTs everywhere except in the U.K., Finland, and Denmark means that there is nothing to discuss in pointing to the competitive relationships within Europe.

2. As noted earlier, however, the relationship among the PTTs is marked by significant rivalry—not only for international traffic, but for retaining or wooing large users who might want to take advantage of favorable rates or conditions for leased lines or interexchange services. This rivalry is carried out in tariff structures, in conditions for the usage of leased lines, in terminal attachment policies, and in overall flexibility and attentiveness to customer needs.

3. Beyond competition in facilities, both satellites and intra-European services are creating opportunities for competitive—and perhaps co-operative—relationships to flourish. Service-based competition, in particular, is the subject of Section V, below. Thus, in its own, unique way competition does exist in Europe. The impact of the Treaty of Rome, and the Commission's efforts to regulate and stimulate such competition, are the principal focal points of the remainder of this paper.

B. Facilities-Based Competition

1. Generally speaking, there is an absence of genuine facilities-based interexchange competition in Europe. There is a consensus that there should be a restricted number of licensed, facilities-based carriers. This view is shared even by the U.K.

a. There are some limited exceptions, however. In the U.K., of course, a duopolistic model has been adopted and the competition between British Telecom and Mercury is increasing in ferocity. The draft legislation in France, which has been scheduled for implementation by the end of 1987, may ultimately result in a facilities-based competitor in Continental Europe.

    b. In Finland, there has been an overlap of facilities for some time between the PTT and the private telephone companies. Moreover, a consortium consisting of the private telephone companies and large users constructed the Dataway network in 1986 for data services. Currently expanding into other areas of Finland, Dataway is introducing genuine and significant facilities-based competition to the country.

    c. Beyond the raw transmission of messages, there is no consensus as to what such carriers should be permitted to do. Some people adhere to the view that carriers should not be restricted to "public utility-like" functions. In their view, there are significant—and usually adverse—financial and entrepreneurial effects of describing carriers or administrations as "utilities". Nevertheless, if the carrier is permitted to provide services other than those of a public utility, one of the central problems in telecommunications policy is raised: how should the line be drawn between the public utility and the other, competitive, services?

  2. Although there is no open entry in the provision of facilities, the limited or sectoral competition that does exist in some countries has had a European-wide impact. As described above in Section II.A, these effects include:

    —driving prices toward costs as a result of competition in the U.K.;

    —making it difficult (though not impossible) for administrations to establish the prices for international services on a basis that is usage-sensitive and not cost-related.

  3. Hub competition is developing for international traffic as London, Amsterdam, Paris, and Brussels all vie with one another to be the terminus for transatlantic traffic. In this sense, of course, there is facilities-based competition for international services. The principal area in which competition is developing is in pricing.

  4. Another arena for the emergence of competition in international services is, however, more regulatory in focus—how restrictively, or liberally, administrations interpret the D-Series Recommendations of the CCITT. These Recommendations, which govern the terms and conditions by which leased lines can be used, are critical to the structuring of international services. More liberal policies toward the application of these Recommendations increase the flexibility of providers of value-added or enhanced services and have become, therefore, a means of attracting new traffic.

C. Satellite-Based Competition

  1. The discussion in Section III.A above explores another arena in which competition is about to emerge—in the provision of satellite

capacity. Such national systems are enabling administrations—such as the DGT—to market services beyond their borders. Many administrations may be motivated by the drive to earn a return from their substantial investments in satellite technology.

    a. Given the surplus of capacity that is likely to develop, intensified competition among administrations to market specialized services to European-wide users is likely over the next decade. In addition, the existence of excess capacity will necessitate actions to increase use in order to defray the infrastructure costs. Thus, such surpluses may be a factor in justifying a more liberalized regime for the implementation of value-added services.

    b. The future of any transnational marketing of satellite services is highly dependent on the regulatory environment. PTTs may be less receptive to satellite-delivered services that originate outside their national territories and compete with a national system. Should such discriminatory practices develop, the Commission may want to take a more active role in applying the non-discrimination provisions of the Treaty of Rome.

  2. Section III.A.11 describes how satellites can be instrumental in the development of services that could not be efficiently or economically provided over terrestrial networks. Satellites permit rate structures that would not be feasible under traditional pricing arrangements. Aside from having to deal with the awkward marketing arrangements described above in Section III.A.14, users may not be able to realize fully the cost savings of using satellite services due to the intermediary role played by the PTTs. Once satellite capacity is marketed effectively, it could exercise substantial pressures on the pricing of interexchange services throughout Europe.

D. Service-Based Competition

  1. Beyond facilities-based competition in international services, a competitive environment is in the process of evolving in the services sector. Here various national approaches are being adopted.

  2. At the outset, however, it is important to note that some observers believe that the focus of European telecommunications policy should not be entirely directed at this time at how, and under what terms, competition should be permitted in the services sector. At present, and in the foreseeable future, the overwhelming bulk of European traffic is and will be in traditional telephony. Thus, instead of focusing on how new business-oriented services might be developed, some experts have said that there should first be a consensus on what they view as the fundamental issue—planning for, and development of, a European network infrastructure.

  3. One of the most important areas for examination, however, should be the national policies toward the development of services, and how

those policies have an effect on other countries. These policies are the principal subject of Chapter II on "Boundary Lines". A review of the changes in policies toward service-based competition, however, suggests that change may be described as "sequential"—as various countries follow the direction of policy elsewhere in Europe.

    a. At the present time the most liberal policies are evolving in the U.K., where there is latitude to use leased lines for protocol conversion and various value-added as well as packet-switching services. The approach is to authorize the use of leased lines for all purposes, except for some specified restrictions on voice resale and telex services, howsoever they are defined.

    b. Due, in large part, to competitive pressures, the U.K. policy is in the process of being adopted in the Netherlands. The Belgians may follow the Dutch, although this may happen at a somewhat slower pace than had been expected. Based on a desire to stimulate the information sector, the Spanish had drafted legislation that would have established a distinction between "transport services"—offered on a monopoly basis— and "final services"—which, with some enumerated exceptions, can be offered competitively.

    c. The French proposal for liberalization of the value-added services sector is perhaps the most significant development outside the U.K. This may have repercussions in Italy. The response in the Federal Republic of Germany is unclear; the governmental commission and other policymakers in the Bundespost are, however, looking at options for liberalizing value-added services in conjunction with the implementation of the TKO.

E. Increased Competitive Pressure

    1. Section III above notes the pressures to which the PTTs are subject, and highlights some of their possible responses. Changes in tariff policies to bring prices closer to costs and to diminish cross-subsidization are squeezing national administrations and could impose severe financial strains.

    2. For better or worse, many PTTs have had historically important roles in carrying out industrial policy objectives. Based on their traditional revenue levels, they have subsidized industrial development in network equipment, satellite technology, and terminals. In addition, as noted above, many PTTs make significant financial contributions to national treasuries. Neither subsidies to industry nor budgetary contributions are sustainable in a cost-based environment. Losses by the PTTs of traditional revenue sources will, therefore, have a significant impact beyond telecommunications services. PTTs will be far less able to fulfill their roles as industrial and social promoters when they are no longer able to enjoy revenue flows from services that have been priced well in excess of cost.

3. The result of these stresses and strains will inevitably cause the PTTs to embark on programs to enhance their competitive position. They are seeking to develop new services with fewer resources. One step might be to have the PTT contributions converted into levies on other services, in order to free capital. Another would be to minimize the significant risks inherent in competing in untested market sectors. Users contend that captive subscribers should not bear those risks and that the private sector should do so by putting up risk capital. PTTs may, therefore, have incentives to shift such risks to private parties by entering into a variety of entrepreneurial arrangements.

V. ROLE OF SERVICE-BASED COMPETITION IN ACHIEVING MARKET INTEGRATION IN EUROPE

A. Service Providers Urging Common Interfaces and Regulatory Policies

1. Even in the absence of facilities-based competition, the onset of service-based competition may have far-reaching consequences for the development of the infrastructure in Europe. One likely development is that new service providers will want to participate in, and exercise pressure for, the emergence of common interfaces and regulatory policies.

2. Service providers may begin to demand that the network itself provide protocol or speed conversion capabilities to make it unnecessary for the service vendors to do so. Vesting such conversion capabilities in the network may be less necessary if the development of the facilities infrastructure is co-ordinated. That is, if there are standardized interfaces common to all PTTs, there will be transparency for service providers. This might well be one of the most important tasks for the Commission. Proper co-ordination among the national administrations would ensure that there would be no need to threaten the autonomy or sovereignty of the PTTs.

3. To the extent that service providers are keen to interconnect with other providers, and are unable or unwilling to reach an agreement among themselves, they may want the PTTs to offer interconnect services. If the Commission achieves its objectives on ISDN services, there should be no need for special interconnect services.

4. If basic services are standardized, value-added service providers could build on the infrastructure and compete on a European-wide basis. A corollary might be regulatory "standardization", some uniformity on policies regarding the provision of value-added services. Again, a European-wide market might be achieved through liberalizing initiatives on the part of the Commission.

B. A Unified Infrastructure

1. As a possible "second best" solution, there have been suggestions that, at the least, a European-wide entity (akin to Eutelsat, perhaps) should be developed to market telecommunications services throughout Europe. This "solution" would not resolve the problem of inconsistent standards or incompatible services. Nevertheless, it might be one way by which small or medium-sized service providers that do not have the resources to implement their own networks could offer European-wide services.

2. The development of a single overlay, broad band infrastructure in Europe may be opposed by some PTTs jealous of their prerogatives in planning facilities. The existing mechanisms within CEPT for facilities planning are not entirely adequate because they exclude bilateral links among administrations.

C. Integration From "Demand" Side

1. Another possible way by which the European telecommunications market might be integrated and facilities co-ordinated may be through pressures from the "demand"—rather than the "supply"—side. Liberalization in the offering of services might facilitate international marketing, which could pull the infrastructure together.

   a. Consider the case, for example, of an Italian company that might want to develop European-wide value-added services. To do so, it might enter into a joint venture with a British company, which could do business in the Netherlands or France. Leaving aside the hypothetical case, companies such as Polycom, through a common business plan oriented at services to users across Europe, will inevitably be making demands for technological and regulatory uniformity. Similarly, European-wide data entry services will exert pressures for similar uniformity.

   b. Some observers believe that service-based efforts at integration may be less successful unless there is agreement on the basic infrastructure. Without first agreeing on standards, it will be difficult for other than the larger enterprises to overcome disparities between national networks.

2. There are different models for European-wide services. As the new joint ventures of Polycom (with the DGT) and Televas (with STET) suggest, PTTs might form marketing ventures with the private sector to develop specialized or value-added services. Alternatively, they could market services jointly with other PTTs. The formation of consortia among a few major administrations or with the private sector could possibly divide the market into large fragments. Nevertheless, such fragmentation would be closer to market integration than the *status quo*, where the only integration of markets is at the national level.

VI. ROLE OF COMPETITION POLICY AND *BRITISH TELECOM* DECISION IN MARKET INTEGRATION

A. Competition Policy

1. Competition policy is designed to ensure that fair conditions of competition prevail in the non-monopoly sector of the telecommunications market. In Europe, such policies are essentially implemented by the Commission.

   a. The problem with the development of a "competition policy" in Europe to date in the telecommunications sector is that decisionmaking has necessarily been *ad hoc*—policies emerge from actions taken in particular cases. There is, therefore, no unified policy perspective on competition policy in the telecommunications industry.

   b. There is another difficulty with the Commission's current approach to competition policy as a means of structuring the telecommunications sector. Although the Commission, and others, are aware of general objectives, they are uncertain about what might be the consequences of a particular decision for the sector as a whole. One example of a not entirely foreseeable result might be the recent restructuring of Bundespost telex tariffs in the aftermath of the *British Telecom* decision.

2. To the extent that there is a competition policy, then, it is largely based on decisions to seek enforcement of the relevant provisions of the Treaty of Rome. The various avenues available under the Treaty are discussed at some length in Section VI.B, below.

   a. The areas in which the Commission has been active are monopolization in the terminal equipment area, value-added services, and the impact of changes in pricing structure. The Commission concedes that it is not entirely clear where the "policy" is headed.

   b. Alternatively, questions of competitive structure and performance can be raised in other fora in which policy is formulated—national governments and regional organizations in Europe, for example. In the United States, by way of analogy, responsibilities for formulating and implementing telecommunications policy may be entrusted, in the first instance, to a single agency, the Federal Communications Commission ("FCC"), but other institutions intervene to enunciate concerns about competitive relationships. In the U.S., the Antitrust Division of the Department of Justice has had a key role in FCC proceedings. Similarly, the European Parliament or other organs within the Community might affect the outcome of Commission policymaking.

   c. With respect to European developments, there are still questions about the fora in which it is appropriate for the Commission's competition policy staff in D.G. IV to offer its views. When national governments formulate competition policies in the telecommunications sector, it is unclear how or whether the Commission should intervene. If so, should it do so only where existing national institutions, such as Oftel, seek its advice? In short, a European "competition policy" is the product of a complex interplay of various organs at different levels within Europe.

B. Importance of the *British Telecom* Decision: Introduction

1. Under the Treaty of Rome, the Commission has several avenues open to it for exercising its authority. The various legal and procedural approaches to opening up competition in Europe depend, then, in large part, on how the Commission chooses to interpret and exercise the authority afforded to it under the Treaty.

    a. How the Treaty applies to PTTs and telecommunications administrations was the subject of the *British Telecom* case, which was decided in March 1985 by the Court of Justice of the European Communities. Case 41/83, *Italian Republic v. Commission of the European Communities*, Judgment of 20 March 1985 ["*British Telecom*"]. In that decision, the Court found that the prohibitions on telex forwarding by British Telecom were an abuse of dominant position in violation of Article 86 of the Treaty of Rome.

    b. The following discussion is intended to examine how the *British Telecom* case, and its implications, might expand the flexibility of the Commission. This section of the paper is not offered to supply anything approaching a definitive legal analysis of the case. Rather, it is submitted as a way of identifying issues that may be the subject of debate in defining the scope of the Commission's authority in embarking on a competition policy.

2. There are three principal approaches that are open to the Commission in the aftermath of the *British Telecom* decision. These will be outlined in greater detail in the subsequent discussion.

    a. First, the Commission may be better able to assert claims directly against PTTs under Articles 85 and 86 of the Treaty. These Articles prohibit agreements that are anticompetitive and abuses by undertakings of dominant positions.

    b. Second, under Article 85 the Commission may be empowered to erect a scheme of regulatory norms by scrutinizing agreements among the PTTs relating to the provision of services and by conditioning any exemption from liability. Such a prior review procedure might affect relationships among PTTs and third-party interests such as customers and providers of value-added services.

    c. Third, on the basis of Articles 59 and 60 the Commission can examine the extent to which PTT tariff restrictions might impede the development of a market for European-wide services. These Articles prohibit one Member State from discriminating against the nationals of another in the provision of a service; they are also intended to remove barriers to the development of integrated markets, regardless of whether the services are provided by nationals or non-nationals of a Member State.

C. Application of Article 86 to PTTs: Prohibiting Abuse of Dominant Position

1. The threshold issue in the *British Telecom* case is whether PTTs, whether integrated in an administration or not, are considered "public undertakings" under the Treaty. The case centered around the interpretation of Article 90.

   a. Article 90(1) states that Members shall not enact or maintain in force "any measure contrary to the rules contained in this Treaty". Thus, it expressly subjects "public undertakings and undertakings to which Member States grant special or exclusive rights" to the competition provisions of Articles 85 and 86.

   b. There is, however, an exception in Article 90(2). This clause provides that undertakings "entrusted with the operation of services of general economic interest" are subject to the competition rules only to the extent that "the application of such rules does not obstruct the performance, in law or in fact, of the particular tasks assigned to them".

   c. The critical question in the *British Telecom* case—a question that would inevitably arise in other exercises of Commission authority under the Treaty—is the breadth of the exception contained in Article 90(2). At the core of the *British Telecom* decision was the conclusion that the British Telecom restrictions were not the equivalent of regulatory policies "assigned" to it by the U.K. authorities. Rather, the Court held, the charges and conditions performed the same function as contractual terms and had been freely adopted by British Telecom—despite the fact that the restrictions had been imposed as part of a regulatory scheme overseen by the British Post Office. *British Telecom*, at para. 17.

   d. The *British Telecom* case and other decisions suggest that the exemption will be interpreted strictly. The Commission had explained in the decision that was appealed to the European Court that the exemption could not be predicated on a showing by the undertaking that compliance with the competition rules would merely "make performance of its duties more complicated". Decision of the Commission No. 82/861/EEC, O.J. Eur. Comm. (No. L 360) 36, 42, at para. 41 (1982). In *British Telecom*, the Court concluded that the Commission's censure of the schemes had not "put the performance of the particular tasks entrusted to BT in jeopardy". *British Telecom*, at 33.

   e. Furthermore, the burden will be on the undertaking of the Member State to demonstrate why it would be virtually impossible for it to comply with the Treaty and its competition rules. *See* Cases Nos. 96 to 102, 104, 105, 108 and 110/82, *AMSEAU/NAVEWA v. Commission*, [1983] E.C.R. 3369; Case No. **127/73**, *BRT and SBACE v. SV SABAM and NV Fonior*, [1974] E.C.R. 313.

2. The *British Telecom* case suggests that it may be relevant to examine the extent to which a particular restriction was expressly mandated by regulation or was adopted by the PTT in an exercise of its commercial

judgment. This analysis may have a parallel in the United States, where an exemption from antitrust liability might turn on the involvement of a government regulatory agency in condoning or requiring the practice.

    a. Even if a practice were explicitly imposed as a regulation, it might not necessarily be exempt, under Article 90(2), from the competition provisions of Article 85 and 86. Article 90(1) prohibits "any measure" of a Member State contrary to the Treaty. Indeed, in the *British Telecom* case, although the restrictions at issue were part of a regulatory scheme overseen by the British Post Office, the Court of Justice affirmed the Commission's finding that British Telecom was engaged in a business activity that was subject to competition rules. *British Telecom*, at paras. 18–20. The Article, therefore, might bar not only discretionary commercial acts of public undertakings, but also regulatory or legislative activities.

    b. In sum, the benchmark for determining whether practices of the PTTs are subject to the standards of Articles 85 and 86 may be whether application of a competition rule would "obstruct the performance, in law or in fact, of the particular tasks assigned to them". This determination, of course, would require examining the "tasks", the overall regulatory scheme, and whether the grant of the requested relief would thwart the PTT in providing telecommunications service. As a practical matter, then, it is difficult to determine whether a PTT would be subject to Articles 85 and 86 in the abstract, without assessing the merits of the particular claim against it and the potential impact of the relief requested.

    c. One related issue is who could bring suit against an undertaking under Article 90. Individuals can initiate complaints at the Commission. It is not clear, however, to what extent individuals can rely on Article 90 in national courts. *See* Case No. 172/82, *Syndicat National des Fabricants Raffineurs d'Huile de Graissage v. Groupement d'Intérêt Economique "Inter-Huiles"*, [1983] E.C.R. 555, 567.

    d. The Commission has taken the view, however, that it could bring suit against a Member State for not causing a public undertaking to end an objectionable practice. Commission of the European Communities, *Sixth Report on Competition Policy*, at para. 274. The European Court has agreed in holding that the Treaty imposes a duty on Member States not to adopt or maintain in force measures that could deprive Articles 85 and 86 of their effectiveness. Cases Nos. 209–213/84, *Ministère Public v. Lucas Asjes*, Common Mkt. Rep. (CCH) para. 14,287, at 16,780 (1986).

    3. Once it is determined that a PTT can be sued (because application of the rules would not be "obstructive" of "assigned" tasks), an even more difficult issue would be the precise legal standards that are to be applied. Article 86 prohibits an abuse of a dominant position by an undertaking; the holding in the *British Telecom* case was that the restriction on telex forwarding was such an abuse. More generally, Article 86 bars:

    a. directly or indirectly imposing unfair purchase or selling prices or other unfair trading conditions;

b. limiting production, markets or technical development to the prejudice of consumers;

c. applying dissimilar conditions to equivalent transactions with other trading parties, thereby placing them at a competitive disadvantage;

d. making the conclusion of contracts subject to acceptance by the other parties of supplementary obligations which, by their nature or according to commercial usage, have no connection with the subject of such contracts.

e. Article 86 might preclude a dominant entity from imposing conditions on access to services for which it is an exclusive supplier. Tying practices barred by Article 86(d) could include conditioning access to communications lines on the requirement that terminal equipment or other services be acquired from the same entity. Such practices might be deemed unlawful *per se*; alternatively, it might be seen as desirable that there be a submission explaining why they were reasonable. The unlawfulness of such tying arrangements has already been tested in the Commission's successful resolution of its complaint against the Federal Republic of Germany; the German Government agreed to amend rules that had granted the Bundespost a monopoly in the supply and maintenance of modems on the ground that they were to be connected to the network. *See* Commission of the European Communities, Information Memo No. IP (86) 379, July 25, 1986, Common Mkt. Rep. (CCH) para. 10,801 (1986).

4. In addition, the Commission may well be able to employ Article 86 in reviewing certain restrictive tariff provisions. Support for this position can be found in the Commission's decision in the *British Telecom* proceeding. The Commission had concluded that certain, never enforced, schemes that would have prohibited forwarding agencies from routing international telex messages more cheaply than if such messages had been sent directly by the subscriber were an abuse because they:

a. prejudiced customers located in other Member States;

b. applied dissimilar conditions to equivalent transactions, *i.e.*, those for onward transmission outside the U.K. must either originate in the U.K. or be charged at a price not cheaper than if they had been sent directly; and

c. made the use of installations subject to acceptance of an unrelated obligation (*i.e.*, to charge prices that had no connection with the type and quality of telecommunications services). Decision of the Commission, at 40, at para. 30.

5. Under Article 86, the Commission might also be empowered to examine the justification for restrictions on the resale of circuits. These restrictions might be regarded as unlawfully conditioning a customer's use of the basic transmission capacity to permit only certain configurations of facilities.

a. One restriction might result in foreclosing the customer from using switching devices to set up its own network. The PTT's prohibition might be regarded as affecting such devices, which are not, by their nature, the subject of the contracts for leased lines.

b. Another approach by the Commission could be to regard restrictions on resale or on other ways of using circuits as attempts to extend the dominance of a PTT. The related, but separate, market that could be affected by such conditions would be the combination of communications and communications-dependent areas. Given the importance of telecommunications in the provision of financial and information-distribution services, there would be at least a basis for claiming that exclusivity in the provision of basic services does not justify dominance in other uses of communications.

c. In evaluating particular attempts to extend dominance, the Commission might rely on the decision of the Court of Justice in Case No. 311/84, *Centre Belge d'Etudes de Marché—Télé-marketing S.A. v. Compagnie luxembourgeoise de Télédiffusion S.A. and Information Publicité Benelux S.A.*, Common Mkt. Rep. (CCH) para. 14,246 (1985) ["*Télémarketing*"]. In that case, the Court held that a television broadcast company with a monopoly could not extend its monopoly to the operation of a telemarketing service: it is an abuse of a dominant position under Article 86 if, "without any objective necessity, an undertaking holding a dominant position on a particular market reserves to itself . . . an ancillary activity which might be carried out by another undertaking as part of its activities on a neighboring but separate market, with the possibility of eliminating all competition from such undertaking". *Télé-marketing*, Common Mkt. Rep. at 16,459.

d. For telecommunications-dependent services, the facts and the language of the Court in *Télé-marketing* are instructive. An abuse of dominant position was found where an undertaking dominant in one market supplies a service that is "indispensable for the activities of another undertaking in another market". *Id.* Thus, the case can be read to suggest that the Commission could take action against a PTT that, "without any objective necessity", seeks to extend its power in the telecommunications sector into the "neighboring but separate" markets for value-added or information-based services.

e. Although telecommunications services are "indispensable" for such services, the *Télé-marketing* case raises significant questions about what would constitute an abuse of a dominant position. To what extent, for example, are value-added services a "separate" market? Can a dominant undertaking supplying indispensable services to another market itself enter that market? If so, under what terms and conditions so that its activities do not constitute an abuse? These issues would have to be worked out by the Commission in the context of specific suits against PTTs.

f. Furthermore, in evaluating particular attempts to extend dominance, the Commission might also usefully examine criteria that are used in the United States for determining whether Section 2 of the Sherman Act, which prohibits monopolization and attempts to monopolize, had been violated. Case law in the U.S. on defining the relevant geographic and product markets, the extent to which the necessary market power is present, and the presence of any requisite intent could be of some assistance in this examination.

6. In determining whether a dominant position had been abused, the Commission would seem obliged to analyze the economic or technological reasoning proffered by the PTT in support of a restriction. Although this inquiry would necessarily be distinct from the threshold determination regarding the Commission's jurisdiction, it is, as noted above, unlikely that the two can be entirely separate.

D. Use of Article 85 to Review and Regulate Agreements Among PTTs

1. A second independent basis afforded to the Commission for asserting and exercising jurisdiction over the activities of the PTTs is Article 85 of the Treaty. Article 85 prohibits "all agreements between undertakings, decisions by associations of undertakings and concerted practices which may affect trade between Member States and which have as their object or effect the prevention, restriction or distortion of competition within the common market". More particularly, Article 85(1) proscribes agreements that:

a. directly or indirectly fix purchase or selling prices or any other trading conditions;

b. limit or control production, markets, technical development, or investment;

c. share markets or sources of supply;

d. apply dissimilar conditions to equivalent transactions with other trading parties, thereby placing them at a competitive disadvantage; and

e. make the conclusion of contracts subject to acceptance by the other parties of supplementary obligations which, by their nature or according to commercial usage, have no connection with the subject of such contracts.

2. Article 85(3) exempts any agreement that "contributes to improving the production or distribution of goods or to promoting technical and economic progress, while allowing consumers a fair share of the resulting benefit". Thus, there must be some showing that the restrictive agreements are necessary to the advancement of some public purpose. And, although not explicitly stated, consistent with the general rules of interpreting the Treaty, the restraint must be the least restrictive possible in achieving its intended purpose. Furthermore, it is significant that the legal framework in which such agreements are made, and the classification given thereto by national legal systems, are irrelevant as far as Article 85 is concerned. *See* Case No. 123/83, *Bureau National Interprofessionnel du Cognac v. Guy Clair*, Common Mkt. Rep. (CCH) para. 14,160 (1985).

3. The Commission's Regulation No. 17/62 implements Articles 85 and 86 and establishes an elaborate set of procedures by which it is to be notified of agreements subject to Article 85. Regulation No. 17 of 6 February 1962, 13 J.O. Comm. Eur. 204 (1962), as amended by Regulation No. 59, 58 J.O. Comm. Eur. 1655 (1962), Regulation No. 118/63/EEC, 162 J.O. Comm. Eur. 2696 (1963), and Regulation No. 2822/71/EEC, J.O. Eur. Comm. (No. L 285) 49 (1971). It is on the basis of this notification that the Commission is to determine whether or not it can grant negative clearance—that there are no grounds for Commission action—or grant an exemption under Article 85(3).

a. The review procedure of Regulation No. 17/62 is potentially comprehensive. The Commission shall act in liaison with authorities of the Member States and can consult with an Advisory Committee on Restrictive Practices and Monopolies. Article 10, Regulation No. 17/62. The Commission may request information from authorities in the Member States and from public undertakings. Article 11. In addition, under Article 14 the Commission has authority to carry out investigations of undertakings, including the examination of books and business records. It can impose fines. Article 15.

b. Finally, the Commission has the authority to conduct general inquiries into an economic sector if it is of the view that competition is being restricted or distorted. Article 12. In so doing, it may request undertakings to supply information relating to price movements, inflexibility of prices, or to any other circumstances that might suggest that Articles 85 or 86 are being violated.

c. When adopted, the reach of Regulation No. 17/62 was viewed as extremely broad. The Council of the Community, therefore, soon exempted the rail, road, and inland waterway sectors. Regulation No. 141, 124 J.O. Comm. Eur. 2753 (1962). Upon the expiration of Regulation 141, Regulation No. 1017/68 was adopted to apply special rules relating to Commission review of agreements in the transport sector. Regulation No. 1017/68, J.O. Eur. Comm. (No L 175) 1 (1968).

d. This comprehensive, sectoral regulation has no parallel in the telecommunications field. Thus, the direct implication is that Regulation No. 17/62 is fully applicable to the telecommunications sector in Europe. The only exemption from Article 85 that would be available to undertakings that offer telecommunications services would be under Article 90(2); this issue has been addressed above in Section VI.C. To date, however, Regulation 17/62 has not been applied to agreements in the telecommunications sector.

4. A fair reading of Article 85 and Regulation No. 17/62, as amended, would be that the Commission has plenary authority to review agreements among undertakings engaged in the provision of telecommunications services. In conjunction with doing so, the Commission could undertake far-reaching inquiries into the entire telecommunications sector. Of course, at the threshold, such agreements would have to be among the

types of agreements enumerated in Article 85(1). They cannot be exempt on the basis of criteria set forth in Article 85(2). The question is what, if any, agreements might be within the scope of the Commission's jurisdiction under Article 85. This matter is not discussed in depth here; rather, only some representative agreements are mentioned.

5. One type of agreement that might be subject to Commission scrutiny could involve an undertaking among the PTTs to offer types of services on a collaborative basis. PTTs might agree to establish a venture or ventures providing data processing services or one or more types of value-added services. Agreements to do so might encompass the services offered, prices, equipment requirements, and conditions regarding the provision of similar services by unaffiliated entities.

a. As discussed below in Section VIII, the Commission is considering a scheme whereby certain services provided jointly and offered on a European-wide basis might be classified as basic services. If it should adopt such a framework, it would at least be arguable that the Commission had established a legal basis for determining that agreements to offer such services would meet the public purpose standard of Article 85(3).

b. Article 85, however, would seem to require the Commission to assess whether any restrictions imposed by the inter-PTT agreements were necessary to achieving the venture's intended purpose. Such restrictions, for example, could be keyed to the rates for underlying services that are available to the venture and the rates charged to unaffiliated entities. Thus, even if the Commission should move toward the proposed regulatory classification, there still might be grounds for its examining the validity of specific provisions.

6. Another important question is whether the Commission would have jurisdiction over the wide range of agreements among the PTTs, made in the context of CEPT, by which they provide intra-European services. Such agreements include those relating to the availability and tariffing of leased lines, the establishment of interconnection arrangements, rates for a range of services, and network structures.

a. The various agreements among the European PTTs can differ significantly among each other. Often, they may constitute simply an understanding as to the establishment of interconnection for a service. In this event, each party to the agreement has its own tariffing practices. Arguably, such national practices, which are not the express subject of the agreement, are outside the scope of the agreement and any Commission review thereof.

b. In a more expansive reading of the Commission's jurisdiction, however, each of the contracting parties could be deemed to concur in—to agree to—the practices of the others. Although there may be no explicit agreement among two PTTs with respect to specific national practices, by jointly providing service, and with each having the capacity to terminate service, a PTT would implicitly be agreeing to the other country's domestic tariffs.

c. In practice, of course, tariffing and rate principles are the subject of collegial discussions within CEPT. Thus, there may be a general convergence of approaches even though there may not be a specific agreement between PTTs with respect to tariffing or conditions on the resale or sharing of leased lines. Such convergence could well be deemed presumptive evidence of an agreement with respect to such practices.

d. The fact that agreements between and among PTTs might be subject to review by the Commission under Article 85 would not, of course, necessarily mean that they were invalid. On the contrary, it is possible that they would be granted an exemption under Article 85(3). The significance of Article 85, however, is that the review procedure affords the Commission an opportunity to focus on contractual provisions or terms that might adversely affect competition in telecommunications services.

E. Use of Treaty Provisions on Free Flow of Services

1. A third avenue available to the Commission in constructing a regulatory framework for the provision of value-added services on a European-wide basis might make use of the Treaty provisions that seek to create a free flow of services. The objectives of the Treaty include the "abolition, as between Member States, of obstacles to freedom of movement for . . . services". Treaty of Rome, Article 3. Article 2 refers to the "establishment of a common market". An entire chapter, Chapter 3, which consists of Article 59 to Article 66, is included in Part II of the Treaty, Foundations of the Community. Article 60 of the Treaty defines services to include activities of "industrial" or "commercial" character, or of craftsmen or of the professions.

2. A threshold question, of course, is whether telecommunications should be deemed the provision of a service. Some argue, it should be noted, that the provision of "international telecommunications" does not involve a national entity in supplying a single service.

a. Those who argue that international telecommunications is not a single service assert that it is provided jointly, through an agreement among disparate national providers. The argument is that no single entity is involved in offering a service to the public or to others beyond national boundaries.

b. Article 60, however, defines "services" broadly: anything that is a "service" provided for remuneration, and that is not covered by provisions relating to goods, capital and persons, is a "service" within the meaning of Article 60. *See* Case No. 205/84, *Commission v. Federal Republic of Germany*, Judgment of the Court, 4 December 1986, para. 18 (with judgments of the same date against France, Case No. 220/83; Denmark, Case No. 252/83; and Ireland, Case No. 206/84) ["*Co-insurance Case*"]; Case No. 279/80, *In re Alfred John Webb*, [1981] E.C.R. 3305. Thus, although the issue has not been tested in Europe, it is likely that telecommunications "services" within a country or within Europe would be subject to the service provisions of the Treaty.

3. Whatever might be the merits of the argument that telecommunications is not a "service" with respect to basic services, undoubtedly a range of activities that make use of telecommunications facilities could be classified as "services". Such activities could include data processing or interactive database services. Even activities such as protocol conversion, which are closely related to communications, would arguably be considered services within the meaning of Article 60. Ultimately, rather than focusing on whether telecommunications is a service, it may be more important to distinguish among types of activities—basic, value-added, and information services. Such differentiation would be necessary for working out international arrangements within Europe.

4. Article 59 of the Treaty states that "restrictions on freedom to provide services within the Community shall be progressively abolished". The heart of this provision is the prohibition of any discrimination against a service provider on the grounds of nationality or on the grounds that it is established in a Member State other than that where the service is to be provided. Case No. 52/79, *Procureur du Roi v. Marc J.V.C. Debauve*, [1980] E.C.R. 833, 856 [*"Debauve"*]. Article 62, which prohibits the introduction of new restrictions on the freedom to provide services after the date of entry of the Treaty, when read in conjunction with Article 59, also might be used to facilitate and encourage services tailored for those residing in other Member States.

5. Article 59 might be used to remove restrictions on procedures for licensing value-added entities that favor nationals of the Member State. If the non-discrimination principle must be applied to applicants, pressures to adopt a relatively liberal entry policy might grow. Of course, with respect to purely national requirements, the Treaty does not explicitly prevent Member States from restricting entry in a particular market. *Debauve*, at 855. It is now well established, however, that any such restrictions would have to be applied so as not to discriminate against service providers of foreign origin.

6. A more expansive reading of the Articles on services, and one adopted by the Commission, is that the scope of the Treaty is not restricted simply to ending restrictions that discriminate against foreign service providers. One of the six foundations of the Community is the creation of a free market in services. Therefore, argues the Commission, the Treaty operates to prohibit all restrictions—not merely those that are discriminatory—on the free movement of services. *See Television Without Frontiers: Green Paper on the Establishment of the Common Market for Broadcasting, Especially by Satellite and Cable*, COM(84) 300 final [*"Green Paper"*].

a. The proposition that the Treaty addresses all restrictions is premised on the notion that a service provider cannot be subject to two sets of inconsistent regulatory restrictions: between the country where the service is provided and the country where the service provider resides. The European Court has acknowledged that the restrictions dealt with in Article 59 include not only discrimination but also "all requirements . . . which may present or otherwise obstruct the activities of the person providing the service". See *Green Paper*, at 145 n.2 (and cases cited therein).

b. Recently, the Court emphasized that the Treaty requires removal of "all restrictions" on the freedom to provide services that are imposed by reason of the fact that the provider is established outside the Member State where the service is to be provided. *Co-insurance Case*, at para. 25. With respect to value-added services, then, inconsistent or conflicting national rules may be viewed as so onerous as virtually precluding the provision of a service on a transborder basis. In this event, Articles 59 and 60 could be invoked by the would-be service provider.

c. In both the *Debauve* holding and in *Cotidel v. Ciné Vog*, however, the Court did appear to limit Article 59 to cases of discrimination. *Debauve*, at 856; Case No. 62/79, [1980] E.C.R. 881, 903. That is, certain national restrictions that are justified by the "general interest" and are applicable to all persons would not be inconsistent with the Treaty. Such restrictions are permitted, however, only if the foreign entity subject to such restrictions is also subject to "similar regulations" when it operates in its own country. The point, of course, is to ensure that a foreign service provider will not have to meet the requirements of a duplicative regulatory framework abroad if it is already subject to a similar framework at home.

d. From a practical standpoint, the Commission might construe "similarity" rather broadly when it comes to assessing the regulatory environment in which value-added services are supplied. The effective provision of such services might be barred if the regulatory requirements were to vary from country to country with respect to services offered on a transborder basis. Consequently, if the Commission were to view a national restriction on the provision of a value-added or other transborder service as serving no additional purpose beyond the purpose served by compliance with a similar regulation in the home country, the Commission might strike such a restriction in an exercise of its authority under Article 59.

7. There are, then, several factors to be applied in determining which national restrictions on the provision of value-added services would be invalidated under Article 59. Given that the freedom to provide services is one of the foundations of the Community, the burden of justifying restrictions based on the "general interest" would seem to rest squarely on the Member State that has imposed the restriction. Furthermore, the restrictions must be both appropriate and proportional, *i.e.*, they must be the least restrictive means of achieving the legitimate regulatory purpose. *See* Cases Nos 62 and 63/81, *Seco v. Evi*, [1982] E.C.R. 223, 237; Case No. 33/74, *van Binsbergen v. Bedrijfsvereniging Metaalnijverheid*, [1974], E.C.R. 1299, 1309.

8. Assuming that the PTTs and the Member States could demonstrate that any restrictions on the entry or provision of value-added services are in the general interest, it would fall to the Council of Europe, acting on a proposal from the Commission and after consultation with the European Parliament, to harmonize differences in national approaches. Article 57(2) sets out the procedure for approximation of national laws to achieve a common market. The process of approximation, however, does not require that a single, uniform, European scheme be adopted. Rather, it might only necessitate the co-ordination of approaches to facilitate the provision of service on a Community-wide basis. The Commission's role in such a co-ordinative process is explored further in Section VIII, below.

9. In removing barriers to the transborder provision of a service, a Member State probably is barred from regulating such activities outside its national territory. Moreover, the Commission's belief is that services can be offered by an entity in a country other than its own without its establishing itself in that country. *See Green Paper*, at 164–65. This view is supported by a holding of the Court which states that a contractor, by complying with the registration provisions of its own state, need not obtain an establishment permit in a foreign country in which the services were to be provided. Case No. 76/81, *Transporoute et Travaux v. Minister of Public Works, Grand Duchy of Luxembourg*, [1982] E.C.R. 417, 427–28.

　　a. The Court has ruled that the condition of permanent establishment may deprive individuals of the right of free flow of services. The Court has reiterated that, given the restrictiveness of requiring permanent establishment as a predicate for provision of service, the condition must be "indispensable" for attaining the legislative objective pursued. *Co-insurance Case*, at para. 52. Such regulation may be justified, however, if necessary to ensure observance of professional rules of conduct. *See van Binsbergen*, at 1309; Case No. 39/75, *Coenen v. Sociaal-Economische Raad*, [1975] E.C.R. 1547, 1555.

　　b. With respect to the provision of a value-added service, the cases addressing the scope of the right to provide a service in a country without an establishment in that country may mean that a provider would not need to maintain a permanent infrastructure in a foreign country in order to provide service. In addition to relying on the interpretation of Article 59 in *Transporoute* and the *Co-insurance Case*, support for this proposition might be found in the Commission's conclusion that broadcasters need not change residences to provide services outside national territories. *See Green Paper*, at 165.

　　c. It should be emphasized, however, that the right of non-establishment does not necessarily mean that information-based or value-added services could be offered in a country without any presence in that country. Similarly, the cases do not suggest that a country is disabled from applying other necessary restrictions (*i.e.*, other than requiring establishment) to such service providers. Such conditions, however, may be applied to foreign entities operating in a Member State only to the extent that the interest of that State is not safeguarded by provisions to which the service provider is subject in the Member State of his establishment. *Co-insurance Case*, at paras. 27 and 33. A Member State may apply an additional condition, beyond that applied by the State of establishment, only if there are "imperative reasons" for doing so. *Id.* at para. 29.

  d. The extent to which an information or value-added service provider has a presence within a foreign country is also determinative of the extent to which national legislation of that country may be applied to it. Temporary or occasional activities of entities established elsewhere may not be subject to the same degree of regulatory control as permanent activities. *Id.* at 26.

  10. As a legal matter, the Commission apparently has two options: using Article 59 to invalidate particular restrictions or approximating different legal schemes. The latter option—harmonization—may be the more cautious approach. Given, however, the amount of time necessary for study, consultation, Commission drafting, and Council action, the use of the approximation approach may gravely delay the introduction of new services.

F. Some Concluding Observations on the Task Facing the Commission

  1. The Commission's task in overseeing and encouraging the emergence of European-wide markets for information or value-added services is formidable. The various national regulatory requirements diverge significantly for different types of services. Determining which requirements would be sufficiently in the general interest and "necessary" to withstand scrutiny under Article 59 will be a time-consuming job, undoubtedly subject to a host of political pressures. In short, the integration of the market in a single, sweeping step will be enormously difficult.

  a. The Commission may be prepared, however, to invalidate restrictions that are impeding the development of a common market for telecommunications-dependent services. Certainly, a coherent, European regime is more likely to emerge if the Commission acts aggressively.

  b. As European-wide services begin to develop, the Commission may choose to have contracts between service providers and their customers address issues that might otherwise be the subject of regulatory concern. If national policymakers, and the Commission, rely too heavily on express legal norms or requirements—and ultimately on a process of approximation—the result may be to mire new services in intergovernmental negotiations.

  2. This discussion of the three legal avenues open to the Commission under the Treaty only highlights the complexity of its future efforts in the field of telecommunications. As a threshold matter, it is clear that the Treaty is only just now beginning to be applied to the sector. To

date, and as demonstrated by the *British Telecom* case, the Commission's approach has been essentially case-by-case.

    a. Nevertheless, if the market for value-added services is to develop in the near future, the Commission will find it necessary to address some of these issues in a broader policy context. In this regard, it would be useful for the Commission to analyze and crystallize its powers under Articles 85 and 86 of the Treaty. By visibly undertaking to assess its legal authority under those Articles, the Commission may help to prod Member States into reaching a consensus on some difficult issues.

    b. This discussion is not meant to suggest that the Commission, in reaching the services sector, might not avail itself of options relating to the provision of goods under the Treaty. For example, Article 37 provides that there can be no discrimination among the Member States as to how goods may be procured or marketed. The Commission might stress that services are dependent on the ability to install and market infrastructure equipment—such as modems and switching nodes. Thus, the Commission might address service-related issues by exercising what is potentially its stronger authority over the provision of goods.

    c. As is suggested in Section VIII below, the Commission may want to define and use newly-established procedural mechanisms as a way of resolving issues. In this way, the Member States might come to accept a more assertive role for the Commission in forging a European telecommunications policy.

VII. EVOLUTION OF REGULATORY MECHANISMS

A. European Regulatory Processes

    1. As nations make changes in substantive policies on industry structure and on the scope of competition, there are concomitant shifts in the policies aimed at establishing the institutions that will regulate in the new environments. In Europe, new substantive policies are gradually forcing new regulatory approaches. The most obvious example of a new regulatory organization is in the U.K., where Oftel was created as an independent entity.

    a. Frequently a critical question is how new entities co-ordinate responsibilities with existing regulatory bodies. In the U.K., there are still some unresolved issues about how Oftel will co-ordinate its role with the Department of Trade and Industry ("DTI"), which shares a role in licensing and in the international arena. As the boundaries between domestic and international services continue to erode, it is likely, for example, that Oftel will have to take a more pronounced role in the international sector than it has to date.

    b. Another development concomitant with the creation of a regulatory body is the formulation of procedures for obtaining the information necessary to make policy. In the U.K., the public comment procedures that were used by the DTI in gathering responses to the proposed VADS license was criticized as superficial and unsatisfactory. Oftel, with its public, consumer-oriented constituency, has been working on the development of a set of procedures to obtain comments. In addition, the flow of information from an agency is equally important in assuring the public that its policies are applied with an even hand; an agency has an interest in developing credibility with the public and a reputation for fairness. In this regard, Oftel has still not made documents that are filed with it available on a broad basis.

        c. Oftel is still somewhat of an arbiter, with less responsibility than the FCC for justifying or rationalizing its administrative determinations. The existence of some administrative procedure—coupled with the flexibility to render *ad hoc* decisions—releases some of the pressure on policymakers and gives them the ability to apply leverage in changing the policies of the government.

        d. Oftel is, nevertheless, a forum in which both British and foreign nationals can state their views on the impact of telecommunications policies. Its procedures allow some imprecision in definitional boundaries or in resolving policy issues: some issues can be dealt with by waivers or postponed until the agency has added experience.

      2. The new French Commission Nationale des Communications et Libertés ("CNCL") is another exemplar of how shifts in policy will necessitate the creation of regulatory bodies.

        a. The independence of the CNCL is a sharp departure from the *dirigiste* tradition and is based on the principle of accountability of entrepreneurial decisions.

        b. The evolution of new institutions to regulate the emerging telecommunications environment in France may have a profound impact on the Italians. Italy has a similar, though distinct, tradition of providing telecommunications services through state-owned companies and their subsidiaries.

      3. In the Netherlands, a new policymaking body in the Ministry of Transport and Public Works will be created, with an appeals process that is outlined in Chapter II on "Boundary Lines".

        a. One concern of users and others, however, is that an open transition process be established as the PTT is transformed from a public agency into a limited liability company. As options are defined, some process of focusing the comments and perspectives of users and other affected interests may be required.

        b. The changes in the Netherlands may parallel the developments of regulatory institutions in the U.K. Just as the Dutch have looked at the British experience with liberalization, so, too, they are likely to examine Oftel as a model for a regulatory agency.

      4. In Germany, the development of any new mechanisms may be more complicated, given the German regulatory tradition. There are, in

the Federal Republic, few examples of mechanisms for independent regulatory controls over industry; one example is the supervision of the insurance industry by the Ministry of Finance. These processes might apply to telecommunications, although it is not clear whether the link has been made explicitly by the government commission or other policymakers.

5. In Finland, the regulatory responsibilities of the PTT will be shifted to the Ministry of Communications. It is not clear, however, what specific mechanisms will be adopted.

B. Relevance of Regulatory Mechanisms

1. Regulatory mechanisms are relevant for several reasons. First, they establish a means by which policies relevant to users and competitors may be implemented.

2. Second, they establish boundaries and referee disputes. These tasks must be undertaken in a new regulatory environment and there must be a process for dealing with the issues. The process allows imprecision and flexibility in definitions, which can be modified or sharpened on the basis of experience.

3. Third, they recognize that diversification of industry structure introduces more players into the game; new institutions must be established to ensure that the interests of these entities are taken into account. An established process may be necessary to distill differing perspectives.

4. Fourth, they are a means of alleviating trade pressures on controversies about market access.

 a. With changes in industry structure, there are new services and new players; different arrangements must be negotiated. Discontinuities in national policies will lead to pressures for market access. Although disputes can be dealt with in bilateral trade discussions, the resulting agreements on general principles still require some entity to implement transitional policies.

 b. Disputes over access may necessitate dealing with long-term structural issues over a substantial period of time. Inasmuch as such issues may not be suitable for resolution in trade talks, the emergence of a regulatory mechanism to assist national and foreign entities may be critical.

5. Ultimately, new institutions may make more complicated the co-ordination of telecommunications policies at the regional and international levels.

 a. New regulatory decisionmakers and institutions are likely to change the role of dominant service providers in the international arena. One example of this development is the involvement of the Department of Trade and Industry in the U.K. in recasting the international institutional and representative responsibilities of British Telecom.

b. As regulatory and operational authority becomes fragmented, more nations will move toward a regulatory regime for international issues that separates "operational" and "regulatory" roles and thus resembles the division of authority in the United States between governmental agencies (the FCC, the Department of State, the National Telecommunications and Information Administration, and the US Trade Representative) and carriers.

6. In Europe, U.S. policies toward competition and industry arrangements are perceived as having a major impact on the structure and liberalization of the European telecommunications sector. In fact, however, it may be that ideas about the regulatory process in the U.S. are more relevant to Europeans, and have a greater impact on the liberalization of telecommunications markets, than U.S. ideas about competition policy. Although procedures in Europe may differ markedly, and may be far less formal than those in the U.S., there are many common issues.

VIII. THE COMMISSION'S ROLE IN INTEGRATING THE EUROPEAN TELECOMMUNICATIONS MARKET

A. Introduction: Shift in Commission's Focus

1. In the 1980s, the Commission has increasingly turned its attention to telecommunications policy in Europe and, most particularly, to how to achieve integration of the European market. At present, it is in the middle of a far-reaching review of the current situation in Europe and of its range of options for the future. Over the last few years, the thrust of the Commission's efforts has differed, taking a variety of approaches that all had the same objective: a single market in Europe. What these policies all had in common, however, was an attempt to co-ordinate more effectively the technical infrastructure for facilities.

2. One area in which the Commission has spent significant resources has been in achieving technical standardization. In this effort it has tried to work in conjunction with CEPT. The RACE program (Research and Development in Advanced Communications in Europe) is an effort to combine various research and development activities into a program that will ultimately both expand the market for European telecommunications manufacturers and manufacturers of semiconductor chips, and benefit European users.

a. The RACE program was discussed in great detail in Phase I of the Study of Telecommunications Structures. Briefly, however, one of its objectives is a program for the design and installation of broad band integrated networks in the mid-1990s. The initial, definition phase has been regarded as a success.

b. For the second phase, a draft workplan was prepared—and an additional communication forwarded to the Council—in June 1986.

See Communications to Council, Community Action in the Field of Telecommunication Technologies, RMC 246 (June 26, 1986). The Commission is now seeking substantial funding (ECU 800 million) to fund the pre-competitive work of the next five-year phase (1987–91) of the program.

    c. Apart from the RACE program, however, the Commission has embarked on a series of steps to bring into closer harmony planning for the various national narrowband ISDN networks that are now being installed throughout Europe. *See* Section III.B.1, above. In furtherance of this objective, for example, it commissioned an elaborate study of the ISDN developments of each country in the Community. It received the report in spring 1985. After the Commission sent a draft recommendation to the Council of Ministers concerning the Coordinated Introduction of Integrated Services Digital Networks in the Member States, the Council adopted the recommendation, committing itself to staying abreast of, and stimulating, technical and regulatory developments taking place across Europe.

    d. In addition, currently pending before the Council is a draft Directive on standardization in the field of information technology and telecommunications. There is some controversy over whether the Council action will be a Recommendation or a simple Resolution, largely spurred by one of the provisions of the Directive, which would oblige Member States to make use of Community standards for public procurement contracts.

    3. Although, then, the Commission historically has focused its efforts on medium- and longer-term plans for the network infrastructure, it has now begun to address more actively the changes within Europe in telecommunications policies affecting the provision of services. Many in the Commission view these policies, which are increasingly liberalizing the use of the infrastructure itself, as both a threat and an opportunity.

    a. The present change in policies across Europe is seen as representing an historic turning point. For the first time in decades national administrations are examining specific policies in the context of their overall regulatory framework for the telecommunications and related services sector. The reasons for policymakers in Europe launching this review process are complex and manifold. They were among the principal subjects of Phase I of the Study.

    b. Such shifts in policy, in short, have been unleashed by several institutional pressures. Several PTTs are seeking greater flexibility in the face of increasing national and international competition. Ministries of industry or economics are focusing on the economic consequences of telecommunications policy. Policymakers are taking advantage of changes in one country to justify a new look at their own national policies.

    c. There is one fundamental aspect of these changes that is highly unsettling to policymakers at the Commission and to others working toward an integrated market. That is, each country in Europe is devising its own national approach to liberalization, and each approach is different from the others. Consequently, the very process of change—which is seen as an opportunity—is also perceived as posing the significant risk of further divergence, not integration, of national policies.

          d. The debate on telecommunications policies, on the future role of the PTTs, and on the conditions, terms, and structure for the competitive entry of value-added and information-based services suppliers has been extremely vigorous at the national level. This intensity has tended to shift the focus of attention away from the Commission and its attempts to develop an integrated market. The reason for this diversion may well be the size of the stakes in the process of liberalization at the national level. The PTTs may see them as too high, and the risks of unrestricted or too rapid movement to competition as too substantial, drawing energy away from debates within their governments toward collaborative activities at the European-wide level. Nor, of course, are they especially receptive to the notion of the Commission acting as a "super-regulator" or as a new, European PTT.

B. New Policy Initiatives: Commission Proposals to Classify Services

          1. The Commission, in the midst of this rapidly evolving situation, has been developing some highly provocative initiatives. In this effort, D.G. XIII has taken the lead, but other directorates, such as D.G. IV, have also been involved and play a critical role in formulating the Commission's proposals. In December 1986, some of these initiatives were discussed with the Senior Officials Group Telecommunications ("SOGT"). As they emerge, the Commission's views will probably become a policy paper—most likely a "green paper"—which will be brought before the SOGT in April 1987. The current objective is to have the Council of Ministers make a decision on a European telecommunications services policy later in 1987.

          2. Some of the core elements of the proposed policy have been the subject of public statements by senior Commission officials. *See, e.g.,* T.M. Schuringa, "The European Telecommunications Services Policy" (Sept. 1986) (contribution to the EUROTELECOM Conference, Madrid) ["*Schuringa Paper*"]. These statements obviously are intended to test the reactions of the Commission's various constituencies to the proposed policies. The policies are, of course, still very much in a state of evolution. Nevertheless, it might be useful to outline and analyze them here.

          3. As a threshold matter, it is important to point out that the Commission now seems prepared to move toward more liberal policies on services, and on the use of the network. One way of doing so is to develop a uniform set of definitions for Europe; this is one of the principal objectives of the policies being tested in the *Schuringa Paper*. The Commission may be prepared to press for such liberalization using enforcement powers afforded

to it under the Treaty. At the same time, however, the Commission does not view competition in the network infrastructure as a probable or likely development, nor does it see the Treaty as compelling such competition. There is, furthermore, no implication that the scale of national markets would make competition in infrastructure desirable—even in the major countries of Europe.

4. The thrust of the Commission's efforts, then, is in the area of services and, more precisely, in seeking to make a clear distinction between basic and "non-basic" services. This distinction, significantly, is not intended to be synonymous with the division between the provision of network facilities and that of services.

   a. As proposed in the *Schuringa Paper*, services introduced throughout Europe, or worldwide, would be called "basic". Such services now include telephony and telex. Eventually, however, because the range of "basic" services is dynamic, they may come to embrace teletex, videotex, electronic mail, paging and several others. The distinction between "basic" and "non-basic" obviously does not parallel the distinction in the United States between "basic" and "enhanced" services, definitions that rely more on the technical than on the geographic nature of the service.

   b. The Commission's proposal would place primary responsibility for the provision of basic, universal services on the PTTs. Nevertheless, the Commission seems open to the possibility that basic services could be provided competitively, so long as the infrastructure of a single PTT is used for that purpose.

   c. All services not provided on a universal basis would be called "non-basic" services. These would comprise value-added services and services to limited groups of users. The provision of such services would, according to the proposals of the *Schuringa Paper*, be left to the initiative of the private sector. Such services would not need to be regulated or licensed.

   d. The intent of the distinction between "basic" and "non-basic" is, of course, to offer some incentives to the PTTs to move toward deregulation, and to work together more closely in offering European-wide services. In the Commission's view, the principal incentive would be to allow a PTT offering a European-wide service certain rate advantages over other, non-affiliated providers of similar services.

   e. The Commission also sees the distinction as permitting it to play a key role in decisions concerning the introduction of European-wide, *i.e.*, "basic", services. With CEPT, the Commission would be in a position to take the lead in co-ordinating the activities of the national providers of basic services.

5. At the core of the Commission's proposed policy are two elements that must be examined carefully. First, the key notion—of European-wide, universal service—remains imprecisely defined. Second, the development of classifications for services would necessitate changes in the pricing of telecommunications services that could be significant. The following discussion reviews these two components of the proposed policy.

6. With respect to the question of what might constitute a "basic" service offered European-wide, several issues are still open. One question is whether a service will be "basic" if it is not initially offered in all twelve of the Community's member states.

    a. The level of development of the telecommunications infrastructure differs significantly throughout Europe. Less sophisticated infrastructures make it less likely that the more advanced services will be introduced. Furthermore, the different levels of economic and industrial development in Europe may make it uneconomic to provide certain services to parts of the Community where demand may be limited or negligible.

    b. What, then, will be required for a service to be considered "basic"? It may be sufficient for the largest countries to agree to the provision of a new service for it to be classified as "European-wide". If so, however, it is not clear how such services can be described and regulated as "universal".

    c. More significantly, determining the scope of what constitutes a "universal service" will be difficult. Although telephony and telex services have high rates of penetration, even telex is concentrated in particular sectors of the business community. In the case of a newer service, it will be difficult to determine what degree of market penetration constitutes "universal". For purposes of declaring that a service is "universal", will it be sufficient, for example, that its intended market is the public at large rather than a small segment of the market? If, however, a service is in fact aimed at a smaller group, such as business users, it will be difficult to maintain the clarity of the distinction between those, arguably "basic", services and other, "non-basic", services that are offered to limited groups or industry sectors, but not to all Europeans.

7. Another problem emerges from permitting the PTTs to agree to a European service and then relying on that agreement for the definition of "basic". Any definitional scheme predicated on such agreements is likely to affect innovative activities undertaken by new service providers. Proceeding to adopt a PTT-driven definition might, for example, allow more risk-oriented ventures to develop new market segments but then find themselves confronting a combination of PTTs offering the same service. Moreover, unless there were a separation between network infrastructure services and new services, such an offering by the PTTs could be made more commercially attractive to the customers than the services offered by the private sector. The possibility of such a responsive entry by PTTs may result in curtailing access to the capital necessary to finance new ventures.

8. Another troubling issue arising from any definition of "universal service" is separating that "basic" service from the larger service with which it may be offered. The PTTs, for example, undoubtedly will want to classify an electronic mail service as "basic". Indeed, the *Schuringa Paper* lays the predicate for this possibility. A mail box service, however, may be an integral, and perhaps almost inseparable, part of a broader

business offering, such as a cash management service for customers of a financial institution. The presence of a "basic" service in a mixed service raises the question of whether the entire offering would be considered contaminated and, therefore, should be reclassified as basic.

9. Concerns about the possible definitions of services have been greatly heightened owing to the second element of the Commission's proposed policy—a scheme for revising rate structures and levels. Commission officials have suggested that pure leased line services, for intra-corporate communications, could be substantially reduced in price. As the *Schuringa Paper* notes, however, simple resale is a cause for some concern by administrations. Thus, the Commission is exploring the introduction of volume-dependent tariffs for third-party uses of leased circuits.

10. Differentials between the kinds of tariff structures that would be applicable to leased lines, and the introduction of volume-sensitive tariffs, would be a critical element of the Commission's definitional scheme. That is, any "basic", European-wide service could take advantage of the lower rate structure applicable to leased lines.

    a. The cause for concern, however, is that there would be some tariff-based discrimination between the PTT and non-PTT entities offering "basic" services. The PTTs or other providers of universal services could take advantage of preferential rate structures based on internal accounting calculations. If, however, the private sector chooses to provide "basic" services, it could do so only by obtaining leased circuits on a non-preferential basis.

    b. By contrast, "non-basic" services could be offered on an equivalent basis by both PTTs and others. With respect to this category of service, the same rate structure would apply regardless of the entity offering the service. For PTTs offering "non-basic" services, it is thought that some financial or other structural safeguards might be imposed to ensure equivalence with the tariffs available to the private sector.

11. The Commission's proposal has several significant problems. These will need to be resolved before, not while, the scheme suggested by Commission officials is adopted. If they are not, any efforts to draft and implement Community-wide regulatory rules are doomed to fail.

    a. First, the Commission does not take adequate account of the fact that many value-added services targeted at businesses make use of leased lines tariffed at a flat rate. By distinguishing between "basic" and "non-basic" services, and then adopting different tariff structures, the Commission's proposal would create substantial confusion with respect to the rates for services that might include a "basic" electronic mail component. If the new proposal were adopted, it could have a highly disruptive impact on existing and emerging uses of telecommunications and information. This result would seem precisely the opposite of the Commission's stated objectives of creating a new, vigorous, and European market for such services.

b. A second major problem is that there is no European institution or mechanism to oversee the repricing process, even though rate restructuring is a significant part of the Commission's plan for Europe. Such rate differentials are the practical manifestation of the proposed distinction between "basic" and "non-basic" services. The rate structure of interexchange services is a critical element of present and proposed new services. Consequently, without a mechanism to supervise the transition and implementation of a European-wide rate structure, many users will be anxious about the proposal.

c. What is likely to happen is that the adoption of the Commission's scheme is likely to precipitate changes in rates on the part of the European administrations. No doubt, the Commission would render some guidance in this process. Although the thought is that the transition should be rapid, it is not clear whether this process of issuing guidelines, PTT action, and eventual harmonization could be accomplished quickly.

d. A third and related problem is that, despite the importance of the rate-related aspects of the Commission's proposal, the Commission itself has neither experience nor expertise in addressing tariffing issues. It has no access to the economic data that would be essential to a rate review process, nor is there any established mechanism by which it could obtain such information.

e. Similarly, many of the PTTs themselves do not have accounting systems that would be adequate for a process that contemplates some review, if not scrutiny, of rates. Moreover, no accumulated expertise exists regarding the types of rate-making methodologies that might be applied in rate restructuring. The transition in the U.K., to oversight of British Telecom by Oftel, suggests that that process can be both imprecise and painstaking.

f. The British experience and the dearth of any national or European-wide institutional expertise in rate restructuring suggest that a European policy that is based on such radical and rapid rate realignment may well be difficult to undertake. Rather, the wiser course may be to rely on a more gradual process of restructuring. Such a process would envision the Commission beginning to develop a perspective on appropriate rate principles, and only becoming involved in disputes as the forum of last resort. This approach is discussed below in some detail in Section VIII.C.

12. An assumption underlying the Commission's proposal is that adequate tariffed services will be available to facilitate service-based competition now and in the future. For new services to develop, new providers of service will have to be able to specify the types of network capabilities they will need; the PTTs will have to identify the facilities they are prepared to make available. The Commission is presupposing that the PTTs will make available all the service elements necessary for the development of value-added and information-based services. The proposal does not focus on any differences of perspective about the services that

might be needed and the facilities that may be made available. Nor has it been anticipated that any dispute-resolution mechanism might be required.

    a. Such assumptions, however, may not be warranted. The PTT or other providers of network services will no doubt want to maintain the maximum degree of control over the development of service-based competition; it is unlikely that many of them will be inclined to make any and all service elements requested available to their would-be competitors. As discussed below in Section VIII.C.6–8. and in Section II.E of Chapter II on "Boundary Lines", there are difficult questions about what types of facilities can and should be made available. Without any oversight mechanism, however, the administrations—many with their own ambitions to be value-added providers—will be able to determine the structure—and the viability—of service-based competition.

    b. Many observers believe that the question of access to network capabilities will become even more important in the future. Some stress that the emergence of PTT narrow band ISDN services will make obsolete the notion of competition offered by suppliers of value-added services. Others argue, however, that the availability of advanced, high-capacity services will only increase the pressures on PTTs to make network elements available in order to encourage new services. Whether such competition will develop may turn on whether such elements (including the signalling capabilities of the D channel of an ISDN) will be available to providers of new services. Some of the issues are explored further below.

    c. The availability of network service elements is likely to be a critical element of any policy of encouraging the development of service-based competition in the present and future environments. The Commission's proposal, however, does not deal explicitly with the question of whether and how the PTTs will make such elements available to others.

    13. The Commission's proposed approach is also likely to meet with resistance from national constituencies with different, though allied, perspectives. National administrations are concerned that a single, European approach may restrict their flexibility to pursue varying domestic policies. Ultimately, countries such as the U.K. and the Federal Republic of Germany, with their divergent views on telecommunications policies, share a common view: a uniform European regulatory policy may well be too rigid to permit the advancement of national interests.

    a. Officials in the U.K. have expressed a concern that the Commission's policy of relying on a single supplier of network facilities might directly or indirectly impair British initiatives to stimulate competition between British Telecom and Mercury. There is some concern that a policy initiated by the Commission might influence the domestic debate over the future of duopolistic competition.

    b. Many policymakers in the U.K. now see Europe as being in the middle of a critical period of transition. The British view the direction of change inside France as being of particular interest and promise. There is a strong interest in such liberalization, which is seen as affording British ventures the opportunity to develop business in Europe. Consequently, several policymakers in the U.K. believe that a clear-cut European policy, which reflects the lowest common denominator, might stabilize the process of change prematurely.

c. By contrast, policymakers in Germany may see the Commission headed in a more liberal direction and at a more rapid pace than might result from solely domestic deliberations. German pricing policies, due to embedded subsidies for postal services and to ensure universal service, have proved quite resistant to debate, if not change. These policies would, however, certainly be under pressure if services were liberalized on an accelerated basis at the European level.

d. As a result of the current process of liberalization within Germany, such pressures may, of course, intensify of their own accord. German policymakers, however, are unlikely to be supportive of radical new directions emanating from Brussels that might accentuate or accelerate this process.

C. Some Suggestions for an Alternative Procedural Approach

1. The Commission's current approach is based on the view that harmonization can and should be achieved. Thus, it is directed at substantive policies and guidelines, and less at procedural vehicles for directing the process of change at the national level. The Commission might, however, look at alternative approaches, which depend on its outlining some general principles, and then on structuring a process in which it could become involved in resolving disputes after they are addressed initially at the national level.

2. The Commission's proposed scheme of substantive harmonization is, of course, entirely consistent with the civil law tradition. It differs somewhat from one used in a common law jurisdiction, where the focus is often on setting out broad guidelines and then using mechanisms to resolve disputes.

a. The utility of this approach, which is more process-oriented than that currently being pursued by the Commission, is that it can be initiated without there being full agreement or a consensus on the issues. Instead, a mechanism is put in place to resolve any substantive differences or disputes.

b. Reliance on such an approach in a political context, where there is a large and diverse number of participants or sovereign entities, is not uncommon. Where the political structure is decentralized and where the polity is characterized by several autonomous centers of decisionmaking, procedural policies can be especially effective.

c. Ironically, then, the political exigencies and configurations of Europe may be well-suited for a more flexible approach.

Nevertheless, the dominant civil law tradition of most of the countries of the Community has militated in favor of a policy of promulgating detailed standards and against one that relies on general guidelines and dispute resolution. In evaluating its current policy proposals for the telecommunications sector, the Commission might examine the utility of a different, more pragmatic, jurisprudential approach.

3. First, a more procedural policy might be less concerned with complete harmonization of the disparate definitional approaches of the various national administrations. In any event, such convergence of policies may be difficult or impossible to achieve. Perhaps the most significant shift, then, would be a more realistic perspective on the part of policymakers on the feasibility of European-wide agreement on substantive issues. Instead, the focus would be shifted to assuring more general agreement on broader principles such as liberalization of service and access to network or other service elements.

4. Second, an approach that ultimately relied on process would, of course, require the formulation of rules that could be applied by the Commission as ultimate arbiter. Thus, the Commission would initially have to define the scope of service-based competition.

   a. The approach that the Commission should emphasize might be the distinction between the provision of facilities and that of services, essentially the line of demarcation adopted by the Japanese in their Telecommunications Business Law. Policymakers in several countries now appear to be gravitating toward that approach.

   b. Service-based competition, it is generally recognized, may be limited in certain special circumstances. Policymakers limit the resale of private line and switched-voice services as a way of easing the realignment in the pricing of these services. By way of example, in the U.K., although simple resale is prohibited, there is some flexibility on sharing or resale of voice circuits to accommodate private network services. Other limits may be appropriate or necessary as the predicate for the offering by dominant carriers of value-added services or to determine the scope of international arrangements for the provision of such services.

5. Third, the Commission would attempt to clarify that the principle of service-based competition, at least on a transborder basis, is required under the Treaty of Rome. The Commission would use its legal authority, as described in Section VI above, to support its initiative. It might also indicate clearly, however, that it would not exercise this authority except to address outright opposition to liberalization on network use.

   a. Regarding the lack of uniformity among the administrations concerning the definitions of services and technical parameters, a more procedural orientation by the Commission might have it promote a consultative process among the PTTs. The Commission would rely primarily on private and public ventures that would, in a bilateral or multilateral way, seek to take advantage of liberalization by offering new European services.

   b. The Commission's policy, therefore, would be demand-driven. Instead of dictating or imposing a particular, detailed regulatory structure at the outset, it would seek to foster a process. Thus, the Commission would only intervene after the fact—once it had been shown that there were national impediments to the initiation of a new service.

   c. Rather than taking the lead in developing a "European" telecommunications policy, the Commission would, in the first instance, defer to private and governmental attempts to establish the arrangements for the provision of new services. The Member States would seek to resolve any outstanding differences on such arrangements in the context of bilateral, trade-oriented discussions.

   d. The role of the Commission in this process would be two-fold: to serve as a multilateral forum for these discussions and to exert leverage through its enforcement powers.

  6. Fourth, the Commission might concentrate its energies on the relationship between the providers of network facilities and the providers of services that rely on those facilities. It might develop options for structuring this relationship, essentially exploring what might be the arrangements for interconnecting facilities- and service-based competitors.

   a. There are a couple of options available to the Commission. First, as noted above, it could examine the tariffed offerings of the PTTs. Second, it could adopt an approach analogous to the regulatory and technology concept that is being developed in the United States—open network architecture ("ONA").

   b. This second approach would not necessarily have to mirror the U.S. concept of ONA, which will be based, in all probability, on a specific elaboration of basic service elements. In a European context, the concept of ONA would not only center around access to the network capabilities of the local exchange, as is the case in the U.S., but also around access in a more conventional sense, to interexchange services and facilities. In the context of integrated digital services, the availability of the signalling channel or other capabilities to entities other than the PTTs may be a hotly contested matter.

   c. In the U.S., the concept of comparably efficient interconnection ("CEI") is developing as a "tariff-like" arrangement that is keyed to the specific service plans of various dominant carriers. ONA is a more comprehensive approach that uses an unstructured set of inter-industry consultations to develop a regime for the increased availability of specific service elements. In Europe, by analogy, the Commission could develop the broad—ONA-like—general principles while the PTTs could be responsible for specific interconnection arrangements.

  7. An important component of moving toward an ONA-like regime would be to supervise the availability and tariffing of the network service elements. With its legal authority under Articles 85 and 86, the

Commission could have the power to act as the final arbiter of tariff structures and levels for such elements.

    a. The Commission might proceed by setting out some general principles for such tariff structures at the outset of its process for formulating a policy. Thereafter, it would accord considerable discretion to the national administrations to implement different plans for interconnection. In Europe, it is likely that a critical element of these plans might rely on contracts, and not tariffing *per se*, to structure the relationships between the network providers and service providers.

    b. Nevertheless, the Commission might become involved, as the forum of last resort, in the efforts to establish rate plans. Its involvement could be predicated on powers that it might have under Articles 85 or 86 to settle disputes over interconnection arrangements and plans. *See* Section VI above.

    8. The development of new arrangements for access, for unbundling of network service elements, and for tariffing capabilities requires the involvement of a diverse group of interests—users, providers of both satellite- and terrestrial-based services, advocates of particular technological capabilities and solutions, manufacturers of network facilities, and representatives of the information-handling and processing sectors. This process of gathering information and of consulting informally across the industry sector is part of the ONA Forum process in the U.S.

    a. In Europe, however, there is no comparable forum. Thus, one of the difficulties that the Commission would face in establishing general principles is obtaining the necessary range of perspectives and expertise.

    b. Currently, the expertise necessary to devise interconnection arrangements is vested in CEPT. CEPT, however, only represents the European national administrations. It has never particularly encouraged the participation of other interests.

    c. In creating a mechanism to develop interconnection plans, the Commission could encourage CEPT to broaden the range of its participants. Alternatively, it could seek to establish a different, but parallel process that would embrace the larger cross-section of interests that must become involved in the formation of European policy.

    d. A new process might facilitate interaction between the Commission and representatives of industries that are dependent on telecommunications services. Currently, as a result of its effort to establish agreements on standards for the network infrastructure, the Commission has well-developed ties with the manufacturing sectors. It has been less active in engaging business sectors in the development of new information-based services.

    e. In addition, the Commission should forge relationships with other groups that are likely to have a strong interest both in how the infrastructure develops and in the relationship of network providers to the emergence of new services. Such organizations as ESA and Eutelsat would be critical to any determination of how satellite facilities would fit into the ONA model, and how their special capabilities could become "unbundled" and tariffed to facilitate the creation of new business services. The Commission should make a special effort to reach out to users, for whom the services would be designed. These steps are essential if European-wide services are to flourish.

D. A Consultative Process Within Europe

1. One issue that the Commission needs to address soon is how best to take account of the rapid development, across Europe, of new regulatory bodies and mechanisms. No longer are the PTTs the sole players in European telecommunications policy. In the U.K., in France, in the Netherlands, and perhaps elsewhere, independent institutions are emerging. These entities are playing an increasingly important role in the development of national, and eventually European, policies. The Commission will need to make efforts to incorporate these regulators into its policy formulation process.

2. At present, with respect to carrying out its function of formulating telecommunications policy, the Commission essentially interacts with two groups—CEPT and the SOGT. The CEPT interests, of course, are those of the national PTTs.

    a. The SOGT is a policy-oriented group; its members are highly placed officials from the PTTs and from national policymaking organs, such as a ministry of communications. One current member of the SOGT, for example, is from the French Ministry, and is on the staff of the Minister. Another is from the Dutch PTT. A third is from the Dutch Ministry of Economic Affairs and represents the interests of manufacturers and users. The head of the SOGT is the Director-General of D.G. XIII.

    b. For the Green Paper that the Commission is drafting on telecommunications policy, D.G. XIII will prepare a draft for review by the SOGT. If the proposal is controversial and is vetoed by the SOGT, it might never be circulated more widely. The SOGT has great influence, therefore, before any steps are taken to seek a decision by the Council of Ministers.

    c. A subgroup of the SOGT is the Groupe d'Analyses et de Prévisions ("GAP"). The GAP principally comprises the staff of those in the SOGT, a group of experts who are detailed from the PTTs to discuss specialized issues. After study in the GAP, an issue may be handed over to the SOGT, although the SOGT can ask the GAP to analyze a particular set of technical or regulatory problems. During 1986, the Commission staff have been studying ONA and related interconnection issues; in the coming months, the GAP may also include ONA on its agenda of issues for study.

3. This internal structure suggests that the Commission has no formal, or even informal, avenue of exchanging information with, or providing advice to, new national regulatory entities. Indeed, one of the

Commission's useful roles could be to act in an advisory capacity to these institutions.

    a. In consulting with its regulatory counterparts at the national level, the Commission's participation might not be limited to the telecommunications and information technology experts in D.G. XIII. It might also involve the experts in competition policy in D.G. IV; their assistance might be regarded as invaluable in a national context because the establishment of service definitions and industry structures inevitably provokes questions about competition policy and inter-industry relationships.

    b. In interacting more openly and directly with national regulators, the Commission could stimulate a dialogue within Europe about different policy options. This role would not, of course, depend on the Commission's authority to impose any particular regulatory solutions. Indeed, in working to establish such discussions with policymakers in Member States on an equal, mutually beneficial, basis, the Commission might want to stress that such a dialogue is useful, and entirely independent of any power that resides in the Commission under the Treaty.

4. If the Commission were to achieve a European "regulatory" process it would do so by first recognizing that the center of regulatory gravity in Europe is at the national level, and is likely to remain there for the foreseeable future. The Commission is unlikely to be successful in developing a model that would have it assume the centralized role of a "European" FCC; indeed, the more decentralized Canadian experience might be more relevant than any federalist paradigm emerging from the United States. Based on the experience of federalist structures elsewhere, and to summarize some of the concepts discussed above, a European process could have several different elements:

    a. First, a European process might contemplate various processes for consultation among national administrations and with service providers. These discussions would embrace the establishment of new services on both a national and a transborder basis.

    b. Second, the Commission should encourage the development of expertise in new national regulatory bodies. This might be accomplished by sharing its own expertise, and by establishing itself as a forum in which regulators from across Europe could exchange ideas and discuss common problems.

    c. Third, when specific controversies arose with respect to particular rate levels, rate structures, and definitional arrangements, the Commission could act as a forum for dispute resolution. The Commission's role would follow, not precede, attempts by the concerned entities to work out a resolution.

    d. Fourth, the Commission could, of course, develop and promulgate broader principles. This task is necessary if there are to be some guidelines for the parties attempting to resolve their differences at the national or intra-European levels.

5. In carrying out this European "regulatory" process, the Commission would reexamine its competition policy and, particularly, the exercise of its enforcement powers. The exercise of such powers could be used to provide the sinew for implementation at the national level of what would be its more process-oriented policy. In its own right, however, the Commission's authority under the Treaty, by empowering it to promulgate regulatory conditions and safeguards as it reviews sectoral agreements under Article 85, would be a useful tool for advancing its goals in the telecommunications sector. *See* Section VI.D, above.

 a. D.G. IV now faces the question of how it should seek to influence the development of the Commission's telecommunications policies. At present, the role of D.G. IV has been to address impediments to competition in an *ad hoc* way.

 b. Many officials in D.G. IV believe that a more studied, planned series of interventions in the European telecommunications sector would be a better approach. To date, however, the traditional approach has not used a sectoral analysis as the basis for enforcement policy.

 c. One of the Commission's concerns has been that acting more assertively in applying competition policy to the telecommunications sector could have broader implications for other sectors of European industry. There is a disinclination, it seems, to act aggressively in the telecommunications sector, if such assertiveness might be read as sending a chilling signal of Commission activism to other industries.

 d. It is important, then, to minimize the risk that an active application of the enforcement authority in the telecommunications area would be read as a threat by other sectors. One way of doing so would be to base an enforcement strategy on a specific, well-planned view of the structure and competitive relationships of the telecommunications industry in Europe. Although it would not be easy to develop this perspective, a more coherent strategy, coupled with economic analysis, would identify the priorities for use of the Commission's enforcement powers.

6. In seeking to achieve market integration, the Commission might take a closer look at the needs and desires of the European user community. As noted above, it may find it prudent to do so in creating a regime in which European services can flourish. European businesses, however, have called for the Commission to focus on technical standards and to bring a more competitive environment to the telecommunications sector. The European business users, through the Union of Industries of the European Community ("UNICE"), has become active in advocating a telecommunications policy that, it hopes, will lead to a common market in services and equipment. In a December 1986 policy paper presented to the Commission, UNICE concluded that national and economic policies must converge, that monopolies should be dismantled, and that competition law should be reformed. Thus, in formulating a policy based on the judicious application of both regulation and competition law, the Commission could

benefit by paying heed to the views of European industry now being articulated.

E. The Commission's Role in the International Context

1. Finally, beyond Europe, it is important that the Commission should assess its place in the international environment. If the Commission is to play certain roles in Europe, it is likely to have certain responsibilities to devise arrangements for new services on an intercontinental basis. Increasingly, new service arrangements will be worked out through bilateral discussions and negotiations. These talks might, for example, involve negotiators from the U.S. and Japan, or the U.S. and the U.K.

2. The Commission has insisted that it should at least have observer status in any bilateral talks involving Europe. The proposed Commission policies on service-based competition seem to welcome the opportunity to participate more actively with Japan and the U.S. to develop worldwide "basic" services. And, of course, the Community has been intensely involved in bilateral discussions with the U.S. over the range of telecommunications trade-related issues.

3. In the future, the framework for international services will emphasize the establishment of arrangements for technical and regulatory compatibility on what will be a link-by-link basis. Consequently, the parallels between the European process that the Commission might initiate and the international process, between Europe and its telecommunications partners, may be striking. Indeed, Europe, with its compact population, its divergent approaches, and its intense industrial base might serve as a test-bed for the rest of the world.

4. The lessons for telecommunications policymakers worldwide that might emerge from European-based processes could well be significant. In guiding the evolution of European telecommunications policy, then, the Commission might have a substantial impact on policies and structural arrangements elsewhere. By adopting a far-sighted policy that fits the unique circumstances of the European case, the Commission has an opportunity, therefore, to take the lead not just in Europe, but around the world.

CHAPTER V
THE CHANGING ENVIRONMENT FOR PLANNING INTERNATIONAL FACILITIES: RESPONDING TO COMPETITIVE PRESSURES IN THE TELECOMMUNICATIONS MARKET

TABLE OF CONTENTS

	Page
I. Introduction	339
A. What Role for "Planning" in a More Competitive International Arena?	339
B. Reasons for Seeking Multinational Processes	342
II. The Evolving International Arena: Its Impact on Efforts to Plan Telecommunications Facilities	343
A. Introduction	343
B. The Growth of International Transmission Capacity: Changing Capabilities and Conflicting Views of Cost Structures	345
1. Increased Availability of Transmission Capacity	345
2. Effects of Price Changes on International Services	350
3. Difficulties of Price Comparison	352
4. Long-Term Impact of the Increased Availability of International Facilities on Service Providers	354
C. Strains in Current Facilities Planning Activities: The NACP and Intelsat Co-ordination Procedures	355
1. North Atlantic Consultative Process	355
2. Intelsat Co-ordination Procedures	356
D. Development of Regional and National Satellite Systems	360
E. Other Important National Developments Affecting International Facilities Planning Decisions	365
1. Japan	365
2. Canada	368
3. United States	369
4. Australia	374
F. Changes Designed to Expose Facilities-Use Decisions More Directly to Economic Pressures	375
G. Summary: Making Facilities Decisions Reflect Market Conditions More Closely	381

			Page
III.	Looking to the Future: The Changing Concept of "Facilities Planning" in the International Market..................................		383
	A.	Is There a Need for Organized Planning Activities Outside of Specific Market Discussions?......................................	383
	B.	Constraints and Opportunities for Multinational Processes Concerned with Facilities Decisions	387
	C.	The Role of Regional Organizations	389
	D.	The Importance of Technical and Technological Concerns ..	390
	E.	Possibilities for Enhancing Intelsat's Contributions to Planning Activities	392
		1. Intelsat's Special Position in the International Market	392
		2. Establishing a "Neutral" Process Within Intelsat for Planning Its System...	394
		3. New Roles for Intelsat: Assessing Pricing and Technological Options and Acting as a Facilities Broker...	398
		4. Process of Participating in Intelsat	399
	F.	Broadening Participation in Multinational Fora That Have Been Limited to Carriers..	401
		1. Involvement of Non-operating Entities........................	401
		2. Special Role for End Users and Non-carrier Service Providers in Multinational Planning Fora	402
IV.	Conclusion: Grappling With the Pressures of New Competition		403

CHAPTER V
THE CHANGING ENVIRONMENT FOR PLANNING INTERNATIONAL FACILITIES: RESPONDING TO COMPETITIVE PRESSURES IN THE TELECOMMUNICATIONS MARKET

I. INTRODUCTION

A. What Role for "Planning" in a More Competitive International Arena?

1. The process of arranging to construct and operate international telecommunications facilities is more complex and volatile than it was only a few years ago. National markets are being restructured as new national telecommunications policies are adopted. These national changes have led, directly and indirectly, to greater competition in the international arena and have drastically altered the environment in which all participants in the telecommunications sector—international carriers, users of international telecommunications facilities and services, and national regulators—must establish the terms by which international telecommunications services are offered.

2. Although policymakers often refer to an international facilities "planning" process, decisions to construct and operate international cable and satellite facilities have always been made in numerous and diverse settings.

   a. Plans for undersea cable are negotiated among the various international carriers and PTTs that intend to construct and operate such cables. These plans are then subject to any necessary independent regulatory approvals—the only significant such requirements being those imposed in the United States by the Federal Communications Commission (the "FCC"). Although the FCC cannot, of course, exercise any jurisdiction over the activities of foreign carriers, it may decide whether or not to accept applications submitted by a U.S. common carrier to construct or to land an international cable. The FCC also has participated in multinational discussions intended to help develop general long-range facilities plans for particular regions of the world.

   b. Plans for international satellites have been developed in a separate process, although there are common participants in cable and satellite planning discussions. International satellites have been provided by the International Satellite Telecommunications Organization ("Intelsat"), a multinational consortium established more than two decades ago to provide a global telecommunications infrastructure. No single national entity directly controls the planning decisions Intelsat must make about its system. The FCC requires that the Communications Satellite Corp. ("Comsat"), the U.S. signatory to the Intelsat Agreement, submit its plans for investment in Intelsat for prior approval. In addition, the FCC, in collaboration with other U.S. agencies, instructs Comsat on how it should vote with respect to Intelsat's system construction plans. Ultimately, however, Intelsat's planning activities (and, therefore, effectively, decisions about future international satellite plans) have rested in the hands of its members, many of whom also are involved in the planning of international cables.

c. Although some entities are involved in both the cable and the satellite "planning" processes, many commentators have viewed the overall international facilities "planning process" as being bifurcated, without any single co-ordinating mechanism.

3. Recently, this already complex scenario has become even more confusing in that it has grown more fragmented.

a. The FCC and other administrations have approved several applications for private fiber optic cables outside the context of established facilities planning processes. In addition, subject to the acquiescence of a foreign correspondent and to adherence to several regulatory conditions (including co-ordination with Intelsat), the FCC has authorized the construction of private international satellite systems. The possibility that other administrations might encourage the use of national or regional satellite systems to offer international or transborder services also seems to have increased.

b. Adding to the potential for confusion has been the injection of trade considerations into facilities construction decisions. For example, in trade talks with the Japanese Government the U.S. and U.K. Governments have advocated the construction of a new private fiber optic cable connecting the U.S. and Japan.

4. In response to many of these recent developments, some policymakers have advocated the need for more co-ordinated, centralized planning of international facilities to prevent any wasteful construction of unneeded capacity. Given the well-established difficulty of integrating cable and satellite planning in more tranquil and less competitive times, however, it seems unlikely that any such comprehensive planning effort will be feasible or successful.

a. In fact, the concept of "planning" seems somehow out-of-step with the realities and rhetoric of the pro-competitive international telecommunications policies now evolving in a number of countries. There may be too much at stake in the rivalry between private cables and cables planned by the major carriers to permit any regulatory handicapping of the contest.

b. Technological and economic pressures may, in fact, be

Chapter V The changing environment for planning international facilities 341

capable of "regulating" the international facilities market, thereby making "planning" unnecessary. Excessive investment in new facilities may well be corrected over time by the laws of supply and demand, if it is not "nipped in the bud" by cautious financiers. Moreover, few users are likely to have regrets about an abundance of capacity. Finally, increasing rivalry among major PTTs seeking to serve as hubs for international traffic could well ensure that deep discounts and flexible usage terms are made available to customers, at least over heavily trafficked routes.

5.   Changes in the market for international facilities, however, do not necessarily mean that "planning" activities have become obsolete. Rather, it may be time to rethink what is meant by "planning" and to explore whether new processes that are better suited to current market conditions can provide some benefit. There may be ways for planning processes to work *with* the changing market to facilitate a transition to a new, more competitive, environment, to reduce the costs of change, and to increase the likelihood that market participants will be able to adjust to new realities. This paper explores such a possibility.

6.   Whereas, historically, planning activities may have protected specific market configurations developed in an era of national monopoly arrangements, planning can no longer involve rigidity and centralized efforts to dictate the amount of capacity that is to be constructed. Planning activities now must be geared toward dealing flexibly with the transition from old to new policies and market structures. They must attempt to fit together the varied pieces of the changing international environment and to remove obstacles (in the form of obsolete regulations or outmoded institutional arrangements). The era in which a limited number of national entities (essentially one from each country) operated a well-defined set of international facilities is rapidly coming to a close. A new era is taking hold in which there is a greater variety of demand for telecommunications facilities and—gradually—a more diverse supply.

7.   This changing environment requires a well-focused effort to rethink regulatory policies and institutional arrangements that were not intended to cope with new technological possibilities and industry structures. Among the factors that must be considered in the development of any new approach to international facilities planning are the following:

a.   The demarcations between the traditionally distinct domestic and international markets are eroding. Satellite systems are increasingly capable of being used to serve both domestic and international markets.

b.   The traditional roles of international underseas cables and satellites also are becoming blurred. Satellites can serve as efficient thick-route trunking facilities as well as network nodes that can distribute communications directly to a small customer-premise earth station. Cables can be branched and used to serve a number of different traffic streams; because of the expanded capacity of cables using fiber optic technology, cables also can carry a broader range of traffic, including international video, which historically was carried almost exclusively by satellites.

   c. Increasingly, the consortium that develops international facilities is becoming more fragmented and competitive. "Private" cables and satellite systems rival similar systems being developed by the major national carriers and PTTs. As a result, major carriers have become more willing to act independently and autonomously than in the past; competitive pressures have increased the likelihood that a company will plan for and construct a facility on its own.

   8. With all this diversification, much of which is still at a relatively early stage, it is virtually impossible even to determine what facilities should be included in any international facilities "plan". For example, "private" submarine fiber optic cables are viewed as somehow being distinct from "carrier" cables; yet, until the first private cable becomes operational, it is difficult to judge how these two types of facilities will relate to each other—if at all. The same difficulty arises in the satellite market, where the relationship between Intelsat facilities, private international satellites, regional satellites, and national satellites with transborder operations is still ill-defined. With all of this uncertainty, it is fruitless to think about setting up a "plan" to be carried out on any broad basis.

   9. Possibly, the market would be better served if the "plan" were to be removed from "planning" activities. What would remain would be fora in which market participants could gather, exchange information, seek to understand more completely the disparate elements of the international market, and possibly develop a broader view of the market that would inform (and enhance) the various autonomous centers of corporate and governmental decisionmaking. Such consultative activities already exist in some regions of the world and within certain organizations; efforts to develop flexible and non-binding procedures to deal with a diverse array of issues relating to the international infrastructure could increase the awareness of many policymakers—particularly in developing countries—about international trends and forces affecting telecommunications facilities.

B. Reasons for Seeking Multinational Processes

   1. Changing national policies and market structures, together with the increasing importance of international telecommunications activities, produce the need for multinational discussion and understanding. Without such discussion and understanding, there is tremendous potential for polarization and conflict that could frustrate the continued development of a varied international infrastructure inherently dependent on cooperation.

   2. Because international networks can—and, in some cases, do—serve as the infrastructures of emerging multinational markets in the service-oriented sectors of major industrialized economies, the flexibility,

availability, price, and performance of telecommunications facilities are seen as vital elements of national economic policies and international trade objectives. National trade objectives have contributed to an atmosphere in which administrations see their own success as paramount, even if that success requires actions that are contrary to the interests of traditional "allies" or "partners". There are increasing signs that future facilities plans may become embroiled in bitter trade disputes.

3. Even overtly multinational initiatives must respond to—and be redefined in light of—development in this chaotic new environment. Intelsat is working to respond to market changes while continuing to fulfill the goals of its charter. This effort is difficult because Intelsat is at once a co-operative organization and an institution with its own perspective. The participants in that co-operative include entities that have differing perspectives.

4. Attempts to respond to expanding and shifting market conditions by constructing new transmission capacity may result in conditions often characterized by an abundance of circuits. Some would argue that market forces will act to correct imbalances in supply and demand, that the risks of overbuild are no longer so great because the market is able to absorb resultant financial losses, and that past centralized planning efforts are responsible for the current excesses (demonstrating the foolishness of seeking to address market imbalances through consultative mechanisms). *See generally* L.L. Johnson, *Excess Capacity in International Telecommunications: Poor Forecasting or What?* (Nov. 1986) (Rand Note No. N-2542-MF) (examining ways in which regulatory and non-competitive social policies may have distorted traffic forecasts and led to overconstruction).

5. A significant question, however, is whether multinational mechanisms can reinforce, rather than obscure, market conditions and thereby assist the market in correcting itself. This paper explores whether, and to what extent, new international consultative arrangements or new institutional arrangements for Intelsat might be useful or necessary parts of the transition to a more competitive environment for the construction and operation of international telecommunications facilities.

II. THE EVOLVING INTERNATIONAL ARENA: ITS IMPACT ON EFFORTS TO PLAN TELECOMMUNICATIONS FACILITIES

A. Introduction

1. Changes in national policies, which—cumulatively—have a dramatic impact on the structure of the international telecommunications arena, affect procedures for making decisions about new plans for international telecommunications facilities. These procedures must be

realistically geared to the changing market environment. If they remain static, they risk becoming unresponsive to the needs of major service providers and users, as well as to the objectives of policymakers.

2. As a backdrop to assessing whether any facilities planning activities could contribute to the increasingly competitive international facilities environment, various developments in the international telecommunications market should be assessed. The relevant aspects of the international market are as follows:

    a. First, there is substantial growth in the availability of international transmission capacity, with accompanying changes in, and a wide divergence of perspectives on, the capabilities and cost structures of undersea cable and satellite services.

    b. Second, two important existing parts of the multifaceted process of planning certain international telecommunications facilities—the North Atlantic Consultative Process (the "NACP") and the Intelsat co-ordination process—are being exposed to strains because of the emergence of private fiber optic cable and satellite systems.

    c. Third, regional and national satellite systems continue to evolve in Europe and in other parts of the world, sometimes competing with each other. Over the longer term, these systems are likely to exert substantial pressure on Intelsat's operations.

    d. Fourth, important national policy developments and trends within countries that are the major participants in Intelsat (*e.g.*, the United States, Japan, Canada, Australia, and members of the European Community) are reshaping the relationship between domestic and international policies and ultimately will have a broad impact on the manner in which multinational facilities decisions are made.

    e. Fifth, changes are being made in satellite and cable investment policies to provide users of facilities (*i.e.*, all non-owners) with new options and to ensure that investors pay for a more substantial portion of the forecasted needs that form the basis for facilities construction decisions.

    i) One impact of some of these changes would be to permit users to obtain satellite capacity on a basis that is more comparable to the manner in which they obtain cable circuits. In the United States, the FCC has authorized users to obtain an investment interest in fiber optic cables similar to the interest held by the carriers that build those cables.

    ii) Intelsat is studying similar long-term investment policies as a way of shifting more of the risks of underutilization of its satellite facilities to the participants in the international satellite system and of enabling system users to obtain capital interests, not just leasehold interests, similar to those that may be available in cable facilities.

3. These policy changes and national and international market developments generally have produced an international market with more options, with greater risks, and with less multinational consensus. As market conditions continue to change, the administrative apparatus designed

to oversee the market must adjust. It remains to be seen whether new mechanisms can be devised to respond to changing market conditions without attempting to control—or to limit—them.

4. A major theme in this period of change is the tension between historic efforts to guard against the construction of excess capacity and more recent attempts to rely on market forces to regulate the balance between supply and demand.

a. This tension can manifest itself in two ways that significantly affect planning activities: (*i*) conflicts over the extent to which facilities planning decisions should be made as part of a multinational, centralized process or be left to decentralized mechanisms (such as national regulatory institutions, organized regional fora, *ad hoc* groups of entities, and individual companies) and (*ii*) debates over the scope of any planning activities (*i.e.*, whether any such activities should be conducted on a regional basis and, if undertaken, should include "private" facilities).

b. Given the strong movement toward promoting competitive market structures and the substantial practical difficulties in any attempt to develop a structured, centralized planning process, any planning activities that are undertaken will inevitably have to be done on a decentralized basis. A question is whether there is some way of making the various decisionmakers sufficiently aware of each other so that any decisions made by any one entity will be made in light of the best available information about market conditions. This goal does not suggest the need for a "master facilities plan" or some mechanism for ensuring adherence to a set of agreed-upon criteria; rather, it merely recognizes that in a system of multiple, interdependent decisionmakers, the decisions of each individual may benefit if they are made with an awareness of the interdependencies and the market conditions being created by other entities' decisions.

c. This tension between centralization and decentralization informs much of the discussion that follows.

B. The Growth of International Transmission Capacity: Changing Capabilities and Conflicting Views of Cost Structures

1. Increased Availability of Transmission Capacity

a. There are a number of reasons for the dramatic increase in the availability of international transmission capacity.

i) Technological progress has lowered the per-circuit cost of constructing, operating, and using telecommunications facilities. The development of fiber optic cables, for example, has stimulated plans to construct a large number of new facilities.

ii) Technological change has permitted the development of more sophisticated transmission facilities; both satellites and cables can be used more flexibly and more competitively.

iii) New national policies supporting the development of privately owned transoceanic cables, international satellites separate from the Intelsat system, and regional satellite systems are setting the stage for the deployment of an abundance of new transmission capacity. Whether that capacity is placed into service will depend, of course, on evolving market conditions, including the ways in which existing facilities providers respond to new demands from service providers and end users.

iv) Current pricing schemes such as Intelsat's global average pricing may well encourage market entry, particularly along heavy traffic routes, where Intelsat's average price is above its costs. Because new entrants are not required to price their services on an average-cost basis, they can undercut Intelsat's prices; in this way, Intelsat's pricing scheme tends to create conditions that may attract new facilities providers to thick-route markets.

  b. The deployment of fiber optic underseas cables, which is planned to begin in 1988, will increase dramatically the capacity available for the transmission of international traffic.

i) New transmission and multiplexing technologies made possible by fiber optic technology have contributed to the increased efficiencies of the cable medium. Thirty years ago, when TAT-1 was placed into service, it was capable of providing less than 100 voice-grade circuits. It is expected that TAT-8 will be capable of providing approximately 40,000 voice-grade circuits when it goes into service in 1988.

ii) Of course, satellite technology also has progressed in recent years to permit satellites to provide an increasingly flexible array of multipoint services and to realize numerous cost savings. Capacity has increased on satellites just as it has on cables. Intelsat's Early Bird satellite, which was launched in 1964, was able to provide approximately 300 voice-grade circuits across the Atlantic. Intelsat has stated that a 48-transponder Intelsat VI satellite will be capable of providing restoration service for a fully loaded TAT-8 cable using just eight transponders (or one-sixth of its capacity).

  c. Over the next few years, a large number of international fiber optic cable circuits will be built and placed into service. These will be owned primarily by AT&T, the U.S. international record carriers, British Telecom International ("BTI"), Kokusai Denshin Denwa Co. ("KDD"), and a number of PTTs in Europe and in the Pacific. U.S. service providers also have agreed to purchase—and are permitted by U.S. law to purchase—ownership-like rights in these cables (known as indefeasible rights of users or "IRUs").

i) The first transatlantic fiber cable, TAT-8, is expected to be placed in service in 1988. AT&T, Teleglobe Canada, BTI and a number of European PTTs are constructing this cable, which will link North America to both the United Kingdom and France, via a mid-ocean branching arrangement. The cable will consist of two 280 Mbps fiber pairs (one each to the U.K. and France) and will employ multiplexing technology capable of providing approximately 40,000 voice-grade circuits.

ii) The Pacific Region will be linked by a similar fiber cable, HAW4/TPC3, which will connect the United States to Japan, Korea, Hong Kong, Guam, the Philippines, and Taiwan. There also are plans to extend the cable into additional areas of Southeast Asia. Australia, New Zealand, and the United States will also be connected by a triangular fiber cable.

iii) Plans for an additional transatlantic cable, TAT-9, also are well under way. An agreement was signed in mid-1986 that calls for a fiber cable with five landing points—the United States, Canada, the United Kingdom, France, and Spain. This cable will also connect with a planned Middle Eastern cable that will bring fiber service to Italy, Turkey, Greece, and Israel. TAT-9 is also expected to involve the first use of a new multiplexing technique (known as wet multiplexing) and new lasers, both of which will expand the flexibility and reduce the cost of the cable.

d. A number of fiber optic cables owned by private companies, rather than by PTTs, also are being planned.

e. Cable & Wireless and Private Transatlantic Telecommunications System, Inc. (formerly Tel-Optik, Ltd.) ("PTAT, Inc."), a U.S. company, are partners in Market Link, a project to construct two transatlantic fiber optic cables (PTAT-1 and PTAT-2) between the U.S. and the U.K. The venture has been granted landing licenses at both ends.

i) Recently, NYNEX, one of the seven Regional Holding Companies (the "RHCs") created when AT&T was compelled to divest its local telephone operations, purchased for $10,000,000 an option to buy all of the stock of PTAT, Inc.

ii) If exercised, that option would make NYNEX and Cable & Wireless 50 per cent partners in the private cable venture. Such a combination would produce a significant new entrant into the international transmission market. Cable & Wireless owns Mercury, the domestic carrier that was authorized in 1984 to compete with British Telecom, and NYNEX owns both New York Telephone and New England Telephone.

iii) U.S. antitrust laws currently stand in the way of NYNEX's active participation in the venture. The Modification of Final Judgment (the "MFJ"), which was entered to effect the divestiture of the old Bell System, restricts the activities of the RHCs and their local exchange telephone subsidiaries, the Bell Operating Companies (the "BOCs"). Under the MFJ, neither NYNEX nor the BOCs that it owns can provide international service; thus, unless this restriction is lifted or unless a waiver of the restriction is granted, NYNEX would not be able to exercise its option for the PTAT, Inc. stock.

iv) Currently, NYNEX's interest in the venture is held in a trust that prevents NYNEX from exerting control over it. Judge Greene has ruled that the trust arrangement is consistent with the present terms of the MFJ. The FCC has approved the trust arrangement, as required by U.S. law.

v) On March 19, 1987, the FCC also approved the transfer of the PTAT, Inc. stock from the trust to NYNEX, an approval that also is required by U.S. law. *Tel-Optik, Limited*, FCC No. 87–98 (adopted March 19, 1987). The FCC found that the transfer would not have anticompetitive consequences because FCC tariffing and access charge policies ensure that Market Link customers pay the same rates as other customers for local services obtained from NYNEX. In addition, NYNEX plans to operate Market Link through a subsidiary structurally separated from its local monopoly telephone operations. Such structural separation is more than the FCC requires, under its *Third Computer Inquiry*, 60 Rad. Reg. 2d (P&F) 603 (1986), *modified in part*, FCC No. 87–102 (released May 22, 1987), to guard against the possibility that an RHC would use its regulated monopoly businesses to benefit its unregulated competitive activities. As discussed more fully in Chapter II, "Boundary Lines", the FCC requires only adherence to certain non-structural safeguards. Thus, in the FCC's view, NYNEX would be acting with particular caution.

vi) Despite FCC approval, the transfer to NYNEX cannot be completed before the MFJ is modified to permit NYNEX to provide international service or before NYNEX obtains from Judge Greene a waiver of the MFJ's restriction on RHC involvement in providing long-distance telecommunications services. NYNEX filed its waiver request in early May 1987; any decision, however, is likely to be delayed until Judge Greene has ruled on the Justice Department's recommended modifications of the MFJ.

f. There are other planned private fiber cables for the North Atlantic region, and Cable & Wireless is working on plans to install a series of fiber cables as part of a so-called "Global Digital Highway". One part of this global cable project is a private fiber cable linking the United States (with landing points in Washington State and Alaska) to Japan (with a landing point on the island of Honshu). To participate in this cable, Cable & Wireless has joined with Pacific Telecom, Inc., which provides local and long-distance telecommunications services in the Pacific Northwest and Alaska, to form Pacific Telecom Cable, Inc. ("PTC"). Cable & Wireless owns 20 per cent of PTC and Pacific Telecom owns 80 per cent. PTC and a consortium of Japanese companies will have equal ownership interests in the international portion of the cable.

i) Although the FCC advocated the construction and operation of the private cable, it granted PTC only a conditional landing license due to the concern about the extent of foreign involvement in the ownership of the proposed cable. *Pacific Telecom Cable, Inc.*, Mimeo No. 2894 (released April 22, 1987). The license is conditioned upon PTC being able to assure the FCC that U.S. entities will be fully involved in the planning, manufacture, installation, operation, and maintenance of the cable. PTC also is required "to make all reasonable efforts to ensure participation by U.S. interests in the ownership of the international portion of the Japanese end of the cable and any cable spurs [that may be authorized

Chapter V   The changing environment for planning international facilities   349

by the Japanese government to extend the cable beyond Japan]". *Id.* at para. 16. The FCC must also give prior approval to any transfer of 5 per cent or more of the stock of PTC from a U.S. to a non-U.S. entity.

ii) In imposing these special conditions, the FCC specifically noted that this was the first private international cable in which there would be non-U.S. ownership of the U.S. end of the cable. *Id.* at para. 16 n.20. It is clear from the decision that the FCC's pro-competitive outlook is tempered by its desire to ensure that U.S. entities receive reciprocal treatment abroad. The cable landing license provides the FCC with the jurisdiction—and the leverage—to see that U.S. policies permitting the involvement of non-U.S. entities in various telecommunications activities do not work to the disadvantage of U.S. entities. This objective gives the FCC's international facilities authorization process some of the appearance of a trade-based initiative, with the FCC working to promote specific market opportunities for U.S. companies operating abroad.

g. If fiber costs continue to decline, as expected, it is likely that there will be an increasing amount of fiber built outside of the traditional market in which national carriers collaborate. Such construction will further expand the amount of available international circuits.

h. In addition to this expected new cable capacity, plans are proceeding for the deployment of new satellites and for the use of some existing domestic satellites in transborder service arrangements. Intelsat, regional authorities, national administrations, and private companies are moving to launch various broadcast and telecommunications satellites that not only will offer additional transmission routes, but also will contain steerable beams and high-power transmission technology which could provide business users that now rely on cable with a more cost-effective solution for their telecommunications needs. Some of the planned systems are described below in Section II.D.

i. The construction of both satellite and cable circuits will almost certainly increase the supply of international facilities that many observers believe already represents an oversupply situation, particularly in the satellite market. Facilities plans now being acted upon were first developed, and are based primarily, on demand forecasts that often have proved over-optimistic. At the same time, the beginnings of a competitive facilities market, which has attracted the interest of new investors, holds the potential to produce a short-term glut before a shakeout in the market prunes away weaker entrants and brings supply back into line with demand, in the view of some observers.

j. Finally, existing regulatory and planning mechanisms (such as the NACP) have not yet determined how to respond to private facilities. The FCC has assumed, and has conditioned its approval of private facilities on the assumption, that such facilities will form a market distinct from the one in which carriers (and Intelsat) operate. These private facilities are to be used for non-switched traffic and are to be made available in bulk, on privately negotiated (not publicly tariffed) terms. Thus, in the FCC's view, these facilities will complement existing carrier facilities. Accordingly, they are treated and regulated differently. They are not subject to rigorous certification and tariffing procedures otherwise applied by the FCC, and they are not subject to consultations in the NACP. However, there is as yet no real evidence as to what impact these private facilities might have on the existing international market. They may provide large users with alternative routings to such an extent that carrier facilities might be significantly underused. They also might ultimately become a source of capacity for carriers offering public switched services.

k. In either case, the FCC has said it might have to reevaluate its posture toward, and its regulation of, private facilities. The FCC—and other national and regional bodies—might look at the facilities market on a more integrated basis. It is difficult to predict, however, what would be the result of such a revised perspective. Would the response be to move further away from regulation and planning on the theory that private facilities had made the international market far more competitive? Would more stringent regulation and planning result from a feeling that carrier facilities deserved protection to ensure their continued economic viability (in the name of the "public interest")? Could significant fractionalization result from divisions between proponents and opponents of competition spurred on by private market entrants?

2. Effects of Price Changes on International Services

a. As discussed below in Section II.B.3, there are a number of difficulties in attempting to compare the costs of using cable versus satellite circuits. Historically, cable circuits have been viewed as more costly for many service arrangements, although due to a variety of factors, including regulatory policies, long-standing investment practices, and technological reasons, international telecommunications traffic has been roughly equally divided between the two media. Fiber optic technology and other new transmission techniques, however, are expected to alter the broad historical pricing arrangements for the two facilities. In most parts of the world, fiber and other technological changes are expected to make the cable medium much more competitive with satellites—in terms of cost—than it is now, when conventional coaxial cables are being used. The expected changes in the relationship of cable and satellite costs could have some significant effects.

b. As the cost of using fiber optic cables declines (relative to the cost of using satellite links) terrestrial carriers will have an increased incentive to use cables. Many of these carriers already have non-cost incentives to use cables rather than satellites (including some inherent operational advantages of cable, and the impact of various regulatory policies, as discussed below in Section II.E). Unless satellite planners anticipate this trend, regional and separate satellite systems might well face severe under-utilization.

Chapter V The changing environment for planning international facilities 351

c. In addition, Intelsat is likely to be forced to price its capacity on a more competitive basis to avoid under-use of its facilities and to deter the possibility of "uneconomic" market entry. Intelsat may have to adopt route-by-route pricing, rather than the average-price scheme that it now uses to maintain uniform global pricing.

d. Intelsat already has begun to respond competitively by developing a "digital bearer circuit" offering. Under this scheme, which the Board of Governors approved in early December 1986, Intelsat will permit its signatories to acquire circuits at a fixed charge and use multiplexing equipment to derive additional channels from the circuits at no extra charge. A 64 Kbps voice-grade-equivalent digital bearer circuit, which could be used to derive up to five voice-grade channels, will carry a $450 per month charge for a minimum five-year commitment. A digital bearer circuit that would support two derived channels will cost $390 per month (also for a minimum five-year commitment). Intelsat will retain the $390 monthly utilization charge for a 4 Khz analogue circuit, although it will offer a discounted monthly rate of $370 for signatories making a minimum five-year commitment.

e. It is not clear whether declines in Intelsat's utilization charges will result in lower per-circuit costs for carriers and service providers and lower communications costs for end users. The result will depend upon whether signatories pass on the Intelsat price reductions.

i) In the United States, it has been anticipated that Comsat will lower its tariffs to reflect the decreased Intelsat charges. AT&T is likely to pass on savings in most of its services, which continue to be subject to full regulatory review by the FCC and therefore subject to cost justification. Other U.S. international service providers, including Comsat's competitive subsidiary (which provides end-to-end services), as to which the FCC has applied less stringent ("streamlined") regulation, will have more freedom to decide the extent to which they pass on savings. However, each service provider's decision will be constrained to some degree by the decisions of its competitors.

ii) In most of Europe, the PTTs will decide whether or not to pass on savings. Although in most countries there will be little or no competitive pricing pressure from domestic sources, each PTT may well have to factor into its own decision the decisions of other PTTs and service providers due to the increasingly competitive nature of the international services market.

f. To a certain extent cost will not affect choice of facilities, because cables and satellites are not always fully substitutable. In many instances, they may be complementary. One impact of the introduction of fiber may be to encourage the respective media to emphasize their technical characteristics, as much as their price advantages: in this event, satellites may increasingly be used to serve thinner traffic routes and to provide networking services not capable of being provided over cables. For example, satellites have inherent advantages in offering distribution from one point to many locations or in collecting data from many locations through a central terminal. Cables, by contrast, may be used more and more to provide thick-route trunking services.

g. As cost ratios of cable and satellite circuits change, and as a greater number of entities compete to market international facilities, price is likely to become a more significant competitive factor. In this event, facilities owners and operators are likely to experience significant pressure to move the prices of the circuits closer to costs. This result could have particularly dramatic consequences for Intelsat.

i) A move toward cost-based pricing has been characterized by some as a move that will necessarily threaten Intelsat's ability to fulfill its role as a provider of affordable universal service. Developing nations are understandably concerned about increased prices that may result from competition between Intelsat and private satellites or cables.

ii) A question, however, is whether repricing will merely minimize the harm from loss of traffic to fiber cables that would result if no such repricing were to occur. Moreover, changes in the configuration of Intelsat's satellite could enable service to be offered more efficiently to users along thin routes or to users seeking service directly to on-premise earth stations.

iii) Even if separate and regional satellite systems are not permitted to compete with Intelsat, fiber optic cables make inevitable the increasingly competitive nature of the international facilities marketplace. Thus, the need for Intelsat to devise a comprehensive new price structure cannot be ignored, although repricing is likely to be controversial and difficult to develop within Intelsat.

3. Difficulties of Price Comparison

a. The difficulty of predicting the impact of pricing changes is compounded by the fact that it is very hard to compare cable and satellite costs. Because many cost elements (*i.e.*, not only the Intelsat portion, but also the ground segment costs) contribute to the price of a particular circuit, one must ensure that comparisons are being made for truly comparable service arrangements. In addition, comparisons are not always valid because (*i*) certain services are typically more economical to provide over a particular type of facility, (*ii*) certain networking services can only be provided over satellites, (*iii*) the technical features of the respective media cause users to prefer one medium or another for certain services, regardless of relative costs, and (*iv*) national regulatory policies or commercial policies of the PTTs may distort the impact of economic signals on investment and use decisions. Despite the admitted difficulty of making such comparisons, it may be useful to note the range of conflicting estimates that have been prepared by a number of sources: Intelsat, AT&T, and the FCC. These estimates are included in the paper to reflect the lines of argument and debate, rather than to attempt to resolve differences among such estimates.

b. According to Intelsat, a comparison of TAT-8 and its Intelsat VI satellite reveals that the per-circuit annual cost of a telephone circuit on the satellite is between one-third and one-fourth the cost of a circuit on TAT-8. This figure, however, does not represent a comparison of the costs faced by carriers or users because it does not include cost elements attributable to expenses not resulting directly from the cost of transmitting information. Such additional expenses include those that result from a carrier's rate-of-return, ground station facilities used in conjunction with satellite circuits, administrative costs and other expenses (such as depreciation and taxes) associated with maintaining facilities, and Intelsat signatory costs included in the tariff for Intelsat circuits.

c. AT&T, claiming to have accounted for these additional costs in the context of the U.S. market, estimated in late 1984 that an annual cost of $9,237 for a half-circuit on the TAT-7 cable (which is not a fiber optic cable) would include costs comparable to those included in the annual tariff rate charged by Comsat for a half-circuit on the Intelsat system. Comsat's tariff at the time was $12,720. AT&T added that, with the addition of certain multiplexing techniques, the per-circuit cost of the cable could be reduced to slightly more than $5,000 annually. AT&T estimated at that time that the annual cost of a derived virtual voice channel on TAT-8 would be approximately $2,500. No figures were provided for the comparable Comsat tariff assuming use of an Intelsat VI satellite.

d. The FCC's Office of Plans and Policy took a slightly different approach to evaluating the relative costs of satellite and cable circuits. It compared the present value of AT&T's investments in various cables, over various time periods, with the present value of lease charges that AT&T would have had to have paid if it had leased the number of satellite circuits that would have been needed to carry the traffic that was loaded on the cable in which the investment was being compared. (The lease amount for each year was calculated by multiplying the average number of circuits in service on the cable during that year by the Comsat charge per half-circuit in that year.)

i) The results varied by region and by time period examined. Between 1970 and 1984, for example, it was estimated that the present value of AT&T's investment in TAT-5 was $39,000,000; the present value of satellite leases needed to carry the traffic loaded on cable by AT&T during those fourteen years is $74,500,000. The FCC's paper noted that these figures understated the savings to AT&T because they did not include the expected benefits of being able to use TAT-5 at minimal cost for the next ten years, and they excluded cost savings that were realized due to the use of multiplexing technology that lowered the per-circuit cost of using TAT-5 during a portion of the relevant time period.

ii) Based on AT&T's forecasts, the FCC projected a much smaller saving to AT&T for using TAT-8 between 1987 and 1991. The present value of its TAT-8 investment during that period is estimated at $150,000,000. Satellite charges for that period (also based on AT&T

estimates of those charges) would be $158,500,000. These figures assume that FCC policies will continue to limit the number of cable circuits AT&T can use during these years; if AT&T were able to use a larger number of cable circuits, the FCC concluded it would save more by using the cable.

iii) Interestingly, the FCC found that AT&T would have benefited by using satellite circuits, rather than cable circuits, in the Pacific region. The present value of expenditures on HAW-3 and TPC-2 between 1974 and 1988 was calculated at $35,400,000; the corresponding present value of satellite leases was $18,800,000. The FCC notes, accordingly, that variations between AT&T's expectations and actual conditions as well as the impact of U.S. regulatory policies were responsible for its decision to use more costly facilities.

iv) One shortcoming of the FCC's analytical method is that it ignores the impact on facilities pricing that might have occurred if AT&T had chosen to shift large amounts of traffic from satellites to cables, or vice versa, during these periods.

4. Long-Term Impact of the Increased Availability of International Facilities on Service Providers

a. As the availability of transmission capacity grows, it will create additional economic risks for individual facilities providers. Some regulatory or administrative bodies may be tempted to minimize these risks by limiting competition (*i.e.*, keeping down the supply of circuits or segregating market segments, such as public-switched traffic and offerings of non-switched bulk capacity). Such efforts would be intended to maintain the market position that PTTs and other "carriers" have enjoyed historically.

b. The under-use of PTT facilities (due to the availability of a large number of new international circuits not owned by PTTs) could have significant consequences. Such under-use will continue to erode international services as a traditional profit center for PTTs and other service providers. Rates for the use of existing facilities already are under pressure due to competition from an increased number of service providers. The construction and operation of additional facilities, however, will soften prices further and enhance the bargaining position of users.

c. In instances where a service provider has a monopoly position, it may be able to maintain price levels. However, reductions on the other end of the half-circuit inevitably will create pressures on the end of the circuit where there is not any significant competition.

d. Moreover, the market for international services is such that the availability of service in an adjacent market at lower cost is likely to exercise a gravitational pull on prices in the market generally. Thus, conditions in the facilities market will have a significant impact on the overall financial condition of service providers—varying, of course, to the extent that such service providers are dependent on international services.

i) Changes in the facilities market may force a shift in marketing strategies as carriers search for ways to dispose of excess capacity. These shifts, in turn, are likely to affect the operational decisions of service providers.

ii) Some degree of polarization between the owners of private cable and of the traditional "public" facilities is also likely to occur. PTTs and backbone carriers will attempt to devise long-term service agreements and, in some cases, to use regulatory processes to concentrate traffic on the cables in which they have invested heavily.

C. Strains in Current Facilities Planning Activities: The NACP and Intelsat Co-ordination Procedures

Some of the existing major mechanisms for developing the international facilities infrastructure are showing strains under the pressures of increasingly competitive market structures. The FCC relied substantially upon the NACP during the late 1970s to co-ordinate satellite and cable plans; lately, however, there have been questions raised about the effectiveness of this process in light of new private cable and satellite plans. Moreover, Intelsat faces a greater burden because of the need to deal with technical and economic co-ordination issues relating to the provision by private, national, and regional satellite systems of international circuits. Both of these processes are examined below.

1. North Atlantic Consultative Process

a. The FCC adopted the NACP as a means of gathering relevant information about the satellite and cable plans of the major U.S. international service providers. Since September 1974, the NACP has consisted primarily of meetings with Europeans PTTs and Canadian telecommunications entities for the purpose of developing long-range facilities plans, not for the purpose of negotiating specific facilities arrangements. Such long-range plans, which the FCC considers and adopts in the course of formal rulemaking proceedings, have become the basis for considering applications for particular facilities, such as new transatlantic cables or requests by Comsat to invest in new Intelsat facilities.

b. The NACP has had many drawbacks. It has been a time-consuming and often cumbersome process that paralleled (and duplicated) operational meetings between major carriers. Although Comsat was included in the process, the NACP could never encompass the Intelsat planning process itself—although some of the major participants in Intelsat were also involved in the NACP. In addition, due to the time and expense imposed on the FCC and the carriers, a similarly rigorous process was never repeated in the Pacific or Caribbean regions. (The planning process in these regions was generally carried out without face-to-face meetings.)

c. More importantly, the NACP has no doubt seemed at odds with the pro-deregulation posture of the current FCC. Although the NACP has been continued as a means of maintaining contacts with other administrations, the current FCC has never really accepted its role as a planning forum.

d. It will be interesting to assess the extent to which the development of a private cable market results in efforts by administrations other than the U.S. to bring private cables within the scope of one or more multilateral planning fora, such as the NACP.

i) Currently, private cables are considered to be outside the scope of the NACP. If private cable capacity begins to affect the use of carrier-constructed cables (either because "public" traffic is "leaked" onto private cables or because carriers make some use of private cable circuits), some participants in the NACP may insist on adding private cables to the mix of issues that are discussed in meetings and evaluated in light of multinational traffic forecasts and facilities plans.

ii) Alternatively, such pressures could prompt a movement away from the NACP and similar processes; participants may decide that if the NACP seeks to operate as a potential obstacle to national plans favoring private cables (or even to plans for new carrier-constructed cables), the potential detriment of the process to national economic interests will have become greater than its possible beneficial effects. Ultimately, the process is likely to remain viable only as a forum for exchanging information about future plans.

2. Intelsat Co-ordination Procedures

a. The decision by the United States to authorize satellites to provide international services separate from the Intelsat system further complicates the market for international telecommunications facilities and any process for planning such facilities.

i) If private satellite systems are constructed and placed into service, they could represent another source of competitive pressure on Intelsat. The pressure could be acute in the lucrative North Atlantic market, where most of the applicants for separate satellite authorizations have focused their attention. Similar authorizations in other countries have yet to emerge, other than the recent approval by the Irish Government of an Atlantic satellite applicant, Atlantic Satellites Ltd. However, other private satellite applicants from European countries might emerge quickly, if these countries perceive that the U.S. is likely to dominate a new market. Any "domino effect" of a single system being authorized obviously would exacerbate the pressures on Intelsat.

ii) A similar situation could arise in the mobile communications market. The United States is moving ahead with plans to develop land mobile satellite services that could end up serving much of North America. In Europe there are ongoing multinational discussions

Chapter V The changing environment for planning international facilities   357

about the development of a more comprehensive pan-European terrestrial and satellite mobile communications network. Both of these developments pose potential new sources of competition for the International Maritime Satellite Organization ("Inmarsat").

iii) Competition could develop relatively quickly in the aeronautical services market. In October 1985, Inmarsat proposed amendments to its convention and operating agreement to permit it to provide aeronautical services; however, the amendments have not yet been approved by members holding two-thirds of the investment shares and, therefore, have not become effective. If a sufficient number of Inmarsat's 48 members approve the amendments, it would be able to enter this market and would be joined by U.S. land mobile satellite service applicants and various European entities that plan (or have discussed plans) to offer aeronautical services. As discussed more fully below in Section II.E.3, the FCC also has proposed altering the scheme by which Inmarsat capacity can be acquired by U.S. entities to promote the development of a competitive aeronautical services market. Finally, Aeronautical Radio, Inc. ("Arinc") has applied to the FCC for authority to launch and operate a six-satellite global system to provide aeronautical services (called "Avsat"). Arinc, a not-for-profit company owned by airline users, also said it would use Inmarsat capacity or capacity from other satellites to meet demand before its satellites became operational. Arinc played a central role in seeking an FCC decision that prevents Comsat from operating as a monopoly provider of aeronautical services in the U.S.

b. The biggest question in the separate satellite "market" at the start of 1987 is whether such systems actually will develop and be used. The U.S. authorizations for fixed services were granted in July 1985, and since that time only one of the applicants, Pan American Satellite Co. ("PanAmSat"), has obtained an agreement with a foreign correspondent and moved deliberately toward a launch plan. Admittedly, the collapse of the shuttle program in the U.S. and the failure of virtually all other U.S. launch vehicles have thrown unexpected obstacles in the path of the applicants. Even with launch capability being available, however, there would still be a number of significant hurdles in the path of aspiring separate satellite operators.

c. In addition to doubts about whether there is sufficient demand to support the operation of new international satellites, a chief obstacle is successful completion of the technical and economic co-ordination procedures required by Article XIV(d) of the Intelsat Agreement.

i) The well-publicized opposition of many Intelsat members toward U.S. separate satellite plans led to an initial expectation that co-ordination procedures would be rancorous. It appears, however, that some of the particularly harsh opposition toward U.S. plans may have moderated, particularly in light of the successful completion of Article

XIV(d) procedures for PanAmSat. Nonetheless, co-ordination efforts are certain to remain controversial.

ii) The sole U.S. applicant seeking a relatively expeditious launch, PanAmSat, which has a June 1987 launch date on Ariane, reached a technical co-ordination agreement with Intelsat in November 1986, after a lengthy series of talks that almost collapsed in October 1986. The agreement did not have the unanimous support of all of the members on the Technical Committee of the Board of Governors.

iii) Following technical co-ordination, the Board of Governors decided in December 1986 to submit a favorable recommendation to the Assembly of Parties on the issue of significant economic harm with respect to the five C-band transponders that PanAmSat will use to provide U.S.-Peru service. The Assembly of Parties voted in favor of the recommendation in April 1987. The favorable consultation will last for five years and is not applicable to the six Ku-band transponders that PanAmSat plans to use to offer transatlantic service. (Nineteen other transponders will be used to provide domestic services in Latin America and the Caribbean.)

iv) According to press reports, the favorable consultation recommendation was somewhat narrow. It read, "any material changes in the technical parameters or operational scope of [the five PanAmSat transponders], or any material extension of the services proposed, will require consultations under Article XIV of the Intelsat Agreement".

v) An initial report on the economic harm question, which has not been made public, is said to have viewed PanAmSat as having a greater potential adverse impact on Intelsat than was estimated by the United States. This finding could have a substantial effect on future co-ordination requests involving systems planning to serve the high-traffic North Atlantic corridor; the economic impact on Intelsat of North Atlantic competition is likely to be substantially greater than the impact of U.S.-Peru competition.

vi) There also had been discussions about Intelsat adopting some kind of cumulative economic impact standard for judging the harm that would be caused by separate satellites. Former Director General Richard Colino reportedly had recommended that all U.S. separate systems be limited to a "cumulative impact" of 10 per cent. The Board of Governors, however, did not adopt any findings with regard to cumulative impact. It remains unclear whether this cumulative impact concept—which has not been well-defined publicly—will resurface in future co-ordination discussions. The election of Dean Burch, a former FCC chairman, as the new Intelsat Director General, could well affect Intelsat's position on separate satellites. Prior to his removal in March 1986, Colino had been a strident opponent of separate systems, contending that they could lead to Intelsat's downfall. At least initially, Burch has declined to express an opinion on separate satellites.

d. A number of issues raised by U.S. support for separate satellites are likely to affect the extent to which these facilities will actually influence the international market. All of this assumes, of course, that U.S. applicants become more active and actually seek to operate viable systems.

i) First, there is the question of what would happen if Intelsat were to issue an unfavorable recommendation on a consultation request. No prior consultation has ever produced an unfavorable recommendation. Although the United States, like other signatories to the Intelsat Agreement, is bound to uphold the provisions of the treaty and to support Intelsat, and although the U.S. repeatedly has affirmed its support for the organization, it is unclear how the government would react if it were to perceive that the Assembly of Parties was effectively blocking the implementation of a U.S. initiative perceived to be important to both U.S. telecommunications and industrial policy agendas. If the U.S. were to act against the wishes of the Assembly of Parties, it is likely that significant turmoil would ensue both within Intelsat and among the U.S. and various other countries in both bilateral and multilateral discussions.

ii) Second, it remains uncertain to what extent the service restrictions that the U.S. has placed on separate satellites in an effort to limit their impact on Intelsat will prove viable or useful. Those restrictions state that (*i*) no separate system may provide services involving direct or indirect interconnection with a public-switched network, (*ii*) no minimum unit of capacity may be established, (*iii*) leases must last at least one year, (*iv*) separate systems may not operate as common carriers, (*v*) interconnection restrictions and minimum lease-term requirements will apply to all levels of user of separate systems (not just direct leases), (*vi*) capacity resale will be permitted only if consistent with the other restrictions, and (*vii*) the use of separate systems by U.S. carriers must be authorized by the FCC. Because no systems have yet begun to operate, it remains to be seen whether these restrictions will be enforceable and whether Intelsat will view them as some reassurance of the U.S. commitment to Intelsat.

iii) Finally, there continues to be doubt about how other countries eventually will line up on the separate satellite issue. As noted above, the U.S. is virtually alone in its explicit advocacy of this policy. Yet, other countries have supported the development of national and regional systems that are or could be used to provide transborder services similar to those being envisioned by U.S. separate system applicants. As competitive pressures build in the international market, these countries may find themselves subject to increased national pressure to permit and to support additional international use of such satellite facilities. Such pressures may result either from concerns about the under-use of existing satellites or from a perception that an increasingly competitive international satellite market is being controlled by other national players. In this event, it is unclear whether the FCC or other administrative bodies would be able to maintain a distinction between the transborder uses of domestic satellites and the international activities of "separate" international satellite systems.

iv) Some movement in the direction of a broader debate on the separate satellite question may follow from Ireland's tentative decision to authorize the operation of a satellite that will serve Ireland, other European nations, and possibly the transatlantic market. The Irish Government has chosen Atlantic Satellites Ltd. as the operator, and plans for a 1989 launch are being made, pending further studies of market viability and the receipt of final government approval. Co-ordination with Intelsat, of course, also would be required. Atlantic Satellites is 80 per cent owned by Hughes Communications, Inc., which also has committed itself to supplying the satellite system that will be used. The remaining 20 per cent of the venture is owned by a noted Irish businessman, James J. Stafford. California-based Hughes acquired its interest in the company in March 1986.

D. Development of Regional and National Satellite Systems

1. Although not typically viewed as "separate international satellites", regional systems that have developed around the world are an additional source of transmission capacity and further evidence of the market's movement away from the days in which Intelsat and the wireline carriers' underseas cables were the only routes for international traffic. Arabsat and the European Telecommunications Satellite Organization ("Eutelsat") are among the most well-known of the regional systems. Each of them has been co-ordinated with Intelsat, but each has also faced operational and political obstacles to their attempts to become established traffic routes.

a. These regional systems may be viewed as evidence that the United States is not alone in exploring the possibility for a competitive international satellite market in which Intelsat might play a very different role from the one it now plays.

b. Regional systems represent a curious middle ground between national systems, national systems with transborder traffic flows (such as those that U.S. satellites provided between the U.S. and Canada), and truly international systems. Regional systems require multinational co-operation, but on a smaller scale than is necessary for operating a system such as Intelsat. Like Intelsat, however, even the regional systems are subject to the impact of competitive pressures that have caused various national administrations to pursue policies designed mostly to bolster national carriers and terrestrial-based services. The tension between national and regional interests can be seen most clearly in Europe. Eutelsat is only slowly establishing itself as a provider of pan-European telecommunications and other satellite-based business services, as discussed more fully below.

2. Because so many entities are moving into the facilities market—usually to promote the national aerospace sector for industrial policy reasons—there is the potential for excess capacity. The consequences for the PTTs could be significant; under-used facilities could result in pressures for revised tariff structures and new services in an effort to cut

losses. Many PTTs will not, of course, feel the financial pinch from excess capacity too directly because other ministries may have contributed to support satellite research and development. These other ministries may not sit idly by, however, to watch their undertakings become "white elephants", particularly when users may be anxious to take advantage of new services and facilities.

    3. Most national governments have sought to protect their PTTs by limiting facilities-based competition, including either the prohibition of pure circuit resale or the revision of tariffs to make such resale uneconomical. It remains to be seen whether such an approach eventually will harm national interests by making a nation's telecommunications industry less competitive internationally.

    4. The PTTs also can be expected to "defend" their viability. As noted above in Section II.B.4, some polarization between the owners of private facilities and of "public" facilities has occurred, and more is likely to take place. In addition, PTTs can be expected to promote the use of those facilities in which they have the greatest economic stake (*i.e.*, their wireline networks). Such a posture can have many consequences.

    a. The current arrangement for marketing satellite-based telecommunications services in Europe is, in part, a result of the desire of European PTTs to control the extent to which satellite facilities will draw traffic away from existing wireline networks. Thus, instead of Eutelsat marketing telecommunications services on an integrated, European-wide basis, entities seeking to provide transborder services must negotiate on an individual basis with each of the PTTs in the countries to be served. Transponders on the three European Communications Satellites ("ECS") of Eutelsat are allocated to national PTTs on a bidding basis, and services are offered to users through the national systems. The PTTs have the responsibility for marketing and pricing services that originate within their jurisdiction.

    b. Earth-station ownership restrictions are another situation that, in part, reflects the concern of European PTTs with competition between satellites and wire networks. Because satellites can be used to provide switched transmissions among customer-premises earth stations, they potentially could be used to bypass significant portions of the PTTs' terrestrial networks. As a result, PTTs have a disincentive to permit the widespread ownership and use of small earth stations. In fact, France is the only European country that permits users to own earth stations; in all other countries, the PTTs own the earth stations, thereby ensuring that the use of such stations will constitute the use of a PTT facility subject to the price and use conditions of the PTTs. This arrangement gives the PTTs some ability to regulate the terms of potential "competition" between terrestrial systems and satellites.

    c. Although the introduction of the Intelsat Business Service ("IBS") has been slow in Europe, the service is beginning to take hold. Administrations are working out different arrangements for the ownership and location of IBS ground stations. The terms of these arrangements vary significantly from country to country. However, the pressures to allow more flexibility are likely to increase.

 d. A number of PTTs also have sought to encourage the development of network configurations in which large, PTT-owned earth stations (teleports) are constructed as central concentration points for traffic using satellite links. The Dutch PTT, for example, has been very active in promoting a teleport in Amsterdam to generate new international traffic. Teleports ultimately may provide an infrastructure for national or regional satellite services.

 i) Teleports ensure that international traffic will transit the national wireline network, rather than connect directly with customer-premises earth stations.

 ii) User demand has been successful in forcing some movement away from the national teleport configuration; it has led to the development of Intelsat and Eutelsat business services that are designed to permit the use of small earth stations. Such demand is likely to increase the pressure for more user involvement in, and more numerous, teleport configurations.

 iii) Overall, teleports are a sign of the increased national rivalries for a larger share of international traffic.

 5. Despite the bias of many PTTs toward terrestrial networks, several national satellite systems are being developed in Europe; many are expected to be used principally for providing DBS services. In Asia and the Pacific, national systems are used for domestic telecommunications or other specialized services. Nonetheless, the launch and operation of these systems will increase the number of available circuits, the likelihood that carriers will face a significant facilities glut, and the possibility that under-used national systems will be used for transborder or international services (rather than remain unused).

a. Europe

Developments in Europe are discussed below relatively briefly. A more complete examination of the evolving infrastructure for satellite services in Europe is contained in Chapter IV, "The Future of European Telecommunications Policy".

 i) In France, the Télécom-1 satellite has been in orbit and operational for more than two years. Of the twelve available transponders, not all are being used; most are being used to provide video services and corporate communications. One transponder is leased to the Deutsche Bundespost and one is reserved for providing European services. The satellite also is used to provide connections between metropolitan France and France's overseas departments in the Caribbean and off the coast of Eastern Canada. There are already approximately thirty earth stations operating in France. Plans to provide DBS services continue to be delayed,

Chapter V   The changing environment for planning international facilities   363

and debate over the appropriate power to be used for the service continues; the launch of the TDF-1 satellite has been postponed at least until sometime in 1987.

ii)   Plans for the DBS satellite in the Federal Republic of Germany, TV-Sat, also have been delayed, and launch is now scheduled for mid-1987. TV-Sat will be able to serve a large part of central Europe, encompassing approximately 100 million people. The first of a two-satellite telecommunications system, Deutsche Fernmeldesatellit ("DFS"), or Kopernikus, is expected to be operational in mid-1988. It will carry voice and data traffic, video-conferencing, and up to five television programs. DFS also is expected to provide business services to up to 30 earth stations at 60 Mbps. Debate over German media policy could lead to further delays in the launch of the first DFS satellite.

iii)   Italy is working on plans for two satellite systems. Italsat is a telecommunications system that is scheduled to be launched in 1989. It is expected to be integrated closely with the terrestrial network, helping to provide services among Italy's major transmission nodes and to develop high-capacity digital services including video-conferencing and certain facsimile services. Four Sarit satellites, which are expected to be launched in the 1990s, will augment the Italsat offerings and provide Italy with its first DBS capacity. It is expected that DBS transponders initially will carry the service of RAI, the Italian state-owned broadcasting company, which is being developed in conjunction with the European Space Agency ("ESA") as part of the Olympus program.

iv)   Plans for DBS in the United Kingdom have fluctuated as greatly—probably more than anywhere else in Europe. A consortium led by the BBC decided in 1985 not to pursue DBS plans. In December 1986, the Independent Broadcasting Authority concluded a lengthy search for a new operator by choosing the five-member British Satellite Broadcasting group, which is made up of two television companies (the Granada Group and Anglia Television Group), a diversified media company (the Pearson Group, which owns the *Financial Times*, Penguin Books, and Goldcrest Films), a record company (the Virgin Group, which also owns a discount airline and a share of a satellite TV venture), and a computer company (Amstrad). The DBS venture will provide four channels of programming on three transponders. No plans for service outside the U.K. have been announced, although it is expected that when launched and in operation a U.K. satellite would have a footprint covering much of Western Europe.

v)   Finland, Denmark, Norway, Sweden, and Greenland have discussed a variety of regional satellite plans in past years, and a Tele-X Nordic satellite is planned for launch in 1988. Both Norway and Finland are supportive of Tele-X; Denmark and Greenland have reserved judgment for the time being. Tele-X will provide experimental DBS and telecommunications services on a regional basis and will be operated by the Swedish Space Corporation, although the satellite's telecommunications functions will be managed jointly by Swedish and Norwegian authorities.

vi) The Société Européenne des Satellites ("SES") is preparing for the late-1988 launch of its Astra satellite on the Ariane space shuttle. Astra will be capable of providing European-wide TV program distribution over its 16 medium-power transponders (45 watts). SES envisions master antenna systems as a major source of demand for Astra services, although it expects to provide direct-to-home service as well. The planned use of Astra on a European-wide basis already has caused conflict with Eutelsat, which argues that Astra will cause it significant harm. SES has contended that Eutelsat's ECS satellites cannot provide the services that will be offered by Astra, although the next generation of Eutelsat satellites are likely to have such capabilities. SES already is in the process of seeking technical co-ordination with Eutelsat. Because Astra will need the support of Eutelsat members to ensure that its signals can be received throughout Europe, discussions between SES and Eutelsat are certain to continue.

vii) Although the PTTs have been reluctant to use satellites, Eutelsat, the ESA, and various national public and private aerospace ventures, such as British Aerospace, are likely to press for the continued development of the technology. These ventures all aspire to participate in international procurements and to gain a share of overseas markets. As the pace of development continues in the U.S. and Japan, it will be necessary for these European entities to have regional or national outlets to evaluate new systems. Thus, it seems likely that there will be continued pressure for innovation in the area of space technology; such innovation is likely to have an impact on Intelsat to the extent that innovative spot beams might be used for transoceanic services.

viii) Despite the rather conservative approach to satellite use that the Conférence Européenne des Postes et Télécommunications ("CEPT") and individual PTTs have adopted, the net effect of European satellite policies—and, ultimately, the lack of an effective planning process within Europe—is likely to be surplus capacity over present forecasts. The potential for such excess capacity ultimately may not have dire consequences; in fact, it might result in a curious repetition of the supply conditions for satellite services that have evolved in the United States. The critical question will be whether the availability of capacity will produce flexible pricing and new services. With respect to pricing, it is difficult to foresee the likelihood of a decision to permit transponders to be sold outright or leased in their entirety. This flexibility in the availability of capacity, however, has been the single most important stimulant of innovative satellite use in the United States.

ix) As discussed at length in Chapter IV on European telecommunications policy, no effective planning process exists in Europe because decisions about the mix of satellites and various terrestrial routes are essentially made in separate fora. Terrestrial links tend to be planned in bilateral situations and do not necessarily involve the same entities that are involved in planning for the future activities of Eutelsat or the ESA.

x) One of the interesting consequences of the European

Commission's involvement in planning for the implementation of integrated services digital network ("ISDN") configurations may be that for the first time there will be a comprehensive examination of facilities planning options.

xi) Satellite uses are evolving relatively slowly within Europe. Nevertheless, as Europeans come to perceive the proper role for and capabilities of satellite technology, their views on the usefulness of satellites will spill over into the international arena and affect the position of European PTTs on Intelsat. It seems inevitable that pressures will build in favor of a more flexible policy regarding the provision of international services by European national and regional satellites.

b. Japan

i) In Japan, a DBS satellite, BS-2a, has been operating since 1984, and a single channel of programming has been provided by the Japan Broadcasting Corporation ("NHK"). BS-2, which was scheduled to be launched in early 1987, will permit the offering of an additional DBS channel. Two telecommunications satellites, CS-2a and CS-2b, have been used since 1984 primarily for communications with remote islands. A CS-3 series with vastly expanded capacity is being planned for a 1988 launch.

ii) Two Type I carriers, Japan Communications Satellite Co. ("JC Sat") and Space Communications Corp. ("SCC"), plan to launch satellites to compete with NTT's terrestrial network. JC Sat, a joint venture of C. Itoh & Co., Mitsui, and Hughes Communications, plans to launch two satellites and to begin operations in February 1988. The Ku-band satellites, which are being supplied by Hughes, will provide a total of 64 available transponders and are expected to be used to provide a wide variety of services. SCC, a joint venture of Mitsubishi Corp. and Mitsubishi Electric Co., plans to launch a Ku-band satellite in February 1988 and to begin providing leased circuit services in April 1988.

E. Other Important National Developments Affecting International Facilities Planning Decisions

In addition to the evolution of domestic and national satellite systems, there have been other important policy developments in several major industrialized countries that are likely to affect the future of the facilities planning arena. These regulatory developments are discussed more fully in Chapter II "Boundary Lines: A Further Exploration of Enhanced or Value-Added Services".

1. Japan

a. In Japan, there has been much speculation about the possible role of having national satellites offer international services.

However, the Ministry of Posts and Telecommunications ("MPT") has been cautiously waiting for the "other shoe" to drop in the United States' dispute with Intelsat over private satellite systems. Much depends on how effectively new national satellite ventures can operate as domestic service providers.

    b. The degree to which national satellites will operate internationally also will depend on the Japanese Government's decision about the type of competition to which KDD will be exposed; this decision has not yet been made. The MPT clearly would prefer to allow only limited competition by an entity that would obtain ownership-like rights in existing cables or in Intelsat transponders. However, it may approve some new entrants with more ambitious plans to construct a new fiber optic cable.

    i) A consortium of more than twenty companies known as Kokusai Digital Tsushin Kikukai (International Digital Communications Planning, or "IDC") is owned in part by Cable & Wireless, but also has had discussions with General Motors, the parent of Hughes Communications, about the potential for becoming a new international operator in Japan. The venture also includes Pacific Telesis, one of the seven RHCs in the United States. Given the interest of Cable & Wireless and Pacific Telesis, and what had been a possible interest by General Motors, this entity could evolve into either a cable-based or a satellite-based competitor of KDD if permitted by the government to compete internationally.

    ii) International Telecom Japan, Inc. ("ITJ") also is a potential entrant into the international market. ITJ was formed as a joint venture of seven private Japanese companies, including Japan's major international trading companies. ITJ added an additional group of Japanese shareholders in the Fall of 1986 and has announced plans to offer shares to a number of foreign investors. Although ITJ is not planning, at this time, to construct new cable facilities, it is keen on developing new correspondent ties, in part to respond to the international communications needs of its major shareholders. Because ITJ plans to lease at least some circuits from KDD and because KDD has provided two of its engineers to ITJ as advisers, some observers have contended that ITJ would not become a vigorous competitor of KDD. However, ITJ's major shareholders, all of whom are large users of telecommunications services, have had long and sometimes difficult experiences with KDD in establishing elaborate international networks that test the boundaries of D-Series Recommendations of the CCITT. Thus, they have committed themselves to providing increased flexibility to users, as well as to offering significant rate reductions to their customers. Such an orientation could produce pressure for a liberalization of circuit-use arrangements.

    c. The potential involvement of U.S. and other foreign companies in the Japanese international facilities and services market has become a focus of debate among Japanese officials and foreign trade negotiators. The MPT has advocated the merger of the two potential KDD competitors. U.S. and U.K. officials have objected to such a plan, characterizing it as an effort to minimize foreign involvement in Japan's international business because ITJ's all-Japanese ownership (at the present time) would dilute the control of foreign companies in a merged entity. U.S. trade officials also have alleged that any merger requirement would have the effect of violating Japan's agreement in bilateral trade negotiations to permit foreign participation in its international market up to a 33 per cent level.

i) The focus on trade issues already has protracted the process of developing a new international telecommunications policy and threatens to embroil the issue in controversy that could further delay a final decision.

ii) The debate over competition for KDD also is having an impact on plans to construct the proposed Private Pacific Area Cable ("PPAC") facility. IDC was to have served as the Japanese correspondent for the cable; neither KDD nor ITJ favor the construction of PPAC, and it remains uncertain whether a merger between ITJ and IDC will evolve or to what extent any merged entity might participate in PPAC.

d. As discussed more fully in Chapter II on "Boundary Lines", the Japanese also are struggling with decisions about how to treat value-added services offered internationally. The D-Series Recommendations, which outline guidelines under which international leased lines may be used to provide third-party services, have been viewed in Japan as an obstacle to the development of vigorous international value-added offerings. In May 1987, the Diet adopted revisions to the Telecommunications Business Law to implement a new arrangement whereby value-added services could be offered over "non-tariff-based" international transmission capacity obtained from international carriers (currently KDD). Such arrangements are thought to be outside the scope of the D-Series limitations because they are not "leased lines". Thus, the usage limits on international leased lines would be inapplicable.

e. Whether this approach proves an effective means for encouraging the development of value-added services internationally may depend in part on the extent to which KDD is subject to competition. Without effective competition, KDD could impose on value-added service providers tariff practices, such as volume-sensitive pricing, that would discourage the development of many international value-added offerings. The details of the new regulatory scheme still need to be worked out in the context of ministerial directives and other implementing regulations. The U.S. also is engaged in talks with Japanese officials about the new scheme for providing value-added services internationally.

f. Future decisions regarding international telecommunications are likely to have a significant impact on Japan's policies regarding Intelsat. Although no clear trend has yet surfaced, it seems reasonable to speculate that Japan ultimately will line up behind the United States in favor of a different approach to Intelsat's future role.

g. Recent deregulatory steps may affect the degree of separation in the control of domestic and international telecommunications, with a more competitive NTT demonstrating a long-term interest in becoming an important participant in the international telecommunications market. NTT already has developed an important role as an adviser to one of the potential new competitors to KDD.

    h. The combination of new service-based competition and the seeds of private satellite and cable undertakings may accelerate a trend toward a more *laissez-faire* approach to the international planning process in Japan.

2. Canada

    a. Teleglobe Canada, the signatory to both the Intelsat and Inmarsat agreements and the exclusive holder of licenses for international earth stations, is the exclusive provider in Canada of international satellite circuits from Intelsat and Inmarsat. The Canadian Government's recent privatization of Teleglobe could lead to widespread changes in the structure and regulation of Canada's international telecommunications market. The discussion that follows is a brief summary of the major aspects of the privatization; a more extensive discussion of the Teleglobe privatization is contained in Chapter II on "Boundary Lines".

    b. On April 4, 1987, the Canadian Government completed the sale of Teleglobe, formerly a Crown corporation, to Memotec Data, Inc., a Canadian provider of data communications and data processing products, for almost $500,000,000. Memotec's shareholders include twenty of Canada's largest pension funds and a number of its largest financial institutions.

    c. As part of the privatization, Parliament adopted legislation authorizing the sale and establishing a new legal scheme to cover international telecommunications activities in Canada. The legislation gives the Canadian Radio-television and Telecommunications Commission ("CRTC") jurisdiction over Teleglobe. Teleglobe was not previously subject to such regulation. Although Teleglobe is still required to provide certain essential international telecommunication facilities and services, it is permitted for the first time to enter into new lines of business, including both telecommunications and non-telecommunications businesses. The legislation authorizes the CRTC to forbear from regulating any activity in which Teleglobe becomes involved that the CRTC determines "is subject to a degree of competition that is sufficient to ensure just and reasonable tolls, rates or charges and ensure against unjust discrimination or undue or unreasonable preference, advantage, prejudice or disadvantage . . .".

    d. The legislation permits Teleglobe to retain cable landing licences, international earth-station licences, and international facilities interests. It also is authorized to continue serving as Canada's signatory in Intelsat and Inmarsat. Although Teleglobe's statutory monopoly in the international services market has been ended, the government has committed itself to using its authority under existing legislation to preserve

Teleglobe's monopoly ownership of international telecommunications facilities for at least five years. The continuation of the monopoly will depend upon the government's assessment of whether Teleglobe is providing Canada with efficient and high-quality telecommunications services.

 e. The government has retained additional supervisory authority over Teleglobe, including the power to request information about international negotiations and agreements, and the right to instruct Teleglobe about certain matters relating to national security, foreign relations, and international telecommunications policy issues.

 f. The legislation also contains restrictions on the ownership of Teleglobe, including a requirement of CRTC approval before control of Teleglobe can be transferred. The ownership restrictions are intended to prevent Teleglobe from becoming subject to the control of foreign individuals, corporations, or governments. The restrictions also operate as a way of segregating the domestic and international telecommunications markets in Canada by prohibiting a list of Canadian telecommunications common carriers contained in the legislation (consisting primarily of Bell Canada and the provincial telephone companies) from obtaining control of Teleglobe. The restrictions on foreign telecommunications common carriers and their "associates" (as defined in the legislation) are more strict; these entities are prohibited from owning any voting stock of Teleglobe, directly or indirectly, except by way of a security interest.

 g. It remains to be seen how the privatization will affect the international services market in Canada. Although the government has committed itself to providing Teleglobe with some "breathing space" by maintaining its monopoly control of international facilities, the privatization has set the stage for the eventual emergence of at least some competition in the international market. As a result, the government may well find itself confronting difficult questions about how many international competitors it should allow (and whether any of these competitors can be "foreign-owned"), how it should manage the country's ongoing participation in Intelsat and Inmarsat, whether it should allow Teleglobe and others to participate in "private" international facilities ventures, and how it should structure competition in the end-to-end international services market between Teleglobe and service providers that do not own international transmission facilities. Chapter II, on "Boundary Lines", contains a more complete discussion of the regulatory issues that Canada is likely to face in the domestic and international markets as a result of the privatization.

3. United States

 a. In the United States, several regulatory developments—other than the authorization of private satellite systems and the generally liberal policies toward satellite use—are likely to have a major impact on the international arena.

b. In 1984, the FCC decided that international earth stations could be owned by entities other than the Earth Station Ownership Committee, which consisted of Comsat (the U.S. signatory to Intelsat) and a consortium of carriers. This step has created a great incentive for the introduction of IBS services around the world.

c. In addition, although the FCC continues to reject a plan that would permit entities other than Comsat to acquire transponder capacity directly from Intelsat, the traditional role of Comsat as the only U.S. representative in Intelsat may be eroding.

i) A proposed merger between Comsat and Contel Corp., the third-largest independent telephone company in the U.S. and the owner of American Satellite Corporation (now Contel ASC), if ever completed, may prompt the FCC to reconsider its view and to alter the way in which the U.S. is represented at, and acquires capacity from, Intelsat.

ii) In addition, the prospects for increased competition between Comsat and the carriers to which it provides Intelsat space segments may subject Comsat to increasing criticism as the sole U.S. representative to Intelsat. This criticism already has intensified in response to the announced Contel merger plans.

iii) A number of parties have opposed the merger on the ground that it would place Comsat in a position where it could not possibly act as a neutral representative of U.S. interests with respect to Intelsat. Comsat already is permitted to provide end-to-end services in competition with the companies to which it supplied Intelsat space segments, although such competitive end-to-end offerings must be provided through a separate Comsat subsidiary and are subject to close tariff and cost-allocation supervision by the FCC. Critics of the merger have contended that Comsat's incentive to act as an aggressive competitor will be increased when it has a ready market of more than 2,000,000 Contel telephone customers to which it can market end-to-end international services. Although Comsat and Contel have said that Comsat's activities as an Intelsat signatory and as the monopoly supplier of Intelsat space segment capacity to U.S. carriers will be kept separate from any competitive service operations, a number of U.S. carriers have opposed the merger on the grounds that it would be anticompetitive.

iv) The end of national representation by an entity formed exclusively as a proprietor of international satellite service also could have a significant effect on decisionmaking within Intelsat. A reconstituted U.S. national representative (such as a post-merger Comsat) is likely to be less focused on buttressing Intelsat and international satellite service and more attentive to strategies for lessening the costs of international facilities.

v) Proposals for direct access to Intelsat facilities by U.S. entities other than Comsat are intended to compensate for or offset an alleged disincentive to use satellite, rather than cable, circuits. This disincentive results, it is argued, because U.S. carriers are able to treat their investments in underseas cables as capital expenditures that can be amortized

Chapter V The changing environment for planning international facilities 371

over the life of the cable and that are considered as part of their rate base (on which they are entitled to earn a prescribed rate of return). By contrast, the cost of leasing satellite capacity is a short-term expense that is not amortized and that is not figured into the rate base. The disparity in treatment provides carriers with a non-price incentive to invest in cables rather than to acquire satellite circuits.

vi) The stability and control inherent in an ownership right is an additional non-cost feature of cable investment that makes it appear attractive. More recently, this disparity in the extent of control over transmission capacity has been extended to users. As noted earlier, the FCC has decided to permit entities other than carriers to acquire IRUs, which are ownership-like rights that will provide users with the stability of long-term investment decisions. Although service providers with IRUs will not have a say in the management and maintenance of cable facilities, they will be protected from price fluctuations and will enjoy the benefits of being able to acquire facilities as long-term capital investments, rather than short-term expenses.

vii) To date, the FCC has concluded that direct access will not substantially change this situation and will not provide U.S. international carriers with additional incentives to use Intelsat space segments.

d. In early April 1987, Contel expressed a desire to abandon the merger with Comsat for a variety of business reasons. Contel requested that Comsat agree to terminate the merger agreement voluntarily, but Comsat has said initially that it has no plans to consent to such a termination. If the proposed merger is abandoned, this source of pressure for revising Intelsat signatory arrangements in the U.S. would disappear.

e. Even if the Contel-Comsat merger is abandoned, developments in the aeronautical services market, discussed above in Section II.C.2, could lead to a reexamination of the way in which the U.S. structures arrangements for access to international satellite facilities and participation in Intelsat and Inmarsat. In January 1987, the FCC denied requests by Comsat to be the sole provider of Inmarsat capacity to be used for aeronautical services. *Communications Satellite Corp.*, FCC No. 87–1 (released January 12, 1987). (Comsat is the sole supplier of Intelsat circuits and Inmarsat maritime service circuits.) The FCC then proposed a scheme that it contends will promote the competitive offering of aeronautical services over the Inmarsat system. *Provision of Aeronautical Services via the Inmarsat System*, FCC No. 87–106 (released March 30, 1987).

i) Under the FCC's proposal, all U.S. entities authorized to provide aeronautical services would participate in a consortium ("Aerocon"), to be organized as a non-profit representative entity that would participate in Inmarsat. The FCC also would seek amendments to the Inmarsat convention and operating agreement (and any necessary new or amended U.S. legislation) to permit both Comsat and Aerocon to serve as signatories to Inmarsat. Each entity would exercise voting power according to the share of Inmarsat capacity that it used. Aerocon would provide entities other than Comsat with direct access to and participation in Inmarsat. The FCC has advocated this approach as the fastest possible way of encouraging competition in the aeronautical services market; new and mobile satellites and Arinc's Avsat proposal, discussed above in Section II.C.2, are likely to be at least several years away from becoming operational—if they come to fruition at all.

ii) The FCC noted that the time-consuming process of seeking amendments to the Inmarsat agreements could be avoided by having either Comsat or Aerocon serve as the sole U.S. signatories to Inmarsat. Relying on Aerocon, however, would alter the arrangements under which Inmarsat's maritime services are provided, effectively introducing competition into that market for the sake of promoting competition in the aeronautical services market. Relying on Comsat (the *status quo*), according to the FCC, "would not be the preferred alternative"; it would deprive new entrants of "a direct voice" in Inmarsat decisionmaking processes and would "deny the U.S. government the opportunity to consider [such entities'] views in the Inmarsat decisionmaking process". FCC No. 87–106, *supra*, at n.18. Reliance on Comsat also would require the U.S. Government "constantly to settle disputes between maritime and aeronautical interests through the instructional process". *Id.*

iii) If the FCC's proposal leads to the establishment of Aerocon and a revision in U.S. arrangements for participation in Inmarsat, the change could spill over into the debate over Comsat's signatory role in Intelsat. The FCC declined to permit entities other than Comsat to acquire Intelsat circuits directly from Intelsat or to participate in signatory functions. *Regulatory Policies Concerning Direct Access to Intelsat Space Segment for the U.S. International Service Carriers*, 97 F.C.C. 2d 296 (1984). Instead, it has liberalized policies governing which entities can acquire Intelsat capacity from Comsat and can own international earth stations, and has relied on its power to supervise and regulate Comsat's signatory functions (including its role as the monopoly supplier of Intelsat circuits) to promote competition in the international services market generally. A move to open up Inmarsat, however, may again invigorate debate over Comsat's Intelsat role and the FCC's policies regarding direct access to Intelsat.

iv) The arguments that the FCC advances for establishing Aerocon and involving it directly in Inmarsat would be applicable to a proposal to involve some consortium of U.S. entities directly in Intelsat. It is unclear whether the FCC would conclude that a change in its direct access policy would add significantly to the degree of competition it believes it is promoting with its other Intelsat and Comsat policies. Its aeronautical services proposal, however, suggests that there are benefits to direct participation in the multinational facilities provider that would not be replicated by rules relating to authorized use of Intelsat circuits, permissible ownership of international earth stations, or the terms on which Comsat can offer Intelsat capacity. Although there are many significant differences

Chapter V The changing environment for planning international facilities 373

between the markets that Intelsat and Inmarsat serve, the FCC's aeronautical services proposal may foreshadow a change in its view of how the U.S. should structure its participation in Intelsat.

   f. Other U.S. initiatives, which are being mirrored or are likely to be mirrored in other countries, will tend to emphasize factors that should lead to a more efficiency-oriented approach to decisionmaking about plans for, and use of, international telecommunications facilities.

   i) Service-based competition between AT&T and other competitive carriers, such as MCI and US Sprint, is having an impact on the international facilities market. With the introduction of these new carriers into the market, along with Mercury from the U.K., and possibly additional Japanese entrants (as noted above), historically simple international correspondent arrangements are becoming more complex and are getting tied up in disputes among participants in the facilities market.

   ii) This competition will have a significant impact on U.S. and international policies toward the use of cable versus satellite circuits. There will be substantial pressures imposed on service providers to identify and use the most cost-effective routes.

   iii) New U.S. service providers are not bound by the balanced loading requirements that the FCC has imposed on AT&T's international message telephone service ("IMTS") and international 800 service. Thus, AT&T's competitors are free to use only the least costly (or most cost-efficient) facilities, which, in many cases, may be fiber optic cables. AT&T already has argued to the FCC with some success that this situation places it at a competitive disadvantage. AT&T asserts that the FCC's circuit distribution policies require it to continue to use both satellite and cable circuits on a proportionate basis, regardless of costs.

   iv) The FCC already has responded to this situation by authorizing AT&T to deviate from balanced loading in the Atlantic Ocean Region by 2 per cent each year through 1988 (without deloading any existing circuits). In the Pacific Region, AT&T is permitted to deviate from balanced loading by a larger percentage annually, primarily because it uses a far greater percentage of satellite circuits in the Pacific Ocean Region than it does in the Atlantic. (The FCC had not adopted formal circuit distribution guidelines for the Caribbean Region.)

   v) The FCC also has initiated a proceeding to develop new circuit-distribution policies to take effect at the start of 1989. In its Notice of Proposed Rulemaking, the FCC has offered three new policies for comment. These policies would be applied worldwide, rather than on a region-by-region basis. One would end FCC involvement in circuit distribution decisions completely at the end of 1988; the other two would phase out FCC involvement in facilities-loading decisions over a certain period of time (each proposal advocating a slightly different mechanism for achieving this phase-out). *Policy for the Distribution of U.S. International Carrier Circuits Among Available Facilities During the Post-1988 Period*, FCC No. 87–96 (released April 10, 1987). Many industry participants, including the CEPT members, are urging the FCC to eliminate all loading requirements.

vi) If these circuit distribution requirements are eliminated as now seems possible, AT&T, which still uses the vast majority of all international circuits between the United States and other countries, will be free to make facilities-use decisions solely on the basis of economic considerations, technical factors, and the preferences of its correspondent carriers.

vii) The elimination of circuit distribution requirements could have the effect of producing a substantial movement away from satellite circuit use—particularly if AT&T is forced to continue dealing with Intelsat through Comsat and is unable to acquire ownership-like rights in Intelsat transponders. However, the commitment of AT&T and many PTTs to Intelsat may well counteract some of the economic pressures for increased use of cable facilities; it is not clear, though, to what extent this commitment will be able to withstand the demands produced by an increasingly competitive market. Of course, continued technical distinctions between satellites and cables, as well as the needs of carriers to provide service to areas reached only by satellites and to maintain service restoration capabilities (*i.e.*, duplicative circuits), will ensure that some mix of cables and satellite circuits is used. It should be remembered, however, that decisions concerning the loading of cable and satellite circuits are not made unilaterally by AT&T; instead, they require the concurrence of AT&T's correspondents overseas.

4. Australia

a. As in Canada and Japan, the Australian telecommunications market is organized to separate the role of the domestic and international service providers. Although these lines of demarcation seem likely to remain intact, some pressures and tensions exist between the Overseas Telecommunications Commission ("OTC (Australia)") and Telecom Australia that might well affect the international facilities infrastructure.

b. One factor contributing to this trend is that OTC (A) is interested in offering its international customers—Australian and foreign companies doing business in Australia—effective and direct access to international cable and satellite services. At present, OTC (A) is dependent on Telecom Australia for providing users with terrestrial connections to its facilities. OTC (A) seems open to arrangements that would change this situation and is pursuing IBS configurations that would permit direct connection of user-premises earth stations with Intelsat capacity supplied by OTC (A).

c. Any overzealous moves by OTC (A) to bypass the domestic transmission network might be met with efforts by Telecom Australia or other Australian entities to gain a more active role in offering international services. As in Japan, Canada, and the United States, there exists some significant interest among domestic carriers for obtaining a long-term role in the international market.

   d. These considerations must be viewed, however, in a broader context. Australia is now one of Intelsat's most vigorous supporters, particularly in dealing with the development of separate satellite systems. How this commitment might evolve in the future remains to be seen. OTC (A) has charted a long-range strategy for positioning Australia as a hub for international traffic; this strategy depends heavily on the development of an infrastructure of fiber optic cables. In the 1990s, for example, OTC (A) plans to deploy a new fiber optic cable to the West Coast of the United States. The capacity of this cable might be so substantial that OTC (A) would have an incentive to price it to encourage transiting traffic into Southeast Asia and even Japan. The movement of such traffic also is being sought to encourage the development of a service-based industry in Australia centered on the financial and information processing sectors. OTC (A) views its role very much as a trading company drawing new business opportunities to Australia.

   e. The eventual role for AUSSAT, the Australian national satellite system, also remains unclear. AUSSAT seems to be positioning itself as a potential competitor to Telecom Australia; it is currently offering private network services to the government of the state of Queensland (Q-Net) and hopes to do so for other state governments, as well as to the private sector. AUSSAT has leased some telecommunications capacity to New Zealand for domestic services. It also has a beam aimed at the islands of the Southwest Pacific. Whether AUSSAT will emerge as a full-service regional satellite carrier, however, is an altogether separate question. It does not seem likely, or feasible, that AUSSAT would become a regional carrier in the near term. However, future generations of AUSSAT satellites may be designed to achieve some of the objectives that are envisioned by a future U.S.-Australia fiber optic cable link.

F. Changes Designed to Expose Facilities-Use Decisions More Directly to Economic Pressures

   1. New options for investing in international telecommunications facilities and changes in the way that costs are allocated among owners and non-owner users of international facilities are altering the parameters by which usage decisions are made.

   a. As preceding sections of this paper have described, traditional pricing structures, regulatory and investment policies, and adherence to historic objectives produce distortions in pricing signals that work contrary to the goals of market competition. In an era of more centralized planning and of relatively little facilities use by non-owners, these pricing signals were less critical to determining the contours of the international telecommunication facilities market. Now, however, as central planning mechanisms have eroded and the number of participants in the international market has increased, strong pricing signals have become vital to ensuring that efficient investment and use decisions are made.

    b. In addition to introducing new investment options and pricing policies, efforts are being made to involve non-owner users more closely in the process of deciding about the need for and the use of international facilities. This involvement, which still is at an early stage in many instances, is critical because it permits a greater interaction among facilities "suppliers" and "demanders"; the effect should be a closer match between the supply of and the demand for such facilities.

    2. Intelsat is considering the introduction of Transponder Rights of Use ("TRUs"), which would be long-term ownership-like rights in Intelsat transponder circuits, as a way of offsetting the disparity in investment incentives between cable and satellite facilities. It remains to be seen, however, how TRUs will be treated by national regulatory authorities. There also is a question of how entities other than Intelsat signatories would benefit from the availability of TRUs.

    a. In the United States, for example, it is not clear how or whether Comsat would be able to pass on the benefits of TRU acquisitions to carriers that must acquire Intelsat capacity from it. It is possible, however, that the availability of TRUs might be an additional factor that could prompt the FCC to change its policy and to permit the direct acquisition of any amount of Intelsat space segment capacity—or of only Intelsat TRUs—by entities other than Comsat. Alternatively, some arrangements may be devised by which Comsat will make TRUs available to carriers under tariff. If only Comsat were able to take advantage of the opportunity to acquire TRUs, it could enjoy a more advantageous investment mode that might allow it to offer lower prices for its end-to-end international services—particularly to users willing to make long-term commitments—than other U.S. carriers that could obtain circuits only on a leased basis.

    b. Outside the U.S., the situation is less problematic because fewer entities are involved. In many cases, the PTTs are either the Intelsat signatories or are the only providers of international services. In addition, service providers—to the extent that third-party providers are permitted— cannot receive the benefits of ownership-like rights in cable circuits. Of course, as national policies change to permit competition in the international facilities or services market, problems more analogous to those being faced in the United States may well arise.

    c. Changing investment incentives are not likely to alter the commitment of many PTTs to ensuring that their existing investments in underseas cables and domestic terrestrial networks are not stranded by a shift to satellite circuits, in which they are likely to have a much smaller economic stake. Although the signatories to the Intelsat Agreement have pledged themselves to supporting Intelsat (and many have reaffirmed that commitment in the wake of recent market developments), and although many of those signatories have made investments in satellite system facilities, economic pressures to guard against the under-use of what typically are more extensive cable facilities should not be underestimated. As competitive pressures force PTTs to reduce the prices of services and facilities along heavily used routes, they will have an additional incentive to prevent under-use of their networks. The ability to subsidize universal services goals through price structures will diminish, and PTTs will have to focus their efforts on maximizing network use to meet overall revenue requirements.

3. At the same time that Intelsat is looking to stimulate a market for new satellite circuit investments, the FCC is exploring new pricing methods that it believes could invigorate the market for IRU purchases in submarine cable facilities.

a. The FCC has proposed a change of its rules that would permit U.S. carrier owners of submarine cables to alter the manner in which they calculate the price of cable IRUs made available to other U.S. companies. *Reevaluation of the Depreciated Original-Cost Standard in Setting Prices for Conveyances of Capital Interests in Overseas Facilities Between or Among U.S. Carriers*, FCC No. 87–71 (released March 9, 1987) (Notice of Proposed Rulemaking). The proposed changes would be applicable most importantly to cable IRUs, but they also could be applied to other forms of capital investments made available by facilities owners (such as satellite earth stations and various radio frequency systems). The FCC will consider issues related to dealings between U.S. and foreign correspondents in its separate proceeding on international regulatory policies. *Regulatory Policies and International Telecommunications*, FCC No. 86–563 (released January 30, 1987) (Notice of Inquiry and Proposed Rulemaking).

b. At present, facilities owners are permitted to convey capital interests at net book cost—the original cost less any accumulated depreciation. Some deviation is permitted, if, in the FCC's opinion, it can be justified by special circumstances. The net book cost standard has been used, however, primarily to guard against two possible results: having U.S. carriers pass on to ratepayers excessive facilities investments, and having them charge prices for capital interests that would be high enough to discourage competition. In transactions between U.S. and foreign correspondents, the FCC has, upon occasion, refused to approve capital interest acquisitions by U.S. carriers in excess of net book cost; the FCC views the pricing standard as a safeguard against playing off one carrier against another, *i.e.*, whipsawing, in the international market.

c. Recognizing that the U.S. international facilities and services market has become more competitive, the FCC has suggested a number of new alternatives. The FCC believes that competitive forces can help to guard against the charging of excessive prices and that a more flexible pricing policy may allow carriers to select prices that they believe will stimulate entry by new investors.

d. The rule change is intended to rectify a perceived deficiency in the net book cost approach. This historic pricing formula effectively burdens original facilities investors with the full costs of carrying capacity sought for future needs. Because depreciation is removed from the price of an IRU or other capital interest upon sale to a third party, original investors necessarily receive less than their original costs; only part of the difference will have been made up by possible tax benefits realized on depreciation charges.

e. The FCC has suggested several new pricing schemes that would permit carriers to recover at least some portion of their carrying costs upon sale of a capital interest. These options include (*i*) placing idle circuits into a pool that would be divided among original investors *pro rata* with their share of allocated circuits (dividing the carrying costs among all original investors), (*ii*) requiring that carriers sell capital interests at net book cost plus carrying charges (imposing on subsequent investors the carrying charges), (*iii*) requiring that carriers sell capital interests at net book cost plus a fraction of carrying charges (dividing carrying charges among original and subsequent investors), and (*iv*) complete deregulation of capital investment prices (allowing the prices to be set in negotiations between buyers and sellers).

f. The three alternative regulatory options recognize that it may be unfair to require the ratepayers of original facilities investors to bear the full cost of carrying circuits that are of value to subsequent purchasers. The Commission's alternatives, however, reflect the fact that it may be difficult to decide who values the excess capacity more—original investors that can guard against unanticipated increases in demand (by purchasing extra facilities that are included in the rate base), or subsequent investors that value the availability of extra circuit construction as an opportunity to enter the facilities ownership market.

g. The FCC's market-oriented option reflects a recognition that as the facilities market in the U.S. has become more competitive there is less chance that prices will be used as a barrier to entry. In fact, permitting prices to be negotiated, the FCC has speculated, may prompt owners to make more circuits available, *i.e.*, they will plan for extra future capacity with the knowledge that a reasonable return will be realized. (Existing idle capacity would not be affected; the FCC would apply new pricing policies only to subsequently authorized facilities to avoid undermining investment decisions made in light of net book cost policies.)

h. FCC Commissioner Dawson has expressed some doubt about the effectiveness of relying on pricing mechanisms to ensure that market conditions—rather than regulatory principles—guide carrier behavior. In a concurring statement, she noted that it might be more appropriate to remove facilities construction from the rate base, so that dominant carriers would not be able to pass the risk of construction on to

Chapter V The changing environment for planning international facilities   379

ratepayers. She suggests that "when and only when real alternatives (competition) exist", it may be appropriate "to move away from rate base regulation". The issue of how rate-of-return regulation may distort market signals is discussed below in Section II.F.6.

    4. New investment options and pricing policies can be offset, at least in part, by historic cost allocation schemes that may shield facilities users from bearing the full costs of their usage decisions.

    5. One major obstacle to strengthening the economic signals in the international facilities market is Intelsat's historic cost allocation procedures.

        a. Intelsat uses a cost-sharing arrangement under which increased use of available system capacity reduces the cost of each member's use of the system. This arrangement, however, does not allocate to individual members the full costs of any decisions by them to reduce their use of the Intelsat system: the costs of such reduced use are spread among all Intelsat members, thus reducing the detrimental impact on the particular member not living up to its use commitment.

        b. The costs set by Intelsat for its circuits are determined by the usage forecasts of its members. The share of total costs that each member must pay, however, is determined by actual use. Thus, if a particular member actually uses far fewer circuits than it had forecast, the total costs to be allocated among all members will increase, but the share of those costs to be paid by the members not using as much capacity as they had forecast will be only a fraction of the full costs attributable to such reduced use. Such under-use by individual members allows them to pay only a small share of any increase in the total cost of operating the Intelsat system.

    6. Rate-of-return regulation, together with other regulatory policies imposed in the United States, also may tend to blunt the impact that non-owners have on international facilities investment decisions. It can be argued that these policies slow any movement toward cost-based pricing and more efficient facilities investment in the international market. *See* L. L. Johnson, *supra*, ch. IV. In the absence of significant competition, the policies may well have the effect of keeping facilities and service prices above optimal levels. As competition in the market develops, these policies will have less of an adverse effect, except that they may delay the competitive responses of regulated entities by insulating them somewhat from the impact of competition.

        a. Rate-of-return regulation has been criticized because it has the potential to encourage over-investment by regulated entities. If the rate of return exceeds a company's cost of capital, and if certain other conditions are present (*e.g.*, as tariffed prices are below the level at which profits are maximized), a company subject to rate-of-return regulation stands to increase its profits by expanding its capital investments, even if those investments are not necessary or particularly cost-efficient. (Over-investment, which increases a carrier's rate base, permits the carrier to increase prices for its services.) *See, e.g., Johnson, supra*, at 24; J. Haring and

E. Kwerel, *Competition Policy in the Post-Equal Access Market* 2 (FCC Office of Plans and Policy Working Paper DA 87–211) (released March 11, 1987).

    b. Regulation is intended to guard against over-investment by requiring government approval for facilities construction plans. In the U.S., for example, the FCC reviews market conditions and attempts to assess the needs for planned international cables as part of its obligation to ensure that construction plans serve the public interest. Without attempting to assess whether or not past cable plans were shown to have been consistent with the public interest, it should be noted that the FCC has approved all of AT&T's new international cable requests, although there was controversy surrounding the FCC's initial denial and subsequent approval of TAT-6 in the early 1970s.

    c. One commentator has suggested that because the process by which traffic forecasts are made typically produces over-optimistic forecasts, the FCC's approval of new international facilities, which relies largely on such forecasts, is virtually assured. L. L. Johnson, *supra*, at 26. If this is true, then the usefulness of the regulatory process as a check against over-investment obviously will be minimal. (The role of traffic forecasting and the criticisms of the current forecasting process will be discussed below in Section III.B.)

    d. In the U.S., it has been asserted that rate-of-return regulation may well prompt AT&T to over-invest in cable facilities because, as noted above in Section II.E.3, only its cable investments go into its rate base; satellite leases are not included. Thus, to the extent that rate-of-return regulation has a distorting effect, it arguably has that effect only with respect to AT&T's involvement in cable construction.

    e. Because Comsat is also subject to rate-of-return regulation, and because Comsat's investments in Intelsat are included in its rate base, Comsat may have a similar incentive to over-invest in Intelsat satellites. Such over-investment would affect not only U.S. carriers that must acquire Intelsat circuits from Comsat, but also users of Intelsat generally, who will have to share the costs of excess capacity in the form of higher prices.

    f. Comsat's incentive to over-invest may be further strengthened by the FCC's circuit loading policies, which, in effect, ensure that regardless of its rates it can be assured of AT&T's business.

    g. A major effect of over-investment by a company subject to rate-of-return regulation, of course, is to increase the price of services provided by the regulated company. In the international cable market, where AT&T gradually has been exposed to some competition, its ability to realize the benefits of over-investment (*i.e.*, higher prices) without losing customers has been, and will in the future be, diminishing. For Comsat, however, the constraints may be slightly less. Although fiber cables soon will offer a very attractive alternative to satellites for many uses (and, thus, may limit the extent to which Comsat can charge higher prices without losing customers), Comsat continues to be assured of AT&T's business due to the FCC's circuit distribution policies. If the FCC continues to relax its circuit distribution rules (or eliminates them altogether at the end of 1988), and if competitive international satellites begin to operate, there will be significant additional constraints on the prices that Comsat can charge.

   h. It must be stressed how difficult it is to assess the extent to which these regulations produce over-investment and excessive prices.

   i) First, it is virtually impossible to predict what facilities would have been constructed and what prices would have been charged in the absence of the existing regulatory scheme.

   ii) Second, it is difficult to determine whether carriers may have overestimated future traffic due to (*i*) a desire to increase their rate bases, (*ii*) an honest error in their predictions, or (*iii*) unforeseen developments that result in less overall demand or in different user preferences between cable and satellite circuits. *Cf.* Johnson, *supra*, at 27–9.

   iii) Finally, one must keep in mind that the decisions of regulated carriers are only half of the story. Decisions on international facilities investment are always made jointly with one or more foreign partners, most of whom are not subject to similar regulatory regimes. Although one would expect that this partnership might tend to reduce the chance of over-investment, at least one commentator has suggested that many PTTs may have an equal or greater incentive—or opportunity—to advocate new facilities construction, whether or not anticipated demand justifies such construction. *See id.* at 34–6 (arguing that because PTTs often are less constrained in the international market than in the domestic market (where the provision of affordable universal service often is required), they might be willing to invest in excess capacity as added insurance against disasters and as a fairly painless way of accommodating important U.S. telecommunications partners). However, many PTTs are facing more intense competitive pressures and, therefore, are more likely to evaluate carefully their future facilities needs.

   i. Although the precise impact of such regulation on the international facilities market may be difficult to document, evidence suggests that the regulation has at least some distorting effect. As the FCC apparently believes, in light of its current inquiry into the elimination of circuit distribution requirements and of less formal investigations of alternatives to rate-of-return regulation, the signals being sent by its policies are somewhat out of step with market conditions and trends.

G. Summary: Making Facilities Decisions Reflect Market Conditions More Closely

   1. The numerous developments catalogued above have the net effect of unhinging what once could have been characterized as a relatively settled set of arrangements for planning the international facilities infrastructure. A range of factors is rapidly changing the international arena and is

producing conflicting pressures. There still is a strong drive to maintain the *status quo*, in particular the stability of existing price structures and international arrangements. At the same time, there are strong pressures to permit at least limited competition and to allow the facilities infrastructure to continue to diversify, both in terms of the types of facilities constructed and the ways in which various entities can participate in the market.

2. Evolution of the international facilities market is a complex process. The changing capabilities of cable and satellite technologies often have both beneficial and adverse consequences for any one participant in the international arena. Many players in this market—particularly those in the U.S.—either sit "on both sides of the fence" (using both cable and satellite facilities) or gradually are finding themselves being moved into such an uncomfortable position. Thus, it often is difficult to evaluate the effects of particular changes in the established environment for making international facilities arrangements.

a. For example, carriers with significant investments in cables need the affordable thin-route services provided by Intelsat to provide users with communications links worldwide. Many of the entities that are Intelsat signatories also are transoceanic cable owners and participants in regional satellite projects.

b. Any discussion of Intelsat solely as a distinct entity (with the ability to respond independently to market conditions) is potentially misleading. Intelsat also is a constituent organization, and its members are mostly the same entities that are participating in and grappling with the effects of the various new ventures that are placing new economic pressures on the organization.

c. For many carriers, new facilities or services represent both a threat and an opportunity. For example, satellite business services might be viewed as potentially detrimental ways of bypassing the wire network and siphoning traffic from that network. These same services, however, also might be seen as a way of quickly meeting user demands for high-capacity, end-to-end services that overcome the problems and expenses of upgrading the "last mile" of an installed wire network. These services could provide carriers with an opportunity to explore the market for integrated digital services without undertaking a massive, risky program of investment in terrestrial facilities until market demand is proven.

3. The potentially conflicting interests of developed and developing nations also must be kept in mind. For developing countries, Intelsat is a particularly crucial organization; it provides many of these countries with their only source of international communication. Intelsat also permits many less developed countries to enjoy a more efficient domestic telecommunications system. The development of high-power satellite services, which can overcome the delay and expense of having to construct expensive and time-consuming local terrestrial distribution networks, also is important to less developed countries.

4. Movement away from Intelsat's policy of providing global

service on an average-price basis also may well be seen as detrimental to the interests of less developed countries, although it is consistent with the cost-based pricing objectives of at least some developed nations.

5. The development of limited competition in the international market has created conflicting pressures and the potential for discord among entities that once carried a set of more common interests into the process of planning international telecommunication facilities, particularly the Intelsat system. Market participants and government authorities face the formidable task of trying to bring the disparate forces into a more harmonious situation. Proponents of free-market principles contend that economic signals produced by competition will organize the market and resolve the conflicts. Skeptics of this notion would argue that some non-market intervention is still necessary, at least during the transitional period, as market participants attempt to grapple with the new pressures of competition.

6. The remainder of this paper examines how—if at all—evolving competitive forces might affect the current processes for making decisions about international telecommunications facilities.

III. LOOKING TO THE FUTURE: THE CHANGING CONCEPT OF "FACILITIES PLANNING" IN THE INTERNATIONAL MARKET

A. Is There a Need for Organized Planning Activities Outside of Specific Market Discussions?

1. Existing multinational processes for planning facilities, which were developed in the light of very different market conditions, are showing strain under the pressure of new competitive conditions. Stress is inevitable because international telecommunications—particularly where satellites are involved—is an inherently transborder activity that is substantially under the control of national authorities. With few exceptions, such as Intelsat, Inmarsat, and a number of regional entities, the development of the telecommunications market is dictated by national priorities. These priorities are not necessarily compatible, but they almost always are interrelated.

a. Disparities between national policies were more easily resolved in an earlier era. Differences in policies toward industry structure and competition were more limited. Demarcations between the domestic and international telecommunications sectors were sharper. A single dominant carrier—or a small number of international carriers—effectively established international telecommunications policy through correspondent relationships.

b. As noted throughout Section II of this paper, the process of policy co-ordination is now more complex. Operational and regulatory functions are being severed in a number of countries, and national priorities are becoming increasingly disparate. Multinational organizations are finding that a global consensus is more difficult to achieve. Intelsat clearly has struggled in its efforts to respond to the new satellite and cable initiatives of some of its members.

2. One option for attempting to minimize polarization among national administrations with differing philosophies is to reevaluate and reexamine thoroughly existing mechanisms for discussing and assessing facilities plans. Any such mechanisms need not—and almost certainly could not—require "global solutions" to market structure issues or prescribe "comprehensive facilities construction plans". Such mechanisms might, however, serve as fora for the multinational *discussion* of broad issues, such as how to provide affordable North-South services in a more competitive market; how the roles of multinational service providers such as Intelsat or Inmarsat might be modified; how potentially competitive national, regional, and international ventures might function in a single market; and whether ISDN plans will or should include both international cable and satellite facilities.

3. One benefit of such fora is that they could provide operational entities with more complete information and additional information about international market conditions than is currently available in bilateral discussions or negotiations.

4. Any multilateral mechanisms, however, necessarily would have to acknowledge the fragmented nature of the international arena—and its many centers of decisionmaking. Such mechanisms would not replace, but would undergird, the complex web of decisions by national authorities and entrepreneurs—sometimes acting unilaterally, and sometimes collaboratively. (This web of decisions really constitutes, and is sometimes described as, the "international facilities planning process".) These supplementary mechanisms would be intended to facilitate decisionmaking in a fragmented and decentralized setting by improving pricing "signals" and by offering an overview of market trends.

   a. Because national industrial, political, and economic priorities are at the core of national, regional, and international telecommunications policies, it is unrealistic to assume that any centralized, authoritarian planning or regulatory process could be workable or efficient—or even agreeable to many market participants.

   b. Decisions about plans for specific facilities or services will remain in the hands of the national or regional authorities—or with the relevant service providers. This "decentralization" of specific facilities decisions also permits users of telecommunications services to exert substantial influence on the service providers and carriers responsible for meeting their market needs. At the international level, user demands are likely to be too diffuse to exert any significant impact on market decisions.

5. Many of the participants in the current international telecommunications market are likely to view any effort to promote new or revitalized consultative mechanisms with skepticism and suspicion. These efforts might be viewed as impeding a transition now under way to a more

flexible, open, and decentralized process by which decisions about future international facilities plans would be made. Proponents of competition believe that economic pressures and market forces will stimulate any corrective measures necessary to counteract imbalances in the supply of and demand for international transmission facilities.

6. Many market participants also believe that the international market is not adequately structured to encourage (or even to require) that planning take place. Thus, additional interventionist policies are viewed as being unnecessary.

a. International cables, for example, historically have involved multinational "planning" discussions as part of the collective process by which such cables are constructed. The correspondent relationships that are central to cable (and to satellite) communication internationally ensure that there are bilateral—if not multilateral—discussions about particular facilities plans. The NACP, discussed above in Section II.C.1, has involved discussions about traffic forecasts, cable routing, and technology. Although the NACP formally involves only certain North American and European entities, participants have invited non-members to join in the planning, procurement, and installation of specific cable systems. Thus, the forum has produced multilateral discussions about facilities issues.

b. However, as new facilities arrangements evolve outside of historic market configurations (*i.e.*, without traditional "correspondent" agreements or outside of the NACP), activities that have acted as explicit or implicit "planning" mechanisms may prove less effective in the future.

7. Any discussion of "planning" in the international arena inevitably engenders controversy, as well as the potential for misunderstanding and confusion. The notion of planning can embrace a multitude of practices. Almost no-one believes that planning can be a prelude to centralized decisionmaking. Yet, it is not entirely clear that existing, fragmented international processes function as a decentralized decisionmaking structure in which market forces act as the regulating influences. Involved decisionmakers continue to be influenced by political pressures and motivated by particular policies and perspectives. Of course, such political and other non-economic considerations do not negate the impact of economic forces on the complex decisionmaking processes. One should not conclude, for example, that the international facilities arena is not a "market" because of the continued effects of non-market pressures. It is simply worth noting that this international arena is not a "market" in the conventional sense of the term.

a. Some believe that arrangements for international telecommunications facilities are best left unmanaged, so that evolving market forces can produce an appropriate state of equilibrium. Others believe that some type of intervention may be appropriate—particularly now, when national telecommunications agendas are so fluid and also so disparate—to help minimize the costs of change.

b. This paper is not intended to suggest that one view, as opposed to the other, is preferable. Rather, the discussion that follows explores whether there may be some usefulness in multinational, multi-dimensional processes that are concerned with international infrastructure issues. Recognizing, of course, that classic centralized planning is at odds with efforts to privatize and deregulate the telecommunications sector, the discussion considers how, if at all, non-market consultative mechanisms might function. The discussion essentially proceeds from the assumption that non-market considerations traditionally have been part of discussions about future international facilities plans. It also assumes that as a transition is made to an environment in which market forces play a more significant role, some intervention in the processes that produce decisions about international facilities will be necessary—at least to adjust and to modify past policies in light of new realities.

8. Thus, multilateral consultations might play a valuable role by focusing participants on how fluid national and regional situations are changing the environment and the context in which decisions must be made. There inevitably will be imperfections in the evolving international arena. Although these imperfections do not necessarily justify intervention, they can dull the impact of "market signals". For example, a political goal or an ideological commitment may cause market forces to go unheeded; in such an event, the market may not adjust itself as quickly or as efficiently as it otherwise might. In other cases, national and regional entities battling to define their spheres of influence in the changing market may pursue a particular result, regardless of market "signals".

a. For example, the U.S. enthusiasm for competition in the facilities market may seem to be generating a rush (or a "planned" rush) to construct new facilities. Such construction might be viewed by some as "unrealistic", in light of the current supply of international facilities. Yet, others view such construction plans as a vigorous entrepreneurial response to new market opportunities. From another vantage point, the approval of such initiatives by the FCC reflects a conscious policy decision to make real for other administrations the pressures of competitive market relationships.

b. Responses from other administrations also are based on a mix of economic and other considerations. In the same way that U.S. actions are driven in part by political and ideological objectives—as much as by "realism" about new forces at work in the international arena—responses from outside the U.S. may be geared to preserving the *status quo* or to slowing movement toward competitive markets. In addition, administrations with still-evolving views about the role of competition may be participating in newly competitive markets through entities designed for an environment of less rivalry.

9. In this situation, multilateral mechanisms may provide a forum for the analysis and discussion of the array of conflicting forces that are reshaping the current international environment. Existing regional and multinational processes, such as the NACP, Intelsat, or Eutelsat, may find

that they can serve as focal points for the consideration of disparate national objectives and transitional measures needed to respond to change. Rather than attempting to "direct" the market, these processes might merely reinforce the directions of the market. They might help market participants sort out which forces are attributable to economic activities and which are the result of other pressures.

B. Constraints and Opportunities for Multinational Processes Concerned with Facilities Decisions

1. If multinational processes can render less bewildering (at least to some players, particularly some of the smaller players) the centrifugal forces and fragmentation inherent in the international telecommunications arena, market participants might view this as a useful endeavor. A goal of any such process is not only to minimize the risk of waste—thereby maximizing the potential for innovation—in a competitive environment that cannot be centrally planned. It is also to remove obstacles to a smooth transition in adapting old procedures and policies to new realities. Over time, market forces are likely to adjust to and correct for imbalances in the supply and demand for international capacity; the process of correction, however, almost certainly will involve an intense struggle for market preeminence and considerable friction among entities with differing perspectives. Existing organizations, such as Intelsat or Inmarsat, which were not conceived as competitive entities, could suffer excessively because they are not, as yet, fully prepared to deal with a surge of competition.

2. Some proponents of a centralized planning forum might argue that one is necessary to guard against overbuilds that will ultimately impose on telecommunications users the costs of stranded investments. A centralized approach also might be useful, it is argued, to manage interconnection arrangements and to co-ordinate technical standards to ensure global connectivity. Technical issues, however, can be addressed by processes that do not mandate a uniform, worldwide array of facilities; linkages are essentially ensured by correspondent relationships that are central to the international telecommunications market. An additional rationale for centralized planning, some contend, is that it can "guide" the market to the most efficient mix of facilities. There are, however, a number of factors that may tend to work against the success of any such endeavor.

a. First, the search for an "efficient" supply of international facilities may be better handled on a decentralized than on a centralized basis. An international body attempting to make decisions about how to match supply and demand would be subject to so many conflicting signals that consensus almost certainly would be impossible to reach.

b. Second, the potential costs of overbuilds may not justify efforts to impose an overall limit on, or otherwise to regulate the construction of, international telecommunications facilities. The under-use of facilities is a concern only to the extent that entities or individuals other than the ones constructing or operating the idle facilities will have to pay for the stranded investment. Thus, for example, if a national monopoly carrier builds a facility that is under-used, there is a risk that the carrier will use its market dominance to charge higher rates as a way of offsetting the costs of the unprofitable facility. As national markets move toward competitive structures, however, excess capacity may induce price cuts and innovative service offerings designed to stimulate greater circuit use as readily as it would prompt price increases intended to cover the costs of under-used circuits.

3. As noted previously, multilateral mechanisms—not necessarily a single central "planning" or "consultative" body—may have a useful role in any transition from a less competitive to a more competitive market structure for international facilities. This is not to suggest, however, that such mechanisms have only a fleeting usefulness.

a. First, multinational discussions may well prove to be appropriate mechanisms for involving non-operating entities, such as regulatory bodies, in the dynamics of the international market. As a result, national regulatory decisions affecting the mix of international facilities may be made on the basis of a more broad-based view. The NACP has provided this benefit to the FCC, which is not involved in carrier negotiations over facilities plans.

b. Second, carriers and non-carriers may find these fora to be useful vehicles for holding exploratory and informal discussions with correspondents and competitors outside the pressures of commercial negotiations.

c. Finally, administrations that function under non-competitive or less competitive national policies may find these processes essential as continuing mechanisms for guarding against the risk of poor decisions on the construction and use of facilities.

4. Multinational fora might focus most productively on serving as collection and dissemination points for information about the international facilities market. They could provide national and regional decisionmakers with more comprehensive information about the economic conditions of the market that might be useful in making decisions about particular facilities. By reinforcing the market information that individual carriers and administrations are likely to have from their own bilateral and multilateral dealings, a co-operative multinational process could help to ensure that a mix of national, regional, and international conditions are factored into individual decisions. Such a mechanism would reinforce the workings of the evolving market, rather than attempt to replace them.

5. A useful objective may be to establish a middle ground between extreme policies, *i.e.*, between *dirigisme* that cannot be acceptable in a pluralistic international industry structure and strict adherence to a philosophy of non-regulation and non-intervention. In the international arena, the latter policy ignores the reality that the very co-existence of policies of regulation and deregulation requires a measured response by

decisionmakers—at least to guide the emergence of new international arrangements.

6. Because any multinational process, no matter how informal, involves some element of "centralization" and some potential to impede or inhibit the autonomy of entrepreneurial decisionmaking, it certainly will encounter resistance in an increasingly competitive marketplace. Success for such a process probably will depend entirely on the degree to which players with a competitive orientation can be persuaded that some multilateral activities will result in longer-term benefits.

   a. The greatest point of resistance is likely to center around efforts to collect traffic data, market projections, and facilities plans. Carriers and administrations almost certainly will consider some or all of this information of competitive significance. They are likely to resist requests to divulge such information to a multinational forum; asking that competitive strategies be shared candidly with competitors and potential competitors is not realistic. At the very least, any multinational process would have to take steps to guard the confidentiality of information, possibly by using a staff with no market allegiances to collect and analyze data that can subsequently be released in aggregate form.

   b. The usefulness of any consultative process in a competitive market would depend, of course, on its ability to gather accurate and comprehensive information from its participants. Given the competitive concerns noted above, some of which already impede the usefulness of processes such as the NACP and the satellite planning activities of Intelsat, future mechanisms certainly will face significant obstacles: competitive concerns will become even more substantial as market competition develops. These mechanisms will have to maintain confidentiality and provide assurances that any collected data would not be used to restrict or restructure the plans of individual participants.

7. The concept of any collaborative activity in a market moving toward a rivalrous mode of operation certainly might be viewed as misguided. However, this paper does not advocate multinational processes that would be either regulatory or *dirigiste* in design. Rather, it suggests that creating some avenues for competitors to enhance each other's market perspectives may help to smooth the transition to a competitive market (in the short term) and permit market participants to evaluate their activities in light of multinational objectives (over the longer term).

C. The Role of Regional Organizations

1. The variety of interests involved in the international telecommunications market almost certainly requires the co-existence of a number of different approaches to multilateral consultations on international telecommunications facilities. Even if a single dominant international process were to be feasible (which it clearly is not), regional bodies almost certainly would have a role in dealing with the economic and industrial goals

of specific geographic areas of the world. National administrations or other national regulatory bodies, of course, also would continue to plan or guide the development of domestic facilities and of certain international facilities.

2. Regional organizations may play an increasingly important role in consultative activities for a number of reasons. Broad-based market analyses almost certainly will have to take account of the possible uses of national or regional systems in providing international services. Regional organizations involved in the operation of such systems may be the best sources of information about the facilities and services offered.

3. Another advantage of regional fora is that they often involve a mix of industrialized and developing countries in a setting where conflicting concerns about pricing policies can be directly addressed. In such a setting, it may be possible to generate a more open dialogue about some of the policy choices that must be faced at the international level. These choices can then be communicated to participants in broader international fora.

4. There are, however, a number of difficulties in relying more on regional processes.

a. Regional organizations often have a special orientation to a particular technology or a specific issue. Eutelsat, for example, focuses exclusively on satellite services from a regional perspective. The European Commission does not deal actively with operational problems involved in international facilities planning. The consultative committee of CEPT, which usually is involved in transatlantic issues, has a perspective isolated from that of Eutelsat or other organizations dealing with intra-European communications issues.

b. Outside of Europe, regional organizations typically have limited resources and often lack any tradition of collaborating on telecommunications planning issues. Telecommunications administrations already have difficulty keeping up with the demands of meetings at the international level; it would be difficult to impose new burdens on these organizations.

5. Despite these possible drawbacks, the potential benefits are numerous. For example, one of the real difficulties faced by telecommunications officials in Southeast Asia, especially among less developed countries, is finding the resources and time to influence important global decisions. It may be useful to hold discussions on some important decisions in places that are easily accessible to policymakers from developing countries and to make available there officials from Intelsat and major national service providers, who can deal authoritatively with future facilities issues in the international arena.

D. The Importance of Technical and Technological Concerns

1. Discussions about the future shape of international facilities markets will have to take into account technical and technology-related concerns. Among these concerns are assessing the role of satellites in future

role of satellites in future ISDN networks and judging the impact of new developments in satellite technology on future facilities plans.

2. Technical issues may be particularly important as ISDN plans are developed.

a. One question is whether the development of national ISDN plans will affect the balance of satellite and fiber optic facilities used to provide international services. Some within Intelsat and other satellite-related organizations have been concerned that ISDN planning might limit the use of high-speed digital satellite services to trunking functions among a few centrally located national switches. For example, some believe that ISDN planning has been based on the premise that national administrations will attempt to use central switching nodes as the only interfaces for international services. In fact, however, IBS arrangements and new generations of satellites are designed specifically to deliver high-speed digital services to small earth stations located on or near the premises of the customer. A failure to anticipate this scenario in ISDN planning efforts could end up inhibiting the use of multipoint satellite networking services.

b. To the extent that digital satellite services are not included in the design and development of ISDN plans, carriers—particularly those in smaller or less highly developed countries in Europe and elsewhere—could be forfeiting a significant asset. These satellite services could foster the spread of ISDN services by allowing PTTs to test market demand without making substantial capital outlays to link together urban centers outside the initial terrestrial-based "islands" of ISDN activity.

3. Technical incompatibilities also could make interconnection of multipoint satellite networks at the international level extremely difficult. In Europe, for example, a large number of different ISDN field trials are being implemented. Many current plans are not fully consistent with the ISDN recommendations of the ITU's Consultative Committee on International Telegraph and Telephone (the "CCITT"). These differences, which the European Commission is working to combat as part of its RACE Program, illustrate the need for multinational co-ordinating efforts. However, co-operation must extend beyond the recent initiatives that the Commission has taken within Europe to promote ISDN standardization and must encompass other regions.

4. Multinational discussions also could examine broadly the future relationships between national terrestrial networks and international satellites. The development of onboard processing being studied in Europe, the United States, and Japan could enable satellites to function as effective links between terrestrial networks. The ability of satellites to allocate transmission capacity flexibly could make them useful switching nodes in network configurations with multiple traffic streams. This capability, which concentrates complex and expensive switching features in a single piece of equipment and permits the use of relatively simple earth stations, also might be applied to encourage the growth of corporate networks. Multinational discussions of these new roles for satellite systems could serve as

information and technology exchanges that would make national decision-makers more aware of the technological configurations being explored in particular markets.

5. As technological development allows satellites and cables to be used in increasingly competitive ways, decisions about the relationship between the two media will be determined substantially by competitive forces. Price and service characteristics, when communicated to users, will influence demand and shape supply. However, as noted previously, the continued impact of non-market forces on facilities decisions could cause distortions that are likely to be more significant—and, possibly, more severe—than they would be when competitive markets evolve more completely. Thus, multinational discussions could play a valuable transitional role.

6. Multinational fora could also study the efficiencies of using certain technologies in certain markets; the findings might assist decision-makers in judging the need for specific facilities. The ESA, for example, is examining the relative roles that mobile satellite services, mobile radio, and cellular communications systems might play in a comprehensive European mobile communications network. It is also looking at similar issues with respect to fixed network architectures. Such inquiries are likely to be the subject of broad international interest.

7. Technological developments can have an important impact on future projections about facilities plans. For example, there must be reliable means for assessing the impact of emerging satellite technologies involving steerable spot beams, onboard switching, and inter-satellite links. Processes that inform carriers about various technological developments can enhance the likelihood that market decisions will reflect market conditions more closely.

E. Possibilities for Enhancing Intelsat's Contributions to Planning Activities

1. Intelsat's Special Position in the International Market

a. Change in the international facilities market poses a unique challenge for Intelsat because, unlike national or regional entities, it cannot respond decisively to such change without broad multinational consensus. Whereas national or regional authorities can sometimes react quickly to changing conditions, Intelsat must first gain at least some consensus among its 110 members.

b. Due to its structure, which requires it to act in this consensus-building fashion, Intelsat functions as one very useful multinational consultative mechanism. It may be possible to augment or to adjust the consultative and planning aspects of Intelsat's existing operations to make them more directly responsive to the changing demands of the current international market. Such change could produce within the organization a capability to contribute to facilities planning activities in a broader international context.

c. This kind of change would not be without its difficulties. Because Intelsat continues to have a specific operational mission—providing affordable global satellite services for much of the world's population—it might have difficulty separating or shielding any planning activities from its own operational predilections or biases. Almost certainly, it will seek to promote the development and use of its own system; indeed, it would argue that the Intelsat Agreement obligates the organization to take such a position.

d. As a result, neither Intelsat nor any other operational entity can be a truly neutral collaborative forum. Nor, in a fragmented, rivalrous marketplace, is it realistic (as already noted) to think that a single forum could be either effective or credible. However, there may be ways to increase the long-range planning capabilities of specific entities such as Intelsat without having to resort to centralized planning efforts that would be destined to failure.

e. At present, Intelsat is focusing on ways to revise or adjust its operations to take account of new competitive forces. In addition to making operational changes, it has reviewed ways in which it might enhance its role as a planning organization. As noted in Section II above, Intelsat is already beginning to make some changes in the price of its transponders and in the form of its service offerings. It is concentrating on technologies and service considerations that it believes will satisfy future user needs. Intelsat is seeking to respond to perceived market needs in part by emphasizing digital transmission and switching features in a satellite-based ISDN and the use of higher-power satellites to communicate with less expensive earth stations.

f. The success of Intelsat's efforts will depend, in large part, on the receptivity of its members to the changes. Although Intelsat is an organization with a separate staff, its activities require consensus among, and the backing of, its members. Therefore, to the extent that members oppose some of the price and service changes being pushed forward, Intelsat—as an organization—is constrained. Some of its members have resisted certain of the proposed changes intended to move Intelsat into a more competitive posture due to fears that a more competitive orientation will jeopardize its role as a provider of affordable global satellite services.

i) Less developed countries in particular have been concerned about the potential impact of repricing and of attention to business services. Such trends reflect moves away from the kinds of subsidized price arrangements and trunk-route links upon which these countries have depended. In many instances, a number of developed nations have supported less developed nations in opposing or questioning moves toward a more competitive orientation for Intelsat.

ii) One question is whether the Intelsat staff, together with those members that support change, can convince the skeptics that change not only is inevitable, but also ultimately is for the best. For example, price adjustments now could well guard against the need for more significant adjustments later that could increase the price of thin-route services much more substantially. In addition, business networking services and other new offerings, although not always relevant to less industrialized regions of the world, may well be beneficial to them. These kinds of services present quick and relatively inexpensive ways for smaller countries to attract and satisfy the needs of larger corporate users. These services also can provide countries that have relatively antiquated local wire systems with a fast way of upgrading their networks to allow for interconnection with more sophisticated networks that offer valuable financial, medical, and educational information and transactional services.

g. The emphasis on the need for change should not be viewed as an argument that change will come easily or that resistance to change can be cast aside. Without a doubt, Intelsat is in a very difficult process of transition. It is an institution formed in an earlier era during which the provision of affordable global services was simpler because competitive pressures did not present as many potential obstacles. Intelsat's formidable task is to reorient itself without abandoning its stated purpose, as defined in the Intelsat Agreement.

h. The discussion that follows considers more concretely how Intelsat might adjust and enhance its planning role. Such adjustment could contribute not only to its effort to respond to the changing pressures of the international facilities market, but also to its value in multinational discussions about responding to changing international conditions.

2. Establishing a "Neutral" Process Within Intelsat for Planning Its System

a. Intelsat historically has functioned as a *de facto* satellite planning forum because its decisions have dictated the contours of the international satellite market. Its satellite circuits, which are planned to meet the aggregate anticipated needs of its members, have constituted the sole supply of international satellite links in an era when undersea cables were not always ready substitutes. But Intelsat has not had any direct input on decisions about the construction of cable facilities. Many Intelsat signatories, however, are also involved in cable construction decisions, creating at least an indirect link between the two facilities markets.

b. It is neither practical nor desirable for Intelsat to attempt to bring the approval of cable construction plans within its mandate. However, there certainly are benefits in an Intelsat strategic planning process that openly and dispassionately assesses the realities of current cable construction plans. By stressing to its members, and in other fora, the potential benefits to Intelsat of taking a more complete account of global

Chapter V The changing environment for planning international facilities

facilities plans, Intelsat might be able to gather more comprehensive information that could improve its system planning activities.

c. The success of efforts to enhance Intelsat's planning activities depends ultimately on its ability to make its planning decisions really matter to its members. Success may also require it to disconnect its planning role from its operational and entrepreneurial roles. Members must be convinced that openness about their facilities plans will not lead to situations in which Intelsat will use the data—wearing its "entrepreneurial hat"—in an "adversarial context" to block new construction initiatives. It may be unrealistic to expect that any institution can separate its planning and operational aspirations; in Intelsat's case, however, it may be useful to try to achieve this separation.

d. To develop a more comprehensive and useful planning function within its organization, Intelsat would have to increase the likelihood that its members will take its planning activities seriously. Intelsat also would have to make itself a more credible and acceptable planning forum. In short, it must foster the perception that it can function as a *bona fide* broker of market information in a complex and fragmented international arena.

e. To encourage its members to take its planning activities more seriously, Intelsat must provide its members with a real economic stake in system decisions. It must work to solidify its members' commitments to using forecast system capacity. As noted above in Section II.F, Intelsat's current cost allocation scheme permits members to walk away from use commitments with relatively little economic pain. This system needs to be changed.

i) A move toward offering TRUs and adopting other long-term commitment strategies would increase the stake that members would have in the Intelsat system. Although such long-term commitments are likely to encompass only a relatively small portion of Intelsat's total system capacity (since long-term commitments for thin-route transponders are likely to be scarce), they would still represent a step in the right direction. They would distribute the risk of under-use more directly to members and require members to evaluate more closely their real needs for system capacity.

ii) Another alternative that has been discussed is the concept of allocating transponder space according to a system of "notional" capacity. Under this scheme, the total anticipated capacity of a system satellite would be allocated to members *pro rata*; any residual capacity would be reserved for occasional use demands. This residual capacity could be sold off by any member, and the money collected for use of the residual capacity would be allocated to all members *pro rata*. The system, therefore, would allocate to members more direct responsibility for system use and would provide a direct incentive for them to promote additional use.

f. It may be more difficult—and more critical—to increase Intelsat's viability as an effective and "neutral" planning forum. Various important players must be convinced that Intelsat's views will not be biased by its entrepreneurial or operational objectives.

i) Achieving this result will not be easy; indeed, it may not be possible. One step in this direction, however, may be for Intelsat to change the tone and style of its participation in recent debates over international facilities authorization and construction decisions. Under its previous Director General, it took an adversarial and aggressively entrepreneurial approach to facilities issues; the approach did not emphasize its unique status as a co-operative organization. It remains to be seen how the new Director General will position Intelsat on these issues.

ii) It may be necessary, in fact, for Intelsat to differentiate more pointedly between its "operational" and its "planning"—or even "regulatory"—roles. It certainly is not necessary for Intelsat to be divided into two separate organizations—one for planning and one for operations—in order to ensure the presentation of distinct perspectives. However, there might be advantages in establishing greater compartmentalization among its various functions.

iii) For example, Intelsat's system planning activities might be separated from its business planning functions. Information gathered on proprietary facilities plans of international service providers might be submitted under confidentiality agreements and held separate from Intelsat's "operational" groups. Facilities planners might be precluded from using their experience and contacts to develop documentation that would be used by Intelsat's operational staff to oppose private satellite applications or to argue against private cable projects.

iv) Intelsat's planning roles might be joined in a separate part of the organization, with Intelsat staff being responsible for preparing recommendations relating to the co-ordination of applications by private satellite systems on technical or economic grounds.

v) The objective of such a reorganization would be to establish an independent process for deciding whether to accept an application for co-ordination of a transborder or transoceanic system. These requests often involve interests independent of, or even potentially in conflict with, one or more Intelsat members. To avoid the perception that the organization is acting to protect its own role as a service provider, rules might be adopted to establish an open and accountable process for handling any such controversies. Likewise, some concrete criteria and procedures could be adopted to facilitate the process of making determinations required under Article XIV(d) of the Intelsat Treaty.

vi) This kind of more formal process would require proponents of separate systems or transborder services to address directly the impact of their actions on Intelsat's operational viability. It could reduce concerns that Intelsat would be acting in an anticompetitive fashion by opposing a co-ordination request. The process also would require opponents of co-ordination requests to make their opposition more specific; general allegations that the viability of Intelsat is being threatened would not be adequate or persuasive. A more objective and formalized process might avoid some of the bitter debate that has surrounded the PanAmSat consultation process discussed above in Section II.C.2.

g. If Intelsat were to distinguish more clearly between its operational and its "regulatory" and "planning" roles, it also could enhance the way in which members and non-members perceive its system planning and regulatory activities.

i) Intelsat might seek to develop more well-defined procedures to adjudicate complaints concerning specific rates that it establishes. Although the Intelsat Agreement provides members with mechanisms for raising such issues, other mechanisms that resemble an independent regulatory process might be appropriate.

ii) More formal rate-setting methodologies, such as are common in certain national regulatory settings, also could be useful. Such a procedure might bring into the open some of the pricing plans and strategies of Intelsat—and the various choices behind such pricing policies. This process might lead to more transparency and predictability in Intelsat's rate structure. As a result, national administrations might be able to respond more directly to proposed pricing changes. The process could also be one way in which system users and entities other than representatives on the Intelsat Board could communicate their particular views to the organization.

iii) These steps would be not intended to transform Intelsat, or a part of it, into a formalized regulatory institution. Nor would such changes be intended to "legalize" its facilities planning activities. Rather, the adjustments are designed to enhance the "objectivity" and "neutrality" of the adjudicatory-type functions and planning activities for which the organization has responsibility under the Intelsat Agreement.

h. An enhanced planning process within Intelsat could well shed light on difficult controversies that affect the functioning of a unified global satellite system. The process might provide an independent perspective that is essential in formulating policy conclusions about the future of the market for international facilities. An improved system planning process within Intelsat also could benefit cable planning activities. If its system plans take into account some or all cable plans—because signatories become more willing or better able to provide cable information to Intelsat—satellite plans, which are relevant to cable plans, may more closely track market demand. If Intelsat's better planning helps to reduce its excess capacity, individual entities or other fora could look to its plans as a source of reliable assessments about future international traffic loads. Such entities or organizations could base their own plans, in part, on Intelsat's decisions, and vice versa. A more vigorous and realistic Intelsat planning process also could play a useful role in disseminating to signatories (and to others) broad-based information on conditions expected in the international market. In this way, changes within Intelsat could have effects outside the satellite system.

3. New Roles for Intelsat: Assessing Pricing and Technological Options and Acting as a Facilities Broker

a. A defined and separate planning process within Intelsat might eventually consider fundamental issues about the system's role in the international telecommunications market. The discussion of such issues would be more productive if held in isolation from Intelsat's entrepreneurial pressures.

b. The planning process could be opened up to new participants. Intelsat might explore new relationships with market players as part of the process of examining the international facilities market from less of an operational perspective.

c. One of the most important steps that might be taken initially would be to air various options for restructuring and de-averaging Intelsat's rate structures. Such a step almost certainly will be necessary to ensure that Intelsat circuits will be viable alternatives to fiber optic circuits. Intelsat, of course, has begun to explore new pricing strategies for particular services and offerings. However, it has been cautious—due to resistance within its organization and its own wariness about "private" systems—about promulgating far-reaching proposals for new rate structures. It might benefit, however, by setting out some of the options in an open process and seeking detailed comments from interested parties. It even might make available to various groups much of its traffic and operational data in an effort to foster the review of various pricing strategies. An operational entity might take such a step only reluctantly; however, a non-operational unit concerned with exploring planning options might find such a step appropriate.

d. Within this defined planning unit, Intelsat also could examine more actively what new system configurations might best serve thin-route traffic streams. In its operational role, it has already begun to explore various new satellite configurations that could serve as an alternative, or complement, to fiber optic cables. Such proposals rely upon high-power Ku-band satellites that would allow direct service to customer-premise earth stations. Intelsat's operational groups are likely to solicit system proposals from aerospace companies to meet specialized system needs. In its non-operational planning role, however, Intelsat might solicit proposals from national or regional systems to meet certain specific service requirements with existing or planned capacity.

e. The development of new relationships with national and regional facilities operators could lead to a fundamental change in Intelsat's role in the market—including its role as an operator. It might begin to move away from a role centering around the procurement of satellite capacity directly from manufacturers and seek to become more of a clearinghouse for facilities requirements articulated by its members. After identifying projected satellite needs, it could act in the role of a market-maker by matching offers of, and bids for, satellite capacity.

Chapter V The changing environment for planning international facilities 399

    f. Although it would not necessarily need to revise its traditional role in such a fundamental way, Intelsat—and its members—might find utility in examining other modes of procuring and planning for future system needs. Such an examination would be intended to develop operational plans that might fit more comfortably into the changing structure of the international arena.
    g. Over time, Intelsat could become less of a satellite system operator and more of a satellite system planner. This is merely one scenario for its future that may warrant closer examination.
    h. To implement this more open process on a broad scale, Intelsat also would have to weave its planning activities into a broader web of direct relationships. Formal input into its system planning decisions by non-members is limited at present; a broader scope of established contacts would be essential to the development of a more vigorous system planning process. Intelsat must have newly structured ties with many of the service vendors that use the facilities it supplies. Closer ties with end users also are important.
    i. The discussion that follows considers how the process of participating in Intelsat may need to be adjusted to reflect new realities of the international market.

4. Process of Participating in Intelsat

    a. To the extent that individual countries permit competition in the provision of international services, the adequacy of existing schemes for participating in Intelsat may need to be revisited.
        i) In the United Kingdom, for example, arrangements have been worked out for the collaborative participation of BTI and Cable & Wireless in Intelsat.
        ii) In the United States, as noted in Section II.E.3 above, there has long been criticism of Comsat's role as the sole representative to Intelsat; this criticism has been particularly pointed since the FCC decided to permit Comsat to offer end-to-end international services in competition with other U.S. carriers. The criticism intensified when Comsat announced its planned merger with Contel. It remains to be seen whether the merger, which appears to have been derailed, will ever be completed; as noted above in Section II.E.3, Contel has announced its intention not to proceed with the merger and, as of early May 1987, there was mounting evidence that the transaction was extremely unlikely to proceed. Comsat's role in Inmarsat could also change, as discussed above in Section II.E.3, due to the FCC's proposal to advocate competition in the provision of aeronautical services via Inmarsat. Although the FCC's proposal has drawn strong criticism from both market participants and the U.S. Government, it has focused attention on Comsat's role as the U.S. signatory to the Inmarsat Agreement. Collectively, these developments could well lead to a fairly broad reassessment of how the United States participates generally in co-operative multinational ventures.

iii) In Japan, KDD has been the representative of the Japanese Government in Intelsat. However, in the event of the approval of a new international carrier—and the authorization of international value-added services on a competitive basis—some new arrangements for representation in Intelsat might be required. In addition, the MPT will have to become involved as a referee of the perspectives of the various interested parties.

iv) A similar situation could develop in Canada, if the privatization of Teleglobe leads to the evolution of a competitive international market in Canada. Although the legislation implementing the privatization designates the privatized Teleglobe as the Intelsat and Inmarsat signatory for Canada, the legislation expressly notes the government's right to replace Teleglobe at any time.

b. The procedure by which its members express their views to Intelsat magnifies their differing perspectives. Intelsat's present structure involves members in efforts to communicate their national policies through their representatives on the Board of Governors. To do so, members must rely on instructional processes, in which various interested government departments and private sector interests arrive at a consensus position and develop a set of instructions that the national signatory to Intelsat is supposed to carry out through its votes within the organization. Because the Board must vote on issues that inevitably will find signatories having been instructed to support conflicting positions, dispute is built into the process; moreover, a signatory's instructions may have left it with little flexibility.

c. Movement by Intelsat toward a more unstructured planning process, in which conflicting views of carriers, non-carrier service providers, and end users may be worked out in an informal international process, could relieve some of this pressure. Such movement might diminish the degree to which entities not well represented by Intelsat signatories would feel excluded from a planning process. It also could increase the willingness of national administrations to broaden the participation in Intelsat, both directly and indirectly.

d. In the past, there have, of course, been barriers to such broadened involvement in Intelsat. For example, many Intelsat signatories believe that the end users are *their* customers—not Intelsat's—and that contact with such users is the responsibility of signatories. From this perspective, Intelsat is not and should not be involved in the direct marketing of its system capacity. However, a broad and non-operational planning process cannot be based entirely upon user and service provider input that is filtered through the perspectives of Intelsat's members, virtually all of whom are carriers.

e. As part of the effort to broaden involvement in planning discussions, efforts might be made to produce an annual report—or set of reports—about the status of the international facilities market. These reports could be forwarded directly to special meetings of the Board of Signatories or the Assembly of Parties. By comparison with the Board of

Governors, these representative bodies reflect the involvement of national officials with policy responsibilities broader than the management of international satellite services. Conveying planning information to these bodies might increase the likelihood that a common set of raw data—as well as an overview of, or even conflicting views on, facilities planning issues—would be put into the hands of a wide number of decisionmakers.

f. The value of broader participation in multilateral fora generally is discussed in the next section.

F. Broadening Participation in Multinational Fora That Have Been Limited to Carriers

1. Involvement of Non-operating Entities

a. Even as the international market moves from an essentially monopolistic to a more competitive structure, existing multinational planning fora still include principally carriers and administrations. This fact is understandable, as these entities are the ones that actually build and operate transmission circuits. However, as a competitive market model makes evident, supply decisions cannot be made by suppliers alone. Even though carriers also use their own circuits, the needs of non-owner users must be taken into account.

b. One important step toward changing this situation would be to include new non-operational entities in multinational planning activities. These entities, which set the policies that shape market conditions, can have as great an impact on the marketplace as operating entities that produce the demand for international facilities.

c. As national administrations have introduced competition into their domestic telecommunications markets, many have separated the regulatory and operational roles of entities that once served as the monopoly providers of domestic telecommunications services. Liberalization plans typically have involved the consolidation of administrative or regulatory functions in a non-operational entity. Thus, the service provider that was once the monopoly operator is not able to take into a newly competitive market the advantage of being the regulator of the terms of competition. Such non-operational entities might benefit tremendously from participation in various multilateral fora. They are not normally involved in actual business negotiations and, therefore, may be isolated from the market pressures being felt by foreign carriers and users. Their views of international developments may be filtered through national carriers, whose operational biases may influence their presentations.

d. The NACP, which involves participants from the United States, Canada, and CEPT, has been particularly useful, at least historically, for the FCC. Unlike European administrations, the FCC has no involvement in the actual business of providing international service; thus, it has not been a party to correspondent agreement negotiations. As a result, the

NACP has been a vital source of contact for the FCC with foreign administrations and carriers.

e. As the operational and regulatory responsibilities of monopoly carriers continue to get separated (having occurred in the United Kingdom and being discussed in France and the Netherlands), the international market may benefit even more by bringing new regulatory or government entities into discussions of international policy issues.

2. Special Role for End Users and Non-carrier Service Providers in Multinational Planning Fora

a. An important aspect of any multinational process is to ensure the effective participation of facilities users (both end users and service providers that do not own transmission facilities).

b. Users can express their preferences regarding the construction and use of international transmission facilities in a variety of ways. They may communicate their views indirectly, through business decisions; a large multinational corporation, for example, may express its dissatisfaction with the regulations or policies of an administration by moving its communications hub or its offices to another country. They can also communicate directly; an end user might select one service provider over another because only one can offer service to a small, customer-premise earth station. In both of these instances, however, market signals are "transmitting" the user's choice. A consultative process intended to be responsive to market signals must take into account more directly the demands and desires of non-owner users of transmission facilities.

c. Users are not directly involved in the Intelsat, the NACP, or the CEPT and Eutelsat planning processes in Europe. Carriers and governments are relied upon to represent the needs and preferences of users in their respective countries. Users' interests, however, may not always be congruent with those of carriers or administrations, although such interests often are quite significant and, ultimately, can have substantial impacts on facilities configurations. For example, if users want to minimize distribution costs or to have greater control over their own facilities, they might advocate the deployment of international satellite facilities capable of serving small, customer-premise earth stations (meaning that higher satellite transmission powers will be needed). Carriers or administrations, however, may want to retain greater control over access points or may have reasons for wanting to have international traffic routed over the public network before being delivered to users' premises.

d. Other user concerns also may be difficult to address. A multinational corporation, for example, may want the option to use a single network for communications among various locations in Europe and North America; it might not want to operate separate networks for international and regional services. Such a desire, however, may run contrary to the wishes of a national or regional authority. If the user's views on network configurations are injected into a planning process only after being "filtered" through the screen of priorities and preferences of a national or regional authority, that user's perspective on the evolving market may never be communicated effectively. As a result, entities other than the national or regional authority contacted by the user could have little opportunity to evaluate and either accommodate or reject the network configuration being requested.

e. User interests might be injected into the planning and co-ordination processes in a number of ways. Large user groups, such as INTUG (at the international level), could be invited to participate in planning fora. Meetings among administrations, carriers, and users also might be structured as part of a formal process; although such meetings certainly would happen in the context of discussions about particular service arrangements, meetings specifically called to address long-range planning issues might be developed as an integral part of some international planning mechanism.

IV. CONCLUSION: GRAPPLING WITH THE PRESSURES OF NEW COMPETITION

A. Existing arrangements for the construction and operation of international telecommunications facilities are being subjected to great strains.

1. Technological developments are changing the capabilities of both undersea cables and satellites. Fiber optic cables can be used as high-capacity links between major traffic centers and can be "branched" to serve a number of countries on both sides of an intercontinental link. Satellites can be used to provide various multipoint business services directly to a user's premises, to accelerate the introduction of new digital services, and even to back up fiber links with high-capacity trunking capabilities.

2. These new technological capabilities are demanding a reassessment of accepted ways of pricing international telecommunications services, particularly those routed over satellite circuits. Fiber optic circuits, for example, constitute a challenge to Intelsat's price structure, which has been based on a commitment to ensuring that universal service is provided at averaged prices. Developments in satellite services also exert pressure on the pricing of cable services. The availability of satellite service directly to a user's premises unsettles long-standing relationships between users and the entities that serve as representatives to Intelsat. Ultimately, these satellite business services offer competition for services provided over terrestrial networks as well, thereby putting pressure on the prices of such terrestrial services.

3. Changes in the policies of a number of countries (including the U.S., the U.K., and Japan) toward competitive entry in the international sector are producing pressures to lower the overall level of

prices of international services. Among other things, these new national policies are encouraging new entities to compete internationally with established carriers through the installation of separately owned facilities, such as the new cable links that Cable & Wireless intends to construct around the world. Proposals for new private fiber optic cables are undoubtedly accelerating plans by groups of carriers for the introduction of new cables, such as TAT-9 and the proposed TPC-4.

    4. At the same time, proposals for new intercontinental private satellite systems and the possibility that various national or regional satellite systems could offer intercontinental or transborder services on a more extensive basis are placing additional strains on the pricing structures and on long-standing relationships in the international telecommunications arena.

    B. Against this backdrop, the means by which countries participate in the international telecommunications market are changing, thus altering the identities of participants and the relationships among those participants. These changes further complicate the process of adjustment in the international environment.

    1. Changes in national industry structures are blurring traditional distinctions between international and domestic service providers. As a result, policymaking is more complex, because once disparate market sectors now are more closely connected.

    2. Also, new entry into the international market has changed the conditions by which business is conducted internationally. As the number of service providers increases, for example, long established arrangements for participation in Intelsat are coming under increased scrutiny. The development of, and the potential for, competition have produced a perceived need to separate operational and policy responsibilities of international carriers, many of whom have served as signatories to the Intelsat Agreement. Once preeminent, or at least highly influential, in the international policy process relating to Intelsat, Comsat, KDD, British Telecom, OTC (A), and Teleglobe (to focus on some major representatives in Intelsat) now are faced with independent government policymakers taking an ever increasing interest in policies in the international field.

    C. Also against this backdrop, facilities owners and operators are being forced to respond to new and more vigorous market demands. Large users of telecommunications services have taken an increased interest in the cost, availability, and capabilities of international facilities. In a number of countries, new types of service providers (described in detail in Chapter II on "Boundary Lines"), that are playing the role of intermediary between users and the providers of underlying facilities, are having an increasing impact on the demand for international services.

    D. Decisions about telecommunications facilities also have become entangled more frequently in disputes over international trade. Thus, the U.S. and the U.K., which have been strong advocates of unrestrained market competition, have been active in urging intervention to remove perceived barriers to competition. Trade discussions have spawned new *ad hoc* negotiating arrangements—some of which have focused on plans for new private cables—that threaten to supplement existing, more established procedures for dealing with facilities plans.

  E. Because all of these factors—and others described in detail in this paper—are changing the environment in which international facilities arrangements have been worked out, it would seem inevitable that existing planning mechanisms, such as the NACP and Intelsat (at least with respect to its own system), would need to be reexamined and reevaluated.

  F. This paper considers a number of approaches for coping with the changing international scene. It assumes that no centralized planning process is likely to be successful. It recognizes that any international facilities "process" has been, and will continue to be, very decentralized. Any "process" inevitably will be influenced substantially by disparate national policies and by distinct centers of entrepreneurial decisionmaking.

  G. It would be difficult, however, to adopt an entirely non-interventionist stance toward the complex web of arrangements that constitute the "process" by which decisions about international telecommunications facilities are made. At the very least, adjustments must be made in many existing national regulatory policies, as well as in some of the arrangements undergirding multinational institutions, such as Intelsat. To cope with just these kinds of adjustments, there may well be a need for some multilateral processes designed to analyze and deal with issues of transition from the old environment in which arrangements and policies were framed to the new environment that is now evolving.

    1. Such processes may help to create consensus—among the diverse group of service providers from industrialized and developing countries—regarding needed changes in existing arrangements for providing and pricing international services.

    2. Such processes would focus their attention on exchanging information concerning traffic projections and facilities plans (for cables, as well as for national, regional, and international satellites). They also would discuss regulatory policies and perspectives that affect decisions about international facilities.

    3. Such processes would not involve formal meetings to make decisions or to bind otherwise independent and autonomous decisionmakers.

  H. An entirely non-interventionist stance also is difficult to reconcile with the growing interrelationship of telecommunications and trade issues. Policymakers will have to look very closely at how they might square *ad hoc* pressures exerted in trade talks with existing, more evolutionary, procedures for working out arrangements to construct and to operate international telecommunications facilities. The right mix of reliance on market forces and of intervention to assure the effective functioning of the international market will almost certainly require a delicate balancing of ingredients. In short, it may be increasingly difficult to discuss issues relating to international facilities planning in stark terms, *i.e.*, a policy of "interventionism" versus a policy of relying on market forces.

I. A number of the proposals outlined in this paper would affect the future role of Intelsat in the international market. Like proposals for multilateral consultations and exchanges of information generally, they may be viewed with skepticism from many quarters. They are intended, however, to respond to the growing tension between Intelsat's operational duties and its responsibilities to deal with sensitive competitive issues relating to the pricing of its services and the relationship between its own system and proposed separate international satellite systems. Due to the extent to which Intelsat is bound up in the many interrelated parts of the international arena, any examination of one also must involve a broad look at the other. This paper is intended to contribute to such a wide-ranging inquiry.

CHAPTER VI
TELECOMMUNICATIONS STRUCTURES IN THE DEVELOPING WORLD: AN ESSAY ON TELECOMMUNICATIONS AND DEVELOPMENT

TABLE OF CONTENTS

		Page
I.	Introduction	409
II.	The Core Problem: A Lack of Resources	410
III.	The Experience of India	413
	A. The National and Sectoral Backdrop	413
	B. A Formidable Set of Obstacles	414
	1. System Deterioration	414
	2. The Strains of Over-Use	415
	3. Unsatisfied Demand Drains Resources	416
	C. Preventing Siphoning: A Hybrid Offering in the Computer Sector	417
	D. Structural Innovations: The Response to Rivalry and to Demands for Efficiency	418
	1. Telecommunications Consultants India Limited	418
	2. New Institutional Structures for Local and International Services	419
	3. New Business Services	421
	E. Responsiveness to Business Users' Needs	422
	F. The Challenge of Network Upgrading: Planning, Finance, and Joint Ventures	424
	1. The Planning Process	424
	2. Finance and Access to Foreign Exchange	425
	3. Joint Venture Activities	426
	G. Some Observations on a Long-Term Strategy	427
IV.	The Malaysian Experience	429
	A. The National and Sectoral Backdrop	429
	1. The Telecommunications Sector	429
	2. Program for Network Upgrading	430
	3. Cellular System	431
	4. The Planning Process	431

		Page
	B. Structural Innovation: Privatization of Jabatan Telekom Malaysia	432
	1. Privatization: The Plan	432
	2. International Structural Issues	434
	3. Flexibility in Structure and Financing	434
	4. Competition in Services	435
	C. An International Strategy: Hubbing	435
	D. Some Additional Observations on a Long-Term Strategy	436
V.	The Experience of Indonesia	437
	A. National and Sectoral Backdrop	437
	1. Physical Obstacles	437
	2. The Five-Year Plans: Catching Up	437
	3. Technological Solutions	438
	B. A Question of Competing Priorities	438
	C. Problems of Financing and Planning	439
	D. A Legal Solution to Conflicting Priorities	440
	E. Relationship of Domestic and International Service Providers	441
	F. Some Concluding Observations	442
VI.	Conclusion	442

CHAPTER VI
TELECOMMUNICATIONS STRUCTURES IN THE DEVELOPING WORLD: AN ESSAY ON TELECOMMUNICATIONS AND DEVELOPMENT

I. INTRODUCTION

As major industrialized nations are reviewing and changing telecommunications policies, their actions are being closely watched in the developing world. Some of the forces that are causing such reviews to take place are also being felt by developing nations. Phase I of the Study of Telecommunications Structures began to document how national developments are interrelated, how national policies both affect the policies of other nations and are felt in the international environment. Phase II has extended that analysis. This essay is a further step in that effort; it begins to suggest how the changes in the industrialized countries are perceived and how they have an impact in the developing world.

The developing world, however, in addition to confronting the pressures that are being faced in the industrialized nations, must also address its own set of issues and problems. Massive and complex problems of underdevelopment, underfinancing, and over-utilization of the network infrastructure do not generally beset the industrialized world. They are, however, as development specialists well know, at the core of developing telecommunications infrastructures in the less developed nations.

Given the magnitude and complexity of these problems, this essay can be only exploratory in nature. Several countries of the developing world were visited in the course of Phase II—India, Malaysia and Indónesia. In these countries and others, global pressures are addressed and solutions adapted to particular national circumstances. Although it would be irresponsible to generalize from those national experiences to describe a set of "Third World" issues, it may be useful to set out some observations that might be relevant to policymakers in the less industrialized world.

In addition, politicians, economists, and decisionmakers in the developed world might find this perspective useful to understanding the particular set of problems outside their immediate spheres. Identification of some differences and common features with regard to problems and approaches facing the developing world may help to narrow the gap between telecommunications administrations of the North and the South, separated as they are by both grand differences in experience and a dearth in the flow of information. This essay then, it is hoped, may stimulate the industrialized world into taking initiatives to assist in enhancing the capabilities and resources of some administrations in the developing world.

II. THE CORE PROBLEM: A LACK OF RESOURCES

It belabors the obvious to state that the core problem in developing a telecommunications infrastructure is the overwhelming lack of resources that are available. Although administrations in the industrialized world are facing budgetary constraints and enormous capital outlays for infrastructure upgrading, their problems pale in comparison with administrations in countries attempting to develop a basic infrastructure.

The overarching question is one of fierce competition for the scarce resources that do exist. The sectors of health and sanitation, transportation, education, agriculture, and housing may all have a claim on funding as good as, if not better than, telecommunications. At some level, of course, this matter of priority is political: people vote or are agitated to action at a fundamental level by starvation and illness, not telephone service.

At another level, however, the question is one of economics: the case can be made that investment in telecommunications is closely tied to improvements in the basic economy, with significant benefits from such investments redounding to the other core sectors. Policymakers from the telecommunications sectors, however, have been hard put, as a qualitative or quantitative matter, to make the connection between telecommunications development and improvement in the economy as a whole.

This is not to say that efforts to draw the linkages between improvements in telecommunications and overall economic performance cannot be attempted or are doomed to be futile. The ongoing work of the World Bank, in particular, has been enormously useful in this regard. The Maitland Commission, in its 1984 report *The Missing Link*, contributed a great deal to the understanding of the complex nature of the relationship between telecommunications and economic growth. *See The Missing Link: Report of the Independent Commission for Worldwide Telecommunications Development*, (1984) Chapter I. Indeed, many of the works cited in Appendix XI of *The Missing Link* have, in specific national or regional situations, traced the economic and social benefits that telecommunications can confer.

More generally, in their World Bank publication *Telecommunications and Economic Development*, Robert J. Saunders, Jeremy J. Warford and Bjorn Wellenius have produced the landmark work in the area. R.J. Saunders, J.J. Warford and B. Wellenius, *Telecommunications and Economic Development* (Baltimore: Johns Hopkins University Press, 1983). Yet, even that book concedes that the complexity of the relationship between telecommunications investment and economic activity is great and that the benefits from a project or investment program cannot readily be quantified. *Id.* at 143. In some parts it proceeds by looking at telecommunications as an input commodity for other sectors (transport and health, for example). And, at one point, given the complex dynamic between overall economic growth and investment in telecommunications, the work comes to focus on the microeconomic benefits of such investment. (The Maitland Commission also acknowledged that it may be difficult to quantify the benefits of an efficient telecommunications system in both individual cases and nationally. *The Missing Link*, at 9–10.)

Apart from *Telecommunications and Economic Development*, however, much of the work to date has not looked at the benefits to an economy, as a whole, from an improved telecommunications infrastructure; the literature, in general, is rather more directed at evaluating the benefits of telecommunications in a project-specific and anecdotal way. Nevertheless, significant work has been done in the area of trying to develop models to quantify the economic benefits from investment in telecommunications. Although it is beyond the scope of this essay to review that literature comprehensively (much of it is cited in the bibliographies of *The Missing Link* and *Telecommunications and Economic Development*), two examples might briefly be mentioned here.

In the early 1980s, British Telecom commissioned a long-range study on the additional benefits for the U.K. from different levels of investment in telecommunications. It was estimated that the productivity gain to business users would grow significantly to the year 2000, with concomitant improvements for employment, the balance of trade, and consumer benefits. The quantitative—albeit very tentative—conclusion of the study was that a high-growth domestic strategy for developing and marketing services could produce a ratio of economic benefits to costs as high as 7:1 in the U.K. *See* J.B. Cowie, "Communications Developments—Some Pointers for Africa", at 2 (Paper presented at the ITU's Africa Telecom '86 conference).

Similarly, for Africa, one study concluded with respect to Kenya that efficient telecommunications could significantly improve revenues for business users by facilitating business expansion. Potential benefits could be realized in other sectors also, including health, transport and agriculture. *See* C. Jonscher, CSP International, "The Contribution of the Communications Sector to African Development" (Paper for the Economic Commission for Africa, July 1983).

Nevertheless, such studies, good as they are, are all too infrequent. Generally, they may be insufficiently relevant in assisting national planners—laboring within precise national constraints—to argue for increasing the allocation of national economic resources to the telecommunications sector. Planners in the developing world are left, therefore, with a lack of data with which they could otherwise appreciate or fully grasp the quantitative benefits of domestic investment in telecommunications for other sectors.

Once funding is allocated to the telecommunications sector, however, additional questions of priority must be faced. The most important of these, it would seem, is one of social equity: how to divide resources between rural and urban areas. The political imperative of universal service may tilt funding toward the areas with no or minimal service; it is costly, and not very remunerative, by and large, to serve these regions. Of course, the most lucrative regions are urban and commercial; service to large businesses and cities is necessary to raise the revenues to fund further infrastructure development. In addition, service to those sectors may be a greater stimulus to economic growth.

Another question of priority is based on the technological choices that may be available. Should resources be spent on cable or satellite? On trunk or exchange lines? On new business services? On developing indigenous switches? The answers to these questions are not so much matters of engineering. Rather, they are closely tied to politics and, more importantly, to specific, overall national development strategies.

Beyond decisions about how the infrastructure should be constructed, the basic question is how to justify substantial investment in the telecommunications sector at all. In many cases, telecommunications administrations must take a nation's scarce foreign exchange to purchase foreign-made network equipment. Decisions to do so must be cleared by ministries of finance or trade—which introduce yet another "non-telecommunications" factor into the determination of whether and how to develop the infrastructure. The involvement of other ministries, however, may also be necessary or beneficial in heightening the level of decisionmaking or raising the amount of political attention paid to the sector.

Once there is a broad, public, and political commitment to devoting resources to the telecommunications sector, policymakers in the developing world are charged with formulating strategies to enhance the effectiveness and value of those investments. To do so, they may embark on a variety of structural models to provide service to the sector. The options that are being debated and implemented are not unlike those being explored in the industrialized countries.

This essay canvasses some of those options. By doing so, however, it neither intends to suggest that this preliminary inquiry is comprehensive nor argues in any way that there is a single correct solution or set of solutions. Instead, this essay is built on the leitmotif of the rest of the Study of Telecommunications Structures; for the developing world, like the industrialized nations, a range of alternatives exists and may be appropriate, depending on geography, culture, political structure, and the organization and health of the national economy. This assessment, then, is intended to explore the relationships between institutional or industry structure, organizational efficiency, and the development of new or additional financial resources.

III. THE EXPERIENCE OF INDIA

A. The National and Sectoral Backdrop

From several vantage points, India is unique in the developing world. Obviously, it has an enormous population: of 735,000,000 people, a full 570,000,000 live in some 578,000 villages. As an historical matter, there has been significant under-investment in the telecommunications sector in India. At the present time, for example, there are four million access lines, with about the same numbers of telephone stations, in the country.

To a degree almost unparalleled among the developing nations, India is endowed with tremendous resources with which it could develop its telecommunications sector. It has a significant industrial base, with substantial government and private enterprise. (Indeed, the Indian GNP is the twelfth highest in the world.) There is, therefore, a relatively large—and essentially untapped—indigenous demand for quality communications services.

India's primary resource, however, is undoubtedly its people. There is a reservoir of highly skilled technical, operational, and managerial personnel throughout much of the country. India has its own satellite system, for example, INSAT, which was developed and launched by the sophisticated Indian Space Research Organization in conjunction with the Department of Telecommunications ("DOT").

India has several domestic manufacturing facilities that produce telephone switching and terminal equipment. The largest of these is Indian Telephone Industries Ltd. ("ITI"), established in 1948, and with a strong research and development base at Bangalore and at Naini in Uttar Pradesh; ITI recently completed a factory in Mankapur to produce E10-B electronic switches under license from CIT-Alcatel. Other large manufacturers include Hindustan Cables, Ltd. and the Electronic Corporation of India, Ltd. The Telecommunications Research Centre ("TRC") focuses on major project and equipment specifications and network planning. The Centre for the Development of Telematics ("C-DOT"), which is jointly owned by the Department of Electronics and the DOT, is developing a family of switches using indigenous technology, including a switch designed to serve rural areas.

In related fields, India is an exporter of software. It has a very visible presence worldwide in telecommunications, where it shares its expertise with other developing countries through Telecommunications Consultants India Ltd., an agency within the DOT. It also has drawn on well-trained engineers to develop a "Silicon Valley" in Bangalore. In short, India has extremely valuable human resources at its disposal.

Another remarkable and important advantage is the fact that the Indian economy is essentially unburdened by foreign debt. Thus, it has the credit rating and the financial standing to borrow from abroad to develop its telecommunications infrastructure. The lack of foreign debt, however, is a product of a fiscal conservatism that makes it difficult for the DOT and some in the Planning Commission to justify increased investment in the telecommunications sector.

Other countries may not have the same opportunities and advantages that India enjoys. But India also faces serious economic constraints in developing a telecommunications infrastructure; these constraints, plus the sheer magnitude of the task, make the Indian experience relevant to other countries in the developing world. New structures and institutional solutions are being devised in India; these may well prove useful paradigms that other nations might be able to adapt to their own national environments.

B. A Formidable Set of Obstacles

Indian policymakers, nonetheless, must confront a set of obstacles that can best be described as daunting, if not formidable. It would be difficult to recount them in detail; such a task is beyond the scope of this essay. Instead, it may be sufficient to recount some of the problems with the infrastructure in an effort to illustrate a set of harsh realities that may be typical of other nations with less- or underdeveloped infrastructures.

1. System Deterioration

About one-third of the telephones in India are concentrated in two of the four largest cities—New Delhi, the capital, and Bombay, the most populous city. (The other two metropolises are Calcutta and Madras, which have approximately another one-third of the country's telephones.) The exchange plant in these two cities is extremely antiquated. Some of the local loops were installed several decades ago under British rule. At that time, the wiring was simply laid under the streets; it was not protected from physical deterioration or damage by enclosure in underground conduits.

In densely populated areas, such as some parts of Old Delhi, for example, the urban congestion is so great that it would be extremely difficult to excavate the streets to upgrade existing plant. Furthermore, such excavation is likely to create practical problems not unlike those faced during the construction of other underground installations; in the outskirts of cities such as Bombay, for example, an itinerant community will gather around an excavation project for an underground sewer. Such projects may, as a practical matter, be required to make use of the labor available in this new community. Undertaking a massive project involving cable installation could well necessitate the expenditure of resources on the local community.

With the passage of time and, in particular, the extraordinary growth of these major cities, the condition of the local plant is grave. Much of it has deteriorated, and the absence of conduits has made the process of supplementing or replacing it quite difficult.

2. The Strains of Over-Use

The most important and overwhelming characteristic of the Indian telephone system, at least in the urban areas, is the extraordinary demands placed on the local plant. This phenomenon of severe over-use is well-known to policymakers in the developing world. The endemic and severe nature of the problem, however, may be less well grasped by those in industrialized countries.

Such over-utilization is, of course, typical of administrations with limited local facilities, particularly those in the developing world. In India, however, with its quickly developing economy, its enormous population, and its rapid urbanization, the strain on the local network has become unbearable.

Operational personnel at the DOT estimate that the use of the Indian local plant is approximately two or three times that of local facilities in major industrialized countries. They note that the calling rate in India might be fifteen calls a day per station, but could be closer to twenty-five or thirty calls. Resources are unavailable to add exchange access lines to the system and, in many cases, the trunk systems could not handle additional lines in any event. Thus, the registered list of those waiting for a telephone (with a waiting list of five years forecast for 1990 and a substantial registration fee to be paid in advance) numbers nearly one million.

The critical problem for policymakers in India, therefore, is how to close the ever-widening gap between pressing demand and scarce supply. What makes the problem even more vexing is that the cycle of demand and deterioration is self-perpetuating.

The shortage of sets and lines creates two situations that encourage over-use. First, because individuals and businesses cannot readily add telephones, each installed station serves a much larger number of people than is the case in the industrialized world. Thus, telephones are, to exaggerate a bit, seldom at rest during the business day.

Second, over-utilization, in turn, breeds conduct that is not unfamiliar to users in industrialized countries who encounter a busy line. The caller begins sequential dialing in an effort to seize the local line once it becomes disengaged. These repetitive calling attempts, but not completions, also generate busy signals that frustrate others attempting to reach the original caller. In an attempt to get through to the party called, some subscribers resort to automatic dialling equipment, which further exacerbates the number of busy signals in the system.

All these calls, of course, rapidly tie up the local circuits. More importantly, they consume the capacity of the local switching facilities. Due to the extremely high calling volume, for example, one of New Delhi's newest and most advanced electronic switches operates at approximately one-half its designed capacity for handling local calls.

The massive congestion of the system inevitably accelerates the deterioration of the plant, which is already at a critical stage. Such sustained use wears out the plant far more quickly than is the case where capacity is adequate.

3. Unsatisfied Demand Drains Resources

The under-financing of the system and the unsatisfied demand exacerbate the difficulties confronting administrations in the developing world in yet another way. As the business sector expands, it requires telecommunications capacity. National administrations, such as the DOT, with competing demands for their scarce resources, may not be able to satisfy those requirements. If those administrations are unable to provide adequate telecommunications facilities, commercial concerns may find themselves having to make alternative arrangements. (The analogy in the developed world, of course, is bypass: if the price of local service is not correlated to cost, large users may be motivated to bypass the local network.)

An inability to devote resources to the telecommunications sector, therefore, may have the effect of further eroding the ability of administrations to obtain revenues from the business sector. In the Indian economy, for example, many industries are public sector enterprises. The Steel Authority of India, Ltd. ("SAIL"), the Oil and Natural Gas Commission, and the Indian Railways are government businesses; they have been able to accumulate the resources that they need to install their own telecommunications systems.

The Steel Authority is proposing a system called SAIL Net, which is now in a study phase. The system would have both voice and data capability.

The Oil and Natural Gas Commission has constructed a fiber optic link from eastern India across the country; due to the low traffic on the route, and the widespread nature of the coverage that was required, the DOT concluded that it could not provide the necessary capacity on an economic basis. Although the cost of the network is tremendous, and far too high to be funded by the DOT, it is a relatively insignificant amount for the company itself.

The Indian Railways has recently awarded a contract to Detecon, the international consulting subsidiary of the Deutsche Bundespost, to design and install an advanced, all-digital communications system. This system is intended to handle and co-ordinate the flow of freight. Some observers estimate that the cost of this network will approach $1.2 billion; with the low traffic volume involved, the DOT again felt that it would be unable to supply the services economically. Nevertheless, the proposed network, which could link manufacturers and their distribution chains, could serve shippers and carry messages not related to freight.

One of the ironies of under-investment, then, is that it tends to breed duplicative investments by the public sector, which can generate and retain resources to install their telecommunications facilities.. There is considerable feeling within the DOT that these private networks are wasteful and should not be permitted. That is, given the scarcity of the resources available to the DOT, the thought is that the amounts expended by public sector enterprises—which are amounts that are part of the national allocation of the Planning Commission—should be allocated directly to the telecommunications sector.

The proposed networks are also criticized for their inefficiency; it is likely that they will be significantly under-utilized unless they are allowed to handle other traffic. The amounts involved may appear small when contrasted, for example, with the total revenues of the Indian Railways; cumulatively, however, the DOT's view is that the expenditures on alternative networks are likely to be huge.

Under Section 4 of the Indian Telegraph Act of 1885, as amended, the DOT has the authority to approve the installation of new lines and interconnections. Certain powers to license telecommunications facilities are retained by the Government of India, but virtually all the powers are permanently delegated to the DOT. The residuum of power retained by the government could be exercised by the Minister of Communications; the DOT is integrated within the Ministry, however, and the prevailing view of those within the DOT is that it could prevent non-DOT public correspondence services from being offered.

Thus, with respect to the proposed Indian Railways network, there would be nothing to prevent a shipper from physically delivering a message to the railway network and having the railway network deliver it to another party. The DOT would have the legal authority to prevent users from attaching their terminals to the network or to prevent the railway from offering a public correspondence service. Its resources for monitoring and enforcement are, of course, scanty at best. Moreover, the DOT does not necessarily have the financial leverage to back up its legal authority.

C. Preventing Siphoning: A Hybrid Offering in the Computer Sector

One of the most interesting developments in India is the offering of a value-added service that combines the telecommunications expertise of the DOT with the interest of the Department of Electronics ("DOE") in advancing the development of the computer and information processing industries. Computer Maintenance Company Ltd. ("CMC"), a Government of India undertaking organized under the DOE, is established in large cities to provide maintenance service to the users of all imported systems of all vendors, including IBM, in case the user does not want to undertake self-maintenance. CMC does not operate any computers unless it is the user of those systems.

Although its expertise is primarily in hardware, CMC is now trying to establish a computer processing network to serve three or four cities across India. Access to this proposed system, called "Indonet", would principally be through the packet-switched public data network.

Apparently, the plan is not to link the CMC agencies themselves through leased circuits. One view of this service, then, is that the CMC would be providing nothing more than remote access data processing capacity on a time-sharing basis. This scenario would not involve the CMC in the creation of a network *per se*.

Others believe, however, that the system being implemented by the CMC is more sophisticated. User computer terminals are to be connected via terrestrial and satellite links leased from the DOT. The CMC will develop software and user access capabilities.

Apparently, the CMC also has been interested in providing services to Indian banks via a proposed "Banknet". The DOT was successful in persuading the CMC not to provide such services, largely on the ground that the DOT packet-switched network costs are likely to be so low that the CMC would not have been able to offer its proposed service on terms that would have been competitive with a comparable service over the network.

The precise relationship between the DOT, which provides the basic network for the transport of data, and the DOE, which oversees the operation of the computer center and provides the enhancements, is still being sorted out. Generally speaking, however, the DOT's perspective is that its function is to provide transport capacity. Thus, it would oppose attempts by the CMC to provide a fiber optic connection directly to a bank for a Banknet or Indonet service; its position would be that such lines would have to be leased from the DOT.

If, however, the DOT cannot supply a particular service, its officials say that it will not stop others from doing so. Between the interests of the DOT and the DOE there is, of course, leeway for rivalry, which may cause the DOT to remain alert to prevent rival networks from emerging.

D. Structural Innovations: The Response to Rivalry and to Demands for Efficiency

1. Telecommunications Consultants India Limited

One of the responses of the DOT to the rivalries between it and the other departments was the establishment of a consulting subsidiary in 1978, a Government of India company called Telecommunications Consultants India Limited ("TCIL"). *See* Section III.A. above. Drawing from the entire range of DOT personnel, including the Telecommunications Research Centre and Indian Telephone Industries, and with a sizeable headquarters staff, TCIL provides consulting and planning expertise in India. One of TCIL's principal functions is to be the DOT interface with some of the Department's major users. In pursuing this objective, TCIL has had nearly forty clients, not just in the private sector, but major state corporations, such as the Oil and Natural Gas Commission, Indian Airlines, Indian Railways, Oil India Ltd., the State Bank of India, and Coal India Ltd., as well.

TCIL also has an important role to play in developing the Indian telecommunications sector. It has assisted in developing the software for, and setting up, the experimental, three-node packet-switched public data network, which will initially serve Delhi, Bombay and Madras. Other projects have included the implementation and operation of videotex services in Delhi, the computerization of subscriber management in one large Indian city, completing an office automation study for the DOT, and conducting a feasibility study for VIKRAM, a proposed national dedicated data network.

TCIL activities outside India are also very substantial; it has been perhaps the preeminent international telecommunications consultancy based in the developing world. Its international mission is to share its expertise in the installation and operation of telecommunications facilities with other developing countries, particularly those in the Middle East and Africa. To date, it has advised in eighteen countries and deployed nearly 1,500 staff worldwide.

2. New Institutional Structures for Local and International Services

One aspect of the complexity of the Indian telecommunications environment is that under-investment can lead to duplicative investments and, therefore, produce some waste and poor co-ordination. The Planning Commission, in the normal give-and-take of the bureaucratic process, is not always able to occupy itself with such inefficiencies. Imperfections in the planning process, however, also tend to produce an intra-governmental, inter-departmental dynamic that keeps the DOT more responsive to users than it might otherwise be.

In response to this multifaceted domestic environment and along the lines of similar national responses in other countries, the DOT has developed a strategy that relies on the formation of new institutions for developing the infrastructure. An earlier aspect of this internal restructuring took place in January 1985, when the postal and telecommunications responsibilities were separated in the New Delhi headquarters; such a split had occurred several years previously in the field.

A second, and far more dramatic, decision was made in the first months of 1986. The DOT decided to establish two new, internal corporate entities— to operate the local services in New Delhi and Bombay and to provide international services.

On April 1, 1986, Mahanagar Telephone Nigam Ltd ("MTNL") was established to run the local services in the two cities. On the same date, the Overseas Communication Service ("OCS"), which historically had been operated separately from domestic services, was reconstituted as Videsh Sanchar Nigam Ltd ("VSNL").

MTNL and VSNL represent an enormously innovative—and still experimental—institutional approach. The two new entities are public corporations, which eventually will have shares that will be held initially by the DOT. There were two principal reasons for establishing MTNL. One was to be able to command additional resources, to obtain much-needed funds on the public market; in this regard, the DOT was attentive to the French model, with its funding source, the Caisse Nationale des Télécommunications. The second reason was to increase efficiency; business decisions that are necessary for operating a commercial enterprise such as a telephone network are difficult to make in a government bureaucracy. If MTNL were operatede more like a business, it was thought, there might be institutional incentives for creating and marketing new services.

The creation of MTNL and VSNL was initially undertaken with some reluctance within the DOT and is still viewed very much as a major experiment. If it is deemed successful, a corporate form could be established for the entire DOT. Undoubtedly, the DOT is thinking about this possibility; whether a corporate DOT would be unitary or subdivided into a "monopoly" division and a "competitive" division (not unlike the Dutch PTT after liberalization) is still not known.

The DOT's institutional strategy is aimed at increasing the effectiveness of the network that is in place, and at developing additional resources. The target is satisfying the goals outlined in its action plan for the year 2000. By that time it hopes to provide connections on demand; to have twenty million exchange lines (or twenty per thousand population, compared with five per thousand today); to provide four telephones per thousand in urban areas; and to have at least one telephone per village. DOT, Action Plan (Aug. 1986); *see also* Planning Commission, Government of India, *Seventh Five Year Plan 1985–90* (New Delhi: Nov. 1985).

The key to having MTNL and VSNL achieve the levels of productivity and effectivity that may be more characteristic of business than government will lie, in great part, with the personnel. At this point, the staff of MTNL largely comprise individuals seconded from the DOT. MTNL is still part of the civil service structure, but eventually new terms and conditions will be developed for its employees and the staff will be transferred to MTNL.

The staff of MTNL are still viewing with some uncertainty the proposed changes in their working arrangements. One positive development might be the evolution of some inter-organizational competition between the DOT and MTNL. It is possible, however, that the staff remaining with the DOT could adopt the bargaining position that they do the same job as the staff of MTNL, but, unfairly, compensation arrangements at MTNL are superior. These possible frictions will need to be resolved if MTNL productivity is to increase.

There is still a common budget for MTNL and the DOT; MTNL remains an agency for which the permissible level of investment is set by the Planning Commission. Where MTNL has additional flexibility, however, is in being able to go into the market for funding. In terms of actual borrowing, MTNL will only be able to do so overseas. It floated Rs 1,500 million (approximately $120 million) in debenture bonds on the domestic market at the end of November 1986, however. MTNL hoped to raise an equal amount with a second flotation in February 1987.

As a result of what appears to have been a political compromise, some substantial portion of the funds that MTNL raises in the financial markets will be passed on to the DOT itself. The prevailing view seems to have been that political problems would have been raised if the infusion of funds to which MTNL could have access were spent only on New Delhi and Bombay. MTNL also hopes, of course, to generate sufficient cash flow to finance its own investment projects. For the future, one critical issue is to what extent MTNL will have ongoing obligations to pass on capital to the DOT or the government.

The DOT has transferred substantial assets to MTNL: the local plant, operator-assisted toll service functions, and control of the toll switch. Interexchange media remain with the DOT. This transfer ultimately will mean that MTNL's local service will have to be established as a profit center. An accounting of the value of the assets transferred will have to be undertaken.

MTNL must now enter into some financial settlement with DOT to obtain compensation for the origination and termination of long-distance telephone calls. The formula by which the DOT will make access payments to MTNL and VSNL is still being worked out. MTNL will have to develop sophisticated cost accounting systems to calculate the costs of providing service to the DOT. The question of how to develop fair and economically-based access charges has been difficult enough in the United States and elsewhere, where local and trunk services are provided by different entities; a similar, if not more, burdensome task will confront analogous structural changes in India and in other countries where services are not provided by a single body.

At present, MTNL bills its subscribers for local, long-distance, and international calls. The process of sharing revenues will require the development of accounting principles. There is some agreement on the broad outline of the access arrangements, however. It is likely that the DOT will keep some percentage of the MTNL revenues that can be attributed to transiting traffic that uses MTNL swtiches; the DOT also may retain a portion of the revenues from local calls.

3. New Business Services

MTNL and VSNL are initial steps toward encouraging efficiency in the DOT. A more far-reaching step will be the provision of sophisticated data services for business users by a "Business Subscriber Network" ("BSN"). To offer BSN services, the DOT is now planning a narrowband ISDN service as a public network overlay on the existing network infrastructure. The network would serve the four metropolises and, perhaps, some other cities. Where possible, the DOT will use existing local loops. In many areas, however, it will have to install new links to the premises of business customers.

The network could be based on fiber optic technology; the more likely development is that the network will be multimedia—microwave, coaxial cable, and fiber optic on most of the main routes. INSAT is a technologically feasible option, but there is insufficient capacity on the satellite system at present.

The DOT has not yet decided on the institutional arrangements through which the BSN services will be offered. The BSN will probably be provided by the DOT; the local loop will be provided by either MTNL (if in Bombay or New Delhi) or the DOT. What is likely, however, is that the network will be developed and managed separately from the existing services of either the DOT or MTNL. There may be an entirely separate group or entity within the DOT that would market the services.

In all probability, TCIL, the DOT consulting arm, will have a major role in implementing the BSN services. The DOT and TCIL have been working very closely with the Committee for Industrial Engineering, a business group with representation from the engineering sector. MTNL is also likely to have a substantial role in the design of the network. The timing of the introduction of the BSN is still uncertain, however.

Another highly innovative aspect of the BSN is the concept of using the new services to raise capital from subscribers. The current plan is to market the services to clusters of users, with the subscribers funding the development of both the infrastructure and the services. Although the investment costs would be borne directly by the DOT, users would pay a certain amount in advance, plus a rental fee, for which they would be provided with a 2B plus D channel. Discussions with potential BSN customers about pricing are now under way.

Advance subscriber contributions to the BSN services would not necessarily be in the form of equity investment; the DOT has not ruled out the possibility, however, that the new venture could be mixed public-private. Given the fact that facilities in India are otherwise scarcely available, this financing scheme, which guarantees digital capacity, might be attractive to large users.

E. Responsiveness to Business Users' Needs

Despite the pressure from the rural sectors for attention to their needs, the DOT has managed to be responsive to the needs of the business sector. In principle, private lines are available for lease. The DOT is flexible with respect to the use of leased lines for information services or data processing. The legal basis for this flexibility is that the Indian Telegraph Act accords the DOT a monopoly only on "communications", which is defined as the "exchange" of intelligence or information. The DOT does not view the retrieval of information from a data base or the processing of data by a computer as an "exchange"; similarly a time-delayed transfer between two banks is not an "exchange" and would be permitted.

The DOT has taken a relatively liberal view with respect to making leased lines available to "closed user groups". Such groups might include an association of government banks that want to engage in interbank clearing functions; not unlike its counterparts in the industrialized world (Telecom Australia, for example), the DOT scrutinizes carefully the *bona fides* of the association leasing the lines. The addition of a private bank to that network, for example, would destroy the integrity of the "closed" user group, unless that bank joined the umbrella association that had leased the lines. If that group wanted to interconnect with the public-switched network, the DOT would be relatively rigid, applying strict engineering standards and taking steps to prevent diversion from the public network.

With respect to data processing networks, the DOT does not permit the transfer of data from one terminal to another; interaction is confined to terminal-to-host transactions. It is, concedes the DOT, difficult to monitor how closed user group or data processing networks are being used, or how information flows once there is interconnection with the public network.

Overall, the DOT seems to encourage the use of leased lines by large business users. In practice, however, such lines are often not available because the shortage of telecommunications facilities necessitates stripping any private circuit out of the public network.

The DOT permits users to select their own terminal equipment, which is supplied by private entities. Users may also install private local area networks; these could be connected to the public network, if the needs of the users so require.

In principle, the DOT indicates that it would be prepared to allow real estate developers to make investments in the telecommunications infrastructures of office or residential complexes. The owners of those buildings could then offer an internal communications service, with the DOT providing access to external lines. To date, however, there have been no applicants seeking to offer this service.

With respect to the interests of the financial community, the DOT is aware of its dependence on information services and data bases located outside India. The DOT understands that restrictive policies will cut off Indian business organizations and governmental entities from international services that may enhance India's competitiveness. For example, the DOT recognizes that there might be advantages in the State Bank of India being able to move funds located in overseas accounts to take advantage of the world money markets. Nevertheless, carriers such as Control Data and GEISCO are not permitted to operate in India and only a few licenses have been issued to permit retrieval of data located beyond the national borders. Aware of the important ramifications for national financial policy, the DOT is trying to develop a coherent policy on access to foreign data bases.

F. The Challenge of Network Upgrading: Planning, Finance, and Joint Ventures

1. The Planning Process

In developing the infrastructure the DOT faces several challenges. The DOT cannot meet demand, which is, it estimates, growing at an annual rate of 11 per cent, of which only 7–8 per cent can be satisfied. One difficulty is that this excess of demand over supply almost requires that steps be taken to repress demand through pricing. This objective is difficult to accomplish through pricing mechanisms. As a matter of cost accounting, it has been difficult to develop a tariff structure that could assist in cross-subsidizing services to and in the rural areas. Furthermore, although the DOT recommends tariff structures and levels, the tariffs themselves are both reviewed and set at the political level.

Given the wide dispersion of the population throughout the countryside, it makes little sense for the DOT to try to tackle head-on the problem of providing or upgrading service for the entire population. The balance between urban upgrading and initial service to rural areas is struck, in the first instance, by the DOT. The decision is ultimately one for the Planning Commission. To obtain a healthy allocation of the national budgetary outlay, however, the DOT must demonstrate that the sector justifies denying funds for other, arguably more immediate, activities.

The planning process takes both political and economic considerations into account. Initially, the DOT draws up plans for overall investment. These are discussed with the Planning Commission and the two eventually achieve a consensus. The political impact of the plan—network extension versus cost constraints and rural versus urban—are often highly significant. In general, however, the DOT has found it quite difficult over the years to justify the importance of the telecommunications sector to the planning group.

India uses a five-year planning cycle. Until recently, telecommunications was not among the country's core sectors. In the planning process, therefore, it would often get a much smaller allocation than might have been appropriate. Now, as a "core" sector, telecommunications is still not treated as the full equivalent of transport or electric power, where shortages can bring industrial development completely to a halt. For example, the current, Seventh Five Year Plan (1985–90) allocates $3.68 billion to the telecommunications sector. This is far less than half of what the DOT had originally requested of the Commission (and only a slight improvement over the $3.18 billion spent by the Government of India on telecommunications during the Sixth Five Year Plan).

Perhaps the principal difficulty is that planning for national development often does not take full or even adequate account of the economic consequences of investing in the telecommunications sector. Despite some of the preliminary work in this area, econometric models tend to underestimate the contribution of telecommunications to overall economic growth. One of the difficult tasks of the DOT and of some people within the Planning Commission is documenting the impact of investment in telecommunications on other sectors.

Despite the studies and other work described in Section II above, the task of documenting the importance of investment is difficult in India and elsewhere in the developing world. Unfortunately, little precise national quantitative information is at hand. Although British Telecom has done some work in the U.K., in many industrialized countries there is scant hard evidence of—though much belief in—the impact of investing in telecommunications facilities. Much decisionmaking in the United States regarding the size of investments, for example, has been based as much on marketplace factors—or unvarnished faith—as on any harder evidence that infrastructure investments produce significant economic benefits.

What there is, by and large, is evidence from Japan and Europe of economic contributions deriving from decisions made in the aggregate—by policymakers, carriers, and other providers of service—to increase investment in the sector. Some Japanese policymakers, for example, have made the point quite forcefully that one important objective of the liberalization in Japanese telecommunications policy has been to drive down the cost of communications and to stimulate economic activity in the industry sectors dependent on telecommunications. In India, as in much of the rest of the developing world, policymakers are faced with the problem of allocating economic resources. Thus, they want more precise factual support for their decisions to allocate economic resources to telecommunications, a precision that may be neither necessary nor deemed prudent in richer, more market-driven economies.

2. Finance and Access to Foreign Exchange

An additional burden for Indian policymakers is establishing that investment should be made in switches, transmission facilities, or other major telecommunications equipment when such purchases will consume scarce foreign exchange. As noted above, Indian economic planners have been exceedingly conservative about their foreign borrowing. They require strict justification for any investment that might require foreign capital.

To prevail in its argument that some foreign exchange must be used for infrastructure investment, the DOT must demonstrate that such investment will generate foreign exchange in return. This is not at all easy. Some areas of domestic activities, such as tourism or financial services, may make substantial contributions to foreign-exchange earnings. By contrast, improvements in the telecommunications sector essentially will only increase domestic revenues, not the flow of foreign exchange into India. The case, therefore, must be made that investments improve efficiency and the capability of Indian industries to compete in international markets.

If it is to receive foreign exchange, therefore, the DOT must make a claim of sorts on the foreign-exchange contributions made by other industry sectors. These sectors also have requirements for foreign-source capital investments; it is unlikely that they will easily accede in any competitive bureaucratic process. Consequently, to gain access to foreign capital, the DOT may want to establish alliances with other business sectors.

The DOT's strategy for convincing planners and the Ministry of Finance that it needs additional resources for investment is two-pronged: first, that considerations of social equity militate in favor of expanding the infrastructure and, second, that investment will stimulate the business sectors and be an engine of economic growth. The creation of an organization to invest in the business sector establishes a basis for delineating between the funding destined for these two different sectors; separate means of raising and using capital make it possible for the DOT to rationalize the allocation of investment funds between expenditures that are mandated by social policy and those that are propelled by commercial imperatives.

Ultimately, the DOT must rely on the fact that the nation's eventual return on investment in new business services will be measured in terms of stimulus and improvement in the domestic economy. It will take a long time, if ever, for the traceable benefits to be measurable. Thus, the economic benefits are likely to be very long-term, and a product of business sector activity, in an environment that is focused on the more immediate issues of poverty and the equitable distribution of wealth. Assuring the flow of funds into services that are part of a long-term strategy is implicit in the structural initiatives that have been undertaken by the DOT.

3. Joint Venture Activities

If government and foreign-exchange funding is scarce, it is possible that there may be some utility in the exploration of joint ventures with the private sector. Such ventures, of course, are among the institutional approaches to stimulating business services. It is possible that such a venture between public and private sector entities could include some foreign investment. The DOT has looked extensively at various models of corporate ventures and is committed to a full exploration of their possibilities. These models might involve different mixes of public and private, foreign and national participation.

Many observers in the DOT are quite skeptical about joint ventures for the development of services; they are considerably more sanguine about joint ventures to produce telecommunications goods, where they point to the presence of several foreign concerns. With respect to joint ventures for the development and implementation of services, however, they first argue that resources are initially needed for infrastructure development, and not for the services that operate over that infrastructure. Second, they point out that the capital for any venture with a domestic partner would come from the same, scarce resource pool as does the allocation to the DOT.

Third, they note that private sector investors might not take a sufficiently long-term perspective with respect to the investment. The administration of Rajiv Gandhi may be prepared for some new openness toward the vigorous private sector interests that are dominated by the Tata group in Bombay; such private interests have managed to co-exist and remain active in the face of a strong tradition of public control over key industry sectors.

The Indian Government has not precluded the possibility of foreign investment in a joint venture. Over the years, in fact, the DOT has been presented with several options for foreign participation in a venture; it rejected one of these, however, that would have turned over management of a cellular radio system, as a sale of spectrum, not a joint venture.

Although joint ventures with foreign entities are not barred, Indian regulations on foreign investment would limit direct foreign ownership of a joint stock company to less than 40 per cent. Clearances are problematic as well. One principal problem with foreign-held equity is the repatriation of capital, interest, or any profits. Such repatriation undercuts the very purpose of the venture—to encourage the flow of foreign exchange into India. Given that current policy does not favor foreign capital investment, and in light of the critical nature of the telecommunications sector, the government may well not encourage foreign equity involvement in any venture.

The DOT will need to identify sectors that are the most promising for joint ventures. Currently, the C-DOT, with its parent DOE and DOT organizations, is engaged in an active research and development program to develop a small switch to be used in rural areas. The DOT perceives the industrialized world as having failed to produce a switch suitable for a small village (where calling patterns are likely to be trunk rather than local). To respond to Indian needs for a rural switch, the C-DOT's program is centered around domestic resources. Another similar effort is under way with Jeumont-Schneider, the French telecommunications manufacturer, as a joint venturer.

G. Some Observations on a Long-Term Strategy

The foregoing discussion suggests that there may be several approaches available to the DOT for obtaining the resources necessary to expand and develop the basic infrastructure and to promote new services. It may be helpful to delineate these vehicles more concretely. An administration might want to avail itself of expertise outside its organization to assist it in bringing some of these options into sharper focus. The DOT relies on the World Bank and other multilateral lending institutions already. Other lending organizations in the public and private sectors, including investment banks, might be able to contribute significantly toward outlining various investment structures.

Eventually, national administrations such as the DOT will need to take a hard look at the broader options for domestic production, as to which there is no loss of foreign-exchange earnings. Where manufacturing and operational interests are combined, as they are in India, the policymakers must balance the objectives of their industrial policy against the imperative of a rapid upgrading of the telecommunications resources. Should the equipment and manufacturing industries represented in the sector be protected, or should telecommunications services be treated as an "input commodity", as an important factor in its own right and likely to influence economic growth? This same dilemma of public policy is, of course, faced in other national and regional contexts, from Australia to many nations in Europe and to the European Community itself.

In addition, the industrialized world should assist in providing evidence of the economic benefits of investments in the telecommunications sector. Admittedly, international organizations, such as the World Bank and the United Nations Development Programme, as well as academics, have attempted and, in some cases, succeeded in linking overall economic development with development in telecommunications. There have also been efforts by some of the foreign assistance or development agencies of the industrialized countries.

Nevertheless, policymakers from the developed world too often adopt a perspective that is far narrower and too short-term. In opening trade discussions with the administrations of other nations, they often characterize the problem as one of market access. The real obstacle, however, in most of the developing world and in much of the industrialized world is not regulatory, legalistic or bureaucratic. Rather, the crux of the problem is often that the nations with "closed" telecommunications sectors are simply unable adequately to justify the need for, and benefits of, additional investments.

From the standpoint of a trade negotiator from the industrialized world, joint activities to assemble the economic data supporting increased investment—and purchases from abroad—might pay substantial dividends. Trade officials might build on some of the preliminary work in this area as part of their argument for expanding the telecommunications sectors in the less developed world. Of course, the argument for additional investment will also make the case for, and open the door to, industrial interests from countries other than the one that had assisted in the economic research.

Adopting a long-term perspective, evincing some understanding of the problems of a developing economy, and being attentive to cultural sensitivities will help to forge relationships which are beneficial from a business standpoint. It is true that specific trade problems with developing countries may need to be addressed directly; paying immediate attention to particular business issues—and resolving problems on an expedited basis—can result in real benefits, and not just for the supplier of services or equipment from the developed world. Nevertheless, at least from the perspective of the developing world, for countries such as the United States, where trade policy is strongly reflective of short-term business concerns, a lack of long-range perspective can contribute to competitive disadvantages vis-à-vis international competitors that do take the longer view.

The telecommunications sector in India can become an important element in a strategy centered around the export of services. The nation, with its outstanding human resources, has great potential to develop value-added services that depend on sophisticated software. India historically has viewed itself as having a critical trading position in the Indian Ocean, with the countries bordering the Arabian Sea, and with the rest of Asia. Thus, the nascent service sector of the Indian economy could offer new software-based value-added services not only in India, but throughout the region.

Indian policymakers have not yet concentrated their policies on a service-based or export-related strategy. This strategy, however, would not be unlike that being pursued in Australia; both Australian policymakers and OTC (Australia) perceive their role as part of an effort to develop an international focus for the Australian financial and services sectors. Although, until recently, Indian policymakers placed domestic priorities at the top of their agenda, the attractions of a trade-oriented approach increasingly may begin to influence their perspectives.

If Indian policies toward its telecommunications or services sectors do become more international in scope, the international dimensions of its telecommunications policies will assume greater importance. Countries in the region will be more attentive to the possibility of INSAT delivering to their territories the new services that could be developed in India. India's role in the regional planning organization, the Asia Pacific Telecommunications group, will also bear some reexamination by Indian policymakers. For, if Indian telecommunications policy becomes more export-driven, the country may find itself having a greater stake in the kinds and uses of the international facilities that are available.

IV. THE MALAYSIAN EXPERIENCE

A. The National and Sectoral Backdrop

1. The Telecommunications Sector

Malaysia is confronting many of the same problems that are facing India: urgency of modernizing and expanding infrastructure, some geographic hurdles, and an unavailability of financial resources for investing in the telecommunications sector. There are enormous differences, however, between the two countries in terms of size and population. The two countries are focusing on parallel, though different, structural answers to the question of how best to make their telecommunications administration more productive, more efficient, and more competitive.

Malaysia shares with India the British colonial tradition. It is a far smaller country, with a population of only 14 million. There is one large city, Kuala Lumpur, with several smaller cities scattered over the country, but no other major urban centers. The focal point of the Malaysian economy is Kuala Lumpur and in a corridor along the west coast from Penang to Johore.

At the end of 1985, Jabatan Telekom Malaysia ("JTM"), which had been the government provider of telecommunications services, had 958,598 direct exchange lines in service. This was an increase of only 12.9 per cent over 1984 (as compared to a 21.3 per cent increase for 1984 over 1983). For the same period, the equipped exchange capacity of the JTM telephone network was almost 1.76 million subscriber lines, an increase of 23.6 per cent over the previous year (and a full 61.6 per cent of which was provided by computerized equipment). *1985 Annual Report*, Jabatan Telekom Malaysia, at 14, 20.

The Kalang Valley, the area immediately surrounding Kuala Lumpur, has between 60 and 70 per cent of the subscribers in Malaysia and generates roughly the same percentage of calling volume in the country. On the east coast, where growth has been slower and the countryside is essentially rural, there is far less penetration of telecommunications service.

Physically, the two states of East Malaysia, Sabah and Sarawak, are separated from Peninsular Malaysia and are located on the island of Borneo. A substantial portion of the land mass of Malaysia is jungle and not easily served by conventional telecommunications services.

Malaysia has moved rapidly to upgrade its network. In contrast to the nearly one million exchange lines now in place, in the early 1980s there were approximately 600,000 telephone subscribers. At that time, the Minister of Communications, Datuk Leo Moggie anak Irok, called for an increase in the number of subscribers to between 1.2 and 1.5 million by the end of 1985. Though falling somewhat short of that goal, Malaysian achievements, in the face of a severe downturn in the national economy, nonetheless have been impressive.

One further goal of telecommunications policy in Malaysia has been improving the staff-to-user ratio. In mid-1984, the Ministry had about 30,000 employees to provide service for the 600,000 telephone lines. Now, however, approximately the same number of employees provides service for the nearly one million exchange lines; indeed, the ratio of staff per 1,000 direct lines improved by 13.8 per cent from 1984 to 1985. *1985 Annual Report*, at 25.

The Malaysia telephone system has, like the Indian, been plagued with congestion and some deterioration in cable facilities. The only place in the country where there is service on demand is Penang, which has expanded as a business center and tourist resort. As of the end of 1985, JTM reported that it was able to satisfy 84 per cent of the demand for telephone service, the best annual performance during the Third and Fourth Malaysia Plan periods. *Id.* at 3.

2. Program for Network Upgrading

Thus, in the face of budgetary constraints endemic to the developing world, the Malaysian Government has tried diligently to follow a three-step program of expanding and upgrading the network. This work began in 1981, and has now slowed down considerably owing to the generally depressed state of the Malaysian economy. The program has cost around M$6 to M$7 billion during the first years of this decade. In 1985, JTM made the largest ever annual capital expenditure—M$1.8 billion.

Another policy followed by the government is to acquire the necessary infrastructure by foreign procurement. In 1982, as part of the first phase of the upgrading program, contracts for switches were awarded to NEC and L.M. Ericsson. The second-phase contracts, for the procurement and installation of local cable networks, were awarded to four local Malaysian firms in October 1983. For the third phase, the installation of an intercity microwave network to link new switching equipment with long-distance lines, a contract was awarded in July 1984 to Standard Elektrik Lorenz.

British Telecom has attempted to become active in Malaysia through participation in a joint venture, Britarafon, which will bid for contracts to provide systems and services in connection with the ongoing development of the telecommunications system in Malaysia. British Telecom has taken three local partners, ETM, Kumpulan AKZ, and Arab Malaysian Development Berhad.

3. Cellular System

One major difficulty in providing universal service in the less industrialized countries is the difficult and often sparsely-populated terrain. Countries such as India have addressed the problem by satellite technology, a solution being implemented aggressively in countries in the industrialized world, such as Australia.

The jungles of Malaysia make it difficult to provide service nationwide. One solution was the installation of a cellular radio network—Automatic Telephone Using Radio ("ATUR") Service—which now covers the entire country. Radio cells overlay the main transport routes and travellers on any road in Malaysia, including East Malaysia, or on any boat, can reach another person anywhere else in Malaysia. The system adopted was that of the Nordic countries.

The system was relatively successful at the outset. Now, after the first two years of operation, there are already 10,000 subscribers. Congestion has appeared in the Kuala Lumpur area. Such congestion may be alleviated by the addition of cells; new infrastructure investment is costly. Therefore, the government is considering a joint venture with the private sector to obtain financing.

Because cellular radio is so costly, it is therefore not viewed as the ultimate solution to the inequities of poor or non-existent rural service.

4. The Planning Process

Five years ago, the government planners finally accepted the proposition that telecommunications is critical to the economy as a whole. This considerably antedated any similar decision by the Indian Planning

Commission. Substantial expenditures on network upgrading have been and are being made as part of the three-phase plan that was approved by the Malaysian planners.

During the course of the current five-year plan it had been forecast that between M$68 million and M$80 million (about US $28–$33 million) would be spent on the telecommunications sector. Owing to the economic downturn, however, this figure may drop to M$50 million or less. As is the case in India, the Ministry has found it hard to argue that the needs of the telecommunications sector should have priority over health, education, or other critical sectors.

Planning is an exceptionally important function within the Department of the Prime Minister. The planners determine sectoral allocations and then the operating ministries reallocate the funds within their own sectors. This process seems to accord some greater flexibility to the ministries than does the planning process in India.

Nevertheless, policymakers in Malaysia, like those in India, complain that the economists in the planning group do not fully appreciate the nature of telecommunications and its impact on the business sector. Often planners support a particular proposal—for switches or for lines—instead of understanding that an integrated system must be provided to the customer if the administration is to earn any revenue from that customer. The process of educating the planners in the developing world will need to be at the top of the list of priorities for those in the telecommunications sector.

B. Structural Innovation: Privatization of Jabatan Telekom Malaysia

Faced with the need to improve the efficiencies of the telecommunications sector, to reduce the staff-to-user ratio, and to develop a financing vehicle, Minister Datuk Leo Moggie a few years ago commissioned a study of the future of Jabatan ("Department") Telekom Malaysia, which was, until the end of 1986, the Malaysian telecommunications administration. The Arab Malaysian Merchant Bank spearheaded a study of the steps necessary to privatize the telecommunications authority.

1. Privatization: The Plan

The plans for privatization of JTM have been developing for several years, with a decision taken on the basic principles in 1984. In 1985, JTM transferred M$1 million to what was to be the new privatized entity, Syarikat ("Company") Telekom Malaysia Berhad ("STM") as an initial contribution to its paid-up capital. STM is a fully government-owned company incorporated under the Malaysian Companies Act. It began operations on January 1, 1987, when it took over what had been JTM's responsibilities.

One of the objectives of the move to privatization was to facilitate the process of raising necessary investment capital. JTM had been severely constrained by investment policies that had limited the flow of capital into the telecommunications sector. In addition, the sector was so closely controlled that there was some risk that JTM might have become a supplier of capital to other sectors of the Malaysian economy. The Treasury has been viewed as playing a key role in deciding which projects to fund. To remove this bureaucratic supervision, the corporate structure was created.

The Treasury will still have some control over off-balance sheet financing by STM. Especially now, with the precipitous decline in the Malaysian economy, the Treasurer is likely to put a cap on the country's total borrowing. It is expected that STM will borrow on the open market, subject to the ceiling; the government will guarantee the borrowings, to enable lenders to offer more attractive terms.

The Malaysians felt it necessary to have a regulatory body oversee STM. They have therefore retained JTM to carry out this function, which has been described as a "miniature Oftel". Although JTM has been separate from the Ministry, in its new regulatory capacity it will become more integrated with the Ministry, and it is thought that it will have responsibility, within the Ministry, for licensing STM.

During the debates on privatization, the recurrent theme of the developing world—how to balance the needs of the rural and urban sectors—was repeatedly the subject of debate in Parliament. In both the developing and the developed world, the fear is that companies which are driven by profit will ignore the rural services. The solution in Malaysia is not unlike that of the Oftel-enforced licence conditions in the United Kingdom; the licence issued to STM will state that the company should invest a set percentage in rural services. This investment expenditure will be monitored by the Minister. It is anticipated that there will be a significant difference of views between STM and the Minister over the size of that percentage.

The Minister will also review the tariffs of STM. A negative veto procedure has been established, with provisions for reconsideration and appeal. What is likely to happen is that the Minister and STM will consult closely prior to proposing any tariff increases. Again, the model of the U.K. might be useful in Malaysia; the tariff increases could be tied to an inflation index, as is the case with the licence issued to British Telecom.

The government's approach to privatizing JTM is modelled to a certain extent on the privatization of the Malaysian Airline System ("MAS"). The shares of MAS were owned by the Governments of Malaysia and the states of Sarawak and Sabah. The government then had to choose between a private placement and a public offering to float the shares; eventually it chose the public market and floated about 40 per cent of MAS's stock on the Malaysian Stock Exchange. Some percentage of MAS stock was acquired by foreign interests.

Similarly, the present thinking appears to be that the shares of STM might be released to the public within two to three years. To fulfill important social and political goals of racial integration and advancement of the Bumiputra population, a certain percentage of the shares will be allocated to that group; other portions will be made available to employees and to the public.

2. International Structural Issues

In the process of reviewing the options for privatization, there was a close look at whether the profitable international sectors should be separated structurally and financed separately. By contrast with India, Indonesia, and Australia in the same region, in Malaysia international and domestic services are provided by the same entity.

The government ultimately rejected the notion of separating the two entities at the time of privatization. The perception was that private companies would only want the lucrative international side. Thus, out of a concern that insufficient capital would be raised to support the domestic sector by itself, it was decided to resist pressure to separate the two.

3. Flexibility in Structure and Financing

The new structure also provides for considerable organizational flexibility within STM. STM is authorized to create separate units ot subsidiaries. As administrations have done around the world, this may be one way of generating internal competition. Alternatively, competitive services might be provided through a separate subsidiary to which strict accounting principles would apply; such a subsidiary might have to deal at arm's length with its parent body.

Minister Moggie believes that the government can assess various joint-venture proposals for business networks in light of the flexible structure of the STM; indeed, ventures between a subsidiary and the private sector might be well received. That is, even though there is no separate international entity, it might be possible to accept foreign or private sector investment with respect to particular services.

The approach that the government might follow would be *ad hoc*. It might, for example, be possible to combine private network facilities of oil companies operating in Sarawak with STM networks. Similarly, in areas such as Terengganu, which is earmarked for increased investment, private sector involvement might permit STM to share a link into a population center.

Another important structural parallel between India and Malaysia is the use of the corporate structure as a vehicle to finance urban requirements separately from those of the politically demanding, but less lucrative, rural sector. There is some interest in Malaysia in addressing the needs of Kuala Lumpur separately from those of the rest of the country. The creation of STM, with the flexibility to create a separate subsidiary (modelled, perhaps, on MTNL in India), might permit the Malaysians to focus on urban needs on a freestanding basis, without having to reconcile them with the demands of the rural areas.

4. Competition in Services

The government's present thinking is to open certain urban, business, and data services to competition. They would be licensed as long as the STM retained its monopoly on the network. (Only the military forces and the police may have their own facilities. The railway is thinking of constructing its own network and there has been some discussion on that question.)

No specific definition of value-added services is evolving in Malaysia. The approach, like that of Australia and other nations, is rather more *ad hoc*. The focus will be practical: if STM does not and cannot offer a proposed service, then private groups will be permitted to provide it. During the two to three-year transitional period, it is especially likely that the approach will continue to be motivated less by the niceties of a precise policy than by the needs of the customers.

No new legislation would be required to license these new services and open them to competition. The existing law already permits the government to license other services.

C. An International Strategy: Hubbing

Like the Australians, the Malaysian Government is keenly interested in the concept of hubbing through Kuala Lumpur. At the least, it believes that international telecommunications companies might be interested in transiting Malaysia to link up with other international facilities. A cable now runs from Malaysia to Madras, and then continues by microwave across India to Europe. The ASEAN cable links up with the Philippines, and also to the A-I-S cable just completed.

A more specific plan is to attract international investment in the upgrading of the cable between East and Peninsular Malaysia, which could be used for international transiting as well. In fact, at the beginning of April 1987, the government signed a memorandum of understanding to allow Cable & Wireless to participate in a joint venture company (51 per cent held by STM, 49 per cent by C&W) to build a $100 million fiber optic link between the two parts of Malaysia. At the time the cable was scheduled to start operations in 1989, and to carry both domestic and international traffic. The joint venture will also be the vehicle for other cable projects based in Malaysia, possibly including cables to the Philippines, Hong Kong, Singapore, and Brunei. The express intent of the parties to the agreement was to make Malaysia a major regional telecommunications center.

The Minister has suggested linking Malaysia to the international network from a branch terminating in the China Sea. In any event, the cable between East and Peninsular Malaysia could become part of the global network being constructed by C&W. Some believe that it might be part of a decision to site the Asian landing point of a C&W Pacific Rim cable system outside Japan. (Such a decision would be taken, of course, only if International Digital Communications Planning, the would-be competitor to KDD in which

C&W has a 20 per cent interest, were unsuccessful in obtaining a Japanese franchise to provide international services.)

The Minister of Communications is also interested in exploring the possibility that Kuala Lumpur could become a regional financial center in competition with Singapore and Hong Kong. As illustrated by the ambitions partly revealed in the participation of C&W in the intra-Malaysian submarine fiber optic cable, communications capabilities could play a role in fulfilling this aspiration. The relatively small size of the domestic economy has made it somewhat difficult for Malaysia to compete with other financial centers in Southeast Asia.

The interplay between Malaysia and Singapore illustrates the broader, global competition between administrations. Singapore has lower prices for its telecommunications services because it is small, compact, and does not have to worry about a high-cost rural network. Singaporean facilities are also superior to those of Malaysia. Telecommunications capabilities are, of course, not the sole reason for Singapore's success as a regional center, but they certainly are a contributing factor. Conversely, the competitive pressure of Singapore is a significant force in motivating Malaysia to modernize and liberalize its network and regulatory structure.

D. Some Additional Observations on a Long-Term Strategy

The ambitions of Malaysian policymakers have been trimmed rather sharply by the severe downturn in the economy. The budgetary austerity imposed by the government has resulted in major cutbacks in the budget of the Ministry of Energy, Telecommunications, and Posts, and at JTM. There is less interest in having non-governmental entities compete for scarce resources. The economic situation has made privatization of less interest now than it was some months or years previously.

A major goal, however, is to adopt more flexibility in managing enterprises in Malaysia. This is one of the core principles of Prime Minister Dr Mahathir Mohamad's proposal for a Malaysia, Inc. Initiatives to achieve this objective are likely to persist even in the face of austerity. At the same time, however, the hard times will also make the government receptive to proposals for specific joint ventures.

The Minister of Communications specifically stresses the problems that JTM and now STM face in developing the infrastructure. He emphasizes less the need for technical expertise in operating telecommunications systems; such expertise is, of course, invaluable for understanding how the system works and for purchasing and tendering. What is important, however, is expertise in managing telecommunications entities. As Minister Moggie sees it, Malaysia needs more managerial and marketing skills.

The Malaysians do not see major industrialized countries, or even suppliers of telecommunications equipment, as focusing on this aspect of the problem of developing the telecommunications infrastructure. Minister

Moggie proposes that there should be a new focus on the transfer of marketing and managerial know-how. This process would require a long-term investment of human resources to work collaboratively with the staff of STM.

V. THE EXPERIENCE OF INDONESIA

A. National and Sectoral Backdrop

1. Physical Obstacles

Indonesia shares characteristics with both India and Malaysia. It is a country that poses significant obstacles of geography and terrain to the provision of service on a national basis: 13,677 islands, 922 of them inhabited, sprawling for more than 5,110 kilometers. Indonesia is the fifth most populous country in the world, with 160 million people. There are 50,000 villages and cities; 80 per cent of the population lives in the rural areas; Java is populated extremely densely. Like Malaysia, there is essentially only one urban area—Jakarta—which has, however, several times the population of Kuala Lumpur.

As a function of geography, Indonesians are more likely, compared even with countries in the developed world, to make telephone calls across the country than they are to make local calls. Thus, the ratio of long-distance to local calls is unusually high.

2. The Five-Year Plans: Catching Up

Indonesia shares with Malaysia and India a planning process for allocating investment resources. Currently, the Fourth Five Year Plan (1984–9) emphasizes the development of industries, including, to a certain extent, the telecommunications sector. The telecommunications sector has been a part of each development plan. In the first five-year plan, priority was given to automatization of telephone services and the construction of a Java-Bali microwave system; in the second plan, the national transmission network was established. In the third plan, telephone facilities were expanded; digitization and manufacturing capabilities are stressed in the current plan.

Telephone density in Indonesia is still among the lowest in the world, approximately 4.4 per thousand at the end of 1984 (an increase from 1.6 per thousand in 1969). *1984 Annual Report*, Directorate General of Posts and Telecommunications, Department of Tourism, Posts and Telecommunications, at 5. The number of telephone stations more than quadrupled, however, from 1969 to 1984. W. Moenandir, "Indonesian Telecommunication Development', at 12 (Paper presented at "Forging a Global Telecommunications Strategy" conference, Washington, D.C., Feb. 25–27, 1985.)

In Jakarta, there are individuals who have been on the waiting list for a telephone since 1981. It is reported, however, that there is no pent-up demand for leased lines. Like India, then, Indonesia has had a long way to come, and has a long way to go in developing its telecommunications sector.

3. Technological Solutions

The special, perhaps ideal, solution to the geographic and demographic problems that beset planners in Indonesia is satellite technology. During the course of the Second Five-Year Plan (1974–9), on August 17, 1976, the Palapa domestic satellite system became operational. Well over one hundred ground stations are now in operation. Domestic services are provided to Malaysia, the Philippines, and Thailand. In addition, Palapa contributes to regional integration by occasionally delivering television signals of special events to the ASEAN community.

Indonesia also has licensed nearly 18,000 non-government radio stations to enable private companies doing business in remote areas (*e.g.*, logging, mining) to communicate internally. Liberal licensing of this non-wireline technology compensates for the distances and the archipelagic nature of the country. These licenses are issued to companies that can use them to form private networks; their use is restricted to intra-company messages. Interconnection to the public switched network is prohibited.

Like India and Australia, Indonesia has separate providers for domestic and international services, Perumtel and Indosat respectively. Not much thought has been given to consolidating the two entities or, in any other way, altering the fundamental structure of the telecommunications sector. Rather, in lieu of structural change, the approach being cultivated in Indonesia relies on legislation to liberalize, in part, the provision of certain services outside Perumtel. *See* Section V.D. below.

B. A Question of Competing Priorities

Like other countries in the developing world, Indonesia faces, perhaps, in some respects, more starkly than either Malaysia or India, a choice between expanding the basic network, introducing new services (principally in Jakarta and internationally), and adjusting to the scarcity of financial resources. As the low level of telephone density illustrates, much work needs to be done on erecting a basic infrastructure; as noted, however, this activity is not likely to be revenue-producing.

The only real interest in new business services will be in Jakarta (and possibly Surabaya), among large financial and industrial concerns, and with multinationals. The predicated market for these services, based on a Detecon study commissioned by the Directorate, is relatively strong. Data communications between banks and money transfers among financial institutions would appear to be attractive to customers.

There would appear to be a substantial market for new services, at least among the multinational enterprises that do business in Indonesia. The international data package communication system that was inaugurated by Indosat in June 1986 already has sixty customers—banks, trading companies, and oil companies.

There is, as yet, no domestic component to this service, largely because Perumtel has not been able to work out certain software-related problems having to do with distribution on Palapa. In 1987, however, Perumtel will begin operation of a domestic, terrestrial packet-switched service. Although new services are being developed, political and social pressures may make it difficult to devote substantial core resources to improving the infrastructure in Jakarta—where the services will be used.

Finally, with the steep decline in the price of oil, Indonesia's economy is not healthy. Budgets are being cut severely; telecommunications, moreover, is not perceived as a core sector. Furthermore, there is not a broad-based political consensus that development of the telecommunications infrastructure is a key to stimulating the economy.

C. Problems of Financing and Planning

More particularly, financing of the sector presents enormous problems. The Ministry of Finance is significantly concerned about the foreign-exchange reserves that are being used to invest in the telecommunications sectors. Telecommunications is, however, being allocated an increasing amount of foreign exchange; this is largely a function of the rebudgeting undertaken as a result of the devaluation of the rupiah.

The Indonesians are most interested in turn-key financing for development of the infrastructure. No foreign company has approached them to offer services in exchange for building up the infrastructure; nor could foreign entities offer any such services.

The planning process seems less intrusive than is the case in India. Perumtel budgets are reviewed first in the Directorate General of Posts and Telecommunications. Perumtel and Indosat, along with the telecommunications manufacturing industry and the postal division, all report to the Directorate. The Directorate, in turn, is responsible to the Ministry of Tourism, Posts and Telecommunications.

After the Perumtel and Indosat budgets are reviewed by the Directorate, they are forwarded to the Ministry of Finance. Thereafter they are sent to the National Planning Institute to make certain that they are consistent with the current Five-Year Plan. Unlike India, there does not appear to be wholesale review at the planning level of each project proposed by Perumtel. This may be a function of the fact that the Directorate acts as an intermediary, as a seal of approval.

D. A Legal Solution to Conflicting Priorities

In Indonesia, one approach to the resolution of the conflicting priorities facing the telecommunications sector is more akin to a model adopted in an industrialized country than to either India or Malaysia, for example. In both India and Malaysia, the model selected was structural—separating activities and vesting them in quasi-public corporate entities.

At present, the Indonesian approach focuses more on legislation. A proposal that is now pending would demarcate industry sectors and stimulate competition. This legislation is a significant move toward liberalization because it would permit the private sector to offer new services, provided that the monopoly of Perumtel and Indosat in facilities is respected.

The cornerstone of the legislative proposal is that any private sector company can provide a new telecommunications service, provided that it "co-operates" with Perumtel and Indosat. It is not clear what is meant by co-operation; the most likely model would appear to be that of a joint venture between the telecommunications monopoly and the private sector.

One service cited as an example of the kind of services that might be offered by a private sector entity under the bill is the paging service that has just been introduced in Indonesia. Perumtel has given the right to offer such services to a private company; in turn, the company returns some profits to Perumtel. Thus, it may be that a cost-sharing arrangement of some sort may satisfy the requirement that there should be an agreement or some degree of "co-operation" between the public and private sector entities.

The legislation is drafted to ensure that Perumtel will remain viable and that no services that are introduced will injure it economically. The view is that permitting the private sector to siphon off lucrative new services may impair Perumtel's ability to attract capital or collect revenues that could be used for the development of the basic infrastructure.

The line between monopoly services—those reserved exclusively for Perumtel and Indosat—and services that can be provided competitively has not been worked out. The legislation was drafted in late 1985 and is now in the midst of an inter-departmental review process. Although it was to have been introduced in the Parliament in Fall 1986, its consideration was postponed until some time in 1987. Its chances of passage are viewed as favorable.

The terms of the law, once enacted, will be implemented through ministerial decrees, which will have the force of regulation. It may be that individual joint-venture services will have to receive the approval of the Ministry. An alternative model would be to issue class licenses for types of services. These issues will be resolved by a team from the Ministry and the Directorate.

The law is designed, therefore, to capture resources in the private sector. It spreads the risk of new start-up services to private companies. Furthermore, it addresses competing priorities: new business services will be provided by the private sector, and resources will be freed for basic infrastructure development.

The Indonesians have concluded, however, at least on a preliminary basis, that foreign enterprises will not be able to enter into joint-venture arrangements with Perumtel and Indosat. Like the Indians and others in the developing world, the Indonesians are rightfully concerned about preserving their sovereignty over the telecommunications network and services. Given, however, the significant amount of external capital that might be available to help finance the new services and, indirectly, the infrastructure itself, they might be moved to re-examine their policy regarding the participation of foreign interests in the service offerings developed under the proposal.

One possible approach is to have private Indonesian companies work with foreign companies—banks, for example—in a joint-venture arrangement with Perumtel or Indosat. The amount of permissible foreign involvement in a venture for new services is not yet fixed; it may be that the Japanese model, which permits one-third of the shares of a Type I carrier to be held by aliens, would be attractive to the Indonesians. Indosat, however, does not foresee substantial demand by foreign companies to enter into joint-venture arrangements with it; nevertheless, it would be quite willing to explore any proposals for such arrangements that are presented to it.

E. Relationship of Domestic and International Service Providers

Indosat, like many international service providers, does not confront the same constriction of resources that besets Perumtel or other domestic providers of telecommunications capacity. The critical question in the developing world (and in the developed world, too, for that matter) is the mechanism for sharing the revenues of the international provider with the domestic provider.

At present, Indosat subscribers pay it directly; Indosat, in turn, compensates Perumtel at a flat domestic rate. When Perumtel subscribers make an international call, Perumtel collects and keeps 25 per cent of the income generated from that call.

Because Indosat is profitable, it pays taxes and dividends to the government. These revenues are not used to help defray some of the investment costs of constructing the domestic infrastructure, but they might be in the future. The theory would be, of course, that Indosat and the country as a whole would benefit by having a more extended domestic network that could be connected to international services.

Indosat has already given substantial thought to how the proposed law will affect its activities or provide entrepreneurial opportunities. The international market for value-added services is not huge, but Indosat seems to have an entrepreneurial spirit that might make it more willing to enter into joint ventures than Perumtel.

In some cases, Indosat might enter into a joint venture and then lease domestic capacity from Perumtel. For such ventures, the Perumtel/Indosat/private sector arrangement will be submitted to the Minister for approval. Indosat does not expect substantial further regulatory hurdles once it agrees to a joint-venture arrangement.

F. Some Concluding Observations

A critical element of future Indonesian telecommunications policy will be how the government implements the legislative proposal to permit new services to be offered under a joint-venture arrangement. The regulatory environment may be liberal, in which case the service sector would be stimulated substantially. Alternatively, if Perumtel and Indosat are seen as having the power of veto over any new proposed service, the growth of the service sector may be stifled. It does seem, however, that Indosat is far keener than Perumtel to enter into joint ventures for international services.

It is quite probable that the Indonesians will be able to work out the regulatory framework when—and if—the law is enacted. This effort is bound to be collegial. Before passage of the law, however, the process of inter-departmental review might be a very useful mechanism for alerting other ministries and the planning commission to the importance of the telecommunications sector and the significance of the legislative approach being initiated by the Ministry of Tourism, Posts, and Telecommunications.

One possible avenue for raising capital—foreign investment—presently seems unavailable in the Indonesian context. As noted above, the Indonesians are concerned about foreign involvement in the activities of a critical sector such as telecommunications. In this they have much in common with the Indians. Nevertheless, Indonesia does seem, as a matter of broad economic policy, somewhat less reluctant to avail itself of foreign multilateral or bilateral financing than does India. An approach that embraced the possibility of using foreign capital in telecommunications services might be a useful starting point for exploring ways in which other, Indonesian resources could be freed for basic infrastructure development.

VI. CONCLUSION

It is increasingly clear that telecommunications policymakers worldwide, regardless of the level of national economic development, face many of the same issues and problems. In the course of the Study of Telecommunications Structures more time was spent in the industrialized world than in the less developed countries. Admittedly, the exposure to the Third World was limited to a discrete set of national circumstances.

Nevertheless, it is fair to conclude that policymakers in the developing nations that were visited during the Study, like their colleagues in the industrialized countries, seek to increase investment, improve efficiency, and reduce staff levels. To achieve these goals in countries of the developed world, a host of structural changes are currently—or soon will be—under way: separate entities are providing network services to different groups or regions, entities are being privatized, and, through new legal or regulatory regimes, the private sector is gradually being allowed to deliver new business or enhanced services, sometime in ventures with the public sector.

As outlined in this essay, very similar structural changes are also taking place in the countries of the developing world that were visited in the course of Phase II of the Study. New corporate forms are being used to experiment and to innovate. More autonomy in operations—one intended consequence of privately incorporating a service provider—can increase the maneuverability of the new organization in capital markets. Thus, structurally separate subsidiaries—or privatized entities—in the developing world (like those in the developed world) are being used to increase accountability to the marketplace and as financing vehicles.

Again, like their colleagues in the industrialized world, the planners in the less developed countries have to pay attention to consumer demand. Consumers want access to basic services, they want flexibility, and they want some new services, too. Thus, the policymakers in the less developed world are under considerable pressure to install new or improved facilities and to develop new services. Similarly, their colleagues in the industrialized countries are attentive to the enormous infrastructure expenditures that must be made for digital networks and for an Integrated Services Digital Networks environment. To accomplish all these objectives, to meet consumer demand while improving the infrastructure, policymakers are, as noted above, turning to new structural arrangements.

Furthermore, given the imperative of delivering new services, of shifting the risk of developing services from the public to the private sector, and of obtaining access to much-needed capital, policymakers in the developing world are looking at ways to liberalize the regulatory regime for providing new services. They are exploring the options for raising capital to launch new business services, perhaps via a separate organizational subsidiary and up-front subscriber financing.

As is the case in the industrialized world, in the less developed countries there is also movement toward permitting the private sector to provide new services through joint ventures established with the supplier of basic telecommunications services. Some entities not affiliated with the service provider may enter into arrangements to provide business, enhanced, or data services. Depending on how profits are shared, and on the extent to which consumer demand is satisfied, the provider of basic transmission services may withhold its objections to such arrangements—so long as it is able to maintain its monopoly.

Policymakers in both the industrialized and less developed worlds are finding that it can be difficult to satisfy the demands of large users. In the developed nations, the concern is with the onset of bypass technologies and with the inability to reprice services to minimize the economic incentives to bypass. In the less developed world, the analogue to bypass emerges from the keen frustration of some large users with telecommunications services that are either unavailable or unsatisfactory. The dearth of services can create significant incentives for such users to develop their own networks, often to the consternation of the national monopoly provider. The result may be a duplicative network—or a legal confrontation that has had its parallels in the United States and elsewhere in the developed world.

As structural changes are implemented, new cost accounting schemes are also being installed. Where separate entities are providing national services, new "access" arrangements and charges must be developed. Where international and domestic services are provided by different entities, policymakers must work out which entity provides which services, how far backward or forward (of the division between domestic and international) the two entities are permitted to do business, and how the international entity shares revenues with or compensates the domestic provider for its origination and termination services.

Again akin to the experience of their counterparts in the more developed countries, policymakers in the less developed nations are beginning to understand the relationship between new substantive policies and the need for other, procedural changes. Thus, they are interested in developing regulatory mechanisms for oversight purposes. Such oversight may be seen as necessary for any number of reasons: to review the performance of a separate subsidiary that has been created to provide urban services, to ensure the adequacy of national services provided by a newly privatized entity, to set policies for tariffing, access arrangements and staffing, or to implement a new framework to encourage the joint, public-private offering of services.

For policymakers worldwide, the external—international—aspects of telecommunications policies are rapidly escalating in importance. Telecommunications facilities and services are increasingly critical to the competitiveness of both the manufacturing and the service sectors. To improve economic performance, investment in telecommunications is becoming imperative. Though policymakers outside the developed world may be faced with immediate domestic concerns that may make this lesson seem less relevant, they are inevitably coming to realize the importance of the trade component of the telecommunications sector.

Therefore, they want to develop export potential—in consulting, switching equipment, and software. They want to be positioned economically—and in terms of an advanced facilities infrastructure—so that they will become a central locus for regional telecommunications or financial activity.

In looking beyond national borders, policymakers in the developing world are noting the importance of being able to negotiate bilateral relations. They want to be able to function in the global environment, to contribute to new fora worldwide. As telecommunications becomes even more tied to other sectors—light industry, heavy manufacturing, banking, insurance, transport, and other services—policymakers in the developed world are beginning to ask whether a new framework is needed for developing trade relationships and new arrangements. Soon, these questions will be at the center of concern for policymakers in the developing world, as they realize that their goals for the telecommunications sector mean more than striving for universal service.

Telecommunications policymakers in the developing world, not unlike their colleagues elsewhere, may want to develop new fora to exchange views on the substantive and regulatory problems that they face. Such fora could be developed on a regional basis; the problems confronting Asia are generally seen as different from those of Africa, for example. Nevertheless, an international forum, at which the experiences of Asia (with its slightly more advanced infrastructures and, in certain countries, more substantial resources) might be shared with Africa, could be an invaluable supplement to the current work of the ITU and the Centre for Telecommunications Development.

Above all, and perhaps to belabor the obvious, it is critical to understand that the problems facing policymakers in the developing world are not merely like those in the industrialized world. True, the developing world does share with the developed nations the range of concerns that have been described thus far in these concluding paragraphs. In *addition* to those concerns, however, the telecommunications policymaker of a developing country faces a much more difficult set of issues.

Far and away the most important of these, it would seem, is the problem of obtaining scarce economic resources in competition with other critical sectors. When truly basic needs like sanitation, health, education and shelter are clamoring for assistance, how can expenditures for a telecommunications infrastructure be justified? Though the literature used to support the argument for telecommunications investment does exist, and much of it is good, it is far from sufficient.

Nevertheless, the crucial issue is how the various arguments for such investment can be better factored into national planning debates. How can policymakers be persuaded that telecommunications can raise the overall level of economic development such that it is not irrelevant to concerns that "basic needs" must be satisfied? For years, the World Bank has worked toward this objective; its activities need to be bolstered by national and other multilateral institutions for the case ultimately to be persuasive.

A second major issue concerns how to make the case for using scarce foreign exchange to invest in telecommunications. Telecommunications (unlike tourism, for example) does not help reap foreign exchange. A third issue is the difficulty of satisfying the competing social, political and perhaps even religious demands of a country's rural sectors for improved telecommunications services. Hard economic realities tend to demonstrate that the commercially viable services—the profitable services—are to be had in investing in urban areas. How can the politician, let alone the telecommunications planner, decide on the proper mix between urban and rural investment?

A fourth issue is how to develop the requisite expertise for managing telecommunications businesses. As telecommunications becomes more central to other sectors, as prices may have to move toward costs, and as new services are brought to the market, knowing how to manage and market the available assets takes on critical importance. The management of telecommunications in the developing world (not unlike the case in some countries of the developed world) is too often left to the engineer or the technocrat. Understanding the needs of the business user and marketing services to that user are at the foundation of the new telecommunications environment to which the providers of today must inevitably adjust.

The problems facing policymakers in the developing world are, in short, awesome. While they can be frustrating, they are always daunting. Given the magnitude of the task at hand, this essay is not intended to be discouraging; rather, the intention is to highlight just some of the difficulties that must be faced.

The point of this essay is, in reality, quite simple: the massive changes of the industrialized world *are* relevant to the developing world. They have an impact on developing countries. The issues and difficulties besetting the developed world have parallels in the developing nations. The substantive and regulatory responses to change that are being developed in the developing world are not unlike those in the industrialized nations.

From its inception, the principal purpose of the Study has been to increase cross-border understanding, to foster the growing realization that telecommunications policies are interdependent, that changes in one country affect and reflect changes elsewhere, and that, therefore, national—and international—policies cannot be developed in isolation. This essay is an effort to expand the reach of that original goal beyond the industrialized world, to highlight the extraordinary—and not often understood—interdependence of the telecommunications policies of every nation on earth—rich and poor, North and South.

ABOUT THE AUTHORS

Robert R. Bruce is a partner in the Washington, D. C. office of Debevoise & Plimpton, which has its principal office in New York and a European office in Paris. From October 1977 to February 1981, he served as General Counsel of the Federal Communications Commission. Before joining the FCC, Mr. Bruce practiced law in Washington, D.C. and, from 1970 to 1972, was Director of Communications Planning for the Public Broadcasting Service. He graduated *magna cum laude* in Government from Harvard College in 1966; in 1970, he received a J.D. from Harvard Law School and an M.P.A. from the John F. Kennedy School of Government, Harvard University. He is the author of numerous articles on communications law and policy.

Jeffrey P. Cunard is an associate in the Washington, D.C. office of Debevoise & Plimpton. He graduated *summa cum laude* in English and Political Science from the University of California at Los Angeles in 1977 and received a J.D. in 1980 from Yale Law School, where he was an Editor of the *Yale Law Journal*. After graduation from law school he clerked for Judge Wm. Matthew Byrne, Jr., in Los Angeles, California. He is the author of and a contributor to various articles on communications law.

Mark D. Director is an associate in the Washington, D.C. office of Debevoise & Plimpton. He graduated *magna cum laude* in English and American Literatures and Language from Harvard College in 1980 and received a J.D. in 1984 from Harvard Law School, where he was Comments Editor of the *Harvard Journal on Legislation*. He is a coauthor of a text on broadcast regulation.

Messrs. Bruce, Cunard and Director are the authors of *From Telecommunications to Electronic Services: A Global Spectrum of Definitions, Boundary Lines and Structures*, which was published by Butterworths in 1986 as the Report of Phase I of the Study of Telecommunications Structures of the International Institute of Communications.

HE 7645 .B78 1988

	DATE DUE		
OCT 1 8 1990			